Software Project Management:

From Concept to Deployment

Kieron Conway

President and CEO
Keith Weiskamp

Publisher
Steve Sayre

Acquisitions Editor
Charlotte Carpentier

Development Editor
Michelle Stroup

Marketing Specialist
Tracy Rooney

Project Editor
Greg Balas

Technical Reviewer
Andrew Indovina

Production Coordinator
Laura Wellander

Cover Designer
Jody Winkler

Layout Designer
April Nielsen

CD-ROM Developer
Chris Nusbaum

Software Project Management: From Concept to Deployment

The Coriolis Group, LLC
14455 North Hayden Road
Suite 220
Scottsdale, Arizona 85260

(480) 483-0192
FAX (480) 483-0193
www.coriolis.com

Library of Congress Cataloging-in-Publication Data
Conway, Kieron.
    Software project management: from concept to deployment / Kieron Conway.
       p.   cm.
    Includes index.
    ISBN 1-57610-807-4
    1. Computer software--Development--Management.   I. Title.

QA76.76.D47 C663 2000
005.1'068'4--dc21   00-064414
                                                                              CIP

Printed in the United States of America
10 9 8 7 6 5 4 3 2 1

The Coriolis Group, LLC • 14455 North Hayden Road, Suite 220 • Scottsdale, Arizona 85260

Dear Reader:

Coriolis Technology Press was founded to create a very elite group of books: the ones you keep closest to your machine. Sure, everyone would like to have the Library of Congress at arm's reach, but in the real world, you have to choose the books you rely on every day *very* carefully.

To win a place for our books on that coveted shelf beside your PC, we guarantee several important qualities in every book we publish. These qualities are:

- *Technical accuracy*—It's no good if it doesn't work. Every Coriolis Technology Press book is reviewed by technical experts in the topic field, and is sent through several editing and proofreading passes in order to create the piece of work you now hold in your hands.

- *Innovative editorial design*—We've put years of research and refinement into the ways we present information in our books. Our books' editorial approach is uniquely designed to reflect the way people learn new technologies and search for solutions to technology problems.

- *Practical focus*—We put only pertinent information into our books and avoid any fluff. Every fact included between these two covers must serve the mission of the book as a whole.

- *Accessibility*—The information in a book is worthless unless you can find it quickly when you need it. We put a lot of effort into our indexes, and heavily cross-reference our chapters, to make it easy for you to move right to the information you need.

Here at The Coriolis Group we have been publishing and packaging books, technical journals, and training materials since 1989. We're programmers and authors ourselves, and we take an ongoing active role in defining what we publish and how we publish it. We have put a lot of thought into our books; please write to us at **ctp@coriolis.com** and let us know what you think. We hope that you're happy with the book in your hands, and that in the future, when you reach for software development and networking information, you'll turn to one of our books first.

Keith Weiskamp
President and CEO

Jeff Duntemann
VP and Editorial Director

Look for these related books from The Coriolis Group:

C++ Black Book
by Steven Holzner

Java Black Book
by Steven Holzner

XHTML Black Book
by Steven Holzner

XML Black Book, 2nd Edition
by Natanya Pitts

Visual Basic 6 Black Book
by Steven Holzner

To my very patient wife, Nazanin, and to my daughters, Sanam and Salma.

About the Author

Kieron Conway graduated from Manchester University in the U.K. in 1971, and worked for six years with the Nuclear Physics Research Group at Manchester. It was here that he learned about real-time computer operating systems and applications. Kieron then spent three years in the Middle East, where he worked as a consultant in areas concerned with mathematical modeling and simulation.

On returning to the U.K., Kieron set up a software support and development facility for a company specializing in total hardware and software solutions. In the mid-eighties, Kieron, with the support of four partners, established and ran a company specializing in technical and scientific solutions for industry.

In the last few years, Kieron has been involved in a variety of health care application developments. He also had an involvement in a revolutionary project to develop a new generation of project management methodology, using an "object" approach, for use by an international organization.

Kieron lives in Derbyshire in the U.K., where he now writes about software development, and provides consultancy to clients.

Acknowledgments

There are many people I would like to thank who helped me in preparing this book. To begin with, I would like to thank my friends at DSP Design of Chesterfield, U.K., for helping to put together the E-MagBook hardware that the software in this book was tested on.

I would also like to thank Andrew Indovina for tech reviewing the book, and Sharon Hamm for copyediting the text. In addition, I would also like to thank the staff at The Coriolis Group. In particular, Charlotte Carpentier, my Acquisitions Editor, and Michelle Stroup for serving as my Development Editor on the book. Also, I would like to thank Project Editor, Greg Balas, Laura Wellander, Production Coordinator, and April Nielsen, Layout Designer at The Coriolis Group for all of their efforts.

Lastly, I also would like to thank Suzanne Kelly for typesetting the book, Mary Millhollon for proofreading the text, and David Astra for indexing the book.

—*Kieron Conway*

Contents at a Glance

Table of Contents

Introduction

Software development is not just about writing code, that's only a part, albeit a very important part, of the overall process. You need to understand what the customer wants, how to analyze the requirements, produce a design, and go about development and testing so that the software you deliver is of high quality, and does what the client wants it to do. The software also needs to be developed to an agreed time scale and a price. The aim of this book is to guide you through all the phases involved in taking a concept and turning it into a deliverable, quality software product. We'll even look at the pre-sales aspects of what you need to do to bid and win an order, without which the project won't get off the ground. We'll study a working methodology used to develop complex systems, and how to go about managing and controlling all the associated processes.

To assist in this task, I'm going to use a single, detailed case study, involving the development of a complete set of software for an electronic book. In this case study, you'll see all the theory put into practice. You'll even see some things go wrong, and what had to be done to recover from these problems. You'll sit in on the experiences of two new employees to my company, K & C Consultancy, as they tackle a software development from concept through to deployment. In other words, we start with the person who has an idea and wants us to turn it into working software, and we end, having designed and developed the solution, setting up a facility to provide all the support logistics for the product we have created.

As a programmer, you are unlikely to get involved in the entire software development process on every project you undertake, but regardless of how much it you are involved in, you need to understand the entire process for creating software.

Meet the Software Developers

K & C Consultancy, set up by myself and my partner, Charlie (The "C" of "K & C"), has a policy of hiring graduates. We don't necessarily look for computer science graduates, we look for problem-solvers, because that's what software development is all about, solving your own and other people's problems. Over the years, we've hired science, engineering, and math students as well as computer people, and also bright individuals who have no qualifications at all. All we ask is that they appreciate that before you start to build something, you must understand what it has to do, and how you are going to do it.

I want to introduce you to two of my latest employees: Archie and Julie. Archie doesn't actually have a degree of any description, but he has already written some really impressive game programs, which he brought to the interview to show me. He's a very confidant individual, and clearly very talented. However, when I asked Archie how he would go about developing a program for a client, Archie's answer was that he'd go and see the client, ask what the client wanted, and that he would go back and write the program, and then bring back his finished product to the client.

Charlie and I asked Archie about the processes in between, and he didn't know what we meant. So we asked him how he would know if what he produced was what the client wanted. Archie's answer did not inspire us with any confidence. He told us that he'd listen to the client, and then go back and develop a solution based on what the client told him. If the client didn't like the delivered product, then the client had not explained his needs properly.

This is actually quite a common scenario: a software house has a client who wants some programs developed, and based on one or more meetings, software is developed. The fundamental problem is that the customers will have all sorts of expectations with respect to what will be delivered. If these expectations have not been understood and managed, then it is very unlikely that the end product will be satisfactory.

We asked Archie how he would go about asking an architect to build a house and Archie, quite rightly, expected the architect to go away and come up with some plans, which would depict what the building would look like. So why should software be any different?

An architect will get the customer to agree to the plans before starting work. The client knows what the end product will look like, and expectations can be discussed and controlled using the plans, drawings, models, and so on. Archie could see how this worked for a house, but wasn't able to see how it applied to software. He had absolutely no experience of writing programs in a commercial environment. Put another way, he did not know how to start developing a system that did what the customer wanted, was produced on time, and in budget. All the games he had written, had been created for his own amusement, and using his own words, "the functionality had sort of evolved."

Despite this lack of worldly experience, we offered a job to Archie on the grounds that he clearly had potential, provided we could get him into a disciplined way of thinking. The games he had produced were very sophisticated, and they demonstrated that he genuinely possessed talent as a programmer, but both Charlie and I knew it was going to be a long haul to get him into the right way of thinking. We anticipated that Archie would become quite frustrated, as the last thing we would allow him to do would be to rush off and start coding at the drop of a hat. Our aim, as a company, is to ensure that we don't cut any code until we know exactly what it is that it has to do and, of vital importance, the customer agrees with our interpretation of what it must do.

In the same batch of applicants, we interviewed Julie. Julie is a couple of years older than Archie, and after we had interviewed her for a while, it was clear that her qualities were quite different from those of Archie. Julie was much more reserved, and initially had to be coaxed into saying anything. For the past two years, she had been working for a small software house with a staff of 25 people. Julie wanted to leave because she was fed up with the lack of planning that resulted in constant failure to meet deadlines, and an ethos that centered on crisis, rather than project management.

We asked Julie to give us an example, and she told us about the project that she'd just completed. At the last minute, the project manager had come to her and asked where the module was to perform the data take-on. This is a phase in which data from an old system is extracted, converted, and then transferred into the new system. Julie explained to him that no one had mentioned data take-on; it was not on the plan. The project manager had taken the news very badly, as had the customer. The result: masses of forced overtime, deadline overrun, disgruntled client, etc.

Julie's company managed to complete the project, with only a month's overrun, but the client hit the company with late delivery penalties, which eat into the profit. Worse still, the customer also demanded all sorts of modifications that were never planned, and of course the software house, who were in a "no win" situation, had to agree to implement the changes at their own cost.

Julie wanted to leave because she felt that there must be a better way of developing software. At college, she had had a very good teacher who had told her all about the System Development Life Cycle, a methodology designed to help people develop complex systems. Unfortunately, she had seen little sign of it in her short career so far, and she was ready for a change. But she wanted to move to a company that had a better idea about how to develop software and manage the associated processes.

The *System Development Life Cycle (SDLC for short)* is the cornerstone of our methodology for developing software of any type. It allows us to define what the customer wants, and how we are going to achieve a solution to meet the customer's expectations.

So, there you have it. You are going to follow the enthusiastic, very talented, but totally undisciplined Archie, and the very battle-hardened, but determined Julie. Quite a contrast, but as you will see as we progress, software development demands a myriad of skills, which very few people possess in total. Successful software houses develop using small teams of developers who work closely together and feed off each other's strengths, supporting any weaknesses.

In line with company procedure, we offered both of them jobs, with a six-month probationary period. Charlie and I figure that you have to give individuals at least six months to prove themselves in the software business, and just as importantly, we have to prove ourselves to the employee. If we don't like the way they work, or if they don't like the way we work, then, after the six-month period is up, either side can walk away. It's a system that has worked well over the years for us. A small company like ours needs people who can work in teams. The majority of employees, who have parted company with us, after (or before) the probationary period is over, have been people who found it difficult to work in a team environment.

Finally, I welcome your feedback on this book. You can email The Coriolis Group at **ctp@coriolis.com.**

Chapter 1
A Methodology for Development

In this chapter, we're going to look at a methodology for developing software, a way of doing things in a structured manner. We'll then begin a case study in the very early stages of the birth of a project, even before the customer has chosen a software supplier.

An Overview of the System Development Life Cycle

As a final part of our company's new-employee orientation process, Charlie and I introduce our new recruits to our development methodology. This methodology is based on the *system* (also known as the *project*) *development life cycle*. We use a methodology that helps us design and develop complex systems using a phased approach. This approach is designed to make sure that we don't move from one phase to another before we have assessed and verified the results of the current phase, and that we have all the necessary information to move on. Our methodology also makes the software project management much simpler. The system development life cycle (or the SDLC, as we will call it from now on) has many variations. The approach presented here is the one our company follows, based on years of experience with successful results. Our company's methodology might not fit every operational scenario you'll encounter. But the presentation of our experience throughout this book—in action, as a full-length case study—will give you valuable information about how to implement a development methodology and manage the resultant processes.

Before programmers can write a line of code, they must understand the client's requirement—in other words, the *what* of "What is this software to do?" Next, they need to know the *how*, from "How will we do it?" The *what* tells them, as programmers, what it is that the customer wants, and the *how* tells them how to go about providing that. And, of course, you need a plan, which defines the *when* of "When does all this happen?"

The SDLC helps you to define the *what,* work out the *how*, and then develop and deliver a quality product by the *when*. System development as defined in the SDLC version we have adopted consists of seven key phases. Following is a brief introduction to these key phases:

- *Phase 1: Capturing the Rquirements*—This phase involves sitting down with the client and doing a lot of listening, followed by a lot of writing. The end result is a document that defines *what* the customer requires in terms that the customer can understand.

- *Phase 2: Analyzing the Requirements*—In this process, we develop a deeper understanding of the requirements and gather as much data about them as we can, to help us to design a solution.

- *Phase 3: Designing a Solution*—After we understand the requirements and have analyzed them in detail, we produce a design. This phase defines *how* the product will be built.

- *Phase 4: Developing a Solution*—From the *what* and the *how*, we now produce and test the individual, self-contained modules that make up the solution.

- *Phase 5: System Integration and Testing*—We now take all the modules developed in Phase 4 and put them together as a complete solution. For the first time, we can test the entire product as a cohesive entity. We confirm that we have a solid product that meets all the original requirements.

- *Phase 6: Implementation and Customer Acceptance*—We now implement the solution and prove to the client that we have met the original requirements. (We are confident from the results of Phase 5 that this is a mere formality.)

- *Phase 7: Support and Maintenance*—After the customer accepts the software, we must support and maintain it. This is the final phase of the life cycle.

To understand the cycle more clearly, take a look at Figure 1.1.

A key point of the SDLC is that you do not go from one phase to another until everything in the current phase has been verified and approved. Just who verifies and approves a phase, depends on circumstances; it may be you, or one of your colleagues, or the customer. For example, you may find that working through one phase leads to a better understanding of what you did in an earlier phase, which you may have to revisit. As we shall see, this iterative nature of the cycle is fundamental to the success of its operation and associated management.

SDLC Phases and Deliverables

For each phase, the goal is to produce one or more *deliverables*. A deliverable does not necessarily need to be something delivered to the customer. The point is that we produce something tangible that we can assess and check. And only when we and/or the client are happy with a deliverable do we move on to the next phase. For example, deliverables from various phases might consist of a requirement specification, design documentation, installation disks and instructions, the source code, user guides, and so on. Figure 1.2 shows the SDLC phases and typical deliverables, or end products.

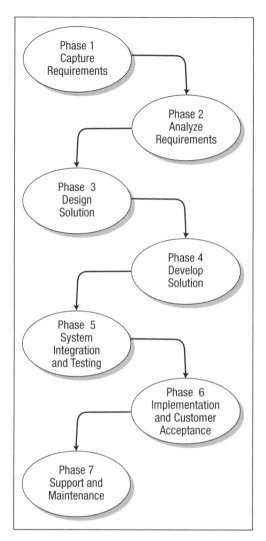

Figure 1.1

Diagrammatic representation of the SDLC phases.

The result of capturing the requirement in Phase 1 is a documented statement of what the customer requires. This statement is the foundation stone of the project—and the sole arbiter in the event of a dispute concerning any matters of functionality. Because of the importance of the approved statement of requirements, the customer is considered the "owner" (regardless of who writes it).

In Phase 2, we analyze these requirements. The result of analysis is that we build different descriptions of the requirements to assist in the design phase. Some of these descriptions take the form of models, such as entity relationship diagrams (showing how data items relate to one another), state transition diagrams (showing the transition from one clearly defined

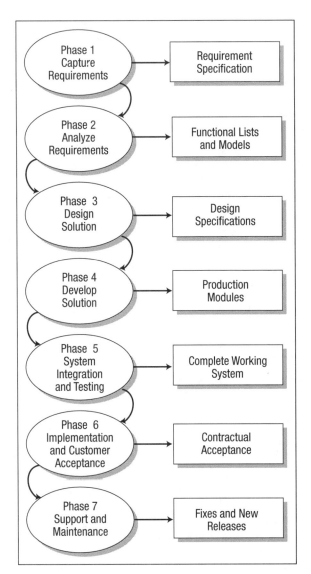

Figure 1.2
Diagrammatic representation of the SDLC phases showing typical deliverables.

operational state of a program to another, and what event triggers the change), and so on. Part of the analysis consists of abstracting the requirements into common descriptions; this abstraction leads to defined lists of generic functionality, from which we can produce designs. In essence, what comes out of analysis is a series of alternative, technical descriptions of the requirements. These descriptions provide views from different perspectives and more detail. The overall aim in Phase 2 is to gain a deeper understanding of the requirements and, in particular, separate out common functionality, in preparation for the design phase. Clearly, this phase is quite complex, and we will spend a lot of time on it later.

Based on the output of the first two phases, we go on to design a solution in Phase 3. Design consists of supplying the detail of how the solution is to be produced. It is the blueprint that informs the programmers how they must go about their task of creating the software components to meet the requirements.

Then, programmers will use the design documentation to develop self-contained software modules in Phase 4. The programmers will develop and test each module in isolation from the rest of the system. This approach allows for significant simultaneous development. If, for example, the design states that Module A must interact with Module B, it is necessary to test Module A as if it were connected to Module B—that hasn't yet been built. Part of the programmer's task will be to build a test harness (extra code that will not be part of the final solution) that lets Module A be tested as if it were interfaced to Module B. Obviously, the programmer needs to understand Module A's requirements in detail, but he or she is concerned only with the *interface* aspects of Module B—not with how it works. Another programmer may develop Module B at the same time, in which case, to develop B as a standalone entity, that programmer needs to understand how Module B interfaces with Module A. If both programmers do a good job (assuming the specs were 100 percent correct), at system integration time, Module A works with Module B—the first time.

This example emphasizes the need to approach software development methodically, with sufficient deliverables to ensure that everyone can work toward the same goals. It also points out that we can manage the project with a well-defined set of definitions.

In the development phase, we construct and test modules. If testing fails, we restart the phase at the appropriate point until our deliverable can be verified as "complete" by passing the designated tests. Clearly, when something goes wrong, we analyze the problem and fix the fault. Then we verify the deliverables again and repeat the process until the output is satisfactory. Once all the modules have passed testing, system integration can commence in Phase 5. In this phase, we put together all the developed modules for the very first time. After they have been integrated, or "bolted together," we can test the system as a whole. Remember, we have tested all the modules in isolation. This is the first time we get to check out the completed system. We can now consider as deliverables both the complete system and the results we achieve when we test it. Only when the system has passed all the tests do we release it. This phase is our chance, as a company, to ensure that we have produced a robust product that meets the customer's requirements in full. Handing the software over to the client is pointless until we are convinced that it is of the highest quality and will do what the client wants it to do.

The two fundamental types of testing for validating deliverables are *formal* and *informal*. Formal testing involves writing down a test specification in detail. We need to define the conditions required before we execute the test, what the test consists of (so someone can execute it), and its expected outcome. If we perform the test and the outcome is as stated, the test is passed. We can check the box, sign the appropriate test sheet, and so on. The end result is an auditable account of testing. If the test fails, we will have an auditable account of what we did to rectify the situation. Informal testing relaxes these constraints considerably, placing an emphasis only on recording what we did at the time and the outcome of the test.

When we are satisfied with the system integration and testing phase, we move to Phase 6, in which we install the programs and let the customer verify that the software meets his or her requirements. Acceptance testing tends to be fairly formal, resulting in a contractual acceptance of delivery by our client. Such customer acceptance provides an essential mechanism for managing the closing of the project's development phase and moving into Phase 7, the support phase.

Quality and Auditing

Nowadays, simply writing and selling software is not enough. Because software plays such a vital role in all walks of life, software quality is a big issue. *Quality* is not just about testing; quality must invade every aspect of the business and the development processes.

Auditing is the process in which an external (or internal) assessor judges whether you are adhering to your quality standards. Auditing also confirms for your customers that you take the correct precautions to ensure software of the highest possible quality is produced. In the context of "acceptance testing," auditing helps validate for your customers that you have actually delivered what is required—or, put another way, that you have supplied everything that was ordered. Auditing also acts as a valuable project management tool to ensure that things are progressing as required.

Quality, auditing, and related subjects are serious issues in the software industry today, where many developers have a reputation for late delivery and failing to meet customers' expectations. In the course of this book, we will show you how you can overcome such problems in a way that provides a high level of accountability—a vital factor in demonstrating that you produce quality software and effectively manage the associated processes.

The Plan

To knit a software development together, you need a *plan*. (The software industry has an appalling reputation for failing to deliver on time. Projects go wrong for lots of reasons, but a frequent source of problems is the lack of a flexible plan that is constantly monitored with respect to progress.) You need to know when you're going to do all the things associated with the life cycle, what resources are needed, when they're needed, and for how long. The secret of a good plan, as you will come to understand, is that it must be both robust and flexible at the same time.

You have to build into your plan a degree of flexibility for contingencies, so you can cope with unexpected challenges the project throws in front of you. Constant—at least weekly—monitoring of the plan is essential. Sometimes, you may have to monitor daily, or even hourly, as circumstances dictate. You should be asking yourself questions such as, How much have we achieved this week? What's left to do? Are we ahead of or behind schedule? We can summarize this process as *progress monitoring*. Progress monitoring will give you early warning if things are going wrong. The aim is to get sufficient warning to recover the situation without having an impact on the master plan.

Before the Project Starts

A *project* can be defined as a temporary set of activities conducted to bring about a defined outcome. In the case of software development, the outcome is usually a product that is developed to meet a requirement. But how does the process that leads to the actual project start?

Can We Meet a Need?

Before the project officially begins, the process starts with someone who has a need. Often, this need is a vague perception of a requirement; or, it can be a very clear, concise definition. And, of course, you'll find every variation in between. If the persons with the need can't fulfill it themselves, they have to look for an organization that can.

As a software company, we are always on the lookout for potential customers who require software developments. How we hear about these potential customers varies a great deal. Some clients approach us directly (having heard about us from elsewhere) and ask us to quote for a job. We read appropriate journals and magazines, in which companies and organizations define a requirement in very general terms and ask for suitable organizations to reply with a proposal for the work. We develop software for a wide range of clients and uses. We also develop a small number of our own software packages, which we sell in the PC marketplace. After we've identified a potential client with a need, the next stage is to start determining what the specific requirements are.

The Case Study:

A Request from Montasana Systems

Quite fortuitously, shortly after I had introduced two new employees, Julie and Archie, to our company's software development methodology, I received a phone call from one of our oldest clients, Bill Montgomery (known to all as "Monty"). Monty is an entrepreneur who specializes in developing high-quality electronic consumer products. Over the years, my company has assisted him with software developments when he was unable to resource them himself.

After Monty and I exchanged pleasantries, he got to the root of his problem. He explained that he had managed to raise a fair bit of capital through a consortium that he'd put together to develop an up-market, electronic book-come-magazine. The product was the sort of thing where you buy the base unit and then purchase or rent removable memory devices that contain one or more books. You insert the storage unit into the book and—presto!—you can read selected titles.

Monty's version was to include full multimedia capability, Web access, family photo album—you name it. He wanted to know if we were interested in quoting for the project. I asked him for some more detail, and he explained that the device would be a miniature PC running standard Windows. It would be smaller than the smallest laptop. Although a standard PC, the unit would be dedicated to booting and running only the electronic book software.

I was a little skeptical, but Monty has developed some very good products over the years, and I agreed to meet with him. As usual, he was in a desperate hurry to get started and suggested that we meet after lunch the following afternoon. We agreed to meet, with the understanding that he would let me bring Archie and Julie. He also made it clear that he wanted a fixed price quotation and that he was inviting a total of three bids from separate companies.

The next morning, I told Archie and Julie about my conversation with Monty and that they were coming with me to listen to his concept. When they both showed surprise that I was going to take two new recruits to this first meeting, I informed them that they not only were coming with me, but they also were going to do the quote. When I explained that the development was to be at a fixed price, Julie was horrified that they were to prepare the quotation. I told them this was an ideal opportunity to expose them to both the SDLC and the pre-sales effort necessary to win the business. If we got the job, they would also design and develop the software.

The first thing we would have to do was to win the order. We would have to do a certain amount of work to be confident that we could devise a justifiable provisional plan, at a reasonable cost. At first glance, getting two novices to quote for a project (something neither had ever done) and develop the software (assuming we would be successful) might seem quite ludicrous. If we had been going to throw them in at the deep end and leave them to swim, so to speak, I would agree. But that was not what we would do. We were going to approach this whole process in a structured, methodical, well-managed manner; and if they got into deep trouble, they would have plenty of support from the rest of the company.

A software house's main asset is the people who work within it. Both Charlie and I believe that we must invest heavily in our staff. For this reason, he and I had talked the previous evening, and we had agreed that, for the next few days, he would take over all of my commitments that could be transferred. I would still handle the rest, but my main task would be to win this contract and then guide Archie and Julie through the development. We would make a final decision about how practical this all was after the initial meeting with Monty.

Describing the Concept

Once you've identified a potential customer who has a need, establishing the overall picture of the concept is essential. The detailed requirements will spring from this viewpoint. Here are some examples: A water treatment company might want to computerize the drinking water purification process by taking automatic measurements of the water's purity and, from the results, control the purification process. A storage company might want to streamline the allocation of storage facilities with automated barcode identification and transportation of goods in and out of a warehouse. Maybe a company wants to develop a business model for predicting its market's behavior. Or, someone might want software developed to handle an electronic book.

An important question to ask at this stage is, Are we capable of doing the job? The second question is, Do we want to do it? Clearly, to answer either question, you may need to do a great deal of work. The goal is to do sufficient work to be confident that the job is worth your while. This initial phase—learning about the overall concept—is crucial. Then, based on an understanding of the concept, a time will come when you must make a commitment to the customer in terms of a price and a timetable.

Identifying Your Customer

When you develop software, you are always doing so for someone who has a need. Identifying the customer is clear-cut when an external customer calls and asks, "Can you build me a widget?" But suppose a software house wants to develop a product. Someone must take ownership of the requirements. Here, the owner—and the customer—could be the marketing department of your own organization. Who you develop for doesn't matter—someone owns the requirement, and that owner is your customer. Whether internal or external, your customer, as owner, must agree to what is in the spec. Who writes the spec (the customer or the developer) also is irrelevant—the customer is totally responsible for its content. Consequently, the spec must be written so the owner can clearly understand it. In project management terms, the customer is one of the project's key *stakeholders*. A stakeholder is someone who has a vested interest in the successful conclusion of the project. To you, as the developer, the customer is one of your most important stakeholders.

Defining Roles and Responsibilities

On an internal project, once the customer stakeholder accepts the completed product, the sales team starts selling the product with a clearly defined functionality to the team's customer base. If any customers think something is wrong with the product's functionality, the feedback should be directed to the instigator of the requirement specification, who must then determine whether to commission more work from the development department. I'm not talking about bugs—customers report these directly to the support desk. I'm talking about issues such as, "This product needs to be able to interface with Microsoft's Access," for example. Marketing might not have originally requested such functionality, and that group must decide if demand is sufficient to justify defining the requirement and asking development to produce it.

Always having a clear demarcation of responsibilities is essential. The developers develop a product for their customer, who might be an external client or an internal department. In the case of mass-market products, sales or marketing people are responsible for handling the end-customers' aspirations and determining what needs to be changed in terms of the product's functionality. At this stage, you might think all this information is very interesting (or not) but it has little relevance to a programmer. The truth is, whether you set up your own business to develop software or you work in a large corporation, you need to understand the way in which the SDLC and its management affects you. A good understanding of the process will allow you to influence the way in which you work to get the most out of your own and other peoples' abilities. Familiarity with the SDLC also ensures that everyone connected with a project understands the situation and that everyone sings from the same song sheet.

Presenting the Concept

Because you are bound to be involved in similar meetings at some stage in your career, I will present our initial meeting with Monty pretty much as it happened. (You need to develop the skills necessary to separate what's relevant from what's not, so your pre-sales work can be done as efficiently as possible.)

The three of us (Julie, Archie, and I) arrived at Monty's offices, a complex of buildings, just on the outskirts of the city. Most of his company's manufacturing is done by contract. Manufacturing companies often commission Monty to design, build, and manufacture the control systems for their own products. So, Montasana has workshops for assembling and testing products. The impressive reception area is large and borders on opulence. The walls are filled with pictures of the products Monty has either made directly or assisted in.

At well over six feet tall, Monty himself is an impressive figure at the best of times, but he looked positively regal that day. Instead of his usual jeans and sweatshirt, he was wearing a three-piece suit. I could see Archie and Julie were impressed. Monty shook everyone's hand and led us to one of his meeting rooms. We took up our places around a huge, polished, mahogany table. Monty shut the door. He thanked us all for coming and then gave us a brief history about his company, which he had founded about 12 years ago. He explained that his mission was to develop interesting, innovative, quality products for the mass markets.

Monty went on to describe the company, its dramatic growth, and so on (Archie and Julie again looked suitably impressed). Although Monty and I are friends, he is, first and foremost, a businessman—and a very successful one, too. Monty is quite typical of the sort of customer you may have to deal with—the owner or manager of some form of business enterprise.

Monty has very rigid principles, and, once he gets an idea, distracting him is quite difficult. In fact, his resolve is quite important to us. For example, after we've developed the requirement specification, it needs somebody to drive it. Remember, we're not going to own the requirement specification. If its contents were disputed, we would need someone to arbitrate. The last thing we want is a committee to decide what should be done. Committee decision-making tends to result in inordinate lengths of time spent waiting for a final decision. Then, the decision is often a bad compromise between two or more opposing factions. To have in place a strong individual who will make decisions for people who can't make up their minds is not just important—it's vital. Too many people are afraid to make decisions; they hide behind group consensus, so, if anything goes wrong, they can direct the blame elsewhere.

Coffee arrived, we chatted about this and that, and then Monty stood up, ready to reveal his concept. He had required all three of us to sign a confidentiality agreement first. Confidentiality agreements are quite common. A company that contracts software development with an outside individual or group must expose a great deal about the proposed project. Much of this information can be commercially very sensitive. Such information in a competitor's hands could give the competitor a valuable insight into what Monty was up to. So, don't be afraid to sign such documents, but understand this: As a computer professional, you must abide by the terms of the agreement. Such agreements are put in place to protect both your customer's and your company's interests.

The Requirements

Monty introduced us to his latest product, an electronic book/magazine that his company called the E-MagBook. The product is a very small laptop. The laptop employs standard PC architecture and has a 300MHz clock, 32MB of RAM, full-color 640x480-pixel screen resolution, and several hundred megabytes of miniature hard drive. From his pocket, he produced a smart, black box, opened it up, and placed it on the table. It was, indeed, a very small laptop. It measured 6 inches wide by 5 inches deep. It possessed a full, miniature keyboard, miniature joy stick mouse, left and right click buttons, volume control, brightness control, and four hours of battery time (from fully charged to automatic switch-off). He showed us the tiny battery unit.

All the laptop components were standard, off-the-shelf items. Montasana had simply created the motherboard. The fixed disk was housed in a 2-inch square unit that was about an eighth of an inch deep. Monty pointed out that the miniature disks were still fairly low capacity—the one he was using was a 200MB version. He explained that the disk needed to hold only a stripped-down version of Windows and the application to be developed. His reference to the application brought us to why we were there. At this stage, we needed to find out whether he wanted the supplier to take care of any necessary modifications to Windows, and he replied that Montasana's developers would take care of those.

Their idea was to strip out absolutely everything that wasn't needed in the operating system. They would take the application and run it on a machine they called "Mother." They would then put Mother on standby. This process would result in Montasana's version of a BIOS (Basic Input/Output System), taking the content of Mother's memory and storing it to disk, in a memory-save type of operation. Their developers would then make a copy of the whole of Mother's system disk and feed the copy onto each electronic book's system disk. When a user switched on an E-MagBook, its BIOS would simply restore the memory and transfer control, and—voilá—the E-MagBook would start up as Mother intended. When the user finished with the book, he or she would switch it off, and the power would be dropped immediately.

This information prompted Archie, who had been quite impressed by the whole idea, to ask how the E-MagBook would recover the next time it was switched on. Monty explained that the PC would simply reinstate memory the way Mother intended, regardless of what the PC was doing when it was powered off. Archie asked about the swap files. Monty told him swap files weren't an issue because the system would be set up so the application would always have enough memory. Swapping would be disabled; in fact, virtually no disk-write access to the system disk would be possible when the system was running. Consequently, when a user switched off the E-MagBook, the software context would be thrown away.

Already, we were getting lots of information from this meeting. As you participate in similar meetings, the critical task will be to focus and sift out what is relevant and what is not.

Prospective customers are usually very enthusiastic about their requirements and want to tell you everything. You have to keep in mind that if you take this on as a project, you will be developing software for an electronic book. In Chapter 2, we'll start to dissect the information, and you'll see the process in action.

Monty continued by telling us that, from a marketing viewpoint, the consumer would make a single purchase of an E-MagBook and would be given a few free books and magazines—a bit like the games console market, where you buy one and select from a series of free titles. The books consisted of miniature disks. Monty took out a removable version of the 2-inch disk. Each disk had a 100MB capacity, and he expected the capacity to increase by leaps and bounds (he was getting the latest developments directly from the manufacturer). He showed us how the disks slid into the E-MagBook. From this point, the application would take over.

Monty explained that his company had planned to develop the software internally because he didn't think it would be a big job. But he then had to apply his entire software development capability to a job for one of his major clients. As a result, he'd had no option but to farm out the E-MagBook software development—which is where we came in. He explained, "What I need are two main programs: a viewer that will go into the E-MagBook, and an editing suite that will allow me to build an electronic title."

Archie had taken no notes at all throughout this presentation, Julie had copious jottings, and I had written a handful of brief notes. At some stage, we would have to sit down together and go over the information we had gathered. We would need to come up with a list of the relevant facts, from which we could plan our project to fulfill the requirements.

Monty continued by defining the two programs as the E-Viewer and E-Editor. Initially, he was contemplating three book formats; ultimately, the sky would be the limit. He needed this prototype up and running eight weeks from the following Monday. (As he gave us this information, three pens wrote, "Eight weeks from next Monday!") He explained that he needed only the E-Viewer fully operational by then. He was quite sure Montasana would find a way to set up the books for the E-Viewer without the editors. (Three pens wrote "E-Viewer only" next to the "Eight weeks…" comment.)

What We've Learned So Far

Let's recap what has come out of this meeting so far. Monty's requirements are as follows:

- A viewer program and editors to accommodate the E-MagBook, a miniature laptop that has the following:

  - 32MB RAM

  - 300MHz processor

  - Miniature system disk using a stripped-down version of Windows (no swapping enabled)

  - BIOS specially developed for the E-MagBook

◆ The system always powers up by reinstating the memory environment from a "Saved To Disk" file, as a typical laptop functions. This file is created back in the workshop on a machine called "Mother."

◆ The E-Viewer must be completed in eight weeks.

In Chapter 2, we'll determine what's relevant and what's not relevant in this list.

The Text Book Format

Monty went on to discuss the formats that the E-MagBook would require. Format 1 is the "Text Book"—that is, a book or a magazine format composed of many pages, each of which contains only text. We discussed what Monty wants on a text-only page. Primarily, this format consists of a scrollable window for the page's contents plus the navigation control buttons that would be required to "turn" the pages. We discussed the main characteristics of a Text Book.

Because this is a high-end product, Monty wants the Text Book to have the capability for narration or for playing background music so that each page could be heard as well as seen—altogether, quite versatile. Not all books would have these capabilities, nor would each page. Talking books are nothing new. But, as Monty agreed, the capacity of the removable disks would have to increase a lot before recording lengthy books using this concept would be possible. However, he is also experimenting with miniature CD drives. Monty drew us a diagram of the Text Book format, using a whiteboard capable of producing an A4 standard paper-sized image of its content, which he could present to us. Figure 1.3 is a copy of what he drew.

Monty asked if everyone was okay so far (everyone seemed to be), and he pressed the button and handed an A4 paper copy of the diagram to Julie.

The Picture Album Format

Monty continued by describing Format 2, the "Picture Album." This format would consist of a picture or photograph album. Monty wants to be able to sell albums containing images with brief descriptive text. For example, an album might contain sites from the ancient world. Each photograph supplied would come with four or five descriptors—for example, a picture of the great pyramids might have descriptions such as "Egypt," "Pyramids," "Cheops," and so on.

Julie asked Monty if he was talking about keywords. Monty explained that we ought to call them "keys," because instead of "Egypt," he might want the description to be "Ancient Egypt." The idea was that users could thumb through the pages, much like they would do with a real picture book—backward, forward, and so on. Or, they could enter one or more keys and home in on a set of related pictures, scanning backward and forward just through that set. This capability would extend the navigation controls a bit.

Monty also wants to sell a kit, consisting of software and hardware, that would allow people to set up photograph albums on their PCs. The albums could be transferred to the removable

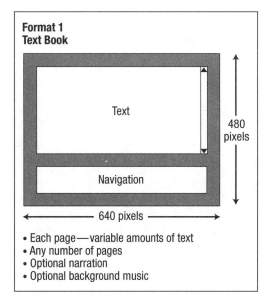

Figure 1.3
Diagrammatic version of Monty's hand drawing of a page from a Text Book.

disks (read/write versions, of course) for use in the viewer. Julie asked if the album was to contain sound and music capability; Monty replied that it would. He then drew a crude sketch of the basic format, as Figure 1.4 shows. This format was very similar to the Text Book, with the addition of information about the picture. Another press of the button and Monty handed Julie the second format.

Monty made it clear that photograph albums on PCs were an extension to the basic project. He wanted us to quote only for an E-Viewer, which would allow an album—regardless of where or how it was produced—to be viewed. He would handle the PC photograph album program development sometime in the future.

The Reference Book Format

Then, we came to the most interesting aspect of the requirements. Monty wants to be able to sell reference books, magazines, and so on. Ultimately (but not for the prototype), he wants a totally free format on a single page. He wants to lay the page out as he would a magazine page or a reference book. He wants the page to be able to accommodate any number of images, text, voice, music, and what he termed "hotspots." We called Format 3 the "Reference Book."

"What's a hotspot?" asked Archie. Monty explained that with a hotspot, when you move the cursor over a page, the cursor could change from an arrow to a hand—the sort of thing you see on Web pages. "Click here," and something happens. On the book page, a hotspot could be anything—more information, text, another picture, or a movie clip. At this point, he realized that he had forgotten to mention movie clips—the album page can be composed of a

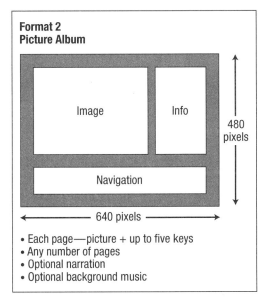

Figure 1.4
Diagrammatic version of Monty's hand drawing of a page from a Picture Album.

single picture or a single movie clip. Monty went on to say, "In fact, the reference page can be any combination of pictures, movie clips, text, sounds, and so on; it also can have a hotspot capability. And I want an editor to be able to create these pages."

There was silence. Monty finally broke the silence by telling us he thought trying to develop a viewer to do all that in eight weeks was too much. So, what he wanted for the prototype viewer was the ability to display a single picture, or a movie clip, unlimited text for each page, and the keys. Navigation capabilities similar to the album would be necessary. But—and this was important—whatever we were to design must not compromise the software's ability to handle the full reference page at a future date.

I was keen to get all this information captured in terms of a picture, and we split the Reference Book format into two types. For the prototype, we defined the "Simple Reference" format, quite simply, as an extension of the album. After several attempts and some haggling, we came up with a drawing for the Simple Reference format, as Figure 1.5 shows. And the ultimate in Monty's E-MagBook we agreed to call the "Extended Reference," or "Composite" format, which we had to be aware of, but not develop. For this format, Monty drew what you can see in Figure 1.6.

"Any questions?" asked Monty.

"Are you going to produce one prototype unit for each book type—I mean one for the Text Book, one for the Picture Album, and one for the Reference Book?" asked Julie after she had scanned through her copious notes. "Goodness no," said Monty. "I want a single E-Book to be capable of showing any format type."

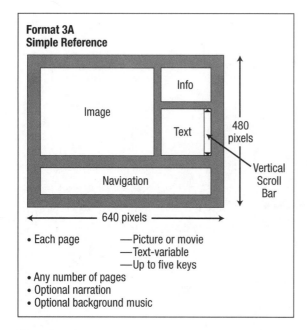

Figure 1.5
Diagrammatic version of Monty's hand drawing of a page from a Simple Reference Book.

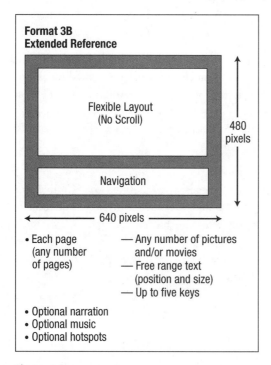

Figure 1.6
Diagrammatic version of Monty's hand drawing of a page from the Extended Reference Book.

What We've Learned So Far

The pictures really say it all. First is the Text Book format, containing a single scrollable text area, then we have the Picture Album format, consisting of an image (or video) only. Finally, within the Reference Book format, we have the Simple Reference and the Extended, or Composite, Reference formats. And, don't forget: Each page, regardless of format, can have a sound or music track associated with it.

Title Selection

Monty next described how a user would select a title. When a customer buys an E-MagBook disk, the disk may contain more than one title. Some titles might be text-only format, some might be albums, and some might be reference works. When the reader first switches the book on, the program will be in a state where the reader can insert an E-MagBook disk and click a button to read the titles on the disk. Up comes a list showing each title and a blurb about each one. The reader can go up and down the list, looking at titles and reading the blurbs, and select one of interest. The title is then read in, and page 1 displays, regardless of what type it is. The software will configure the screen according to the appropriate format type. At any time, the reader can request the titles and select another book. In fact, the reader can change disks and reread titles.

Julie asked if she was right in saying that once a reader selects a book and its format is determined, the format remains in effect until another title is loaded. Monty confirmed that was correct and stressed that the same must be true when we introduce the Extended Reference format. An E-MagBook running the old program will simply state that it cannot read the format and suggest that the user upgrade the software. A book with the new software will read all four format types.

Future Requirements

Monty continued, "I've outlined the job, I hope, and we've considered the extended format. But it won't end there. I want to be able to handle local Web pages as well as online Web pages." Archie gasped. "Don't panic, Archie," said Monty. "This is all in the future, but you have to think about it now. I don't want to throw all the software away and rewrite it each time we want to add new capability."

Archie asked how the system would be able to connect onto the Internet. Monty stated that he was going to build a mobile phone into the E-MagBook. Now, even I was impressed. He intended to make the unit bigger, allowing its display resolution to be increased to 800x600-pixels, but he indicated that it would still not be much larger than the prototype box that sat on the table.

"We want the book to operate within a number of different levels. From a standalone "take anywhere" book (within which you have a stack of E-disks containing hundreds of books, albums, and reference works), to the knowledge base (from which you pick a subject and obtain locally stored information with interactive ability; in addition, you have the capability to automatically go to the Web). When we get that far, we'll also be marketing it as a full-blown wireless Web browser. But that's another story."

As far as Monty was concerned, for HTML/Web-based books, where a page came from shouldn't matter. The page could be read from the removable disk, or it could come from a Web site in Outer Mongolia. We would need to come up with a structure that would allow the book to access the data it needs from wherever it is told to get the data.

At this stage, Monty thought that wrapped up requirements for the viewer. Next, he would get his graphic designer to talk to us about what she wants from an editor. He summarized that he wants the viewer eight weeks from Monday, and the editor could follow later. Monty disappeared to fetch his graphic designer.

So far, we had amassed a lot of information—some relevant, some not. We were now going to meet a second person, and a key aspect would be to ensure that her understanding of the requirements matched Monty's.

Different Presentation Forms

In our case study, we have a verbal presentation with notes, as well as diagrams, being generated on the fly. This example is one extreme of a presentation. At the opposite end of the scale, you can be presented with a huge document that describes the requirements in great detail. However the presentation happens, your introduction to the requirements is a very crucial time. This point is where you are obtaining new information—usually in large volumes—and you must come up to speed as swiftly as possible. You must be able to ask sensible questions to clarify issues that may arise as a result of the vagaries of language, either written or spoken.

The quality of the information you receive in a presentation varies enormously. Hopefully, the information is reasonably free of jargon. And where jargon is unavoidable, definitions assist in your interpretation. As we mentioned earlier in the chapter, your aim is to ensure that your interpretation of the requirement, in terms of the big picture, is the same as that of the customer. This agreement is crucial, because you will use this information to come up with a price and a timetable for turning the concept into working code.

The Responsibilities of Quoting

Where your customer gives you a large amount of prepared text—sometimes called a "statement of need," or an "operational requirement," or some other term that implies a list of requirements—you have to study this information in depth. If you become involved in providing a quote to a customer, you are responsible for committing your company to the project. Get the quote wrong, and you could put your company in jeopardy.

"But, surely, that's the job of the sales staff," I hear you say. Our company doesn't employ any salespeople at all. We have a handful of senior consultants—as well as the company's directors—who are allowed to make such commitments. These people are all software developers, and they can verify commitments they or others have made, based on their experience. In other words, we let only people capable of doing so provide quotes for work. In our experience, sales staff are very good at selling well-defined products (those that have a specification, can already be used, and are available off-the-shelf). A computer-literate salesperson can identify with, learn about, and then talk sensibly about such products to potential buyers.

Quoting for software development, however, is a completely different ball game. This process requires someone who is steeped in the development process and methodology, and who can assess situations quickly. Developments are all different, and it's unfair to expect a salesperson who has never developed a line of code to be able to quote for software development. Therefore, at some stage in you career, you have a very good chance of becoming involved in the work that must be done before the project starts. Companies that recognize this reality employ *sales engineers* to assist the sales staff in assessing potential business, responding to invitations to submit a quotation, and so forth. A sales engineer is someone with a lot of technical expertise and development experience who can provide all the assistance required to bring in a sale. That way, the sales staff can concentrate on the commercial aspects of the work.

In one company where I worked, we had such a problem with salespeople making technical commitments to clients that we reached a stage where an authorized technical resource had to evaluate every quotation. That person was responsible for ensuring that, first, what was being quoted was technically feasible, and, second, the timetables were not works of fiction. When we began that approach, a great number of quotes were rejected, until the sales staff appreciated that, if they made a commitment to a customer concerning a technical aspect of a project, the people who would have to carry out that work must be involved in the loop.

How much work must be done "up front," before a project actually starts, often surprises people. Even worse, you're quite often not paid for this effort—it's all part of the pre-sales cost of the market in which you operate.

Return to the Case Study:
The Editors

Getting back to our case study, we'd learned all about what was required of the viewer program, and Monty had gone off to find his graphic designer. He was soon back and introduced us to Samantha. She had worked for Monty for some years and now headed the graphics department. She was responsible for a whole range of things, from how a product should look, to the advertising that went with it. Her brief today was to explain to us what she needed an editor to be able to do. The floor was hers.

"Monty no doubt has explained to you what the three main formats are, and, hopefully, our ultimate goal of the free-format page, as I call it." Julie produced the A4 copies. Samantha cast a critical eye over the diagrams and then said she thought they summed up the basics. She looked up at Monty, "Did you mention pull-down menus?"

This was something Monty had forgotten to tell us. Simply stated, the display on the viewer was too small to provide pull-down menus, as the font would be difficult to read. So, all commands needed to be available on the navigation control area, with big font sizes on the captions. Once this had been explained, Samantha continued to inform us that she needed two editors: one to make up the E-MagBook Title Index that is resident on each removable disk, and one to make up the Page Index, for the books themselves. She pointed out that she had no idea how we would design these editors, but, clearly, she felt we needed something that defined each page's content. The editor would allow her to set up a given page in terms of the image, text, mini-descriptor, and so on.

When she mentioned the term *mini-descriptor*, Julie interrupted her. "The mini-descriptor?" queried Julie. Samantha glanced at the diagrams that Monty had produced. "Sorry, the keys."

"Okay," I said, "please excuse me for a moment, but can we make sure we all have the same definition as Samantha? A given page can have up to five keys. Each key can consist of one or more words to an unlimited number."

"Yes," responded Samantha, "although, because it's a miniature description, we can limit each line to, say, 20 or 30 characters. The keys will be used for searching as well, so each one shouldn't be too long." I checked—Monty was in agreement, and he nodded.

We went over the example that Monty had given us on "Ancient Egypt," and Samantha was quite comfortable with all that. So, we appeared to agree that the definition of *keys* was the same as what she had called the *mini-descriptor*, and we sized the key to something like 20 or 30 characters.

When more than one person becomes involved in any human endeavor, the problem of interpretation exists. Each person has an interpretation of the requirements, and that interpretation may or may not be the same as another person's. Part of our job is to look for potential disagreement and get it out into the open, so we can identify the true requirement. Samantha then produced a diagram of what she regarded as the book-creation process that was relevant to the editor she wanted us to develop. Samantha produced the diagram shown in Figure 1.7.

Samantha continued her description. Basically, Montasana would produce all the images (some might be JPEG; some might be BMP). They would use a variety of sources, scanners, digital cameras, library images, and so on. Each book would be composed of a collection of images of different formats; some images would be very high quality.

The Forgotten Workbench Functionality

Samantha asked if Monty had mentioned the capability to blow up, or enlarge, the images on the viewer. Clearly, Monty had forgotten to mention this vital piece of functionality. Samantha explained that this functionality applied to Picture Album and Reference Book formats only. This capability would let readers use simple controls to manipulate the dimensions and posi-

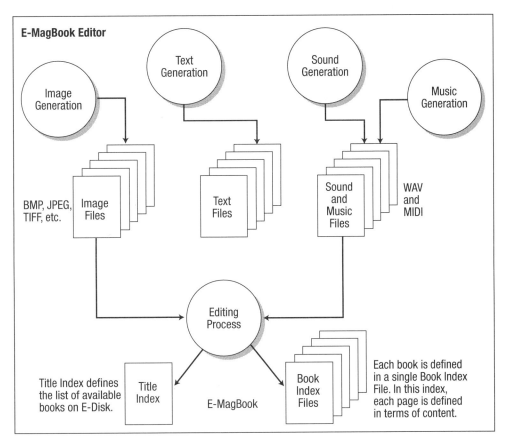

E-MagBook Editor

Image Generation

Text Generation

Sound Generation

Music Generation

BMP, JPEG, TIFF, etc.   Image Files

Text Files

Sound and Music Files   WAV and MIDI

Editing Process

Title Index defines the list of available books on E-Disk.   Title Index

E-MagBook

Book Index Files

Each book is defined in a single Book Index File. In this index, each page is defined in terms of content.

Figure 1.7
Diagrammatic representation of the E-MagBook creation process.

tion of a single image within the viewer—including enlarging the image any number of times—to have a detailed look at the picture (the sort of thing most paint and graphics software packages let you do).

For example, the E-MagBook might have a high-quality image of a famous painting on view, and a narration instructing readers to enlarge the picture. Then, readers could look at a segment of the canvas in more detail while the narration talked about it. I asked if this function was separate from the standard page viewer. Samantha confirmed that it was, and she envisioned a button on the navigation controls that would let readers switch to what she termed a "Workbench" screen, where they would see the image at full size. They would be able to shrink, expand, or move the image around, doing whatever necessary to look at any portion in detail. For Reference Book pages, she also wanted the text to be displayed as an option in this mode, with a text on/off switch control. She wanted readers to be able to set up the image on the screen, together with the text, for a hard-copy print out.

"Is this for a printer connected directly to the E-MagBook?" asked Archie. (He still hadn't written very much, whereas Julie was on to her sixth page.)

"That's right. It will act as a hard-copy function. We hope to use some of the miniature printers currently available, with a parallel connector between them."

Samantha asked us if this had been an adequate introduction to the Workbench format. We all agreed that it had been, and she went on with the editor.

Returning to the Editor

Returning to her diagram, Samantha explained that they would go through a number of processes to produce the images, text, and sounds. For example, they had all the facilities to scan and process images, as she had mentioned before. They had digital cameras for both stills and movies. They intended to build a sound studio for any recording they needed to produce, although they would probably commission—or buy—the majority of music and specialized sound files they needed.

They would set up text files using word processors, so they could spellcheck the content. But, if it helped us, she said they would be glad to produce a single text file for each page. In fact, doing so would make life easier for them. Having a self-contained collection of files per page would simplify the logistics of handling the files. They could then use the editor to "sew" the files together in a structure that defined the content of each page for a given title. They intended to use standard files for multimedia: BMP, JPEG, and so on for the stills; AVI for the movies; WAV for the sound; and MIDI for the music. Archie and I knew what all these things were, but Julie clearly did not; we would go over the details with her later.

Samantha continued, "We have made a decision that the E-MagBook will be composed of standard components and run standard Windows—even though Monty will work some magic on it and the BIOS (whatever that is). We will use only standard graphics and multimedia file formats. The editors will run on a standard PC, with a minimum screen resolution of 800x600 pixels, but probably higher. Because most of us have 800x600-pixel laptop screens, however, it is important that the software works at that resolution as well."

Julie asked if the editor would need to run on the E-MagBook hardware. Samantha explained that a 640x480-pixel screen wouldn't be big enough to accommodate the editor, because it needs to provide all the necessary facilities to build a page. That is, they would need the editor to string together all the components—the image, text, sound, and so on—and see the end result as it would look on the viewer. They would need to set fonts, and so forth. They would also need to manipulate the text so they could format it as it would look on the viewer. In other words, how a page looks in the editor must be identical to how it would look on the viewer. And, of course, they'd want a facility to type in the five keys.

They also needed an editor to let them create and amend the Title Index structures on each removable disk. The Title Index would contain a title in free text and a short description. For example, the title might be "The Complete Gardener's Reference," and the description might tell you what a wonderful reference book this is for gardeners. The decision about whether this facility would be part of the page editor or a separate facility was left to us.

Samantha looked at Monty. "I think that's about it, unless you have anything to add, Monty." He didn't. "Are there any questions?" she asked.

"Only about a million," said Julie, "but I think we need to go away and digest all this."

"Good idea," said Monty. "Today's Tuesday. I want the quotes in by close of business Friday evening, if that's OK?"

"Have you met with the other companies yet?" I asked.

"No, you're the first. I must apologize for being so disorganized. We've simply not had time to produce any decent documentation, apart from Samantha's diagram, because we want to give you the maximum time to quote before the end-of-the-week deadline. You must appreciate that we decided to go out to tender bids only yesterday. One of the other two companies is coming in this afternoon, and the other this evening. We'll go through the same process with them. And don't worry, Kieron; if anything else crops up that we've forgotten to tell you, I'll be on the phone to you."

"Thanks, Monty," I said. As I mentioned earlier, the quality of information that you will get at an initial meeting of this sort varies enormously—for example, from the quick sketches of Monty's format requirements, to the more formal diagrams of Samantha's editor. In our situation, a minimum of documentation was available to us, with Monty and Samantha imparting most of the information verbally. In some situations, the presentation might even include a detailed requirement specification, so you can start from Phase 2 of the SDLC. The possibilities all make for rich variety.

I asked when they would make a decision, and Monty told me he and Samantha intended to review all the quotes over the weekend and then have an early morning session on Monday to make a final decision. He would telephone the result to all three potential suppliers at 9 A.M. Monday morning.

So, by Monday morning, we would know the outcome of the next few days' efforts. All we had to do was take the information that had been fired at us and convert it into a quotation that would let us do the job on time, within budget, and with a reasonable profit. As we came away, both Archie and Julie were bubbling with excitement. When we got back to the office, they still had a final orientation session with Charlie. We agreed that we would start the presales drive to win the E-MagBook project the following morning.

Later that evening, Charlie and I discussed the situation. We went through all the things I was supposed to do for the next three days and released as much time for me as possible. I had to confess that I also wanted this project—not just for Archie's and Julie's sake. Some of Monty's enthusiasm had rubbed off on me as well. We had three days in which to estimate the size of the job, produce a proposal and a plan, and price the work so that Monty would choose us as his supplier.

A Recap

We learned about this potential project in the following stages:

1. We heard about the E-MagBook in general terms.

2. We received more detailed aspects of the requirements for the viewer.

3. We obtained some diagrams that neatly illustrated how the viewer was to handle each of the different page types. (These diagrams actually gave us quite a good feel for the requirement already.)

4. The explanation of the editors' functionality clarified for us the requirements for designing and developing the Title Index and the Page Index that are components of an electronic book.

The Next Step

We'd now looked at a methodology for software development that involved the system development life cycle, or SDLC. We'd been introduced to the concept of an electronic book, and we'd listened to a big-picture description of the software requirements to make this concept come to life. So, what were we to do next?

Monty wanted us to quote for the work, in competition with two other companies. We needed to assess the project's complexity, determine how much time and effort it would take to complete, see whether we could meet the requirement to complete the viewer in the time imposed, and determine whether we could make a profit.

Quite a tall order, really. But we'd employ our methodology to help us in the pre-sales phase. In the next chapter, you'll see what we did in the three days at our disposal to complete the quotation and deliver it to Monty.

Chapter 2
The Proposal

In this chapter, we're going to look at what we need to do to win an order once the customer has presented the initial concept and asked for a quote. We need to perform a very preliminary pass of Phases 1 and 2 from the SDLC—that is capture the "big picture" requirements and perform a preliminary analysis on them to gain a reasonable understanding of the project's complexities. We will then make a full list of the activities that we need to complete to turn the concept into software. From the result of all this work, we will (hopefully) obtain sufficient information to come up with a proposal for the customer that includes a timetable and a price that ensures our selection as the supplier.

We'll use the case study that we started in Chapter 1 to illustrate all this, showing what happened in the three days after the concept talk with Monty and Samantha. We'll also look at risk analysis, and we'll take some time to perform a feasibility study to assess what we consider, at this stage, to be the main risk factor in the case study—our ability to meet the multimedia requirements. It's a tight schedule, and, if we don't get the job, all our investment in the time we've spent will be lost.

The Pre-Sales Effort

First, you need to determine how long you want to spend on any *pre-sales effort*. The time needs to be long enough for you to make a good assessment of the complexities of the project, so you can come up with a valid quotation. However, this effort shouldn't take up too much time, because, if you don't win the contract, you don't get paid for any effort you have put in. Clearly, you will have a number of considerations—most importantly, answers to the questions, Can you do the job if you get it? and Do you want the job in the first place?

The pre-sales phase of a prospective project includes the following:

♦ *Preliminary capturing of the requirements*—You will go through all the information you have, to come up with a list of the high-level, or overall, requirements.

- *Analysis of the captured requirements*—You will analyze the high-level requirements in an attempt to produce enough information about the complexities of the software to be developed so you can make a realistic quote.

- *Assessment of risk*—What you have learned to date will let you assess the areas of risk and possibly do some work to minimize the impact of those areas—or at least highlight them in the proposal.

- *Production of an activity list*—Based on your methodology for development projects and the results of the analysis, you will come up with a list of activities that you must complete within the project.

- *Estimates*—From the activity list and the level of understanding that you have gained from your capture of the high-level requirements, your analysis, and any risk assessment you have performed, you will attempt to estimate the time each activity will take to complete.

- *Production of a plan*—You convert the activity list and estimates to a project plan.

- *Costing*—You can take the estimates and cost them according to a variety of criteria.

- *Production of a proposal*—You produce a proposal, with cost estimates and timetables, for the client.

If this all sounds like a tall order, it is. But you must remember that, without it, you may be putting yourself, your company, or both at serious risk. Following this methodology at least ensures that you proceed in a structured and coordinated manner, so that your estimates are based on sensible criteria. Assuming you think you can do the job and you want the work, the next step is to come up with a plan of action for the pre-sales effort.

Requirements and Analysis

You will need to perform one pass of Phases 1 and 2 in the SDLC (capture the high-level requirements and perform some analysis on them). As we mentioned, the purpose of this analysis is to give you sufficient understanding of the project's complexities. Without an analysis, you can't possibly estimate the amount of work that will be involved, unless the project is very similar to one you have already done. That's not usually the situation, but if this project is like a previous one, you already have a model from which to price the new project.

Completing the preliminary capture and analysis phases will be an enormous help in identifying and analyzing the project's risk. Simply because you are thinking about and analyzing each requirement, any areas of technical risk should become evident. For example, if the requirements demand integration with a virtual reality package, with which you have no experience, then the risk to you is in finding a suitable package. You will need to evaluate the software to see that it matches the requirements, can provide an acceptable level of reliability, and will integrate with your solution.

Activity Estimates

After you complete your analysis, the next step is to make a list of everything that needs to be done to complete the project. You will need to provide estimates for each single activity on the list. List items might involve any of the following:

- Detailed requirements capture
- Analysis
- Design
- Development
- Testing
- Installation
- Review time
- Iteration time

You will encounter many unknowns here. In the case study, we'll look at ways in which our company tackled such problems, either by doing some extra work or by estimating in a way that took into account our level of uncertainty.

Timetables

From the estimates you produce, you can see what sorts of timetables are involved, tempering them by a measure of the uncertainty you determined from the estimating techniques. The result of all this work is a plan for the project and a qualified estimate of the effort required, from which you can calculate costs. Finally, you can put together a proposal for the customer. This proposal can address both the positive and negative parts of the project; it can even present a case for some paid feasibility work to be a part of the job.

In large projects, this pre-sales phase can be a mini-project all its own, involving many people. Although this activity encompasses two phases of the SDLC—capturing and analyzing the overall requirements—you are conducting those phases at a superficial level. All you need at this point to turn the concept into the software is sufficient information to make an estimate of the work involved. Let's see how all this information applies to our case study.

The Case Study:
Plan of Action

To begin with, we were restricted to a maximum of three days to complete our pre-sales effort (we met with Montasana Systems on Tuesday afternoon, and Monty required the quotation by the end of Friday). For this pre-sales phase of the project, our initial plan was to do the preliminary capture of high-level requirements and their analysis on Day 1. Neither Archie nor Julie had any experience handling images or multimedia. So, in terms of risk analysis, the three of us had already determined that we wanted to do some feasibility work in this area to gauge its complexity. Doing all this the first day would be good progress, so we set that as a target.

We reserved the second day to build a list of the activities that we needed to perform, from which we would estimate the effort required. Based on these estimates, we would produce and verify our first version of a project plan. Achieving all this in the second day would be excellent progress.

For the third day, based on the estimates, we would produce a proposal and come up with a quote. Preparing the proposal and quote shouldn't take us the whole day, so we would use any spare capacity as contingency time. In other words, if we started losing time in Days 1 and 2, we would have a cushion of half a day to absorb any overruns. Because this plan was for pre-sales effort and of short duration, it was very basic. We would gauge progress each evening simply by whether we had accomplished our designated tasks for that day. Figure 2.1 outlines this plan.

To recap, Figure 2.1 shows the three-day period in three equal sections. Within each day, thick black lines mark the activities. We had allocated a third of the day to each activity. This time frame was an arbitrary figure. At this stage, we would be quite happy if, at the end of each day, we had completed the allocated tasks for that day. Finally, we built contingency time into the final day, in case we overran any of the planned activities.

Capturing the Requirements

When you are gathering a list of your project requirements, go through any notes you made at the preliminary meeting (like the meeting we depicted in the first chapter) as soon as you can, while the information is still fresh in your mind. As I've mentioned, you should come up with a simple, descriptive list of the overall requirements. Usually, the time frame for performing this activity is very short in the pre-sales stage. And, it's essential that you avoid too much detail. A good test of the completed list is to scan through the notes you have made and be sure that you can categorize each reference to a piece of the functionality into one of the items in your top-level list.

Identifying Areas of Risk

Be on the lookout for areas of functionality that you think might represent severe risk to the project, particularly from a technical point of view. Such an area might be one in which you and the rest of the company have little or no experience, or it might be one that involves new and untried technology.

For example, component technology is an area of enormous potential to developers, because it offers building blocks that let you develop software with vastly reduced development times. However, the promises that components offer can lull you into a false sense of security. As an example, consider a set of requirements in which one requirement is to produce graphs in realtime that show the state of a number of physical processes. One graph might represent temperature; another, pressure; another, humidity, and so forth. A wealth of graphics components is available that you can slot into your program, assuming you are using a development

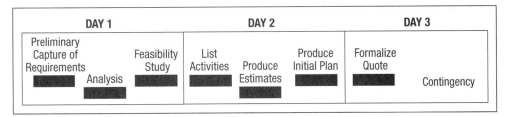

Figure 2.1
The plan for the pre-sales effort.

language that is capable of interfacing to components. The risk with this approach is that you choose a component that can't do exactly what you require. The component may have limitations you are unaware of, but which mean, when you put it into use, it doesn't meet the detailed requirement.

Here's the problem. You won't know what the detailed requirement is until you start Phase 1 of the project, and you won't know exactly what the component can do until you've fully evaluated it. If you have extensive experience in graphics components, you probably won't have any trouble; if you've never used such components before, then you need to be wary. Clearly then, using a component to address part of the requirements is a potential area of risk.

Return to the Case Study:
A Project Title and Some Hardware Constraints

We described the project in this case study as the *E-MagBook Software Development* project. If you recall, we talked a lot initially about hardware. The E-MagBook would consist of standard PC architecture, and it would include a 300MHz clock, 32MB RAM, and a full-color 640x480-pixel screen. What was the most relevant specification here? From a programming point of view, memory and clock speed were totally irrelevant. The standard PC architecture was important. Also, the screen size would place a limitation on the GUI (graphical user interface) design and was, therefore, an important requirement.

We summarized the previous points as "standard PC architecture with a 640x480-pixel screen size." We weren't interested in physical dimensions or battery time; we were interested in summarizing only the elements that would affect the software we had to write. Although disk size didn't directly affect the software, the disk volumes were quite small by modern PC standards, so including that information in the summary points might be a good idea—just to keep attention on the fact that we couldn't develop huge volumes of code.

We summarized the disk situation as "200MB system disk with 100MB removable E-disk." The disk situation triggered a discussion about storing the data that describes the book pages, the multimedia file components, the text, and the book Index structures. We toyed with the idea of using Microsoft's Access database to store all the keys, text, and pointers to the multimedia files. (To store a sound track, an image, or a video clip in a database would require

BLOB [Binary Large Object] support, which would let the database store large binary data objects as records. Most low-cost database systems don't have this type of support, so our idea was to store only the file references and keys in a database.)

A New Constraint

We were halfway through the discussion, having determined that using a database might require a substantial amount of disk—on both the system and removable disks—when I received a call from Monty. Coincidentally, he wanted to inform us that, yesterday evening, one of the other companies had brought up the subject of a database. The company representatives had asked Monty if he had a preferred database. He said that under no circumstances was a proprietary database to be involved, because that approach would hit his unit costs too hard. However access to the page descriptions and multimedia files would occur, it must not involve a database that would incur unacceptable license fees. Fortunately, we hadn't yet gone very far down the database discussion route. Clearly, this requirement formed a major constraint: Use no proprietary database packages.

As you'll recall, in the original meeting, Monty had talked about how Montasana was going to set up Windows and the BIOS to load the application from power-up, so that the E-MagBook would always start in a consistent state. He had described this approach as "how 'Mother' intended it." If you recall, Mother's copy of memory, set up running the viewer and all ready for action, had been saved to disk. Montasana would then copy this "memory-saved image" to all E-MagBooks' system disks. The system would then use this "restore" image to load the operating system and application at start-up time, from the E-MagBook's system disk. Monty would handle all the required modifications to the BIOS to make it work, and he would be in charge of Mother. So, interesting though this part of the process may be, none of it affected what we had to write.

Summary of Hardware Constraints

Already, we're building a picture of summary requirements for the E-MagBook Software Development project, as determined so far. We can define these requirements as follows:

Hardware
Standard PC architecture with a 640×480-pixel screen size.

200MB system disk with 100MB removable E-Disk.

No proprietary database packages to be used.

The Main Programs

As we hunted through our notes, we were able to define three basic program requirements. Monty wanted a viewer that would run on the E-MagBook and allow users to read a book. The E-MagBook's hardware would be a constraint on this program, which we called the E-Viewer. Then, Samantha had defined the need for two programs: an editor to create and edit page descriptions for a book, and a Title Editor to create the title Indexes for each removable disk. These two programs could run on standard PCs, and they would not execute on the E-MagBook. Furthermore, their minimum screen size would be 800x600 pixels. We'd call the programs E-TitleEditor and E-PageEditor.

Imposed Time Schedule

A major project constraint was that we must complete the E-Viewer by eight weeks from the following Monday. The editors, which could follow later, had no such constraint. We can summarize all this as follows:

Programs Required

E-Viewer to run on E-MagBook (fixed screen: 640×480 pixels), delivery required in eight weeks.

E-TitleEditor and E-PageEditor (minimum screen: 800×600 pixels) to run on standard PCs.

Page Format Types

Next, we looked at the book format types. Fortunately, we had Monty's drawings captured on A4 (8.27×11.69-inch) sheets of paper. In terms of the requirements, these drawings succinctly defined each format type. The five E-MagBook format types were Text Book, Picture Album, Reference Book (which, in turn, includes the Simple Reference and the Extended, or Composite, Reference formats), and HTML/Web. The first drop of the viewer (required in eight weeks) required only the first three formats (Text Book, Picture Album, and Simple Reference). However, we needed to keep the future requirements in mind, to ensure that nothing we did now would compromise our ability to extend the software in the future. Monty wanted to avoid having to throw away the programs we developed now and start over again, just to accommodate the Extended Reference format or the Web-access requirements.

(If you recall, the Picture Album and Reference Book formats could either display an image or play a video clip. The drawings do not depict these options, because they developed from discussions that followed the drawings.) At the end of our deliberations, we summarized the formats as follows:

Text Book Format

Variable amount of text for each page.

Any number of pages.

Optional narration for each page.

Optional background music for each page.

Picture Album Format

Single image or movie clip for each page.

Up to five keys per page.

Any number of pages.

Optional narration for each page.

Optional background music for each page.

(Simple) Reference Book Format
Single image or movie clip for each page.

Variable amount of text for each page.

Up to five keys per page.

Any number of pages.

Optional narration for each page.

Optional background music for each page.

These are the three formats that the viewer must support at the end of eight weeks. We summarized the Extended Reference format and the HTML/Web format as follows:

Extended Reference Format (Future Requirement)
Any number of pictures and/or movies.

Any number of independent text blocks.

Up to five keys per page.

Any number of pages.

Optional narration for each page.

Optional background music for each page.

Hotspot capability.

HTML/Web (Internet) Access (Future Requirement)
Ability to view HMTL pages on removable disks or as Web pages.

Any number of local HTML pages or remote.

Automatic Internet access.

Up to five keys per page.

Any number of pages.

Optional narration of each page.

Optional background music for each page.

Browser controlled.

As you can see, from just the few notes we had made so far, a reasonable high-level picture of the requirements was developing.

Viewer Modes of Operation

The viewer needed to operate in one of the three modes Monty and Samantha had defined. In the first mode, a reader could select a title from a removable disk. At that point, he or she could view the book and turn the pages. Finally, the reader could invoke the "Workbench" mode, as Samantha defined it, in which the reader could expand an image and move it about. This mode also would allow the reader to set up the text and picture for a printout.

The editors would function, primarily, in a single "edit" mode. However, the Page Editor must be able to run all three viewer modes so the operator could see what had been done to a given page he or she was creating or editing. We can summarize all this as follows:

Viewer Operational Modes
Title selection

Page view

Workbench

Title Index Editor Operational Modes
Edit mode only

Page Index Editor Operational Modes
Edit mode

Title selection

Page view

Workbench

Both Archie and Julie had lots of questions about how we were going to accomplish various tasks. For example, How would we implement the Workbench in the viewer program? How were we going to manage without a database? And so on.

At this stage, we are concentrating on capturing the requirements—that's our goal, and we don't want to be side-tracked. (This focus can be quite difficult because, as programmers, we are always thinking about how we are going to meet a particular requirement.) At this stage, we had to be objective and totally dedicated to the purpose of capturing requirements.

As we go on, you will see how, in real life—and to minimize risks—looking at how you can do things is perfectly acceptable. The important point to remember is that the how-to's must not get in the way of capturing what the user requires.

Summary of Notes

Having combined all the preceding notes with the format diagrams Monty produced, we had a succinct version of the high-level requirements at this stage. We had also converted the hand-written diagrams to something a little more formal:

Summary Points for E-MagBook Requirements—Part 1

Hardware
Standard PC architecture with a 640×480-pixel screen size.

200MB system disk with 100MB removable E-disk.

No proprietary database packages to be used.

Programs Required
E-Viewer to run on E-MagBook (fixed screen: 640×480 pixels), delivery required in eight weeks.

E-TitleEditor and E-PageEditor (minimum screen: 600×800 pixels) to run on standard PCs.

Book Formats to Support

Text Book Format
Variable amount of text for each page.

Any number of pages.

Optional narration for each page.

Optional background music for each page.

Picture Album Format
Single image or movie clip for each page.

Up to five keys per page.

Any number of pages.

Optional narration for each page.

Optional background music for each page.

(Simple) Reference Format
Single image or movie clip for each page.

Variable amount of text for each page.

Up to five keys per page.

Any number of pages.

Optional narration for each page.

Optional background music for each page.

Extended Reference Format (Future Requirement)
Any number of pictures and/or movies.

Any number of independent text blocks.

Up to five keys per page.

Any number of pages.

Optional narration for each page.

Optional background music for each page.

Hotspot capability.

HTML/Web (Internet) Access (Future Requirement)
Ability to view HMTL pages on removable disk or as Web pages.

Any number of local HTML pages or remote.

Automatic Internet access.

Up to five keys per page.

Any number of pages.

Optional narration for each page.

Optional background music for each page.

Browser controlled.

Viewer Operational Modes
Title selection

Page view

Workbench

Title Index Editor Operational Modes
Edit mode only

Page Index Editor Operational Modes
Edit mode

Title selection

Page view

Workbench

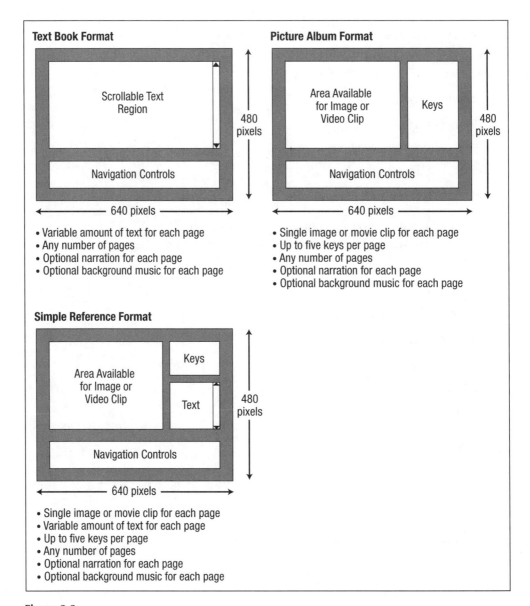

Figure 2.2
The Text Book, Picture Album, and Simple Reference formats for the E-MagBook.

You can see the modified diagrams in Figures 2.2 and 2.3. Note that we added one diagram to show how a browser would integrate into the viewer.

Don't forget, this was only a first pass at capturing the requirements. All we were interested in here was getting enough information from which to make a proposal and quote an "informed" price and timetable.

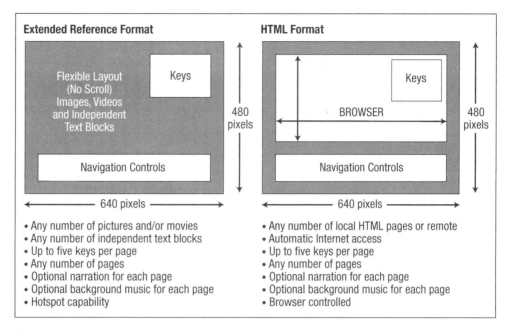

Figure 2.3
Extended Reference and HTML/Web formats for the E-MagBook.

Risks of Leading-Edge Technology

All software development projects contain risks. Even when you're working in a totally familiar area, you are bound to come across something new—something you have never done before. If you are developing software for a living, steer clear of leading-edge technology. For example, the customer for whom you are trying to build an inventory control system will not thank you if you base your solution upon a brand new technology (hardware or software). Such technology is bound to be a bit unreliable, and if it affects the customer's software—in terms of either robustness or performance—in a negative manner, you could be in serious trouble.

This principle applies to operating system environments, development languages, and hardware platforms in particular. Use technology that's been around for a while. One thing I dread to hear when I call a supplier is, "That's interesting; no one's ever done that with our system before. I can't really say I'm surprised it doesn't work!" If your solution is going to rely on third-party hardware or software, you need to be sure that hardware or software is up to the task. If determining its appropriateness involves doing some extra work, cost that work into the project. And if no other solution is available to you, make the customer aware of the risk.

Using Leading-Edge Technology

Sometimes, a client may even demand that you employ a given piece of leading-edge—or "bleeding edge," as it's often described—technology. If the client is forcing this option on you, make sure that you identify the risks to the client and leave a contingency in the plan for having to cope with problems. Using any third-party products can represent a significant risk factor to the project, not only in terms of whether the products are up to the task, but also in terms of the support you are likely to get from the supplier if something goes wrong. This risk factor applies to components as well.

And even though a technology has been around a fair while and its capabilities have been proven, you and your team may be totally unfamiliar with it. It is risky to base quotations on technology with which you have no experience, and you need to identify that risk. Clearly, as you list the requirements at this top level, you can ask yourself Does this requirement and its likely solution pose any risk? For example, in the case study, we had two people (Archie and Julie) involved in estimating for a project that would involve heavy use of multimedia technology. They had no experience with such software. Consequently, designing any functionality associated with image, video, or sound handling placed us at risk, and we needed to find a way to minimize the risk so we could make a reasonable quote.

Minimizing Risk

How you minimize risk depends on the nature of the risk itself, but doing so frequently involves evaluation exercises or feasibility studies. You will hear a lot about these activities in the near future. If you can overcome an area of concern by imposing a restriction on the functionality involved, seek the customer's approval for the restriction, and put it in writing. You can place such restrictions in the proposal at the pre-sales stage. That way, the restriction is out in the open, and the customer can either accept the proposal with its restrictions or reject it. The important factor is that you don't hide the issue. Hiding issues simply to win the job usually has a way of catching up with you in the end—often with a vengeance. By then, the sentiment "If only we'd addressed this issue when it first came to light, in the pre-sales stage…" is irrelevant.

Return to the Case Study:
Viewer and Editor Requirements

Next, we decided to look at the viewer's modes of operation in a little more detail and make a list of key requirements. When we had completed those evaluations, we moved on to requirements for the Title Index Editor and Page Editor.

Viewer Workbench Requirements

If you recall, the Workbench was quite an important piece of functionality that Monty had forgotten to tell us about. To review, he wanted to display the image, on its own, for the Picture Album format and the image plus text for the Reference Book mode, on the Workbench screen. He wanted to be able to move the image and/or the text around the screen; he also wanted to be able to change the size of the two objects.

We decided to extend this facility to the Text Book format, to allow the text to be printed, because printing was defined as a function of the Workbench mode. This extension would provide a standard printing method for all three initial format types. Printing would consist of producing a bitmapped representation of whatever was on the screen. In theory, this approach meant we would also be able to print Extended Reference and HTML/Web pages using the Workbench concept. (The only difference would be that those pages would not require the functionality to change size and position screen objects.)

Already, we were starting to impose restrictions on functionality. (Such restrictions are acceptable at this stage, provided you make them clear to the customer in the proposal, and the customer accepts the limitations.) We could consider an image and a text box as screen objects. Each entity would have a length and a height (the dimensions) as well as a coordinate position on the screen. We could manipulate these attributes to change the size and position of the image. Consequently, we could summarize the functionality required for the Workbench as follows:

Workbench Requirements for Text Book, Picture Album, and Reference Book Formats
Allows screen objects to be sized and positioned on screen.

Allows content of screen to be printed as a screen dump.

Workbench Requirements for Extended Reference and HTML/Web Formats
Allows content of screen to be printed as a screen dump.

Viewer Navigation Requirements

Next, we looked at the requirements for what we have described as "navigation," available only in view mode. We needed to be able to navigate through the pages backward and forward—that is "turn the pages"—and we needed to be able to use the keys to search.

The search facility was centered around the keys that could be assigned to each page of a book, with the exception of the Text Book format. To review, each page would have a maximum of five keys, each of which could be 20 or 30 characters of totally free text. In other words, the key could consist of one or more words.

We summarized navigation as follows:

Viewer Navigation Requirements
Ability to turn the pages of a book backward and forward.

Ability to access pages by searching on keys.

Keys (All Formats Except Text Book)
Each page has up to five keys.

Each key is free format up to a maximum of 30 characters.

As you can see, at this stage, we imposed an absolute maximum per key of 30 characters, a figure mentioned at the meeting.

Image and Multimedia File Requirements

In terms of requirements, we need to be able to display images and video clips, and to play sound tracks and music. Samantha had mentioned a whole range of image and multimedia file formats they would use to create the page content: BMP, JPEG, AVI, WAV, and MIDI files. Archie knew what most of these formats were, but Julie was in the dark. As we've already discussed, they both recognized that the whole area of multimedia file handling was a big risk in the project because of their lack of experience. As a result, we decided to leave that issue for the time being and get on with capturing more requirements. We would look at the multimedia aspects in more detail at a suitable time and conduct some feasibility work to see what these requirements demanded from a technical standpoint. Remember, our quotation would need to take into account our assessment of how much work we would need to do to meet the project requirement for handling multimedia files. We would have to do some work to gauge this aspect of the project. As part of our initial capture, we summarized image and multimedia requirements with the following statement:

Image and Multimedia File Requirements
Display images and video clips.

Play sound and music.

IDENTIFIED AS MAIN AREA OF RISK—Requires some feasibility work.

Title Editor Requirements

The Title Editor must allow an operator to create a list of titles—i.e., a Title Index—from scratch; it also must allow the operator to amend an existing or newly created Title Index. This Title Index would define the disk's content in terms of available books of any format; it would appear on a removable disk. Each entry in the Title Index would define a single title in more detail. We specified the required functionality as follows:

Title Index Editor Requirements
Must allow creation of a Title Index.

Must allow amendment of an existing Title Index.

Each entry consists of the following: Book Title, Description, Reference to Page Index (for the book).

At this stage, this definition of the Title Editor requirements is sufficient.

Page Index Editor Requirements

The high-level requirement for the Page Index Editor was essentially the same as that of the Title Index Editor. We summarized this basic requirement list as follows:

Title Page Editor Requirements

Must allow creation of a Page Index.

Must allow amendment of an existing Page Index.

Must allow viewing of the edited page in the same manner as that available on the viewer.

Each entry consists of the following: up to five keys, text, image, video, sound, and HTML/Web references, according to format.

Enough Capturing for Now

Putting everything together, we could now add the following to our summary list of requirements:

Summary Points for E-MagBook Requirements—Part 2

Workbench Requirements for Text Book, Picture Album, and Reference Book Formats

Allows screen objects to be sized and positioned on screen.

Allows content of screen to be printed as a screen dump.

Workbench Requirements for Extended Reference and HTML/Web Formats

Allows content of screen to be printed as a screen dump.

Viewer Navigation Requirements

Ability to turn the pages of a book backward and forward.

Ability to access pages by searching on keys.

Keys (All Formats Except Text Book)

Each page has up to five keys.

Each key is free format up to a maximum of 30 characters.

Images and Multimedia File Requirements

Display images and video clips.

Play sound and music.

IDENTIFIED AS MAIN AREA OF RISK—Requires some feasibility work.

Title Index Editor Requirements

Must allow creation of a Title Index.

Must allow amendment of an existing Title Index.

Each entry consists of the following: Book Title, Description, Reference to Page Index (for the book).

Title Page Editor Requirements
Must allow creation of a Page Index.

Must allow amendment of an existing Page Index.

Must allow viewing of the edited page in the same manner as that available on the viewer.

Each entry consists of the following: up to five keys, text, image, video, sound, and HTML/Web references, according to format.

Lessons to Learn

The process you've seen in action in the case study—that of extracting the key requirements from a mass of information and documenting those requirements—illustrates a number of points:

♦ Unless you are very experienced in going to meetings and extracting the key points for a software development project, go with at least one other person—preferably someone who has more experience than you.

♦ Take notes. What format these notes take is really a matter of personal preference. I prefer to make bullet points, with small amounts of descriptive text—often just a few words (not full sentences).

♦ Perform the capturing session as soon after the meeting as you can so its contents are still fresh in your mind.

♦ Don't get bogged down by detail. You are simply listing the main requirements.

♦ Don't get side tracked by considering how you will address the requirements in code.

♦ Be on the lookout for areas of high risk, and mark those areas clearly so you can consider them in more detail later.

♦ For commercial projects, where your profit and reputation are at stake, steer clear of leading-edge technology, unless you have no choice. Such technology always increases the risk factor. If the client is forcing you down a particular path, you need to make sure that your company doesn't carry the responsibility for someone else's problems. You can handle projects that use state-of-the-art technology in other ways, and we'll look at that subject in more detail later.

♦ Above all, don't take everything that you have been told as 100 percent accurate or final. People are fallible and can make mistakes. You may even develop a better definition of a requirement than the customer does—just try to keep your enthusiasm inside commercial boundaries.

♦ Never lose track of the fact that the customer must pay for the work you will do, and customers want value for money.

The Preliminary Analysis

In our case study, we performed a preliminary capture of the requirements, at the highest level, producing a list of *summary points*. This list was our first piece of project documentation. For a large project, this preliminary list might be quite substantial. The list serves as a focus for all the subsequent activities you undertake; you can add to and modify the list as things progress.

Analysis is the process whereby a complex situation is broken down into its constituent components. Initially, you can concentrate on analyzing the data entities, then you can analyze the requirements in terms of basic functional components; you also can do some calculations on data associated with the requirements. For example, the rate at which the solution will have to process inputs and provide outputs as well as data volumes that must be handled.

Breaking Down Requirements

You must now perform a preliminary analysis of your initial requirement list. This means you need to look at the requirements from a different perspective. First, you'll try to determine the key data requirements. Doing so will give you a view of the requirements in terms of data components only; from that view, you will work out how the data-component requirements relate to each other, based on your current understanding of those requirements. You can sum all this up in a simple diagram known as an *entity relationship diagram*, which shows each data entity and how it relates to the others. (We used very simplistic forms of these diagrams in our case study.)

In the full analysis, you also can produce diagrams that show how programs will move from one operational state to another and what events trigger such changes. These diagrams present another view of the requirements, as do diagrams that show input and output to a program. All these different viewpoints help you to better understand the requirements.

Functional Requirements

In the case study, another of our tasks was to look at the requirement list and see whether we could come up with an alternative list of self-contained functional requirements that related more to the nature of the software we must design than to the requirement definitions. Our real aim in all this was to come up with an activity list for developing the software. For example, we had a requirement for the Page Editor defined as, "Must allow amendment of an existing Page Index." After analyzing that statement, we could see that it actually consisted of a number of functional requirements:

- The ability to select a Page Index file from the file store.

- The ability to read a selected file into the program.

- The capability for the records of the Page Index to be modified.

- The capability to write the modified Index back to disk.

So, at a simple analysis level, the single requirement contained four functional requirements. The beauty of this process is that it let us identify functions that other requirements would also need. For example, we have another top-level requirement—"Must allow creation of a Page Index"—which can also be split into a number of functional requirements, one of which is the ability to output the Index to a disk file. Both our top-level requirements posses this same functional requirement, the ability to output a Page Index to disk. If this requirement were met by developing a single software module to output the Page Index to disk then, provided that the file name could be supplied to the module, it could be used to meet the file output needs of both our top-level requirements. From the point of view of our pre-sales effort, this software-focused information is extremely valuable. It means we have a piece of reusable, self-contained functionality that we need to design and develop only once, but then we can use twice. Without such information, we might estimate for development of the same function twice, or possibly even more. If we want to make our quote competitive, then breaking down the top-level, general requirements into self-contained functional requirements to make our estimating process as accurate as possible is essential.

Data Volumes and Data Rates

Another aspect of analysis is calculating volumes, data rates, and so forth. If your project demands high-speed response to external events, for example, you need to do some calculations to determine how much time you have to respond to an event before the next one is due. Maximum data rates are key parameters in such projects; so are data volumes. For example, if you know that once every minute a program is going to receive 5MB of data that needs to be graphed, you must be reasonably confident that the hardware and software you will propose can handle these specifications.

Where speed, response times, data volumes, and other such factors are involved, defining the maximum—and possibly minimum—operating parameters at this early stage is important (if the customer hasn't already done so). Such analysis might mean the difference between making completely inaccurate cost estimates and at least having your estimates in the right ballpark. We'll come back to analysis in much more detail when the project starts up. However, the case study also will give some valuable insight into the analysis process.

In summary, the results of analysis are alternative requirement descriptions of a much more technical nature than the high-level list. Among other things, analysis helps us to identify commonality in the functional components we will need to meet the overall requirements.

Return to the Case Study:
Data Entities

The two principal data entities were the Title Index (which describs the contents of a removable disk, book by book) and the Page Index (which describs the content of a single book, page by page). An Index is just a list of entries, and each entry consists of a number of data entities.

The Title Index, for example, consists of a list of title entries, each of which in some way defines a book. The Page Index consists of a number of page entries, each of which describes the contents of a given page. Put another way, the Title Index defines all the books available on a single removable disk. The Page Index defines all the pages available in a single book.

We can also say that the Title Index links together all the Page Indexes available on a single, removable disk.

Depicting the Relationships

A page could consist of text, images, videos, sounds, and music. We described each of these elements as a *data entity* for the appropriate book formats. A given page might or might not have text, an image, and/or a video clip—again, depending on the page format. In the same way, the page might or might not have a sound or music track. We designated this collection of data objects as *multimedia data entities*, and the Index entry simply consisted of references to these data entities.

Now, at this stage, we could provide a useful diagram showing the relationships among each data entities. Figure 2.4 shows this relationship; this figure is a simplistic form of an entity relationship diagram. In a single picture, Figure 2.4 summarizes what I have described and also indicates that a single disk could contain only one Title Index. A single Title Index could refer to one or more Page Indexes, and each Page Index could refer to one or more of the multimedia data entities. This example clearly illustrates the key relationships.

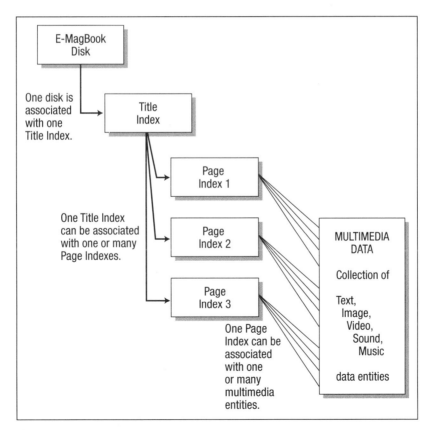

Figure 2.4
The relationships among the various data entities.

Because we would not be using a database, the Title Index would have to be a single file located on the removable disk. The Page Indexes were also likely to be individual files located on the removable disk; and the collection of multimedia objects would consist of text, image, video, sound, and music files, all also on the removable disk.

Data Volumes

Now was also a good time to consider the volumes of data we were likely to encounter. While I was on the phone with Monty, I asked him how many titles he thought they'd have on a single removable disk; he speculated that it would vary—from a single title, to perhaps as many as 20 or 30 titles. A Page Index might contain hundreds of pages. The question I was interested in answering was, Can we load a complete Page Index into memory at one time so every page entry is available to us? Being able to do this would greatly simplify our ability to meet the requirement and would keep the cost down. Consequently, Monty agreed that a limit of 1,000 pages per Page Index would be acceptable.

Let's take things a step further. A Title Index would consist of a series of references to the Page Index files, one Page Index File reference per Title Index entry. Each Page Index would consist of a series of entries, each of which would define a page of the book. A single page entry must contain the five keys and pointers to all the multimedia files required to construct the page. This information was telling us that, apart from the keys, the data we would store in these Index files would be references to other files.

Separating analysis and design is sometimes difficult, and the temptation arose to start being much more specific about these file structures. We didn't need that specificity for our current purpose, which was to size the job. For now, we'd done enough with data entities to provide an alternative view to the requirements and help us better understand them.

Let's go back to the issue of memory versus disk-based data. We would use a Page Index entry to construct the current page. We assumed an entry would be read from disk, the keys would be used to set up the screen, and the file references would be used to load in the image and/or multimedia files. When the operator requested another entry (page), the program must read the new entry from disk. A much slicker facility would have been to have the whole Index simply read into memory arrays when the operator first selected the book. Then, "turning the pages" and searching would be much swifter because the keys and multimedia file references would all be available from the arrays. The question was, Can we store an Index of 1,000 pages in memory?

A simple calculation pointed the way. A given entry might contain five keys—each 30 bytes, and up to three file pointers, each of which was a string that contained the file name and path—say, another 30 characters each, worst case. This combination would give a total Page Index record size of eight data items (five keys+three file references) by 30 byes each, or 240 bytes. A book might contain as many as 1,000 pages, in which case, the Index would amount to 240KB of storage—a small fraction of the 32MB available to us.

This analysis immediately let us determine that we could simplify navigation and searching that involved only in-memory data structures—we wouldn't need to page data in and out of Index files from disk. We summarized this piece of information, valuable for the estimating we had to do later on, as follows:

Page Index Handling
All entries to be loaded into memory when the book is "opened."

(Maximum capacity=1,000 pages, each of five keys (5×30) and three file refs (3×30)=240KB bytes).

Inputs and Outputs

If we considered each program, we could provide a list of *inputs* and *outputs* to give us an indication of how the data entities related to program functionality—another alternative view that would help further our understanding of the requirements. For example, What were the viewer's inputs? They were the Title Index, the Page Index, and all the images: multimedia, HTML (remember, future requirements), text files, and, of course, a possible Web site. Other inputs were the list of titles and details, the current page contents, and so on.

Again, we came up with a simple diagram that showed the primary inputs and outputs to the viewer. We could show all the different inputs—predominately a variety of files—and the program would convert all this input to one of two principal outputs—either a page display or a printout of a displayed page. Figure 2. 5 shows the viewer inputs and outputs.

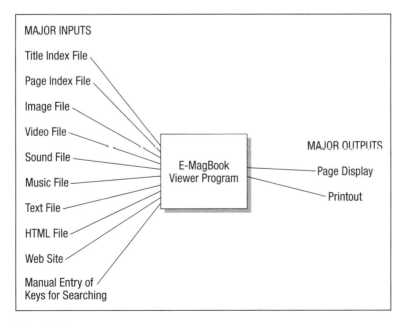

Figure 2.5
Main E-MagBook Viewer inputs and outputs.

Once again, the diagram helped to consolidate our understanding of the viewer using the alternative description. As for the editors, we would draw a single diagram (see Figure 2.6) to reflect both editors; we would leave the detailed split between the two editors for the full analysis. Our inputs for the two editors were the same as those for the viewer. The editor outputs consisted of either the Title Index entry display or the Page Index entry display, but they also consisted of a Title Index file and a Page Index file, because these editors could create or update the Index files. The viewer's diagram made obvious the fact that the viewer was a read-only facility, while the editors were read/write enabled.

A List of Basic Functional Requirements

Until now, we'd looked at the high-level, or "big picture," requirements. From the work we'd done so far, we should be able to make a list of self-contained functional requirements that the software must meet. We would now be analyzing the requirements at a deeper level.

If you look at what we had determined about all three programs, you see that they all must let the user select a title from the Title Index—that is, select a book. We summarized the requirement for this functionality as follows:

Functional Requirement
To read a Title Index, display the list, and let the user select a title.

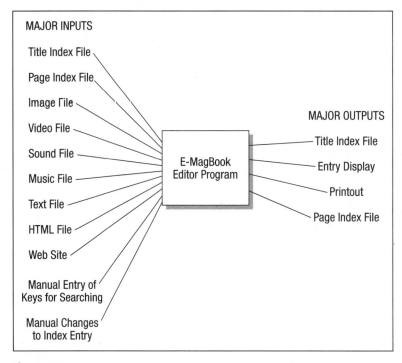

Figure 2.6
Main E-MagBook Editor inputs and outputs.

We'd defined a self-contained piece of functionality that any or all programs might require. Now, we had to develop a software entity to accommodate this requirement. And, if we would develop generic and independent code, we could use it anywhere and in any way. However, the three programs would all have different interfaces to the user. For example, the Title Editor might use a pull-down menu to activate the typical Windows "Open file" option to load a Title Index, whereas the viewer program couldn't use a drop-down menu because that was one of Monty's restrictions—no pull-down menus. So, in addition to isolating functionality, we needed to isolate the *interface-dependent* and *interface-independent* (or, as we'll call it, *pure*) functionality.

Interface Dependent vs. Pure Functionality

Next, we looked at the Title Index functionality statement we'd written to see whether we could make it clearer. The statement currently read, "To read a Title Index, display the list, and let the user select a title." As we analyzed deeper, we found that the statement contained three functional requirements. The first requirement was to read a Title Index into the program from disk. If we assumed that a file name and path were supplied, this requirement became a completely interface-free function in its own right. The software would take the file name supplied, open the file on disk, and load the contents into memory—end of function.

We looked at the second requirement: "display the list" Now, that requirement was, clearly, interface specific. To display, the function must have knowledge of the screen objects used to hold the title and the description, and these objects would be different from program to program. So, here, we had GUI-dependent functionality.

The next requirement was "let the user select a title." This requirement was interface related, because it needed a list box, a combo box, or something to select from. We now had three, self-contained functions: read a specified Title Index into memory, display Index list, and let the user select a title. But, in fact, these three boiled down to two. When we re-analyzed the situation at a deeper level, we realized we would never have a requirement to display the list without being able to select from it. The end result of a bit of careful thinking was that we had two clear functional requirements:

Functional Requirements

Read a specified Title Index into memory (pure functionality).

Display a list of titles and let the user select a single title (GUI-bound).

But, what about the requirement for supplying the file name to the first function? The system couldn't load the Title Index file until someone had specified what that file was, via the interface, could it? Right. But if we considered the viewer first (recall this from our data entities), each removable disk was to contain a single Title Index. Given that, the Title Index could always have the same name, because the requirement was that if you inserted a new E-disk, then you simply requested the E-MagBook to read the new Title Index. Consequently, the Index was likely to be hard coded in terms of path and name. This setup might not be the case with the editor. But as long as we had a generic, self-contained functional entity that only needed access to a file name to function correctly, how that name was derived didn't matter. The name could be hard coded, it could be selected from another list, or it could be obtained from a screen list. The infrastructure of the program itself would determine which approach would be used. In essence, the file name was just a call parameter. Of course, we had other requirements to let the user select Index files, as follows:

Functional Requirements

Select a Page Index file for input (GUI-bound).

Select a Title Index file for input (GUI-bound).

These GUI functions would use standard Windows dialog boxes to solicit the file name from the user. After the file had been selected, then, we could use the generic function to read the selected file into memory.

We were defining here the basic functional requirements of the software that we would need to develop. To make these requirements work, we would still need to produce some code to glue everything together; that code was the infrastructure code. We didn't need to define the code here in terms of a requirement—it would develop out of the process as we continued.

Taking this process a stage further, after the user had selected a title, then the program had a file name for the selected book. That name could be used to load the book's Page Index into memory; this requirement was self-contained, independent of the GUI, and exactly equivalent to the Title Index read function. We now had a functional requirement:

Functional Requirement

Read a specified Page Index into memory (pure functionality).

Just as for the Title Index, this requirement needed only the name of the file to load. What we were doing now was building up a shopping list of items that we needed to develop, and this list would form a vital input to the estimating process.

The Lists Grow

As we continued with the analysis, to expand the functional requirements list, we determined that we needed the following:

Functional Requirement

Page Index navigation functionality (GUI-bound).

The navigation controls that appear on the screen of the viewer would drive this functionality, which consisted of a set of sub-functions to support movement to the next page, previous page, start of book, end of book, and so on. The viewer and the Page Index Editor would require these functions. An equivalent set of navigation functionality would be necessary for the Title Index Editor:

Functional Requirement
Title Index navigation functionality (GUI-bound).

When a user encountered a given page, regardless of how he or she got to it, the program must be able to display a page according to format—clearly, a self-contained, GUI-dependent function:

Functional Requirement
Display page (GUI-bound).

Both the viewer and the Page Editor had this requirement.

Some functions might be specific to the editors. For example, the Title Index Editor will require the following function:

Functional Requirement
Display contents of current Title entry (GUI-bound).

Then, the Workbench facility for the viewer must allow a user to manipulate the image or text block:

Functional Requirement
Workbench functionality (GUI-bound).

When you are looking for common functionality, it's sometimes not easy to see. For example, Julie came up with a function to "Display Result Of Search," a GUI-related function. On closer analysis, this function turned out to be "Display Current Page." Provided that a mechanism existed for "telling" the functional component which page to display, the code had everything it needed to extract the data from the Index and load all the page components. It would make no difference whether the function was invoked because the user requested "Next Page" or because the program was to show the next result in a search.

In terms of searching, we split the functionality required into the following:

Functional Requirements
Set up for search (GUI-bound).

Perform search (pure functionality).

Setting up for the search involved entering the strings to be searched for using the GUI, and searching involved scanning the in-memory Index looking for an entry that matched the selection criteria the user entered.

I cannot overstress the importance of looking for common functionality—it keeps the shopping list down and, therefore, keeps the job small. A collection of well-defined, generic components is easier to write, easier to debug, easier to maintain, and more robust that just taking each piece of functionality directly from the requirements and coding for that piece. Finding common functionality does, however, require a degree of abstraction to interpret the requirements.

Index Functions

Each editor would require a set of common Index functions to process an entry. In fact, all the editors supported were add new entry, delete old entry, insert new entry, and overwrite existing entry; these functions constituted a typical set of data-access functions. The most likely way to provide an "add" function was, first, to let the user set up the screen with all the required items for the new title or the new page and then click a button to add the screen layout to the Index. So, at this level, the function was GUI-bound. When we analyze deeper, we might determine that the function should be split into sub-functions, but that's a level of detail much deeper than we needed to go at the time. We could say at this stage that each Index consisted of a record containing a number of data items that were character strings. In the case of the Title Index, these data items would be the name of the Page Index file, a book title, and so on. For the Page Index, the data would consist of the five keys and file descriptions of the multimedia components. Consequently, the required functions would be similar for the two Indexes. This information would be important to us when we estimated the amount of effort for each function. Once we'd designed the code for one program, we would be able to reuse much of the code in the next program, making the overall burden less onerous in terms of required effort. We summed all this up as follows.

Functional Requirement

Add/Delete/Insert/Overwrite Page Index functionality (GUI-bound).

Add/Delete/Insert/Overwrite Title Index functionality (GUI-bound).

After an Index had been modified, we would need the software to write it back to disk. First, we needed to define the file name that would contain the Index:

Functional Requirements

Select file name for Page Index output (GUI-bound).

Select file name for Title Index output (GUI-bound).

Both requirements were GUI-bound because a dialog box would be used to let the user define the name of the relevant output file. We could also define a totally generic, pure functional requirement to output the contents of the Index to the specified disk file. How the file name would be selected was irrelevant—a matter for the infrastructure. And, in the case of the typical menu Save functions, only the file name selection process was GUI-related. So, we defined two pure functional requirements:

Functional Requirements
Output a Page Index to selected disk file (pure functionality).

Output a Title Index to selected disk file (pure functionality).

Again, these requirements would be similar to each other, a fact we needed to remember when we estimated the effort they would require.

The editors also required editing functions whereby the user could change the content of an entry. We would have to look at these functions in much more detail later. For this exercise, we classified the functionality as follows:

Functional Requirements
Page entry edit functionality (GUI-bound).

Title entry edit functionality (GUI-bound).

Both these functions were GUI bound and might be relatively involved—something we needed to be aware of (this has to do with GUI functionality).

Let me explain. Unlike with traditional sequential code, in an event-driven GUI environment, the programmer has no way to know what will happen next. In the example, the user might alter the description of the current title and then, suddenly, decide to move on to the next title in the Index. Our question was, What do we, as programmers, do with the changes that have been made on screen? Do we assume they are good and modify the current entry before moving on, or do we ask the user if they should be saved? Making sure that the GUI is "friendly" and doesn't allow the user to do silly things would require a fair bit of thought and code. We would have to leave this work until later, if we got the job. For now, when we estimated these tasks, we must merely appreciate that they are likely to be more complex than a first glance might indicate.

Enough Analysis for Now

We now had two lists of functional entities that needed to be developed, and we had isolated the lists sufficiently so they were self-contained. (As you will see, we cannot overemphasize the importance of this self-containment.) The first list was for what we had termed pure functionality; the second list defined functionality related to the GUI. The lists are as follows:

Functional Requirements Lists for E-MagBook Development

Page Index Handling
All entries to be loaded into memory when book is "opened."

(Maximum capacity = 1,000 pages, each of five keys (5×30) and three files (3×30) = 240KB bytes).

Pure Functional Requirements
Read a specified Title Index into memory.

Read a specified Page Index into memory.

Perform search.

Output a Page Index to selected disk file.

Output a Title Index to selected disk file.

GUI-Based Functional Requirements
Display list of titles and let the user select a single title.

Select a Page Index file for input.

Select a Title Index file for input.

Page Index navigation functionality.

Title Index navigation functionality.

Display page.

Display contents of current Title entry.

Workbench functionality.

Set up for search.

Add/Delete/Insert/Overwrite Page Index functionality.

Add/Delete/Insert/Overwrite Title Index functionality.

Select file name for Page Index output.

Select file name for Title Index output.

Page entry edit functionality.

Title entry edit functionality.

To achieve these lists, the three of us went through a brainstorming session. The result was two lists that were not particularly well structured—that structuring would come later. From our understanding of the requirements and a bit of analysis, we'd identified self-contained functional components, which now gave us a functional requirements list that we needed to develop. Don't forget, we didn't have the job—we needed to do only enough work to ensure that we were comfortable with the quote we produce. This time was all *our* time. We were not making any money yet, and, if we lost the contract, the effort would have been all for nothing anyway.

To give you some idea of time schedules, we took an entire morning to get this far—that is, to capture the basic requirements and analyze them to this level. From the point of view of progress, that timing gave us the afternoon to conduct a feasibility study on image and multimedia functionality. If we could complete that study by the end of the day, we would be on target, according to our plan for the three-day pre-sales effort.

Risk Assessment

We'd identified handling multimedia files as the biggest technical risk area, from our point of view as a supplier. As we discussed earlier, the risk was that Julie and Archie had no experience in this type of software, and, because this project was at a fixed price, we needed to gauge as accurately as possible how much work would be required. We must be able to display images and play video, sound, and music files. As you can imagine, because they'd never programmed such facilities before, Julie and Archie had no possible way to estimate how much effort would be required—which left us wide open in terms of risk.

The Feasibility Study

How do we go about assessing our risk? In this particular case, we needed to come up to speed quite rapidly about how to handle images and multimedia files. A *feasibility study* would help us do this. If the study indicates how we can deal with these entities, then we have immediately minimized the risk factor, because we can make the subsequent quotations from a position of understanding rather than complete ignorance.

The aim of a feasibility study is to determine whether something is possible. What we needed to do first is define what we wanted to check out—that is, define a goal. Then, we needed to do enough work to confirm that we could accomplish the goal we set. But—and this is critical—we must do only enough work to satisfy ourselves that we can meet our goal. We could get carried away and end up developing a complete solution (unfortunately, programmers are a bit like that).

In our case study, we needed to address the following issues:

♦ How could we easily load and scale images onto defined screen areas?

♦ How could we easily load and run video clips on screen?

♦ How could we easily load and play sound and music files?

In a situation like this, you can either bring in an expert to bring you up to speed rapidly, or you can conduct a feasibility study. The study involves learning all about, and trying out, the technology available to you. As you can imagine, this approach could take considerable time.

So, in the case study, we decided to use my experience in multimedia handling to get Julie and Archie up to speed, and to develop enough code to determine how we could achieve the basic requirements. You can see the details of what we did in the case study to assess the image and multimedia handling complexities (with a view to answering the preceding questions) in Appendix A. The outcome of our study was that we developed sufficient code to show how we could handle each aspect simply. We tested the feasibility using Visual Basic (VB). Provided we would then choose a development environment that contained similar components to those we used in VB to perform the study, we were all confident we had minimized our risk. If you are also unfamiliar with image and multimedia handling, refer to Appendix A.

Progress Monitoring

At this point, our progress monitoring for the pre-sales effort in the case study was very straightforward. We were defining a list of tasks to do, none of which would require more than a single day. At the end of each day, we simply looked at which task had been completed and which had not. That information provided us with a simple, early warning system if things were going wrong.

In any project work, pre- or post-sales, it is vital to have early warning when the plan is not going according to schedule. From a management perspective, you need to know whether you are on, behind, or ahead of schedule. If you are behind schedule, the earlier you find out, the sooner you can do something about it. Again, the key to progress monitoring is to get as early a warning as possible that something is not right.

Let's look at the current situation in the case study as an example. By the time we had finished everything we have discussed so far, a full day of the three available to us had gone. However, we had achieved a great deal. We had performed the first iteration of the first two phases of the SDLC, capturing the top-level requirements and performing some useful analyses. We had also minimized the greatest risk factor we had identified so far by performing enough of a feasibility exercise (the details of which are available in Appendix A) to see how VB could meet the multimedia requirements.

In terms of evaluating our progress, we had originally defined that we would accomplish three tasks in Day 1—complete the preliminary requirement capture, perform an analysis, and assess the feasibility for image and multimedia handling. We had accomplished all three tasks and were, therefore, on schedule. Clearly, this was a simplistic situation to monitor. As the project started up, progress monitoring would become much more complex.

Breaking Down Tasks

Our next task was to develop a complete list of activities that we must accomplish to meet the project's software design and development requirements. This list would act as the key input to our estimating process.

SDLC Phase 1 and 2 Activities

If we got the job, the first project phase would be to capture the requirements. To achieve this goal, we would have to perform a similar, but much more detailed, exercise than what we had done in the pre-sales phase (where we were interested only in the top-level aspects). From this work, we would then need to produce a requirements document—the main product, or deliverable, from Phase 1 of the SDLC process. And don't forget: The client will own the requirements document, which defines what the software we develop will do. This document will be the customer's most important project document.

Remember from Chapter 1 that, after we'd produced the requirements document, and before we handed it over to the client, we would need to review it as objectively as possible. Only when the review process was complete, and we were all happy with the document's contents, would we move on to the next phase—analysis.

We would then perform a more detailed analysis and produce a number of viewpoints of the requirements as well as expanded lists of self-contained functional entities. This analysis would be a far more rigorous version of what we had done at the pre-sales level. The end result would be what we've termed a series of models. These models would be analogous to an architect's plans and models. When we'd produced the models, we'd need to review them.

Because the whole purpose of analysis is to deepen our understanding of the requirements, our review of the models might highlight a deficiency in the requirements specification. Consequently, we would require time to reiterate both Phases 1 and 2. We needed to take this time into account when we quoted for the amount of effort we'd expend to perform the following activities for Phases 1 and 2 of the SDLC:

- Capture requirements

- Produce requirements document

- Review requirements document

- Analyze requirements

- Produce models

- Review models

NOTE: *Remember to include time in reviews for iteration of phases.*

Phase Iteration

Getting the requirements 100 percent right the first time is almost impossible. Through the iteration of phases, as you discover more and more about the requirements, you can correct any misconceptions, add detail to make things clearer, and so on. The example in Figure 2.7 shows how verification of the deliverables can affect what you do next.

To make everything crystal clear, let's go back to the beginning. You start capturing requirements—in detail this time—and, once you are ready, you produce a requirement, or specification, document. Then, you review this document. If you are not happy with it, you go back and update the document, having captured more of the requirements where necessary. When you believe you have documented all the requirements, you move on to analysis, during which you produce one or more models. In their simplest form, these models consist of diagrammatic descriptions and lists of common functionality, similar to what you produced in the pre-sales

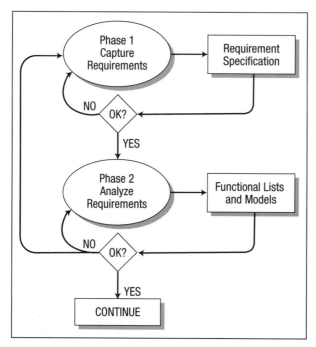

Figure 2.7
SDLC Phases 1 and 2 showing verification and iteration (where verification has failed).

phase, but in much greater detail. You then review these models, cross-checking them with the requirements. Now, at this stage, you might highlight discrepancies in, or issues with, the requirements document; if you find such problems, you go back to the capture phase and update the requirements document accordingly. When you are happy with the update, you come back to continue your analysis. After you are satisfied that the models reflect the requirements and that all the descriptions are consistent, you can continue to the design phase.

When the output fails validation, two paths are available out of the analysis phase. If the requirements document needs updating, you go back to the capture phase. If the models are not right, but the requirements document is, you should go back to the analysis. You continue to go back, then forward, until you have total consistency between the two sets of output, and you regard both as acceptable.

Milestones

From a project management point of view, deliverables and their validation are essential. To facilitate the successful movement from one phase to another, you must declare someone as the verification authority. When that stakeholder has authorized the deliverable, the project can proceed to the next phase. This verification provides an event you can set as a project *milestone*, so that verification must be complete by a given date. If you reach the date and verification cannot be given, the project is in trouble. Consequently, the project needs milestones, set at regular intervals, so that you can make undisputed measurements of progress.

When the project runs into trouble because you cannot meet a milestone, the plan needs to be flexible enough and contain sufficient contingency time so you can bring the project back on schedule without affecting the next milestone event.

SDLC Phase 3 Activities

At this stage, you can define the activities required at design time quite simply. You need to design data and file structures that we will classify together as *common data structures*. Such structures are data entities that all programs might require. Then, you will need to design individual programs as well, although your goal will be reusability of software modules where possible, based on the list of functional requirements you developed in analysis. The result of the design phase will be a design document that contains all design specifications. We can list the activities that you need to perform as follows:

◆ Design common data structures

◆ Design software modules

◆ Review designs

NOTE: *Remember to include time in reviews for iteration of phases.*

Of course, we include iteration so that, if your review of the designs fails to validate them, you will restart the design phase at the appropriate point to make necessary modifications. The design process might reveal a fundamental flaw in the analysis, or even in the requirements specification. If this happens (and depending on the nature of the issue you unearth), the project could be in serious trouble—you might not be able to meet the projected timetable.

The purpose for reviewing the design specifications is more fundamental than just to ensure that the deliverable from the current phase is valid. You are also ensuring that you are introducing no discrepancy with the outputs from previous phases. You are looking for total consistency across the project. You are constantly challenging the requirements, the results of analysis, and so on.

This brings us to another vital aspect of quality assurance: Where possible, validate each deliverable in the context of the project as a whole—not as an isolated entity The iteration process becomes particularly important here. If you find something wrong in an output from an earlier stage, you need to go back and rectify the output from that stage.

Even when a requirement specification has been accepted and signed off, it's not cast in stone. You can modify the specification, but you must do so in a highly controlled manner that includes an audit trail of events. Any decision point in a project requires some form of project documentation to indicate what happened and who was responsible. Hopefully, this documentation just supports the fact that a deliverable was found to be acceptable. When the deliverable is not acceptable, however, you need to make a note that identifies why it was not acceptable, and what action you will take to rectify the situation.

Always learning from your mistakes is vital. Good project auditing lets you review a completed project to see where things went wrong, why, and what was done to get the project back on track—and, above all, helps you learn from experience.

SDLC Phases 4 and 5 Activities

After the design phase, which encompasses design of the complete system, you will start Phase 4, software development. As we've discussed, the design will be for modular-based software development; so one of the activities must be to develop the individual, self-contained modules. You must validate each module by testing it as an independent, standalone unit. That means testing each module will also be part of the process. After all the modules are complete and have passed the tests, they need to be integrated as a whole. So, you also have a system integration activity to consider.

Next, you will need to test the entire system, in SDLC Phase 5. Any iteration should go back only as far as the design. At this stage, you are in deep trouble if you go any further back in the process. (You can, however, accept very minor design modification.)

I also want to add an activity called *rework* here. Rework is when the system testing identifies bugs, and you have to go back and fix the fault. Adding rework as an activity ensures you don't forget to account for it in your estimates.

We have now added the following to the activity list:

♦ Develop and test software modules

♦ Integrate software modules and test whole systems

♦ Verify software and perform rework where necessary

NOTE: *Remember to include time for iteration of phases.*

Figure 2.8 demonstrates the iterative nature of Phases 4 and 5, and includes going back as far as design. This figure also indicates that, where you must do iteration, the plan is at risk. We've made a point to put notes in the lists to remind you to allocate time in your estimates for iteration for this reason. Clearly, if the iterations become numerous or extensive, the plan is exposed to greater and greater risk.

When all the modules have passed their individual tests, you will integrate them and test the system. You will move on only when the result of testing is a 100 percent pass. And, as before, you have to loop back, first to development, then to design, if you unearth some design flaw.

Once again, how much risk is involved depends on how far back in the process you have to go and how much time it takes you to get back to where you were. If you've tested all the modules, you're bolting together tested modules, and nothing should go wrong. However, as we discussed when we looked at SDLC in Chapter 1, some modules, when developed in isolation, still need to be tested as if they were connected to other modules that have not yet been produced. In such instances, the programmer needs to understand how his or her module is supposed to interact with the external module, and he or she must simulate the

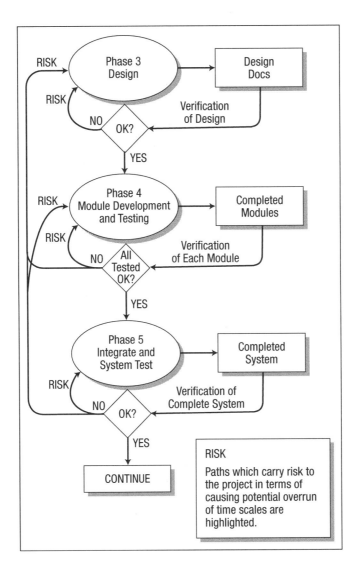

Figure 2.8
Iteration in SDLC Phases 4 and 5, highlighting its risky nature.

interface. If the programmer gets that bit wrong for any reason, then system integration and testing will be in jeopardy—even though the module testing worked. Fundamentally, if the design specs are not good enough, and the module testing involves interfaces to other software not yet developed, the capacity for error is considerable.

The design spec is where you need to make sure that any interfaces between the modules being developed in isolation are well defined. A programmer doesn't need to know how another module works, but understanding what that other module requires in terms of input and what it produces in terms of output is vital. Get that part right, and the system testing should be a breeze.

Production of Test Specs and User Guides

Testing includes three areas. First, at development time, you will test each module. Then, at system integration time, you will test the whole system or program. Finally, at acceptance testing time, the customer gets a chance to check out the complete system.

You can come up with formal test specifications for each aspect of testing, but (except on really big projects) that process can be onerous. To save duplication, you can develop one set of formal acceptance tests that you can use for both the integration testing and acceptance processes. These formal tests will include test specifications that detail how to set up a test, what to do for the test itself, and what to expect as a successful result. You will need at least one test per item of defined functionality.

You can leave the module testing to the developer. However, I must say that developers are not the best people to test their own software. In fact, at system testing and acceptance levels, it's vital that they not be involved in the testing at all. For module testing, you can relax the formal nature of testing somewhat, to make life easier. You can place the onus on the programmer to test the module to his or her satisfaction. You should require that the programmer describe in writing how the tests were performed and document the results, for accountability.

For this process to work, you must provide adequate guidance notes for the developers; such notes should explain how to go about module testing and validation. The acceptance tests, on the other hand, will be much more detailed. I've been describing a pragmatic approach. Ideally, you would have a test supervisor whose job is to review the programmers' testing and provide final authorization that they have satisfactorily tested a module. You must also allocate time to develop user guides and Help facilities. These are somewhat specialized activities that, again, developers aren't typically very good at.

We now have the following to add to the activity list:

♦ Development of informal module test logs and guidance notes

♦ Development of formal acceptance test specifications

♦ Development of user guides and Help facilities

Installation and Acceptance Testing

Next, you will install the entire system on the customer's site and let the customer rerun the acceptance tests. We can add "acceptance testing and remedial work, if necessary" to the activity list. You need to be on hand to guide and manage the customer through the whole process and to analyze any issues of functionality and the like. If any issues come up that require remedial action, you need to be able to do the necessary rework. But, if you've done your job correctly, no remedial work should be necessary.

Summary: The Basic List of Activities

Based on the SDLC, we now have a complete list of activities for which we must produce estimates. As a summary, here is the complete list:

List of Activities: SDLC Phases 1 and 2, Requirement Development and Analysis
Capture requirements.

Produce requirements document.

Review requirements document.

Analyze requirements.

Produce models.

Review models.

List of Activities: SDLC Phase 3, Design
Design common data structures.

Design software modules.

Review designs.

List of Activities: SDLC Phase 4 and 5, Develop, Test, Integrate / Test, Verify, and Rework Software
Develop and test software modules.

Integrate software modules and test whole system.

Verify software and perform rework where necessary.

> **NOTE:** *Remember to include time for iteration of phases.*

Test Specifications and Documentation
Development of informal module test logs and guidance notes.

Development of formal acceptance test specifications.

Development of user guides and Help facilities.

Acceptance Testing Activities
Acceptance testing and remedial work, if necessary.

> **NOTE:** *Remember to include time in reviews for iteration of phases.*

A Costing Strategy

In an ideal world, you would prefer, for a fixed price, to complete the capture of the fixed price requirements and their analysis. You would then work out an estimate, based on all the resulting information, to design, develop, test, and deliver the software. Some customers are quite happy with this approach; you can perform the first two phases of the SDLC for a fixed price or (possibly) even be paid according to the time those phases take. Once you have all the data, you can quote from a position of real understanding.

Unfortunately, most customers want a fixed price from the start. We've developed a strategy over the years to accommodate that expectation and minimize our risk, because the risks involved with quoting a fixed price for a development based only on the pre-sales effort are high. We quote a fixed price for the completion of the requirement specification and its analysis, and then we provide a range of prices for the rest of the project. We provide a minimum and a maximum quote, and then we tell the customer we will establish a fixed price for completion after we have completed the analysis phase. We guarantee the price will be between our minimum and maximum quotes—that's our risk. We'll explore this concept further in the case study.

Return to the Case Study:
The Activity List

At this point in the case study, we had to come up with a list of activities for the project. We would base the list on the lists that we presented earlier. We also were going to adopt the minimum-maximum (min-max) pricing strategy. We would quote a fixed price for development of the requirements specification and its analysis, and then we would quote a min-max price for completion of the project. First, we split the project into three main project phases (not to be confused with SDLC phases):

- *Phase 1*—We will produce the requirement specification and its analysis and then requote for completion of the project. We called this phase *Completion and Delivery of Requirement Spec, Analysis, and Requote*.

- *Phase 2*—This phase includes design of the complete system, but development and delivery of just the viewer. We called this phase *Design of Complete System, Development and Delivery of the Viewer Program*.

- *Phase 3*—In this phase, we complete the development and delivery of the editors. We called this phase *Development and Delivery of the Editors*.

At this stage, I asked Archie and Julie to set up a spreadsheet with all the activities we had recognized so far. Next to each item, I wanted three sets of two columns. Each column pair would include a minimum and a maximum estimate. Each of us would be providing the figures to fill in both columns.

A Spreadsheet Approach

Figures 2.9, 2.10, and 2.11 show the empty table, split into the three phases. Items 1 through 6 are from the basic model we discussed earlier. Items 7, 8, 9, and 10 are specific to this project, in which we were adopting the min-max pricing strategy. We would revisit the plan and quote (the ones we were currently producing) and produce a fixed price for project completion. We would then submit this new quote and plan to Monty. We even put in an activity to wait for approval, which could serve as extra contingency time to handle any issues that might arise.

We based this approach on our standard model made specific for the development of the viewer and editors. Note that we planned to complete the full system design in Phase 2.

E-MagBook ACTIVITY ESTIMATES—PROJECT PHASE 1

Item	Kieron		Archie		Julie	
	Max	Min	Max	Min	Max	Min
1 Capture Requirements						
2 Produce Req Doc						
3 Review Req Doc						
4 Analyze Reqs						
5 Produce Models 6Review Models						
7 Revisit Plan						
8 Revisit Quote						
9 Submit New Plan and Quote						
10 Wait for Approval						
Totals:						

Figure 2.9
Blank form for estimates in Phase 1.

E-MagBook ACTIVITY ESTIMATES—PROJECT PHASE 2

Item	Kieron		Archie		Julie	
	Max	Min	Max	Min	Max	Min
11 Design Data Structures						
12 Design Viewer						
13 Design Title Editor						
14 Design Page Editor						
15 Review Design						
16 Develop and Test Viewer Modules						
17 Integrate Viewer Mods and Test						
18 Rework of Viewer						
19 Dev Accept Specs for Viewer						
20 Install/Accept Viewer						
Totals:						

Figure 2.10
Blank form for estimates in Phase 2.

E-MagBook ACTIVITY ESTIMATES—PROJECT PHASE 3

Item	Kieron		Archie		Julie	
	Max	Min	Max	Min	Max	Min
21 Develop and Test Editor Modules (Informal Testing Logs)						
22 Integrate Editor Mods and Test						
23 Rework of Editors						
24 Dev of Editor Accept Specs						
25 Install/Accept Editors						
Totals:						

Figure 2.11
Blank form for estimates in Phase 3.

Designing part of a system and then completing it after some of the development has been done is not advisable. You are more than likely to compromise the design if you don't consider all its aspects at the same time. Finally, we would complete the editors. We had defined a total of 25 activities.

Estimating

We've now come to the difficult bit. You have a set of activities that you need to perform to complete a project. You have a breakdown of the requirements, you have some alternative descriptions of the requirements, and you have a list of functional requirements. Using all this information—and your experience and gut feelings—you have to provide a minimum and maximum (min and max) estimate, usually specified in days of effort, for each activity.

Each min and max will be an estimate of how long a given individual thinks he or she will take to perform that activity. The range between the min and max values represents the degree of uncertainty the person has about the activity. Even when you are forced into providing a fixed price from the outset, still present your estimate as min-max values; this approach will help you identify any areas of risk. Where you have wide min-max spreads, you have major risk. Having two or more people go through the estimating process is essential; that way, you can spot and investigate anomalies between different people's figures.

Validation

Someone who has relevant experience needs to validate the estimates. Unless you have that authority, you should never be placed in a position where your estimate commits the company. Unfortunately, this situation happens a great deal. The classic example is that of a project manager taking a junior programmer along to a meeting with the client, with the junior programmer to act as a technical backup. At some stage during the meeting, one of the customer's managers asks how long performing a given development task that has suddenly been required is likely to take. The project manager turns to the programmer and asks him how long it will take. The programmer, without thinking very hard, and eager to impress, blurts out, "Three days." And there you have it. From that day on, "three days" is cast in stone in the customer's eyes. Unfortunately, I have seen this situation often.

So, how do you handle such a scenario? First, you do your very best to avoid giving a time frame off the cuff. You explain that you must take all the implications into account, and you have procedures that you will need to invoke to get an authorized estimate.

The customer laughs and says, "Come on; you must have some idea."

Gently explain that to give an estimate without going through all the appropriate procedures—designed to protect both supplier and customer—is not really professional. And, besides, you must consider the impact on the project plan.

Then, when the customer gets cross and says, "I just want an estimate, a ball park," give a minimum-maximum estimate. Such an estimate should truly represent your inability to gauge under the given conditions. The customer is trying to make you give a figure, preferably one that he or she wants to hear, and, regardless of what assurances the customer provides that he or she will not hold you to your quote, I can almost guarantee that there is a very strong likelihood of the figure being quoted back at you at some future stage. If you can get your qualified response into the meeting minutes in full, you have some protection. But don't be overly eager to impress or please the client. It's just not worth it. The worst thing you can ever do in a situation like this is to come out with the immortal phrase, "Oh, it's easy; just a couple of lines of code will sort that." The statement might well be true, but you must develop a methodical way of working, in which you consider any requirement sensibly and in the context of the project as a whole.

Unfortunately, at the end of the day, estimating is dependent on your level of experience. To repeat: Always think and quote min-max, unless you are forced into a fixed price; use the min-max approach to calculate all the figures from which you must provide a final price.

Return to the Case Study:
The First Estimates

Archie and Julie both indicated they were glad we were doing this estimating after the feasibility study we did yesterday about images and multimedia. The result of that single session had made a substantial difference in their estimates of the project's complexities.

Archie brought up the subject of user guides and Help facilities, which we had not included in our list of activities. Developing those components was something our resident author would do, so Julie and Archie didn't have to worry about it. But we did need to include those activities in the plan and cost estimates. One author would also produce any Help files the editors required—another issue we had avoided.

Because developers are not normally good at producing either user guides or Help systems, those tasks are best left to the experts. Forgetting something is easy; consequently, a template to remind you of things to include is very useful.

What followed next was a long session, in which each of us studied the notes we had—the lists of functionality, the result of our analysis and feasibility work—and, based on each person's experience and "gut" feel, we came up with the estimates that follow. Clearly, I was asking Archie and Julie to provide figures for things they had never done before. In Archie's case, he had never written a requirement document or a set of acceptance tests. As a result, we had to spend considerable time discussing what we would need to do for each activity. This example highlights that you should never be placed in a situation where you must go through an exercise like this without at least one person with extensive experience in the process to provide guidance—and a set of estimates. My view is that involving Julie and Archie was fully justified, despite their lack of experience at this level of project work. Being involved, under supervision, would allow them to appreciate the entire SDLC concept. Throughout their careers as developers, they will have to provide task and job estimates, whether for an external customer or an internal project manager. In either case, they will need to understand how to estimate. By the way, a word of warning: The people who ask for estimates will tend to hear only what they want to hear.

A key advantage to using a spreadsheet to develop your estimates is that you can set up the columns to automatically total the number of days. This means that, if you want to play around with the figures, you don't have to keep recalculating the sums. The spreadsheet offers you a neat modeling tool with which you can answer questions such as, What would happen if I added this activity and reduced the number of days in these three activities by 50 percent? and the like. You can see the result of our deliberations in Figure 2.12.

Because I had suggested that we set up Items 9 and 10 in the same way for each of our estimates, these items are identical. These items include submitting the new plan and quote, and waiting for approval of the requirements specification.

Can We Deliver the Viewer in Time?

We'd now reached the point where we had to commit to a timetable—in particular, the eight weeks in which we had to produce the viewer. Let's see what our commitments were. First, we had to capture the requirements, analyze them, submit our quote to Monty, and requote a fixed price for design and development. All that's what we've called project Phase 1. Then we would start project Phase 2, which consisted of designing the whole system and developing the viewer. The restriction placed on us was that we must complete project Phases 1 and 2 in just eight weeks. In terms of design, we could concentrate only on the viewer, but that would almost certainly cause problems when we were ready to design the rest of the system. So, we were committing to designing the complete system in the eight weeks and developing and delivering a working viewer. From my experience, I felt quite comfortable that all this was achievable. I asked the other two what they felt. Archie had no idea. Julie felt the answer lay in the spreadsheets, but she wasn't sure how to extract the data.

Let's take this process stage by stage. To be honest, if Archie and Julie hadn't admitted to such misgivings, I would have been worried. The project was clearly in three major phases—the two I've just described, and development and delivery of the editors (Phase 3). We first needed to be confident that we could complete Phases 1 and 2 in the eight weeks Monty had forced upon us. A total of 40 working days would be available in eight weeks, assuming each week consists of 5 working days. (We didn't forget to check for national holidays, and so on.) We had a total of 40 working days in which to complete the work.

Next, we made a list of suitable personnel, and the numbers of days those people would be available. Because Julie and Archie were new employees, they were not yet entitled to any time off, and they did not anticipate having any time off in the 40 days of the project. In theory, both would be available for the full 40 days. Let's assume that in each week, both will be available for four days. So, in each week, we have eight days of effort that the two developers, Archie and Julie, can expend. "Why 8, not 10, days?" I hear you ask. We based these calculations on 80 percent availability, to take into account such things as dentist appointments, sickness, forced leave of absence, and so on.

E-MagBook ACTIVITY ESTIMATES—PROJECT PHASE 1

Item	Kieron		Archie		Julie	
	Max	Min	Max	Min	Max	Min
1 Capture Requirements	4.0	2.5	10.0	5.0	6.0	4.0
2 Produce Req Doc	2.0	1.0	3.0	1.0	4.0	3.0
3 Review Req Doc	1.0	0.5	4.0	2.0	2.0	1.0
4 Analyze Reqs	2.0	1.0	8.0	4.0	4.0	2.0
5 Produce Models	2.0	1.0	3.0	1.0	2.0	1.5
6 Review Models	1.0	0.5	2.0	1.0	1.0	0.5
7 Revisit Plan	1.0	1.0	1.0	0.5	1.0	0.5
8 Revisit Quote	1.0	0.5	1.0	0.5	1.0	0.5
9 Submit New Plan and Quote	1.0	0.5	1.0	0.5	1.0	0.5
10 Wait for Approval	5.0	3.0	5.0	3.0	5.0	3.0
Totals:	20.0	11.5	38.0	18.5	27.0	16.5

E-MagBook ACTIVITY ESTIMATES—PROJECT PHASE 2

Item	Kieron		Archie		Julie	
	Max	Min	Max	Min	Max	Min
11 Design Data Structures	2.0	1.0	4.0	2.0	2.0	1.0
12 Design Viewer	3.0	2.0	5.0	3.0	4.0	2.0
13 Design Title Editor	1.0	0.5	3.0	1.0	1.0	0.5
14 Design Page Editor	3.0	2.0	5.0	3.0	4.0	3.0
15 Review Design	1.0	0.5	2.0	0.5	2.0	1.0
16 Develop and Test Viewer Modules	10.0	5.0	15.0	10.0	12.0	5.0
17 Integrate Viewer Mods and Test	4.0	2.0	3.0	2.0	3.0	1.0
18 Rework of Viewer	3.0	1.0	1.0	0.5	2.0	1.5
19 Dev Accept Specs for Viewer	3.0	2.0	1.0	0.5	2.0	1.5
20 Install/Accept Viewer	2.0	0.5	1.0	0.5	1.0	0.5
Totals:	32.0	16.5	40.0	23.0	33.0	17.0

E-MagBook ACTIVITY ESTIMATES—PROJECT PHASE 3

Item	Kieron		Archie		Julie	
	Max	Min	Max	Min	Max	Min
21 Develop and Test Editor Modules (Informal Testing Logs)	10.0	5.0	12.0	6.0	10.0	6.0
22 Integrate Editor Mods and Test	4.0	2.0	3.0	1.5	4.0	3.0
23 Rework of Editors	2.0	1.0	2.0	1.5	3.0	2.0
24 Dev of Editor Accept Specs	4.0	3.0	3.0	2.0	3.0	2.0
25 Install/Accept Editors	4.0	2.0	5.0	3.5	4.0	2.0
Totals:	24.0	13.0	25.0	14.5	24.0	15.0
Grand Totals:	76.0	41.0	103.0	56.0	84.0	48.5

Figure 2.12
Completed activity estimates.

So, when you're planning projects of this sort, declare each full-time person as being available for four out of five days. This method acts as a safety net—it provides contingency time for unforeseen eventualities that have nothing to do with the project. If you schedule someone into a project for 100 percent of his or her time, you are asking for trouble.

Julie appreciated this approach, pointing out that, in her last company, such calculations—when the company bothered to do them at all—always assumed you were free five days a week, plus the weekend.

I intended to be involved in the project for 50 percent of my time. As you probably recall, I had discussed this with my partner, and we had both accepted this schedule. My involvement would likely be higher in the early stages of the project and then drop off. At this stage, we assumed 50 percent availability for me. All this information meant that in the 40 available project days, we had a total of 32 days available from Julie, 32 days from Archie, and 20 days from me—a grand total of 84 days of manpower. I've summed this up in Figure 2.13. This information told us that within the 40 days available, we could put in a total of 84 days of effort.

Now, let's look at the cost estimates we each gave and calculate the totals for Phases 1 and 2. Each person's estimate consisted of a minimum and maximum duration, within which that person believed he or she could complete the project single-handedly. Archie estimated between 41.5 and 78 days to complete Phases 1 and 2 if he worked on his own—but, as he put it, "with a lot of guidance." Clearly, because of his lack of experience, he would require considerable assistance and management.

Julie estimated a total of between 33.5 and 60 days to complete Phases 1 and 2, and I came up with 28 to 52 days. We were looking at the estimates of three people with three different sets of experience and ability. If we took the extremes, we would have a minimum of 28 days and a maximum of 78 days. Would you believe it? That range falls neatly inside the manpower availability figure of 84 days we had calculated. See Figure 2.14 for a complete summary.

Archie was convinced the result Figure 2.14 showed was a fluke, but those figures genuinely point to the conclusion that all three of us felt reasonably comfortable with the overall schedule being imposed upon us. Remember, however, that we were basing our estimates on scant information, which the wide range between min and max for each estimate reflects. Nevertheless, I felt quite confident. The outside range falling inside the available manpower is clearly a good omen.

E-MagBook ACTIVITY ESTIMATES—PROJECT PHASES 1 and 2—Availability Figures

Total number of working days available = 40 days

STAFF AVAILABILITY

Archie (80% utilization) = 32 days
Julie (80% utilization) = 32 days
Kieron (50% utilization) = 20 days

──────

Total manpower available to project = 84 days

Figure 2.13
Project Phases 1 and 2 availability figures.

```
┌─────────────────────────────────────────────────────────────┐
│  E-MagBook ACTIVITY ESTIMATES—PROJECT PHASES 1 and 2—Estimates │
│                                                               │
│              Archie  =  41.5 to 78 days effort                │
│               Julie  =  33.5 to 60 days effort                │
│              Kieron  =    28 to 52 days effort                │
│                                                               │
│     Combined range:  Minimum of 28 days                       │
│                      Maximum of 78 days                       │
└─────────────────────────────────────────────────────────────┘
```

Figure 2.14
Project Phases 1 and 2 estimates.

Archie wanted to know what we would have done if the overall range had not fallen inside the available person-day figure. In that case, we would have had to add more bodies to increase the manpower availability figure.

You have to be careful here. Writing software is not like digging holes. You can't judge software development from the same premise that, if one man takes a day to dig a hole, then two men will take half a day. With software, you must be very cautious, because, sometimes, adding more people can actually slow things down. You must bring new people up to speed, train them, manage them, and so on. In software developments, you are frequently dealing with the need to impart lots of information, and the information might sometimes be quite complex. Also, different people have different abilities—one person may have a flair for programming, but be totally incapable of designing a matchbox.

The general consensus among the three of us was that project Phases 1 and 2 were achievable in the imposed time frame. We would monitor progress daily if we needed to. If we ran into trouble, I would just have to find extra time or second someone else if worst came to the worst. We had not included any management time in these calculations. Phases 1 and 2 were to be completed in 40 days. Primarily, management would consist of assessing progress and handling milestone events.

A reasonable rule of thumb for calculating management time is to estimate that management can account for a minimum of 10 percent of the total manpower figure. So, our 84 available man-days would require something on the order of 8 days of management effort. Those days would fall to me and come out of my 50 percent availability. Of course, if the project ran into trouble, this management-time figure could skyrocket.

Project Phase 1 in More Detail

Having determined that the imposed timeframe was probably adequate to complete project Phases 1 and 2, we needed to look at each phase in more detail. In Phase 1, we would capture requirements and analyze them. We then needed to hand over the documentation to Monty for acceptance, and we needed him to complete that process in a maximum of five days. That figure was mine, and, if you recall, we all used it in our calculations (three to five days to wait for approval). See Figure 2.15 for E-MagBook Activity Estimates for Project Phase 1.

```
┌─────────────────────────────────────────────────────────────┐
│                                                               │
│    E-MagBook ACTIVITY ESTIMATES—PROJECT PHASE 1—Availability  │
│       and Estimates for Capturing Requirements and Analysis   │
│                                                               │
│       Total number of working days available = 10 days        │
│                          (+5 days wait for approval)          │
│                                                               │
│                        AVAILABILITY                           │
│                                                               │
│              Archie (80% utilization) = 8 days                │
│               Julie (80% utilization) = 8 days                │
│              Kieron (50% utilization) = 5 days                │
│                                                               │
│       Total manpower available to project = 21 days           │
│   ─────────────────────────────────────────────────────────  │
│                        ESTIMATES                              │
│                (less waiting for approval time)               │
│                                                               │
│                 Archie  15.5 to 33 days effort                │
│                  Julie  13.5 to 22 days effort                │
│                 Kieron   8.5 to 15 days effort                │
│                                                               │
│         Combined Range: Minimum of 8.5 days                   │
│                         Maximum of 33 days                    │
│                                                               │
└─────────────────────────────────────────────────────────────┘
```

Figure 2.15

Figures for capturing requirements and analysis.

A "gut" feeling was that we should be able to capture requirements, analyze, and perform any iterations between SDLC phases in two weeks. Then, we would have a week in which Monty reviewed and then accepted the requirement specification. During that time, we would have to be on call to assist and manage the process. So, let's say we had 10 days for capturing and analyzing, and five days for Monty to accept the specification. I believed this goal should be achievable, but how did it tie in with the estimates? When I transferred the figures from the spreadsheet to a table, I would deduct three days from each min and five days from each max, so we would be looking only at the work we had to do in the first two weeks.

In the 10 days we had imposed, we had 21 days of effort available from the three of us, based on the use figures. The estimates ranged from 8.5 through 33 days of effort required. All three minimum figures fell inside the available manpower effort of 21 days, but only one of the maximum figures did. However, we needed to temper this information a little with experience. As you can see, Archie was quite a way from 21 days on his max, but Julie was not. Based on the information we had—taking all things into consideration—the risk was reasonable that we could complete in the 10 days.

Archie thought that the assessment process we used was "almost scientific," as he put it. I wouldn't go quite that far. To be honest, estimating is a bit of "black art," but we were making it as scientific as we possibly could. It all had to do with feeling comfortable, and there's no substitute for experience.

Both Julie and Archie admitted that the min-max approach really helped, and they decided they would approach estimating that way in the future. Archie had never done anything like this before, but he could see how sensible it was. We were narrowing the risks all the time, something Julie could appreciate from her previous experiences. We might still be wrong, but our approach forced us to stop and think at every turn, instead of charging onward regardless of the information available to us.

Seeing such a positive response from Archie was pleasing. Both Charlie and I recognize that imposing a working methodology on talented programmers can be difficult for them, because doing so means their creative urges must wait to be unleashed. The benefit, however, is that once unleashed, that creative ability will be channeled in exactly the right direction.

After some discussion and reassurance that I would not leave Archie and Julie in the lurch if things went wrong, we were happy that we had a minimum risk in completing project Phase 1 on time. We had good contingencies built in, and options existed for me to find more time if I needed to. And, if the worst happened, we might have to shorten the time Monty had to approve the requirements (remember, we quoted this time as ranging from three to five days). Monty wouldn't like that change—nor would I—but we had a potential option if things went wrong.

Project Phase 2 in More Detail

We'd accounted for three of our eight weeks. We now had five weeks left to design the entire system, and develop, test, and complete client acceptance testing for the viewer. Let's say we would have the software ready for installation at the end of Week 7, which would give us a week for acceptance testing with the client. That gave us four weeks—or 20 available days—to complete Phase 2. Figure 2.16 summarizes the results.

Figure 2.16 confirms that we had 20 days to complete Phase 2. Within that 20-day period, we had 42 days of effort available from the three of us. Looking at our estimates, we had a range from 16.5 days to 40, all of which was inside the available manpower (looks good). However, Julie spotted that the figures included installation and assistance in acceptance testing, for which we had already allocated one whole week, separate from the 42 days' effort-available figure. This discovery meant we had even more contingency built in than we had planned. The figures were telling us that we could complete all of Phase 2, including acceptance, in four weeks. With that, we all felt much more confident that we could bring in Phase 2 on time.

So, based on these figures, we could actually deliver and have the client accept the software in four weeks instead of five. We had to make sure Monty was ready for acceptance, however. I would feel much more comfortable if we told him we would be ready at the beginning of Week 8, and so he must be ready. The extra time would give us extra breathing space—never a bad thing with such a vital milestone.

At this stage, we had a list of activities and min-max estimates. We could lay out these details in a plan, taking into account that we could conduct some activities in parallel; some we would have to do in sequence. We might also have to fit in activities according to time frames forced by the customer.

```
┌─────────────────────────────────────────────────────────┐
│                                                           │
│   E-MagBook ACTIVITY ESTIMATES—PROJECT PHASE 2—Availability │
│      and Estimates for Design Total System, Develop Viewer │
│                                                           │
│        Total number of working days available = 20 days   │
│                                                           │
│                        AVAILABILITY                       │
│             Archie (80% utilization) = 16 days            │
│             Julie (80% utilization) = 16 days             │
│             Kieron (50% utilization) = 10 days            │
│                                                           │
│       Total manpower available to project = 42 days       │
│   ─────────────────────────────────────────────────────  │
│                         ESTIMATES                         │
│                 (less waiting for approval time)          │
│                 Archie    23 to 40 days effort            │
│                 Julie     17 to 33 days effort            │
│                 Kieron   16.5 to 32 days effort           │
│                                                           │
│        Combined Range: Minimum of 16.5 days               │
│                        Maximum of 40 days                 │
│                                                           │
└─────────────────────────────────────────────────────────┘
```

Figure 2.16
Availability and estimates for full system design and viewer development.

The Project Plan

At this stage in your project, you need to determine what the time frames will be. The simplest approach is to take the maximum estimate for each activity and plan accordingly. But this method usually results in an unacceptably long project. You have to make a judgment call at this stage—this is where experience is essential. Look at each set of figures and determine a time value for the plan that makes you comfortable.

Be sure that your project plan contains contingency time, so that, if things go wrong, you have some slack. Never plan human resources in for 100 percent availability; plan them for 80 percent maximum. So, in a working week, you will expect to get four days of effort from the people involved. As we discussed earlier, this plan accounts for things such as funerals, dentist appointments, sickness, and so on. Always establish what everyone's available vacation times are before you plan them into a project, and make sure they aren't scheduled on another project (this might sound silly, but it does happen).

The Importance of Milestones

As we talked about earlier in the chapter, *milestones* are the critical points in a plan that designate when you must complete certain tasks, or when certain events must occur. If a deliverable is involved, a milestone also serves as a point in the project where you can send out an invoice. For example, a critical delivery is the completed and analyzed requirements specification. After the customer signs off on this, you can invoice for the work done—which brings cash into the company during the project life. Whether you like it or not, cash flowing into the company is essential to pay your salary. Consequently, you should assume a responsible attitude toward the need for milestones that result in payments.

It's important that you clearly mark milestones on the plans and define them in writing. Equally important are both the supplier's and customer's responsibilities to meet these deadlines. Remember that, if a customer must be ready to review and accept a document by a certain date and fails to do so, this failure will put your plan at risk.

Return to the Case Study:
The First Draft of a Plan for Phases 1 and 2

Let's split up the eight weeks according to what we've discussed so far. Figure 2.17 illustrates the first version of a plan for project Phases 1 and 2. On the left, you can see manpower, specified by name, and the project weeks across the top. Each major activity is marked as a black line to indicate where the activity starts and ends. All the activities shown occur one after the other. This progression defines a *critical path*. On this critical path, one activity cannot start until the previous one has been completed.

In Weeks 1 and 2, we would capture requirements and analyze them. At the end of Week 2, we had a milestone: We must complete the requirements document by this date. We would submit the document to Monty at the start of Week 3. He must be available to verify the document and accept it. We had a week for that process and any necessary rework.

Milestone 2 would occur at the beginning of Week 4—we must have the go-ahead from Monty. If we didn't get it by then, we couldn't guarantee to deliver on time. To summarize, we must meet Milestone 1's target date, Monty must be ready to start verifying the documentation, and he must have completed verification by Milestone 2.

In Week 4, we would design, which we would need to complete by the end of the week. We then had two weeks to develop and test all the viewer's modules. We would have a little

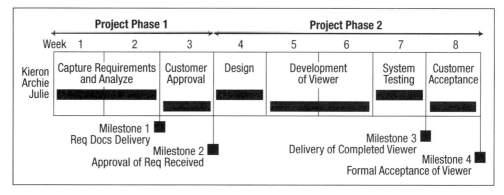

Figure 2. 17
First attempt at a project plan for Project Phases 1 and 2.

flexibility in those three weeks—that is, Weeks 4, 5, and 6—but we must start system testing in Week 7 (although, because this was an internal deadline, we didn't classify it as a milestone). The final milestone was that we would have to deliver the software, ready for acceptance testing, to Monty at the start of Week 8. Remember that these milestones are major events, usually signifying completion of something—and they were dates we must meet.

Project Phase 3: The Editors

All that was left for us to plan was the development of the two editors. We could approach this phase from a different point of view. We had to fit Project Phases 1 and 2 into an imposed time frame. But for Phase 3, we could look at our estimates and determine how long we needed to complete it. That approach represents quite a big difference, we could work from a clean slate.

In fact, if we had decided to use more manpower, we would probably have been able to complete the editors as well as the other scheduled activities in the eight weeks. Completing all that would have meant a lot of parallel activities after design and a great deal more project management. The way we had set up the schedule, Archie and Julie could take part in almost every aspect of the project, which was one of my goals. Monty said he could wait for the editors, so I was quite happy to produce them in Phase 3, which would minimize the management complexity. This time, we could work from our estimates rather than from an imposed time frame.

Figure 2.18 tells us that we needed between 13 and 25 days of effort to complete the editors and have them up and running. For each project week, we could put in four days of Archie's time, four days of Julie's time, and 2.5 days of my time. That meant we could supply a total of 10.5 days of effort per week, given our utilization figures of 80 percent for Julie and Archie, and 50 percent for me. Let's assume we needed all 25 days of effort, our worst-case estimate. We could comfortably supply that effort in four weeks, with lots of extra contingency time. We'd give ourselves another week to do the customer acceptance. All three of us felt confident with this figure. However, we were not just giving ourselves plenty of time for fun. You need to remember that, in this phase, the viewer would be in operation, and we might have to support it if any problems occurred. So, our proposed time scale gave us plenty of slack, which we might need to take up if issues arose with software out in the field.

A Plan for Project Phase 3

We then drew up the plan to complete the project, which you can see in Figure 2.19. We would start when the viewer was completed and accepted. If all had gone well, we would be in project Week 9. We had 15 days to complete the editors, five days for integration and testing, and then we would reach our final milestone: We must be ready to hand over the editors for acceptance testing. And, of course, Monty must be ready to do that work.

After two days of hard work, we had a plan. Tomorrow, the final day, we would write up a proposal and produce a quotation. Again, we had managed to complete all the planned activities in just two days, although we didn't finish until quite late in the evening on the

E-MagBook Project Phase 3—Estimates for Development of the Editors

Archie = 14.5 to 25 days effort
Julie = 15 to 24 days effort
Kieron = 13 to 24 days effort

Combined Range: Minimum of 13 days
Maximum of 25 days

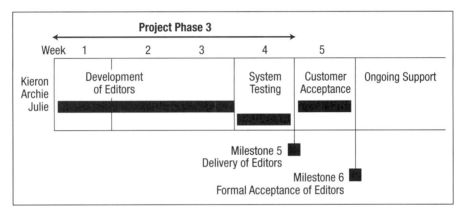

Figure 2.18
Estimates for developing the editors.

Figure 2.19
The Initial plan for completing Phase 3 of the project.

second day. The two days had been hard, and we had covered a huge amount of ground. Had our efforts all been worthwhile? Julie and Archie certainly thought so, but the big question was, Would Monty?

The Proposal and Quotation

The proposal is your chance to put in writing a high-level description of the requirements against which you have quoted. The proposal gives you the opportunity to lay down any restrictions, reservations, and even recommendations. This document is your chance to define precisely what you will be supplying against which your quote is valid. The customer has to approve the proposal. In the quotation, you commit yourself to a price—either fixed or a min-max range to be firmed up at a later date.

Return to the Case Study:

The Proposal

All we had to do on the final day of the three allocated to the pre-sales effort was to put together a proposal that contained some suitable words, formalize the plan, define the milestones and related time elements, and add a quotation. We had loads of raw material at our disposal, which we reviewed to help us in the process. We sat and thrashed out the wording for a proposal that described to Monty what we considered to be the scope of the project. Here is what we came up with:

Proposal to Develop Software for the Montasana E-MagBook

1. Introduction
This proposal is based on the information Montasana Systems provided at a meeting held in their offices to discuss the design and development of software to support the E-MagBook concept.

We propose to design and develop three programs, as described next.

2. Program 1: The E-MagBook Viewer
Consists of the program that will run on the E-MagBook. This viewer will allow a user to select a title from a Title Index contained on each removable disk. After the user has selected a title, a Page Index will be read into the program, which defines the content of each single page.

2.1. Viewer Format Types
A single Page Index will be one of three format types:

2.1.1. Format 1—Text Book
Contains only text pages.

2.1.2. Format 2—Picture Album
Contains a single picture or movie clip (AVI file) per page as well as up to five descriptive keys, each ranging from 0 through 30 characters in length (multiple words allowed).

2.1.3. Format 3—Simple Reference Format
Consists of a single picture or movie clip, a block of unlimited text, and up to five keys, each ranging from 0 through 30 characters in length (multiple words allowed).

2.2. The Page
After a Page Index has been read into the program, the format remains fixed for each page. Each page, of any format type, can have an optional sound source associated with it. This sound takes the form of a wave audio (WAV) file or a MIDI sequencer (MID) file.

2.3. Future Requirements
Another requirement is that a page may consist of a composite of many images, videos, and text blocks. This format is referred to as the Extended Reference format. Another alternative is that a single page may be composed of HTML content, available locally or via the Internet. This content will be displayed using a browser object. These are future requirements that we need to consider at this stage to avoid compromising the design in the future.

2.4. Viewer Modes of Operation
The viewer works in one of three operational modes:

2.4.1. Mode1—Title Selection
For each removable disk, a list of titles is presented, from which the reader can select a single title.

2.4.2. Mode 2—Viewer Mode
The program displays pages from the selected title according to the format type of the Page Index read. Navigation controls allow the user to "turn" pages. For the Picture Album and Reference Book formats, a search capability is also provided to allow the reader to select pages based on their key contents.

2.4.3. Mode 3—Workbench
In this mode, the program allows a page to be displayed such that the reader can position and size the image. If text is present, the reader can position the text and size the container to change the amount of text on view. The resultant layout can then be printed, in every case, as a screen dump.

The composite and HTML pages are required only for printing in the Workbench mode—again, as simple screen dumps.

2.5. Viewer Restrictions
The viewer will be the only program running on the E-MagBook. The display available to the viewer has a resolution of 640¥480 pixels. Because of the physical size of the display, there are to be no drop-down menus.

3. Program 2: The Title Index Editor
This editor will allow Title Indexes to be created using manual data entry. The content of a single entry will consist of a file reference to the Page Index, a free-format title, and a free-format description. Facilities will be available to create a new Index file or edit an existing one. Each entry can be created or amended. The Title Index Editor will run on a standard PC with a minimum resolution of 800×600 pixels. This program does not need to run on the E-MagBook.

4. Program 3: The Page Index Editor
This editor will allow a Page Index to be created or amended. The program will allow the contents of an individual page to be created or amended, and for the resultant page to be viewed in the same manner that the viewer will accommodate, using an area equal to 640x480 pixels of the screen. This program will run on a standard PC, with a minimum configuration of 800x600 pixels. This program does not need to run on the E-MagBook.

This was a preliminary, high-level requirements specification that defined the scope of the project as a whole. The specification did not contain enough information to program from, but it indicated that we had thought about and understood the concept.

The Plan

In addition to enclosing the two plans that you saw earlier (Figures 2.17 and 2.19), we also specified the phases, duration, milestones, and responsibilities (particularly those Montasana Systems demanded) in writing. Here's what we came up with:

Proposed Plan to Develop Software for the Montasana E-MagBook

The fundamental criterion is that a working E-MagBook Viewer is available to Montasana Systems eight weeks from receipt of order. The proposal is to implement the project in three phases.

Phase 1—Expected Duration: Three Weeks

This phase will commence upon receipt of order from Montasana Systems. Phase 1 will consist of the production of a requirement document, which Montasana Systems will need to verify and sign off on as well as an analysis of the requirements.

    Milestone 1: Delivery of the completed requirements specification, beginning of Week 3.

    Milestone 2: Formal acceptance of the requirements specification by Montasana Systems, end of Week 3.

Phase 2—Expected Duration: Five Weeks

This phase will commence at Milestone 2. Phase 2 will consist of the design of the entire system (viewer and editors) and the development and testing of the viewer. The completed viewer will be delivered to Montasana Systems, who will then be required to verify its functionality according to test specifications agreed upon between the two parties.

    Milestone 3: Delivery of fully working E-MagBook Viewer program, beginning of Week 8.

    Milestone 4: Formal acceptance of viewer by Montasana Systems, end of Week 8.

Phase 3—Expected Duration: Four Weeks

This phase will commence at Milestone 4. Phase 3 will consist of the development and testing of the Title Index Editor and the Page Index Editor. Once both editors are completed, they will be delivered to Montasana Systems, who will then be required to verify their functionality according to test specifications agreed upon between the two parties.

    Milestone 5: Delivery of fully working Title Editor and Page Editor programs, beginning of Week 13.

    Milestone 6: Formal acceptance of both editors by Montasana systems, end of Week 13.

Warranty

Warranty of the software will commence from Milestone 6, for a period of three months. After this time, it is expected that either Montasana Systems will take up a support contract for maintenance of the software or support will be supplied and charged for as required.

This proposal defined the phases and deliverables as well as the responsibilities of both parties, according to milestone events. Coupled with the two plans, the proposal would provide Monty with a very clear picture of the project.

The section on warranty indicated that we would offer warranty support, as part of the package, for three months after the final delivery. After this period, Monty would have to make arrangements with us for continued coverage. If he wanted the warranty to last longer, say 12 months, then we could accommodate that, but at an increased price.

The Quote

Because the sums, terms, and conditions are beyond the scope of a book like this, I won't show you the actual *quote*. However, I'll go through what we did to develop the quote. We started with the fixed price for the development of the requirement specification and its analysis. We costed the maximum and minimum days effort values we obtained for project Phase 1. From those, we determined a suitable price that Charlie and I felt comfortable with. We then presented this as a fixed price. The quote took into account the fact that we would have two junior people working full-time, one senior person working part-time, and that we were also treating this as a training exercise. Training is a cost that, quite clearly, we couldn't pass on to Monty. The rates we charged obviously would need to reflect the expertise being called upon and for how long. Then, we needed to make a commercial decision to increase or decrease the price according to a variety of factors, such as, How badly do you want to get the job? Will it lead to further work? Is there a potential product in it? (I could easily write a whole book based solely on setting a price.)

We then looked at the max-min figures for the remaining two phases and costed them according to a formula our company uses for type of effort required. For example, a senior consultant costs three times as much per day as a junior programmer. These are commercial figures, based on overheads, expected profit levels, and so on.

We presented Monty with a minimum price and a maximum price to complete the project. We then stated that, at the end of Phase 1, we would reassess our quotation and produce a fixed-price quote to complete the work involved in Phases 2 and 3. We would guarantee this price to lie between the minimum and maximum prices. Again, we arrived at the final figures based on a variety of business decisions specific to the company involved and to the operating environment.

We also identified the requirement for a Web browser in the future as an issue for which some feasibility work would be necessary. We could conduct this feasibility study while we were capturing and analyzing the requirements, and we could make a report at the end of project Phase 1. We also costed this study as a separate item.

Finally, we put in a payment schedule that followed milestones—provide a deliverable that can be signed off on, and you have an ideal invoicing point. Use these invoicing points to keep cash flowing into the company while you are engaged in the work. As I explained earlier, we determined the amount of management required as a percentage of the total effort. In this case, we used a figure of 15 percent, to compensate for the fact that Archie and Julie would require more assistance than highly experienced staff. In other words, for every 10 days of effort quoted, we added 1.5 days for management. Management of a project depends on many factors and can vary from 10 percent to 30 percent. Management depends on the project's complexity, the number of overlapping activities, the number of milestones, the number of personnel, the amount of customer involvement, and so on. Because we would be monitoring progress daily much of the time (as we looked for early warning signs of problems), progress monitoring would be our biggest activity.

To summarize the costed items, we provided a quote for the following:

♦ Fixed-price quotation for the development and analysis of the requirements.

♦ Minimum-maximum price for the design of the complete system, and development and testing of all three programs (including installation, assistance with acceptance testing, and three months' warranty on delivered software).

♦ Fixed-price quotation for the feasibility study concerning use of a browser for the E-MagBook concept.

Delivering the Proposal, Plan, and Quote

And that was that—the end product of three, very long days of unpaid effort from three people. Clearly, we would like to recoup that cost if we won the job (and we embedded the cost in the overall figures—that is, it was part of our "business" decision-making to set the final prices).

We sent the paperwork to Monty by email, and I called his secretary at 5:00 P.M. to make sure that everything had arrived. Monty called back at 5:30 P.M. to say he had everything he needed, and he thanked us for all the hard work we had put in. He said he would be in touch again on Monday morning, so all we had to do was wait.

The Next Step

We'd now done everything we could, and it was time to wait. However, we would know the result after the weekend. If you're really confident you are going to get the job, there's no harm in making an early start. But my experience says to wait for the order to arrive before committing any resource whatsoever.

Chapter 3

Capturing the Requirements

In this chapter, we'll look, in depth, at capturing requirements and why requirements are so important to a project. We'll also look at a variation of *use cases*—an *object-oriented programming (OOP)* concept that we can usefully employ in non-OOP projects as well—to provide alternative definitions of requirement. In the case study, we'll start to develop the requirements specification for the E-MagBook (completing our first attempt at that document) and the associated use cases, or scenarios (which we will define shortly).

Project Startup

Once you have an order to begin the work for a software development project, your first task will be to develop the requirements specification. You might, however, be involved in a project that starts up with a requirements specification already in existence. In that case, provided the specification's quality is suitable, you can go straight to the SDLC Phase 2 and begin the analysis.

The Startup Meeting

Before you start work on a new project, you must call a startup meeting. The key elements for a startup meeting are as follows:

- *Stakeholders*—All the relevant project stakeholders who will be involved in the project (usually excluding customers) must be present in the project startup meeting.

- *Presentation*—Here, in a short introduction, you present the general nature of the project and the terms of reference of the order.

- *Time frames*—You present overall time frames for the project.

- *Responsibilities*—You make clear the responsibilities of each stakeholder, both to the individual concerned and to everyone else.

- *Chain of command*—You inform all stakeholders of the chain of command and, in particular, whom they are responsible to.

- *Quality plan*—You introduce a quality plan that clarifies the standards you will adhere to and when you will schedule quality audits.

- *Concerns and queries*—You address concerns and queries without getting involved in a detailed discussion. Where discussion is necessary, you urge the appropriate parties to meet separately at another time.

Stakeholders

You will call all the company's stakeholders (remember, these are people who have an interest in the successful conclusion of the project) together for the startup meeting. You will give a brief presentation of what you know about the project (gleaned from the presales effort) and the details of the order. This overview puts the project into context for the interested parties.

Responsibilities

You then need to clarify each person's responsibilities, first to the person concerned, and then to the rest of the team. In a big project, you initially discuss these responsibilities with the key stakeholders, who then pass the information on to other team members directly under their control.

Because all the different disciplines come together for the first time in the startup meeting to discuss a project, the meeting is quite crucial. For example, you might invite support and training staff, even though you might not require their involvement for some weeks (or even months) to come. These people need to be aware that you will require their time. If they have a reasonable description of the project, they can start to consider what they will need to do to prepare for their eventual involvement. At this stage, you should also be able to give them a reasonable idea of when you will need their help.

The startup meeting places the first pegs of the project in the ground, outlining the plan. The goal is to ensure that everyone likely to be involved in the project is aware that the project is starting and knows when you are likely to need him or her on the project.

Introducing the Quality Plan

A vital component at the start of a project is the *quality plan*, which you introduce at the startup meeting. Companies use many written standards; the job of the quality plan is to indicate which of these standards you will use for this particular project. Indeed, a customer might demand that you adhere to *its* standards, so the standards you will be working to might not always be clear-cut. As a result, the quality plan must make the designated standards obvious, so people don't start working against the wrong set of quality criteria.

The purpose of this book is not to go into detail about standards. Suffice it to say that you should write standards clearly and avoid ambiguity. You also need to avoid being too dogmatic or verbose—a fine balance is necessary. You must remember that, if a standard states something must be done, a quality auditor will look for evidence that it has been done.

The quality plan must also designate when you will perform internal quality audits. Through these audits, you can gauge whether everyone is adhering to project standards. This function is vital for proving to the world (both customers and external auditors from standards bodies) that you have a quality system and that you adhere to it. We'll talk more about quality as we go on.

Keep 'Em Brief

Project startup meetings need to be relatively short. In fact, that's true of all meetings. Most people can cope with one to two hours—at the most—of fairly intense information dissemination. After that, concentration starts to wane quite dramatically. If you can, keep the meeting to an hour, and then let the participants take away summaries of the key points. Remember, the main goal of a startup meeting is to make sure all participants know what their responsibilities are, to whom they are responsible, and when they are likely to be involved.

To keep meetings short, particularly where large numbers of people are involved, good preparation work is essential. If you can predetermine peoples' concerns, you can do your best to ensure that you accommodate those concerns within the agenda of the proposed meeting—or even beforehand.

Keep 'Em in Line

Having a tough chairperson who can bring the meeting together when it starts to go off track is also vital. Like so many aspects of complex human endeavors, you can easily become involved in the minutiae of detail, and the meeting will bog down. After all, meetings might be the only time certain stakeholders have to air their views on various subjects. A good project manager will encourage people do this *before* the meeting—and put people together who can resolve issues ahead of time—to avoid having the issues brought up in the meeting itself.

Tip

Meetings such as the startup meeting are to disseminate information, not to carry on a detailed discussion.

External Stakeholders

If the project involves outside contractors, the startup meeting is a good time to introduce those contractors to all the relevant players. Even for the people who are not likely to work together, the introductions will make it easier for them to at least identify each other and understand the other persons' responsibilities.

The Case Study:
Project Startup

True to his word, on Monday morning, Monty was on the phone at 9:00 A.M. (give or take a few minutes) with good news. Against the opposition, he had unreservedly accepted our proposal, plan, and quote. After further questioning, we learned that we were not the cheapest, but we were the only ones who had clearly looked at the job and given it thought. He said that was evident from the detail that appeared in the proposal. One of the other companies had provided a price, stated it could deliver the entire system in eight weeks, and would start *programming* on receipt of order. Monty was not impressed, even though that company's quote was a good 30 percent cheaper than ours.

The order we had received was for "The development and analysis of the requirements specification, Phase 1 of the E-MagBook software project, and a feasibility study into the use of a Web browser for the E-MagBook." This description would form the primary terms of reference for the order. From a project management point of view, the first task on the agenda was to have a startup meeting.

The Startup Meeting

I invited the heads of our support facility, quality assurance (Q/A), training, documentation, and testing departments. Apart from the Q/A people (who had already been busy drawing up the quality plan), these people would not be involved for a while. But, they must know what their responsibilities would be and when we would be likely to require their involvement. For developers, we had Archie, Julie, and myself. I would be serving as the main project manager, and Julie and Archie, under my technical guidance, would be doing all the work for project Phase 1.

In terms of the quality plan, the order was specifically for project Phase 1, so we had drawn up a plan that covered aspects of requirement capturing and analysis. I introduced Charlie as the auditor, and we allocated dates within the plan on which he would assess whether we were adhering to the company standards.

The introduction I gave about the project was based entirely on the proposal we had developed in the previous week. After the introduction, we let the people leave who would not be directly involved in the requirement capturing and analysis. In the next part of the startup meeting, we would come up with a more detailed plan for project Phase 1.

Activities for Project Phase 1

In the plan we produced in the pre-sales effort (Figure 2.17 in Chapter 2), we set aside a two-week period for the "Capture Requirements and Analyze" phase. We now needed to produce a more detailed plan that would let us monitor our progress. We first defined a list of activities that we needed to accomplish to complete the requirements document.

Our task was to physically capture the requirements on paper. This process was the first pass through the SDLC Phase 1 to determine the requirements for the viewer program and the two editors. For each of these, we would then develop a series of descriptions about how a user would use the final product. In OOP, these descriptions are known as the *use case*; we would use a less formal version, which we called the *use scenario*. These scenarios would be simple descriptions that would serve as alternative views of the requirements. These alternative views would allow us to challenge the requirements. Only when we had total consistency between the requirements specification and the use cases, or scenarios, would we have a completed requirements document. We'd look at use cases and scenarios in more detail at the appropriate time.

We'd also agreed to do the feasibility study for integrating a browser into the E-MagBook concept, so that would be another activity in its own right. For the time being, we'd not break down analysis any further, but we needed to remember that analysis would raise lots of issues within the requirements document—issues that we must address to achieve total consistency between requirement descriptions, scenarios, and the results of our analysis.

In project Phase I, we needed to perform the following activities:

♦ Capture requirements for the viewer

♦ Capture requirements for the editors

♦ Develop scenarios for the viewer

♦ Develop scenarios for the editors

♦ Complete the requirements document

♦ Review the requirements document and rework (iteration)

♦ Complete the feasibility study—browser

♦ Analyze requirements

The Plan for Project Phase 1

We had a maximum of 10 working days to produce the requirements document, analyze the content, and to do the feasibility study on integrating a browser with the E-MagBook. We had 21 days of effort available among us: 8 days from Archie, 8 days from Julie (both at 80 percent availability), and 5 days from me (at 50 percent availability). If you recall, we summarized this information in the top half of Figure 2.15, in the previous chapter.

We had extra contingency time available—we had set up all allocations for four days out of each week for Julie and Archie—and we had tried to plan the amount of effort we would require with contingency in mind anyway. We started by splitting the workload among tasks. We'd allocate half the available effort for the capturing process, half for the analysis, and try to fit the feasibility study into Week 1 of the 2 weeks. We'd do the feasibility study using VB again, very much along the lines we followed to explore the multimedia control in Appendix A. VB has a browser control, and I knew a little bit about that, so we estimated half a day to complete the study. Again, we were relying on my expertise to help us; otherwise, the time frame would be much more difficult to gauge.

We'd made a split—50 percent of the effort for capturing requirements and doing the feasibility study, and 50 percent of the effort for analysis. (Every project is different, but, if you're in doubt, I think that approach offers a good starting point.) If everything went like clockwork, we would have the requirements document completed by close of day on Thursday. We could start the analysis early Friday (assuming we had people available) and complete the analysis Tuesday afternoon. That would give us Wednesday to review and do any iteration required, with two days of contingency time left over. We drew up a simple plan based on the activities we had listed for the completion of the requirements document, as shown in Figure 3.1.

Risk Assessment

We'd allocated a whole day to handle the requirements and scenarios for the viewer, but only half a day for the two editors. We had determined those allocations on the basis that the viewer was more complex, and we were producing the requirements for the first time. We had determined in the presales work that the two editors' functionality was similar.

This schedule might be too ambitious; if we were wrong, the feasibility study might have to slide into Day 3. That wouldn't be too disastrous, because one day to complete the document and one day to review and rework was generous—and we also had a whole day of contingency time. As long as we had some staff available on that day, we could make use of those people if we had to. It's also worth pointing out that we had lost a couple of hours on Day 1 getting the project started up, so we no longer had a whole day for the viewer. However, at the time, the risks looked minimal, and, should they arise, we could deal with them using project contingency time.

Progress Monitoring

Because we had a clear goal to achieve every day, we'd review our progress at the end of each day. For the time being, monitoring our progress remained quite straightforward. We'd look at the list of activities for each day and decide whether we had completed them. If we ran ahead of schedule, then we'd start analysis early. If we ran behind, we would have to move activities on the plan. We'll discuss progress monitoring in more detail as the project progresses.

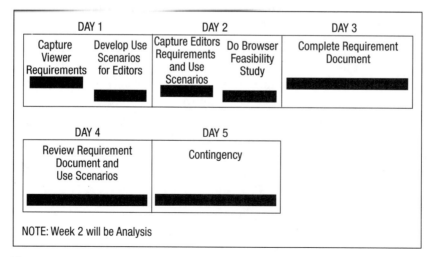

Figure 3.1
Plan for project Phase 1, first week, showing detailed activities.

The Project Begins

From a project management perspective, the project had now definitely started. We had an order for work against a fixed price. The work had to be accomplished in 10 working days so we could meet the first milestone—delivery of the fully analyzed requirements documentation to Monty. We'd had a startup meeting, so everyone was clear about the terms of reference, each person's responsibilities, and who would be supervising whom. We also had a detailed plan to monitor.

The Requirements Specification

The document you have to produce for your project will define all the software requirements—everything it must be able to do. A *user guide* defines what a product does and, in essence, is a requirements document, but you write the user guide after you have completed the development. Conversely, if you think of a requirements document as a user guide you write *before* you develop the system, you won't go too far wrong. Clearly, because the system does not exist, the style of the requirements document can't be the same as a user guide, but, fundamentally, the requirements specification will explain what a customer wants the software to do.

You must make sure that the requirements specification doesn't become highly technical in terms of computer jargon. Never lose track of the fact that the customer will own this document, so you must write it in language the client fully understands.

The Application Domain

The *application domain* refers to anything to do with the nature of the business or activity for which the software is required. For example, in our case study, the application domain is electronic books; for an inventory control system, the domain is inventory control. Any application domain will have its own language, and that's the language of the requirements document.

As a software engineer, your task in producing a requirements document is to go to the domain experts to learn about their domain and then document their requirements. Obviously, the best people to write a requirements document are the domain experts themselves, but, often, they don't have the time, the inclination, or even the ability, to do so.

Where the requirement contains a real complexity, such as data processing algorithms or *business rules* that you must meet, you must document the complexity in a form that domain experts and software engineers alike can understand. Business rules define what the software must do with data according to how the application domain works. A very simple example of business rules is how interest rates are calculated for bank accounts. The full definition of how the calculation must be performed and how often, taking all possibilities into account (positive and negative balances), needs to be set down in writing before you contemplate coding for such functionality.

Unless you happen to be a domain expert, you cannot possibly know about the business complexities—or, indeed, about any aspect of what the domain is all about. You must extract all that knowledge from someone who does know. In Chapter 1, I defined the activity of capturing the requirements as sitting down with the customer and doing a lot of listening, followed by a lot of writing—and that sums it up. You have to learn about the application domain and then document the requirements for a specific development to address specific needs.

Communication Skills

You must be a proficient communicator to extract from clients what they need. You must ask questions to clarify issues you might have. Domain experts can easily intimidate you. Just remember, they might have worked in their own area of expertise for many years. They will talk glibly about concepts that are second nature to them. As a result of their familiarity with the concepts and/or the situation, however, they often overlook the obvious.

Ask Questions

Try not to feel self-conscious about asking your client what you fear might be stupid questions. If the client refers to acronyms, ask what they stand for—you can't be expected to understand domain acronyms if you are not a domain expert.

Use Diagrams

Ask the customer to assist you by drawing relevant diagrams for the customer to review, and, every now and again, offer a summary of what you believe the situation is. You'll find that, if you pick things up quickly and provide some feedback to the client that you have assimilated the content, a healthy respect will burgeon.

Get Constant Feedback

Communication is a two-way process. If you sit and do nothing but listen, chances are that you are missing a great deal. By asking questions, you are doing two things: The nature of your question gives the other party an indication of your level of understanding, and you also are indicating your ability to grasp the key points. Without this feedback, the client will draw one of two conclusions: Either you understand nothing, or (possibly more dangerous) you understand everything.

Another important fact is that the customer doesn't always *know* what is required and needs help to extract the information. Often, a customer has a vague perception of what he or she needs, but can't explain it in depth. Here, the feedback between the person developing the requirements specification and the domain expert is extremely important. The very act of explaining your perception of a requirement to a potential user suddenly clarifies what he or she is trying to get across.

Keep It Simple and Specific

Because languages are so rich, the same thing can be said in many ways. Unfortunately, the same thing can also be interpreted in many ways. Those variations are why we will be looking at scenarios later to augment the requirements specification. As you will see, things don't really start to sort themselves out and make sense until the analysis.

You'll be wise to stick to reasonably short sentences in the requirements specification. The longer a sentence is, the more open to different interpretations it can become. You don't have to be a literary genius to write good requirements documents, but you do need to be methodical and as precise as possible.

Independent Reviewing

The most important aspect of writing a requirements document is to get at least one other person—and preferably more—to review it. Other readers will help you to find any vague statements.

Different Views

In truth, no simple way exists to specify a software development that meets all the needs of all the players within a project. Consequently, you must rely on a number of views of the requirements. Written in plain English, the requirements document is just one view and will be open to misinterpretation. Scenarios will contain very specific definitions of how the system is to be used; these scenarios will clarify much vagueness. From analysis, you will define models that provide more alternative views of the requirements' component structure. Taken together, requirements statements, scenarios, and models narrow the vagueness considerably. Unfortunately, only you, as a software developer, will posses the skills to understand all the different views—from the verbose English descriptions to the more technical models (quite a responsibility, really).

Functions of the Requirements Document

You might be surprised at just how many ways you can use the requirements document. The following uses make the requirements specification the key element of the project:

- *Extent of supply*—Defines exactly what functionality the software you develop will provide, which can be used as a contractual document to determine if you have fulfilled the customer's order.

- *Arbiter of disputes*—Acts as an arbiter if of disputes arise concerning delivered functionality.

- *Early learning*—Allows nontechnical and technical people to come up to speed with the product before it has been produced.

- *Expectation control*—Allows the developer to control the customer's expectations by defining restrictions in detail.

Extent of Supply

First and foremost, *extent of supply* describes what the customer wants out of the development—it represents the definitive terms of reference for the project's software requirements. The customer can order software to be developed according to the content of the requirements document, which means you have a contractual framework against which you develop the software.

Arbiter of Disputes

As contractual terms of reference, the requirements document is only as good as its content. If an issue arises concerning functionality, everyone will refer to the requirements document. If the customer tells you he or she expected to see the developed software produce export files that could be read into Microsoft's Access database system—and it clearly doesn't—the answer to the discrepancy lies in the requirements specification. If the document doesn't mention export facilities, then such facilities are not part of the extent of supply. If the specification includes a reference, you should have supplied a facility. It's as simple as that.

Early Learning

Assuming that the requirements document lacks ambiguity—or at least that ambiguity is minimal (because the document is written in English and is devoid of computer jargon)—a whole range of people will be able to understand it. You can use the document to introduce the end product to anyone who joins the project. For example, our testing people use the requirements specifications to come up to speed on what the software does, long before we have produced the software. This means that, with this document and the test specifications, they can be ready to start testing as soon as the software is ready. Without a completed requirements document, they would have to start up the learning curve only when the software was handed to them, which would delay the start of testing.

The same principle applies to the documentation people—they can study the requirements specifications, so that, by the time they have the software to document, they are already quite knowledgeable about its functionality from the application domain's point of view. Support staff will eventually have to gear up to support the application. Again, the requirements specification gets them well on their way to understanding the software before the system is available.

Expectation Control

Customers have expectations about what the software will do. You must control these expectations, and that's also a function of the requirements document. You must use your skill to help ensure the customer doesn't misinterpret your original meaning.

Finally, the primary function of the requirements specification is (obviously) to define what the customer wants from the software, but you can also use the document to define what the software can't do. To repeat: The requirements specification is your tool for controlling the client's expectations.

Return to the Case Study:
Capturing the Viewer's Requirements

We would now define the requirements for the viewer in detail. We already had a good, high-level definition of requirements, produced in the presales phase. Next, we started expanding the level of detail. We'd look at various aspects and produce detailed descriptions. Remember that our understanding of the requirements would evolve throughout the allocated two-week period. As a result, the definitions would change, expand, and possibly be completely rewritten—this was all part of the process. During this capturing process, one of us always wrote the outcome of any discussion directly onto a laptop.

You won't see the final, completed, and accepted version until Chapter 5, after we've done the analysis. In Chapter 5, we will review the requirements in detail, and you will be able to see how our understanding evolved.

Page Format

As you can see from the proposal, key aspects of the requirements were the formats to be handled and the three modes in which the viewer program could run. We started with those requirements as the basics. Obviously, we'd add an introduction (and so on) later, but, basically, here is what we decided would be a reasonable description for formats:

E-MagBook Formats
The E-MagBook viewer program will be capable of initially reading three types of book format. These formats are defined as follows:

Format 1—Text Book
The Text Book consists of any number of pages, to a maximum of 1,000, each of which is referenced by page number. A single page consists of an unlimited block of text.

This was our current perception of a text-only book. (As the analysis unfolds, watch how this view changes.)

Format 2—The Picture Album
The Picture Album consists of any number of pages, to a maximum of 1,000, each of which is referenced by page number. A single page contains a single, static image, which will be positioned on the screen and scaled to fit into a defined *Album picture area*. Alternatively, the page can contain an AVI movie clip instead of a static image. Each page is completely independent of any other page. Any of the pages can be image or video pages in any sequence. The image can be of any size and must be scaled so that the entire picture is always on view and so that the aspect ratio is as defined in the full-sized image.

The primary image file formats to be used are BMP and JPEG, although the following file types will also be available, if required:

- BMP   Windows Bitmap

- DIB   Device Independent Bitmap

- GIF   Graphics Interchange Format

- JPEG Joint Photographic Experts Group

- WMF   Windows Metafile

The video file format will be the Windows AVI (Audio Video Interleave) format.

Each page can be associated with up to five keys (as defined later) and can also be accessed by a search on one or more of its keys.

Our description was starting to be very specific. Thanks to the feasibility work we had done earlier (described in Appendix A), the requirements definition should be perfectly understandable to you. Again, watch how this definition changes during our analysis phase.

Format 3—Simple Reference Book Format
The Simple Reference Book format consists of any number of pages, to a maximum of 1,000, each of which can be composed of a single static image, a block of text, and up to five keys. The image is viewable in a manner similar to that described for the Picture Album format, but it will be scaled and placed in an area of the screen defined specifically for the Simple Reference Book format. Alternatively, an AVI movie clip might replace the static image. Each page will also have an unlimited block of text, which users can view in a text scrolling area adjacent to the displayed image or video clip. The keys can also be displayed on a page together with the image/video clip and text.

As with the Photo Album format, users can access the Simple Reference Book format page by page number or by searching for one or more of its keys.

Future Format Requirements

At this stage, we could add definitions for the future page requirements.

Extended Reference Book Format

The first of the future requirements was for an Extended Reference Book format, also known as the Composite format:

Format 4—Extended Reference Book Format (Future Requirement)
The Extended Reference Book format consists of any number of pages, to a maximum of 1,000, each of which is composed of a composite image layout. This composite can consist of any number of images, in any position and size. It can also contain any number of text blocks, each of which can be positioned anywhere on the screen and in any size. Each block of text can also use any font type and attributes. The composite can also contain a single video clip and static images.

This composite structure of images, text blocks, and video clips uses the full screen layout, except for the area used by the navigation controls (defined later). Each page can also possess up to five keys.

A single page can be accessed by page number or by a search on one or more keys (as defined later).

Note that we'd set a limit of a single video clip. Monty would have to approve this limitation, of course. As we discussed earlier, the requirements specification is the ideal place to put in restrictions—and even definitions of what the software won't do. Remember, this document is the tool by which we would curb the customer's expectations—our attempt to avoid the words, "But I thought it was supposed to do that!"

HTML Format

We needed to think a little about HTML pages. We were talking about a Page Index that would contain any number of pages; each page would be an HTML file resident on the removable disk or on an Internet Web site. Within one book, the pages could even be a mixture of local HTML files and remote Web sites. For example, a local page reference might look like "E:\DIRECTORY\FILE.HTM", whereas a remote reference would look like "**http://www**…". These alternatives meant that the program could strip off the first characters up to the colon (**:**) and then know immediately what to do—go straight to the file on the disk, or access the information via the connection that Monty would provide with his built-in telephone. That was all we needed to worry about at this stage, because the HTML pages were outside the scope of the current project.

Tip

Although SDLC purists will tell you that doing so is wrong, we were actually touching on design phase here. (Purists believe that you should not consider design until the design phase.) But asking yourself, How on earth am I going to do this? as you go through the requirements is a natural human response. And, in truth, if considering the answer to this question makes you comfortable, to do so is a good thing. The point is this: Don't get bogged down in anything else at this stage except capturing those all-important requirements.

The Browser

To view an HTML page, we would require a browser, and part of our feasibility study scheduled for this project phase would be to see how we could incorporate a browser into the E-MagBook viewer. Again, as a reminder, we would do the feasibility in VB.

Even though the browser integration was a future requirement, we spent some time discussing it in depth. VB had a browser control that we could employ. The control provides a browser form, which we could size and to which we could pass the Web reference. The pages of the Web site would then be displayed on the available screen via the Internet Explorer browser, whose components the VB browser uses. One question we had was, Are the navigation controls still to be present on the screen? The basic concept was that, even though the pages would be in HTML format, the entity was still a book. So, navigation would still be required, even for Web sites.

An Issue Identified

This discussion raised an important requirements issue: Once connected to a Web page, can the user then surf the Net? Because we would be using a browser, there would be nothing to stop the user from surfing. From the point of view of the E-MagBook's functionality, we could treat the browser as an independent facility with which the user could access other Internet sites, but as soon as the reader used a navigation control, he or she would be pulled back into the index. We wrote this up as follows:

Format 5—HTML Format (Future Requirement)
This format consists of any number of HTML pages, to a maximum of 1,000, which can be accessed by page number. Each page is viewed through a browser, which occupies the entire screen, except for the navigation controls. A single page can be held locally on the removable disk, or it can be accessed via an Internet Web site reference.

After an HTML page is placed on the screen, the reader can use any hot links present to bring up any other HTML page accessible to the browser. Alternatively, the reader can use the navigation controls to navigate through the Index and bring up HTML pages according to the Index entry. Use of the navigation controls overrides any links the reader might have made outside the Index.

Up to five keys can be attached to each page. One or more keys can be used to search for an HTML page in the Index.

We would revisit these descriptions when we created the application scenarios and again when we performed the analysis. Consequently, the descriptions were likely to change.

VB as the Development Environment

We keep mentioning VB—something the purists would not approve of, because system developers shouldn't make a decision on platform until they have the requirements and have analyzed them. Again, life's just not like that. VB kept screaming at us, "I can do this!" I was quite comfortable that we could complete the project using VB, but the all-important requirement was that we leave our options open. We wouldn't make the final decision until the right time. But, if considering VB made us comfortable at this stage, then that was fine. We would be able to prove that we could integrate a browser into the program to our satisfaction, and, if we didn't use VB, we could use the feasibility study as a model to show what functionality would be necessary in whatever environment we chose.

In an ideal world, you look at all the requirements, you analyze them, and you design a system that is independent of platform (that is, independent of hardware, operating system, and language). But again, life is not that simple. Monty had no idea what we were going to use, and he didn't much care, either. As long as the product we delivered met his requirements, consisted of software that was easily maintainable, and could be further developed over a period of at least five years, then he'd go along with whatever we chose. The system also would have to be cost-effective. Remember, Monty didn't want lots of third-party license fees to pay out for each E-MagBook he sold.

On a big job, you might devote an entire project phase to evaluating platforms, to pick the one that best suits your requirements and design. My motto is "Be comfortable with what you're doing." If you hit a sticky patch, where you're uncertain how to proceed, take some time out to think about it. But, as I said earlier and will no doubt say again, don't get bogged down. Just do enough extra work to minimize the risks and confirm that you have a possible way forward—even though it may not be the final route.

Document Status

Like all project documents, the requirements document must be drafted and then accepted by the client. During its development, this document can be changed any number of times and by a variety of individuals. For example, in our case study, Archie, Julie, and I might well be modifying it.

Eventually, we will reach a point at the end of SDLC Phase 1 where we will believe the requirements document is complete. At this point, we will classify it as "Completed Draft Version 1." We will still maintain the document at draft level, which means the customer has not yet accepted it. We expect that the document *will* likely change as a result of what we would unearth in analysis. Consequently, we continue to classify it as a draft document that any one of the three of us could change.

Once we complete our analysis and have total consistency between the results of analysis and the content of the document itself, we are ready to submit the requirements document to the client. At this stage, its status changes to "Completed" and we drop the "Draft." However, Monty has not yet accepted the document, and, in the course of acceptance, he might demand changes. From now on, we will have to control changes carefully, and changes must be authorized.

We must implement a system that allows us to track the reason for a change as well as details about the change itself. Version numbering now becomes very important, so that, at any given time, we know the latest, completed version number and how it differs from the previous (lower-numbered) versions.

A Procedural Approach

If you think this is all starting to get to be too much to ask, let's look at an example. A customer signs off on a requirements document, and you start design. Halfway through the design phase, the customer suddenly remembers that the software must link to a remote system to receive data on a regular basis. You did not include this requirement in the specification—indeed, you knew nothing about it. You look at the changes required and agree to include them. You produce an addendum to the requirements specification, and the client signs off on the addendum. You continue with development.

Three memos arrive from the customer referring to this extra functionality; these memos go directly to the developers. One of these memos defines a requirement that contradicts the information in the addendum, one requests extra functionality not previously defined as a requirement, and the third removes a small requirement. The developer doesn't tell anyone (I've seen it happen).

You create test specifications that relate to the accepted requirements document and the addendum. When the time for testing arrives, the software functionality, which the programmer developed, does not relate to the requirements documentation from which you produced the test specifications. In a big project, this discrepancy could have a serious impact on delivery. In other words, the developer took it upon himself or herself to produce functionality according to the memos from the customer, and the functionality turned out to be substantially different from the accepted, documented definitions.

To prevent such a possibility in our projects, we require two procedures: one to control requests for change, and one to implement those requests. We'll look at this subject in a much wider context later.

Tracking Changes

Customers might demand changes to the completed requirements document before they are prepared to accept (and take ownership of) the document. Each change—or batch of changes—will result in a revised "Completed" document, an addendum, or even both. You must change the document's version number so that project management can track its status. You might have a situation, for example, where five changes are demanded, each of which is quite substantial. You would then reissue the document as "Completed Version 2." The acceptance process then begins again.

Another example—and variation—might be that the customer is satisfied but wants some minor changes. You can define these changes on a couple sheets of paper, which you then add to the completed document as addenda, and you change the document's version number to 1.1. (We use the first digit before the decimal point to indicate a major change and the figure after it to indicate minor changes.)

Within the project management files, you will have a reference to the requirements document as Version 1 (status=Completed), delivered to the customer on a certain date. The next reference might be to Version 1.2 (status=Completed), delivered at a later date, and acceptance of Version 1.2 logged on a third date. At a glance, anyone can see the document's history. To obtain the detail, you will need to read the first section of the document itself, into which you have placed a change history (whether the change was a change to the document content or merely the inclusion of an addendum).

Your goal is an auditable trace of what happens to a document in its lifetime, from its first "Completed" status to its final "Accepted" status, with corresponding version numbers. Later, we'll look at how you can extend handling a document this way to accommodate subsequent changes, after the first customer acceptance.

Return to the Case Study:
Modes of Operation

We captured details about page formats and some future requirements in our first-draft requirements document. We then moved on to describe the operational mode requirements. If you recall from the proposal, we would have three modes in which the viewer could operate: Title Selection, View, and Workbench. Here are the first detailed descriptions:

Required Modes of Operation for the E-MagBook Viewer

It is required that, at any given moment, the viewer be operating in one of the modes defined in this section.

Mode 1—Title Selection

When in this mode, the program presents a list of titles to the reader from the removable disk that is currently inserted into the E-MagBook. The reader can select any of the listed titles, and the following information is then displayed:

- A free-text title, of unlimited length.

- A free-text description of the book's contents, of unlimited length.

The limiting factor for the length of each of the above will be the display space provided on the screen.

Optionally, the reader may remove the disk and replace it with another one. On request, the new Index is presented to the reader.

Optionally, the reader may select a title from the displayed list and request that the title be loaded into the program. At this stage, the program will revert to the Page View mode.

What, Not *How*

Up to this point, I had assisted Archie and Julie; now, it was their turn. I left them to continue on their own. After an hour, I went back to see how they were faring. They had become caught up in how things would look on the screen, and they were talking a lot about screen controls in VB. Where they were was such an easy trap to fall into. I reaffirmed that what we were doing was capturing the requirements. What they had started to do—in depth—was determine *how* things would be done in the software. They had started to move away from the *what* to the *how*, and they were getting bogged down. We discussed the issues for a bit, and then I left them to redo what they had done. I gave them another hour, and I saw a vast improvement. This time, they had concentrated on only functional requirements. We had a lot of debate about what they had defined as requirements, and we made modifications as we reached agreement among us about what the requirements ought to be.

Modes of Operation Completed

By now, you should understand the process—going through the details of how Julie and Archie arrived at the final version isn't necessary. Using all the documentation produced in the presales effort, they produced the following:

Mode 2—Page View

The program can be placed in this mode only after the reader has requested a valid title from a removable disk, using the Title Selection mode. When the reader invokes the Page View mode, the program determines which format type is in use and sets itself accordingly. All pages in the selected title must conform to this format. The program starts by displaying the first page of the title in the appropriate format, as already specified.

In this mode, the full range of navigation and search facilities (as detailed later) are available. The reader also has the option to request that the program mode be changed to Workbench.

When the reader has finished using Workbench mode, he or she can reselect the Page View mode, and the current page that was on view at the time the reader invoked the Workbench mode is then reinstated, according to its format type.

At any time, the reader may reinvoke the Title Selection mode.

Mode 3—Workbench

The Workbench mode is invoked only from the Page View mode. The Workbench mode uses the full-screen availability (that is, no navigation controls are on screen). The requirements for the Workbench mode of operation depend on the format type.

Format 1—Text-Only Pages in Workbench Mode

A text-only page is displayed as a single block of text on the Workbench screen. Text for a text-only page can be of any length. Requirements are that the textbox can be moved around the screen for positioning purposes and it can be resized in terms of its height or width. The purpose of these requirements is to allow the reader to set up the block as required for printing purposes. A print request will direct a copy of the text, exactly as it appears on the screen, to the E-MagBook's default printer, if present.

At any time, the reader can invoke the Page View mode of operation.

Format 2—Picture Album Pages in Workbench Mode

The picture from a Picture Album page is displayed at full size on the screen in Workbench mode. The top, left-hand corner of the image will be present on the screen. The rest of the image may or may not be present, depending on whether the image is bigger or smaller than the available space.

It is required that the image can be moved around the screen for positioning purposes.

The user will be able to alter the dimensions of the image by shrinking or expanding the height and width together so that the aspect ratio is always preserved.

An alternative method of changing the image's dimensions—by expanding or contracting just one of the dimensions (height or width)—is also required. This method does not require preservation of the aspect ratio.

Changing the image dimensions and ignoring the aspect ratio is not an actual requirement Monty had mentioned. We had decided to include a bit of extra functionality here to make the program more versatile, because we could easily do so. The Text Book functionality already required this functionality, so it wouldn't be a big job to include it for the Picture Album format as well. Monty could always reject the addition if he didn't agree.

After the reader moves the image and manipulates and increases its size, only a small portion of the bitmap might be present on the screen. This portion could be any part of the enlarged image.

At any stage, the reader can request a print of the image, exactly as it appears in the viewing area. The output will be directed to the system's default printer, if there is one. And at any stage, the reader may reinvoke the Page View mode, in which case the page that was current when the Workbench was invoked will be reinstated on screen.

Format 3—Reference Book in Workbench Mode
The picture from a Reference Book page is treated in Workbench mode in exactly the same manner as that described for the image of a Picture Album page in this mode.

The text from a Reference Book page is treated in the Workbench mode in exactly the same manner as that described for a Text-Only format in this mode.

The image and text display must be treated as completely separate objects in the Workbench mode, with the following requirement: Where the image and text block overlap, the text block always appears in the foreground, overlaying the image.

Format 4—Extended Reference Book in Workbench Mode (Future Requirement)
The Extended Reference Book format will be displayed in the Workbench mode in exactly the same way that it is displayed in the Page View mode, except that the navigation controls will be removed. Neither the Composite, nor its components, can be moved or have their dimensions manipulated in any way.

At any stage, the reader can request a printout of the screen content. This printout will be directed to the system's default printer, if one is attached.

Format 5—HTML Pages in Workbench Mode (Future Requirement)
Navigation controls are removed and the browser is extended to cover the available screen. No screen objects can be manually manipulated or resized. The content of the screen may be printed to the system's default printer, if there is one.

Who Is the Document For?

It's worth recalling at this stage that the document is being written as if Monty had actually put pen to paper. He was paying us to do the work, and we were second-guessing a lot of what he required because he was too busy to be involved. Hopefully, you can now see why we were giving Monty a whole week to go over the documentation we produced here—so he could be sure *we'd* captured what *he* wants!

You may well be involved in many projects where the customer hands over a completed set of requirements, and you are just told to get on with it. Personally, I prefer to be involved in capturing the requirements, because we can add lots of elements to the list that perhaps the customer hasn't had time to think about. In really big projects, the requirements capture can be a massive undertaking all its own. (I've known such exercises to take more than 12 months.) I hope you are beginning to appreciate that, without this process, it's very difficult—if not impossible—for either side (customer or developer) to really know what's wanted.

Requirements for Navigation

Next, Archie and Julie moved on to navigation in Page View mode:

Navigation (Page View Mode Only)

A requirement is that, when the program is in Page View mode for any book format, the reader can request a page number at any time, and the page will be brought up on the screen and formatted accordingly. This is defined as a **Go To Page Number** function. Two special variants of this are also requirements, defined as the **Go To Start Page** and the **Go To End Page** functions. Also, at any time the E-MagBook is in Page View mode, the user may request the next or previous page in the sequence, and this request may be performed any number of times until the user encounters either the last page or the first page. Any subsequent attempt to navigate beyond the first or last pages is blocked, and an appropriate message is delivered to the reader.

Here, they'd specified the requirements to let a user "turn" the pages of a book. Note that they also added **Go To Page**, **Go To End**, and **Go To Start Page** facilities—all nice and specific.

Requirements for Keys

And then they moved on to keys:

Keys

Each Page (except Text-Only) can have up to five keys associated with it. A page may have no keys or any number of keys, to the maximum of five. Each single key consists of totally free-range text, to a maximum length imposed by the size of the screen display reserved for each key. If required, a key may consist of more characters than can be displayed. Keys can be composed of one or more words, and any mixture of uppercase and lowercase is permissible. Only printable characters are acceptable (that is, no control codes).

We talked about keys quite a lot. We were allowing them to be of any length, but, clearly, from what Samantha said about them, they would have a finite size of about 20 to 30 characters. We'd specified that the actual requirement would be what was sensible in terms of the display area allocated to each key. Because readers would use the keys for searches, from a practical viewpoint, it seemed sensible to keep them relatively short. Otherwise, who would remember them? Nevertheless, we included built-in flexibility so the keys could be long if they needed to be used as mini-descriptors (a term that might be relevant in Picture Album mode). This flexibility was no extra effort to us, and it gave the designer of the page the choice to use the keys as mini-descriptors, simple search keys, or even a mixture of both.

Requirements for Searching

Searching was a piece of independent functionality that required only the selection criteria and the Page Index with which to work:

Searching

A requirement is that, at any time in Page View Mode (except in Text-Only format), the reader can specify one or more keys, to a maximum of five, which he or she can then use to locate a page that contains the same keys. We refer to the collection of requested keys as the *search selection criteria*. A requirement is that a user be able to set up or modify the criteria at any time, and that the defined criteria will remain in force until they are next modified. The criteria are also preserved across the three program modes of the viewer, even though searching can be instigated only in the Page View mode.

At any stage in Page View mode, the user can request a search. It is required that two variants of this request are available:

Search from Page 1

Whenever a reader requests this option, the program will examine the keys for Page 1, then Page 2, and so on, looking for a match between each page's keys and the search selection criteria. This process continues until a matching entry is found, at which point the entry is displayed and made the current page. Alternatively, if no match is found, the program supplies an appropriate message to the reader and makes the last page available.

Find Next

Whenever a reader requests this option, the program will examine the keys of the page next to the one currently on screen. If the program finds no match, then it will continue searching each entry, up to the last page, until it has either found a match or failed to find one. If the program finds a match, it brings the associated page onto the screen, and the page becomes the current one. If the program finds the last page and no match ensues, the program supplies an appropriate message to the reader.

Type of Search

Two types of search are required. In the first type, all the keys defined in the selection criteria must be found—that is, if three keys are defined, those three keys must exist in their entirety on a page. It does not matter how many other keys exist on the page. In the second type, a match requires that only one or more of the selection criteria are present on a page's list of keys for a match.

In summary:

Search Type 1—All keys defined in selection criteria must exist on the page.

Search Type 2—One or more keys from selection criteria must exist on the page.

From a functional point of view, this information defined, in detail, how the search engine would operate. As a programmer, you must know this level of detail; otherwise, you will develop what you think is a search facility, but which might not come anywhere close to what the customer expects. You might well design a search facility infinitely better than the customer expected, but don't forget—you are trying to make a profit as well. With the preceding requirement definitions, you know exactly what is needed from your code for this functionality.

Requirements for Sound

Finally, Julie and Archie defined the requirements for the WAV and MID file types:

Page Sound Track

Each page may have a single sound track associated with it. This sound track is in the form of a WAV file or a MID file. Only one file type is required per page. A page may or may not contain a sound file. When a page that does contain a sound file is brought up onto the screen, any sound track currently being played is terminated and the new sound file is played immediately.

If subsequent pages selected for viewing contain no sound file, the last loaded sound continues to play.

It is also required that a sound being played can be manually stopped and restarted.

Diagrams

In addition to all the descriptions, we had the screen layouts that we produced and included in Chapter 2 (Figure 2.2)—shown here in Figure 3.2. We would include these layouts in the appropriate places in the final document. You can see the final result in Chapter 5, where we review the specification in its final form.

All this work had brought us to a very late lunchtime. It looked like the morning's work had been very fruitful. Because we had been entering all the descriptions into a word processor, we printed out copies of the document so far and broke for lunch.

Use Cases and Scenarios

As I mentioned previously, a very useful tool developed specifically for object-orientated programming (OOP) development is the *use case*. The use case defines how an "actor" interacts with a system; it helps to establish the identity of users and what they are allowed to do to fulfill their needs. We will use a simple form of use case—the *application scenario*—to help clarify the requirement specifications. These scenarios will be a part of the final document in the case study.

A scenario needs a name—something that allows us to reference it. For example, in the case study, we developed a scenario for "Selecting A Title"—that is, a definition of how a user would select a title from the E-MagBook removable disk. We would employ scenarios to describe how an actor interacted with the system under a specific set of circumstances. We

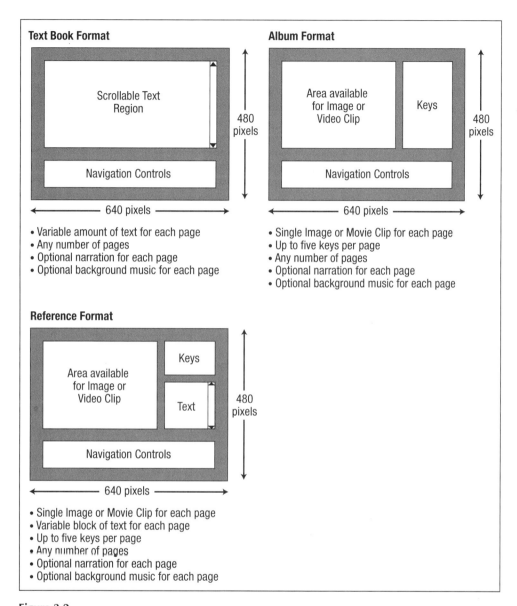

Figure 3.2

Text Book, Picture Album, and Simple Reference Book formats.

also needed to define the type of actor associated with a scenario. For the case study, we had three actors: a *reader*, someone reading an E-MagBook; a *Title Editor*, someone who could create and edit Title Index; and a *Page Editor*, someone who could edit or create a Page Index.

We must also define any preconditions that must be met before the scenario is relevant. For example, a scenario that defines how an invoicing clerk submits an invoice might be applicable only if a client has placed an order and work for that order has been completed. Post conditions might also apply.

A number of entities are required in the OOP use case to assist in the analysis when objects and their characteristics are to be established. How we used the scenarios in our case study is not quite the same as the way we would use them in the more rigid OOP approach. Ideally, we would require one or more scenarios for each piece of required functionality. The scenarios would provide an alternative description of the requirements, and they would have to be consistent with the definitions that constitute the requirements document. Table 3.1 shows the template we used to define our scenarios.

Example Scenarios

Your goals in defining scenarios are to enhance your understanding of the project requirements, test the requirement definitions you have produced so far, and provide straightforward descriptions for the customer to verify. Let's consider an example. A storage facility exists, into which a manufacturing plant places its products until it needs them. At that time, the plant removes the products from storage.

Before Computerization

For the existing system (before computerization), we can define two scenarios—one for goods into storage and one for goods out of storage.

Scenario Name: *Goods into Storage*

Preconditions: Production has produced an item, and the item is to be stored until required.

Description: The item is brought to storage and measured by the storekeeper. The storekeeper assigns an identity to the item and allocates a free storage location that will accommodate the item, given its dimensions. The storekeeper records the item identity and its storage location in the storage register and also on a tag placed on the item itself. The item is then moved to the Goods In area. A *store person takes the item and places it in the required location.* This is a very high-level description of what happens to an item that needs to be booked into storage. The "Goods Out of Storage" scenario might look like the following summary.

Scenario Name: *Goods Out of Storage*

Preconditions: An item held in storage has been allocated to a customer order.

Description: A request arrives at the Goods Out section of storage for a given item. The storekeeper looks up the item in the storage register and identifies its location. A store person is then dispatched to the location to remove the item, which is taken to the Goods Out area. The storage location is then marked "empty" in the storage register. *When the item is removed from the Goods Out section, its entry in the storage register is marked "collected."*

These two simple descriptions define how an item gets into storage and is subsequently removed as a result of manual operations. Suppose you are asked to computerize the process to include automated conveyor belts and stacking cranes.

Table 3.1   Scenario template for the case study.

Scenario Name	Descriptive Name for the Scenario
Preconditions	Conditions that must be met before the scenario applies.
Description	The description of how an actor interacts with the system.

After Computerization

The first thing you need to do is see how the manual scenarios will change as a result of implementing an automated process. The two scenarios for the final system might now read something like the following descriptions.

Scenario Name: Goods into Storage

Preconditions: Production has produced an item, and the item is to be stored until required.

Description: The item is brought to storage and placed on the input conveyor. The input conveyor automatically moves the item to the measuring bay, where it is automatically measured. The computer uses the measurements to determine what sort of storage bay is required and allocates a free, suitable location for the item. At the same time, the computer generates a bar code identity for the item. The bar code is printed on a label and attached at a designated location to the standard pallet that holds the item. The item is then automatically transported to the crane pickup point. Once free, the crane returns to the pickup point and loads the item. The crane reads the bar code identity and looks up the allocated storage location. *The crane then moves the item to the location and automatically deposits it.*

As you can see, the manual process has given way to a much more sophisticated, automated process that involves conveyors and a stacker crane. The "Goods Out of Storage" scenario might well have changed to something like the following summary.

Scenario Name: Goods Out of Storage

Preconditions: An item is required from storage.

Description: An electronic request arrives for the crane. The crane, when available, looks up the storage location identity for the requested item and travels to it. The item is automatically extracted and placed on the crane. The crane then moves to the Goods Out location and deposits the item on the output conveyor. The item is then automatically transported to the pickup point for goods out, for subsequent collection. *After the item has been picked up, the recipient wands the bar code to clear the item from storage and indicate that it has been collected.*

The two sets of scenarios tell an interesting story of how the system functions before computerization and how it will function afterwards. In OOP, we would further break down these use cases, to allow us to define objects and verbs that we could then analyze to assist us in the development of *objects* and *classes* (the templates from which common objects are created).

Challenging the Requirements

To recap, the business of defining scenarios focuses our attention on how the user will interact with the system. It is, therefore, likely that we will encounter a number of deficiencies in the requirement definitions as we probe deeper into them, using a viewpoint that is specific to the operators of the final solution. Scenarios supply us with alternative views of the requirements, letting us probe them in greater depth. One extremely useful aspect of use cases, or scenarios, is that they provide invaluable raw material for developing test scripts, as you will see later on.

Return to the Case Study:
Scenarios for the Viewer

Each of us—Julie, Archie, and I—armed with a copy of the requirements specifications produced so far, met on the first afternoon to begin developing a series of scenarios; that is, we were going to try to describe how a reader would operate the viewer. Our aim was to challenge the requirements and provide a different perspective of them.

Selecting a Title

Let's start with a scenario of someone selecting a title in Title Selection mode.

Scenario: Viewer Title Selection

Preconditions:
No E-MagBook removable disk is present in the E-MagBook.

Description:
The reader switches on the E-MagBook and is informed that no Title Index is available. A disk is inserted and the user requests that the system try again.

An Index is successfully read into the program, and a list of titles is presented to the reader. The reader scans each title to examine each description. He or she then selects a particular title and requests that the system load the title. The system now enters Page View mode.

The reader abandons Page View mode and again requests Title Selection mode. The original set of titles is redisplayed, and the user makes another selection and enters Page View mode once more.

The reader changes the removable disk while in Page View mode and then returns to the Title Index. The newly inserted Index is then available for selection.

This is a simple description of how a user might go about using the E-MagBook; this description provided us with a valuable crosscheck of the requirements. This scenario already brought up the fact that we didn't have a description of how to handle a situation in which the reader encountered no Title Index. Where such revelations occurred, we noted the discrepancy for inclusion in the first iteration of the requirements document, as follows:

NOTE: *Requirement to handle "No Title Index Present" to be documented.*

And that last bit was food for thought. If a user removed a disk while the system was in View mode, what would happen when the system tried to load the next page entry? We couldn't physically stop someone from removing the disk while in Page View mode, could we?

Bingo! Scenario justification. Considering how a user might select titles had uncovered a weakness in the concept. Another note resulted from this:

NOTE: *Page View mode—disk must be present all the time.*

This limitation was not too much of a constraint to place on the user, but we needed to highlight it as a requirement of the user. We also needed to define what we wanted to have happen if the system suddenly couldn't find its page files:

NOTE: *What to do if View mode can't find page data.*

Another Scenario for Title Selection

The second scenario we came up with was as follows:

Scenario: Viewer Title Selection—2

Preconditions:
A removable disk is present in the E-MagBook.

Description:
Reader switches on the E-MagBook. The Title Index is read and displayed for the user.

The reader scans each title to examine each description. The reader selects a particular title and requests that the system load the title. The system then enters Page View mode.

The reader removes the removable disk while in Page View mode and selects the next page. The system produces a suitable message indicating that the page can no longer be found. The reader immediately returns to the Title Selection mode. The program informs the reader that no Title Index is available. The reader inserts a new disk and requests that the program read the new Title Index.

The reader selects a title and requests Page View mode. The reader then immediately requests Title Selection mode once more, and the Title Index is reshown. The reader changes the disk and requests that the system show the new Title Index.

This example provides a few variations that describe how a reader might operate the E-MagBook, including removing a disk while the system is in Page View mode. In addition to helping cement everyone's ideas about the requirements, these scenarios also were providing us with the raw material for acceptance test specifications. At this stage, we decided we had enough descriptions for title selection, so we moved on to the View mode.

View Mode with a Text Book

Here was our first attempt at describing how a reader might view a Text Book:

Scenario: Text-Only Book, Viewer Page Handling

Preconditions:
A removable disk with a variety of Text Book titles is loaded.

Description:
The reader selects a text-only title and enters Page View mode. The system displays Page 1 of a 250-page book. The volume of text is sufficient to be displayed on the screen without the need to scroll. The user attempts to modify the text by placing the cursor on the text and typing. Nothing happens. No way exists for the user to change the displayed text content.

Thinking about how the program would be used led us to write the following note, which we clearly needed to include in the requirements specification:

NOTE: *Text display must be bombproof.*

And, as Julie reasoned, the same was true for the Workbench text display and all the keys:

NOTE: *Workbench text must be bombproof.*

All keys must be bombproof.

Now, let's go back to the scenario:

Scenario: Text-Only Book, Viewer Page Handling (continued)
The reader now uses navigation to go forward through the pages until he or she finds a page that cannot fit on the available text display. The user scrolls through the text, both up and down, so that he or she can read every portion in turn.

The user now requests a random page number and reads the page presented. The reader repeats this process a number of times, selecting different pages totally at random.

The user selects a page number that is greater than the last page. An appropriate message appears.

The user types in garbage for a page number—that is, not numbers—and the system produces an appropriate message.

This scenario led to another note:

NOTE: *Require bombproof page-number entry.*

This need might seem obvious, but including it as a requirement leads to no doubt whatsoever. Let's move on:

Scenario: Text-Only Book, Viewer Page Handling (continued)
The reader can move sequentially through the pages, forward or backward. The end conditions of "first page" and "last page" cannot be overcome, and appropriate messages warn the user.

The reader can see the page number of each page.

We had never thought about the page number appearing on the screen, but, clearly, when you describe how a user reads a book, whether electronic or otherwise, the presence of a page number is fairly significant.

NOTE: *Requirement to put page number on screen.*

We seemed to have a reasonable amount of functionality defined in scenarios for handling the Text Book format, so we moved on to Picture Album use.

View Mode with a Picture Album

Here's what we produced, describing how a reader might use the Picture Album:

Scenario: Picture Album Handling

Preconditions:
A removable disk with a variety of albums is loaded.

Description:
The reader selects an album from a Title Index and enters Page View mode. Page 1 of a 12-page album is displayed. The system automatically sizes and positions the image to use the maximum amount of available screen space. The user attempts to move the picture using drag and drop, but the picture is immovable.

From this scenario, we determined that the first point we needed to included in the requirements specification was the following:

NOTE: *Images in View mode are not movable.*

Scenario: Picture Album Handling (continued)
The reader now uses navigation to go forward through the pages, and all images he or she encounters are automatically sized to fit on the screen. Some of the images are bigger than the available image area and need to be scaled into it, while others are smaller and are shown at full size.

The user now requests a random page number and views the image presented. He or she repeats this request a number of times.

The reader selects a page number that is greater than the last page. An appropriate message appears.

The reader types in garbage for a page number—that is, not numbers—and the system produces an appropriate warning.

The reader can move sequentially through the pages, forward or backward. The end conditions of "first page" and "last page" cannot be overcome, and appropriate messages warn the user.

The reader can see the page number of each page.

The reader can see the keys.

Questioning the Requirements

When we got this far, the scenario we'd just completed caused a small debate. Archie wanted to know if the keys for the album remained onscreen all the time. When I asked what he was getting at, he wanted to know why we had to sacrifice screen space so the keys would be in view all the time. We looked at the screen diagrams (which we had produced at the time of the proposal and were now part of the requirements documents). The diagrams clearly showed a required block on the album to hold the keys. The Simple Reference Book format also required a similar facility. (We showed these diagrams in Figure 3.2 earlier in this chapter.)

Archie continued his argument by saying that the box reserved in the Picture Album format for the keys takes up a third of the available area, whereas in the Simple Reference Book format, the box is much smaller. In fact, the space required to show the five keys would be the same in both cases; it would more likely require the sort of dimensions you see marked out in the Simple Reference Book format. Archie suggested that we use the Reference Book dimensions for keys as the basis for displaying keys in general and allow their display to be turned on and off. In that way, when the keys were switched on in the Picture Album mode, they would simply overlay the top, right-hand edge of the image. For the reader to view the whole image, the keys would be switched off. That definition would give us a nice, standard layout for both formats.

Julie then suggested we take this requirement further, because the amount of text space available in the Simple Reference Book format was quite small, even though a given page might contain masses of text. Why not allow the text area to expand up to the top of the page when the keys were not in view? That way maximized available text space when the keys were not showing.

Improved Specifications

All these suggestions sounded sensible and led to commonality in handling keys. Remember that word—*commonality*? The result of this process was that, in the proposal, we redefined the screen layouts for the Picture Album and Reference Book formats, as you can see in Figure 3.3.

Redefining the screen layouts would also mean updating some of the requirements specification we had produced so far. We had, however, started to improve the specification quite dramatically. What we'd done was to give the Picture Album format much more screen for

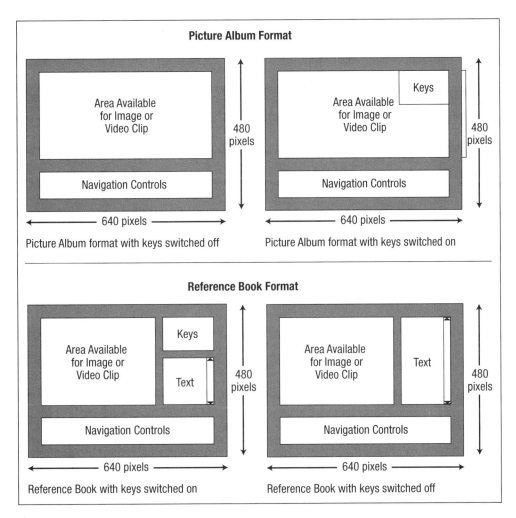

Figure 3.3
Picture Album and Reference Book formats showing common key panel configuration.

the image by allowing the keys to overlap a small fraction of the image space. That we could turn the key display on and off meant that we could use screen space more efficiently on the Reference Book format; the added functionality would let us extend the size of the text object when the keys were not in view.

We were tampering with the requirements as Monty had specified them, but we had difficulty seeing how he would object to the improvements. The revisions would also make our life easier in the respect that we now had a similar screen object to handle keys in both format types. To remind us to update the requirements, we noted the following:

NOTE: *Image/keys/text layout requirements (see new diagrams).*

Julie commented at this stage how valuable the scenarios had been, forcing her and Archie to think about how the program would be used.

Using the Reference Book Format

Next, we needed a scenario for the Reference Book format. (We wouldn't bother with the Extended Reference or the HTML formats. They weren't in this project, and we'd done enough on them already to achieve our objective—to understand them sufficiently to avoid compromising the design with their subsequent inclusion.) I left Archie and Julie to their own devices again, and they came up with the following scenario for a reader handling a Reference Book:

Scenario: Reference Book Handling

Preconditions:
A removable disk containing at least one Reference Book is present in the E-MagBook.

Description:
From the Title Selection mode, the reader selects a Reference Book and enters Page View mode. Page 1 of a 789-page Reference Book is displayed. The image is sized and positioned to use the maximum amount of available screen space after the text and keys have been displayed. The reader attempts to move the picture using drag and drop, but the picture is immovable. Any attempts by the reader to change text or keys fail.

The reader now uses navigation to go forward through the pages, and the system sizes all images the reader encounters to fit into the available screen area. The reader can view or remove keys. When he or she removes the keys, the system makes the extra space available to the text display. Where a page contains more text than can be displayed, the text display is set to "scrollable."

The reader now requests a random page number and views the image, keys, and text presented. The reader repeats this request a number of times.

The reader selects a page number that is greater than the last page of the book. An appropriate message appears.

The reader types in garbage for a page number—that is, not numbers—and the system produces an appropriate warning.

The reader can move sequentially through the pages, forward or backward. The end conditions of "first page" and "last page" cannot be overcome, and appropriate messages warn the reader.

The reader can see the page number of each page.

Clearly, Archie and Julie had taken on board the new layout that would let us make best use of screen space for the text object. We were now developing substantial discrepancies between the scenarios and the requirements specification as it currently stood. The first iteration of the requirements document must address all the issues, so we would have consistency between the two sets of descriptions. Validation could not occur until we had achieved this consistency.

Workbench for Text Books

Julie and Archie then moved on to scenarios for the Workbench mode of operation. Using the Workbench would require one scenario per format type. Here's the first scenario:

Scenario: Workbench Mode (Text-Only Format)

Preconditions:
A user loads a text-only book into the E-MagBook and selects Page View mode.

Description:
The user selects Workbench mode. The screen is cleared, and only the text block appears at a default size and position. The user then drags the block of text around the screen and drops it in the required position. The user then changes the height and width of the text display. As the user makes the text box bigger, more text appears if it could not be accommodated in the previous size.

When the user shrinks the box, less text appears.

When the user sets the text object on screen as desired, he or she then requests that the text be printed. The printer produces an exact copy of what appears on the screen.

This description defines WYSIWYG printing. If you haven't come across the WYSIWYG acronym before, it stands for "What you see is what you get." WYSIWYG printing implies that the printout on paper will emulate exactly what is set up on the screen. The emphasis on WYSIWYG was the result of a debate about how we would print what was on the Workbench. To make all three formats operate in a similar manner (and include the Extended Reference and Web pages later), we decided we would print exactly what was on screen for each format. We needed to ensure that criterion was reflected in the requirements document. Consequently, the following appeared on our "To Do" list:

NOTE: *Detail "Print Screen" definition must specify WYSIWYG.*

Workbench for Picture Albums

Here is our Picture Album scenario for the Workbench:

Scenario: Workbench Mode (Picture Album Format)

Preconditions:
The reader has selected a removable disk containing at least one Picture Album, and the program is in Page View mode.

Description:
The reader selects Workbench mode. The screen is cleared and only the image appears at full size, with its top-left corner—and whatever else can be accommodated by the available screen size—on screen. The user then manually resizes the image to appear in the available viewing area, and then he or she drags the image around the screen to the required location. All changes made to image dimensions keep the aspect ratio constant. When the user has set the image object on screen as desired, he or she then requests that the image be printed. The printer produces an exact copy of what the user sees on the screen.

The user then expands the image until a blown-up portion of the image fills the screen. The user drags and drops the image until the appropriate detail is centered on screen, and then he or she requests a print.

The user then alters the image dimensions so that the image displays in whole on the available screen. The user then alters the image so that its width is expanded, but without preserving the aspect ratio. This action leads to a distorted image that the user then prints.

As you can see, when you start trying to describe what a user can do, it becomes clear that he or she can manipulate the image quite extensively.

Workbench for Simple Reference Books

The Simple Reference Book, when in Workbench mode, requires features from both the Picture Album and Text Book scenarios:

Scenario: Workbench Mode (Simple Reference Book Format)

Preconditions:
The reader has selected a removable disk with at least one Reference Book on it, and the program is in Page View mode.

Description:
The user selects Workbench mode. The image appears at full size on the screen, and the default text display appears on top of the image.

The user manually sizes the image with suitable dimensions to display the image in full. The user manually manipulates the text object until all (or sufficient) text is displayed; then, he or she positions the text as required. The user makes further adjustments to the size of the image so that image and text appear on the available screen without any overlap. When the user has set the text and image objects on screen as desired, he or she then requests that the image be printed. The printer produces an exact copy of what appears on the screen.

The user then expands the image, and a section of it fills the entire screen. The user then moves and resizes the text so that it overlays a portion of the image. The printer again produces an exact copy of what appears on the screen.

The user sets up the image as required and completely removes the text object. Once again, the printer produces an exact copy of what appears on the screen.

Both Archie and Julie determined that situations would occur where only the picture would be printed without its text. This conclusion also led to a question about what should happen if there was more text than could be printed at one time. We decided that the text could be printed in sections, according to what was placed on the screen at any given time. This decision required us to make changes to the specification to ensure that the requirement was clear, as the following note indicates:

NOTE: *Detail "Print Screen" definition.*

Workbench and Keys

Julie also brought up the fact that we hadn't mentioned the keys anywhere in the Workbench. To be on the safe side, they called Monty and asked him if he wanted keys to be printed out. He consulted with Samantha, and they decided printing the keys was not necessary. They thought that we should reflect this preference in the specifications, in case they forgot what they had agreed to. (I knew Samantha wouldn't forget, but Monty might, and, if we specifically stated in the requirements specification that key printing wasn't necessary, the issue would be resolved after Monty signed the document.) Archie and Julie made a note:

NOTE: *Specification needs to state no keys in WB mode.*

Receiving an answer to a question such as this by phone is all well and good. Just remember that you might ask a question of someone who is very busy and who, therefore, might completely forget the call later. Make sure you document the result of the call in the requirements specification so no argument develops at a later date.

A List of Modifications

By the end of the day, we had done a considerable amount of work. We had produced the first draft of a requirements specification for the viewer, for which we also had a series of scenarios. We had inserted some of the changes; some we had not. Our list of things to change was as follows:

NOTE: *Requirement to handle "No Title Index Present" to be documented.*

- *Page View mode—disk must be present all the time.*

- *What to do if View mode can't find page data.*

- *Text display must be bombproof.*

- *Workbench text must be bombproof.*

- *All keys must be bombproof.*

- *Require bombproof page-number entry.*

- *Requirement to put page number on screen.*

- *Images in View mode are not movable.*

- *Image/keys/text layout requirements (see new diagrams).*

- ◆ *Detail "Print Screen" definition must specify WYSIWYG.*

- ◆ *Specification needs to state no keys in WB mode.*

This list defined what we needed to do with the requirements document in the first iteration. All the points arose from our development of the scenarios.

Progress Monitoring

We'd reached the end of Day 1 in project Phase 1, and we needed to assess our progress.

End of Day 1

We ran out of time to get all the changes into the specification. That meant we were now slightly behind schedule. We had originally planned to complete the first draft of the requirements specification for the viewer and complete its scenarios on Day1 (Monday). We couldn't do all this. Archie and Julie wanted to continue into the evening, but I stopped them. They were both tired, and I felt their efforts would be unproductive. I ordered them to go home, have a relaxed evening, and be ready to catch up in the morning.

Tip

Knowing when to stop is quite difficult for developers. A driving force tends to make us work for ridiculously long periods of time, often without realizing it. When we are tired, we don't work as efficiently as when we are fully alert. Although stopping is sometimes difficult, doing so pays dividends in the long run in terms of efficiency. Often, especially when we're debugging code that we've just written, stepping away from a problem and leaving it for a while—concentrating on something completely different—has a truly dramatic effect. What was a major problem before we took a break suddenly becomes something so obvious that we can't understand why we had an issue. Taking a break kicks off an "uncluttering" of the brain, and it works well.

We now must try to assess how much we'd dropped behind our initial plan. Archie and Julie both estimated that they would take a whole morning to complete the viewer specifications to a satisfactory level, and to make further verification between the requirements specification and the scenarios. So, we apparently had half a day left to complete.

Until we had verification between requirements and scenarios, as project manager, I wasn't happy continuing with the editor definitions. Our original estimate of completing the viewer's specifications in one day was out. We needed to make a mental note of that fact so we could learn from our experience. This experience also did not bode well for the time we would need on the editors.

However, I was not particularly worried at this stage, despite the fact that we'd overrun our schedule by 50 percent of the original estimate. The project had a lot of contingency time built in, and we still had a full four days if we needed them. If we were still working on the requirements specification and scenarios on Friday afternoon with no sign of completing them, then we'd be in trouble.

I think both Archie and Julie appreciated my calling it a day the previous afternoon. They were now refreshed and ready to start again. I reminded them of our goal, which was to have requirements fully captured before Monday.

We don't need to go through all the details of Tuesday morning's work, throughout which Julie and Archie modified the requirements specification and reviewed their work, added more bits and pieces, and reviewed again. You'll see the end results in Chapter 5 (although, by then, they will have been influenced by the analysis).

Archie and Julie took all of Tuesday morning to complete the first draft of the viewer specification and scenarios. That meant we were then, as predicted, half a day behind schedule. As soon as they had completed their final validation, we were ready to start on the editors.

Test Scripts

In the case study, as I mentioned earlier, the scenarios we had been developing would also form the basis for our *test scripts*. As part of our commitment to testing—and a vital component of quality assurance—we would have to produce a range of formal test scripts for the software we had to develop. We would use these test scripts for acceptance testing. Because we could base the test scripts on the scenarios, we had already done some of the work.

Test Scripts in a Nutshell

We can summarize what comprises a test script as follows:

♦ *Based on Scenario*—The tester can generate test specifications from use cases or scenarios.

♦ *Requirement Being Tested*—Each test must identify the requirement being tested, either with a direct reference to the requirements specification or through a clear description of what functionality is being checked.

♦ *Preconditions*—Each test must have a set of preconditions that define to the tester what he or she must set up before the test can be executed.

♦ *Execution*—The steps for execution of the test must be clear and, where necessary, describe validation.

♦ *Repeating*—One step can be an instruction to repeat previous steps until a defined outcome occurs.

♦ *Conclusion*—After the tester has completed all the steps, he or she provides a final conclusion.

As you can imagine, even a small project such as the case study will have a lot of test scripts.

Defining the Functionality Being Tested

A test script must do a number of things. First, it needs to define the area of functionality being tested—an important condition for auditing. Auditors from external standards bodies are eager to see a link from the test specification back to the requirements document. This is all part of the trace capability that makes for good quality assurance. Such a link makes it possible to determine whether each aspect of functionality, defined in terms of a requirement, has a test specification to validate that the function has been produced according to specifications.

Formal acceptance test specifications also let us give the customer a mechanism to check that the software we provide is robust and meets the agreed-upon extent of supply or functional requirements—another good reason for the link back to the requirements specification.

Preconditions

The specifications must define the conditions that set the stage for the tester. These preconditions are a definition of everything to be done before you can execute the test. Such a precondition might be an instruction to modify an already completed test file, or it might be a condition that Tests 1 through 10 must be completed before a specific test—for example, Test 11—can be executed. Quite often, you might perform a batch of tests that make up a complex test scenario.

You use the preconditions to set the framework for the test, and, of course, you must remember that you write these test specifications in plain English so that someone who only understands the application domain can follow them. Do not assume the tester is a programmer—this is quite an important point. For testers to be able to check the software, all they need is a copy of the requirements document to get them up to speed in the application domain and a set of instructions on how to go about testing.

Test Steps

You define the test in a series of executable steps. For example, in the case study, Step 1 might be to run the viewer and let it load the Title Index, which has been set up according to the preconditions to contain one book of each type. The next step might be to check each title and description. You might have a whole series of steps to execute, and you might require that, along the way, certain details must be verified. Suppose you want the tester to check out that a Picture Album format reads correctly. Step 1 might be to run the program and load the default Title Index. Step 2 might be to select an album and request that the program open it. In Step 3, you might be asked to verify that the program has selected the Picture Album format and is displaying Page 1 of the selected album correctly. Clearly, if you select a Picture Album and a Text Book appears as Page 1, either the Index is at fault or the program has failed. The tester needs to verify correct operation before proceeding.

Test Conclusion

Finally, when you have defined all the steps and checks required on the way, you can set up a conclusion. Quite often, this conclusion might read, "If you have accomplished and successfully verified all the preceding steps, the test is completed." Alternatively, the conclusion might be a more detailed account of what you are supposed to observe. For example, "If you have successfully completed all the preceding steps, the screen display goes blank, and the following message appears: 'You may now shut down the computer.'"

Test Scripts and the Contract

The test specifications, in conjunction with the requirements document, give you a powerful contractual framework within which to run the project. The requirements document defines the extent of supply, and the acceptance test scripts provide a formal mechanism for both you and the customer to verify that the delivered software meets the extent of supply.

These documents are a means by which you can obtain the customer's formal acceptance of the supplied software, leading to the customer's sign off on the project. Without such a procedure, the customer can string you along forever. Having the customer sign off on these documents formalizes the process whereby you can close the project once you have the customer's acceptance.

Not all customers may have the same commitment to testing. Because testing is quite a resource drain, you always need to clarify from the outset that acceptance testing is the customers' chance to ensure that they are getting what they asked for. As a supplier, you can certainly assist them in performing the tests, but, at the end of the day, they are the people doing the validation.

Some customers provide their own acceptance criteria. If that is the case in your situation, make sure you have a good look at the criteria at the start of the project, so you can determine whether they're adequate. Also, ensure that you adopt your customer's test criteria as part of your own system testing, together with any other testing you feel you must conduct.

A Commitment to Testing

Testing is a demanding activity that requires considerable commitment from the testing team and the verification authority. To illustrate the importance of commitment, let's look, for a moment, at an example of a badly managed project.

The customer takes delivery of the software, which has been carefully set up in a test environment where a failure of the software can't do any harm to the customer's business. (The customer's business might, for example, involve some form of process control on the factory floor.) Testing is to occur on weekends, only when the plant is not in production.

This particular client suddenly decides that running through formal scripts for three or four weekends is a waste of time; the client decides that it's only going to accept the software after it has lived with it for a month. The customer abandons testing halfway through the first weekend and forces the supplier to put the software into a live environment on the following Monday morning. Chaos ensues.

Education and an Incremental Approach

As the preceding example demonstrates, you might need to educate clients about testing early on in the project. The pitfalls of going live in complex environments with sophisticated software are all too apparent in the press. An incremental approach that builds up everyone's confidence in the software over a period of time is essential. The customer gets to know the new system and check it out in a highly controlled manner. That way, you can deal with issues as they arise, without having to worry about the customer's business suffering.

Testing is a major commitment in time and effort on the part of the client, and you must ensure the client understands this reality from Day 1. You even have to be quite firm at times. If the customer bullies you into going live early, and things go wrong, more than the customer will suffer—your reputation will suffer, as well.

Hopefully, your module and system testing lead to a solid, robust product. However, your test environment might not be able to emulate the live environment 100 percent. Remember this: Never, ever, throw software—no matter how well you think it has been tested—into a live environment without making sure you have a good fallback position, which allows the customer to regain its business activity as it was being conducted before testing of the new system was introduced.

The essence of good testing is to define tests that precisely check given bits of functionality. Testing can become more and more sophisticated as it progresses, until the environment becomes as close to a live environment as you can make it. You build the complexity incrementally by building on the successful outcome of previous tests. However, be aware that you often cannot create a live environment; no matter how hard you try—particularly where many asynchronous events trigger your software. So, after you've completed formal testing, you need to start live testing—also in a highly controlled manner. Treat live testing initially as an extension to formal testing but, above all, ensure that you have a fallback position to which you can return in a hurry. You will hear a great deal more about testing later in this book.

From Scenario to Test Script

Let's take our first scenario and see how we can convert it into a test specification. Here is the first scenario we came up with for the viewer in the case study:

Scenario: Viewer Title Selection

Preconditions:
No E-MagBook removable disk is present in the E-MagBook.

Description:
Reader switches on the E-MagBook and is informed that no Title Index is available.

The reader inserts a disk and requests that the system try again.

The system successfully reads an Index into the program and presents a list of titles to the reader. The reader scans each title to examine each description. The reader then selects a particular title and requests that the system load the title. The system then enters Page View mode.

The reader abandons Page View mode and requests Title Selection mode again. The system redisplays the original set of titles, and the reader makes another selection and enters Page View mode once more.

The reader changes the removable disk while the system is in Page View mode and then returns to the Title Index. The newly inserted Index is now available for selection.

Here's the preceding scenario converted into a simple test specification:

Test 1: Viewer Title Loading

Functionality Tested
Initial loading of E-MagBook Title Index.

Preconditions:
The E-MagBook is powered off, and the removable E drive: is empty.

Two test disks are available—Test Disk 1 and Test Disk 2.

Each test disk contains one of each type of book format—that is, one Text Book, one Picture Album, and one Reference Book.

The two disks contain different titles.

Execution

Step 1
Switch on E-MagBook.

Verify that the program starts up and informs that no Title Index is available.

Step 2
Insert Test Disk 1 and request that the new disk be read in.

Verify that the correct Title Index is loaded by examining the list of titles available, together with the descriptions.

Step 3
Select each title, in turn, from the Index, and verify that the title and description presented on screen are as expected.

Step 4
Select a title from the Title Index and request that the book be opened.

Verify that Page 1 of the requested title is displayed in the correct format.

Step 5

Return to the Title Selection mode.

Step 6

Repeat Steps 4 and 5 for each title on the test disk.

Step 7

Select one of the titles and request that it be opened. While in Page View mode, remove the test disk.

Verify that preceding actions have no immediate effect on the program.

Step 8

Insert Test Disk 2 and return to the Title Selection mode.

Verify that the new titles are available.

Conclusion

If you have executed and verified all the tests as described, then this test is deemed to have been passed.

The test script consists of clear instructions and details of what to expect. The only knowledge the tester needs is a good understanding of the requirements specification.

As you will probably realize, it's virtually impossible to come up with a test specification that covers every possible combination of events that a Windows GUI program can encounter. You must target as many events as you think practical. Testing is a tedious business. You can automate much of the process, but you still need the test specifications to define how you must set up the automated testing. We will look at this subject again when we come to *regression testing* (testing of the software after you have modified it, to ensure that its original functionality has not been affected by the changes), a vital part of quality assurance.

Test Records

You must record the results of testing; these results, together with the specification of what the test consisted of, become important project records. Each test specification needs a simple record that lets you capture basic information, such as who performed the test, on what data, and at what time; whether the software passed or failed the test; and a comment (if necessary). Figure 3.4 shows a very simple layout of a test record.

As you can see in Figure 3.4, the test record should include enough room for three or four occurrences of the test being executed. As a company, we have standards for defining test specifications and the paperwork that accompanies them.

Project Name:					Project Ref No:		
			Test Records				
Test No	Date	Time	Comment	Fail X	Pass +	Signature	
1							
2							
3							
4							

Figure 3.4
Test Record.

The Testers

In our company, anyone who has knowledge of the requirements specification, and access to the scenarios and our standards, is equipped to develop test specifications. In fact, we have two, full-time testers and a number of others we can call in on short- or long-term contracts to help develop and execute testing for a given project. Testers are logical and methodical professionals. Some testers are (or were) programmers; some testers have never programmed a computer in their lives. All testers become application domain experts in the respect that they develop an understanding of the software and what it does from a user's perspective.

System Testing

If you recall, system testing is where you, as the supplier, check out the complete software after you have developed and integrated the various modules into a cohesive system for the first time. You can use the acceptance test scripts to perform your own system testing after the developers are satisfied that the system is ready. The big difference between this stage and the client's acceptance-testing stage is that, when you do system testing, you expect to find bugs; when you conduct acceptance testing with the client, you don't want to see any bugs.

Return to the Case Study:
Requirements for the Title Index Editor

We had started capturing the detailed requirements for the editors on Tuesday afternoon. Don't forget, we were half a day behind schedule. Here is the first draft of our detailed requirements, together with notes on how we arrived at some of the content for the editors:

E-MagBook Title Index Editor

It is required that a program be made available that allows a user to create a Title Index from scratch or to modify an existing Index.

This program does not run on an E-MagBook. This editor will run from a minimum screen size of 800×600 pixels.

Each entry in the Title Index will hold a single, free-text title; a single, free-text description; and a single Page Index reference. None of these data entities may be blank. The Title Index can contain any number of such entries.

The editor must be capable of displaying the details for each entry as well as a numerical entry number. The user can then insert, modify, or add text to any of the three data fields.

The user can modify the Index by appending entries to the end, inserting entries at any point, or changing the content of an existing entry. Entries may also be deleted from an Index. The user can write changes made in an Index back to the same file used to load the Index, or he or she can create a completely new file.

Before they are committed, changes made to an entry can be aborted without having any impact on the original content.

At any stage, the user can update the disk file version of the Index with changes he or she has made since the file was last updated.

Additions, deletions, modifications, and insertions are not stored to disk as they are performed. These changes are written to disk only when the user issues an instruction to do so, as in a **Save File** operation. Until that stage, the user can abort all such changes. If a user aborts all changes, then the Title File Index reverts to the state it was in when the file was last saved.

This specification was not particularly big, but here again, the program didn't do a fantastic amount from a requirement's point of view. However, the specification would evolve when we started our analysis and probed more deeply.

Scenarios for the Title Index Editor

We needed a series of simple scenarios that covered the main features of creating and amending the Index files.

Creating Titles

Here's a scenario for creating a title from scratch:

Scenario: Creating a Title from Scratch

Preconditions:
The Title Index Editor is running.

Description:
The user elects to create a new, empty Index.

The user then enters a title, description, and Page Index Reference for Entry 1. The user then enters a title, description, and Page Index Reference for Entry 2. The user repeats this process until he or she has produced an Index of 12 titles.

The user inputs a thirteenth title, but without a description, and the program refuses to add this title to the Index until the user supplies a description. The user rectifies the error. The same thing occurs when the user creates a fourteenth entry with no title. Again, the user corrects the error. Finally, the same thing occurs when the user creates a fifteenth entry without a Page Index Reference. Again, the user corrects the error.

When the user has created the final entry, he or she then saves the Index file, giving it a user-defined name.

Modifying the Title Index

After we had dealt with creating a brand-new Index, it seemed sensible to construct a scenario in which the user opens an existing Index, modifies the Index, and then the program writes the modifications back to the original Index.

Scenario: Opening and Modifying an Existing Title Index

Preconditions:
The Title Index Editor is running.

Description:
The user runs the program and opens an existing Index. The user modifies the contents of selected entries—the title, the description, or the Page File reference. The user adds a new entry to the end and another new entry halfway through the Index file. The user deletes one of the old entries.

The user instructs the program to write the modified Index back to disk to overwrite the original Index.

Aborting the Operation

We'd specified in the requirements that, when modifications to an Index had not been stored to disk, the user could abort the operation. The equivalent scenario is as follows:

Scenario: Title Index Entry Manipulation and Abort

Preconditions:
The Title Index Editor is running.

Description:

The user opens an existing Index.

The user selects a random entry and modifies data. The user then aborts all such modifications, and the system reinstates the original entry content.

The user modifies the contents of selected entries—the title, the description, or the Page File reference. The user adds a new entry to the end and inserts a new entry halfway through the Index. The user deletes one of the old entries.

The user then aborts these changes, and the system reinstates the original Index structure.

These scenarios represented a good start to our defining the requirements and scenarios for the Title Editor, but we still had some way to go before we were 100 percent done. We'd get closer to that figure after we started analysis, because the Title Editor and the Page Editor would be very similar entities—just how similar wouldn't be apparent until we had learned a bit about the Page Editor requirements and had done some analysis.

Requirements for the Page Index Editor

Archie and Julie moved straight to the Page Index Editor requirements and produced the following:

E-MagBook Page Index Editor

It is required that a program be made available that lets a user create a Page Index from scratch or lets a user modify an existing Index.

This program does not run on an E-MagBook. This editor will run from a minimum screen size of 800×600 pixels.

The content of a Page Index depends on format type. The editor must be able to display the data fields, according to format type, in a manner totally consistent with how the viewer displays the data. The editor must have all the functionality available in the viewer. Additionally, the editor must let the user create and modify data items as defined next.

Formats that show data items the user can modify, and that are to be supported initially, are as follows:

Format 1—Text Book Only

Each page consists of:

• A block of text of any length.

• An optional sound-track file reference.

Format 2—Photo Album
Each page consists of:

- Either a static-image or a movie-clip file reference.

- An optional sound-track file reference.

- Up to five keys of any length.

Format 3—Reference Book
Each page consists of:

- Either a static-image or a movie-clip file reference.

- A block of text of any length.

- An optional sound-track file reference.

- Up to five keys of any length.

When creating an Index, the user must declare which format type to apply. This Index can then be populated with the data items defined above, according to format type. The Index can include any number of entries, to a maximum of 1,000.

The user can modify the Index by appending entries to the end, inserting entries at any point, or changing the content of an existing entry. Entries may also be deleted from an Index. The user can write changes made in an Index back to the same file used to load the Index, or the user can create a completely new file.

Before the user has committed changes, he or she can abort the changes made to an entry without causing any impact on the original content.

At any stage, the user can update the disk file version of the Index with changes that he or she has made since the file was last updated.

The program does not store additions, deletions, modifications, and insertions to disk as they are performed. The system writes these changes to disk only when the user issues an instruction to do so, as a Save File operation. Until that stage, the user can abort all such changes. If a user aborts all changes, the Page File Index reverts to the state it was in when the file was last saved.

Commonality

Some of the descriptions for the Page Editor were the same as—or slightly modified from—those that appeared for the Title Editor. This commonality shouldn't be too surprising, because both were editors. It became clear to us that we could improve these definitions by taking out the common elements and defining the functions once. In the final version of the specification, you'll see how we made the definitions for the two editors much more generic, splitting the description into one description that defines common functionality and two descriptions that define specific requirements.

Page Editor Scenarios

In the same way that we developed scenarios for the Title Editor, we must now develop scenarios for the Page Editor.

Creation

We started by creating a scenario that described the building of a Page Index from scratch. This approach seemed logical because it had worked for the Title Index.

Scenario: Creating a Page Index from Scratch

Preconditions:
The Page Index program is running.

Description:
The user elects to create a new, unnamed, and empty Index. The user then sets the format type. According to format, the user then enters data (keys and allowed file references). The user stores this data as Entry 1. The user then enters data for Entry 2. The user repeats this process until he or she has produced an Index of 12 pages. For Picture Album or Reference Book formats, some entries contain a movie clip rather than a static image. In all format types, some entries have no keys; other entries have from one to five keys.

The user has, on occasion, used the same key in more than one entry.

The user inputs a thirteenth entry, but without any text or sound, and adds one key to the entry.

After the user has created the final entry, he or she saves the Index file to a disk file, giving the file a user-defined name.

As we've already seen, creating a scenario for every combination of uses a user might require clearly was not possible. The best we could do was to aim for a reasonable mix of scenarios, and include as much variation as possible. This is a particular problem common with event-driven programs in which you are never quite sure what the user will do next.

Modification

Modifying the Index was our next scenario:

Scenario: Opening and Modifying an Existing Index
The user runs the program and opens an existing Index. The user modifies the contents of selected entries—picture, video clip, text block, keys, or sound—according to format type. The user adds a new entry to the end of the Index and another one halfway through the Index. The user deletes one of the old entries.

The user specifies that the program write the modified Index back to disk using the original name.

The user then makes further modifications to the entries and outputs the result to a newly named file rather then the file originally loaded into the system.

Aborting

Finally, we developed the scenario that defined how the user could abort a series of changes:

Scenario: Page Index Entry Manipulation and Abort
The user runs the program and opens an existing Index.

The user selects a random entry and modifies data. The user aborts all such modifications and reinstates the original entry content.

The user modifies the contents of selected entries—either the keys or any of the file references. The user adds a new entry to the end of the file, and inserts a new entry halfway through the file. The user deletes one of the old entries.

The user then aborts these changes and reinstates the original Index structure.

As you can see, the specifications and scenarios for the two editors were quite similar, differing only when it came to the references about entry content. Note that the descriptions were very high-level—for example, they talked about adding a sound or a movie clip. But those details were sufficient at this stage. When we began to analyze the requirements, our details would become much more specific.

Verifying Viewer Functionality in the Editor

One requirement for the Page Editor was that the user be able to see the content of a page on the editor in the same way the content would appear on the viewer. This requirement led to another scenario:

Scenario: Viewing the Index in the Editor
This scenario consists of all the viewer scenarios.

Archie and Julie were eager to show here that the user could navigate and search through the Index in exactly the same way as he or she could navigate and search through the viewer. The editor requirements were those of the viewer, plus the capability to manipulate the Index and page contents. Although creating these scenarios might not seem like a great deal of work, by the time they were done, it was late Tuesday afternoon.

Progress Monitoring

We'd now completed Day 2 of project Phase 1. At this point, we needed to monitor our progress once again.

End of Day 2

We had started the day behind schedule. Archie and Julie had taken all morning to complete the requirements and scenarios for the viewer. They started on the requirements and scenarios for the two editors that afternoon.

By the end of Day 2, we had completed the work for the editors, so we were still half a day behind because we had not yet started the feasibility study. So far so good—we hadn't caught up, but we hadn't slid backward either. We still had no real cause to worry, given the level of contingency we knew existed.

Start of Day 3

Today, we were going to look at using VB to enable the application for the Internet. As you might recall, this process represented a feasibility study Monty had commissioned us to do as part of the order. We were half a day late. In our original plan, today we were to review the work we'd done so far, and tomorrow we were to produce the final version of the requirements specification.

Keeping Programmers Content

The SDLC Phases 1 and 2 can be tough going. Some people take to these phases very well; some don't. Our company's strategy is to vary project involvement (in terms of what the programmers will be doing) as much as possible and program this variation into the project. As I've said before, programmers like to program. So if you ask them to spend time on capturing requirements, developing use scenarios, cross validating, and writing up all the results, you really need to let them do some programming as well.

In the case study so far, we'd managed to do quite a lot of programming in the form of feasibility studies, evaluation exercises, and so on. These activities had also been a good learning experience for Archie and Julie. So we'd managed to break up the monotony of the project work, we'd managed to improve their knowledge (which they would need in the development phase), and they'd both experienced programming with some powerful VB components.

Balancing Project Activities

Getting the right balance of activities in a project is not an easy matter, but doing so is essential for a successful project. Provided you build plenty of contingency time into the plans, you will have sufficient flexibility to manage the project in a way that accommodates the need to keep talented programmers relatively happy.

The last thing you want to do is obligate a programmer to continue capturing requirements for months on end. (That's a classic way to make a useful member of your staff feel it's time to leave.) Without variety, you also can become stale with respect to what you are currently working on. When you take a break from an activity (and do something completely different), you can come back to the original task refreshed—which can have very positive results on the project. Taking breaks is particularly helpful when you are reviewing documents. You can become stale very quickly if you spend hour after hour reading—and you might miss important information.

People Are Your Assets

Projects are all about people doing activities in a team environment, and software development projects are no different. In the software industry, people are the major asset of companies like ours. The way a company treats its people reflects in the quality of their work, their enthusiasm, and their desire to succeed.

Also remember that some people might be very good at capturing requirements. This component can be quite a challenge, and you might find people asking to be part of the process. Developing software consists of much more than just writing code, and you'll be wise to let your staff members find their areas of interest. Foster any budding aspirations that programmers might have in project areas other than coding.

Balance Starts at the Top

You might be tempted to maintain the *status quo* when things are going well on your project. Putting individuals on a project that lasts for years is all well and good from the company's point of view, but that approach is not so healthy for the people concerned. The *ethos* (culture) that surrounds a company environment must come from the top. If "variation" (and the balance that results) is not on the agenda from the highest level within the company, then implementing variation at the bottom of the organization is difficult.

Software solutions at the application level are often quite complex. For example, how many of us know all the functionality available in our favorite word processor? When project managers make decisions about what manpower to put on an aspect of a project, they often make the safe decision to use people who've been there before. That approach can be counterproductive in the long term—sometimes, it can be positively unhealthy. Few of us really enjoy working on the same thing day in and day out. If you require that of your project staff, it probably won't be long before you'll find people reaching for the job advertisements.

Constant Learning Is Key to Variation

The key to supplying enough variation to your staff is to ensure that people are constantly learning new things. The statement "Variety is the spice of life" did not come about on a whim—it's part of what makes us tick.

If programmers feel that their career is going nowhere because they've been working on the same project for two years, how can you be surprised when the resignation letter arrives? But if you take those same people out of the project for a week or two every couple of months to work on something completely different, you'll find they might even do another three months on the project without complaint. Companies struggle to accommodate the need for variation, particularly small companies. But my advice is that they fail to consider the need at their own peril.

Return to the Case Study:
A Diversion—The Multimedia Control

Although we were behind schedule, I felt that, with all the contingency time at our disposal, we had sufficient time to learn a little more about the multimedia control before embarking on the feasibility study. After all, knowing our components would be vital in being able to interpret the requirements in terms of the technology they required.

So, before doing the feasibility study, I thought we might explore the multimedia control further. We used the multimedia control to play CDs, and then we went over its general functionality in depth. You can see the work we did in Appendix B. (And if you fancy a break from capturing requirements, why not go and do a bit of programming?) Appendix B also contains much of the information you need so you can understand how we will be using the multimedia control in the E-MagBook project; finally, Appendix B introduces a variety of other ideas we will employ in the project.

The Web Browser Study

When we had finished evaluating the multimedia control in more detail, we tackled the subject of the Web browser. The basic question we needed to answer was, Is it feasible to integrate Web browser technology into the E-MagBook concept?

We didn't want to reinvent the wheel and develop a browser just so it could work within E-MagBook software—that would have been ridiculous. We wanted a browser component to knit into our own software.

Again, VB provided a solution. We could explore the feasibility of integrating browser technology with the E-MagBook using a VB platform and, if this proved successful, offer that approach as a model for our way forward on the project. That's not to say VB *would be* the way forward, but any development platform that could emulate the way in which VB accommodates the requirement would be suitable. You can see the work we did in Appendix C.

A Feasible Conclusion

The work shown in Appendix C demonstrates that we'd proved we could accommodate the requirement for browsing in VB with the Microsoft Internet controls. We could say with a reasonable degree of confidence that we could meet Web page requirements—and, indeed, any HTML requirements—using VB. Because we were invoking an instance of the object on a form over which we had total control, we could position the object, size it, and so on. Don't forget, the browser would be running on an 800x600-pixel, mark 2 E-MagBook, not the current one. From this exercise, I was, therefore, quite confident that we could meet the future HTML—and, specifically, Web-based—requirements (provided, of course, Monty would supply us with a reliable connection capability).

Because we were being paid for this job, we needed to prepare a more formal write-up. This document would be a deliverable that simply stated the preceding information in a more formal manner. The document would conclude by saying that, although we had used VB for the feasibility study, VB was serving as a model, and any development environment that met the specifications implied by the model would be adequate.

Progress

Completing the CD exercise and the browser feasibility study, and writing the result in a more formal report, had taken all of Wednesday morning. Referring to the plan, we should have completed the feasibility study on Day 2. We were now in Day 3, and we should have been completing the documentation, with Day 4 available to review and rework what we had done.

We were still an estimated half-day behind the schedule, although we wouldn't know for sure where we were until the end of Day 3. So, we had a day and a half to complete the requirements document and the scenarios, review these documents, and perform any necessary rework. We still had Friday as contingency time, provided someone would be available to work. I was still confident we could meet the deadline to complete by Friday night at the latest and be ready to start analysis on Monday.

Review

We were now ready to go through all the documentation, updating it from notes we had produced along the way, checking for consistency between requirements and scenarios, and modifying any conflicting aspects. We did manage to complete the first draft and review the requirements specification. Although we completed the work late on Friday morning, I was quite delighted with the progress Archie and Julie had made. They never managed to make up the half-day they had lost early on. But the contingency factor helped, and they completed before the end of the week, which was the bottom-line completion date. They were now really beginning to understand what this project was all about in terms of Monty and Samantha's requirements.

End of the SDLC Phase 1

We were still in *project* Phase 1, but we'd reached the end of Phase 1 of the SDLC. Before we could go on to the SDLC Phase 2, on Monday, we needed to validate the output. According to our quality plan, the project manager must sign off on this process as complete so we could record the validation. Without this formality, an external project auditor had no way to know that we had followed our quality procedure. In reality, because I was heavily involved in the project, this was not a big issue.

But for a project manager who is not involved in the detail of something he or she must validate, his or her cooperation with the people who work on the project is vital. The project manager needs assurances from all involved that they are satisfied that the work has been validated. At this stage, if anyone has any reservations, they can record those reservations in writing.

In some situations, proceeding from Phase 1 to Phase 2 might be quite practical and sensible, even though validation of the Phase 1 output has not been 100 percent successful. Clearly, this situation depends on the nature of the project and the issues involved. But if you find yourself in such circumstances, recording those circumstances is important. In addition to following the quality plan for validating outputs, you are also writing down the project's history, so, if anything goes wrong, you can learn from your mistakes. A vital management responsibility is to ensure that the documentation about decision points is sufficient for good auditing. That record might only amount to something like the following:

Project team interviewed, and all approved that the requirements document, scenarios, and results of feasibility study are valid.

Alternatively, you might have a record such as the following:

Requirements document and scenarios validated by project members. Feasibility study is not complete and is still being worked on. However, this situation does not affect analysis, which will commence on schedule.

Another, more serious, outcome might be this:

Requirements document and scenarios validated by project members. Outcome of feasibility study recorded. Some project members have expressed concern that insufficient scenarios are completed. Time frames do not permit any further work. Analysis will commence on schedule.

These examples give you a taste of what I mean by recording the validation. If the project goes seriously wrong, you might possibly trace it back to the fact that people were pointing out there wasn't enough time allocated for scenario development. This sort of information helps you assess where projects have gone wrong. If you can't make such assessments, you can't guarantee the same problems won't happen again—and if they do, an external auditor could call you on this. As far as the E-MagBook was concerned, the three of us were happy that we had sufficient data captured to progress to the analysis phase. The big question was, What will analysis reveal?

The Next Step

At this point, we'd done a first pass at capturing the requirements and had them documented in draft form. (The draft wouldn't become completed until it had been validated again after analysis.) We'd augmented the requirement specification itself with a series of what we'd called scenarios, based on the OOP use case. These scenarios had been invaluable for checking the requirements specification itself. As part of our commitment to acceptance testing, the scenarios could also furnish us with test scripts. We'd officially validated the requirements document. We were now ready to start analyzing the content in detail, but we must be prepared to change the requirements definition in light of what we might discover in the analysis process.

Chapter 4
Analyzing the Requirements

In this chapter, we will look at analysis in detail. As I mentioned in Chapter 2, *analysis* is the process whereby we break down a complex entity into its simpler, component parts. Another way to look at analysis in the SDLC is that we put the requirements under the microscope. For a software development project, analysis results in a series of more precise requirements definitions that are much more technical—preparing the way for design.

In the case study, you will see how we performed our analysis of the requirements and how we constructed the various technical descriptions as a result of the process. In line with our management philosophy of supplying programmers with plenty of variation, and in an attempt to address another area of concern in the project, we also did some feasibility work on *drag-and-drop* handling (which I explain in Appendix D).

Analysis vs. Design

Programmers often confuse the terms *analysis* and *design*. In fact, determining where analysis ends and design begins is sometimes quite difficult. With analysis, you are clearly engaged in discovering more about the *what* of the question, What is this software to do? With design, you are interested in the *how* of the question, How do we produce a solution?

As analysis proceeds, however, design considerations keep popping up, making it easy to get sidetracked into following up in depth on such issues. Dealing with design issues at a superficial level at this stage helps minimize the technical risks, but you must temper any time you spend on design with the realization that any effort directed toward design can put your schedule at risk. Like so many things in software development (or in life), a fine balance is essential. Remember, every time you stop to answer the question How will we provide a solution?, you are failing to address the main theme of analysis, which is still What must the software do? Hopefully, the balance required on time spent answering both questions, at this stage of the project, will become more evident from the case study.

The Case Study:
Preparation for Analysis

We had taken four-and-a-half days to capture the requirements and perform the browser feasibility study. We all decided to finish early on Friday, so the team could have a good break from the project over the weekend and start fresh on Monday morning of the second week.

We had to deliver a complete, fully analyzed, requirements specification to Monty and Samantha in one week's time. We hashed out a plan for analysis; once more taking into consideration the iteration we would need to do to ensure that the requirements specification and the results of analysis were consistent with each other.

Based on what we had learned to date, I asked Julie and Archie to tell me what they considered to be the next technical area of risk. Julie expressed some concern about a facility required for the Workbench. She wasn't sure how to accommodate the drag-and-drop requirements for the text and image objects. Consequently, we decided to include a bit of feasibility work. That work would be a useful exercise in its own right, and it would help to break up the analysis so Archie and Julie could do a bit of programming—consistent with our philosophy of variation.

Activity List and Plan

The activities that we must perform for analysis were the following:

♦ Analyze data requirements

♦ Analyze viewer requirements

♦ Analyze editor requirements

♦ Do feasibility study of drag-and-drop requirements

♦ Complete models

♦ Review models and requirements document (iteration)

Figure 4.1 shows the plan we agreed upon.

Plan Management

From a management perspective, the plan was straightforward. Once again, we would monitor our progress daily. After we handed over the requirements document to Monty, we would need to monitor the situation carefully. If he came up with any issues, we must assess and address them swiftly. We could deal with minor issues by updating the supplied document, using our change-control procedure. But we would have to identify, assess, and address any substantial issues that would have an impact on the project in a way that would not require us to make major changes to the project plan. That approach might involve negotiating with Monty and Samantha.

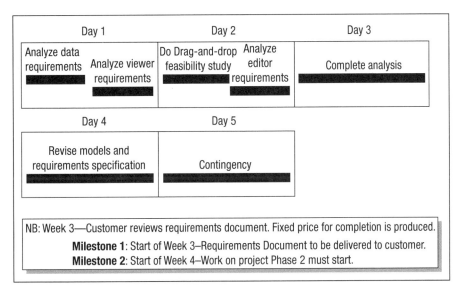

Figure 4.1
Plan for project Phase 1, second week, showing detailed activities for analysis.

We had again given ourselves a total of four days to complete analysis and the all-important verification and possible update to the requirements document. However, the four days also included the feasibility study. The study was not essential, and we could, therefore, postpone it if we ran into problems the first day of analysis. We'd allocated a whole day (Day 3) for completion of the analysis, which helped to reduce the risk factor considerably. We also had a whole day for reviewing. By the end of Day 3, however, we would have considerable documentation to review. We might need to split the documentation review among the three of us to ensure we could complete it.

We needed to remember that the time frame we had imposed wasn't rigid. Whether we completed the analysis of the editors in half a day was not the important factor. The milestone we had to meet was to produce the completed requirements document by the end of Friday—ready to ship to Monty so he had it Monday morning.

If things really got tough, the whole day Friday was contingency time, so the plan looked good. We had a lot of flexibility and contingency time available to help minimize the risks. However, our first week's experience—in which four days proved to be inadequate—tempered our positive outlook a bit. As a last resort, we could work the weekend, which would still let us get the documentation to Monty Monday morning.

Sign-Off

We'd allocated a whole week for the client to review the output of project Phase 1, address issues, and have the client sign off on the output. The sign-off was critical, because we must have it at the beginning of Week 4, together with a new order, so we could proceed with design. We had made Monty fully aware that he had a commitment to complete his work by then. Once we had the signed agreement, we could invoice for the work we had completed to that point.

Feasibility Study

I'd try to make both Julie and Archie comfortable with how to implement the drag-and-drop requirement, so they'd have good background knowledge with which to tackle design and then development. In fact, the drag-and-drop function was possibly the most complex thing about this entire project, and some feasibility work on the subject would minimize our risk in trying to give an accurate quote for that requirement.

Re-Quote

As part of project Phase 1, we also needed to re-quote for the design and development of the software, providing a fixed price for what we had quoted only as a minimum and maximum price so far. However, we could leave that quote until Week 3. We could do that while Monty was looking at the documentation we would deliver in one week's time.

Getting Started

First, we would take stock of the data entities that made up the requirements. In the analysis we did, for the case study, in Chapter 2, we produced a very simple version of an entity relationship diagram. This diagram showed all the data objects in the project and how they relate to one another.

The Entity Relationship Diagram

The entity relationship diagram provides a real-world model of just the data requirements. We can use this model to create and develop a relational database in which entities are defined in tables.

We can describe the characteristics of an entity relationship diagram as follows:

- *Represents a data model*—Models the requirements from the point of view of the data entities.

- *Defines data entities via data items*—Defines each data entity in terms of its constituent data items.

- *Depicts simple relationships*—Easily depicts one-to-one and one-to-many relationships.

- *Identifies complex relationships*—Easily identifies many-to-many relationships, although these often can be broken down into simpler relationships.

- *Defines a relational table structure*—Can be used directly to design the table structure of a relational database.

Data Entities

The purpose of this book is not to provide a detailed description of entity relationship dia-grams, but, for those who have not seen such a diagram before, this discussion will serve as a brief introduction. A *data entity* is a collection of one or more things related to the real world. For example, consider this requirement:

Requirement: *A person can request an appointment with any of the company's consultants. The receptionist takes the demographic details about the person, and the staff member on duty conducts the interview and produces notes. After the person has been interviewed, his or her demographic record and the notes that were taken will be permanently available.*

If you analyze the above in terms of its data requirements, you can identify these data entities just from what is written here: the "company consultant," who conducts an "interview," of a "person," in an "appointment," the outcome of which is a set of "notes." Figure 4.2 Illustrates this relationship in a simple diagrammatic form.

Reading the Diagram

You can read the diagram in Figure 4.2 as follows: A person can have one or many appoint-ments, but an appointment can relate to only one person. An appointment is associated with one consultant, who can relate to none, one, or many appointments. An appointment can have one appointment note, and a given appointment note relates to a single appointment.

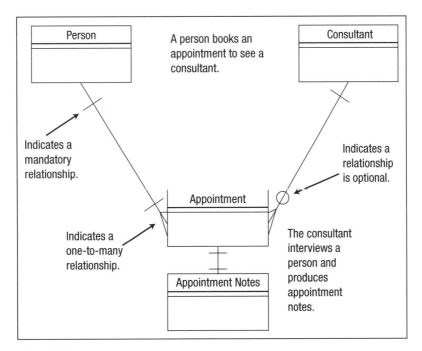

Figure 4.2
Simple entity relationship diagram.

The preceding description defines the relationships between the data entities. Explained on the diagram, the same thing is more elegant, more meaningful, and far more practical as a description. The diagram defines each data entity—person, appointment, consultant, and appointment note—each of which is a collection of such records. The diagram uses one of three types of relationships to show how a given entity is related to another:

- One to one

- One to many

- Many to many

Clearly, a single person can be associated with many appointments (one to many), but a single appointment can be associated only with one person and one consultant (one to one).

Using the line and circle, as the diagram shows, you can also depict whether a relationship is mandatory or optional. The diagram provides a simple model of the data entities and the relationships that define the requirement.

NOTE: *We have produced a diagram based on the single requirement we gave earlier. In reality, the picture will take into account other relationships that undoubtedly will be defined in other areas of the full requirements document. Therefore, the diagram is likely to be more complex than what you see in Figure 4.2.*

Data Items

You can define a data entity in terms of the basic data items that it holds. In our example, the "person" record might consist of the following:

- Last name

- First name

- Sex

- Date of birth

- Phone number

- Address

And so on. Likewise, the "consultant" entity might consist of the following:

- Consultant's last name

- Consultant's first name

- Sex

- Department

- Home address

- Contact number

The "appointment" entity might be defined as containing the following:

♦ Date

♦ Time

♦ Reference to consultant identity

♦ Reference to person identity

♦ Reference to notes produced

Note that the appointment contains references to other data entities; namely, the person, the consultant, and the notes. You can consider that the notes consist of a single, variable-length report. Figure 4.3 shows a more detailed diagram, in which the data items are also defined in each data entity for our example.

Relational Database

In the preceding example, we would define person, consultant, appointment, and note tables for a relational database. Tables consist of the data items, and links from one table to another

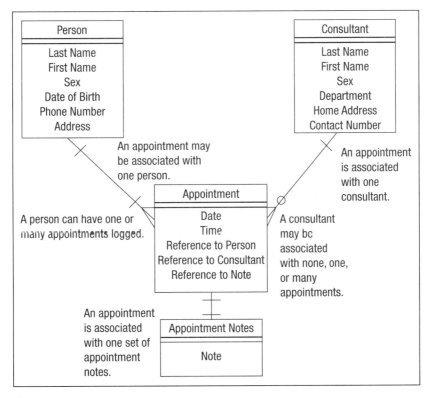

Figure 4.3
Entity relationship diagram showing detailed structure of each entity.

fulfill the relationships. For example, you do not need to store the person's name in the appointment table. All you need is a link from the appointment table to the person table, where the details are. The advantage to a relational database is that you store the main data entities and their items only once.

Return to the Case Study:
Basic Data Entity Definitions

We would start the analysis of the E-MagBook software by looking at the data entities in more detail. We'd split the data entities into two groups—basic and high level. We would classify a basic data entity as one that consisted of a single data item, whereas a high-level entity would consist of a number of data items. We wanted to achieve definitions of data entities and their associated attributes, and their relationships to other entities. We'd start with the basic data entities of the E-MagBook.

From our understanding of the requirements, the E-MagBook would use the following basic data entities: images, video clips, text blocks, sounds, HTML files, and Web sites. The Composite Descriptor would likely be a complex entity with more than one item, but we'd include it as a basic entity for the time being because it seems to be more akin to the components already listed.

Each basic entity consists of a single, self-contained item. For example, an image consists of a bitmap stored in a single file; text consists of a single block of text stored in a file; sound consists of a single WAV file or MID file, and a Web site—as far as this project is concerned—is simply a URL. (We'll come back to composites a little later.)

NOTE: *The book page and book title are the two remaining data entities, but they are not basic because they each consist of a number of items. The book title, for example, consists of at least a description and a title.*

We'd now consider each of the basic data entities individually; you'll see how our analysis expanded our perception of these objects.

Image File

We began by producing a definition of each data entity, starting with the image file.

Basic Data Entity Definitions

Image File
A self-contained file that contains a bitmap.

Attributes: **Drive, directory path, file name, bit map type, size.**

The file attributes you see resulted from a deeper analysis of the term *file reference*. At first sight it might appear a bit of a diversion, but, in reality, it homed in on some key issues.

File Reference in Depth

We'd been using the term *file reference* a great deal. The two Index files contained specific references to data entities that also happened to be files. We determined that splitting file reference into three attributes—**drive**, **directory path**, and **file name**—might be useful. For example, we'd already specified that the E-MagBook would look for a Title Index on the E: drive. We would hard-code this attribute into the software, provided Monty approved. Consequently, we could say that, for an E-MagBook removable disk, all file references contained within the disk must have the **drive** attribute set to **E:**.

This evaluation of file references made us stop and think about the Page Index Editor program for a moment. That program would operate on a standard PC, not the E-MagBook. Theoretically, the Page Index Editor could make up an Index anywhere on its file storage system and reference files anywhere. However, at some stage, the Title Index, Page Indexes, and basic data entities that constituted the full collection must be transferred to a removable E-MagBook disk. If the file references had been set up with drive attributes that were not set to **E:** they would be incorrect when the removable disk was created and run on an E-MagBook. For example, suppose that the Title Index, the Page Indexes, images, videos, text, and so on were all created on the C: drive of the editing PC. All references created would be to files on drive C:. That arrangement would work fine on the editing PC. For the E-MagBook, all the files that made up the book collection must be transferred to a removable disk. The user would access the removable disk on drive E: of the E-MagBook. If the **drive** attributes of all file references stored in the Title Index and Page Index files were still set to **C:**, the viewer would not find any files at all!

At this stage, we reached for the use cases for the Title Index and Page Index, and realized that we had simply not considered this situation.

Some File-Handling Rules

We decided to establish some rules for file handling. We could have been clever and made all file references relative to the drive that contained the Title Index, but that approach started to get quite complicated, so we opted for a simple solution. We developed the following rules to define the requirement for file handling in the three programs:

Rules for File Handling

- Any data entity that is a file (Title Index, Page Index, image, video, text, WAV or MID) has three attributes that define its location absolutely:

  - **drive**

  - **directory path**

  - **file name** (includes extension)

- All the Index files and the basic data entities that are files, which together constitute a single removable disk collection of books, must be resident on the removable disk located on drive E: for an E-MagBook that is viewed by the E-Viewer.

- The **drive** attribute for all file references on the removable disk must be set to **E:**.

- The drive can be any logical or physical drive on a PC that the E-Viewer, E-TitleEditor, or E-PageEditor accesses, but this reference is applicable only to running the three programs on the PC.

- If a working book collection is to be transferred from a PC to an E-MagBook removable disk, all **drive** attributes in all file references must be converted to **E:** without exception.

- The Title Index is always set up on the removable drive such that its **drive** property is set to E:, its **directory** property is set to **\E-MagBook**, and its **name** property is set to **Title.idx**.

NOTE: *In a typical commercial software project, part of the analysis would consist of developing the business rules of the software. These rules would define how the software would handle the various data entities. For example, we could define what needs to be done to an invoice before it can be completed as a set of business rules for invoice handling. What we've defined for file reference is equivalent to the E-MagBook's business rules.*

The simple act of defining a file's attribute—**drive**—had suddenly made us think about how the three programs would use file references and led us to establish a set of rules for file handling.

To keep the software simple and, thus, keep the cost down, we had defined a set of rules that we wanted to impose on the people who would edit the E-MagBook content. We knew Monty would approve, provided he and Samantha could live with the restrictions that resulted. Therefore, the rules must appear in the requirements document so Monty could verify them.

Changes to Scenarios

We also decided to modify the existing scenarios to reflect the rules we had just defined, and to create two more scenarios that would define the full book-creation process. Here are the scenarios:

Scenario: The Book-Creation Process—Mode 1

Preconditions:
The PC on which the book will be created contains a removable disk drive on drive E:.

Description:
The editor (an actor) creates a directory called E-MagBook on drive E: of the PC that is running the Title Index Editor and the Page Index Editor.

The editor creates a Title Index called Title.idx on E:\E-MagBook\ with a single reference to a Page Index file called TestBook1, which is set up as follows: E:\E-MagBook\BOOK1\TestBook1.Idx.

Using the Page Index Editor, the editor creates the Page Index: E:\E-MagBook\BOOK1\TestBook1.Idx.

The editor copies the files that make up Book 1 to the following areas:

> Image files to E:\E-MagBook\TestBook1\Images
>
> Text files to E:\E-MagBook\TestBook1\Text
>
> Sound files to E:\E-MagBook\TestBook1\Sounds

Using the appropriate file references to drive E:, the editor adds pages to the Index to create the book.

The editor then removes the disk and places it in an E-MagBook for user access.

In the first scenario, the editor makes up a book using a removable drive attached to the PC on which the book is being created.

After a lot of discussion, we decided to include the following scenario to clarify the situation as well as to indicate another way to execute the creation process:

Scenario: The Book-Creation Process—Mode 2

Preconditions:
The PC on which the book will be created contains a removable disk drive in drive E:.

Description:
The editor (an actor) creates a directory called E-MagBook on drive C: of the PC that is running the Title Index Editor and Page Index Editor.

The editor creates a Title Index called Title.idx on C:\E-MagBook with a single reference to a Page Index file called TBook1, which is set up as follows: C:\E-MagBook\TEST1\TBook1.Idx.

Using the Page Index Editor, the editor creates the Page Index: C:\E-MagBook\TEST1\TBook1.Idx.

The editor copies the files that make up Book 1 to the following areas:

> Image files to C:\E-MagBook\TBook1
>
> Text files to C:\E-MagBook\TBook1
>
> Sound files to C:\E-MagBook\TBook1

Using the appropriate file references to drive C:, the editor adds pages to the Index to create the book.

The editor then places a removable disk in drive E: and copies the directory C:\E-MagBook\ to drive E:.

The editor changes all the **drive** attributes of file references in E:\E-MagBook\Title.idx from C: to E:.

The editor changes all the **drive** attributes of file references in any Page Index files on drive E: from C: to E:.

The editor then removes the disk and places it in an E-MagBook for user access.

The second scenario demonstrates the capability to run E-MagBooks from a PC with all files resident on the PC's hard drive. If the editor then transfers these files to a removable disk, he or she must convert all Title Index and Page Index file references to designate the removable disk drive. The editor can either do this manually using a text editor, or the requirements specification can incorporate a conversion function that scans an E-MagBook's Indexes and converts any **drive** attribute to **E:**.

Changes to the Requirements

Clearly, we would have to verify that the requirements document reflected all these new findings, add the extra scenarios, and so on. The value of iteration between Phases 1 and 2 of the SDLC becomes quite apparent.

NOTES: *Update requirements document with file-access rules.*

Add new application scenarios.

Define requirement for **drive** *attribute conversion.*

All this came about because we started to define the image file data entity in more detail and assign it some attributes. But that's how analysis works—you drill more deeply into the requirements and ask new questions, challenging the requirement definitions all the time.

Video Clips

We then went back to defining the basic data entities, moving on to video clips.

Video Clip File
A file that contains a video data stream and an optional sound track.

Attributes: **Drive, directory path, file name, sound track, size.**

Sound track present is simply a *logical attribute* (that is, it's either set to **True** or **False**)—the file either does or does not contain a sound track.

Text Files

For the Text Book and Reference Book formats, we defined the files that hold text as follows:

Text File
A file that contains a block of text of any size.

Attributes: **Drive, directory path, file name, character size, font type**—size and font type are inherited from the Page Index format.

The word *font* led to another lengthy discussion before we arrived at the preceding definition. The font issue was something we had never really faced up to in full before then.

Font

The first question was Are we talking variable font, fixed font, or what? We realized Monty and Julie might have an expectation here. Did they want totally free font capability—so that each page of a book could be set using **font** attributes in the way a word processor allows? Or, would they be happy with a fixed font for each book page? We searched through our notes, and the only references to font we could find were that the font size on the viewer buttons needed to be large, and the text in each text block in a composite was to be independent of the other blocks. We clearly had not addressed the issue of font for the text blocks in the Text Book and Reference Book formats.

If Montasana wanted variable font throughout the block of text, the file had to contain both **font** attribute information and the raw text, and the file would become complex and large. We could use Microsoft's *rich-text format (RTF)* to define the data—most word processors will output RTF—but then we would have to find a component that could handle rich text. Because we were developing a prototype, we decided to go with a fixed font for all pages. We could always expand the functionality later, but fixed font was clearly the simpler option to get the prototype up and running. We'd have to get Monty's approval first; however, if he was adamant about having variable font throughout the text, then we'd have to think again.

Inherited Font Option

We could vary the font between books. If we made the font type an attribute of the Page Index, every text file in a given book would inherit the font type. In other words, we didn't have to define font in the text entity—we could define the font in the Page Index entity, and all text files used would inherit the font. That approach would give some flexibility, for example, for Samantha to set up large text for a child's storybook and smaller text for a technical reference book. In fact, different books could use the same text file displayed with different font characteristics set by the book in question.

Both Archie and Julie were surprised that the issue of font had not surfaced before, but we hadn't analyzed to this depth. When we'd talk about text, we'd just taken it for granted. (Only when you start to analyze a requirement at this level of detail do these kinds of issues come to light.) At this stage, we called Monty to seek approval. He was comfortable with our defining a fixed font in the Page Index for each page of a particular book, but (as usual) he didn't want that requirement to compromise the capability to make a future change. Clearly, we needed to reflect this deeper understanding of font in the requirements document:

   NOTE: *Define text font requirements in detail.*

And that's how *font characteristics (inherited from Page Index)* came into being. Monty approved the wording, but he stressed that the Composite format must use variable font on a single page. We agreed to incorporate that as a future requirement. We would handle the Extended Reference, or Composite, format differently than we would the standard Reference Book page. We would use a descriptor file for the Composite format. We could deal with that issue when (and if) Monty commissioned us to develop that functionality—without any compromise to the software we had to design now.

Sound File

The next basic data entity we defined was the sound file.

Sound File

A file that contains either a WAV audio data stream or MID event stream.

Attributes: **Drive, directory path, file name, size, data type** (WAV or MID).

The Self-Contained Composite Descriptor

Up to this point, we hadn't thought much about composite images (Extended Reference format), other than to identify the possibility that they would be quite complex. Here's the definition we developed:

Composite Descriptor File

A file that contains a full description of a composite image layout.

Attributes: **Drive, directory path, file name, size.**

Fundamentally, a Composite file would consist of none, one, or many images; optionally, a video; none, one, or many text blocks; and possible hotspot definitions. Clearly, the Composite format would not be a basic data entity, which we'd defined as comprising a single item. What we needed was a data entity (in this case, a file) that contained references to all the basic entities that made up the Composite format, (image, video, text, etc.). This data entity must also contain information about where each object was to be placed on screen, the dimensions required and—for text—the font characteristics, and so on. We could define all this in a single descriptor file. The Page Index reference, therefore, would need to point only to this descriptor file.

The Composite Descriptor file would be a completely self-contained description of what a composite image comprised, and how to construct a composite image on screen. For example, a Composite format might consist of two images and a block of text. The descriptor would contain the three file references for the images and text, and the details about how to place those elements on screen. As long as this descriptor was a self-contained entity and could make use of the basic data entities as they were currently defined, we could accommodate the descriptor in the future without compromising the initial design we had to develop. In fact, instead of introducing new data entities, we'd be including additional data items that would be part of the descriptor.

Unlike the data entities we had defined so far, the Composite Descriptor file would consist of a variable number of data items. We decided that, at least for this project, we would draw up an entity relationship diagram (which you will see later) to indicate the complexity of the Composite Descriptor file.

HTML Files

We moved on to HTML files and Web sites, which we defined as follows:

HTML File

A file that contains HTML formatted data.

Attributes: **Drive, directory path, file name, browser required, size**.

We'd added a **browser required** attribute to indicate the HTML file's special status.

Web Site

An Internet/Web site.

Attributes: **Browser required, remote access required, URL**.

The URL is the *Uniform Resource Location*, or Internet address. In addition to the **browser required** attribute, we'd also added a **remote access required** attribute to further distinguish this data entity from the simpler HTML file.

Basic Data Entities Completed

We now had a set of definitions for our basic data entities. The analysis phase had required us to ask lots of questions and raise some important aspects of the requirements. We had also reclassified the Composite Descriptor file as a more complex, high-level, data entity because it clearly contained a variable number of data items and references to genuine *basic* data entities.

High-Level Data Entities

In our preliminary analysis (in the presales phase), we had identified the Title Index and the Page Index as the E-MagBook's two primary data entities. We drew a crude, entity relationship diagram, which showed that a single E-MagBook removable disk consisted of one Title Index and many Page Indexes. You can see this diagram, which represents a top-level view of the data relationships, in Figure 4.4.

The Page Index and the Title Index were the high-level data entities that pulled the E-MagBook data objects together to provide the book structure. Each data entity consisted of a number of data items. We now needed to delve deeper into the data entities, and we started with the Title Index.

The Title Index

Each title record consisted of three basic data items: a title, a description, and a reference to a book (or what we called the Page Index in the requirements). So, here's our official definition:

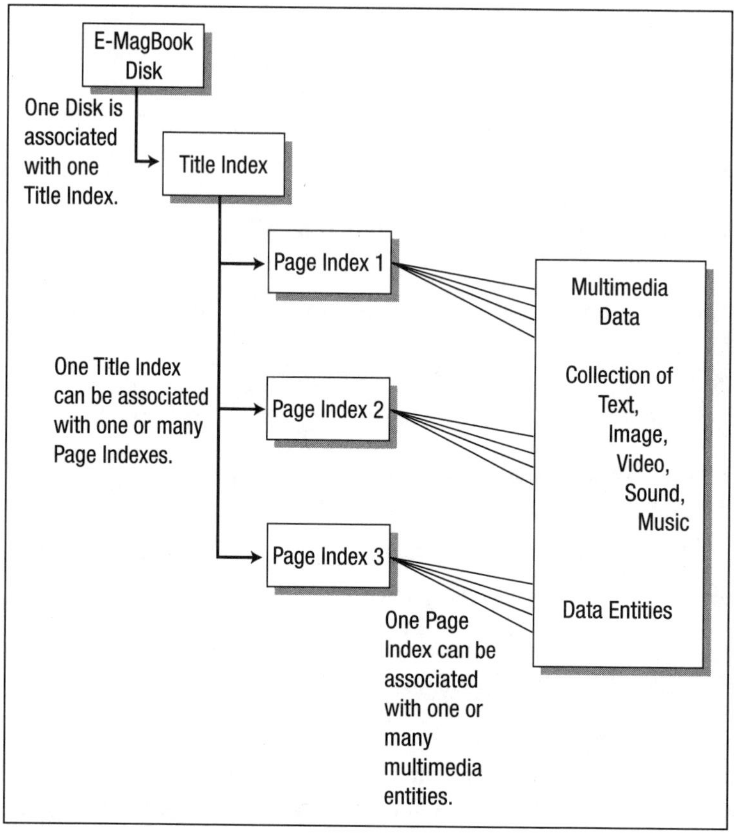

Figure 4.4
Relationships among the primary data entities.

Title Index
Consists of a collection of title records.

Title Index Record
Defines a single E-MagBook book in detail.

Attributes: **Record number.**

The content of a Title Index record consists of the following items or references to basic data entities:

Title (may not be blank)

Description (may not be blank)

Page Index file reference (may not be blank)

This example shows how each Title Index record consisted of two items and one reference to a basic data entity. We could also depict this in a diagram, as you can see in Figure 4.5.

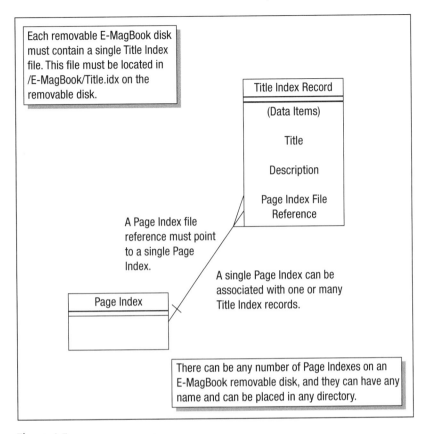

Each removable E-MagBook disk must contain a single Title Index file. This file must be located in /E-MagBook/Title.idx on the removable disk.

Title Index Record

(Data Items)

Title

Description

Page Index File Reference

A Page Index file reference must point to a single Page Index.

A single Page Index can be associated with one or many Title Index records.

Page Index

There can be any number of Page Indexes on an E-MagBook removable disk, and they can have any name and can be placed in any directory.

Figure 4.5
Title Index entity relationships.

The Page Index

We could define the Page Index similarly to the Title Index. Our definition was as follows:

Page Index
A collection of page records that make up a complete book.

Attributes: Format (that is, Text Book, Picture Album, Reference Book, Extended Reference, or HTML), font type, font size.

Page Record

Contains all the details of a single page in a book.

Attribute: Page number, format (inherited from Page Index).

The content of a Page Index record consists of the following items or references to basic data entities:

Keys

A collection of five items, Key(1) to Key(5) (each key may or may not be blank).

Reference to an image or video clip data entity (may or may not be present, dependent on the **format** attribute).

Reference to a text data entity (may or may not be present, dependent on the **format** attribute).

Reference to a sound file (may or may not be present, and is not dependent on the **format** attribute).

Reference to a local HTML page or reference to a Web site (may or may not be present, dependent on the **format** attribute).

Reference to a composite descriptor data entity (may or may not be present, dependent on the **format** attribute).

We also drew an entity relationship diagram, as you can see in Figure 4.6.

Indexes Modeled

The three diagrams—Figures 4.4, 4.5, and 4.6—model the relationships we had defined in the requirements specification in a highly visual manner; the diagrams would clearly be a major input to design. Note, however, that the diagrams also need the description to back them up, and vice versa—one would not be complete without the other.

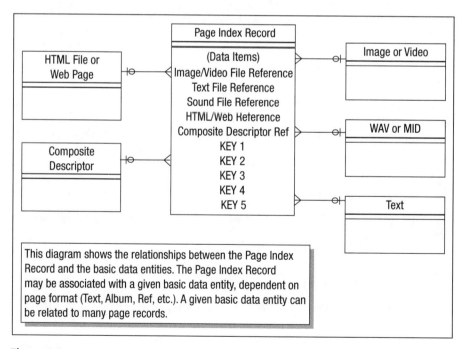

Figure 4.6

Page Index entity relationships.

An Extra-High-Level Entity

We now must turn our attention back to the Composite Descriptor file. We'd already decided the file was a high-level entity because it contained many data items and references to basic data entities. We summarized the Composite Descriptor file in another diagram that defined the relationships, as you can see in Figure 4.7.

Figure 4.7 defines the Composite Descriptor file as a single entity, which contains a number of lists, a sound reference, and a video reference. These elements indicate that the file has a more complex structure embedded within, which will require a much more detailed analysis when the time comes. We placed the items of the Composite Descriptor file into compartments and drew the relationships right into the compartment to indicate the item each relates to. This approach is not standard, but it indicated to us the nature of the relationships as we had defined them in the text on the diagram.

The diagram in Figure 4.7 reflects the one restriction we had introduced—that, optionally, only one video could be related to a Composite Descriptor, a restriction we established when we were capturing requirements. We thought it sensible to apply a similar restriction to the sound reference because we could play only one sound at a time. Don't forget, Monty still had

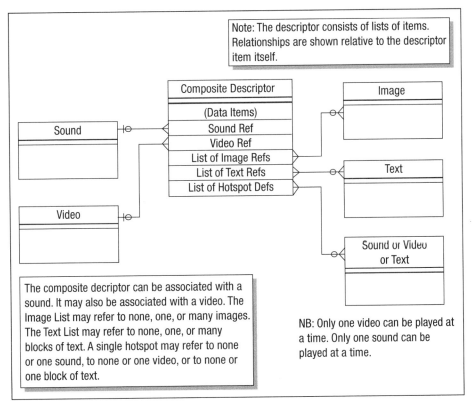

Figure 4.7
Entity relationship diagram for the Composite Descriptor file.

to approve these restrictions. Each hotspot, however, could be associated with a separate video, sound file, or text block; the important requirement was that only one video or one sound would be played at a time. We had put all this information into the diagram.

We ran the risk of moving into too much detail for functionality that we didn't need at the time. Our brief was to ensure that we could accommodate composites without compromising the design we were currently establishing. The entity relationship diagram contained sufficient detail at this stage to help ensure that we would avoid any compromises.

We now had descriptions, together with relationship diagrams, of all the data entities. The process had definitely expanded our understanding of the requirements, and it would also lead to modifications and additions to the requirements specification and the scenarios.

Procedure-Driven vs. GUI Programming

In Chapter 2, as you might recall, I mentioned that the E-MagBook project would incorporate a GUI design. GUI programming is quite different from conventional procedure-driven programming—a difference we needed to understand as we continued with our deeper analysis. The most notable differences relate to how the user interacts with the program and to how data is stored in memory.

In a procedure-driven program running on a conventional terminal, the program can either force a user to enter data in a particular order or monitor where the user is moving the cursor and act appropriately, disallowing certain locations if appropriate.

The big difference in GUI (event-driven) programming is that the program has no way to know what will happen next—a GUI program must accommodate the fact that the user is in total control over what happens to data on the screen. This difference is inherent in the way the user interacts with a keyboard and mouse. The user can manipulate the data any old which way, changing any field, in any order, at any time. For example, if a screen shows 10 input fields, all of which the user needs to fill, he or she can place the cursor on any of those 10 fields, click the mouse button to place focus there, and start entering data. For the next field, the user can go to any one of the remaining nine input fields.

This setup has implications on the data and the way in which we (as programmers) handle the data, because we have no control over what the user does on the screen. To understand this fully, take a look at Figure 4.8, which represents a typical GUI program environment from a data point of view.

To verify individual field data, we could put validation into the **change** event of a given screen object so we could check the object's content as it changes, or we could put the validation in the object's **LostFocus** event (triggered when the cursor is moved onto another screen object)—whichever would be more convenient. The most sensible way to proceed would be such that changes made to the data on screen had no effect on data held in memory and no effect on data held on disk. To accomplish that, we must keep the data on three separate levels—in the screen objects, in memory variables, and in disk files—all independent of each

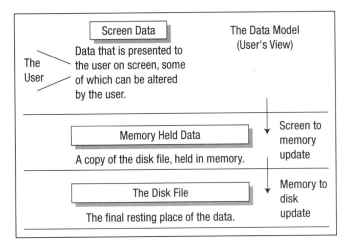

Figure. 4.8
The GUI data model.

other. (This approach is in stark contrast to a conventional, sequential programming module, in which the programmer solicits data input for one item at a time, usually building an in-memory picture of the data.)

An Example

As an example of the freedom the GUI offers to users, suppose you, as a user, are reading in a record from a database file in a GUI data model. You read the record into a set of in-memory variables of some type. The program now has two sets of data: the data on disk and the data in memory; initially, these data sets are identical. Next, the program copies the data from memory variables into screen objects. The program now has three versions of the data: the copy on screen, the copy in memory, and the version in the disk file. The program is set up such that changing the data on the screen objects has no effect on the memory data or the disk data—that is, the program does not intervene to update the other two levels as data entry occurs.

In typical database systems, programmers provide some form of Commit button, which lets the user commit to the disk, all the changes he or she has implemented on screen. When the user selects the Commit button, the program performs a final validation, and, if the data on screen passes, the program writes the data into the database. The operator is in total control. He or she can take as long as necessary to set the screen up from scratch and then commit all the changes together. In this example, the program is likely to keep the memory data in phase with the disk data at all times.

As a programmer, however, you might decide to update only the memory variables when the user makes the commit. In the case study, where we were not using a database, this option had particular relevance. All the data from a Page Index would be resident in memory and on disk. The screen would contain the contents of just a single page record. Each time a page record was updated on screen, that data could be used to update the appropriate memory record. The advantage of this approach would be that the user could make a series of data updates, all of which the program would hold in memory, and which could be aborted or transferred to disk as a further, single, commit action. This method provides much greater flexibility than that in which all changes are committed at once, because here a user can abort a whole sequence of changes that are held only in memory, providing a useful back-out function, or second-level commit. We'll look at this subject again in the case study.

Program States

Most programs work in a variety of *states*, each of which is usually associated with one or more self-contained requirements. For example, the case study's viewer program can operate in a state whereby its sole function is to solicit a title name from the user. Once the user has selected a title, the program can be moved into the Page View state, from which the user can view the selected title's pages. Within this program state, the user can also elect to return to the Title Selection mode, or, alternatively, the user can select the Workbench state to set up the content of a page for a hard copy.

State-Changing Events

When a program can operate in many different states, of great interest in the requirements is what allows the program to *change state*—that is, what events let it change from one operational state to another. This information is particularly important in GUI programming, wherein many external events can be involved in changing a program's operational status.

Understanding the way in which a program changes its states is particularly important in terms of design. The state transition diagram becomes very useful when you're trying to extract the information from all the combinations of a verbose requirements specification. In the case study, you will see how effectively we used the state transition diagram to define all the possible permutations of the viewer and editor states—and how each program moved from one state to another. Such a diagram clearly indicates what events do what and—just as importantly—what they can't do. The state transition diagram gives us, yet again, a model that describes the component structure of the requirements from a different point of view—in this case, the operational states of the programs required.

State Transition Diagram Example

As an example, suppose we have a program that can operate in one of five states, labeled A, B, C, D, and E. Theoretically, a program can move from one state to another in all sorts of ways, but analysis of the requirements shows which ways are relevant. Figures 4.9 and 4.10 show two quite different operational scenarios, each indicating how a program could move from one state to another. In terms of design, the state transition diagram succinctly illustrates a key aspect of program behavior.

We would use state transition diagrams in the case study to show how the viewer and editors changed from one state to another and what events caused those changes.

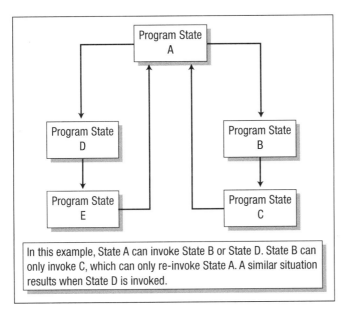

In this example, State A can invoke State B or State D. State B can only invoke C, which can only re-invoke State A. A similar situation results when State D is invoked.

Figure 4.9

State transition diagram for Application 1.

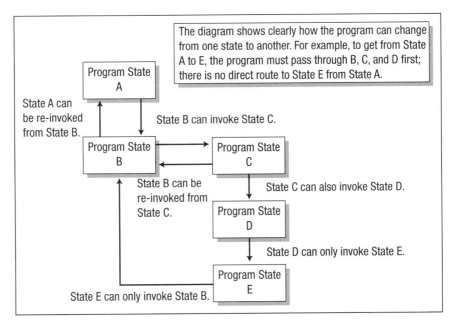

The diagram shows clearly how the program can change from one state to another. For example, to get from State A to E, the program must pass through B, C, and D first; there is no direct route to State E from State A.

State A can be re-invoked from State B.

State B can invoke State C.

State B can be re-invoked from State C.

State C can also invoke State D.

State D can only invoke State E.

State E can only invoke State B.

Figure 4.10

State transition diagram for Application 2.

I/O Diagrams

I introduced inputs and outputs in Chapter 2. The I/O (input/output) diagram treats the program like a black box, showing what inputs the black box can accept and what outputs are produced after the black box has performed its function. I/O diagrams are extremely useful in depicting what data a program handles under specified conditions.

In the case study, I added a little more detail to the diagrams we had produced at the time of our original proposal, to provide another viewpoint of the requirements. Once again, this additional perspective related to the detailed breakdown of components.

Return to the Case Study:
Analysis of the Viewer Requirements

After we had dealt with the data entities, we looked at the viewer from a number of different standpoints. First, we looked at the different states that the program could find itself in. Then, we looked at what inputs and outputs related to each of these states.

Viewer States

If you recall from our previous work, the viewer would operate in one of three modes, or states—Title Selection, Page View, and Workbench—as Figure 4.11 shows.

In Figure 4.11, you see the three states, or modes, and the events that cause a change of state. The event **Switch on E-MagBook** would cause the program to invoke the Title Selection mode. When the user selected a book and requested that it be opened, that event would change the state of the program to enable Page View mode. The user could then trigger an event to go back to Title Selection or to move on to Workbench mode. Again, the user would trigger a return from Workbench mode to Page View mode.

The key points to note are that the user causes all the events that trigger state transition changes. Note, also, how clear it is that the user couldn't get back to Title Selection directly from Workbench mode; he or she first must go back to Page View mode. This limitation was a direct interpretation of the requirement, and the resultant model made that point most succinctly. The viewer was not a particularly complex program, but, when a multitude of states and events could trigger changes, state transition diagrams could be very useful, as we'd see when we created them for the editors.

I/O for Each State

We could now take each state of the viewer and draw its main inputs and outputs to complete the picture. We managed to depict the three states in a single I/O diagram, which you can see in Figure 4.12.

Starting with the Title Selection mode depicted at the top of the diagram, the Title Index would be the primary input to this mode of operation. Manual Title Selection would act as

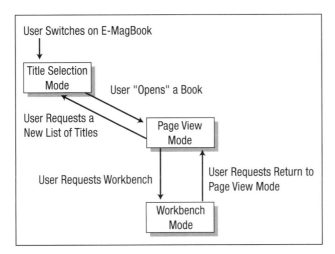

Figure 4.11
State transition diagram for the E-MagBook viewer.

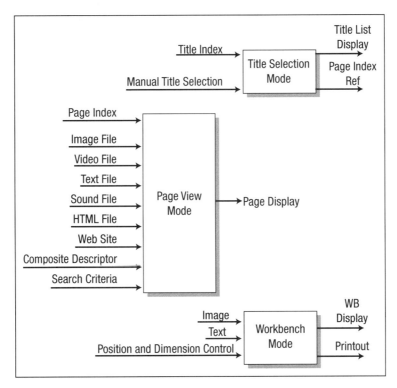

Figure 4.12
Inputs and outputs for each state of the E-MagBook Viewer.

the second input, and the Title List presented on the display—as well as the reference to a Page Index that had been selected—described the outputs. The reference to a selected Page Index also would serve as one of the main inputs to the Page View mode.

Page View mode would be a bit more substantial, as the center of the diagram shows. The output would be a page displayed on screen, while inputs consisted of the basic data entities or multimedia files, the user's search criteria, and the Page Index itself.

For the Workbench mode, the image and text would serve as input, and the output would be a Workbench display of those objects. The user would supply secondary input, which would consist of position and dimension changes. Position changes would be input via drag-and-drop, using the E-MagBook's mouse, and would be the subject of our next feasibility study. And, of course, we would have a possible hard-copy screen dump as output.

Form Modeling

Form modeling consists of modeling the screen layouts for the programs. At one time, screen modeling consisted of drawing screen objects on graph paper, labeling all the objects, and writing a brief description of their functions. This exercise provided a paper model of the user interface. Form modeling serves as a superb focus for discussions with the user concerning the requirements, because it focuses attention on how the user will interact with the completed system.

VB's design-time environment is extremely powerful and acts as an ideal prototyping environment for form layout, thanks to OOP. By this, I mean that all the VB screen controls are self-contained objects in the true sense of the word. You can create an instance of one object on the form and—from the design-time environment—manipulate the object's properties. This manipulation has an immediate effect because objects are "live" in the VB design environment. Consequently, you can set up a screen layout as if the application were using it. If you then run the program, the objects are all shown the way you set them up, just as they will appear in the completed program. However, no application-level code exists behind the screen—it's quite amazing what you can accomplish without writing a single instruction.

The Value of Form Prototypes

Providing some form layouts at this stage of the project does two things: First, it lets you redefine the requirements in terms of what happens on the GUI screens. Second, by allowing the customer to get close to the user interface, the prototypes help him or her begin to understand, from a functional viewpoint, how you will meet the requirements.

With VB, you can build a shell of the complete solution. From this shell, you can demonstrate both how the screen functions and how the user interacts with the screen, which provide a superb crosscheck on the requirements. Remember, we're looking at the requirements only from a functional point of view.

Creating of a VB-Generated Prototype Form

No matter what development environment you end up programming in, you can still model the forms using VB. For example, here's a requirement:

Requirement: *The data files from the company's field loggers will arrive at head office on 3.5-inch diskettes. Files are standard ASCII/DOS-type structures. Each file consists of from 10 through a maximum of 200 data points, 1 datum per line. The file also contains a single line of header information. The files will be transferred from diskette to the main server data area. The data preparation user will be able to select a data file and request the program to show the data in graphical form on screen. After visual inspection, the user can then transfer the data to the logging database or discard it. If the user discards the data, an entry is automatically made in the database concerning the data rejected. The entry consists of only the original file's header and an operator's reason for rejection.*

Prototype Form

Using VB to come up with a prototype, we can model the form that allows a user to select a data file, read it in, and display a graph. In our company, we have a standard component that we use to draw graphs in VB projects, and we can manipulate this component at design time to produce graphs. The component even has the capability to generate random data points. All we have to do is set the properties that define the number of data points to generate, the type of graph we want, and some scaling information. We set all this up using the property box of the graph control. We can set up the labels at design time by entering text directly into their captions. When the program runs, the graph control automatically generates data, providing the screen shot you see in Figure 4.13. Not one line of code needs to be generated to produce this screen shot.

Initial Definitions

The following definitions also accompany the first attempt to produce a prototype form:

Data Selection Screen Objects

- *File Name*—Name of file opened by the operator.
- *File Header*—Copy of exact content of Line 1 of data file.
- *Graph*—Representation of data points (minimum of 10 to a maximum of 200).
- *Accept*—Button to accept data for automatic input to logging database.
- *Reject*—Button to reject data for automatic input to logging database.

Customer Feedback

We showed the prototype form in Figure 4.13 and the initial requirements description to the user, whose first question was "How do I get a bar chart?" This question led to a discussion about what formats the user required. It turned out the user needed a line graph and a bar chart. The user also wanted to see a number, which defined how many points had been

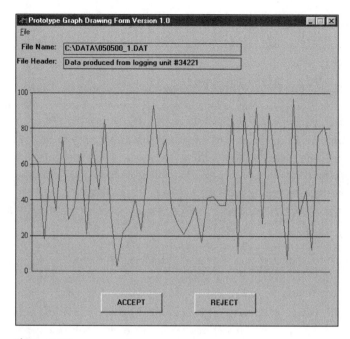

Figure 4.13
Prototype form for accepting/rejecting data.

plotted on the chart. In terms of modeling the process, the requirement was for three possible user actions after the graph was on the screen. The first requirement was to accept the data and transfer the file to the database. If this process was successful, the program was to delete the original data file. The second requirement was to reject the data, log that fact in the database, and then delete the original file. The third option was to allow the user to clear the screen and do nothing with the data that had been displayed.

A Second Version of the Form
The customer feedback highlighted deficiencies in the requirements statement, which we would obviously have to rewrite. However, before we did, we made another attempt at the form prototype based on our new understanding of the requirements. Figure 4.14 shows the final version of the form.

We also needed a way to switch between the line graph and bar graph styles.

A Second Version of the Definition
We then modified the definition to reflect the new prototype form layout as follows:

Data Selection Screen Objects

♦ *File Name*—Name of file opened by the operator.

♦ *File Header*—Copy of exact content of line 1 of data file.

- *Number of Data Points*—The number of points read from file and being displayed.

- *Graph*—Representation of data points (minimum 10 to a maximum of 200), shown as a line or bar graph, selected by user.

- *Accept Button*—Button to accept data for automatic input to logging database.

- *Reject Button*—Button to reject data for automatic input to logging database.

- *Abort Button*—Data is abandoned, no automatic action is taken, and screen is cleared.

Iteration of Requirement Capture

With the form layout in front of the customer, finding out the customer's expectations was easy—just by trying to model the process involved in meeting the requirement. The result was that both the customer and we now had a much better understanding of the requirements. As a result, the requirements statement might now read as follows:

Requirement: *The data files from the company's field loggers will arrive at head office on 3.5-inch diskettes. Files are standard ASCII/DOS-type structures. Each file consists of from 10 through a maximum of 200 data points, one datum per line. The file also contains a single line of header information. The files will be transferred from diskette to the main server data area. The data preparation user will be able to select a data file and request that the program show the data in graphical form on screen. The data can be presented either in the form of a line graph or a bar chart. Once data has been placed on screen, the operator requires three options:*

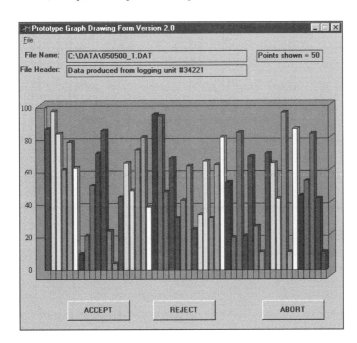

Figure 4.14
Final prototype form for accepting/rejecting/aborting data.

(a) The operator may accept the data, which is then automatically input to the logging database. Upon successful input, the original data file is automatically deleted and the graph on screen is then cleared.

(b) The operator may reject the data. An entry containing the header of the file and a comment from the operator concerning the reason for rejection is automatically inserted into the logging database. Upon successful input of the rejection information, the original data file is deleted, and the graph on screen is cleared.

(c) The operator may abandon the data. No action is taken, and the screen is cleared.

As you can see, analyzing the form requirements in detail led to many questions—from both the user and us. The result was that the customer's expectations, which we had clearly not captured in the original requirements statement, came out into the open, and we then captured them.

Yet Another Alternative View

By setting up form prototypes and defining the objects on the GUI, you are building another view of the requirements—but one that, for the first time, focuses the client's attention on the requirements like nothing else can. In the case study, you will see just how effective form prototyping using VB can be, where all the forms required were modeled to great effect.

VB as a General Form Modeling Tool

As I said earlier, what software development platform you ultimately use really doesn't matter—you can still employ VB as your form prototyping environment. Provided the final environment has screen objects similar to VB, any specifications you put together using the form prototypes are valid.

As a company, we have used a variety of programming languages for large database applications. Quite often, we can use third-party components (that the programming language can support) to meet requirements. However, we can also run these components in VB. A typical programming language might require 100 lines of code before we can even run a set of screens with no functionality behind them. Consequently, we tend to model using VB. Because VB lets us do the job far more quickly (thanks to its powerful design-time environment), we also use it to evaluate third-party components. (You might also be interested to know that we have people who are not programmers at all, but who are capable of designing form layouts in VB.)

Return to the Case Study:
The Viewer GUI Models

We were now going to produce a series of GUI form prototypes that reflected our understanding of the requirements for the viewer program in each of its operational states. *We would not write a single line of code.* We produced all the forms you see next in the VB design environment, manipulating only the screen objects' properties. The effect is quite dramatic—the viewer will suddenly start to come to life.

Title Selection Mode

Now what requirements did we have of this mode? The user needed to be able to view a list of titles, select one, and see the description. Then, the user needed to be able to open the relevant Page Index file. So, we needed a "list" object—something to show a selected title and its description—and a button to open a selected title. We'd need a second button to repopulate the list after a disk had been changed. That was apparent from reading the use case that specified the following:

User switches on the E-MagBook without any removable disk on board and is informed that no index is available.

User inserts a disk and requests that the system try again.

The Prototype Screen

We had some idea of what was required on screen, so we made our first attempt to build a form to accommodate the Title Index mode. (Don't forget, too, that the Title Index format needed to be set in a 640×480-pixel screen size.) We used VB to come up with a form that would accommodate the requirements, as we understood them. You can see the result in Figure 4.15.

Creating Your Own Sample Prototype

All you have to do to achieve a prototype like the one in Figure 4.15 is start a new VB project and follow these instructions:

1. On the form, create a label and set its caption to "E-MagBook." Set the font to match what you see in Figure 4.15.

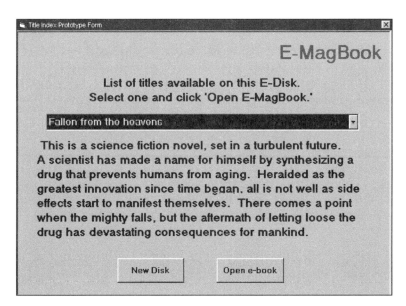

Figure 4.15
Viewer GUI form model for Title Selection mode of operation.

2. Place a combo box on the screen, and set a single entry (as shown in the figure) with the background color set to black and foreground color set to white and large font.

3. Above this box, place an information label with its caption set up as shown. Below the combo box, create a big label and set the caption with plenty of text, as you can see in the figure.

4. Place two buttons on the bottom of the form and label them accordingly. When you run the program, you will see the screen, as depicted in Figure 4.15, with whatever variation you may have introduced to the text content.

5. You can then capture this as a screen shot and make it part of your specification.

Title Selection Form Requirements

Next, we wrote a set of requirements that matched the ones we had already produced but, this time, according to the screen model. Clearly, as we were going to a much deeper level of detail, we would also have some new requirements.

Title Selection Form Requirements

Title Label
A title label is required to indicate "E-MagBook".

Help Text
To hold the following as a Help message, a hard-coded block of text is required: "List of titles available on this E-Disk. Select one and click 'Open E-MagBook'."

Title List
A screen object is required to hold the list of titles and allow one to be selected.

Description
When the user has selected a title, the associated description is placed on the screen.

New Disk Button
It is required that, if a new E-Disk is inserted into the E-MagBook, the user can request the new Index to be read into the program.

Open E-MagBook Button
It is required that a selected title can be loaded into the program and Page 1 displayed.

Until now, we hadn't said anything about Help text and title labels in the requirements document, but we were starting to drill deeper and deeper into the requirements, and Monty clearly needed to decide what we should put there.

NOTE: *After we had produced this form, Julie said she thought the project was really starting to come to life. The more we defined, the less ambiguity the specification had. It was hard work, but the payoff would come when we developed the software—development would take only one round. Remember what we were trying to eliminate: Monty looking at the completed software and saying, "But that's not what I wanted...."*

GUI form models are comparable to an architect's drawings of the building that will be constructed. You can sit down in front of these forms and discuss the functionality as you would with a building model. This process tests, validates, and enhances everyone's understanding of the documented requirements.

Page View Mode—Text Book

Using the same approach as we did for the Title Selection form, we could now define a series of form prototypes and descriptions for the viewer's Page View mode of operation. The only complication was the fact that three formats changed the layouts. We needed to define a form for each separate format type. We started with the Text Book format.

The Text Book Prototype Form

The prototype form we developed for a Text Book-formatted page shown in the viewer's Page View mode is displayed in Figure 4.16. The form shows the text display area and the navigation controls, which will be common to all the other formats.

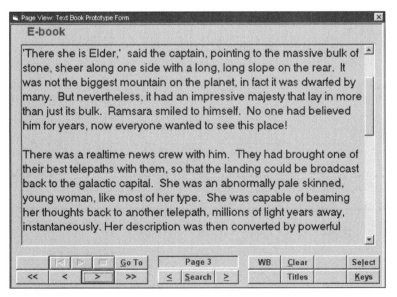

Figure 4.16
Viewer GUI form model for Page View mode, Text Book format.

What you see in Figure 4.16 required a lot more work to produce than the layout for Title Selection mode, but note how this figure reflects the original, very crude drawing Monty had done for us. We had filled in the detail on the navigation control area and set up what we believed was a suitable set of button controls. We'd split the controls into a set for navigating through the pages—remember, Go to start (<<), Go to end (>>), Next (>), Previous (<), and one that would be used to request a page number from the reader (Go To). We'd also placed the multimedia control there for stopping, starting, and rewinding the sound files. This provided a sensible subset of controls. Next to those controls were the search controls. We had some discussion about searching and decided to add a Previous search button as well. This button made the search more functional (as you will see), but it required an addition to the requirements specification. Then, we placed all the other buttons we needed (to invoke the Workbench and so on) on the right. It was our first attempt at designing the GUI, and it might be subject to change, but, as a way to focus on functional requirements, we couldn't beat it. We'd populated the text box with plenty of text and set the font large.

The Description

I'll not bore you with all the discussions that led to the definitions you see next for the text format. Suffice it to say that we had some debate. However, both Archie and Julie were now steeped in the requirements of the project, and this part of the analysis went very well:

Viewer—Text Format, Form Requirements

E-Book Format Specifier
"E-Book" is placed in the top left of the form when "text-only" books are loaded.

The Text Display
For "text-only" format, the text display area is maximized as the prototype form layout shows. Text is displayed so that it can be scrolled up and down to accommodate large volumes. The font characteristics of a page are inherited from the **font** attribute set up for the Page Index.

NOTE: *We now had a simple description for defining the font characteristics of the text display, thanks to the work we had done on data entities (that is, "the text display's font characteristics are inherited from the Page Index").*

Next, we defined the requirements for the navigation controls:

Navigation Controls
This section describes all the functionality required from the button controls located at the bottom of the screen in all book modes:

<<	Go to Page 1.
>>	Go to last page.

<	Go to previous page.
>	Go to next page.
Go To	Go to a user-selected page number.
MM Sound	(Multimedia control).
	Rewind current sound.
	Stop playing current sound.
	Start playing current sound.
Page no.	Shows current page number.
Search	Search for first match starting from Page 1.
>	Search from current page for next matching page.
<	Search from current page for first previous matching page.
WB	Select Workbench mode.
Clear	Clear selection criteria.
Titles	Return to Title Selection mode.
Select	Show selection criteria panel.
Keys	Display keys.

We'd defined two button controls: one to switch on the keys and one to switch on the selection criteria panel. Going back to the scenarios, we suddenly realized that we didn't have a scenario to explain how searching was to work.

The Forgotten Scenario

Embarrassing as it was, we'd forgotten to create a scenario for searching. This oversight was typical of what analysis might dredge up. We couldn't think of everything, and overlooking the scenario was a classic example of how useful the SDLC's structured approach is to developers. We had already added an extra requirement, too—the capability to search back from the current page to the beginning of the Index. We needed a scenario that told us how searching involving the selection criteria would be conducted. Here's what we came up with (note that we made it generic in the respect that it does not refer to any page format type):

Scenario: Searching a Page Index

Preconditions:
The user loads an E-MagBook with a selection of titles.

Description:
The user selects a title and views Page 1. The user then clicks the Select button control and the selection criteria panel appears on the screen. The user enters a single search parameter into a randomly chosen selection field. The user now clicks the Search button control.

The display changes to that of the first entry that meets the selection criteria. The user clicks Keys to see the keys for that entry. The user then clicks on Search Next (>) and the next matching entry is shown. The user repeats this process until he or she is informed that he or she has encountered the end of the Index, and no more matches have occurred.

The user then clicks the Search Previous button (<) and the previous match is displayed. The user then clicks the Selection button; and enters a second key into another empty field. The user then requests that both the defined keys must be present for a match.

The user then clicks Search, and the first page containing both these keys is located. The user clicks Next and Previous to step backward and forward through the collection of entries containing both keys.

The user then requests that the search criteria be changed so that only one of the keys needs to be present. The user views matching pages as before, noting that more matches are now available because only one key needs to be present.

Repercussions

After we had developed a scenario for searching, something occurred to Archie. We'd defined requirements to switch on the key display panel or the selection criteria panel, but not to switch them both off. Switching the panels off must surely be a requirement, because we had indicated in the requirements that, in Simple Reference format, the text box could expand to full height if neither key panel nor selection panel was required. We needed another button control that switched off whichever panel was on and left just the text. We had a few spare button controls, so we could easily add that.

NOTE: *By this stage, Archie and Julie were becoming quite despondent that we had missed so much out of the requirements capturing. But that happens. The important point for you to take away from all this is that you plan the project with iteration of the SDLC Phases 1 and 2 in mind. What you learn from Phase 2 you must use to improve the output from Phase 1. But, to do this properly, you must allocate time for the iteration.*

An evolutionary process was at work here. From knowing nothing about E-MagBooks, we were becoming domain experts in our own right. The more we learned, the more we challenged our previously acquired knowledge. Without a structured methodology for handling this apparently haphazard evolution, we would have had much more difficulty capitalizing on this learning process and producing the definitive statement of requirements.

Making the Keys More Generic

When we were capturing the requirements, we had made an assumption that we wouldn't have keys for "text-only" pages. We made that assumption because we had been influenced by Monty's original drawings of the formats. His drawing of the Text Book format didn't have any keys on it, so we'd assumed it didn't need any. But why shouldn't a Text Book have keys? When we thought about it, a text page was no different from any other page. Its keys could be the page number, the chapter name, and the section name—there must be all sorts of keys relevant to text-only pages. And of course, users didn't *have* to use the keys if they didn't want to (which defaults to Monty's apparent lack of interest in them for textbooks). In fact, adding keys to the Text Book format would make everything much more generic. Although we'd have to update the requirements specification, we'd now introduced a much more unified way of looking at pages.

NOTE: *Make keys available to text-only format.*

That good bit of analysis had fallen out from our delving deeper into the requirements—and a scenario we'd forgotten about.

Page View Mode—Picture Album

After the diversion the missing scenario caused, we moved on to the Picture Album format prototype form. (Now, you will really start to see how powerful the VB design-time environment is.)

The Prototype Screen

We were able to load a picture into the image control object, just by setting its **picture** property. As long as the **stretch** property was true, the user could then resize the object to the desired dimensions and position it, as we would expect to see it work if the program were running. You can see the result in Figure 4.17.

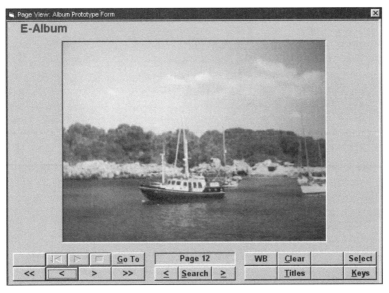

Figure 4.17
Viewer GUI form model for Page View mode in the Picture Album format.

Creating Your Own Picture Album Prototype

If you want to set up the album form, take the preceding text form layout and remove the text box. Add an image control, and load a picture into the form by clicking the **picture** property. This action results in a file dialog box appearing. Select a suitable image and load it. Set the **stretch** property to **true** and manipulate the image until you get the desired effect. You can directly modify any labels that have changed from the text layout. Run the program, and it should look like Figure 4.17—with your own image, of course.

The Picture Album Form Description

Everything was suddenly starting to come together in a big way. Here's the detailed description of the functional requirements we developed for this form:

E-Album Format Specifier
"E-Album" is placed in the top left of the form when the Picture Album format is loaded.

The Image
For the Picture Album format, the available area for image display is maximized to occupy the entire screen, from the navigation controls up to the format specifier. Any image is first sized and then scaled to fit into this area, preserving its aspect ratio.

Keys
Keys can be viewed as an overlay in the top right-hand corner of the display using the same panel layout as shown for the Reference Book format screen. This panel can be switched on and off as required.

Navigation Controls
The requirements are the same as those defined for the text-only format.

Page View Mode—Simple Reference

We had now come to the more complex Reference Book format. At this stage, I left Archie and Julie to get on with the work. They decided that, for the final version of the form model descriptions, they would separate and define all the button controls generically, rather than embed them in the Text Book format prototype form. (You'll see the final result in Chapter 5.)

The Prototype Screen

After Julie and Archie had analyzed the requirements and had a bit of healthy debate, we developed the first prototype screen, which you can see in Figure 4.18.

The Description

The description of the screen objects is as follows:

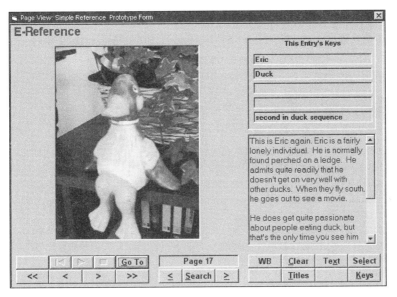

Figure 4.18
Viewer GUI form model for Page View mode, Reference Book format.

Reference Layout 1
This example shows the required layout for the Reference Book mode when the image, text, and keys are all in view.

E-Reference Format Specifier
"E-Reference" is placed in the top left of the form when a Reference Book is loaded.

The Image
For the Reference Book format, the available area for image display is maximized to occupy from the left-hand side of the form to the start of the text area. The area extends from the top of the navigation controls to below the format specifier. The image is loaded, sized, and centered in the available area with the aspect ratio preserved.

The Text Area
Text is placed in a fixed area as shown. In this mode (display image, text, and keys), the text area extends vertically from the top of the navigation controls to just below the key panel.

The Keys
When the user requires seeing the keys for a given entry, the keys are required to be displayed above the text box to the top of the form as shown.

Navigation Controls
The requirements are the same as those defined for the text-only and Picture Album format.

Page View Mode—Simple Reference 2

Archie and Julie felt it would be prudent to produce a prototype of the Simple Reference format with the text box expanded. (You will see the result they produced in Chapter 5 when we review the final requirements document.)

The Selection Criteria Panel

Julie and Archie hadn't yet shown the selection criteria panel. They decided to mock up that panel as a prototype and make it the same size as the key panel. Only one of these two panel objects is ever present on the screen at any give time, so, if they made each panel the same size and placed each panel at the same position on screen, one panel just hid the other one. That way, they could use the same position for all book formats. (Again, you will see the final result in Chapter 5.)

The Workbench Interface Mode

Quite pleased with what they had achieved, Archie and Julie set about producing form layouts and descriptions for the Workbench mode of operation. (You will see the results of these endeavors in Chapter 5.)

Functional Lists

You now come to a critical part of the analysis phase. (In fact, in the case study, we performed much of this exercise at the time as the presales effort.) You need to look at the requirements and extract self-contained, functional entities, or *functional lists*. This time, you will use the following template to expand the definitions of the entities:

- *Functional Requirement Name*—A name that identifies the requirement.

- *Description*—Detailed description of the requirement.

- *Inputs*—List of inputs required.

- *Outputs*—List of outputs required.

Black-Box Approach

A *black box* (which I mentioned earlier) is a description of something that performs a given function; how the black box goes about performing that function you neither know nor care. All you need to understand to use a black box is to know what it does, what inputs you must supply, and what outputs you will get back. If you think this description sounds remarkably like *objects*, that's not a coincidence.

You can take the black-box approach to all sorts of situations. For example, you can consider a factory that produces plastic ducks as a black box. The inputs are the raw materials to make plastic; the output is a plastic duck. How the raw material is converted to a plastic duck is of no interest to us. To get the factory to make plastic ducks, we need to supply it with the appropriately defined inputs, and, after the process has been completed, we can then receive a specified duck. By "specified," I mean a designated color, size, and so on. We can use this approach in software. If we can define a lump of self-contained functionality in terms of inputs—*what* (not *how*) that functionality does to those inputs, and what the resultant outputs are—we can create a series of building-block definitions.

Encapsulation

Encapsulation is another OOP term. An object has characteristics that its users need to understand to employ it—just as a black box does. The actual workings of the object and its internal data structures are completely hidden from the user—they've been "encapsulated" into the body of the object.

VB is an object-based environment in the respect that programmers can incorporate objects into their VB programs. To do this, programmers need to create an instance of the object or control and then use its properties to obtain the desired effects. We've used text boxes, picture boxes, labels, and button controls in the work we have done so far in our feasibility studies. We had no idea how a picture control works or what its internal structure looks like because all that is hidden away from us by encapsulation. To change the size of a viewed picture, we just reset the height and width properties of the control. If we set the **auto-stretch** property to **true**, the image is reconfigured by the object's internal code to fit the width and height exactly—in response to our changing one or more of the object's properties. We just set the specified inputs to produce a desired output.

Functional Requirements

If we can define lumps of functionality as black boxes—specifying inputs, outputs, and what the black box will do to the inputs to create the outputs—we can leave the programmers to encapsulate all the necessary code to perform the desired function. Because ours is not a true OOP project, we can go only so far with this approach. Our aim is to define building blocks for development that will be robust, self-contained, and reusable.

Reusability

Reusability is one of the main requirements for successful software development. We want to define building blocks that we can reuse in many different contexts. We can provide reusability in conventional software with subroutines and functions. (In OOP, the reusability comes from classes). Our aim, therefore, is to define functional requirements that we can identify as self-contained, functional components of the system. We're looking for entities that we can develop in isolation, test, and then integrate into the whole. We're looking for many black boxes that we can use in lots of different circumstances, simply by setting the inputs appropriately to achieve the desired output. We put all this theory into action in the case study.

Return to the Case Study:
Viewer Functional Requirements

We now needed to define self-contained, functional requirements for the viewer. Remember this from the proposal? We produced these requirements in preparation for estimating how much effort the project would take. Here is the list we produced from that exercise, but, remember, this list includes aspects of all three programs:

Functional Requirements Lists for E-MagBook Development

Page Index Handling:
All entries are to be loaded into memory when the book is "opened."

Pure Functional Requirements:
Read a specified Title Index into memory.

Read a specified Page Index into memory.

Output a Page Index to selected disk file.

Output a Title Index to selected disk file.

Perform a search.

GUI-Based Functional Requirements:
Display list of titles and allow user to select a single title.

Select a Page Index file for input.

Select a Title Index file for input.

Select file name for Page Index output.

Select file name for Title Index output.

Page Index navigation functionality.

Title Index navigation functionality.

Display page.

Display contents of current title entry.

Workbench functionality.

Set up for the search.

Add/Delete/Insert/Overwrite Page Index functionality.

Add/Delete/Insert/Overwrite Title Index functionality.

Page entry edit functionality.

Title entry edit functionality.

This time, we went through each of the preceding items and redefined the requirements in terms of inputs and outputs, and in terms of the function required. Initially, we did this only for viewer-related items, starting with the GUI-bound list. Our aim was to put more "meat" around the specification for what would become a self-contained, development module. (As you consider our doing that, keep in mind the comment at the top of the list about the Page Index being in memory.)

Title Selection

We started with the GUI function described as **Display List Of Titles And Allow User To Select A Single Title.** First, we gave it a simpler title, **Title Selection**, and then we defined it as follows:

Requirement: **Title Selection**

Function: To display list of titles from memory and allow user to select a single Item.

Inputs: Memory-held Title Index, user-selected entry.

Output: Record number of selected title.

Julie questioned the output, believing that it should be the selected title. Let's consider the situation. If the title is returned from this functional component, the title is just a string—all we can do is display it. The associated Title Index record number is far more useful. With that, we can get at all data items relating to the selected title whenever we want, just by extracting them from the Title Index. At this point, we decided that it was sensible to hold both the Title Index and the Page Index in memory (something we had determined right back at the proposal stage). So, in essence, if the functional requirement was to supply the record number of the entry the user selected, all we had to do to access the detail was to use the value as an array pointer to the title record.

Julie realized that this approach let us define a standalone requirement or function that we could program as a module, which is what we were after. We would call the function whenever we wanted the user to make a title selection. Upon return from the function or subroutine, the programmer would have the record number of the selected title. One important point we needed to remember was that, for the function to work, the Title Index must already be in memory.

NOTE: *This was our first "black box": Supply it with a Title Index (memory based), point to a title, and it would return the corresponding record number of the title record.*

Selecting a Title Index

The next item we considered from the GUI list was **Select A Title Index File For Input** because that item looked like it was relevant to the first item we had looked at. However, in the viewer, the user was not allowed to select a Title Index. The program would be hard-coded to read the Index from E:\E-MagBook\Title.idx. All the user could do would be to remove an E-MagBook disk, insert another one, and click on the Open E-MagBook button, which would simply read the file using the above reference. If the program couldn't find a Title Index, then it would simply inform the user to try again with another disk. So, because **Select A Title Index File For Input** was not one of the viewer's requirements, we'd leave it until we got to the editors.

Selecting a Page Index

We then went back to look at **Select A Page Index File For Input**, the second item on the GUI list. This, too, was not actually a viewer requirement. The mechanism to select a Page Index in the viewer would consist of selecting a title from the list of titles presented in the Title Selection mode of operation and, using the resultant record number, to extract the desired Page Index reference from the title record. So, we didn't ask the user explicitly to select a Page Index. Once again, we'd leave this functionality until we looked at the editors.

Index Output Functions

The viewer did not require the next two functions in the GUI list, **Select File Name For Page Index Output** and **Select File Name For Title Index Output**, because we had established that the viewer could not output any files.

Navigation

That brought us to **Page Index Navigation** functionality, which the viewer *did* need. This functionality would be accommodated by the button controls on the viewer, so we'd just make a note as follows:

Requirement:	**Page Index Navigation**
Function:	To turn the pages of a book. Specifically:
	(a) Go to Page 1
	(b) Go to end page
	(c) Go to next page
	(d) Go to previous page
	(e) Go to user-defined page number
Inputs:	Page number for (e)
Outputs:	Page display on screen; new page number

Clearly, the button controls would service all these functions. All the functions would result in a new page number being defined and the contents of the page being displayed.

This definition for a navigation requirement also applied to the Page Index Editor. We had already established that the Page Index Editor must contain all the functionality of the viewer, plus its own editing capability—that's reusability across programs. The Title Index Editor required the next function, **Title Index Navigation Functionality**, so we moved on to the **Display Page** function.

Page Display

The **Display Page** function was possibly the most important viewer function, and we needed to analyze it in more detail. I asked Julie and Archie what displaying a page was all about, and, because they were now so knowledgeable about the requirements, they rattled off the following description easily.

Displaying a page depended on format and could involve one or more of the following: read and display an image, read and run a video clip, read and play a WAV or MID file, and read and display text. For the Composite and HTML/Web pages, we would have something similar, but we wouldn't worry about the detail. All we were concerned with was that those formats would fit into this page-display functionality.

Clearly, displaying a page involved invoking all the functions just described, on an individual basis, depending on the format type. In other words, **Display Page** must invoke **Read And Display Text** if the format was either Text Book or Reference Book, but not Picture Album. The **Display Page** function also had to determine whether an image reference was for an image or a video, and then invoke the appropriate function.

We were saying that **Display Page** would provide the overall functionality based on format and other criteria, and we could define a set of self-contained, functional entities to meet the lower-level requirements. We defined a batch of requirements based on page handling as follows:

Requirement:	**Display Page**
Function:	According to format, display all the contents of a given page number.
Inputs:	Page number, Page Index record, page format, basic data entities.
Outputs:	Static image on screen, moving image on screen, scrollable text on screen, sound played on speaker, music played on speaker.
Requirement:	**Load and Display Image**
Function:	To load, scale, and position an image into the available image area on screen.

| Inputs: | Image file reference, image file, image area definition. |
| Outputs: | Static image on screen. |

Requirement: Load and Play Video Clip

Function:	To load and run a video clip on screen.
Inputs:	Video clip file reference, video clip file, image area definition.
Outputs:	Moving image on screen.

Requirement: Load and Display Text

Function:	To read in and display text in a text display area with correct font characteristics.
Inputs:	File reference, text file, font characteristics, text area definition.
Outputs:	Scrollable text on screen.

Requirement: Load and Play WAV Sound File

Function:	To read in and play a WAV sound file.
Inputs:	WAV file reference, WAV File.
Output:	Sound played on speaker.

Requirement: Load and Play MID Music File

Function:	To read in and play an MID sound file.
Inputs:	MID file reference, MID file.
Output:	Music played on speaker.

Subcomponents

Displaying a page would require all the listed functionality; so, we reasoned, Why not embed it all in one functional requirement—Why split it up? The advantage of splitting the functionality into smaller, self-contained subcomponents (and isolating those, as we were doing) was that we could use the components anywhere their particular function was required, and not just to display a complete page. This approach gave us a number of advantages. First, if we designed them appropriately, we had some modules we could use in any application in which we needed to display an image, play a sound, and so on. Second, we did not restrict ourselves to requesting all functionality through the **Display Page** function in any of the three programs. We had kept our options open. Third, we were starting to define building blocks that more than one person could develop and test simultaneously.

Parallel development was vital to us. If we couldn't have at least two people working in parallel on the project, we were unlikely to meet the deadline. We needed to define functional requirements so they led to the development of a series of independent, self-contained units that we could develop and test in parallel and then integrate.

Developing a small, self-contained piece of software that you can fully verify before you put it into the whole system leads to improved reliability and easier maintenance—and it eases further development.

Parallel development also would let us much more easily "slot in" Composite image and HTML/Web functionality, which we must keep in mind. All we needed to do was define self-contained requirements to service each type, and then make a minor modification to the **Display Page** module to invoke the new, self-contained functions for Composite and HTML handling.

The next functional requirement in the list was **Display Contents Of Current Title Entry**, which only the editors required, so we left that alone for the time being.

Workbench Functionality

We could expand the Workbench functionality into three separate requirements: a requirement to set up the Workbench, similar to the **Display Page** requirement, but specific to the needs of the Workbench; the functionality involved in manipulation of the screen objects; and, finally, the printing requirement.

The **Display Workbench** requirement must also include video clips, which prompted Archie to ask what we would do with a video if the user requested Workbench mode. Again, that functionality had fallen through the net. As the specification stood, what a user was to do with a movie in the Workbench mode wasn't at all clear—in fact, we hadn't mentioned it anywhere. Archie pointed out that users couldn't really print a video, and printing was one of the main functions of the Workbench mode. They could print a snapshot of the current frame, but to be honest, overlooking videos in the Workbench was a bit of an embarrassment. Nevertheless, we had to do something about the situation.

I decided to call Monty and see how critical putting videos into the Workbench mode was to him. Monty forwarded me to Samantha because he wasn't sure what they required. Samantha was quite unconcerned and said she couldn't, at that moment, see any point in having a video in the Workbench mode other than for printing any text associated with the video. So, we agreed to place the video on the screen together with the text; a print would capture only the text. This modification required an update to the specifications:

NOTE: *WB and videos.*

Altogether, our definitions for the Workbench functionality amounted to the following:

Requirement:	**Display Workbench**
Function:	To set up image at full-size, video, and text in Workbench mode, according to format.
Inputs:	Page number, Page Index record, image, video, text.
Outputs:	Static, full-sized image on screen, video on screen, text on screen.

Once the program was in the Workbench mode, then according to the requirements, a toolbar would let users manipulate the image or text object's dimensions. The toolbar would consist of a series of buttons. We skipped that section in the requirements, but you can see the form layouts in Chapter 5, where we have defined the Workbench mode in detail.

In Workbench mode, the user could also move the objects around the screen using drag-and-drop. We took the following definitions directly from those we produced for the Workbench form layout, which you will find in Chapter 5. Even without reading the requirements in detail, you should recognize these definitions from what you already know:

Requirement:	**Workbench Screen Object Positioning**
Functions:	(a) Drag and drop image object.
	(b) Drag and drop text box object.
Inputs:	Image and text screen objects.
Outputs:	Image and text screen objects.
Requirement:	**Workbench Screen Object Manipulation**
Functions:	(a) Increase width and height of image by fixed amount, preserving aspect ratio.
	(b) Decrease width and height of image by fixed amount, preserving aspect ratio.
	(c) Increase height of image only, by fixed amount.
	(d) Decrease height of image only, by fixed amount.
	(e) Increase width of image only, by fixed amount.
	(f) Decrease width of image only, by fixed amount.
	(g) Increase height of text box only, by fixed amount.
	(h) Decrease height of text box only, by fixed amount.
	(i) Increase width of text box only, by fixed amount.
	(j) Decrease width of text box only, by fixed amount.

(k) Switch text on and off (if present).

(l) Return program to View mode at last current entry.

Inputs: Image reference, image file, text reference, text file, video reference, and video file.

Outputs: Image on screen, text on screen, and video on screen.

This block of functionality is likely to use the functions to load and display an image, load and display text, and load and play video.

Finally, we defined the Workbench print requirement:

Requirement: Print Content of Workbench
Functions: Prepare screen (remove unwanted objects), and produce a bitmapped representation of the screen content for images and/or text only.

Inputs: Image on screen, text on screen.

Outputs   Printed screen dump.

The analysis, so far, had raised a host of issues. We were constantly deepening our understanding of what was required and challenging what we had already defined.

GUI Definition for Search

Next on the GUI list was **Set Up For Search**. Here's our definition:

Requirement: Set Up For Search
Function: Handle user entry of up to five selection keys for searching, and define search type.

Inputs: Selection words, search type choice (all keys present or any key present).

Outputs: Search selection criteria.

Completion of GUI Definitions for the Viewer

All the rest of the items in the GUI functional list were editor requirements. We now had a more comprehensive list of self-contained GUI requirements for the E-MagBook Viewer, and we had also gone down to a deeper level, defining components such as **Load And Display Image** and so on. We could now move on to the non-GUI requirements for the viewer by scanning the list we had created at presales time.

Read a Specified Title Index into Memory

Read A Specified Title Index Into Memory was the first function in the pure functionality list. The viewer would require this function, even though the action would be to open and read E:\E-MagBook\Title.idx in every case. The editors also required this function, but in the case of the editors, the name might be variable. We defined the functional requirement as follows:

Requirement:	**Read a Specified Title Index into Memory**
Function:	To open a named Title Index on disk and read the Index into memory.
Inputs:	Title Index file reference, Title Index file.
Outputs:	Memory version of Title Index.

This was a black-box definition that we could use in all three programs— the viewer and both editors. Supply the black box with a Title Index file name, and it would load that file into memory.

Read Page Index into Memory

The Page Index requirement was similar to that of the Title Index. Both the viewer and the Page Index Editor would need this requirement. We defined the functional requirement as follows:

Requirement:	**Read Specified Page Index into Memory**
Function:	To open a named Page Index on disk and read the Index into memory.
Inputs:	Page Index file reference, Page Index file.
Output:	Memory version of Page Index.

This black box functions like the Title Index version, but this one works on different inputs and provides a different output.

Perform a Search

Finally, we came to the search functionality. (Don't confuse this with defining the search criteria, which is a GUI-based requirement independent of performing the actual search. If we have set up no criteria and the user invokes the **Perform A Search** function, the program will simply search for entries with no keys.) First, we needed to make this requirement bi-directional because we'd added a **Previous Search** facility to the requirements.

I asked Archie and Julie to try to write up a requirement for performing a search that took everything into consideration but was generic, self-contained, and free from the GUI. Julie wanted to know how to make the requirement free from the GUI when the selection criteria were defined in five screen objects. I explained we could do this by copying the objects' contents to internal variables and passing them as arguments to the function for searching, and that we could do the same with a search direction indicator.

We made a few attempts before we got the following requirement written up:

Requirement:	**Perform a Search**
Function:	Three separate functions are required:
	(a) Search from Page 1 to end of Index for a match.
	(b) Search from current page +1 to end of Index for a match.
	(c) Search from current page −1 to start of Index for a match.
A match is found if, according to search mode, the selection criteria match the keys found in a page.	
	Search Mode 1 requires that all the selection criteria match.
	Search Mode 2 requires that one or more of the selection criteria must match.
Inputs:	Page number, in-memory page keys, selection criteria strings.
Outputs:	Matching page number, or start or end of Index indicator.

Clear Page Index

With respect to the last set of requirements in the non-GUI functional list, it was obvious that we would need a **Clear Page Index** requirement for the viewer to prepare the in-memory Index data structures for a new Index, but the **Save Index To Disk** functions were for the editors.

We defined the **Clear Index** requirement as follows:

Requirement:	**Clear Page Index**
Function:	In-memory Page Index is completely cleared.
Input:	In-memory Page Index.
Output:	In-memory Page Index.

Completing this specification brought us to the end of a long day.

Progress

The analysis we'd just been through took a whole day because much discussion accompanied it. We looked at progress in the evening. Our goals were first, to analyze the data requirements for the project as a whole, then to analyze viewer requirements specifically. We had completed both tasks; therefore, we were on target. In fact, we had spent about 2.5 man-days working on this (we had two people for the whole day; I popped in and out, and must have spent about half my time on the work).

So, although we were talking about one day in elapsed time, we'd actually supplied 2.5 days of effort. However, Archie and Julie were also using this as a training exercise, so they were learning at the same time they were working. That fact implied that, instead of 2.5 days of effort, we were instead probably looking at between 1 day and 1.5 days.

NOTE: *This level of detail illustrates how you need to qualify the effort you cost to a project. A realistic cost for the day's work we had completed would have been 1.5 days of effort, as opposed to the 2.5 we actually spent, including training. (We couldn't really charge the training time to the customer because it would likely make our costs too high in a competitive situation.)*

Prototyping Software

In the case study, to help us to capture the requirements at a very detailed level, we used VB to produce prototype forms that related to the final solution. The prototype forms were a direct by-product of our analyzing the requirements from the GUI point of view. Hopefully, you can see what a fantastic difference the forms make to your understanding of the requirements—confirming the saying that "a picture speaks a thousand words." But the benefits of using the prototypes don't necessarily stop there. If you have a really complex set of requirements to determine, a sensible strategy might be to prototype the requirements using a form of rapid development tool—which we can consider VB to be—and develop code as well as the forms.

In a situation where you want to clarify complex functionality, without a great deal of design, you can build software that explores the requirements. You need to do enough design to meet the objectives of the prototype, but you can do the design without having to consider the complete solution, which gives you considerable freedom and makes the task much easier. You can develop prototypes to test the requirements, help develop everyone's understanding, and, from the results, construct a definitive requirements specification.

Limitations of Prototyping

You must keep in mind one fact whenever you engage in writing prototype code: You (and the customer) must be prepared to throw the code away at the end of the exercise and design the functionality into the full system from scratch. This limitation might not fit in every case, but you must be prepared to accept it if it applies in your situation.

We use prototypes to explore the unknown. Once the unknown becomes understandable, many of the premises on which you developed the prototype might no longer hold true. You might be able to salvage bits of the prototype work, but the point is that you must be prepared to sacrifice that effort when you move to the final solution, start again, and build on the experiences you gained from the prototype. Software systems can evolve from prototypes in one of two ways—directly or indirectly. Let's take a look at each means of evolution.

Direct Software Evolution

As we've discussed, you build a prototype to explore a given requirement. The customer looks at the prototype and requests all sorts of changes, which you implement directly into the prototype. You show the prototype to the client again, the client requests more changes, and you repeat the process—development, demonstration, feedback. Eventually, the client decides he or she now properly understands the requirement, which the prototype has met.

This evolutionary development of code is in stark contrast to the formal methodology that we imposed on the case study, but we might as well have developed a working solution that the customer was happy with without all the formality of a structured methodology. All might have ended well and good, with the customer happy and us paid.

Then again, the end of the story might have been quite different. As time went on, the customer demanded more changes, we modified the programs, and they started to grow. Soon, as we added more functionality, the system became sluggish. We had to make compromises between existing design (assuming there was one) and new requirements. The software became more and more top-heavy. Changes took longer and longer to implement.

Support had become a nightmare because the code had *evolved* rather than been *produced* through a well-disciplined methodology. The code had become intensely difficult to follow, and the design documentation was conspicuous by its almost total absence. But we had developed the system in a very short time frame. And the system did what the customer wanted...for a while. It wasn't long, though, before adding new functionality became impossible without compromising the rest of the system. The result: For short-term gain, the price was long-term loss.

Indirect Software Evolution

Prototyping is one of the best ways to determine requirements, particularly when you are exploring new frontiers with new technologies. But, as I already mentioned, you and the customer must understand that, to get the best out of a methodology based on "try it out and see what happens," you must be prepared to throw away the result and start again to avoid the long-term pitfalls of an unstructured development.

Removing the formality of a structured approach can lead to innovating and exiting discoveries in terms of the requirements—but at the expense of software quality. By quality, I don't just mean that the software doesn't keep breaking down; quality is much deeper than that. Quality is all about accountability, traceability, adherence to standards, and a working methodology that provides a consistent approach.

Prototyping can still fit into our methodology, provided we use it to build *from* rather than build *upon*. By this I mean that we learn from the results of the prototyping and plan subsequent work correctly, rather than turn the prototype into the final solution. This process is what I term *indirect* evolution.

A Case in Point

In the case study, we had performed a number of feasibility studies and evaluations. The code we produced as a result of these studies was prototype code, but that didn't stop us from using elements of the code directly. That approach was valid, provided those elements fit the requirement specifications—which they helped develop—and were integrated in a manner consistent with our overall philosophy of a structured approach to the final solution.

An Alternative Approach

You can base a development methodology on prototyping, provided you appreciate that you will have to reengineer the end result to provide the final solution. In the next chapter, we'll explore an alternative form of development based on *iterative prototyping*.

Return to the Case Study:
Drag-and-Drop Feasibility

At the start of Day 2, project Week 2, we had a bit of a diversion. I reviewed drag-and-drop functionality with Archie and Julie to help them appreciate what that required from a programming point of view. We developed a simple prototype to explore the requirements in detail.

If you want a bit of a diversion from analysis before you start looking at the editors, you can see the result of that work in Appendix D. The drag-and-drop capability is quite crucial to the Workbench functionality, so, if you're not sure about how to go about implementing drag and drop, Appendix D is well worth a visit before we start coding.

The Title Index Editor

To quickly review, we had started analysis by considering the data entities for all three programs. Then, we looked at viewer states, I/O, form requirements for the main modes of operation, and, finally, black-box functional requirements. Archie and Julie decided they would develop the form prototype for the Title Index Editor first because that seemed to serve as such a good focus for everything else. You can see the form layout they produced for the Title Index Editor in Figure 4.19.

Once again, the form was very simple to set up and populate with text to emulate actual usage. Julie and Archie completed the form by defining the functions of each of the screen objects, providing another view of the requirements.

The Title Index Editor Main Form Layout
This layout allows the user to see the contents of a Title Index record.

Title Index File
This is the file reference of the Index file currently opened. It is a read-only data field.

Figure 4.19
The Title Index Editor main form layout.

Current Entry Number
This is the number of the record currently on display.

Page Index File
This is a text box that displays the Page Index file reference from the selected record; it can be used for manual input.

Free Format Title
This is a text box that displays the book title from the selected record; it can be used for manual input.

Free Format Description
This is a text box that displays the title's full description from the selected record; it can be used for manual input.

Index Manipulation Functions
These are the Add, Insert, Overwrite, and Delete buttons, which are used as follows:

Add   Adds content of screen to end of Index in memory.

Insert   Inserts content of screen at current position, increasing size of Index by one.

Overwrite	Overwrites current entry in memory with screen content.
Delete	Deletes current entry from memory.

Index Navigation
These are buttons used to step backward and forward through the Memory Index.

<<	Go to Entry 1.
>>	Go to last entry.
<	Go to previous entry.
>	Go to next entry.

File Drop-Down Menu
This is used for the following functions:

New	Create a new, empty Index.
Open	Open an existing, disk-based Index.
Save	Save Memory Index to currently opened disk file.
Save As	Save Memory Index to a named disk file.
Exit	Exit from program.

Because the Title Index is not huge (Monty had suggested 20 to 30 titles), we had no need for a **Go To Entry** facility. Julie and Archie were adamant that, because these form layouts were so focused on what was required of the programs, they would include all the layouts in the requirements specification. In the next chapter, when we review the document in its completed form, you will see the impact that had.

Title Index Editor States

The Title Index Editor was more complex than the viewer, which had three clearly defined states. The states of the Title Editor are defined from the GUI data model we developed earlier and relate to the state between screen data and memory data as well as memory data and disk data. We started by defining the possible operational states for the program:

Title Index Editor Operational States
At any given time, the Title Index Editor is in one of two Alert 1 states and one of two Alert 2 states.

Alert 1 Normal State:	Screen and memory data are the same.
Alert 1 Change State:	Screen and memory data are different.
Alert 2 Normal State:	Memory and disk data are the same.
Alert 2 Change State:	Memory and disk data are different.

At any given instant, the Title Index Editor could be in one of the two Alert 1 states, which related to the screen and memory data. Coupled with this, the program could also be in one of two Alert 2 states, which related to the memory and disk data. The program could, therefore, exist in one of a total of four combined states, as depicted by the state transition diagram you can see in Figure 4.20.

The four possible states were the following:

♦ *Combined State 1*—(Alert 1 Normal State+Alert 2 Normal State)—that is, screen is same as memory, and memory is same as disk.

♦ *Combined State 2*—(Alert 1 Change State+Alert 2 Normal State)—that is, screen is different from memory, and memory is same as disk.

♦ *Combined State 3*—(Alert 1 Normal State+Alert 2 Change State)—that is, screen is same as memory, and memory is different from disk.

♦ *Combined State 4*—(Alert 1 Change State+Alert 2 Change State)—that is, screen is different from memory, and memory is different from disk.

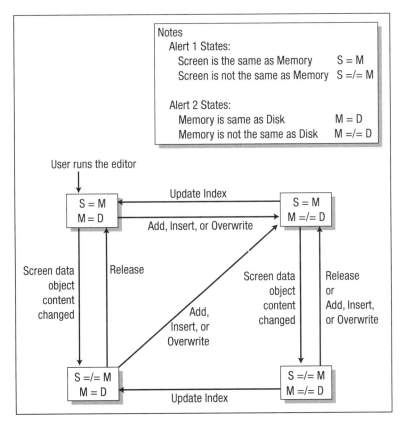

Figure 4.20
State transition diagram for editors.

The state transition diagram really came into its own when we started to define the events that triggered changes to the different combined states. The diagram took quite a while to produce and required a lot of thought. Archie and Julie realized quite quickly that this diagram was applicable to both the Title Index Editor and the Page Editor, so they made the definition generic.

Events

An editor clearly could be in four combined states, as defined earlier. Let's start with the state where the screen was the same as the memory and the memory was the same as the disk. This state could change when the user modified the content of a data object on screen. In that case, the program would change to the state where the screen content no longer reflected the memory content, but memory and disk were the same. The change was triggered by the content of a screen data field changing. Also, as Archie and Julie discovered by analyzing the situation, the **add**, **insert**, **delete**, or **overwrite** functions could be used while the editor was in the first state. Using any of these functions would cause the program to change to a combined state in which the screen was still the same as the memory but the memory no longer reflected the disk data.

The completed diagram (see Figure 4.20) defined exactly how the program moved from one state to another and which events caused the transitions. It defined quite a complex set of possible changes in a succinct form and—even better—it applied to both editors. The diagram also helped Julie and Archie to appreciate that they needed a way to get back from a screen change that didn't update the memory—that is, they needed a release mechanism to let the user back out of a possible change. They could meet this requirement with a button control that would become evident only when the program was in the change state.

A User-Friendly Interface

We needed a simple-to-use and "user friendly" GUI. For illustration, look at this scenario:

Title Index Editor Scenario
The user loads an Index. Entry Number 1 appears on screen.

The user modifies one of the screen data fields. The data on screen no longer reflects what's in memory.

The user forgets to add, insert, or overwrite, and navigates to the next entry.

This situation actually could create quite a serious nuisance. The user had lost the input and would have to do the process all over again. For this reason, Julie and Archie decided that, once a screen object had been changed, the program must disable navigation until the user had done something with the changed screen data or aborted the change using the release button. Otherwise, the potential existed for the user to lose all the screen changes he or she had made. (Hopefully, you can now see the value of that data model we produced showing the three levels of data.)

Alert 1 Change State Handling

In addition to stopping the user from navigating in the previous situation, we also needed to make him or her aware that the program was in Alert 1 Change State. We'd already decided to lock the user onto the screen until he or she had decided to add, insert, or overwrite, or (alternatively) abort the screen changes. We had also decided to use color to indicate Alert 1 Change State. That's how the layout you see in Figure 4.21 came into being for the Title Index Editor in Alert 1 Change State, which it would enter every time a screen object's contents were changed manually. The program would remain in this state until the change was accepted (Add, Insert, or Overwrite) or aborted (Release).

Note how the navigation buttons had been disabled. The user was being forced into either accepting the changes on screen or aborting the operation. The Release button had taken the place of the **delete** control (deleting was clearly not an option when the program was in change mode). We were striving to create an interface that was friendly for the user and prevented changes from inadvertently being discarded—clearly a key requirement.

Alert 2 Change State Handling

We also needed to ensure that the user knew when the memory data was not in phase with the disk—that is, Alert 2 Change State. We could indicate this by changing the background of the Index file name field to what we'd call the "Alert" color. When Alert 1 Change State changed to normal, if the memory and Index were still out of phase, then an indication of this condition

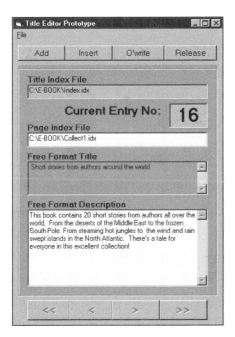

Figure 4.21
The Title Index Editor in Alert 1 Change State (that is, the screen is not the same as memory).

would be visible on the form. Most of what I've said up to this point is neatly encapsulated in the state transition diagram that applies to both editors (again, see Figure 4.20).

Menu Options

We required the capability to open an existing file and read it in for editing, and the capability to create a file from scratch. Coupled with these requirements, we needed to be able to save an in-memory Index to a new file, to an existing file (overwriting it), or to the same file we'd opened in the first place. We could meet all these requirements with the typical New, Open, Save, and Save As menu options that you see in the majority of GUI-based applications. All these options appear under the drop-down File menu.

Functional Requirements for the Title Index Editor

Now, we could go through the original list of functional requirements applicable to the Title Index Editor and establish the following detailed functional requirements:

Title Index Editor Functional Requirements List
Requirement: Read a specified Title Index into memory.

This Function Is Being Developed for the Viewer

Requirement:	**Output a Title Index to Selected Disk File**
Function:	Outputs the memory Title Index to a specified disk file.
Inputs:	Memory Title Index, output file reference.
Outputs:	Specified disk file.

Requirement:	**Select a Title Index File for Input**
Function:	Allows the user to select a file reference from the file store.
Inputs:	Directory lists.
Outputs:	Selected file reference (drive, directory, and name).

Requirement:	**Select File Name for Title Index Output**
Function:	Allows the user to select a file reference from the file store.
Inputs:	Directory lists.
Outputs:	Selected file reference (drive, directory, and name).

Requirement:	**Title Index Navigation Functionality**
Function:	Allows the user to move through the Index entries.
Inputs:	Memory Index.
Outputs:	Record number of selected entry.

Requirement:	**Display Contents of Current Title Entry**
Function:	Displays strings from entry.
Inputs:	Memory Index record.
Outputs:	Record data fields.
Requirement:	**Add/Delete/Insert/Overwrite Title Index Functionality**
Function:	Allows manipulation of Title Index records.
Inputs:	Screen data.
Outputs:	Memory Index record.
Requirement:	**Title Entry Edit Functionality**
Function:	Handles changing screen content.
Inputs:	Data entered directly into screen object(s).
Outputs:	Screen objects.

The Result of Analysis

The process we used to analyze the Title Index Editor was very similar to that we had employed for the viewer. Much of the outcome ended up in the requirements specification, which we will review in full in the next chapter.

Analysis of the Page Index Editor

A prime consideration for the Page Index Editor was that it must contain all the functionality of the viewer. So, everything that we had specified for the viewer must apply here as well, without exception. As I've already said, Archie and Julie had realized quite early in the proceedings that much of what we had developed for the Title Index Editor applied to the Page Index Editor. Consequently, they restricted themselves to developing a couple of screen models. Then, they rewrote all the definitions and related details of the Title Index Editor in a generic way to describe both editors where they could, and they left specific elements behind in a section for the Title Index Editor. Then, they would build a specific description for the Page Index Editor. For one thing, the resulting specification would be much shorter, with all common functionality defined once. Of course, this approach also reflected the way we would design and develop the software.

The Page Index Editor View Functionality

One of our goals was to ensure that the Page Index Editor had all the functionality of the viewer as well as page editing capability, so whatever a user set up could be viewed exactly the same as it would be displayed in the E-MagBook's 640×480-pixel viewer. Figure 4.22 shows the basic layout we developed for the Page Index Editor, incorporating the viewer form layout. The figure shows an 800×600-pixel screen shot—the minimum screen size the editor

Figure 4.22
Basic Page Index Editor layout.

had to run on. As you can see, we placed the editor controls up on the top of the main form; the viewer functionality was provided in a 640×480-pixel portion of the screen that precisely emulated the viewer. In fact, in the figure, you can see one of the prototype forms developed for the viewer.

File Reference Data Fields

At the bottom of the viewer form, you can see the main data items of the Index entry, shown in text boxes. There are four labels: One holds the Index name of the Page Index file that has been opened for editing. The one below that contains the name of the picture that is loaded. Another label indicates the name of the text file, and a fourth label is for the sound file if there is one. These labels are the data fields of the page, which the editor needs to be able to create or modify. Clearly, if a label's content changes, the associated screen object must be updated as part of the process. For example, if the picture file reference is changed, the new image must be loaded onto the screen. We would need to expand this area in the future to accommodate the HTML, Composite, and Web references. In essence, all we'd done was extend the viewing capability to include the text strings associated with the data items located in the Page Index record.

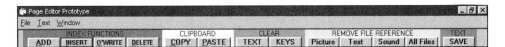

Figure 4.23
The Page Index Editor's main button controls.

The Page Index Editor Basic Functionality

Figure 4.23 shows the Page Index Editor's basic controls. This figure shows the top portion of the main form. You'll be able to see the formal description of the Page Index Editor's basic functionality in the next chapter when we review the requirements document in detail. What follows are notes on how the analysis unfolded.

Basic Index Manipulation

If you look at the top portion of Figure 4.23, the first buttons represented on the left of the screen are Add, Insert, Overwrite, and Delete. The functional requirements for these buttons are the same as those we defined for the Title Index Editor, with the exception that these buttons work on a Page Index rather than a Title Index. When the program is in Alert 1 Change State, a release button will replace the Delete button, exactly as determined for the Title Index Editor.

Copy and Paste

The Copy and Paste buttons indicate a requirement that Archie came up with. We had thought about moving entries from one place to another in an Index, and Archie put forward a very simple idea: provide the capability to copy a page and paste it onto the form for entry into another part of the Index. To clarify the functionality, we developed the following simple scenario:

Scenario: Copy and Paste

Preconditions:
A Page Index is loaded into the Page Index Editor program.

Description:
The user selects Page 12 for viewing. When the screen has been set up with the content of Page 12, the user clicks the Copy button. The user now clicks the Delete button, and the previous content of Page 12 disappears. What was the content of Page 13 now becomes that of Page 12.

The user now moves to Page 55 and clicks the Paste button. The content of what used to be Page 12 now appears on the screen, and the program goes into the Alert 1 Change State—that is, all navigation is now disabled. The user now clicks Insert. The screen content is moved into Page 55, and that page's previous content is moved up one page (that is, to Page 56) as are the contents of all subsequent pages.

This scenario defines a very useful capability—to be able to move the contents of entries around an index. The requirement came about because Archie felt something was lacking with the **add**, **insert**, **overwrite**, and **delete** functions. He wondered how a user would rectify a mistake, particularly in a very large Page Index. He considered the case in which the user had created a page in the wrong place and needed to move it. The introduction of a simple copy and paste requirement allowed movement within the Index without the need to redefine the page. We also decided that, because the Title Index was fairly small by comparison, the copy and paste requirement would apply only to the Page Index Editor.

Clear Functions

The next button controls following the Copy and Paste pair were the Clear buttons. Clear Text allows the content of the text block (as a whole) to be deleted, and Clear Keys allows the five keys to be cleared in one action. Don't forget that the text-block and key fields in the viewer form are now data-entry fields.

File-Reference Functions

We decided that we would not let the user enter data directly into the four text boxes at the bottom of the viewer form—that is, in the Index, Picture, Text, and Sound labels. Instead, these contents would be accessible only from the file-selection functions we still needed to specify. We would, however, require functions to clear these fields (with the exception of the Index file-name field which could only be changed by using the New, Open, or Save As menu options).

We had specified a requirement for a Clear button to clear the picture file name and unload any image on display. Another button would clear the text box and remove the text file reference. We needed a third button to eliminate the sound and remove the file references. In some situations, the user might want to clear out all three references, so we'd also added a fourth button to clear all file references (except the Index file name). Together, these buttons fulfill the requirement that enabled editing the contents of a page to remove file references.

Text Functions

A user would be able to create a block of text by typing directly into the text box in the viewer portion of the editor. Alternatively, the user could modify existing text. To accompany this functionality, the user must also be able to save text—that is, copy the content of the text box back to the file. We suspected this would be a frequently used option, so we defined the requirement for a button control to execute the save. We also needed to define requirements so that the user could create a text file from scratch or modify an existing file. These cases involved only two instances of the data: on screen and in the disk file (that is, we were not also holding a copy in memory).

Menu Options

The menu options for the Page Index Editor were predominately the same as those we had defined for the Title Index Editor. However, for the Page Index Editor, we also had a requirement for a **Save Text As** file function to allow a newly created block of text to be stored for the first time. We also required a function to let us set the font for the Page Index. That was the font all the pages of the Index inherited once the font had been defined.

File Selection

The only real issue concerning the Page Index Editor was how to provide an efficient method to set up file references for each page. Initially, we had three such references—image or video, text, and sound. Setting up a single page would involve invoking a file dialog box three times, switching file extensions on each occasion, and possibly even switching directories. The process was totally unfriendly. Introducing HTML, Composites, and Web references would make it even worse.

So, we decided to use a separate form that contained permanent selection boxes for the **device, directory path** and **file name** attributes of any file to be loaded. We could have done this three times—once for the image/video file, once for the text, and again for the sound—with the prospect of having to add even more later. This approach would have made a very large form. Our restriction was that the Page Index Editor must run on a minimum screen size of 800x600 pixels. So, we devised a form with a single set of Device, Directory Path, and File Name selection objects permanently on screen, but with the capability to define which type of file reference was being created—image, text, or sound. We could easily extend this functionality in the future. With the aid of color, we determined this would be a friendly way to let the user select files to load into the viewer, thus creating page descriptions. The file-selection process would then consist of defining the file type (image/video, text, or sound), switching to the correct drive, and directory path, and then selecting the appropriate file by name.

File Selection Form

Archie and Julie set up a new, independent form within the Page Index Editor for file selection. (Remember, the user needed to be able to specify an image or video clip file, a text file, or a sound file as page data items.) The form housed a selection box to set each file attribute (that is, one box for the drive, another box for the directory path, and one box for the file name). You can see the file selection form they designed in Figure 1.24. In the next chapter, when we review the completed requirements document, we will examine the specifications for how the form was to be used.

Functional List

Scanning down the functional requirements list, we saw only five requirements that we had not yet defined; they were all Page Index Editor requirements. Of course, we had already associated some Page Index Editor requirements with the development of the viewer or the Title Index. We'll list here only those we hadn't yet defined.

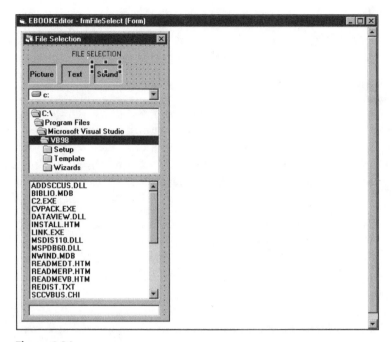

Figure 4.24
File selection form layout.

Page Index Editor Functional Requirements List

Requirement:	**Output a Page Index to Selected Disk File**
Function:	Outputs the memory Page Index to a specified disk file.
Inputs:	Memory Page Index, output file reference.
Output:	Specified disk file.
Requirement:	**Select a Page Index File for Input**
Function:	Allows user to select a file for input.
Inputs:	Directory lists.
Output:	Specified disk file reference (drive, directory, and name).
Requirement:	**Select File Name for Page Index Output**
Function:	Allows user to select file reference for output.
Inputs:	Directory lists.
Output:	Specified disk file reference (drive, directory and name).

Requirement:	Add/Delete/Insert/Overwrite Page Index Functionality
Function:	Allows manipulation of Page Index records.
Input:	Screen data.
Output:	Memory Index record.

Requirement:	Page Entry Edit Functionality
Function:	Handles changing screen content.
Input:	Data entered directly into screen object(s).
Output:	Screen objects.

Completion of Analysis

I've quite deliberately not shown you much of the formal specifications we produced for the editors' requirements, although we did look at the Title Index in detail. The end product (which you can see in the next chapter) evolved quite dramatically from the analysis of both editors.

At the end of Day 2 (another long day), we had accumulated a vast amount of information. Archie and Julie were both feeling a little nervous about whether they could complete the specification in time because they had both been surprised by the volume of information that had come into being. Our progress monitoring showed that, although we were on schedule, we had reservations about completing on time.

Disaster Strikes

To make things worse, on Tuesday night, disaster struck the office. The building was a very old lace mill. At the top of the edifice, on the sixth floor, was a huge, ancient, water tank. That night, the main inlet pipe to the tank had burst, mainly due to old age, and we arrived on the Wednesday morning to find most of the office soaked. Water was running down the walls and had pooled on the carpets. Every floor was in the same condition, right down to the basement.

As you can imagine, we were somewhat preoccupied for most of the day trying to salvage computers, files, furniture, and all the things that make an office run. The situation was almost literally "all hands to the pump." We had to bring in dehumidifiers, and all sorts of chaos rained down on us for the rest of the week. After Archie and Julie had managed to salvage their bits and pieces, I sent them home to work on their laptops. Consequently, Wednesday was not as productive as it should have been.

We didn't meet again until Thursday. We now had only two days left to complete the analysis and draw up the final version of the requirements specification. As soon as we could, we set up a meeting room for Archie and Julie in the location furthest from the end of the building that took the brunt of the flood. Archie and Julie spent Thursday and Friday reviewing and checking all the information, and modifying it here and there according to their newfound understanding. They had a lot to do.

Tip

As this story warns, when you are planning contingency time into your project, that time is not only to accommodate things that go wrong in the normal course of work in progress. Contingency time might also have to accommodate situations completely external to the nature of the work and absolutely outside your control.

Delivery to the Client

Not until Friday afternoon did Julie and Archie have a complete draft for me to go through and authorize. The draft, however, was very good. It contained a requirements specification with scenarios, all of which we would send to the client. Some of the results from analysis—in particular, the form layouts and their descriptions—had been amalgamated into the requirements document. They had put the remaining diagrams and descriptions from analysis into another document. I was so impressed with their final products that I decided to send everything to Monty—the requirements specification and the results of the analysis. Normally, we would send only the requirements specification with application scenarios and possibly the GUI models with their definitions. We delivered the package to Monty by email very late on Friday evening.

Post Mortem

By the end of Friday, we had used up all our contingency time, but, as I pointed out to Julie and Archie, they had been on a learning curve—a steep one—and fate had played a cruel hand as well. So, with the help of our built-in contingency time, and having accomplished the task at hand, they had learned a great deal about capturing and analyzing requirements, and building on the knowledge they gained in the process. We had also done a lot of coding in the feasibility work. So, all in all, the result was good.

If the water disruption had been worse, we still would have had a weekend in which to try to recover. However, building weekend contingency time into a project is not a good idea. Weekends are important breaks when the pressure is off and you can unwind. The software industry makes substantial demands on an individual's time, and frequently unwinding and uncluttering the brain are important to avoid becoming stale. Maybe the most important lesson to learn from project Phase 1 is that contingency time is a key aspect of a good plan that we should never take for granted. We never know what Fate holds in store.

The Next Step

In the case study, we had completed the requirements document and delivered Version 1 to Monty and Samantha for their assessment. Our goal was Montasana's formal approval of the requirements specification, at which point Montasana would become the owner of the document.

Monty and Samantha now had a week to review the documentation and approve it. During that week, we would be on hand to clear up any issues and resubmit the documentation with any required changes (having implemented them using our change-control procedures). We also had to produce a fixed price for the design and development of the software. The price we would submit must be between the minimum and the maximum that we had quoted at the time of the proposal.

Chapter 5

Reviewing and Re-Quoting

You have completed the requirements document and submitted it to the customer. Your knowledge of the project is now quite substantial—you are becoming a domain expert as far as the application requirements are concerned. Assuming your customer agreed to let you quote a minimum and maximum (min-max) price for design and development at the proposal stage, you are now in a much better situation to quote a fixed price for the project itself. The fundamental criterion is that your quote must fall between your original minimum and maximum values. Your analysis has led to a good understanding of the component structure of your requirements. You have lessened the risks, and you are now at an advanced level of understanding. You can quote from a position of strength this time around. (Even if your customer did not allow you to quote min-max from the outset, a useful exercise in financial risk assessment at this stage is to check the validity of the fixed price you gave to win the order.)

In this chapter, we'll discuss reviewing in general terms and use the case study to review the completed and accepted requirements documentation. You'll see the requirements document in its final form for the first time. I will provide comments after each document section to let you see how the specification ended up the way it did. How the document evolved through the two SDLC phases that helped shape it will become apparent. Finally, we'll go through another estimating exercise to establish a fixed price for the design and development of the E-MagBook software.

Although the chapter is predominately about reviewing the requirements document and providing a more detailed quotation, we'll also look at a completely different methodology for development—*iterative prototyping*—based on the "try it and see what happens" principal.

Independent Reviewing

Whenever you complete an output from the SDLC (a requirements specification, a design specification, a software module), you review your work and eventually determine that it is satisfactory. Unfortunately, from a quality viewpoint, all that is seldom sufficient. Having an independent person review the work as well is imperative.

We will consider two types of review, both of which contribute to the quality of the output. The first is a review designed to check adherence to standards—a form of verification that, as an organization, you are doing what you claim you do. This review can be internal or external, performed by a standards authority or your client. In the second, purely technical type of review, someone checks your work for accuracy, clarity, and so on.

Adherence to Standards

Standards are a necessary nuisance that provide a high level of consistency across a wide range of activities. In terms of quality assurance, when you have two different people producing similar outputs from a process, you want those outputs to be as uniform as possible. The benefits of such standards are obvious: Numerous people are usually involved in a project, and standards serve as a template to guide them in their different activities toward a consistent goal. Individuals who weren't involved in the process can easily recognize the products and check them for adherence to the standards.

Accountability

Quite possibly, the customer may require you to follow its standards and not your own. Consequently, it's not always obvious what standards are being used until a reviewer checks the quality plan to find out. The next task is for the reviewer to become familiar with the standards if they are not ones he or she has employed in the past. Then, the reviewer can start checking for compliance. For example, one of our quality assurance people might be asked to review the requirements specification. One standard we employ in our company is that sections in the document must be numbered—it is, after all, a key reference document. So, the first thing the reviewer will check is that all sections are numbered.

A good standard will provide a checklist template, which the reviewer/auditor fills in as he or she checks each aspect. The reviewer normally files the result from a review or audit for standards adherence in the project file. When an independent assessor from an external standard's body arrives at your establishment, his or her aim is to see what standards you employ and how you go about policing them. The project files tell the auditor a great deal. From them, the auditor can create a list of activities that have been (or are being) performed, and then, from the quality plan, what standards are being applied. The auditor will ask to see evidence that an internal review/audit has been performed, and what the result was.

Content Review

A *review of content* is quite different from checking on adherence to standards. In a content review, the questions are, Does this make sense? Is the content technically accurate? For example, in terms of software, you are probably already familiar with a code review. Another programmer who knows what your code is supposed to accomplish looks at your code and checks it for error. This review contrasts sharply with a standards review of code, in which the reviewer is checking for headers at the start of code sections, a reasonable level of comments, adherence to variable nomenclature standards, and so on.

In terms of the requirements specification, the reviewer needs to come away from the document with a good understanding of the requirements, without ambiguity. If the reviewer simply can't understand sections of the document, that's an indication that the customer will struggle as well.

Traceability

In terms of *traceability*, auditors are interested in three things:

- They want to see that scheduled reviews are actually performed.

- They want to see a written statement of the outcome of the review. This statement doesn't have to be an essay, but something must indicate that the reviewer has done his or her job—even if it's only to say how wonderful the content is.

- They want to see evidence of remedial action where problems were reported.

With respect to the requirements document, traceability is in place if the review is performed after you have completed the document and before you send it to the client. If the review demands a change, then you can record that change using your change-control procedure and increasing the document's version number to 1.1 before you submit it to the client. The auditor can then see a chain of clear evidence: A reviewer noted a deficiency in the requirements specification, and the review report detailed the deficiency. This report led to creation of a *change request* for the document. The change request is a piece of paper that details the necessary change required and provides authorization to proceed. The requirements document was then updated, its version number was changed from 1.0 to 1.1, and a change log in the document's first pages ties the change to the change request. The chain is complete. From the reviewer's report, the auditor can ask to see any appropriate change requests. The auditor can check the change log recorded in the document to look for references to the change request itself.

This level of traceability is important, but it's also vital that it doesn't hamper a project by creating so much official red tape and so many complex procedures that traceability takes over the project. Consider the following example: A reviewer notes in a requirements specification that, although the document frequently refers to "the backup procedure," no definition exists of what this procedure is. The review might read as follows:

Review Report Ref: R_6: Frequent references are made to "the backup procedure," but this procedure is not defined anywhere.

The project manager then creates a change request:

Change Request Ref: CR_12: The requirement specification needs to define "the backup procedure" referenced throughout. See Review Report Ref R_6.

This change request clearly develops as a result of a review. Someone is then tasked with creating the appropriate section, which is added to the specification. The Change Log in the specification reads as follows:

Requirement Specification Change Log:

Version 1.0   *First completed release.*

Version 1.1   *Section on Backup Procedure added in response to Change Request Ref: CR_12.*

The references ensure traceability. Provided all reviews have a unique reference number, all change requests have a unique identity, and sufficient detail is entered concerning what sparked the event, you have total traceability within the project. For example, CR_1 to CR_11 might be change requests involved in other aspects of the project and not at all related to the requirements specification. In the example, the first project change request applicable to that document is identified as CR_12. If you've never been involved in the level of formality that we've been discussing, then it probably looks very daunting. It's not really. And, once you get into the habit, the process becomes second nature. But the really important fact is that it becomes second nature to *everyone* on the project.

Standards Should Help, Not Hinder

When people think about standards, they often think of punitive statements that dictate exactly how everything must be done. Unless such an approach is totally necessary, such rigidity can often be counterproductive.

If a standard states that A=B, an auditor will look for random occurrences of A and check that they are, in fact, equal to B. If the auditor finds an instance in which A is not equal to B, he or she has uncovered a breach of standards. Always setting A to B may actually be a real nuisance at times for very good reasons. Consequently, if a standard states that, under *most* conditions, A=B, but exceptions might occur where A≠B, you have the flexibility to set A to something else. Provided you can give the reviewer/auditor a good reason for setting A≠B, you have not breached your standard.

In software development, standards should be designed to make your life easier, providing flexibility where it is needed. Standards should never be used to regiment your work to an unacceptable degree.

Reviewing the Case Study

I have devoted most of this chapter to reviewing the case study's requirements document. Throughout the process, look at the document from a number of viewpoints, which the following questions summarize:

♦ Does the document clearly define the customer's requirements?

♦ Is the document easy to read?

♦ Can you easily use the document as a reference work?

♦ Can someone with no knowledge of the application domain read the document?

♦ Are acronyms and jargon explained?

♦ Is the detail sufficient to allow you to develop detailed costing for the project?

If you can answer "Yes" to all these questions, then we achieved what we set out to do for project Phase 1; that is, we successfully captured and analyzed the requirements of the E-MagBook.

The Case Study:
The Review

We were going to review the completed and accepted requirements document. We were looking at the final version against which Monty would place his order to complete the project. Consequently, you will see many differences between this version and the portions of the document that we developed and modified in Chapters 2 and 3. From the moment we completed the document, it was—and still would be—subject to formal change control. We could now modify nothing you see here without going through our full change-control procedure, which involved creating an authorized change request, scheduling the work, updating the document's version number, and entering the detail in the document's Change Log.

Introduction

A Table of Contents and the all-important Change Log that we have discussed were part of the introduction to the document. We started our review with the Introduction to the requirements document as a whole. We aimed this introduction at the reader who had no idea what the project was about; the introduction would provide enough information to put the rest of the specification into context.

The E-MagBook Software Development Requirements Specification

1. Introduction

This document describes the requirements for software to view, create, and edit the multimedia book formats for use in Montasana Systems' E-MagBook concept.

The E-MagBook is a miniature, but standard, multimedia PC that uses a 640×480-pixel display and functions as an electronic book. Books will be available in the form of removable media, each of which is a self-contained entity that houses a collection of books. The collection consists of a Title Index that pertains to books on the removable disk, the page definitions for each book, and the mass of supporting files that make up the book content in terms of images, videos, text, and sounds. Users will always access the removable disk on drive E: of an E-MagBook or of any PC used to create books.

The specification herein also encompasses the need to develop the software further at a later date to handle more advanced book formats, including links to Web sites.

The general requirement is for the development of three programs, summarized as follows:

1.1. The E-MagBook Viewer
The program that runs on the E-MagBook hardware and allows users to select "books" and view pages.

1.2. The Title Index Editor
The program that allows users to create and edit lists of titles for use on the E-MagBook's removable medium.

1.3. The Page Index Editor
The program that allows users to define in detail the page content of a book.

Comments on Introduction

Section 1 serves as a succinct introduction to the whole project. Julie pointed out that she had seen complete project specifications that weren't much more than this (and that begged more questions than they answered). Unfortunately, such specifications are not too uncommon in my experience. Every document you produce should always have some form of summary or introduction at the front. Quite often, the summary or introduction is all most people will read, so that portion must contain enough information for readers to appreciate whether they need to read the rest of the document at all.

Note how we forced the issue about what drive letter would be used for accessing removable disks. We did confirm our decision with Monty before we submitted the completed version, and he agreed that mandating that both E-MagBook hardware and editing PCs specify drive E: as their removable drive was not an issue.

Formats

Section 2 of the document describes the formats of the various books.

2. E-MagBook Page Formats
The E-MagBook viewer and editors will initially be capable of handling three types of book format. Further formats will be required in the future. When viewed, the page from a book consists of the page objects, which are specific to the format of the selected book; the navigation controls, which allow the user to "turn" the pages; and a panel to show the keys. Each page, regardless of format, can be qualified with up to five keys. The keys describe the page precisely. Users can use the keys to search for that page via the navigation controls. All format requirements are defined in detail in the following sections.

2.1. Format 1—Text Book
The Text Book consists of any number of pages, to a maximum of 1,000, each of which can be referenced by page number. A single page consists of an unlimited block of scrollable text and up to five keys. Each page must conform to a single font type and size, which are defined for the book as

a whole. Optionally, each page may have its own sound track. Users can view a text page as shown in Figure A, either with or without the keys displayed.

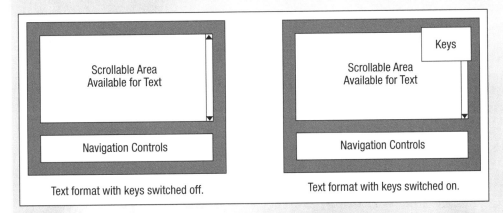

Figure A
Text Book page viewing requirements.

2.2. Format 2—The Picture Album

The Picture Album consists of any number of pages, to a maximum of 1,000, each of which can be referenced by page number. A single page contains a single, static image (which will be placed in a defined album picture area) and up to five keys. Alternatively, the page may use an AVI (Audio Video Interleave) movie clip instead of a static image. Any of the pages may be image or video pages in any sequence. The image may be of any size and must be scaled accordingly so that the entire picture is always on view, and the aspect ratio (ratio of width/height) is as defined in the full-sized bitmap. Optionally, each page may have its own sound track. Users can view an album page as shown in Figure B, either with or without the keys displayed.

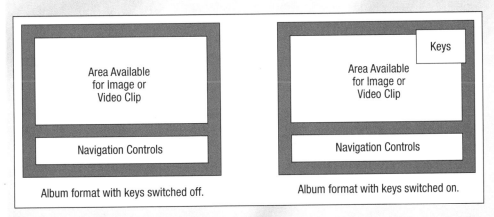

Figure B
Picture Album page viewing requirements.

2.3. Format 3—Simple Reference Book

The Simple Reference Book consists of any number of pages, to a maximum of 1,000, each of which can comprise a single static image, a block of text, and up to five keys. The image is placed in an area of the screen defined specifically for the Simple Reference format. Alternatively, an AVI movie clip can replace the static image. Each page may have an unlimited block of text, which the user can view in a text scrolling area adjacent to the displayed image or video clip. The font type and size of the text will be determined by the reference book selected and is then the same for all pages. Optionally, each page may have a sound track. The user can view a Simple Reference page as shown in Figure C, either with the keys or without them (in which case the area available for the text content is increased, as shown).

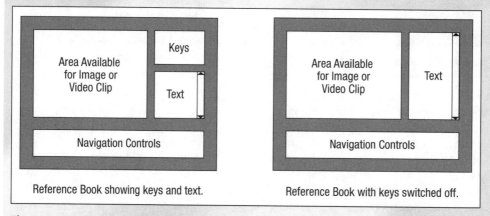

Figure C

Simple Reference page viewing requirements.

2.4. Format 4—Extended Reference or Composite Book (Future Requirement)

The Extended Reference Book consists of any number of pages, to a maximum of 1,000, each of which consists of a Composite layout. This Composite can consist of any number of images at any position and size. It can also contain any number of independent text blocks, each of which can be positioned anywhere on the screen and at any size. Each block of text can also use any font type and attributes independently of the others. The Composite may also contain a single video clip, the static images, and, optionally, a single sound track.

This Composite structure of images, text blocks, and video clip uses the full-screen layout except for the area used by the navigation controls. Each page also can possess up to five keys, which optionally the user can view over the Composite.

It will also be required that rectangular areas of the Composite act as *hotspots*, such that when the user moves the cursor onto them and clicks the mouse, extra information (in the form of text, an image, a video clip, or a sound track) then becomes available. When activated, each hotspot will be independent of the others in terms of its location and function. If a video clip is already playing, activating a second clip will cause the first to be terminated. This sequential action is also true of the sound tracks. However, the program can play a single video at the same time it plays a sound track.

A user can view an Extended Reference page either with the keys or without them, as shown in Figure D.

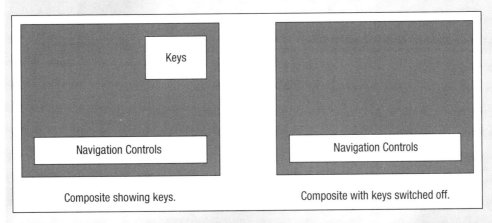

Keys	
Navigation Controls	Navigation Controls
Composite showing keys.	Composite with keys switched off.

Figure D
Extended Reference (Composite) page viewing requirements.

2.5. Format 5—HTML/Web Books (Future Requirement)

This format consists of any number of HTML pages, to a maximum of 1,000, which can be accessed by page number. The user views each page through a browser, which occupies the entire screen except for the navigation controls. A single page can be stored locally on the removable disk, or it can be accessed via an Internet/Web site, using a standard Internet URL (uniform resource locator, such as **http:www.coriolis.com**) reference.

Once an HTML page is placed on the screen, the reader can use any hotspots present to bring up any other HTML page accessible to the browser, locally or on the Internet. At any stage, the user may return to the pages of the "book," request the next page, and so on. Optionally, the page may possess a single sound track.

The user can view a local HTML page or Web site page with the keys on or off, as shown in Figure E.

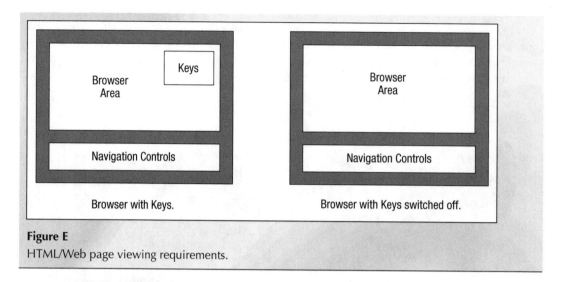

Figure E
HTML/Web page viewing requirements.

Format Comments

If you recall, our first attempt at defining a text page had no keys available. That effort had been influenced by Monty's original diagram of a text page. As we analyzed the requirements, we realized that a text page could have keys to allow the user to search for specific pages, just as any other format allowed. Adding keys to the text page definition also allowed us to create a more general page definition. To ensure that we "managed" Monty's expectations, we had specified that a font type was defined for the book as a whole and was applicable to each page within that book. If you recall, we had a discussion about font type being a book attribute that each page inherited. Without the specification being explicit, Monty might well have expected to see full word-processing capability within the text blocks for text and reference books. Note that for the Composite page format, we were stating that each text block could be a different font and size on the same Composite.

We had also woven the simplistic diagrams neatly into the text to summarize the viewing requirements for each format. Although the diagrams we used in the preceding descriptions were quite satisfactory, both Archie and Julie were adamant that the entire specification was vastly improved by including the form layouts (developed in analysis) within the body of the text.

You'll encounter those layouts later in the specification and see how they crystallize all the verbal definitions. No matter how hard one tries, words are far too open to interpretation, and the pictures clarify much of the description. Neither picture nor text on its own is totally adequate, but, taken together, they complement each other's strengths.

Supported File Formats

In this section, we make clear what we will support.

3. Supported File Formats
Pages of an E-MagBook consist of a collection of images, videos, text, and sound tracks, depending on the page format. Required formats for the associated multimedia files are as follows:

3.1. Image Files
These files are predominately BMP and JPEG formats, although all the following file types will be available if required:

BMP	Windows Bitmap
JPEG	Joint Photographic Experts Group
DIB	Device Independent Bitmap
GIF	Graphics Interchange Format
WMF	Windows Metafile

3.2. Video Files
The video file will use the Microsoft AVI format. All videos will conform to a standard height and width for the initial viewer development. It is required that, in the future, variable-sized videos will be available.

3.3. Text Files
These are standard, fixed-font, ASCII text files, carriage-return/line-feed delimited, with no stored attributes. The files can be read by a standard DOS editor.

3.4. Sound Track Files
A page's sound track may be composed from either a Microsoft WAV (WaveAudio) file or, alternatively, from an MID format.

Supported File Comments

In Chapter 3, we started off by defining image file formats under the heading of "Format 2—The Picture Album" because that's where we first encountered the image file formats. Archie and Julie decided having a single section on format types would be better; that way, we could make the section more general to encompass the video, text, and sound files as well.

Julie pointed out that her software development experience had taught her to appreciate that what you leave out of a specification—not what you say—causes the trouble. If we had not bothered to state which file formats we would support, you can almost bet a format would have turned up that we were "expected" to support. We had defined the requirement clearly for Monty in our definitions; if he came up with another format later that must be supported, we had a clear-cut case for treating the request as a new requirement.

The essence of capturing the requirements is to be as precise as possible about what the customer wants. At the very least, such precision gives a reasonably solid contractual platform from which to develop. Always remember, no matter who wrote it, the customer owns the requirements specification.

Finally, note that we had specified a fixed format for the video's dimensions, thereby simplifying the requirements. We had checked with Monty that this was acceptable for the prototype viewer, and he had agreed—provided, as usual, he had the option to expand the requirement in the future.

What the Viewer Must Do

As you will see, we had substantially enhanced the sections describing the requirements for the viewer by introducing the form prototypes that we developed in analysis.

---

4. Required Modes of Operation of the E-MagBook Viewer
It is required that, at any given moment, the viewer be operating in one of the modes defined in this section. Regardless of which mode the program is in, it is required that the program contain no drop-down menus.

4.1. Viewer Mode 1—Title Selection
The required form layout is presented in Figure F.

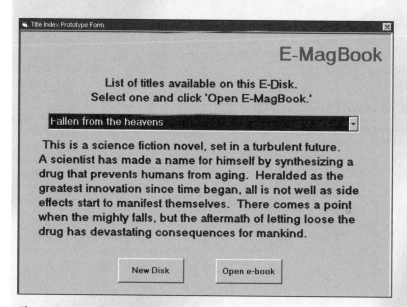

Figure F
Required Title Selection form layout.

When in this mode, the program presents a list of titles to the reader from the removable disk that is currently inserted into the E-MagBook on drive E:. The titles are presented to the reader via a drop-down list screen object, as shown in Figure F (in the layout, the object is shown with a currently selected title "Fallen from the Heavens"). The reader can select any of the listed titles, and the program then displays the following information:

Title —A free-text title of unlimited length (as shown in the drop-down box).

Description—A free-text description of unlimited length of the book's contents (as shown below the drop-down box).

The limiting factor for the length of each of the above will be the display space provided on the screen.

The reader may remove the disk and replace it with another one. By clicking the New Disk button, the reader requests the program to read in the Index of the new book.

The reader may select a title from the displayed list and request that the title be loaded into the program by clicking the Open E-MagBook button. At this stage, the program will revert to the Page View mode.

4.1.1. Title Selection, Required Screen Objects
Specifically, the Title Selection mode screen contains the following elements:

(A) Title Label

Indicates "E-MagBook".

(B) Help Text

A hard-coded block of text is required to hold the following as a Help message: "List of titles available on this E-Disk. Select one and click Open E-MagBook.

(C) Title List

A screen object is required to hold the list of titles and allow one to be selected.

(D) Description

When the user has selected a title, the program places the associated description on screen.

(E) New Disk Button

It is required that if the user inserts a new E-Disk into the E-MagBook, he or she can request that the new Index be read into the program by clicking the New Disk button.

(F) Open E-MagBook Button

It is required that the user can load a selected title into the program and display Page 1 by clicking the Open E-MagBook button. The program then enters View mode.

Viewer Comments

Julie and Archie's decision to include the form layouts and screen-object definitions (developed in analysis) into the main body of the specification had quite clearly paid off. They argued that these descriptions provided enormous clarity to the requirements specification. (You can't always do this in a project, but these additions certainly made a difference here.)

What had impressed both Archie and Julie was how we were able to produce such detailed forms without writing a single line of code, simply by manipulating screen objects in the VB design environment. As I've already said, you can use VB to model the forms regardless of the final language you will be using. You must remember that all the VB controls are genuine objects with properties, methods, and events. The objects are "live" in the design-time environment; in other words, if you change one of the object's properties, the object will behave in the same way as if you had done so in runtime mode. For example, if you set the **.left**, **.top**, **.width**, and **.height** properties of a text box and load it with text, the text box takes on those attributes. If you run the program, you see the text box in the right place, at the right size, and showing the text you typed in. The same is true with the image; you can set it up by defining the **.left**, **.top**, **.width**, and **.height** properties and then load a picture into it, all from the Properties window. When the program runs, it looks just as it would if you had defined the properties with code.

More on What the Viewer Must Do

Let's continue with the definitions of viewer requirements.

4.2. Viewer Mode 2—Page View

The program can be placed in this mode only after the user has requested a valid title from a removable disk, using the Title Selection mode. When the Page View mode is invoked, the program determines which format type is in use and sets itself accordingly. All pages in the selected title must conform to this format.

All functions are available from a collection of control buttons, which will be placed at the bottom of the Page View screen. (See format diagrams in Section 2, where this collection is referred to as "navigation buttons".) The required functions of these buttons are the same, regardless of format, for Page View mode of operation. The functions are defined in a later section.

Once the program enters Page View mode, the program starts by displaying the first page of the selected book. The reader also has the option of requesting that the program be changed to Workbench mode. When the reader has finished using Workbench mode, the reader can reselect Page View mode. At that point, the page that was on view at the time the reader invoked Workbench mode is reinstated according to its format type. At any time, the reader may re-invoke the Title Selection mode.

Initially, the three formats to be supported are Text Book, Picture Album, and Simple Reference Book, as specified in Section 2. How Page View mode of operation handles each of these formats is defined next.

4.2.1. Page View Mode—Text Book Format

The required layout for the Text Book format is shown in Figure G. The primary screen objects are the text block and the keys (which the user can switch on and off, as indicated in Section 2).

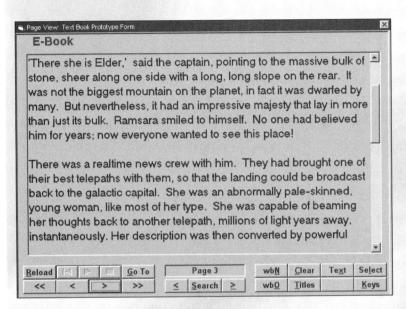

Figure G

Page View mode for Text Book format.

4.2.1.1. Viewing a Text Page, Required Screen Objects

The following elements are required:

(A) E-book Format Specifier

"E-book" is placed in the top left of the form when textbooks are loaded.

(B) The Text Display

The text display area is maximized, as shown in Figure G. Text is displayed such that the user can scroll up and down to accommodate large volumes. A single font type is used, inherited from the **Font** attribute set up for the Page Index as a whole.

(C) Navigation Controls

Located at the bottom of the screen, these common controls are defined later.

(D) Key Panel (Not Shown in Figure G)

The user can display the keys for a given page in a panel overlaying the text box, as defined in Section 2.

(E) Search Selection Panel (not shown in Figure G)

The user can display search selection criteria in a panel overlaying the text box (in a similar fashion to the key panel) and employ those criteria, as defined later.

4.2.2. Page View Mode—Picture Album Format

The required layout for Page View mode is shown in Figure H. The primary screen objects are the image or video clip and the keys (which can be switched on and off, as indicated in Section 2). The program plays a video clip in its own form, centered in the available image area.

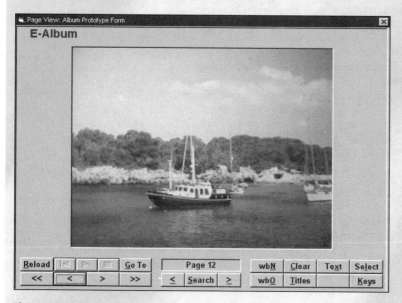

Figure H
Page View mode for a Picture Album.

4.2.2.1. Viewing a Picture Album, Required Screen Objects

The following elements are required:

(A) E-Album Format Specifier

"E-Album" is placed in the top left of the form when Albums are loaded.

(B) The Image

The available area for image display is maximized to occupy the entire screen from the control button collection up to the format specifier. The program first sizes any image, then scales it to fit into this area, preserving the image's aspect ratio. If the image is a video clip, the playing window is loaded into the same area and centered before playback starts.

(C) Navigation Controls

Located at the bottom of the screen, these common controls are defined later.

(D) Key Panel (not shown in Figure H)

The user can display the keys for a given page in a panel overlaying the image, as defined in Section 2.

(E) Search Selection Panel (not shown in Figure H)

The user can display the search selection criteria in a panel overlaying the text box (in a similar fashion to the key panel) and employ the criteria, as defined later.

Comments about the Viewer

I was quite impressed with what Archie and Julie had done here. They'd set up definitions for each viewing mode and, where there was a common requirement, simply made a reference to a more detailed description that would follow. For example, they referred to the navigation controls, the key, and the selection panels, but they didn't define them in more detail until later because they were essentially the same in each format. Julie and Archie were concentrating only on defining differences in Page View mode for now.

They had avoided a lot of duplication and made the whole document much tighter. Your first attempt at a requirements specification will typically repeat definitions of functionality. As you start to understand the requirements better—and particularly during analysis—you may see far better ways to define the requirements so that you define common elements once and refer to them many times. This clarification occurs as you iterate between the SDLC phases. What also becomes more apparent is that a page is just a page—whether it's a Text Book page, a Picture Album page, or whatever. Although the page looks different in each case, it's still a page of a book.

An Interruption

At this point in the review process, I received a call from Monty. He had opened the specification and seen the screenshots. He told me he and Samantha were "over the moon" about the form layouts, but the layouts had also led to him making a demand on us.

Monty explained that Samantha wanted to come over to our office and try out some ideas she had for layouts. She wanted to see what we could do in terms of loading some images onto the forms as background and playing around with a few of the screen objects. From our point of view, this could develop into quite a burden, but Monty said he would pay for any company staff time this used. That offer put a slightly different complexion on the issue.

Samantha wanted to come the next day. Monty and Samantha had become so exited because they could now fiddle with the prototype forms, which would let them get some screenshots off to their financial backers way ahead of schedule. They were convinced that the backers would be just as excited when they saw the screenshots Samantha would "manipulate." In fact, Monty was convinced their backers would be on the next plane if they could see only what we had produced in the draft specification. But Samantha would be able to apply some "real magic" using background images on the forms.

More Prototyping

Monty wanted me to supply someone to help Samantha get started with the VB design environment so she could access the prototype forms. As far as I was concerned, if he was going to pay for any time used, and the assistance we gave did not have a serious impact on something else we should be doing, then, of course, giving our help was okay. We had dedicated this whole week to reviewing, re-quoting, and addressing any issues that Monty or Samantha might have with the specification's content, so we had ample flexibility. We agreed that Samantha would come to our office first thing the next morning.

When I told Archie and Julie what Monty had said, they were ecstatic. I had to agree to let both of them help Samantha, although I would charge Monty only for one person's time. We decided to set Samantha up with a VB design environment and all the prototype forms we had produced. Julie and Archie would show her around the layouts and then let her make the modifications.

A Good Sign

The enthusiasm Monty and Samantha exhibited was clearly a good sign. Both had fully appreciated the prototype forms, and Samantha was keen to use her influence as a graphic designer to produce something even better.

Tip

In the course of a project, you may well find that the customer starts to make all sorts of demands on your time. Monty was aware of the commercial repercussions of such interruptions, but many customers are not. Don't let yourself be bullied. Quite often—but not always—mentioning a cost for time involved in providing assistance will deter a customer from continuing. It's up to you to make sure that such demands don't interfere with the project. If they do, then you must make sure you are compensated for the effort, and that you can control the impact it might have on the project. If you inform the client that his or her actions might delay delivery, you'll be amazed how many urgent demands suddenly evaporate.

Continuing the Review

We were now ready to look at the Reference Book format in Page View mode.

4.2.3. Page View Mode—Reference Book Format
Two layouts are required for this format, as depicted in Figures I and J. The primary screen objects are the image, the text block, and the keys. The alternative video clip is played in its own form, centered in the available image area. Figure I shows the layout when the keys are on screen. Figure J indicates how the text block expands in height when the reader removes the keys.

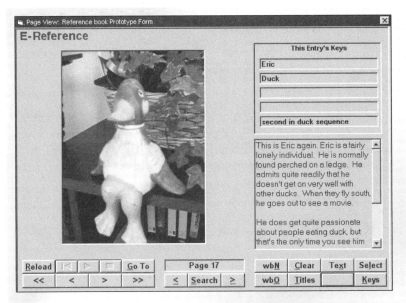

Figure I

Page View mode for a Reference Book with keys switched on.

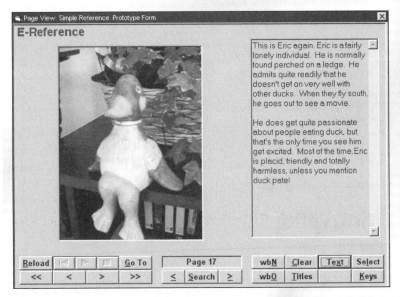

Figure J

Page View mode for a Reference Book with keys switched off.

4.2.3.1. Viewing a Reference Book, Required Screen Objects

(A) E-Reference Format Specifier

"E-Reference" is placed in the top left of the form when Reference Books are loaded.

(B) The Image

The program loads, sizes, and centers the image in the available area with the aspect ratio preserved. If a video is present, the video is first placed in the center of the available image area and then played. The available area for image display is maximized to occupy from the left-hand side of the form to the start of the text area. The image extends from the top of the navigation controls to below the format specifier.

(C) The Text Area

The user places text in a fixed area, according to the condition of the key panel, as indicated in Figures I and J.

(D) Navigation Controls

Located at the bottom of the screen, these common controls are defined later.

(E) The Key Panel

The user can display keys in a key panel, as shown in Figure I.

(F) Search Selection Panel (not shown in Figures I and J)

The user can display and use search selection criteria in a panel that exactly replaces the key panel, as defined later.

Reference Format Comments

Julie considered that making up the forms was actually fun as well as useful. However, she found it a bit frustrating to run the forms and start clicking on buttons, expecting to see things happen, and nothing did. (Actually, you do have to be a little cautious here—screen prototyping with VB can be a double-edged sword.)

The Perils of Prototyping

You can use prototyping for all sorts of reasons. We used form prototypes in the case study analysis to help determine the requirements themselves. As we discussed in the previous chapter, you can use prototypes that involve code development to model the requirements. You can use these models to gain feedback from the user to help establish the true requirements. In general terms, as we've discussed, you use prototyping to explore the unknown.

The VB design environment provides a brilliant modeling facility. You don't even need to be a programmer to use it. The speed at which you can produce prototypes, with or without code, using a powerful design environment such as VB can lead an uneducated customer to think there's really nothing to software development—all you have to do now is put some code behind the forms and—Presto!—out pops the solution.

Blame the GUI

The problem is that, because the GUI looks so complete, the customer has difficulty appreciating that you can produce such sophistication that does nothing. You've seen the effect the layouts had on Monty, and he's highly computer literate. Customers often have difficulty appreciating all the work required to take the prototype forms on to a completed system. You might find they are startled by your time frame and price—after all, haven't they seen the project almost complete?

Education

You must educate uninformed customers that form prototyping, in particular, is a simple exercise. Show them how form prototyping works in VB, and explain the advantages of an object-based design environment. Architects have been using object-based environments for years—indeed, many application domains are looking to objects to make their lives easier. Explain that you have a library of screen objects at your disposal. Show how you can create an instance of one and manipulate its properties to produce the required effects. Then, show how the program can't do anything when you run it. You might even be wise to take an example program and give an indication of the amount of code that lies behind it.

A Model for Iterative Prototyping

I've indicated that prototyping has a place in the scheme of professional software development, provided you understand that you may need to throw away the prototype and start over to provide the final solution. So, let's look at a methodology for developing software that uses prototyping in direct opposition to the formal, methodical SDLC approach. We can define a model for prototyping as detailed in Figure 5.1.

Capture Requirements—A Rough Idea

You can't start to develop code unless you have some idea of what the code's supposed to do. In a genuine prototyping situation, this process usually involves sitting around a table with the interested parties and hashing out a set of requirements, but at a very superficial level. The size and complexity of the project largely determines the degree of informality possible. The bigger the task, the more formality you'll need to maintain control of the project. Overall, the process leads to a loosely defined set of requirements.

Design and Develop Prototype

Next, we embark on a design and development phase—again, largely unshackled from a formal approach (the degree of informality is, once more, a function of job size and complexity). As software engineers, we may well throw in lots of clever ideas of our own, based on our understanding of the requirements. The whole process is much looser than the one we defined for a structured methodology. This loose approach is highly conducive to innovation and flare, provided the project doesn't go off on too many tangents for too long. The end result is a prototype program.

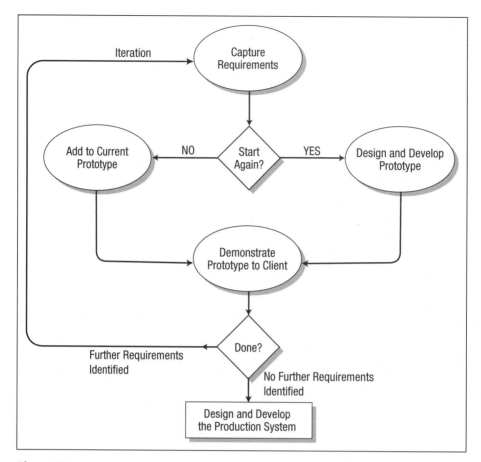

Figure 5.1
Model for developing by prototyping.

Demonstrate to Client

When you are ready, you come back and show the prototype to the client. This demonstration leads to more discussion, and further requirements materialize.

Iteration

Based on the results of the demonstration, you may decide to develop the prototype further. At this stage, you must ask the question, Should we start again? The prototype you have developed may be unsuitable for further expansion because of design constraints. After all, you designed and developed the prototype with only a limited understanding of the true requirements. If the design is lacking, you need to go back to the drawing board and redesign the prototype to accommodate the old and new requirements. Alternatively, you may be able to bolt on the new requirements without starting design and development again from scratch. Every circumstance will be different.

Whichever route you take, you meet the new requirements and produce the next level of prototype. Eventually, you are ready to demonstrate to the client once more. This iteration (development, discussion, and refinement) continues as the requirements evolve.

Completion

You typically reach completion when the client decides the prototype meets his or her requirements, or the money runs out, whichever occurs first. This brings up the point that prototyping can be very expensive. Because the process is so open-ended, identifying and defining completion events is often quite difficult. In terms of software development, prototyping is the path of least risk to both client and supplier, but it carries a high price.

An Unstructured Approach

To a large extent, the way in which we developed the requirements document in the case study follows the relatively unstructured approach of the prototyping model described here. We wrote what we thought were the requirements, then we reviewed and improved them. Next, we looked at the requirements from a different viewpoint (scenarios) and tried again—amending, improving, and sometimes throwing away what we had completed in the first attempt (such as the descriptions of the Title Index Editor, whose formal specification changed substantially from the first attempts). The really important aspect of the iterative prototyping model is what happens at the end—the prototype is converted to production software.

Production Software

If your prototype software has been developed with a loosely structured approach, it's not production standard. The prototyping process quite possibly included little accountability, traceability, and so on. Because you added to the prototype over and over again, its design might be suspect. You must consider support, training, further development, and the like for software the client is going to use in earnest. And the only way to provide production software is to follow a structured methodology that leads to a robust, well-documented, well-tested product. That process is in direct conflict with what you develop a prototype for. As I've said, in the majority of cases, you must engineer the prototype from scratch using a formal methodology. However, because you have a working model of the requirements, you can develop the final solution much faster than if you were starting from scratch, as the case study demonstrates.

Prototyping Has Its Place

To summarize, when neither you nor your client has a clear understanding of the requirements, or knowledge of how you might engineer a solution, prototyping is a sensible way forward. You can explore the unknown and develop your understanding gradually. Iterative prototyping is, however, an expensive approach. And to construct production-standard software, you and the client must be prepared to start over after the prototype has shown the way.

You will meet customers who insist that the prototype is suitable for their use. The challenge you face is to convince them of their folly and if that doesn't work, I would advise getting something written down on paper to the effect that the software may not be suitable for long-term expansion in its current form.

Return to the Case Study:
Continuing the Review

Both Archie and Julie wondered what Samantha would do with the layouts they had produced. I suspected she would come along with a collection of background images that she'd want to use to create a style for each book type. She'd almost certainly want to experiment with the fonts and sizes for text displays. And she might want to try to change the position of elements such as the image and the text block. That wouldn't be a problem because those things were just properties that we could capture and set up when the program loaded.

I also pointed out we couldn't afford too much of a diversion, even if Monty was paying for the time. Our main purpose this week was to review the documentation and come up with a new quote. From a project-management point of view, we could accommodate Monty's request, but we must not let it get in the way of our schedule.

Future Formats

We were now ready to see how we had dealt with future requirements in the final document.

4.2.4. Page View Mode—Extended Reference (Composite) Format (Future Requirement)
It is required that a display consisting of the Composite format described in Section 2 be made available in the future. As used in the other formats, the navigation controls, keys, and selection criteria will also apply here, as indicated in Section 2.

This is a future requirement and will be specified in more detail at the appropriate time.

4.2.5. Page View Mode—HTML/Web Format (Future Requirement)
It is required that a browser be used to display a page defined as an HTML file or from a Web site via a TCP/IP socket connection that Montasana Systems will make available. As used in the other formats, the navigation controls, keys, and selection criteria will also apply here, as indicated in Section 2.

This is a future requirement and will be specified in more detail at the appropriate time.

Future Requirements Comments

Notice how we clarified that the connection to the Internet for the browser was not our responsibility, but Monty's. Making clear statements about such details pays so they don't become issues in the future. The browser connection was a requirement, but not one that we had to address.

Don't forget, the clients are examining this document before they take ownership, and if you feel responsibility needs to be defined in any areas, you can put necessary statements in the document. Then, it's up to the client to argue if something's unacceptable (after all, Monty didn't have to sign off on the document until he was happy with it). If you're unsure about any demarcation of responsibility in your project, then define who has what responsibility in the requirements document, and negotiate with the client until you are both happy with the definition. Never sweep such issues under the carpet if you feel strongly about them.

Restrictions

As I've said before, defining what a program is *not* going to do is often just as important as describing what the program *will* do. Remember, you are trying to control the customer's expectations. This section of the requirements document is another good example of how we defined such software restrictions—here, with respect to Page View mode.

4.2.6. Page View Mode—Restrictions

When the program is in Page View mode, the reader must not remove the disk containing the selected title. If this should happen, any subsequent failures by the viewer to locate files as the user tries to navigate through a book should initiate an appropriate message to notify the user. Recovery will be automatic if the reader reinserts the correct disk. Alternatively, the reader can invoke the Title Selection mode to view a new disk's contents.

A further restriction is that when the program is in Page View mode, the user is unable to modify or relocate any image, video, text, or keys.

Restriction Comments

If you remember, a scenario necessitated these definitions. We were contemplating how a reader would switch on the E-MagBook, select a title to go to a book, and then pull out the removable disk. Those scenarios were useful exercises that helped us to challenge the requirements.

Julie came up with a profound comment at this stage. She reasoned that the whole process of defining requirements, producing scenarios, and doing the analysis—as well as constant reviewing—takes away much of the mystique about software development. The process becomes a much more comprehensive exercise to the person who wants a program written as well as to the programmer. The process also particularly helps the nontechnical people involved in management of the project.

NOTE: *Julie's point was that many people regard software development, and programming in particular, as a mystery. What we were doing here was putting software development (and programming) in context. Programming is simply the means by which to solve a set of problems or furnish a list of requirements.*

Control Buttons and Sound Tracks

By taking common elements out of the descriptions of the View modes and simply referring to the generic single description, Archie and Julie improved the specification considerably, as the following shows.

4.2.7. Page View—Summary of Control Button Collection (Navigation Buttons)

This section summarizes the functionality required from the button controls located at the bottom of the screen in all Page View modes of operation. The buttons are visible at the bottom of each form layout provided for Page View mode. They are referred to as "navigation controls," although that is only one of their functions. (Subsequent sections, such as "Searching," "Workbench," and the like contain further details describing specific functional requirements.)

4.2.7.1. Page Navigation Controls (Left-Hand Side of Collection)

These controls are the button controls the user uses to move to other pages in the currently loaded E-MagBook title:

Reload	Reloads current page.
<<	Go to Page 1
>>	Go to Last Page
<	Go to Previous Page
>	Go to Next Page
Go To	Allows user to select page number

4.2.7.2. Multimedia Controls (Left-Hand Side of Collection)

These controls are located above the page navigation controls. From left to right, they are:

Rewind current sound

Start playing current sound

Stop playing current sound

4.2.7.3. Page Display and Search Controls (Middle Set of Collection)

These controls consist of a page-number display and three search buttons (the user sets up the search criteria using the search criteria panel, as defined later):

Page no.	Shows current page number on view
Search	Search for first match starting from Page 1
>	Search from current page for next matching page
<	Search from current page for first previous matching page

More details concerning searching are supplied later.

4.2.7.4 Miscellaneous Controls (Right-Hand Side of Collection)

These controls, located on the right-hand side of the collection, provide the following:

wbN	Select Workbench mode, reset settings
wbO	Select Workbench mode with previous settings
Clear	Clear selection criteria
Titles	Return to Title Selection mode
Text	For Text Book and Picture Album modes: Removes key panel or selection panel, if present; otherwise, has no effect.
	For Reference Book mode: Remove key panel or selection panel, if present, and extend text display in height; otherwise, has no effect
Select	Displays selection criteria panel
Keys	Displays key panel

The relevant sections that follow contain more details on the requirements of these buttons.

Control Button Comments

Archie confessed that he had thought we would have masses of different code to handle the various page formats. But just from the descriptions we'd been through, it was already evident that a lot of the functionality we had to develop for the page handling would be the same for each page, whatever its format.

Again, the analysis helped to identify the commonality. We should always be on the lookout for a generic description of a requirement that handled many different instances of the same thing. Rather than having a requirement to handle the control button collection for a Text Book format and then another requirement to do the same for the Picture Album format, and so on, we only had one requirement to handle any page.

4.2.8. Page View Mode—Sound track Requirements

A page of any format might or might not contain a sound track. When the user brings a page that does contain a sound track onto the screen, any sound track currently being played is terminated and the new sound track is played immediately. If subsequent pages selected for viewing contain no sound track, the last loaded sound track remains playing. After the sound track has completed, it remains loaded and can be manually replayed at any time. The user can manually stop, play, and rewind loaded sound tracks.

Sound Track Requirement Comments

Archie also admitted that if it hadn't been for the depth of probing we'd been involved in, he would have assumed that the user would play a sound file, and that was it. But, of course, we needed to define the requirement if a sound was already playing and what would happen if the user moved to another page that didn't have a sound. As Archie had always worked, he would have encountered these situations as development progressed, and he would have made decisions "on-the-fly" about how to handle the various situations. (That was not really a brilliant approach because, as he admitted, he'd usually missed some repercussion that implementing functionality on-the-fly might have on software he'd already developed.)

NOTE: *The preceding comments emphasize the difference between a structured and nonstructured approach to software development.*

The Workbench

The Workbench was not particularly easy to define in terms of a requirement. But what a difference the two screenshots made. We had developed them as part of the analysis to help define in more detail how the Workbench was to function. We glossed over Workbench analysis in the previous chapter, but here you can see what a profound effect the analysis had on the requirements specification.

4.3. Viewer Mode 3—Workbench
The Workbench mode is invoked only from the Page View mode. The Workbench mode provides a facility for exploring images in Picture Albums and Reference Books, and in setting them up, together with any text, for print output. For Text Books, the Workbench allows the text to be printed on its own. In all cases, regardless of format, the printout consists of a screen dump of the object(s) in the Workbench. The Workbench facility will ultimately include the Extended Reference and HTML/Web formats.

Workbench uses the full screen availability (that is, the navigation controls are not on screen). At any time, the user can reinstate the Page View mode. The detailed requirements for the Workbench mode of operation depend on the book format type.

4.3.1. Workbench for Text Book Pages
A Text Book page is displayed as a single block of text on the Workbench screen at a default font type and size defined by the program. Although the text can be of any length, no scroll bars are available. The user can scroll by placing the text cursor on the last line and using the down arrow key to scroll to the next line. It is required that the user can move the text display around the screen for positioning purposes, and that text can be resized in terms of its height or its width. The purpose of this functionality will be to allow the reader to set up the block as required for printing purposes. A print request will direct a copy of the text, exactly as it appears on the screen, to the E-MagBook's default printer, if present.

4.3.2. Workbench for Picture Album Pages
The picture from a Picture Album page is displayed at full-size on the screen in Workbench mode. The top, left-hand corner of the image will be present on the screen. The rest of the image may or

may not be present, depending on whether the image is bigger or smaller than the available space. It is required that the user can move the image around the screen for positioning purposes.

The user will be able to alter the dimensions of the image by shrinking or expanding the height and width together so that the aspect ratio is always preserved. An alternative method of changing the image's dimensions by expanding or contracting just one of the dimensions (height or width) is also required, where the aspect ratio need not be preserved.

It may be that after moving the image and manipulating and increasing its size, only a small portion of the bitmap image is present on the screen. This portion can be any part of the enlarged image.

At any stage, the user can request a print of the image, exactly as it appears on the viewing area. The output will be directed to the system's default printer, if one exists.

If the page contains a video clip, the clip will be placed in the Workbench, but the clip will not be available for printing.

4.3.3. Workbench for Format 3 Reference Book Page
The picture from a Reference Book page is treated in Workbench mode in exactly the same manner as that described for the image of a Picture Album page. The text from a Reference Book page is treated in the Workbench mode in exactly the same manner as that described for a Text Book page.

The image and text display must be treated as completely separate objects in the Workbench, with the following requirement: Where the image and text block overlap, the text block is always shown in the foreground, overlaying the image.

4.3.4. Workbench for Extended Reference Book (Future Requirement)
The Extended Reference Book format will be displayed in the Workbench mode in exactly the same way that it is displayed in the Page View mode, except that the control button collection is removed. Neither the Composite nor its components can be moved nor have their dimensions manipulated in any way.

At any stage, the reader can request a printout of the screen content. This content will be directed to the system's default printer, if one is attached.

4.3.5. Workbench for HTML / Web Pages (Future Requirement)
The browser used to display an HTML / Web page will be displayed in the Workbench mode in exactly the same way that it is displayed in the Page View mode, except that the control button collection is removed.

At any stage, the reader can request a printout of the screen content. This content will be directed to the system's default printer, if one is attached.

4.3.6. Invoking the Workbench
The user invokes the Workbench by clicking on the wbO or wbN buttons of the Page View mode's control button collection.

Control button wbN invokes the Workbench and requires that the program set up the objects on view with default, program-defined settings for position and dimension. These positions and dimensions are stored for subsequent use on exit from the mode via use of the wbO button.

Control button wbO invokes the Workbench with the last object settings for positioning and dimensions. In this way, the user can use a preferred setting multiple times without having to position and resize the screen objects each time the Workbench is invoked.

4.3.7. Workbench, Required Screen Objects

Required screen objects for Text Books, Picture Albums, and Reference Books are the appropriate combination of text and image objects. Figure K shows a reference page in the Workbench set up with the default program locations and object dimensions. The figure also shows the toolbar at the top of the form, which is used to manipulate object dimensions. Figure L shows the same two objects as Figure K, but after they have been moved and their dimensions have been modified.

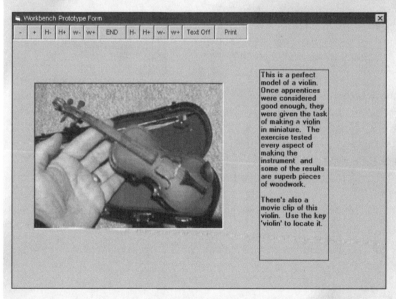

Figure K
Reference Page in Workbench with default load settings for objects.

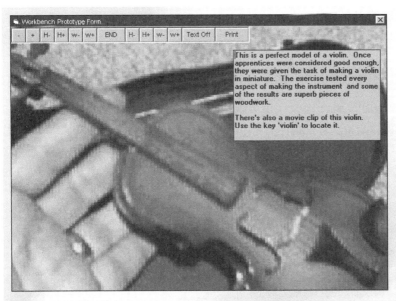

Figure L

Reference Page in Workbench after manual manipulation of objects.

The required screen objects can be defined as follows:

(A) The Image Container

For Picture Album and Reference Book modes, the image is initially placed on the Workbench at full size, with the top, left-hand corner guaranteed to be clearly visible. Videos are centered in the available area.

(B) The Text Container

The text from a Text Book or a Reference Book is placed in a text box of fixed default size and position with a fixed default font, as defined by the program.

(C) The Button Toolbar

This toolbar consists of a series of button controls that can be used to alter the dimensions of the image and/or the text box for Text Book, Picture Album, and Reference Book formats.

A summary of the required controls is as follows:

Picture Controls

In text-only mode, the picture controls are disabled:

+ Increase width and height of image by a default, fixed amount, preserving aspect ratio.

-	Decrease width and height of image by a default, fixed amount, preserving aspect ratio.
H-	Decrease height of image only, by a default fixed amount.
H+	Increase height of image only, by a default fixed amount.
W-	Decrease width of image only, by a default fixed amount.
W+	Increase width of image only, by a default fixed amount.

Text Controls

In Picture Album mode, the text controls are disabled:

H-	Decrease height of text box only, by a default fixed amount.
H+	Increase height of text box only, by a default fixed amount.
W-	Decrease width of text box only, by a default fixed amount.
W+	Increase width of text box only, by a default fixed amount. Text Off switches off text. It is required to change the caption to Text On so that the same button may be used to make the text box visible again.

General Controls

End	Returns program to Page View mode at last current entry.
Print	Prepares the screen for printing with the current layout and asks the user if it is okay to continue. If "Yes," a printout of the screen (exact screen dump) is produced, and the program returns to Workbench mode. If "No," the program remains in Workbench mode.

Workbench Comments

The two screenshots made such a difference to the description of the Workbench requirements. According to Archie, the screenshots took only about 20 minutes or so to produce, and they gave even more support to the statement that a picture speaks a thousand words.

Note that we had used the word *default* quite a lot. We were indicating that certain constants were defined internally to the program. These constants were, for example, the default values for increments to the height and width of the image. Another set of constants defined the increments for the text box, and so on. We were making clear to the client that these were internal constants. A likely future requirement was that these default values would become user configurable. At this stage, to lessen the workload, we were explicitly defining them as default constants. Without the word *default*, the descriptions could lead to an expectation that the user could define the values. This might seem a trivial point, but to develop user configurability for setting default parameters could turn into a lot of work.

Navigation and Searching for Pages

As you will see, the navigation and searching descriptions had undergone quite an overhaul from our first attempts. As our understanding grew deeper, then, too, our definitions became better.

---

5. Navigation and Searching in the Viewer
The user may navigate through a loaded book in Page View mode by "turning pages" or by searching for specific keys.

5.1. Keys
Each page, regardless of format, can have up to five keys associated with it. A page may have no keys or any number up to the maximum of five. Each single key consists of totally free-range text, to a maximum length as imposed by the size of screen display reserved for each key. A key may consist of more characters than can be displayed, if required. Keys can be composed of one or more words, and any mixture of uppercase and lowercase characters is permissible. Only printable characters are acceptable (for example, no control codes).

Keys are displayed on the key panel, which the user can bring on screen by clicking the Keys button in the control button collection. The key panel is depicted in the screen layout as shown for the viewer's Reference Book mode of operation, and, regardless of format, this is the position and size that the panel will adopt when requested by the user. The panel will overlay the text for a Text Book display, the image in a Picture Album display, the Composite in an Extended Reference display, and the browser in an HTML page. In all cases, the user may remove the key panel by clicking the Text button control. For Reference Book formats, this has the effect of stretching the Text Box, as defined earlier.

Keys can be used as search entities or as mini-descriptions of the page on view.

5.2. Navigation
It is required that when the program is in Page View mode, for any book format, the reader can request a page number at any time, and that page is then brought up on the screen and formatted accordingly. This can be described as a **Go To Defined Page Number** requirement. Two special variants of this are also required, defined as a **Go To Start Page** and a **Go To End Page** function. Also, at any time, in Page View mode, the user may request the next or previous page in the sequence, and this may be performed any number of times until the user encounters either the last page or the first page. Any subsequent attempt to navigate beyond the first or last pages is trapped, and an appropriate message is delivered to the reader. These functions are to be accommodated in the collection of navigation button controls, as defined earlier.

5.3. Searching
It is required that, at any time, in Page View mode, for any format, the reader can specify one or more keys, to a maximum of five, which the reader can then use to locate a page that contains the same keys. These requirements are referred to as the *search selection criteria*.

5.3.1. Search Selection Criteria Panel

The required panel to be used for entering search criteria is shown in Figure M. This panel is the same size as the panel used to display keys and is located in exactly the same location. The buttons Keys, Select, and Text, present on the control button collection, will be used to select and remove the criteria panel, as described earlier.

Figure M

Search Selection Criteria panel.

5.3.1.1. Search Selection Criteria Panel—Required Screen Objects

(A) Selection Input Fields

There are five data entry fields. The user may enter keys to be searched for in any order into one or more of these fields. The set of five fields makes up the selection criteria.

(B) Radio Buttons: Match All Keys and Match Any

The two radio buttons define whether all the selection criteria must be met (Match All Keys) or one or more of the criteria must match (Match Any).

5.3.2. Searching

It is required that a reader be able to set up or modify the criteria at any time, and that the defined criteria will remain in force until they are next modified. The criteria are also preserved across the three program modes of the viewer, even though searching can be instigated only in the Page View mode. On power up, the fields are blanked.

Three variations of a search request may be made.

5.3.2.1. Search from Page 1

Whenever the user requests this option (Search button on the button collection in Page View mode), the program will examine the keys for Page 1, then Page 2, and so on, looking for a match between each page's keys and the search selection criteria. This process continues until a matching entry is found, at which point the page is displayed and made the current page. Alternatively, if no match is found, an appropriate message is supplied to the reader and the last page is made available.

5.3.2.2. Search for Next Occurrence

Whenever the user requests this option (> button next to Search on the button collection), the program will examine the keys of the page next to the one currently on screen, looking for a match between its keys and the selection criteria. If there is no match, the program will continue searching each entry up to the last page until it has found a match or failed. If a match is found, the associated page is brought on screen, and this page becomes the current one. If the last page is found, and no match has ensued, an appropriate message is supplied to the reader, and the last page is made available on screen.

5.3.2.3. Search for Previous Occurrence
Whenever this option is requested (< button next to Search on the button collection), the program will examine the keys of the page previous to the one currently on screen, looking for a match with the selection criteria. If there is no match, then the program will continue searching each entry back to the first page until it has found a match or failed. If a match is found, the associated page is brought on screen, and this page becomes the current one. If the first page is found, and no match has ensued, an appropriate message is supplied to the reader, and Page 1 is made available.

5.3.2.4. Types of Match
It is required that there are two types of search. The first type is where all the keys defined in the selection criteria must be found. That is, if three keys are defined as the search criteria, then those three keys must exist in a page in their entirety. It does not matter how many other keys exist in the page. The second type of match is one that requires only one or more of the selection criteria to be present in a page's list of keys for a match to be deemed true. In summary:

Search Type 1—All

All keys defined in selection criteria must exist in the page.

Search Type 2—Any

One or more keys from selection criteria must exist in the page.

Matching is independent of uppercase and lowercase conditions.

Navigation and Searching Comments

Defining requirements isn't difficult. You have to put in a lot of detail, which can be very tedious, but extremely necessary. All the time, you are trying to be precise and avoid ambiguity. Ambiguities can cost you dearly, which is why getting other people to review your written work is important. All the descriptions must be in plain English, with as little computer jargon as possible. Never lose sight of the fact that many people who will read this document will not know how to program—why should they? You are describing functional requirements; how they are achieved and what underlying technology is being employed is of little interest to most clients. The important question to ask is, Does the program do what the client needs it to do? If it doesn't, then the latest, most up-to-date programming environment with the greatest features on earth is of little consolation to the client.

The Viewer Completed

And that is the viewer's requirements definition in full. If you look back, first to the original proposal we put together, then at the first attempt at a specification and the results of the analysis, you can clearly see how this specification evolved as we gained a better and better understanding.

Julie noted she was fascinated at how, just over two weeks ago, they were introduced to what she thought was an incredibly complicated project, with lots of image and multimedia functionality—she simply didn't know where to start. What she had seen and been a party to was a logical process whereby we had captured and formalized the required functionality. With all the understanding she now had, and with the results of the feasibility work, she felt much more confident that the project was totally achievable.

Chicken and the Egg

Someone once told me that one couldn't possibly program an application unless one was an expert in that application field. So, if one wanted a banking system, one would have to go to a banker to get the software written. Or, if one wanted a multimedia presentation program, one would have to go to a multimedia expert.

If everyone could rely only upon domain experts to develop software for the application domain, then no software would ever have been written. When banks first started to computerize, no bankers understood computers, and no computer experts understood the world of banking. That's what the SDLC is all about. Capture the requirements—learn from the application experts what the application domain comprises. Learn the business rules. In the process, you may well become a banking expert, or an expert in automated warehousing, or an expert in whatever the application area covers. But only when you understand the requirements can you engineer a computer solution.

However, understanding the requirements is not enough to move forward; you also must understand how to program computers. You must know how to program a computer to change a concept into reality. We are really software engineers who take a concept, define it in terms that both the domain experts and we can understand, and, from those definitions, engineer a solution—as you'll see when we start the design process.

Programming by Nonprogrammers

As programming becomes easier, particularly with the advent of component technology, you will see more and more application experts doing their own programming—and why not? Programming is only a means to an end, after all, and the sooner we realize that, the better.

A Final Review of the Editor Requirements

Based on the way in which we had gone about defining the viewer, Archie and Julie developed the requirements for the editors. However, quite early on, as they were documenting the Title Index Editor, they had realized the two programs would have a lot of common functionality. Consequently, they decided to define a specific set of requirements for each editor, and then a general set of requirements that would apply to both, which would keep the descriptions tighter and more readable. And, of course, they just had to include all the forms.

General Requirements

Julie and Archie produced an initial, introductory section to define the data model and the operation of an editor in general. This section would make the specific definitions that followed much easier to write.

---

6. Editor Data Model, States of Operation, and File Rules

This section describes the data model required for use by the Title Index Editor or the Page Index Editor, and the states of operation required in both programs. The final section defines rules for file handling.

6.1. The Data Model

It is required that, at any given time, three versions of the data exist for the editors. This representation is shown in Figure N.

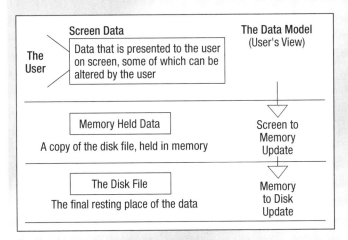

Figure N

Representation of the three levels of data accessible to an editor.

Data is present on screen in the screen objects; it is also present in the memory and on disk. This arrangement provides three levels of data storage that need to be understood. The data on screen amounts to a single entry from the Index. When the editor loads an Index, it loads a complete copy from disk into memory, and places the content of Entry 1 on screen. At this stage, the data on screen is the same as the data in the memory record for Entry 1, and the complete Index in memory is the same as that on disk.

6.2. States of the Editor

It is required that a user can directly modify the screen data. To modify the corresponding memory entry, the user must *commit* the change. Alternatively, the user can abort the change. This arrangement leads to two, well-defined program states. In normal mode, the screen data is the same as the corresponding entry in memory. This state is referred to as **Alert 1 Normal State**. When any part of the screen data is modified by user intervention, the program goes into **Alert 1 Changed State**. The program must remain in this state until the changes have been committed to memory or aborted.

Regardless of what **Alert 1** state the program is in, it can also be in one of two **Alert 2** states. These states refer to the state of memory and disk data. If the memory data and disk data are the same, the program is in **Alert 2 Normal State**. When memory and disk data differ, then the program is in **Alert 2 Changed State**.

At any given time, the program is in a combined state indicating the **Alert 1** and **Alert 2** conditions.

In summary, an editor can exist in one of the following states:

> **Alert 1 Normal State**=Screen data is the same as the corresponding memory entry.

> **Alert 1 Changed State**=Screen data is not the same as the corresponding memory entry.

An editor can also exist in one of the following **Alert 2** states, regardless of the **Alert 1** condition:

> **Alert 2 Normal State**=Memory Index is the same as the disk Index.

> **Alert 2 Changed State**=Memory Index is not the same as the disk Index.

An editor is always in one of the four possible combined states at any time. The color used to represent the change state will be referred to as the *alert color*.

6.3. Rules for File Handling

Both the Title Index Editor and the Page Index Editor use file references to point to images, videos, text, and sounds, and (in the case of a Title Index Editor) to the Page Index itself. This section defines general rules for file references.

(1) Any data entity that is a file (Title Index, Page Index, image, video, text, WAV, or MID) has three attributes that define its location and name absolutely:

> **Drive**   Drive on which file is located.

> **Directory Path**   Full directory path on which file is located.

> **File Name**   Name and extension of file.

The full file reference is made up from the following:

> **Drive\Directory_Path\File_Name**

(2) All the Index files and basic data entities that are files which constitute a single removable disk collection of books must be resident on the removable disk located in drive E: for an E-MagBook viewed by the E-Viewer.

(3) **Drive** attribute for all file references on the removable disk must be set to **E:. That is**, all file references must therefore become:

> **E:\Directory_Path\File_Name**

(4) **Drive** can be any logical or physical drive on a PC accessed by the E-Viewer, E-TitleEditor, or E-PageEditor, but this is only applicable to running the three programs on the PC.

(5) If a working book collection is to be transferred from a PC to an E-MagBook removable disk, all **Drive** attributes in all file references must be converted to **E:** without exception.

(6) The Title Index is always set up on the removable drive such that its **Drive** property is set to **E:** and its **Directory Path** property is set to "**\E-MagBook**" and its **File Name** property is set to **Title.idx**.

General Requirements Comments

This section sets the stage for the descriptions of the two editors by defining their operational states and rules for file reference handling. The specific requirements of each editor are then defined, followed by a general section defining all the common aspects. This format produces a much more readable and concise set of requirements.

The Title Index Editor

Now I'll discuss the Title Index Editor in greater detail.

7. E-MagBook Title Index Editor Requirements

The requirements for this program fall into two categories: general editor requirements, defined in sections 6 and 9, and specific requirements, defined in this section. This program does not run on an E-MagBook, but from a PC with a minimum screen size of 800×600 pixels.

It is required that the program allows a Title Index to be created from scratch or allows an existing Index to be modified. Each entry in the Title Index will hold the following:

Title   A free text title for a book.

Description   A free-text description of a book.

Page Index Reference   The name and location of the corresponding book's Page Index file.

None of the data entities may be blank. There can be any number of such entries, to a maximum of 50 per Title Index.

7.1. Program in Alert 1 Normal State + Alert 2 Normal State

The required form layout for the Title Editor in normal mode (screen content is the same as the corresponding memory entry, and Memory Index is the same as the disk version), is shown in Figure O.

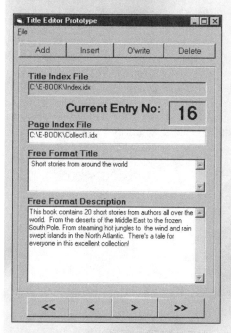

Figure O

Title Editor in normal mode of operation.

7.1.1. Required Screen Objects

The following elements are required.

(A) File Options Drop-Down Menu

This provides New, Open, Save As, and Save Index file options, as defined in more detail in Section 9, "Common Requirements for the Editors."

(B) Add, Insert, Overwrite, and Delete Button Controls

These buttons are used to modify the Memory Index as described in Section 9, "Common Requirements for the Editors."

(C) The Title Index File

This is a read-only data field used to display the name of the Index file that is currently opened. If no file is open, the text *No Index File Opened* appears in the field. The background color of this field can be used to indicate the **Alert 2 Changed State**.

(D) Page Index File

This is a file reference consisting of the full drive, directory path, and file name of the file that contains the page definitions for the title.

(E) Free-Format Title

This is the title of the book to which the Page Index file reference points.

(F) Free-Format Description

This is the description relevant to the above title.

(G) Navigation Controls

These controls provide the page-turning features, defined in Section 9.

7.2. Alert 1 Changed State

When the user manually changes the content of one or more screen fields, the program enters the **Alert 1 Change State**, as defined in Section 6. For the Title Index Editor, this state is engaged when the title, description, or Page Index reference is changed. The screen layout then becomes as shown in Figure P.

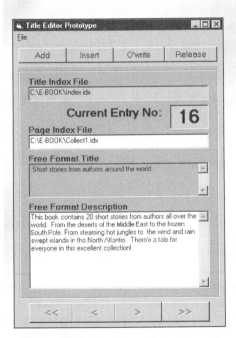

Figure P
The Title Index Editor in the Alert 1 Changed State indicating, in this case, that what is on screen is not the same as the content of the current memory location. In the figure, the form's main panel and the free format title data field have all had their background colors changed to the alert color.

It is required that color be used to make clear to the operator that the screen does not reflect the current memory entry. Navigation and all functions associated with opening or saving a Title Index file must be inhibited. The user may only add, insert, overwrite, or release the current change, as defined in Section 9.

7.2.1. Screen Objects

Apart from the **Release** button, all required screen objects are as defined in Section 7.1.1. Presented here are notes concerning the screen objects in the **Alert 1 Changed State**.

(A) File Options Drop-Down Menu

These options are all disabled in this mode.

(B) Add, Insert, and Overwrite Button Controls

These buttons are available, as described in Section 9.

(C) Release Button Control

This button replaces the **Delete** button in this mode and is used to abort a screen change, as defined in Section 9.

(D) The Index File

Note that this field can be in **Alert 2 Changed State** or **Alert 2 Normal State**, as defined in Section 6. The alert color can be used to set the background color of the data field to indicate the **Alert 2 Changed State** condition.

(E) Page Index File

If the user has modified this field, its background color can be changed to that of the alert color.

(F) Free-Format Title

If the user has modified this field, its background color can be changed to that of the alert color.

(G) Free-Format Description

If the user has modified this field, its background color can be changed to that of the alert color.

(H) Navigation Controls

These controls are all disabled.

7.3. Alert 2 Normal State and Alert 2 Changed State

It is required that the **Alert 2 Changed State** is indicated by changing the color of the read-only Index file data field to the alert color. A Save, Save As, or New menu option will then change the state back to normal. The functional requirements of this state are independent of the **Alert 1 State**, and vice versa.

7.4. Remaining Requirements

These requirements are described in Section 9, which deals with common aspects of the two editors.

Title Index Comments

With just two screenshots, Archie and Julie felt they had managed to define the real essence of this editor's two main modes of operation. Archie felt that separating the requirements for change handling, Index updating, and file options really made the difference. When they had started, they hadn't realized how similar the requirements for the two programs were, even though they looked so different in terms of their form layouts.

NOTE: *When you have more than one "chunk" of functionality that may or may not have common definitions, start by defining one portion in detail. When you start to do the same with the second chunk, keep referring to the first to see whether, by changing some of the words, you can achieve a single definition for both sets of functionality. In the case study, loading and saving an Index, whether it is the Page Index or the Title Index, will be the same from a requirements point of view. The only difference will be the type of record that is input or output. The same principle applies to navigation— both programs simply allow the user to step through entries, forward or backward.*

The Page Index Editor

What you see next is the specific definition of the requirements for the Page Index Editor.

---

8. E-MagBook Page Index Editor

The requirements for this program fall into two categories: general editor requirements, defined in Sections 6 and 9, and specific requirements, defined in this section.

This program does not run on an E-MagBook, but from a PC with a minimum screen size of 800x600 pixels.

It is required that the program allows a Page Index to be created from scratch or allows an existing Index to be modified.

The content of a Page Index entry depends on format type. The editor must be capable of displaying the data fields, according to format type, in a manner that is totally consistent with the way in which the viewer displays the data. All the functionality available in the viewer must also be present in the editor. Additionally, the editor must be able to let the user create and modify data items, as defined in the following sections.

Page formats to be supported initially are defined next. Note that, in all cases, a file reference consists of the drive, directory path and file name that specifies the location and identity of the file on the PC running the editor. Listed here are the data items, which can be created and edited for each format type.

Format 1—Text Book

Each page consists of the following data items:

A text file reference

An optional sound track file reference

Up to five keys of any length

Format 2—Picture Album

Each page consists of the following data items:

> Either a static image file reference or a movie clip file reference
>
> An optional sound track file reference
>
> Up to five keys of any length

Format 3—Reference Book

Each page consists of the following data items:

> Either a static image file reference or a movie clip file reference
>
> A text file reference
>
> An optional sound track file reference
>
> Up to five keys of any length

When creating an Index, the user will be forced to declare which format type is to apply. The blank Index can then be populated with the data items defined above, according to format type. There can be any number of entries, to a maximum of 1,000, in each case.

8.1. Form Layout—Alert 1 Normal State + Alert 2 Normal State

The required basic layout of the Page Index Editor is as shown in Figure Q.

Figure Q

The Page Index Editor in **Alert 1 Normal State** and **Alert 2 Normal State**.

The form is split into the editor's main control button collection, located at the top of the form, and a replica of the viewer's layout, as defined in this section, with the addition of four read-only text boxes at the bottom of the viewer display.

8.1.1. Screen Requirements for Normal Mode

(A) The Viewer Area

The viewer's Page View mode form layout is required on the Page Index Editor, configured according to format type. This layout is exactly the same as that of the viewer itself. This layout supports all three modes of operation: Title Selection, Page View, and Workbench. In every aspect, the layout performs and behaves as described in the viewer specification.

(B) Keys

In addition to their standard functionality, it is also required that the keys in the viewer area can be modified. As soon as any input is received in any of the key fields, the program switches to the **Alert 1 Changed State**.

(C) Text Block

When a text block is present (Text Book and Simple Reference formats), the user can modify the text block. Any such change causes the program to switch to the **Alert 1 Changed State**.

(D) Index File Reference

Full drive, directory path, and file name of currently loaded Page Index is displayed here in a read-only field. If no file is loaded, the box contains *No Index File Loaded*.

(E) Picture or Movie Clip File Reference

Full drive, directory path, and file name of image or video currently on screen is displayed. If no file is loaded, the field is blank. This is a read-only field.

(F) Text File Reference

Full drive, directory path, and file name of text file currently on screen is displayed. If no file is loaded, the field is blank. This is a read-only field.

(G) Sound File Reference

Full drive, directory path, and file name of sound file currently being played is displayed. If no file is loaded, the field is blank. This is a read-only field.

(H) Index Button Controls: Add, Insert, Overwrite, and Delete

These are the button controls used to change the contents of the Memory Index. They are described in detail in Section 9.

(I) Clipboard Button Controls: Copy and Paste

The Copy button allows the contents of the screen display to be copied to the clipboard. The Paste button transfers the contents of the clipboard to the on-screen viewer and switches the program into the **Alert 1 Changed State**. Together, the two button controls allow any entry from the Index to be copied and placed somewhere else in the Index.

(J) Clear Text and Keys Button Controls

These button controls allow either the text display or all five keys on the viewer layout to be cleared. Each button causes the program to enter the **Alert 1 Changed State**.

(K) Clear File Reference Button Controls

These button controls clear the file reference data fields (with the exception of the Index file reference) on the viewer layout. Clearing any of these items causes the program to enter the **Alert 1 Changed State**. Specifically, these buttons are Clear Picture Reference, Clear Text Reference, Clear Sound Reference, and Clear All Three.

(L) Text Button Control

This control allows the user to save the content of the text display, usually after it has been changed, to the currently referenced text file, indicated in the text file reference box. If there is no such reference (that is, the box is blank), the Save button must solicit a file name for output from the user.

(M) File Drop-Down Menu Options

This menu contains options to handle the main Page Index requirements:

> New, Open, Save, Save As

These options all refer to the Page Index file and are defined in full in Section 9.

(N) Text Drop-Down Menu Options

This menu contains options to handle the text display for Text Book and Reference Book formats:

Save text

This option allows modified text on display to be written back to the currently opened text file (that is, the one named in the text file name box).

Save Text As

This option allows text on display to be written to a named disk file, either to create a new file or to overwrite an existing one. The file name is solicited from the user via a dialog box, and this name then appears in the file name text box.

Font

At any time, the user can use this option to change the font settings for a page file Index. Once set, the font characteristics apply to every single page of the Index.

(O) Window

This menu option lets the user reinstate the File Selection form if it has been closed down. Otherwise, it places focus on the selected form.

Showing a Change

Now that we had defined all the screen objects for the Page Index Editor, it was time to define the form in the **Alert 1 Changed State**.

8.2. Form Layout for Alert 1 Changed State

When any of the data fields have been modified, (text display, any of the keys, image file reference, text file reference, or sound file reference), the display takes on the form shown in Figure R.

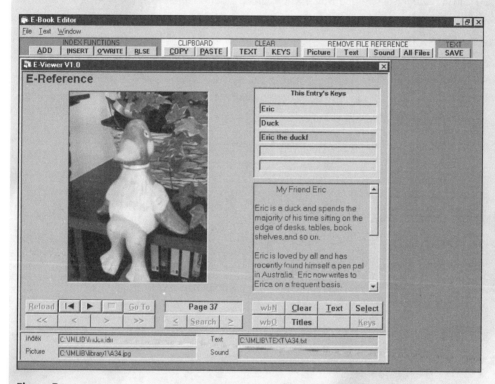

Figure R

The Page Index Editor in **Alert 1 Changed State**. In the figure, the color of the viewer form and the text box have been changed to that of the alert color.

8.2.1. Screen Requirements for Alert 1 Changed State

(A) The Viewer Area

When the program is in the **Alert 1 Changed State**, it is required that this mode be made evident on the viewer form by use of an alert color in the background.

(B) Keys

Each key that has been modified has its background color set to the alert color.

(C) Text Block

When a modification has been made to the text block, its background color is set to the alert color.

(D) Index File Reference

This field cannot be changed in **Alert 1 Changed State** because the New and Open file menu options are disabled.

(E) Picture or Movie Clip, Text, and Sound File References

The content of these fields can be changed only via the File Selection form. The background color of the appropriate field is changed to the alert color.

(F) Index Button Controls: Add, Insert, Overwrite, Delete, and Release

In **Alert 1 Changed State**, the Delete button is replaced with the Release button. When any of these buttons is used as defined in Section 9, the program reverts to **Alert 1 Normal State**.

(G) Clipboard Button Controls: Copy and Paste

These functions are as described in Section 8.1.1.

(H) All Clear Button Controls

These functions are as described in Section 8.1.1.

(I) Text Button Control

Use of this button changes the text background color to the normal color after the file has been saved. **Alert 1 Changed State** remains operative.

(J) File Drop-Down Menu Options

The file options New, Open, Save, and Save As are all disabled in **Alert 1 Changed State**.

(K) Text Drop-Down Menu Options

These functions are as described in Section 8.1.1.

(L) Window

This menu option functions as described in Section 8.1.1.

8.3. Form Layout for Alert 2 States

It is required that the **Alert 2 Normal State** is indicated by setting the background color of the Index file reference to a neutral color. The **Alert 2 Changed State** can be identified by setting the background color of this field to the alert color. This is totally independent of whatever the condition of the Alert 1 state.

The Add, Insert, and Overwrite button options switch the program to **Alert 2 Changed State**.

The menu options Save and Save As switch the program back to **Alert 2 Normal State**.

Comments about Form Layout

Archie and Julie created the Page Index Editor prototype forms by taking the viewer proto-type and adding to it. We added the editor's controls to the top of the form and the main data fields (file references boxes) at the bottom of the viewer layout. The real problem centered on where to put the file-selection controls.

Selecting Files

Here's the requirement for multimedia file selection specified.

8.4. Multimedia File Selection

This section defines the requirement for selecting an image or video file reference, a text file refer-ence, and a sound file reference. The file is selected from the File Selection form (as shown in Figure S) that exists in the editor as an independent form.

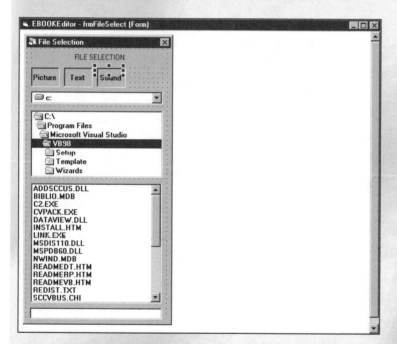

Figure S

The independent File Selection form.

8.4.1. Screen Object Requirements

The form must be set up for selection of a specific file type, of which there are three: image/ video, text, and sound. For each file type, there is an associated context consisting of **Drive**, **Directory**, and **Filter**. When the current file type is changed, then it is required that its context is preserved so that, when it is recalled at a later time, the applicable **Drive**, **Directory**, and **Filter** can be reset.

The objects used on the File Selection form are as follows:

(A) Picture

This control is located at the top, left-hand side of the form (labeled *Picture* in Figure S). When clicked, the control causes the context for the form to be reinstated for image and video selection. The color of the file-selection controls and filter, and the Picture command button, are switched to a default color designated for picture/video selection.

(B) Text

This control is located at the top of the form, in the middle (labeled *Text* in Figure S). When clicked, this control causes the context for the form to be reinstated for text file selection. The color of the file selection controls and filter, and the Text command button, are switched to a default color designated for text file selection.

(C) Sound

This control is located at the top, right-hand side of the form (labeled *Sound* in Figure S). When clicked, this control causes the context for the form to be reinstated for sound file selection. The color of the file selection controls and filter, and the Sound command button, are switched to a color designated for sound file selection.

(D) Drive Box

This box allows the user to define the **Drive** attribute of a required file using a typical Windows-type drop-down list capability, as seen on a standard File Selection dialog box. When the user changes the content of this box to another drive, the contents of the Directory Path box and the File Selection box must be updated automatically to reflect the new **Drive** setting.

(E) Directory Path Box

This box allows the user to define the directory path of the required file using a typical Windows-type drop-down list capability, as seen on a standard File Selection dialog box. When the user changes the content of this box, the content of the File Selection box must be updated automatically to reflect the new **Directory** path setting.

(F) File Selection Box

This box allows the user to define the required file to be loaded onto the page currently in view. If the file is of the wrong type (that is, not an image when an image is being selected), an appropriate message is required. The content of the File Selection box is automatically governed by the content of the File Filter box—only files with the specified extensions are displayed.

(G) File Filter Box

This box allows the user to specify a list of file extensions that can be displayed for the selected file type. This list box can be used to edit or create a list of applicable extension types.

8.4.2. File Selection

Figure T shows the File Selection form set up to allow a user to select an image or video clip. Figures U and V show the equivalent setups for text and sound files.

Figure T
The Page Editor with File Selection form set for picture/image selection.

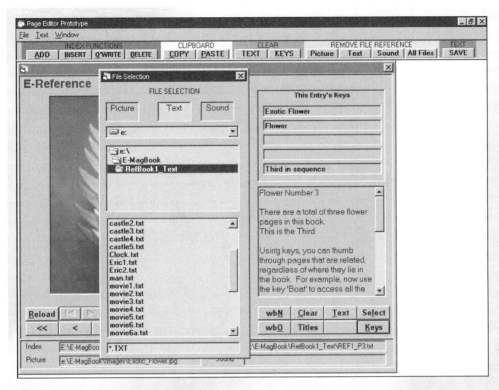

Figure U

The Page Editor with File Selection form set for text selection.

Figure V

The Page Editor with File Selection form set for sound selection.

The requirement to select a file, regardless of type, is as follows:

The user defines the file selection type by clicking Picture, Text, or Sound, located at the top of the form, as appropriate. This action turns all the form's screen objects to the default color defined for the file type. The content of the **Drive**, **Directory**, **File**, and **Filter** screen objects are then set to each of their previous settings, applicable to the file selection type. From this point on, the user can select any file on the file store system, and, by double-clicking on a file's name, the full file reference is placed in the appropriate file-reference data field beneath the viewer form. The object contained within the file is then loaded onto screen and/or played as appropriate (image, video, text, or sound). If the user selects an inappropriate file, a message is required to indicate that the format is unknown.

Multimedia File Selection Comments

We could link the file-selection controls available in VB to provide the functionality defined in the specification—that is, when one box was changed, the others would automatically be updated to reflect the change. You can see in the figures that accompany the File Selection option how the drive, directory, and file names look real. You can't input into these fields directly; you can manipulate them only in the same way that you would the equivalent controls in the standard file dialog box. To achieve the desired effect, Archie and Julie wrote a minute amount of code to make the boxes work in the desired way. You can see this work in Appendix E.

General Editor Requirements

Both the Title Index Editor and the Page Index Editor now have their specific functionality defined. Next comes the definition of general requirements for both editors. This example illustrates a very good principle for specifications: Where you can, be general, and be specific only when you have to be. Even in a general section, there's nothing wrong with introducing specific instances. As long as the information flows and doesn't contradict the earlier specifications, you have no problem. Always remember that we're talking about good and unambiguous communications.

---

9. Common Requirements for the Editors
This section describes requirements that are general to both the Title Index Editor and the Page Index Editor.

9.1. Navigation Functions
At any given moment, in **Alert 1 Normal State**, the editors are displaying a current entry from the Memory Index. Navigation requirements are as follows:

<<	Go to Start Entry; causes entry 1 to become the current entry.
>>	Go to Last Entry; causes last entry to become the current entry.
>	Go to Next Entry; causes current entry +1 to be displayed and become current.
<	Go to Previous Entry; causes current entry −1 to be displayed and become current.

If, during the **Next** and **Previous** navigations, the user encounters the last or first entry, a message indicating start or end of index, as appropriate, is required.

Note that the Page Index Editor's navigation functions are the same as the viewer program's functions.

9.2. Index Manipulation Functions
The Add, Insert, Overwrite, and Delete buttons control these functions.

9.2.1. Adding an Entry to the Index
At any stage, in any combination of alert states, it is required that the user can request that the screen contents be added to the current Memory Index. The Index is increased in size by one, and the data fields of this newly created last entry are updated from screen. The screen display then indicates the last entry number of the Index. The disk version of the Index remains unchanged. The program now returns to the **Alert 1 Normal State** if it was not already in it. If the program was in **Alert 2 Normal State**, it is switched to **Alert 2 Changed State**.

9.2.2. Inserting an Entry into the Index

At any stage, in any combination of alert states, it is required that the user can request that the screen contents are inserted into the Memory Index at the current entry number. Before this action is performed, all the entries from the current entry number to the end of the Index are moved one entry up (that is, the content of entry number *n* is moved to entry number *n*+1 and so on). The screen content is then moved into the current entry number. This has the effect of increasing the Index by one entry and inserting the new entry at the current position, pushing all other entries up one place. The program then returns to **Alert 1 Normal State** (if it was not already in it), displaying the newly created current entry. No change is made to the disk Index file; consequently, the program is switched into **Alert 2 Changed State**.

9.2.3. Overwrite an Entry in the Index

At any stage, in any combination of alert states, it is required that the user can request that the screen contents are used to overwrite those of the current entry number in memory. The program then returns to **Alert 1 Normal State** (if it was not already in it) and shows the new content of the current entry number. No change is made to the disk Index file; the program, therefore, switches to **Alert 2 Changed State**.

9.2.4. Delete the Current Entry

The **Delete** function is available only when the program is in **Alert 1 Normal State**. When the program is in **Alert 1 Changed State**, the Delete button is replaced by the Release button. When Delete is requested, the current entry is removed from the Memory Index. The program remains in **Alert 1 Normal State** but is switched into **Alert 2 Changed State**. The function results in the Index size being reduced by one, and all entries after the one being deleted are reduced by one entry. The new current entry is then displayed on screen.

9.2.5. Release

When the program is in **Alert 1 Changed State**, the Delete button is replaced with the Release button. The user can abort the changes that have been made to screen objects by clicking the Release button. The Release button causes the program to switch into **Alert 1 Normal State**, and the screen is updated from the current entry in memory. No change occurs to whatever is the current **Alert 2** state.

9.3. Index Updating

Additions, deletions, modifications, and insertions are not stored to disk as they are performed. These actions are written to disk only when the user issues an instruction to do so, as an **Index Save** file operation. Until that stage, all changes that have occurred in the Memory Index since it was loaded, or since the previous disk update, can be aborted, if required, by the user reopening the Index file. The Index is then reinstated to the condition it was in after the previous save to disk. The disk Index requirements are detailed in the next section.

9.3.1. New Index

The user may elect to create a new, blank Index, in which case the program is cleared and made ready to accept data. The Index File Name box is set blank. Program states are set to **Alert 1 Normal State** and **Alert 2 Normal State**. This function cannot be used when the program is in **Alert 1 Changed State**.

9.3.2. Open Index

When the program is in **Alert 1 Normal State**, the user is allowed to search the file store and select any file to be input as an Index file. If the file is not the correct type, an error message results, and the Index is cleared. If the file is of the right type, it is read into memory, and the contents of Entry 1 are displayed. The program is then made ready to accept changes. Program states are set to **Alert 1 Normal State** and **Alert 2 Normal State**. This function cannot be used when the program is in **Alert 1 Changed State**.

9.3.3. Save Index As

When the program is in **Alert 1 Normal State**, the user can save the contents of the current Memory Index as a named file. The user can select a file from the file store, and this file will be overwritten by the contents of the in-Memory Index. Alternatively, the user can create a new file to hold the Index. Program states are set to **Alert 1 Normal State** and **Alert 2 Normal State**. This function cannot be used when the program is in **Alert 1 Changed State**.

9.3.4. Save Index

When the program is in **Alert 1 Normal State**, the content of the in-Memory Index can be saved to the file named in the **Index File Name** data field. The content of the in-Memory Index overwrites the current content of the disk file. If no named Index file is open, then the Save Index As option is automatically invoked. Program states are set to **Alert 1 Normal State** and **Alert 2 Normal State**. This function cannot be used when the program is in **Alert 1 Changed State**.

Common Requirements Comments

The last set of definitions is all very straightforward and easy to read—there's just a lot of it. Have you noticed how the requirements specification often reads like a user guide? In fact, it will be used as the basis of the user guide, which will follow its content quite closely (nice bit of reusability).

At long last, we'd come to the end of the requirements specification. You should now have a good understanding of what the software we will design and develop in the rest of this book must do. Our next task was to do some detailed planning. We now had all the information we needed to begin work on drawing up a detailed plan to complete a project. We had to produce a fixed-price quotation to design the complete system, develop and test all the required modules, integrate them, and test the system.

We'd already committed to a plan, based on the work that we had done in the presales effort, so it would be hard to change any of the milestones, but, between milestones, we had some flexibility.

Detailed Planning

Before you start any detailed planning, it is vital that you review all the documentation you have produced so far in the project. This review ensures that you have all the required details fresh in mind before you start the plan.

Juggling

Planning a software development project is a real juggling act. You must juggle resources and activities to fit into the initial plan around the milestones you have already established. You produce a plan that ensures that resources are available when required and they are kept busy when they're engaged on project work.

Development Tasks

You've now reached a stage where you need to define a set of development activities or tasks. Each task should consist of the development of one or more of the self-contained functional modules that you defined in analysis. Wrapped around this will be a *test harness*, which is code developed to glue the module(s) together in a standalone test environment. Ideally, a single programmer can complete each task.

Let's use an example from the case study. We needed to develop a search facility for the viewer. We'd defined two modules that related to searching: **Set Up For Search**, a GUI-based module using the search criteria panel, and a pure module called **Perform Search**. If we developed both together as a single development task, we could create a test harness that would check searching fully as a standalone test program. We would need to supply a Memory Index that contained entries with lots of test keys, and this would serve as the test bed. We could run the test program, set up selections, and perform searches through the test Index.

Definition of Development Task

We must define a set of development tasks that would let us develop each functional module and test it, either on its own, or in conjunction with other modules. To create a development task, we needed to define the following:

- ◆ The modules that we would develop.

- ◆ The modules already developed that we needed to embed in the test environment.

- ◆ Relevant notes, particularly concerning verification of functionality.

List of Modules

We listed all the modules that would be developed as part of the programmer's task. These were the modules we defined in analysis. As you probably recall, we had given each a title, a description, and a list of inputs and outputs. Each module was a self-contained entity (remember the black-box concept) that we could test and verify in isolation from the rest of the system.

Dependencies

We defined any dependencies on other development tasks. Continuing with the search example I started earlier: The search development task could make use of a test Index that we created artificially and installed as part of the test environment. However, a much better idea would be to embed the modules that allow the user to select a Page Index file for input and the module that allows the user to input a specified Page Index file. The likelihood was high that these modules would be developed in another development task. Consequently, if we placed a dependency on the task that developed those modules, we could plan the search module in such a way that it would start after the Index file modules had been developed. That would let us pick up the newly developed and tested modules and integrate them into the test environment for checking search functionality. We now had a much more comprehensive testing capability that would let us load different Index files that could be created using standard text editors.

For each development task, then, we must list all the other tasks on which that task was dependent. The task could not be started before the required dependent modules were available because we would need them to complete the test program.

Notes

As part of the definition for a development task, we would jot down any notes that were applicable and relevant to planning. Of particular importance was how we would verify the functionality being developed in the various modules. Other aspects might be to indicate that a number of test files would have to be created. Basically, we would add anything that would affect the estimates for the task or its planning.

Scheduling

After we had established a complete list of all the tasks and activities that we needed to conduct to complete the project, we would need to schedule them. In the simplest form of schedule, a single person performs each activity, and no activities are performed in parallel. You start performing the first activity; when it's finished, you move on to the second activity; and so on. If you are ahead of schedule, you move on to the next activity and start it early. If you're behind schedule, you must try to make up the time lost by finishing subsequent activities early. This situation is quite straightforward and similar to how we'd planned and executed the case study up to the end of analysis. Even though we had three people working on the project, we were executing none of the activities in parallel—we were performing them one after the other.

The planning now started to become more complex because we were going to run activities in parallel, with more than one person involved. We also had dependencies to consider. You can see our planning and scheduling in action in the following sections.

Return to Case Study:
Development Tasks for the Viewer

Our first job as part of the planning exercise was to form the lists of GUI and pure functionality modules into development tasks. Each would be a self-contained development activity for a single programmer to take on. The result would be a test program that would let the developer verify the developed modules' functionality. In this section, we'll look at the reasoning we used for setting up the self-contained development tasks for the viewer.

Title Handling

We started by defining a development task called *Title Handling* for the viewer. To make the enterprise sensible, we made it up from the GUI-bound function **Title Selection** (selecting a title from the list of available titles) and the pure function: **Read a Specified Title Index Into Program,** which was a general, non GUI requirement. These two modules together gave us a self-contained chunk of development. We would have to set up a test harness that would let the tester select a test file and feed this name to the module that read in a Title Index file. The test harness would then invoke the **Title Selection** module to display the titles in a combo box. When a title was selected, the test harness would then be used to place the strings that define the content of the selected entry in view.

We'd defined a self-contained development task with no dependencies (that is, it could be developed without having to wait for anything else to be completed). Because the task was producing a fairly key general module—the ability to read a specified Title Index file—other modules might depend on its completion.

Our goals were to make any code we developed as a test harness as simple as possible—to require a minimum of code to coherently check out the functionality of the modules. We defined the development task as follows:

Development Task Name: Title Handling

Component Modules:
Read a Specified Title Index into Program, Title Selection (display list of titles and allow user to select a single item).

Notes:
(a) Test harness required to allow selection of test files.

(b) Test harness required to display strings from selected Index entry.

(c) Need to prepare test Title Index files.

(d) Visual inspection of title, description, and Page Index file reference strings will verify operation.

As it stood, we believed that a single programmer could develop the above task quite easily. We had defined our first development task.

Page Index Handling

For the viewer, Page Index handling would amount to two functional modules: **Read A Specified Page Index Into The Program** and **Clear Page Index**. We would require a test harness that would let us select a test file for input and some simple code to let us navigate through the Memory Index, displaying the strings of each entry, in turn, for verification. This procedure would let us confirm that each entry of the test Index had been read correctly into memory.

We'd defined another self-contained development task to select a Page Index and read the named file into memory, having first cleared the Index. This single development task allowed us to develop all the required modules and check them out in a self-contained manner. We would, of course, have to create a few Page Index test examples. Here's the definition of the development task:

Development Task Name: Read Page Index

Component Modules:
Read a Specified Page Index into Program.

Clear Page Index.

Notes:
(a) Test harness required to select test Index files.

(b) Test harness required to navigate through Index and show each entry's strings—this will allow verification of functionality.

(c) Need to prepare test Page Index files.

We also believed that a single programmer could accomplish this task.

Display Page

The Display Page functionality would provide a fairly meaty task if we threw in all the modules to load and display the basic data entities. As a single development task, the programmer would have to develop each module in turn before the Display Page function could be completed. We wanted to be able to develop the modules in parallel, so we had to define each as a development task in its own right. Consequently, the task to develop Display Page functionality couldn't be started until we had completed those modules. That task was, therefore, dependent upon those modules. We could indicate this dependency by listing the modules as dependent development tasks rather than modules for development within this task. Here's the definition:

Development Task Name: Display Page

Component Modules:
Display Page.

Dependent Development Tasks:
Load and Display Image.

Load and Display Video.

Load and Display Text.

Load and Play WAV Sound File.

Load and Play MID Music File.

Notes:

(a) Test harness required to emulate Page Index structure for calling Display Page function.

(b) Test images, videos, text files, WAV files, and MID files will be required.

As note (a) indicates, we would have to emulate an Index entry structure that contained the appropriate file references to supply to the module.

Dependent Tasks

We could now define all the development tasks on which Display Page was dependent. Remember, we were defining them as separate tasks so different people could develop them in parallel.

Development Task Name: Display Image

Component Modules:
Load and Display Image.

Notes:

(a) Test harness required to let user select an image for display.

(b) Will require test images of varying sizes (BMP and JPEG).

Development Task Name: Play Video

Component Modules:
Load and Play Video.

Notes:

(a) Test harness required to let user select a video for playing.

(b) Will require test videos with and without sound tracks.

Development Task Name: Display Text

Component Modules:
Load and Display Text.

Notes:

(a) Test harness required to let user select a text file for display.

(b) Will require test text files of varying text volumes.

Development Task Name: Play Sound

Component Modules:
Load and Play WAV Sound File.

Load and Play MID Music File.

Notes:
(a) Test harness required to let user select a sound file for playing.

(b) Will require test WAV and MID files.

A single person could develop each of the above tasks. When the tasks were all complete, they could be integrated into the Display Page task, which could then be completed.

Workbench

The Workbench formed another development package with possible dependencies. However, in this case, we decided there probably wasn't sufficient work to run the development of the component modules in parallel, so we lumped it all together as a single development task:

Development Task Name: Workbench

Component Modules:
Display Workbench.

Workbench Screen Object Positioning.

Workbench Screen Object Manipulation.

Print Content of Workbench.

Notes:
(a) Test images (BMP and JPEG), videos, and text files will be required.

(b) Printer required.

Clearly, Display Workbench is the functionality invoked when the user switches the viewer from Page View mode to Workbench mode. The other modules will involve setting up full drag-and-drop capability for the image, text, and main form; and the sizing functions will involve setting up the toolbar display. We had another self-contained development task that would provide us with full Workbench capability, and it was suitable for development by a single programmer. If our estimates indicated that doing the component modules in parallel was sensible, they would become development tasks in their own right, and the preceding references would change to "dependencies" of the task to develop Display Workbench.

Searching

Searching would consist of setting up search criteria and then actually performing a search. However, we really needed a Page Index to work from. Consequently, we could make the search dependent on completion of the Read Page Index development task. With this task available to us, we could develop a full-scale search module:

Development Task Name: Search

Component Modules:
Set Up Search Criteria.

Perform Search.

Dependent Development Tasks:
Read Page Index.

Notes:
(a) Test Page Index set up with keywords will be required.

(b) Verification achieved by visual inspection.

This dependency would affect when this task would be performed relative to the other tasks in the plan.

Navigation

We could define a navigation development task as follows:

Development Task Name: Page Navigation

Component Modules:
Page Index Navigation.

Dependent Development Tasks:
Read Page Index.

Notes:
(a) Test Page Index will be required.

(b) Verification achieved by visual inspection.

Making this module dependent on the Read Page Index module seemed sensible because doing so would save a lot of effort building code to populate an in-memory Index to test navigation. The test only needed to take the requested entry's data and display the strings on screen or in the debug window. All we needed was to produce something that we could check against the content of the test file we used.

Ready for Integration

We now had a comprehensive set of self-contained development tasks, with clearly defined dependencies for building the components of a viewer. If we thoroughly tested each task, then integration would be a breeze. However, we would still have code to develop in integration—code to glue the modules together.

Development Tasks for the Title Index Editor

Let's now discuss the development tasks we established for the Title Index Editor.

Open Command

According to the requirements specification, the user would be able to open and load a Title Index file by using an Open command from a drop-down menu (see the description of the Title Index Editor's form layout in Chapter 4). This description provided a useful piece of self-contained development that we could define as follows:

Development Task Name: Load Title Index

Component Modules:
Select a Title Index for Input.

Dependent Development Tasks:
Title Handling (Module: Read a Specified Title Index into Memory) (developed for viewer).

Notes:
(a) Test harness required to check whether Title Index contents are read in correctly.

(b) Need to prepare test Title Index files.

(c) Verification of functionality can be achieved by navigating through Index and displaying strings of each entry.

Save

Two types of Save functions would be required: a save to the currently opened file and a save to a file named by a user, usually referred to as Save and Save As functions. Together, these functions would form a self-contained development block. However, to make the block more meaningful, we'd place a dependency on the first task we defined, Open Title Index. Within the Save development task, this would allow us to open a file, read it in, and then output back to the same file, or to another one, to test all the combinations of the Save functionality. We could verify the functionality by checking the input and output files for consistency.

Development Task Name: Save Title index

Component Modules:
Select a File Name for Title Index Output.

Output a Title Index to Selected Disk File.

Dependent Development Tasks:
Load Title Index.

Notes:
(a) Title Indexes can be read in using Open, and combinations of Save and Save As tested.

(b) Need to prepare test Title Index files.

(c) Verification achieved by checking input and output files.

Navigation

We could define the navigation module in a similar manner to the definition we had used for the viewer:

Development Task Name: Title Navigation

Component Modules:
Title Index Navigation.

Dependent Development Tasks:
Load Title Index.

Notes:
(a) Test Title Index will be required.

(b) Record content can be displayed as strings to verify that navigation is correct.

Just as with navigation for the viewer, we could set up a test program that used the code module developed in the Load Title Index development task to allow the tester to define a Title Index file, which would then be read into the program data structures. We could verify navigation by selecting the required entry and displaying the strings that made up its data fields.

Change Handling

We'd defined what the Title Index Editor form must look like when a change on screen or the like would occur. We could set up a self-contained development task to perform Change Handling, as we'd call it.

Development Task Name: Change Handling

Component Modules:
Title Entry Edit Functionality.

Notes:
(a) This will require dummy operation of all buttons and drop-down menus required by Title Editor.

(b) Only code required will concern change handling.

(c) Verification achieved by monitoring alert color changes.

(d) Includes **Alert 1** and **Alert 2** state handling.

Change Handling is concerned with changing the program's state when a screen object is modified, disabling the navigation controls, and handling an Index request in terms of returning to the normal state.

Index Manipulation

The editor needed to be able to let a user add to, delete from, insert into, and overwrite the current content of the Title Index. These were standard Index manipulation functions that we could constitute as a single development, which we defined as follows:

Development Task Name: Index Manipulation

Component Modules:
Add/Delete/Insert/Overwrite Title Index Functionality.

Dependent Development Tasks:
Load Title Index.

Change Handling.

Notes:
(a) Test Title Index will be required.

(b) Index can be loaded and Memory Index can be modified.

(c) Verification provided by simple navigation and display of entry strings.

(d) Title Index test files will be required.

Clearly, we needed to be able to load an Index file; hence, the dependency on Load Title Index. We could build a test harness that showed the current record's three fields, allow us to modify them, and then let us use one of the Add/Insert or Overwrite functions to modify the Index. Verification could come from stepping through the Index, or even printing it in the debug window and checking the strings held after one or more operations had occurred. Because we were changing data fields on screen, having another dependency on Change Handling seemed sensible. That way, we could build required functionality more efficiently, integrating it at development time. Leaving the required functionality to system integration could cause more work than necessary for such a simple set of functionality.

And that defined the modules for the Title Index Editor development. Now, we had to do the same thing for the Page Index Editor, but, clearly, that would follow quite closely what we had already done here.

Development Modules for the Page Index Editor

The first thing we needed to do was set up the viewer functionality within the editor.

Viewer Functionality

We could define a development module to set up the viewer functionality within the page editor as follows:

Development Task Name: Set Up Viewer Functionality

Component Modules:
Complete suite of viewer modules.

Notes:
(a) Testing will consist of showing that complete viewer functionality is available within the editor environment.

Once we had completed this task, it gave us all the functionality of the viewer embedded into the editor.

Tasks Similar to Title Index Editor

The rest of the development tasks required for the Page Index Editor, apart from file selection, were based on those we had defined for the Title Index Editor, as follows:

Development Task Name: Load Page Index

Component Modules:
Select a Page Index File for Input.

Dependent Development Tasks:
Read Page Index (developed for viewer).

Notes:
(a) Test harness required to check that Page Index contents are read correctly.

(b) Need to prepare test Page Index files.

Development Task Name: Save Page Index

Component Modules:
Select a File Name for Page Index Output.

Output a Page Index to Selected Disk File.

Dependent Development Tasks:
Load Page Index.

Notes:
(a) Page Indexes can be read using Open and combinations of Save and Save As tested.

(b) Need to prepare test Page Index files.

(c) Verification achieved by checking input and output files.

Development Task Name: Change Handling

Component Modules:
Page Entry Edit Functionality.

Notes:
(a) This will require dummy operation of all buttons and drop-down menus required by Page Index Editor.

(b) Only code required will concern change handling.

(c) Verification achieved by monitoring alert color changes.

(d) Includes **Alert 1** and **Alert 2** handling.

Development Task Name: Index Manipulation

Component Modules:
Add/Delete/Insert/Overwrite Page Index Functionality.

Dependent Development Tasks:
Load Page Index.

Change Handling.

Notes:
(a) Test Page Index will be required.

(b) Index can be loaded and Memory Index can be modified.

(c) Verification provided by simple navigation and display of entry strings.

(d) Page Index test files will be required.

Navigation

We established a development task called Navigation for the Title Index Editor. The equivalent Page Index Navigation would be supplied by the viewer functionality embedded in the Page Index Editor. Therefore, we had no need to develop an equivalent task.

File Selection

If you recall, file handling consisted of the functions required to select and load one of the multimedia or text files from the File Selection form. We could define File Selection as a single development task that could make use of the some of the basic modules that we would develop to accommodate the Display Page development task. File Selection really defined the development of the form itself, with the code required to select files and view the resultant object. Here is the definition:

Development Task Name: File Selection

Component Modules:
File Selection from Associated Code.

Dependent Development Tasks:
Display Image.

Play Video.

Display Text.

Play Sound.

Notes:
(a) The development module consists of the code to "glue" together the main functions of file selection, and to load and display objects.

(b) Test files will be required for images, text, videos, WAV files, and MID files.

Copy and Paste

Then, we had a very specific Page Index Editor development task: the capability to copy and paste an Index entry.

Development Task Name: Copy and Paste

Component Modules:
Copy.

Paste.

Dependent Development Tasks:
Load Page Index.

Save Page Index.

Change Handling.

Notes:
(a) Full access to Page Index will be required such that an entry can be copied and pasted at different points.

(b) Verification can be achieved by reading in an Index, performing a number of copy-and-paste functions, and then outputting the resultant Index for comparison with original.

(c) Test Page Indices will be required.

This task would give us the capability to move entries around in the Index.

Text Handling

We also had to develop some text-handling capability. One development task was, first, to produce text Save and Save As facilities and, second, to produce a capability to set font. Because these would be fairly simple tasks, we'd also include functions to clear keys, text content, and file references.

Development Task Name: Text Save

Component Modules:
Select File Name for Text Output.

Output Content of Text Object to Specified File Name.

Dependent Development Tasks:
Display Text (developed for viewer).

Notes:

(a) Set up a text box into which input can be directed and then request this input to be saved to a named file.

(b) Verification achieved by comparing output file with text box.

Development Task Name: Text Font and Clear

Component Modules:
Font Set.

Clear Text.

Clear File References.

Clear Keys.

Auxiliary Tasks

In your software development project, you've now established a comprehensive list of development tasks/activities. To complete a plan, you need to add all the auxiliary tasks that make up a software development project. These are as follows:

♦ Production of test specifications

♦ Production of user documentation

♦ Integration of all developed modules

♦ System testing

♦ Installation and setup

♦ Acceptance testing

♦ Support

Production of Test Specifications

Although you can create test specifications by converting the scenarios, you must schedule someone to do the work. Armed with the requirements specification and scenarios, a competent tester can create all the required test scenarios. (This work was particularly easy for the case study because the requirements specification contained screen layouts.) You will typically schedule this activity in parallel with development activities.

If it's feasible, show the requirements specification to the person who will do the job of producing test specifications and ask for an estimate of how long that person believes it will take. Add a bit of contingency time to whatever quote you receive.

Tip
Remember when you are scheduling time for the development of test specifications to include the time it will take the person tasked with the job to get up to speed (that is, read the requirements specification and become reasonably proficient in the domain).

Production of User Documentation

To a large extent, producing user documentation is much like developing the test specifications. Where possible, show the technical author the specifications and ask for a time frame. User guides are best done after the software is stable enough to hand over to the customer.

NOTE: *The software doesn't need to be 100 percent robust for documentation to begin; in fact, the documentation people will serve as more testers for the software.*

Integration of All Developed Modules

After you have developed, tested, and verified all the software modules as complete, you can integrate them. You will almost certainly have to write some code to knit together all the components. We will refer to this process as *infrastructure code development*.

During the integration process, you might discover problems associated with the interfaces between modules, so you'll need to schedule some rework time at this stage—as well as that all-important contingency time.

Tip
You might be able to integrate collections of modules as and when they become available, rather than wait until all the modules have been completed and verified. Where possible, this approach is recommended, because it lets you keep ahead of the situation. If you leave everything until the end, you risk the possibility of being overwhelmed with integration issues. The importance of part integration increases according to the size of the project, but, for large-scale projects, being able to perform integration in a series of phases (rather than all in one go) provides a clear advantage.

System Testing

The amount of system testing you have to do depends on how well the modules were designed, developed, and tested. The more care and attention to detail given at these earlier stages, the less system testing you are likely to have to perform. In an ideal world, after the system was bolted together, all you would have to do would be to run the acceptance tests. However, life is seldom that simple.

Again, on large-scale projects, phased integration and testing enormously eases the pain of system testing. Whether large or small, the system is being exercised for the first time; consequently, you *expect* to find bugs. This is when you want to see faults. The minimum testing you should perform is based on the acceptance tests. In reality, you should be inventing new tests and trying out combinations of usage all the time. Because you are expecting bugs, you need to schedule time for performing the tests; discussing, reporting, and fixing bugs; and then testing all over again (*regression testing*). (We will discuss regression testing in more detail in a future chapter.)

Installation and Setup

After you have a system up and running and fully tested, you need to take it down and install it on the customer's site. You set up the system there and make it ready for acceptance testing.

Tip

Running through as many of the acceptance tests as you can as part of setting up at the customer site is well worth the effort. The final environment on which the system is to run may well be impossible to emulate in full back at the factory. Consequently, a run-through of all—or well-targeted—aspects of acceptance testing is well worth your while.

Acceptance Testing

We don't want to see any bugs here. You need to schedule time to help guide the client through the testing, and to handle issues if and when they arise. If any bugs do materialize, you need to handle them formally and not, under any circumstances, on-site in an ad hoc manner—that would be a recipe for disaster. Consequently, you need to put plenty of contingency time into the plan so you can be available on-site to manage and guide the acceptance process.

Tip

Acceptance testing on big or complex projects can run into a series of phases, such as controlled acceptance testing, alpha testing on a genuine live environment, and beta testing (We will look at alpha and beta testing in detail later). Always remember to ensure that if anything goes wrong you have a fallback position to allow the client to recover his or her business operation if the new software fails catastrophically. (A later chapter will include more on this topic.)

Support

Once you make it through acceptance testing, you will still have a development involvement in support. For a new system, the developers are the best people to support the *software—not* the *application*—(a subtlety software houses often miss) until such time you can hand over a fully documented system to support. This is a big subject we will discuss at length in a later chapter. It is important that this involvement is accounted for in the master plan.

Return to the Case Study:
Working Out the Plan

We'd now produced three lists for development tasks to build the viewer, the Title Index Editor, and the Page Index Editor. Most of the tasks were familiar from the presales phase, when we had determined standalone functional requirements. Due to the results of analysis and the development of the requirements specification in general, we had added more development requirements. Those requirements were now defined in the lists that we completed in the last visit to the case study. We also had a list of auxiliary activities that we needed to schedule.

To build a plan, we needed to do the following:

♦ *Place all the activities and tasks on a spreadsheet*—Into which we could place our min-max estimates, similar to what we did in the presales phase, but with a much more comprehensive list of activities.

♦ *Produce a plan for design*—To encompass design of the entire system.

♦ *Produce a plan for completion of the viewer*—To be done by the end of the eighth week in the project.

♦ *Produce a plan for completion of the editors*—To follow the viewer after the eighth week in the project.

The juggling process of trying to come up with a plan commenced on Wednesday afternoon, and we had a plan by mid-morning Thursday. We had juggled time schedules, resources, and dependencies, and produced a detailed plan of action.

The Spreadsheet Estimates

We filled in the spreadsheet with the activities to complete all three programs—as well as the auxiliary tasks. All three of us did our min-max calculations and arrived at numbers with which we felt comfortable. (You've seen the process before, so I won't go through it again.) The end results will be apparent from the plans you will see.

Design and Test Scripts

The first thing we established was that design would take three to four days. To be perfectly safe, we settled on three days, with two days for contingency time. That process would take up the whole of the project's Week 4, consistent with the time we had allocated in the presales phase.

We would start the design process by defining the Index file layouts, and then proceed with viewer functions, followed by editor functions. Figure 5.2 shows this plan, together with a schedule for producing the test specifications.

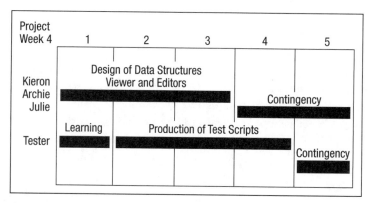

Figure 5.2

Plan for E-MagBook design and test specification production.

We had allocated five days to complete both tasks: design and test-specification production. For test-specification production, we had one day to get up to speed, three days for production, and one day for contingency time. We had not yet named an individual to do the work, but, at the start-up meeting, we had made the head of the testing team aware of that group's likely involvement.

Risk Assessment

We had two days' contingency time for design, and three people would be involved, so there was a good chance one or more person would be available during the contingency time, should the three days prove to be inadequate. We also had a weekend as a last resort. The risk lay in the fact that the design must be complete by the start of Week 4 so development could begin.

The production of the test specifications was far less of a risk. Not completing them by the end of the week would not be a problem because they wouldn't be required until system testing.

Tip

When time schedules are not critical, I advise not to broadcast that fact to the project team. Doing so can result in complacency setting in. If people think that completing a task by the designated deadline isn't vital, the task has a good chance of dropping in priority in their eyes. Give people deadlines, and expect them to meet those deadlines.

If mitigating circumstances arise, make sure you are party to the decision-making process to slip the schedule. When a noncritical time frame is slipped, increase its priority to avoid having it slip again. Slippage, even in noncritical paths, is unhealthy.

Viewer Development

Development of the viewer required scheduling the development tasks such that they would have built-in contingency time. We must allocate sufficient time to test the module and have

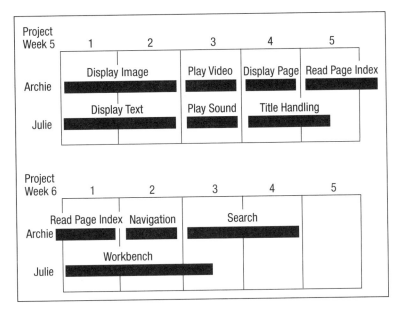

Figure 5.3
E-MagBook plan for development of the viewer.

it verified. (We'll look at testing requirements in development in the next chapter.) Figure 5.3 shows the plan required to develop the viewer modules by the end of Week 5, in accordance with the initial plan we had developed during the pre-sales effort.

We had Archie developing the Display Image and Play Video modules, while Julie was working on Display Text and Play Sound. If all went according to plan, both should be finished at the end of Day 3, and Archie could begin the Display Page module, which was dependent on all the aforementioned modules. Meanwhile, Julie started work on the Title Selection module. Archie then moved on to Read Page Index, followed by Navigation and Search. After Julie completed Title Selection, she would move on to Workbench.

Risk Assessment

As you can see in Figure 5.3, we had varying degrees of contingency time available—one day for Archie and almost three total for Julie. If Archie ran into any problems, or we couldn't get the required availability from him, we could use Julie's contingency time to assist.

If things went very badly, we could extend development into Week 6 because the milestone was an internal one. However, this would have an add-on effect to integration, system testing, and acceptance. The bottom line was that we must deliver a completed system, fully tested, to the client at the start of Week 8. We could, therefore, manage any issues by sliding around schedules, with the proviso that we must meet the drop deadline at the start of Week 8. Together with built-in contingency, we believed we had minimized the risks.

Viewer Integration and Testing; Start of Documentation

To be honest, we had little idea how long integration would take and how long we would need to test the functionality using the acceptance tests. We were all reasonably comfortable that we could achieve both in one week. So, we'd allocated just two-and-a-half days for each activity, as Figure 5.4 shows. In fact, when we completed integration, we would move on at once to system testing. We anticipated that both Archie and Julie would be working at 80 percent availability on each activity. Also as indicated in Figure 5.4, we started the production of the user documentation at this stage.

Risk Assessment

This level of testing was vitally important. We couldn't afford for the activities in this week to slip (with the exception of documentation) because we must deliver the tested software at the start of the following week. We would need to monitor progress carefully. Our developers would do initial testing, but Julie and Archie would not conduct the first pass at system testing. They would be totally free to handle all issues.

NOTE: *Letting developers system test the software they developed can be a disaster—they know too much. Use independent testers—people who have no knowledge of the code, only of the requirements. (More on this subject later.)*

Installation and Acceptance Testing; Completion of Docmentation

Once again, we were unsure about how much time acceptance testing would require. We had allocated a whole day to installation and setup, which gave us plenty of contingency time. The rest of the time, we needed to be available to address issues and assist in the acceptance-testing process. We should also complete the documentation for the viewer in this week. Figure 5.5 shows all activities.

Risk Assessment

Contrary to what you might think, this was not a time to relax. The customer might well be doing the testing, but this was the first time Montasana would have access to the system. Consequently, we needed to be ready to do a lot of hand-holding in the form of guidance and

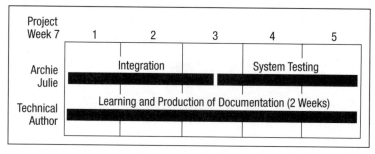

Figure 5.4

E-MagBook viewer integration, system testing, and start of documentation.

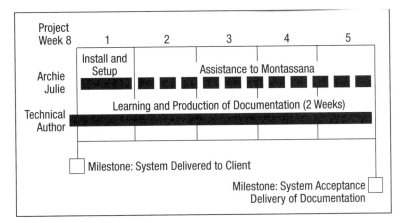

Figure 5.5
Installation and acceptance testing of the viewer, and documentation completion.

assistance. However, we must be careful not to perform the acceptance testing—the client needed to do this. Managing the client during this process was vital so that time was not wasted and the client felt able to sign off on the testing at the end of the period. We must record and address all issues. We didn't expect bugs. We did, however, expect to have issues concerning functionality. (More on this later.)

Editor Development

Development of the editors would occur over a three-week period, in project Weeks 9, 10, and 11, as Figure 5.6 shows.

In the Page Index Editor plan, we decided that change handling was a little more than a day's work, but, when we put the plan together, we found that we would have to do change-handling development in two rounds. The first round would involve the data fields, and the second round would include the file-selection change handling, which wouldn't be finished until the end of the penultimate day—hence, our reasoning behind splitting up change handling as you see it.

Editor Integration and Testing

We were now into Week 12, as Figure 5.7 shows. We'd set up a similar plan to the one we had for the viewer. If you recall, we had some spare time in the first week of editor development, and we might well be able to use that time for Title Index Editor integration, because it was a relatively simple program.

Editor Installation and Acceptance

The final week, project Week 13, as Figure 5.8 shows, was identical to the plan for the viewer's integration.

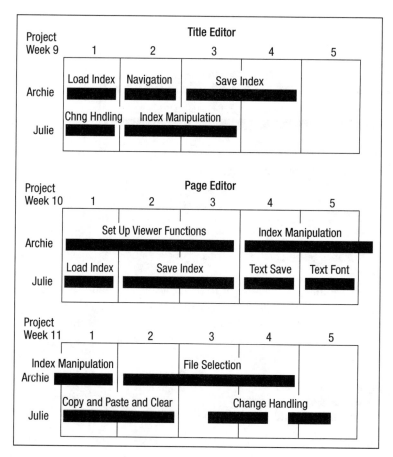

Figure 5.6
E-MagBook Editor development plan.

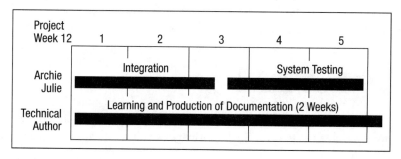

Figure 5.7
Editor integration and testing.

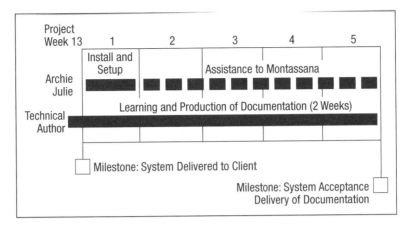

Figure 5.8
Editor installation and acceptance.

Buying In

Both Archie and Julie had been involved in the production of the requirements specification, its analysis, and the construction of the plans. Now, I wanted *them* to be responsible for the plan. But, first, I needed to ensure that they were both comfortable with this request.

Julie felt confident because she now knew so much about multimedia handling that she didn't have any real misgivings about the project. The plan had flexibility and contingency, we had looked at the risks, and we always had expertise in the rest of the company to fall back on. Archie also felt comfortable. All the preparation had made him feel that he really understood what he had to produce.

We had built in contingency to each module (possibly some more than others) and had free time in the plan as well. Both programmers agreed that they accepted the plans and would be responsible for making sure the milestones were met. I had a "buy in" to the project from my programmers.

So what's my point here? All too often, programmers have time schedules imposed on them. Sometimes, before they even start work, they know they don't have a hope of meeting the schedules. Charlie and I try to get the programmers to come up with their own time estimates (possibly negotiating and guiding here and there, but at the end of the day getting them to "buy in" to the process). We don't pay any overtime unless something happens over which they have no control and overtime is demanded. If the project they have bought into runs late, we expect them to do something about it. We monitor progress tightly, as you will see. But it's down to Archie and Julie now. The reward? If they deliver on time or early, then they have a great sense of satisfaction. We pay above-average salaries, and we expect commitment. Motivation is very important—but so, too, is this concept of the "buy in."

NOTE: *Bonus payments can help to motivate, but you need to make sure you're not using bonuses to compensate for poor basic salaries. If you regularly hand out bonus payments, people will start expecting them as a matter of course, not as a reward.*

Return to the Case Study:
The End of Project Phase 1

It was now late Thursday morning, and we had a plan and a new quote for Monty. He and Samantha were still going through the requirements specification. We received another call from Monty, who wanted to know if we could help Samantha set up some examples of the browser in action and also display a couple of composites. To display composites, Samantha simply created a single bitmapped image from a number of others and placed text across it. (Provided we did this very carefully so that the image onto which we placed the text was the same size as it would be when we viewed it on the E-MagBook, the quality of the combined bitmap—image plus text—would be acceptable. If the image had to be compressed to fit into the E-MagBook's image area, the text would become corrupted and difficult to read.) This extra work took up most of Thursday afternoon and a little of Friday morning, but, once again, Monty was paying for the time.

Both Monty and Samantha accepted the specification without reservation, agreed to the plans, and gave us the go-ahead to start design. This approval arrived late Friday morning as Samantha was packing up to return to her office with prototype screenshots of composites and Web pages. Because we had worked hard to get to this stage, Charlie and I took Archie and Julie out to lunch—a very long lunch, and they did no further work that day. They deserved the break.

The Next Step

The requirements document was frozen. Changes would be accepted only through our change-control procedure. The same limitation applied to the models we had produced in analysis. Our plans were in place, and we had all the knowledge we needed to start the design.

Chapter 6
Design

Y ou've now reached a stage in your software development project where you can, at last, start asking the question, How do we produce a solution to meet the customer's requirements? You have defined the *what*; now, it's time for the *how*.

We'll start by looking at platform considerations before we move on to actual design. After that, we'll consider a testing strategy for development. Finally, we'll look at how we'll manage the development in terms of monitoring the progress of a number of parallel activities.

In the case study, we'd come a long way since the afternoon when we met Monty and Samantha. We'd captured the requirements in a specifications document, produced scenarios, and analyzed our findings. With the possible exception of the analysis, we'd done everything so far with the customer in mind—we'd written the requirements specification in plain English that anyone could understand.

All our hard work so far had paid off: We'd captured the concept on paper, and the customer had "signed off" on the specifications. We had a sound, contractual basis from which to proceed. It was the beginning of the fourth week of the project and time to start the software engineering process to turn the concept into code.

Choice of Platform

Ideally, you can determine the hardware and software platforms on which an application will run after you have completed the design. This ideal implies that the design is independent of platform—a truly noble aspiration. In reality, design centers on the chosen platform because that approach makes the process much easier and less risky. From analysis, you should have sufficient information to make a reasonable decision about what hardware and software to employ. Certainly, in the case study, the customer's requirements (PC-type hardware running Windows) tied us to a hardware and operating system platform.

One drawback of designing in a platform-independent manner is that you might need to do a lot of extra work to ensure that a particular platform can accommodate the entire design, including further detail about specifically what a programmer must do. The benefit of developing a platform-independent design, however, is that you can move between platforms without undermining the design itself.

A number of factors govern whether you choose platform-specific or platform-independent design. Such factors include the size and complexity of the project, the required database package (where one is needed), the anticipated lifetime of the application, the type of technology demanded, and so on. For enterprise solutions, in which the projects are large and the software will perform well into the future, a platform-independent design becomes not only more practical but also essential. Platform-independent design helps protect what is likely to be a substantial investment by the customer.

Choosing the Familiar

The temptation to choose what you are familiar with, particularly in programming languages, is difficult to avoid. After all, if you choose your favorite language, for example, you can see how you will implement a project from very early on. While your favorite language might well be suitable, don't assume so from the outset. Although you sometimes might find it difficult to make an objective platform decision, doing so is very important. Consequently, getting other peoples' opinions—and, for those opinions, trying to select individuals who don't have exactly the same preferences as you—is always a good idea.

Future Proofing

The lifespan of a typical database application might be from 3 years to 10 years, although I know of systems that have been running considerably longer than 10 years. The computer industry moves fast in terms of hardware improvements, but much more slowly for software innovations. Nevertheless, for a long-term application, the design must embody a high degree of future-proofing, which, in this context, implies the ability to survive and make use of new innovations that are likely to appear in the future. For example, you need to ask yourself, if you choose a product that's available from a single supplier, what's the likelihood of that supplier still being around in 5—or even 10—years? This thought can be quite sobering, and it lends a lot of support to the idea of platform-independent design.

Changing Technology

Database applications were initially developed around a large computer with many terminals connected to it. The next fundamental, evolutionary stage involved client/server applications, in which the terminals became PCs and much—if not all—of the application's "intelligence" moved out of the central machine to the terminals. Then came the ultimate client server, the Web.

You can see at least three major redesigns resulting from the above description. Clearly, an application based on a large mainframe will have to be redesigned to accommodate the client/server environment—or *will* it?

Modularity

The key to keeping pace with changing technology lies in an accurate analysis of the functional requirements. Let's look at an example. If you consider a simple inquiry system, in which a user logs onto a server and requests information, you can specify that requirement, whether the solution comes from a mainframe with lots of dumb terminals connected to it or from Web access via the Internet. What will change dramatically, depending on which of these solutions you choose, is the user interface—but not the basic requirements.

Consequently, you design with a high degree of modularity and try to encapsulate each module so that it presents a well-defined interface to the world. Everything else is hidden away. This approach provides a good chance that you can accommodate changing technology by simply unplugging one module and replacing it with another that makes use of the new technology. Provided that the single component that interfaces directly to the new technology services all the new requirements, you have *plug-compatible modules*.

Simple Model

The model shown in Figure 6.1 is a gross simplification of an application environment. The application has been split into four, clearly defined, functional entities: an input module and an output module that handle the user interface, a database-access module that handles all data requests, and, at the heart of the system, the data-processing module. Within the data-processing module lies all the business logic that dictates what is done with the input data to create output.

All the domain-specific functionality lies in the processing module. Clearly defined interfaces exist between the input and output modules to this processing unit as well as to the database module. Figure 6.2 shows the simple model running on a client/server database platform, using what's termed the *thick client* model. In the thick client model, the majority of the application exists and runs on the client. The database module is communicating with a

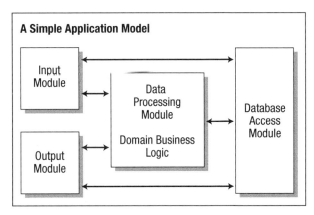

Figure 6.1

Simple four-module application model.

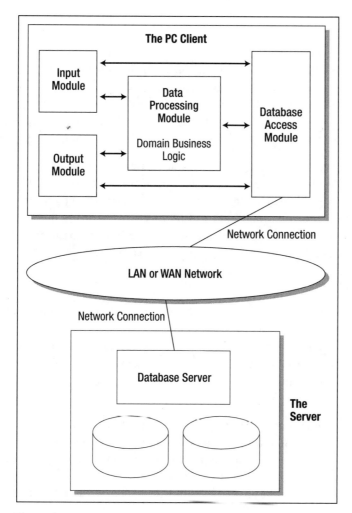

Figure 6.2
The simple application running on a client/server platform.

proprietary database package across a local area network (LAN) or wide area network (WAN). Clearly, to maximize performance, the interface between the database package and the database module is likely to be specific to the package you purchase. In theory, if you change the database, you need to change only the database-access module to accommodate the new database server, preserving the interfaces between the other modules and the high-level, database-access interface.

Figure 6.3 shows the simple model running on a Web-based platform. A browser running on the PC (which is communicating with a Web server that drives the input and output modules of the application) now handles the front-end interface to the user. We are using the same database as in Figure 6.2, so we have had to change only the input and output modules to accommodate the new technology interfacing to the Web server.

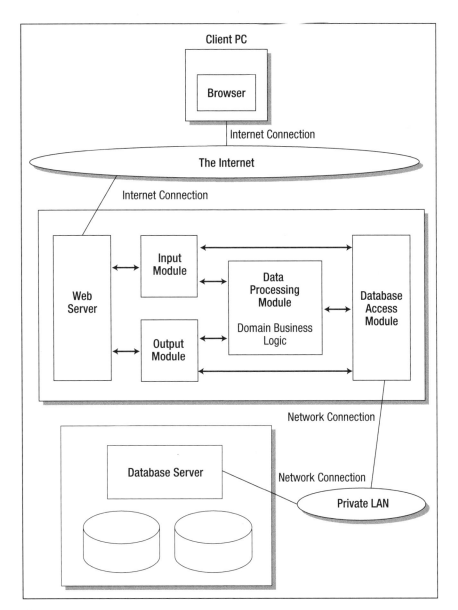

Figure 6.3
The simple application model running on Web technology.

Reality is never quite as simple as the theory dictates, but you can—and always should—employ the general principles of modularization that this simple model exhibits. One reason why object-oriented programming (OOP) has become so successful is that it inherently provides such modularization, together with the highest degree of encapsulation (hiding the inner workings of the object from the user as we discussed in "black boxes" in Chapter 4).

VB for the Case Study

In the case study, as we commenced the design phase, Julie, Archie, and I had decided that we would develop the application in Visual Basic (VB). All our prototyping experiences had confirmed that, for this type of multimedia application, VB was a suitable choice because it was a well-established, reasonably stable product likely to be around for some time to come. We were committed to a hardware and software platform, and we would design around that platform. Had the project been substantially larger, we would have opted for a platform-independent design to more completely protect the customer's investment. Nevertheless, our decision would not prevent us from producing a modular design.

Robust Technology

For a commercial application, the hardware and software technology you choose as a solution for running the programs you will develop must be robust. No matter how great your urge to go out and buy the latest gizmos, resist the urge. The risk factors rocket skyward when you choose brand-new technology.

Just consider what you are doing: You must write software to build a product. You'll have your hands full making the product solid. The last thing you need is a flaky software or hardware environment. Otherwise, when you have a problem, you'll never be sure whether the cause is your code or the operating environment (hardware and/or software), and you may waste considerable time finding out.

Getting the supplier to support you on a brand-new platform is another problem. These issues all add up to headaches you can do without (and believe me, you'll have enough from the work you have direct control over). When you must take on suspect technology because you have no other alternative, you must ensure that you isolate the software that will use that technology from the rest of the design as much as you can. With a clearly defined interface to the rest of the system, you can always unplug the module and replace it with something better when that comes along. (This is a good example of isolating an area of technical risk at the design stage.) Creating a modular design with a high degree of encapsulation for each component will give you a product that can readily adapt to changing requirements and technologies.

Top-Level Design

Design has two aspects—*top level* and the *low level*. Top-level design provides a view of the whole system, which lets you put all the component parts in context. At this level, you see the basic building blocks and how they relate to each other. The simple model we looked at in the last section (involving input, output, processing, and data-access modules) provided examples of top-level design views.

In analysis, you will have identified the main functional components that make up the top-level design. You will have defined each module's function, its inputs, and its outputs. From this information, you can specify a module's interface to the rest of the world.

Design for Future Requirements

In the case study, we made a big thing about composites, and HTML and Web access. We had to design for both immediate and future requirements because, if we hadn't, we might well have to start all over again to accommodate those future requirements later. The customer would not accept that approach, because the cost for future expansion would likely become excessive.

The case study demonstrates why you need to extract from the client what the future needs will likely be. Although you usually can't initially accommodate every possible requirement (that's likely to produce an unacceptable timetable), always design with the future requirements clearly onboard. Incorporating future needs is the big difference between our chosen approach to development in the case study and the less rigid methodology based on prototyping. Remember that prototyping allows for development without the need to understand the requirements fully, but it accommodates the possibility of starting all over again after you fully appreciate the requirements. A typical commercial project involves planned phases of development, all of which you must take into account at design time. Ignore this advice at your peril.

Design for Exceptions

The easy part of design is designing a system to cope with the expected. However, you also need to design programs that include provisions for unexpected situations. Many programmers neglect this part of the process because correctly designing for exceptions can more than double the size of the job.

For example, if part of the requirement is to open a file and read in its contents, what happens if the file doesn't exist? What happens if the file is of the wrong format? What happens if the file has been truncated and most of the data is missing? You must accommodate exceptions and error conditions in the design. You will see much of what we've discussed to this point put into action in the case study.

The Case Study:

Top-Level Design

From our analysis in the case study, we had identified self-contained, functional modules, which are listed in Figure 6.1.

What we needed to do now was create a *view* that showed the context in which all the functional components would operate. If you recall, some of the modules would be used only in the viewer, some only in the Title Index Editor, and some only in the Page Index Editor. But some modules would be shared. From a top-level design perspective, indicating which modules were shared was important.

The Viewer

Figure 6.5 shows the top-level view of the viewer. The figure depicts all the modules and the key data entities—the two in-Memory Index files. First, we had a collection of input modules

**List of Functional Modules Required
for the E-MagBook Software Mark 1**

Title Selection
Page Index Navigation
Display Page
Load and Display Image
Load and Play Video Clip
Load and Display Text
Load and Play WAV Sound File
Load and Play MID Music File
Display Workbench
Workbench Screen Object Positioning
Workbench Screen Object Manipulation
Print content of Workbench
Set up for Search
Read a Specified Title Index into Program
Perform Search
Read Specified Page Index into Program
Clear Page Index
Output a Title Index to Selected Disk File
Select a Title Index File for Input
Select File Name for Title Index Output
Title Index Navigation Functionality
Display Contents of Current Title Entry
Add/Delete/Insert/Overwrite Title Index Functionality
Title Entry Edit Functionality
Output a Page Index to Selected Disk File
Select a Page Index File for Input
Select File Name for Page Index Output
Add/Delete/Insert/Overwrite Page Index Functionality
Page Entry Edit Functionality
Copy and Paste
File Selection Form's Associated Code
Output to Selected Text File
Select Text Font

Figure 6.4

List of E-MagBook functional modules.

that let the user interface directly with the viewer. These modules were the **Title Selection**, **Page Index Navigation**, **Set Up for Search**, and all the Workbench-associated modules, of which there were four (**Display**, **Manipulate**, **Position**, and **Print**), lumped together in a module called **Workbench**. These components were all GUI based, directly handling user input. For output, we had all the modules associated with displaying the page content, im-

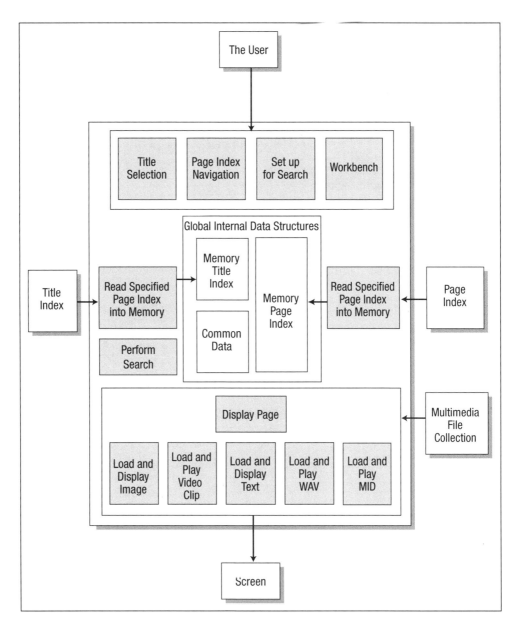

Figure 6.5
Top-level view of the viewer program.

ages, videos, and text, and playing sounds. In the figure, these are depicted together as a block and connected to the screen, to indicate their GUI nature.

In the heart of the program, we had the in-Memory Title and Page Indexes. The pure function modules—**Read Specified Title Index into Memory** and **Read Specified Page Index into Memory**—were used to get the content from the outside world (disk files) into program memory. We'd also indicated a common data block, which we could consider as an in-memory database of global parameters that the program as a whole used. For example, the current page number was a global data parameter in which many of the modules would have an interest. One other pure module was the **Perform Search** component.

In this simple diagram, we placed all the top-level components in context, centered on a set of global data structures. An immediate fact was that the viewer could not change the contents of any of the external files (Indexes or multimedia files).

The Title Index Editor

Selecting all the modules that made up the Title Index Editor, we could now easily see which modules were common to the viewer as well. This process highlighted reusability. We designed and developed the common module once and used it more than once. Figure 6.6 depicts the Title Index Editor. Again, several modules are associated with GUI input, one module is associated with GUI output, and, this time, an input module and an output module exist for the Title Index disk file. The central, in-memory data component houses the Title Index and global parameters suitable for Title Index handling.

Page Index Editor

The Page Index Editor is the most complicated of the three programs. This program must have the viewer's entire functionality embedded in it. From a design point of view, the simple way to embed that functionality is to take the viewer form and make it a child form of the editor, which is pretty much how we achieved the prototype form back in Chapter 4. Figure 6.7 illustrates the module configuration for the Page Index Editor. The module consists of a mixture of viewer and Page Index Editor modules, with a central data area similar to that of the viewer. We'd now specified the top-level modular makeup of the three programs.

Tip

It's very useful to place a top-level, diagrammatic representation of the program's component structure on the office wall or keep the diagram close at hand. Whenever you need to see the global picture, you just glance at the diagram. Such representations are also very useful for explaining things to people, especially when you're trying to get new programmers up to speed on the project.

Code Organization

In your project, you need to consider how you will organize the various modules you produce so that you can share them across programs. The top-level design has already identified where the reusable elements lie. Now, you need to set up module libraries, that more than one program can use. The key to setting up module libraries is to remember that any shared modules are independent of the program in which they run. This arrangement immediately provides two definitions of code and data: *program-specific* and *program-independent*. We can define the following design features that you will incorporate:

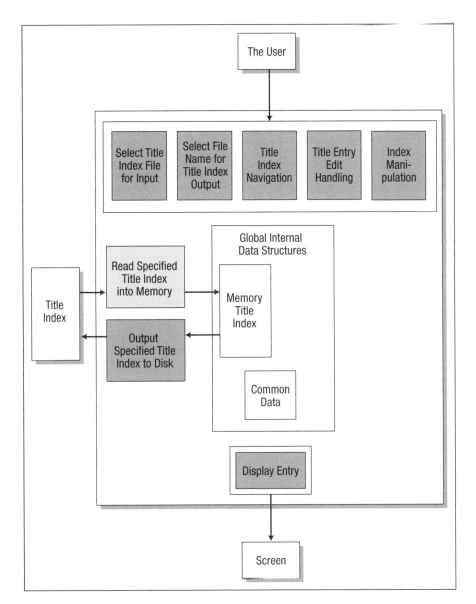

Figure 6.6
Top-level view of the Title Index Editor program.

♦ Program-specific code or data is made "private."

♦ Private code or data constitutes the program's infrastructure.

♦ Any code or data that other programs can use is made "public."

♦ Public code must be designed to be independent of the program in which it is used.

♦ Public code and data must be installed in a module library.

♦ A program can use none, one, or many module libraries.

♦ Infrastructure routines can call any public routine from any library.

♦ Infrastructure routines can access private or public data.

♦ Public routines may not access private code or data, which is part of the program's infrastructure.

In the case study, we had a collection of self-contained modules and three programs that made use of these modules. Each program would have what I've previously termed its own infrastructure code and also data. Because this code and data would be private to the program—no other program would use it—it would be "program specific." The code and data would consist of all the glue to make the program function, and it would use the library modules wherever it needed their functionality.

Private and Public Code

You can implement a given functional module identified from your analysis either as an infrastructure routine specific to the program in which it is required, or as a general module you locate in a module library, where it must be program independent. While the library modules are available to the infrastructure code, the infrastructure routines will not be available to the library code (that is, an infrastructure routine will be classified as private and cannot therefore be called from inside one of the library modules).

The same is true about data. Infrastructure code can access its own private data and the global data of the libraries, but the library modules can access only the public data. These principles define a clear architecture for our programs that you can see in Figure 6.8.

The first program in Figure 6.8 illustrates the simplest situation, which consists of infrastructure code and data alone (that is, no library modules are present). The second program uses a single library of modules, together with its data. The infrastructure code can call upon the routines in the library and manipulate the library's public data directly. The library routines, alternatively, cannot call the private routines of the program, and they cannot access the program's private data.

In the third program in Figure 6.8, we see a situation similar to the case study, in which a program includes more than one library. Routines in any of the libraries can access all public data, including data in other libraries.

Forms

Another aspect of a program that we must consider is the *form*. A program can be made up of one or more forms. A form acts as an independent entity, and each form can have its own set of infrastructure code and data. The routines in any form of a program can call any of the public routines and can also access any public data.

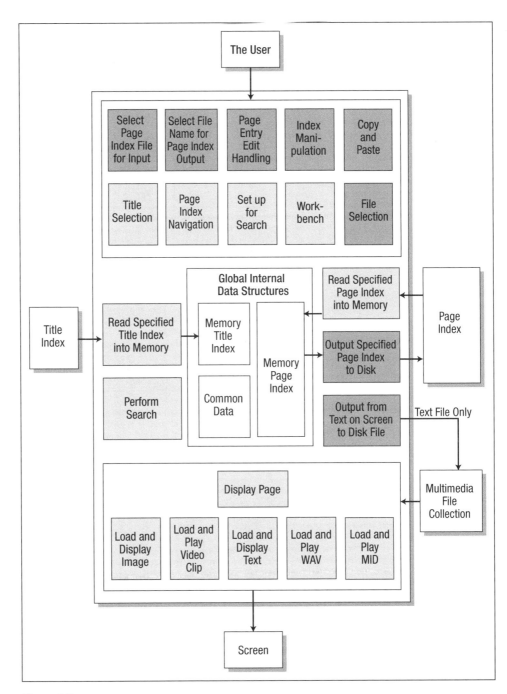

Figure 6.7
Top-level view of the Page Index Editor, showing the split between viewer and page modules.

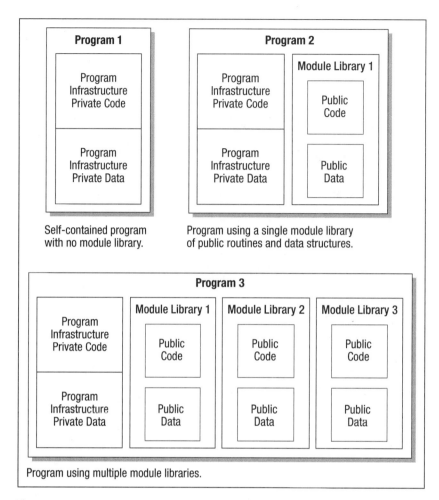

Figure 6.8
Design architecture for the case study.

Because a form contains private code and data, the form cannot access another form's private code or data. This limitation might be too restrictive in certain situations. Consequently, you'll want to modify the architecture so that code from one form can access code in another form. You do this by explicitly declaring the target routine as public, even though it is embedded in a form's infrastructure code. Even so, to ensure that the libraries are independent of program or form, you still will not make this public infrastructure code accessible to any public routines from the libraries.

Let's clarify this point with an example. Suppose we have two forms in a program: **frmA** and **frmB**. Let's say that one button on **frmB** is required to clear both forms. **frmA** has a private routine called **ClearFrmA**, and **frmB** has a private routine called **ClearFrmB**. Our architecture will not let us create a library routine that has direct knowledge of a form, so we can't create these routines as public and place them in a library. The simplest solution is to let

frmB call **ClearFrmA** directly, even though **ClearFrmA** is in another form. To do this, we have to declare **ClearFrmA** as public and call it as **frmA.ClearFormA** from **frmB**'s private code. (This construction is known as *object dot notation*. **ClearFormA** is present in form **frmA** and can be called from outside **frmA** by specifying the form name followed by a dot followed by the name of the routine.)

GUI Library Modules

The architecture we are defining implies that a GUI functional module may be installed in a program only as a private routine in the infrastructure. This restriction exists because the module accesses a form's screen objects directly and is, therefore, program specific. We can remove this restriction if we declare that, for a GUI module to be a general routine, the identity of screen objects must be declared when calling the routine at runtime.

Let's look at an example from the case study. We had a module to load and display text. We needed to define to the module the name of the file to open and read, as well as the text object on screen into which the module would place the data. If that text object was called **txtText** in one program and **txtTextBox** in another, then we could define the call as

```
Call LoadAndDisplayText(strTextFileName, txtText)
```

in one program and

```
Call LoadAndDisplayText(strTextFileName, txtTextBox)
```

in the other.

To make this work, the definition of the library module **LoadAndDisplayText** would be as follows:

```
Sub LoadAndDisplayText(strName as string, txtTXT as control)
```

This definition identifies the second argument as a VB control. In this way, we could turn a GUI-specific module into a public routine that would be independent of program. The stipulation to its use is that the second argument in its call must be a text box name.

The public GUI library routines that we would create would be independent of the screen objects in a program until they were called at runtime. At that point, the routine would be linked to a specific screen object via the call. The link would thus be dynamic, and it could be different from one call to the next and from one program to another. The only "knowledge" required by the routine would be that one or more of its arguments would contain screen-object identities.

We'd now defined an architecture into which we could design and specify routines that were either private (program-specific infrastructure) or public (general-purpose library modules) for the development of E-MagBook software.

Return to the Case Study:
Module Libraries

From the top-level diagrams of the viewer and editors, we could identify three sets of modules: those of the viewer, those of the Title Index Editor, and those of the Page Index Editor. A key point was that the editors required modules from the viewer. If we defined three module libraries, **ViewerLib**, **PageLib**, and **TitleLib**, then we could depict another top-level view of each program that showed how the programs related to code libraries. This relationship would substantially affect how we would develop source code.

ViewerLib

Figure 6.9 shows the viewer, composed of two basic units. The first unit is the viewer library, **ViewerLib**. This unit contains the common data entities and the functional routines that would be required in other programs and the viewer. The second unit consists of the infrastructure code that we needed to write to glue the modules together and make them function from the viewer program the way we wanted them to. We also declared any parameters specific to this code as private infrastructure data. Infrastructure code might also consist of modules that we decided were specific to the viewer only and that would not be used in any other program.

One example of infrastructure code was the **Form_Load** event handler, which is a critical piece of code in any GUI program because it's always the first code the form executes. In the case of the viewer program, all the **Form Load** event handler might do would be to invoke a module from **ViewerLib**, but, more than likely, a bit of code would be required first. For

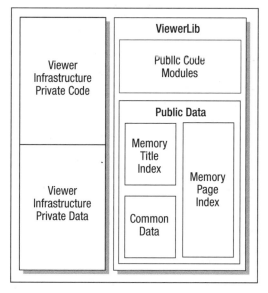

Figure 6.9
Top-level view of the E-MagBook viewer.

example, we would use the viewer's **Form_Load** event to invoke the public module **Read a Specified Title Index into Memory**, with a hard-coded file name of **E:\E-MagBook\Title.idx**.

We had a clear demarcation of reusable public code modules, with their common data structures, program-specific infrastructure code, and its related data. Remember the basic rules imposed by our design: Infrastructure code in the viewer form could invoke public modules from **ViewerLib** and could also access common data values in the library. **ViewerLib** modules could not invoke infrastructure code in the form and could not access the form's data. (Without this criterion, we would not be able to use **ViewerLib** in another program because we might introduce a dependency into the library on an item of infrastructure specific to the viewer program.) If we adhered to the rules, the library code would remain independent of the program in which it resided and could therefore be reused in many different programs.

TitleLib

Figure 6.10 shows the Title Index Editor composed of private infrastructure code, **TitleLib** and **ViewerLib** (even though the Title Index Editor would call only one routine from the code and access only the Memory Title Index). We could have broken down the library structures even further to provide less redundancy but, on a project of this size, doing so wouldn't have been worth it. Redundant code or data in a program does no harm other than make the program larger than it needs to be.

Any common data the Title Index library modules required that was not already available in the viewer library would be placed in **TitleLib** so that, should the need arise, another program could use the data.

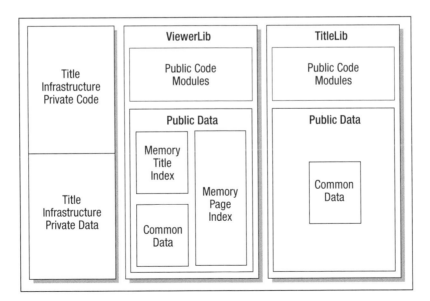

Figure 6.10
Top-level view of the Title Index Editor program showing library structure.

Write the Code Once

The Page Index Editor required all the functionality of the viewer. The last thing we wanted to do was develop all the viewer code twice—once for the viewer itself and again for the Page Index Editor. So why not consider the whole of the viewer program as a black box? If we designed the viewer as a single form (plus the form in which videos would be played), that form could be run as a program, or it could be embedded into another program as a child form. Although this process was becoming very VB specific, it was of tremendous value to us.

The implication was that we would develop the viewer once and then embed the whole form into the Page Index Editor to provide viewer functionality. Because the form was now a child form within the editor program, all its screen objects were available to the editor, which could access them directly using object dot notation defined earlier. For example, if we had a screen object called **txtText**, a text box on the viewer form, the editor's infrastructure code could access the object by referring to it as **frmViewer.txtText**, assuming the name of the viewer form was **frmViewer**. Exactly the same GUI interface would be presented to the user as from the viewer program, so all the viewer's functionality would be available. The beauty was that, if we changed anything in the viewer form, the updated information would automatically be available to the viewer program or the Page Index Editor program after a recompile—a small price to pay for such reusability.

Tip

Wherever possible, design in such a way that you write a specific aspect of functionality once and make that functionality available in a suitable manner to any other context that requires it. You can accomplish this reusability in many ways other than the way we chose for the case study—for example, using DLLs, OCXs, and so on.

PageLib

Finally, we came to **PageLib**, which would contain specific modules for Page Index handling that were not available in **ViewerLib** or **TitleLib**. However, the structure of the Page Index Editor was more complex than the other two programs in that it would require a total of four forms—the editor form, the viewer form, the file-selection form, and the video form. We'd embed the entire viewer form into the editor as a child form. This arrangement implied that all the viewer's infrastructure code and data would be available in the Page Index Editor, to be executed as required when the user invoked the viewer functionality. Figure 6.11 shows the structure of the Page Index Editor program.

This time, we had three sets of private code and data—one set for each form present in the program. Once again, only the forms in which the code and data were defined could use that code and data. (This restriction did not include the video form because that form would contain no data and no code—it would function purely as a window in which to play the video clip.)

If we encountered a situation in which private code needed to access a routine in another form, we would have made provision for this by declaring that we could upgrade the private

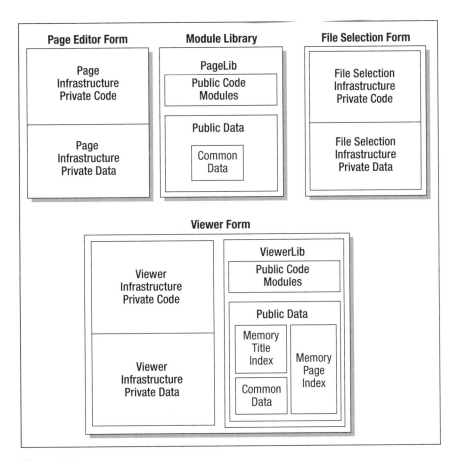

Figure 6.11
Top-level view of the Page Index Editor showing library structure.

routine in question to public status. We could do this only with the proviso that the module in question must never be called from a library module.

Further Top-Level Design

After you have established the overall top-level design, it's time to look at the key data structures.

Data Structures

Data structures are of three types:

♦ *Database*—External structures that permanently house data items and are accessible via a database interface package.

♦ *Internal Global Data*—In-memory data structures that house temporary data relevant to the running the program.

◆ *External File Structures*—Files (other than database files) that permanently hold data the program can use.

Database

For an application that involves a database, most of the work has been done in analysis, where you have defined the data items and their relationships. All that is left to design are the database tables themselves.

Internal Global Data

The key to a program's functioning is the common data structure used across all the modules and possibly even across programs. From the definitions of the inputs and outputs the functional modules require, which you established in analysis, you can now design a common data structure that will furnish all the runtime requirements.

We'll refer to these data structures as "global" in the sense that they will be accessible to infrastructure code and across all library modules. For example, in the case study, if we had a data entity to define the current page number, and we declared the data entity as a public global data entity, this variable would be available to page navigation, searching, the display modules, and so on, regardless of whether they were private or public routines. We could encapsulate any variables that did not need to be global within the infrastructure code for use by infrastructure routines, or we could even declare the data structure as private in the library in which it would be used (in which case, only that library's routines might access it).

Because all programmers might have to use the key data structures, even though they are working on independent development modules, those data structures need to be in place before anyone starts to program. Don't forget, all the modules must be integrated at the end of development, and, if they haven't been integrated using the same data declarations, you will fail to integrate the modules until they are rewritten correctly.

External File Structures

In addition to database and global data structures, the program might demand that you define file structures before work can start. This is certainly true in the case study, where we had two critical files—the Title Index and the Page Index.

GUI Design

If you haven't already designed the screen forms, now is the time. I've put forward a case for doing this at the requirements stage for the simple reason that doing so helps to focus attention on the requirements in a way that nothing else can.

Return to the Case Study:
Data Files

It's now time to look at designing a structure to accommodate the Page Index and the Title Index records.

The Title Index File Format

We had carte blanche to design any format we required for the Title Index because we were also going to design and build the Title Index Editor. First of all, what did the Title Index file need to do? The Title Index file would reside on each removable E-Disk, and it would hold the details about each title available on the E-Disk. For each title, the file must contain a single Title Index record, which would consist of the free-format title and description, and the file reference of the Page Index that contains the book's page definitions.

Actual Title Indexes needed to be available as soon as the viewer was completed, but we wouldn't have developed a Title Index Editor by then. If we designed the file structure sensibly, then we could use a standard text editor to create and amend Title Index files to assist us in testing the viewer's modules.

Identity

The format of the Title Index file must allow us to do two things. First, it must allow the software to verify that it was indeed a Title Index, and then it must provide a format that the software could understand. If we did this right, we could use a standard text editor to create and edit Title Index files long before we developed the Title Index Editor.

To identify the file type, we needed a header line. This header line would allow any program to open the file and read Line 1 to determine whether the file was the correct type. For example, the bitmapped files we read into the picture and image controls in our feasibility studies could have extensions of .bmp, .jpg, and so on. But we could change these extensions, which meant a program couldn't normally rely on a .bmp extension being present to indicate that the file was a Microsoft bitmapped file. Instead, the file contained an identifier in the first two bytes of its content in the form of the ASCII characters **B** and **M**. A program could read in these bytes, and if they were **BM**, it could assume that the file was in Microsoft bitmap format. If the characters were not **BM**, then the program would look for whatever other header it was capable of handling.

We needed something similar to indicate the program was opening an E-MagBook Title Index. Let's say the first line of the file must contain the string **E-BOOK TITLE INDEX**. This identifier would also make obvious what the file was when we examined it with an editor, and any program we wrote could read Line 1 to see whether it contained that exact string. We could do the same for the Page Index file. We could start that string on Line 1 as **E-BOOK PAGE INDEX**, so we would have a method to tell the two Index files apart.

Future Requirements

We could leave Line 1 at that—simply a text string that indicated this was a Title Index, but we needed to think about possible future requirements. Introducing the idea of *field separators*, also called *delimiters*, would provide a more flexible design.

Field separators, or delimiters, would let us have more than one data entity defined on a single line of the file in such a way that we wouldn't have to worry about the length of the data field, its position on the line, or the total number of data fields present.

We could use a specific pair of characters to denote the start and the end of a data string. You can do this in all sorts of ways, but we chose an approach that encloses all text that can be defined as a single field in square brackets. The file header now became the following: **[E-BOOK TITLE INDEX]**. This format did, of course, mean that we could never use a square bracket as part of a data string. The advantage of encapsulating a field between delimiters is that we could add other fields to the line for later developments.

We would design the programs to read in the whole line in one action and then use code to extract the content of Field 1, Field 2, and so on. If the program didn't yet know about Field 3, Field 4, and so on, no harm would be done, and we would have a high degree of future-proofing.

Let me give you an example to demonstrate why this design might be useful. We started with Line 1 of the Title Index containing a single field, **[E-BOOK TITLE INDEX]**. All the programs that needed to access a Title Index were written so that the first thing they would do was read Line 1 of the specified file and extract Field 1's contents. They would then check to see whether the data entity was an "E-BOOK TITLE INDEX." If it was, all was well and good. If it were not, then the program would provide an error message. Now, let's suppose that, six months later, Monty wanted us to include some new feature in the E-MagBooks, such as a classification for the content of a removable disk that might be *Gardening* or *Science for the novice*. In other words, he wanted a basic description that would qualify all the books on the removable disk. We could accommodate such a description by adding an extra field on Line 1. The new Line 1 would then read, for example:

```
[E-BOOK TITLE INDEX] [Gardening]
```

Backward and Forward Compatibility

Backward compatibility refers to the capability of newer software and/or hardware to operate correctly with (and within the limitations of) previously developed software or hardware. *Forward compatibility* refers to the capability of previously developed software or hardware to continue to function to its fullest extent with updated software or hardware. Let's look at more detailed explanations of each.

In our example, programs knowledgeable about the extra field would read Line 1 and extract two fields. The older programs would read the whole line but extract only one field because they wouldn't know about the second field. This capability of the older program to read the line and extract the known field correctly represents forward compatibility.

Old programs could still read the new formats, and the new program could also read old Index formats (in which it won't find a second field, so it must leave the description blank). This capability of the new program to read old Index formats correctly (although it will provide no description) represents backward compatibility.

We could add as many fields as we liked at later stages. The only criterion would be that the added fields must appear in the correct order, and, if a field contained blank data, the field must still appear so that the program extracting the field data could count fields correctly. This required structure will become more apparent as we go on.

Specification for Line 1

We developed a formal design specification for Line 1 as follows:

Title Index File Format
Line 1: Contains a single field, fixed format, file identifier starting in character position 1.

Field 1: [E-BOOK TITLE INDEX]

Provision is made for additional, delimited fields to be added in the future.

The Data Record

The first data record starts at Line 2 of the file. This specification made the assumption that we could accommodate all future requirements for expansion of the Index header in one line. Because text files could have very long, single lines, that would not be an issue.

Line 2 could contain the start of Record 1. Each Title Index record needed to contain three data entities—the free-text title, the free-text description, and the Page Index file reference. We could put all the data entities on one line in three fields, but the description could be quite lengthy. And remember, we would initially be using an editor, so we would be wise to avoid lengthy data lines. Consequently, we defined a record as consisting of three lines. The first line would include a single field containing the Index file reference, the next line would contain the title, and the third line would hold the description. Here's an example:

```
[E:\GARDENING\WINTER1.IDX]
[Preparing your garden for winter]
[This book tells you how to prepare the soil, ready for winter. It tells
you...]
```

NOTE: *The third line can be quite long, so I've included an ellipsis to indicate that before the final field delimiter.*

We'd defined a record structure that consisted of three lines, each containing one field. We could just as easily have set up the file reference and title on Line 1 with the description on Line 2, eliminating the need for three lines. But we stuck to three lines. Line 1 must contain the Page Index file reference, Line 2 the title, and Line 3 the description.

Extensions to the Data Record

In terms of future expansion, we could add fields to Line 1 and Line 2; Line 3 was likely to be a bit on the big side to consider additions. But, if we defined an end-of-record marker as a single line, we could make a record from as many lines of text as we required. This option would give us substantial future-proofing. We could design a program to read data lines until it thought there were no more, and then it would read in any extra lines that might be present and discard them (forward compatibility) until it found the end-of-record marker. Future programs reading old formats simply would find a premature end-of-record indicator and blank off the corresponding global data entities for which no data was present on the input line, (backwards compatibility). We formalized the design as follows:

Title Index Record Structure, Format 1
Record 1 starts at Line 2 of the file.

For Version 1 of the format, all records must consist of three lines plus an end-of-record marker, as follows:

Line 1: [*File Reference of Page Index*]

Line 2: [*Free-Format Title*]

Line 3: [*Free-Format Description*]

Line 4: [END OF RECORD]

All data lines must start in character position 1 of the line.

From Version 1 of the file structure, any number of lines may be inserted between Line 3 and the end-of-record marker. Any program capable of decoding only Format 1 will ignore such lines. Subsequent additions to the file record format can be accommodated using these additional lines.

Future formats could even use variable-length records. The first three lines would conform to the preceding description, and the end-of-record marker could come after any number of additional lines. The last line of a record must contain [**END OF RECORD**]. We'd set up the program so that it would read three lines and then keep reading until it found an end-of-record marker. That way, it would automatically be future-proofed.

We needed to design the program so that it continued reading in records until an end-of-file was indicated, at which point the file would be closed. We defined this as follows:

The end of data is indicated by a standard end-of-file maker as used by DOS ASCII files.

So, there was our format specification for the Title Index file structure with a comfortable degree of future-proofing.

Page Index File Format

We followed similar arguments when we designed the Page Index file structure. We needed a header line to define the file type, just as we had for the Title Index file, and we needed to add font type and font size because these were fixed for a book (remember, a page's font characteristics would be inherited from those defined for the book). We also needed to show what type of format the book was—Text Book, Picture Album, or Reference Book. So our first line took on the following structure quite quickly:

Page Index File, Format 1

Line 1: Contains header field and font data

Field 1: Contains one of the following:

    [E-BOOK PAGE BOOKS]

    [E-BOOK PAGE ALBUM]

    [E-BOOK PAGE INDEX]

Field 2: [*font type string*]   (for example, [Times New Roman])

Field 3: [*font size integer*]   (for example, [12])

We'd defined three headers—one for the Text Book, one for the Picture Album, and one for the Reference Book. We decided that should do for the time being; we could always add fields at a later date. Again, this approach gave us future-proofing. We would have a situation in which we would want to define composites and HTML books; in those cases, the program we developed now would not be able to read those formats. As long as the current program could handle the error and provide a suitable message to the user, that would be satisfactory. If an old version of the program would find a new file with more than three fields, the program would read the whole line, but unpack only the first three fields because it wouldn't know about any other fields. So, we'd achieve some forward compatibility.

The Page Record

The data records of the Page Index file needed to hold the five keys, a picture or movie-clip file reference, and the sound and text file references—eight fields in all—for the initial program. In this case, we decided to put all eight fields onto a single line and impose the restriction that all Page Index records were accommodated in one ASCII line. The main reason we had split the Title Index record into multiple lines was that the description could be quite long. But we didn't have any really long fields in the Page Index. Even if we set each key to 30 characters, the total length would not contain more than 200 characters. For future expansion, we could add fields to the end of the line. Old programs would ignore the added fields; new programs would act upon them.

Composites

One other thing we considered was the composite page descriptor. This descriptor had to define an unlimited number of image and text file references; the positions and dimensions of all images and text file blocks; and all text file content, font, and size. The result could be a colossal volume of data. If we intended to place the data on a single line, the line might go on forever. We had already determined, however, that a composite descriptor would be defined in its own file. The Page Index record would simply hold a data field that contained the name of the required file. (In the future, that field was likely to be Field 9 of the data record.)

Page Record Specification

We'd done sufficient work to prevent compromising the design in the future. We could expand the design by adding extra fields to our single-line Page Index record, and we could make any of the new fields a file reference. Using a format to be designed at a later date, we could make the file reference point to a file that contains another description. This approach would allow the program to build a complex composite or anything else that Monty might come up with.

The formal design specification for the Page Index file became the following:

Page Index Record Structure, Format 1

All records consist of a single data line that contains eight data fields. If a data field is blank, it must still be present with nothing between the delimiters.

Field 1 must start at character position 1 of the line, and the fields must be in the order specified here. Otherwise, the placement of fields or delimiters has no restrictions. Likewise, there is no restriction on what is contained between fields. Any data that is present between fields, however, is ignored.

The format is as follows:

Field 1:   [*key 1*]   string (must start at character position 1)

Field 2:   [*key 2*]   string

Field 3:   [*key 3*]   string

Field 4:   [*key 4*]   string

Field 5:   [*key 5*]   string

Field 6:   [*picture or video file reference*]   string

Field 7:   [*text file reference*]   string

Field 8:   [*sound file reference*]   string

Any future requirements can be met by adding delimited fields after Field 8. Format 1 programs will simply ignore any fields after Field 8.

Here's an example:

```
[Picture Framing] [canvas] [ ] [ ] [ ] [E:\PICDIY\P34.JPG] [E:\PICDIY\P34.TXT] [ ]
```

In the example, two keys are defined and three keys are blank. Then, a text reference follows an image reference, with no sound file. A future ninth field could be the file reference to the composite description. New programs will open the descriptor and build a composite from Field 9. Older programs could continue to use the text and image fields if that was a sensible alternative. This arrangement provides many options for future expansion.

Browser Pages

We'd dealt with standard entries and future composites, but what about the browser pages? We needed to define an HTML file reference or a Web site URL. We could introduce a tenth field that was either an HTML file reference or a URL (the difference being that a URL would begin with the string **http:**—something we talked about some time back). If future programs detected content in Field 10, they would either load an HTML file into the browser directly or they would hand the file the URL, and so on. Once again, we were providing options for the future, but we did not have to consider the details at this stage—we just needed to provide the options.

File Termination

The final question was "How do we terminate the file?" We could rely on the DOS end-of-file marker, like we had with the Title Index. But we decided to add some more future-proofing capability. Let's suppose we were to use a line that contained the word *END* in each field as an end-of-data marker. The program would read lines until it found this special record, at which point it would stop reading, close the file, and continue. We could then add data lines after the end marker at a later date and treat these lines however we might require. Earlier programs would read up to the end marker and stop. Later programs would treat the end marker as an end of Phase 1 read, and go on to read whatever other format we had defined for the second part of the file. That method could enormously extend the capability of the file. We could have a multipass structure and define as many structures as we needed.

In conclusion, we added the following:

End of Data Determined by Setting Each of the Eight Fields to Hold the Word *END*
For Format 1, the program will ignore any data that appears after this line, and this data can be used for future expansion using any format required.

We now had two well-defined, flexible format designs for our key data files. Next, we must take each of the modules from the top-level design, identify subroutines and functions, and specify the design for each module. In essence, we were ready to begin the low-level design.

Low-Level Design

Many design tools are available nowadays to help with software design. Many design methodologies, or ways of designing, also exist. In Archie and Julie's first project, we would use two very simple tools—the pseudocode description and the flow diagram. These two tools provide a good starting point for our discussion of low-level design.

Pseudocode

By *pseudocode*, I mean a code that is not a real computer language—it's more like English, but structured. For example, suppose we are defining the code to ask the user to specify a file name and then read in that file. We can do that with pseudocode, as follows:

EXAMPLE OF PSEUDOCODE
FUNCTION: SelectAndReadInFile(StrFileName) as Boolean

DESCRIPTION: Let user select a file and read its contents into memory.

ARGUMENTS:

    StrFileName   returned if a file read OK containing the name of
                    the file read in; Blank otherwise.

    Function result = True if file read OK,

                = False if failed to read.

ACTION:

    Get file name from user.

    If canceled, then **EXIT**, setting function **FALSE**.

    Open file.

    If error, then close, report error on screen, and **EXIT**, setting function **FALSE**.

    Check file is of correct format.

    If not, then close, report error on screen, and **EXIT**, setting function **FALSE**.

    Read file into memory.

    If error, then close, report error on screen, and **EXIT**, setting function **FALSE**.

    EXIT, setting function **TRUE**.

We start by defining whether the module is a function or a subroutine. If it's a function, we need to specify the return type, in this case Boolean. We provide the programmer with a short description, followed by a definition of the arguments that have been defined in the call. Finally, we define what we want the code to do, but we use high-level English sentences—for example:

```
Get file name from user
```

Attention to Detail

Note that we have defined all the possible error conditions. This attention to detail is vital for producing good software. Programmers are usually very good at programming for the expected, but they frequently don't have the time, inclination, or experience to consider all the possible error conditions.

By using pseudocode, you can be quite pedantic about error handling, ensuring that you have considered all possible cases. Because you are writing in English in a freely structured manner, you can quickly rattle off these specifications. But, at the end of each statement, you must consider the possible outcome. If you open a file, what happens if the file does not exist? If you read in a file, what happens if it fails? At this level of design, you are concentrating on the different possible outcomes of each action. The programmer's job is to convert these possibilities to code. You will witness the simplicity of pseudocode in the case study, but also note how much information the pseudocode imparts to the programmer.

Go To

Generally speaking, you should avoid the **Go To** statement. Instead, the code you write should be structured, using conditional statements and loops, just as in VB code. When a program uses **Go To** statements to pass control backward and forward, the code becomes a complete tangle and difficult to fathom.

Within our company standards, we reserve **Go To** statements for passing control to error handlers. We also stipulate that a **Go To** can transfer control only in a forward direction. VB uses the **On Error Go To** construction to trap errors, as well.

Caution

You can easily get carried away with pseudocode and start writing volumes of it. You have to ask yourself, Would it be quicker to write the actual code? If the answer is "Yes," you are wasting your time with pseudocode. The real purpose of pseudocode is to define the required code in shorthand—in fact, that's a good analogy. People use shorthand as a quick way to capture what someone is dictating (the alternative, writing out in full, slows down the speaker). You need to ensure that pseudocode is your shorthand description of how you want the programmer to provide a solution.

Flow Diagrams

Flow diagrams are useful when the logic of the solution is complicated. Pseudocode is excellent for defining sequential processes and their exception handling (for example, "If read fails, then report error"), but for more complex structures, the flow diagram is invaluable.

Figure 6.12 shows a flow diagram that represents the same definition we produced in pseudocode. As you can see, the flow diagram shows the decision points and the result of various conditions more clearly.

In a flow diagram, simple sections of sequential processing are defined in a box with one or more high-level, English-style statements. If a decision point occurs after this box, (for ex-

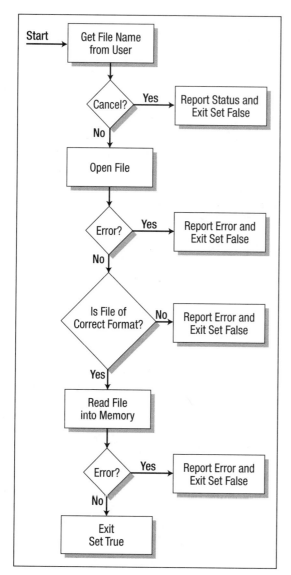

Figure 6.12
Flow diagram for **SelectAndReadInFile** function.

ample, Did the file open successfully?) you use a diamond shape to represent the decision point. The flow indicates movement from the box downward to the decision point. Using a diamond provides three possible routes out of the decision. A logical decision has a "Yes" route and a "No" route out. A numerical decision point might have three routes—one for "greater than," one for "equal to," and one for "less than." You can depict a series of decisions by cascading more diamonds, one under another.

A flow diagram is an effective tool with which to design a complex algorithm. Using the diagram, a programmer can easily identify loops, decision points, exception conditions, and their handling. If a particular algorithm proves to be so complex that the flow diagram becomes impossible to read, you can split the diagram into a series of views. You can identify an overall flow pattern at the top-level, and then supply finer details for the more complex elements from the top-level diagram.

How Much Detail?

The amount of detail you need to go into for low-level design depends on many factors. The bigger the project, the more vital the design documentation is, because many people will be relying on it. When hordes of programmers work on a project, everyone must work from the same, clearly defined specifications.

When fewer programmers and smaller projects are involved, the amount of low-level design you must supply depends on the caliber of the programmers. Some may well argue that the high-level design is perfectly adequate for a high-caliber programmer, taking into account the level of detail that the requirements specification and related information provide.

The poorer the communications between programmers, the more important detailed design is. Suppose that you work on a project with two programming teams, if a large physical distance separates your two teams, communications are more likely to be poor, and the teams will need to rely more on the design documents. A team working together in the same room should mean good communications, and team members can quickly clarify aspects of the design and make the results available to everyone.

You also must take into account the financial context of the project. If you didn't budget for sufficient time in design, you might have a problem if you can't overcome the deficiencies that lack of detailed design will cause. The overriding factor you need to consider is that you are designing not only for the programmers who will create the product, but also for the support people who will have to look after the software when it's established. After support programmers have become proficient with the requirements specification, you can't expect them to wade through masses of code to become familiar with the workings of the software. They need a top-level view to help them identify how the components are bolted together, and they need design specifications that tell them what to expect when they look at the code. (Forewarned is forearmed.)

And remember that traceability is also an issue. An auditor is entitled to see the design criteria upon which a section of code is based. Of particular interest will be the defined criteria for exception, or error, handling. Unfortunately, the question of how detailed a design should be has no simple answer. You must gauge the average ability of the available programmers and then ask yourself, Is there enough information here for a programmer with this level of ability to code?

Return to the Case Study:
Screen Objects

The next thing we did in the E-MagBook project was to formalize the identities of the screen objects for all three programs. We had good definitions of the layouts in the form prototypes, so the task was relatively simple. We needed to formalize the screen object identities now because we would have two programmers working in parallel on the code. Therefore, we needed to set up a naming convention from the outset to which both programmers would adhere. If we didn't establish a convention, they would invent their own names, and we'd have a problem trying to integrate the code each person developed.

We would use what is termed *Hungarian notation* to give a name that also defined its type to every screen control. Hungarian notation defines a set of three character prefixes for variables as well as screen controls that identify the parameter's type. We'd already done this with **txtText**, **imgImageIt**, and with the keys and selection criteria panels; **txt** for text box, **img** for image control, **pic** for picture box, and so on.

Container Controls

I want to introduce something at this stage that we discussed only in passing when Monty hit us with the request for Samantha to play with the layouts—*containers*. We could use picture controls as containers for screen objects, and picture controls provide us with two very useful capabilities. One was that picture controls could hold a picture as a background image underneath the controls contained within, and the other was that we could remove all the objects on the picture control by simply making the picture control itself invisible.

We needed two such panels—one for Title Selection mode and one for Viewer mode. When the Workbench mode was invoked, we'd place the image and text controls directly on the form. In this way, Samantha could stylize the other two modes as she saw fit, and the modes could be switched on and off just by setting the appropriate panel's visible property.

Categories

We needed to define three lists of screen objects—one for the viewer, one for the Title Index Editor, and one for the Page Index Editor.

NOTE: *Any programmer setting up code, whether in a test harness or for inclusion in the final version of the integrated system, must use these screen object lists to ensure that the infrastructure code written employs the correct object names and types.*

The Viewer Screen Objects

We simply used the form layouts developed for the requirements specification to define the viewer screen objects needed, and then we listed the objects.

Title Selection Objects

The Title Selection objects are as follows:

DESIGN SPEC: E-MagBook Viewer Screen Objects
MENU OPTIONS: **None**

Title Selection Mode	Screen Objects:
picTitle SelectionPanel	Main panel and container for Title Selection mode screen objects.
cmdLoadIndex	Open E-Magbook button.
cmdLoadNewTitles	New Disk button.
comTitleIndex	Combo list box for titles.
lblSelectedTitle	**DEBUG AID:** Contains title of selected record.
lblAboutSelectedTitle	Contains detail of selected record.
lblSelectedFileName	**DEBUG AID**: page file reference.

We'd defined the container control first and then all the objects that were contained within it. To leave Title Selection mode, the program only had to make **picTitleSelectionPanel** invisible.

Note that we'd added a debug aid, **lblSelectedFileName**. The operator could make this aid visible and use it to help debug the program by showing the selected file reference on the layout when necessary. We might find this aid useful in testing. After the function worked, we could just make the debug label invisible.

Tip

*Debug controls can be extremely useful. You can write code that outputs to screen controls that are set up with their visible properties set to **FALSE**. Under normal conditions, these controls are not visible to the user, but, if you have a problem to debug, you can make them visible. Then, you can watch the data the controls provide as the program functions. After you've fixed the problem, you can make the controls invisible again.*

You can even activate debug controls without recompiling code. If you have a data-entry field, you can set the program up so that, when you type in a special code, it switches on all the debug objects visible. As long as the code is something a normal user would never enter in the data field, you have a neat method to automatically switch on your debug controls at runtime.

Page View Objects

The page view objects are as follows:

Page View Mode, Screen Objects:

picFrontPanel		Main panel and container for Page View mode
cmdClearCriteria	**CLEAR**	Clears selection criteria text boxes
cmdGoEnd	**>>**	Go to End of Page Index
cmdGoStart	**<<**	Go to Start of Page Index
cmdNext	**>**	Go to Next Page
cmdPrevious	**<**	Go to Previous Page
cmdGoToPage	**Go To**	Solicit Page and Go to It
mmcSoundPlayer		Multimedia Control, Stop/Rew/Play
cmdSearch	**Search**	Search from Page 1
cmdSearchNext	**>**	Search from Current+1
cmdSearchPrevious	**<**	Search from Current−1
cmdShowCriteria	**Select**	Display Selection Panel
cmdShowKeys	**Keys**	Display Keys
cmdSizeText	**Text**	Show Text Only
cmdWorkBench	**WbN**	Invoke WB, Default Settings
cmdOldWorkbench	**WbO**	Invoke WB, Old Settings
cmdLoadNewTitles	**Titles**	Return to Title Selection Mode
cmdReLoad	**Reload**	Reload current page
imgImageIt		Main image control
txtText		Main text control
lblCurrent		Shows page number
lblTitlebar		Contains E-MagBook title
lblCommentLine		Located at top of form; set to hold any message
picKeyPanel		Key panel container
txtKeyView(5)		Control array; holds keys of current page
picSelectionPanel		Search criteria selection container
txtSelect(5)		Control array; holds selection strings
rdoAll		Must match all criteria

rdoAny	Must match any of the criteria
LblIndexFileName	Needed by Page Index Editor; shows Index name
lblPictureFileName	Needed by Page Index Editor; shows current picture reference
lblTextFileName	Needed by Page Index Editor; shows current text reference
lblSoundFileName	Needed by Page Index Editor; shows current sound reference

Note that **picKeyPanel** and **picSelectionPanel** are two more containers, contained within **picFrontPanel**. Each has its own group of controls embedded within.

We added the last four items because we needed them for the viewer to work inside the editor. If you recall from our earlier discussion, the Page Index Editor needed to be able to load files onto the viewer screen from the file-selection process. We also wanted to be able to display the strings that made up the Index file reference and the image, text, and sound references. (You can see these references at the bottom of the embedded viewer layouts, on the prototype form layouts of the Page Index Editor in Chapter 5.) Our reasoning was that, because the viewer had total control of what was read onto the screen, we would add four text controls to the viewer. When the viewer was running standalone, the controls would be hidden. When the Page Index Editor was using the viewer, then, as part of the Page Index Editor setup, the controls could be made visible on the viewer form.

Workbench Objects

The screen objects required for the Workbench mode of operation in the viewer would be as follows:

Workbench Mode, Screen Objects:		
imgImage2		The WB drag/drop image control
txtText2		The WB drag/drop text control
picPictureToolBar		Toolbar container for WB button controls
cmdIm2ExpandDown	-	Reduce; Preserve Aspect Ratio
cmdIm2ExpandDownH	H-	Reduce Height Only
cmdIm2ExpandDownW	W-	Reduce Width Only
cmdIm2ExpandUp	+	Increase; Preserve Aspect Ratio

cmdIm2ExpandUpH	**H+**	Increase Height Only
cmdIm2ExpandUpW	**W+**	Increase Width Only
cmdText2ExpandDownH	**H-**	Reduce Height Only
cmdText2ExpandDownW	**W-**	Reduce Width Only
cmdText2ExpandUpH	**H+**	Increase Height Only
cmdText2ExpandUpW	**W+**	Increase Width Only
cmdPrint		Screen Dump
cmdTextButtonOnOff		Toggle text2 On and Off
cmdToolEnd		Return to Viewer Mode

We placed two objects directly on the form—the image control and the text box. All the button controls were contained within a single toolbar object, made up from a picture control. To place the toolbar on screen, all we had to do was execute the following line:

```
picPictureToolBar.Visible = True
```

To remove all the button controls, we simply set the toolbar to **FALSE**. (The alternative was to toggle 13 controls' visible properties.)

The Title Index Screen Objects

You can find the list of Title Index Editor screen objects in Appendix F.

The Page Index Screen Objects

You can find the list of Page Index Editor screen objects in Appendix F.

The Viewer Screen Layouts

One area of relative complexity was the viewer's screen layout, which could consist of five possible configurations, depending upon the program's operational state: the Title Index Editor layout, three screen layouts for Page View mode (according to book format), and the Workbench layout.

We had to be able to format these screens on-the-fly. In other words, if we opened a Picture Album, we needed to be able to format the screen to handle the Picture Album format. We might then go back to Title Selection mode and open a Reference Book, and so on. The format type would be defined in the Page Index file itself. After we had opened a book, we needed to set the viewer screen objects accordingly.

Main Objects

The first thing we needed to do was to specify the principal screen objects that needed to be repositioned and sized when a format change occurred:

Viewer Screen Objects Requiring Dynamic Positioning and Sizing at Runtime

imgImageIt	The object that will hold an image in Picture Album and Reference Book formats.
txtText	The object that will hold the variable text in Text Book and Reference Book formats.
picKeyPanel	Panel container object used to display the keys of a page.
picSelectionPanel	Panel container object used to display selection criteria objects.

The image will be placed in the center of the image container area. One such area is defined for the Picture Album format and a different one is defined for the Reference Book format. For each book type, we need to define the position and dimensions of the text box. The key panel will always appear in the same place, as will the selection criteria panel. Remember, only one of these two panels can be on view at the same time. In Picture Album and Text Book formats, the panels overlay the main image or text box. In Reference Book mode, a small text box can exist when the selection or key panels are in view, or a large text box can exist when they are not present.

All this information comes from the requirements specification, and you can see it in the screenshots and layout diagrams in Chapter 5.

Origins and Dimensions

We needed to define all the format possibilities as part of the design. Figure 6.13 illustrates the viewer's form layout with four origins defined. From this diagram, we could define a data structure that could be used to set up all the relevant objects when a format change occurred.

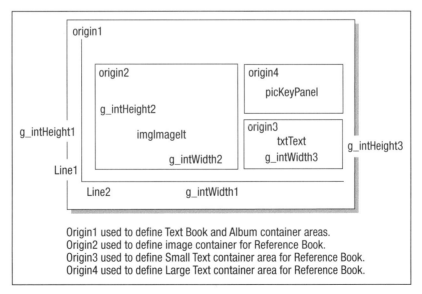

Origin1 used to define Text Book and Album container areas.
Origin2 used to define image container for Reference Book.
Origin3 used to define Small Text container area for Reference Book.
Origin4 used to define Large Text container area for Reference Book.

Figure 6.13
Viewer screen origin definitions.

Any of the screen objects (image, text, or panels) would require an origin that would provide the **.Left** and **.Top** values for the object, together with a width and a height for the **.Width** and **.Height** properties. Each object's origin and dimensions could be set up initially with a default value. When the program changed state, the code would merely select the appropriate new origin and dimensions to reset the principal screen objects. This arrangement would allow dynamic screen reconfiguration. But it would be even more useful to have a mechanism that was dynamic at design time and that would let us define the default origin and dimension values.

Data Structure

We started by defining the data structures we needed for dynamic screen layout, based on the content of Figure 6.13:

Viewer Default Screen Object Origin and Dimension Data Structure
These variables will be used to hold default values for **txtText** and the area that defines the maximum possible extent for **imgImageIt** (that is, the image must be scaled to fit inside this area). This area is referred to as the *image container area*. One such definition will exist for Picture Albums and another one will exist for Reference Books.

g_Origin1_Left and **g_Origin1_Top**

Integers defining **txtText.Left** and **txtText.Top** for Text Book format. Also used to define the top, left-hand side of the image container area for Picture Album format.

g_intOrigin2_Left and **g_intOrigin2_Top**

Integers defining the top, left-hand side of the image container area for Reference Book format.

g_intOrigin3_Left and **g_intOrigin3_Top**

Integers defining **txtText.Left** and **txtText.Top** for small version of **txtText** in Reference Book

g_intOrigin4_Left and **g_intOrigin4_Top**

Integers defining **txtText.Left** and **txtText.Top** for large version of **txtText** in Reference Book. Also defines position for either key panel or selection panel.

g_intHeight1

Integer defining **txtText.Height** in Text Book format and height of image container area for Picture Album format.

g_intHeight2

Integer defining height of image container area for Reference Book format.

g_intHeight3

Integer defining **txtText.height** for small text boxes in Reference Book format.

g_intWidth1

Integer defining **txtText.width** in Text Book format and width of image container area for Picture Album format.

g_intWidth2

Integer defining width of image container area for Reference Book format.

g_intWidth3

Integer defining **txtText.width** for Reference Book format.

A programmer could use this table to construct the common data structure and then set the various properties of **txtText** and **imgImageIt** according to the format context.

Variable Defaults

We could define all the preceding parameters as constants in the data declarations. However, a much more flexible way of doing the same thing was to make use of the VB design-time environment. Remember, we could manipulate objects at design time so that their **.Left**, **.Top**, **.Height**, and **.Width** properties were set as we required. So, why not use screen objects at design time to define the parameters' values? If we could do this, all we had to do to change the image container area for a Picture Album was modify the object that defined its location and size at design time. When the program was recompiled, all the constants would automatically be set up from the screen objects' new design-time values.

That reasoning is why you see two objects in Figure 6.13 called **Line1** and **Line2**. VB has a series of shape controls that do nothing other than let you set up shapes on the screen. The two line objects could be used to define the left-hand side and bottom of the area that would be used for both **txtText** in Text Books and the image container area in Picture Albums.

When the program loaded, it would need to run a routine that stored the positions and dimensions of the objects defined in Figure 6.13 in the relevant default variables defined earlier. This facility would provide dynamic reconfiguration of the format default values using the design time environment. The program only had to be recompiled to make any changes effective.

To set up each format, we could define a set of three viewer infrastructure subroutines that would run at program load time to set up all required constants to handle format changing. These subroutines were as follows:

Viewer Format Set Up Infrastructure Routines
Subroutine: SetupFormat1

Description: Called to set up the Text Book screen format.

ARGUMENTS: None

ACTION:

Set any relevant data for Text Book format.

Enable **txtText**.

Set origin of **txtText** to origin 1.

Set dimensions of **txtText** to Line1 height and Line2 width.

Remove **imgImageIt**.

END:

Subroutine: SetupFormat2

DESCRIPTION: Called to set up the Picture Album format.

ARGUMENTS: None

ACTION:

Set any relevant data for Picture Album format.

Enable **imgImageIt**.

Set origin of Picture Album image container to origin 1.

Set dimensions of Album image container to Line1 height and Line2 width.

Remove **txtText**.

END:

SUBROUTINE: SetupFormat3

DESCRIPTION: Called to set up the Reference Book format.

ARGUMENTS: None

ACTION:

Set any relevant data for Reference Book format.

Enable **txtText**.

Set origin of **txtText** to origin 3.

Set dimensions of **txtText** to **g_intHeight3** and **g_intWidth3**.

Enable **imgImageIt**.

Set origin of Picture Album image container to origin 2.

Set dimensions of Album image container to **g_intHeight2** and **g_intWidth2**.

END:

A programmer now had sufficient design details to create all the necessary code to handle dynamic screen configuration.

Title Index Input and Output

In Chapter 4, we defined modules for the entire project. In Chapter 5, we defined development tasks based on the need to complete the viewer first and the editors at a later date. From the design perspective, we would first look at all aspects of reading in and writing out the Title Index, regardless of which program was involved.

The modules for title handling, defined in Chapter 4, would be the following:

♦ **Read A Specified Title Index Into Program**—Required by all three programs.

♦ **Output A Title Index To Selected Disk File**—Required by the Title Index Editor.

We defined each module's function and the inputs and outputs each required. Then, we'd use pseudocode to turn the definitions into module specifications.

Title Input

This module, **Read A Specified Title Index Into Program**, was supplied with the Title Index file name as an argument. All the module had to do was open the file, check that it was a genuine Title Index by examining Line 1, and read in each record until it hit the end-of-file designator. The file format had already been defined. Using pseudocode the specification would be as follows:

FUNCTION: **ReadInTitleIndex(StrFileName) as Boolean**

DESCRIPTION: To open a named Title Index on disk and read into memory.

ARGUMENTS: StrFileName   Name of Title Index file to be loaded.

                    Function Result = True if file input OK.

                                = False if not able to read in file.

ACTION:

START.

Open **StrFileName**.

If failed, then go to **FATAL ERROR 1**.

Read Line 1, extract Field1, and verify header.

If file is not a Title Index then go to **FATAL ERROR 2**.

START LOOP:

    Read next line in file.

If **END OF FILE**, then **END LOOP**.

Extract page file reference and place in memory.

Read next line, extract title, and place in memory.

If **END OF FILE**, then go to **FATAL ERROR 3**.

Read next line, extract description, and place in memory.

If **END OF FILE**, then go to **FATAL ERROR 3**.

Read all lines until [**END OF RECORD**] is located.

If END OF FILE read, then **END LOOP**.

End loop.

Close file and **EXIT**, setting function **TRUE**.

ERROR HANDLING:

FATAL ERROR 1—Close file; inform user file cannot be opened.

EXIT, setting function **FALSE**.

FATAL ERROR 2—Close file; Inform user file is wrong type.

EXIT, setting function **FALSE**.

FATAL ERROR 3—Close file; inform user file has been truncated.

EXIT, setting function **FALSE**.

The specification was very "basic-like," using high-level statements. A programmer should have no problem coding from the preceding pseudocode and filling in any obvious gaps.

We defined the function name, its description, and its arguments based on what we determined at analysis. We added that the result of the function was a Boolean **TRUE** or **FALSE**, so that the calling code could check the result of the function. We'd also tried to use a name that was meaningful—we couldn't make it much clearer than **ReadInTitleIndex**.

We then had a description of its action. The file would be opened (remember, the file name would be supplied as an input argument) and the program would read Line 1, the first line of the file. According to the format specification, the program would extract Field 1 and check to see of it contained **E-BOOK TITLE INDEX**. If it did not contain the required text string, the module would declare an error as defined in **FATAL ERROR 2**. If Line 1 was OK, then the program would start a loop.

In the loop, the program would begin by reading the next line in the file. If this line was an end-of-file marker, the program could **EXIT**. If the line was read in, this must be Line 1 of the next Title Index record. The program would extract the file reference, then the title and description, from the next two lines and feed them into the memory variables that made up the Memory Index. If any of the reads encountered an end-of-file, a fatal error would occur because the file had been truncated before a record had been completed.

If all was well and the program had successfully read in three lines, it would continue to read in lines until it encountered [**END OF RECORD**]. When the program located the end of the record, it would go back to the start of the main loop to read in Line 1 of the next record, and so on.

Title Output

The specification for the output function is very similar to that for input:

FUNCTION: WriteOutTitleIndex(StrFileName) as Boolean
DESCRIPTION: Outputs the Memory Title Index to a specified disk file.

ARGUMENTS: StrFileName   Name file to receive Index

                    Function Result = True if file output OK.

                                        = False if not able to output file.

ACTION:

Find out if file exists.

Inform user of situation and seek authorization to proceed.

If authorization is not given, close file, **EXIT** setting function **FALSE**.

If an error occurs, at any time, then go to **FAILED TO OUTPUT**.

Open file for output.

Format header line and output to file.

Loop from start of Index to end.

      Format Lines 1 to 3 and output to file.

      Format [**END OF RECORD**], output to file.

End Loop.

Close File.

EXIT setting function **TRUE**.

ERROR HANDLING:

FAILED TO OUTPUT.

Close file.

Produce appropriate error message.

EXIT, setting function **FALSE**.

The output function was fairly dramatic in the sense that if a file name was supplied that was already in use, the code would overwrite a file's contents. This would be quite a devastating action, particularly if the user accidentally supplied the wrong file name. Consequently, the first section of the module would determine whether the file existed. The program then would inform the user of the situation and ask whether the program should proceed with the output. The two possible scenarios would be the following: "A file exists—should it be overwritten?" and "Do you want to create a new file?" The rest of the description needed no explanation—the opposite of the "read in" module. This example demonstrates the need to design with a high degree of user friendliness. We had identified the possibility of the user accidentally overwriting a file, and we had designed in some protection from that possibility.

The In-Memory Title Index

To allow a programmer to develop the input and output modules for title handling, a data structure to hold the Index was required. This couldn't have been much simpler. We'd use arrays to hold the three strings—**Title**, **Description**, and **Page Index Reference**. Now, we came to a major design issue.

In the requirements specification, we had defined a Title Index as having a maximum of 50 entries and the Page Index as having a maximum of 1,000 entries. That definition clearly provided us with a fixed size for the arrays. But we decided to implement *dynamic arrays* instead. A dynamic array initially has no memory allocated to hold it. Each time you want to add an element, you ask VB for space. When you want to remove an element, you can ask VB to drop its memory allocation. In this way, the memory requirement grows and shrinks according to demand. The main advantage in using dynamic arrays here is not that we use space efficiently, but that we don't have to worry about hard coding upper limits into the program, which have to be checked all the time. With dynamic arrays, checking can be done by using the Basic function **Ubound**, which will automatically return the highest element of an array.

The Page Index could be very large, so, if we made both title and page Indexes dynamic, they could grow and shrink as demand dictated, and we could probably accommodate more than the 50-entry and 1,000-entry limitations we had imposed on the files.

Here's our definition for the Title Index:

Title Index Memory Data Structure
Global, dynamic arrays

g_intCurrentTitle	Pointer to current title
g_strTitleTitle( )	Contains title string
g_strTitleDescription( )	Contains description string
g_strTitleFileName( )	Contains Page Index file reference

A given entry is obtained from:

g_strTitleTitle(g_intCurrentTitle)

g_strTitleDescription(g_intCurrentTitle)

g_strTitleFileName(g_intCurrentTitle)

Note that global variable names are prefixed with **g_** to indicate their global, or public, nature.

We added a pointer, **g_intCurrentTitle**. This would serve as a pointer to the current title record at any given time. The memory record would then consist of the three elements referenced by **g_intCurrentTitle**, as shown in the definition.

Page Index Input and Output

As we've discussed, the Page Index would be a much bigger file than the Title Index, but we could approach the code design in exactly the same way for both. We already had a file design around which the specifications were based.

The Page Index Input Module

The design for the Page Index input module followed what we had done for the Title Index—the two requirements were, after all, very similar. Here's what we produced:

FUNCTION: **ReadInPageIndex(StrFileName) as Boolean**
DESCRIPTION: To open a named Page Index on disk and read into memory.

ARGUMENTS: StrFileName   Name of Page Index file.

                     Function result = True if file read OK

                                  = False if file not read OK

ACTION:

Open file for read access; if error, then go to **FATAL ERROR 1**.

Read Line 1; extract Field 1.

If Field 1 is not recognized, then go to **FATAL ERROR 2**.

Set global variable format specifier, according to header type, in global memory.

Extract Fields 2 and 3 and place in global variables for font information.

On any error, go to **FATAL ERROR 3**.

START LOOP.

Read next line of file.

If **END OF FILE**, then go to **FATAL ERROR 4**.

If all fields are [**END**], then **EXIT LOOP**.

Extract Fields 1 to 8 and place in memory structures.

End loop.

Close file.

Exit; set **TRUE**.

ERROR HANDLING:

FATAL ERROR 1—Report file open failure, **EXIT**, setting function **FALSE**.

FATAL ERROR 2—Report file not Page Index, close and **EXIT**, setting function **FALSE**.

FATAL ERROR 3—Report error reading file, close and **EXIT**, setting function **FALSE**.

FATAL ERROR 4—Report file truncated, close and **EXIT**, setting function **FALSE**.

Again, you should be able to make sense of this quite easily. Note that the header line yields three variables that would need to be accommodated. The first was the book format specifier, used to indicate book type—Text Book, Picture Album, or Reference Book. This format would be determined from the header line's Field 1 (see the Page Index file specification for detail). The next two fields contain text format type and size details, which would also need to be stored. We'd define these three variables together with the Page Index structure.

The Page Index Output Module

The specification for Page Index output should be perfectly obvious, because it is a modified version of the Title Index Output module:

FUNCTION: **WriteOutPageIndex(StrFileName) as Boolean**
DESCRIPTION: Outputs the Memory Page Index to a specified disk file.

ARGUMENTS: StrFileName   Name of Page Index file to create or overwrite.

Function result = True if file output OK.

= False if file output not OK.

ACTION:

Find out if file exists.

Inform user of situation and seek authorization to proceed.

If authorization is not given, **EXIT**, setting function **FALSE**.

If any error occurs, then go to **FAILED TO OUTPUT**.

Open file for output.

Format header line and output to file.

Loop until end of Index.

Format Fields 1 to 8 and output to file.

End Loop.

Format **[END]** record and output to file.

Close file.

EXIT, setting function **TRUE**.

ERROR HANDLING:

FAILED TO OUTPUT.

Close file.

Produce appropriate error message.

EXIT, setting function **FALSE**.

The only difference between the Title Index and the Page Index Output module is that, for the Title Index, we had to output an end-of-file marker record containing eight fields, all set to **[END]**.

Page Index Data Structure

The Page Index data structure had to house the in-Memory version of the Page Index. Remember that this structure would also be a dynamic array.

Page Index Memory Data Structure
Global, dynamic array

g_intFormatType	Format specifier: 1=Text Book, 2=Picture Album, 3=Reference Book
g_strFontType	Contains font type string (for example, Palatino)
g_intFontSize	Contains font size as integer
g_intCurrentPage	Always points to current page record
g_strKeys( )	2-dimensional array
g_strPictureFile( )	1-dimensional array
g_strTextFile( )	1-dimensional array
g_strSoundFile( )	1-dimensional array

At any time, the contents of the current page are defined from:

g_strKeys(1,g_intCurrentPage) accesses key 1

g_strKeys(2,g_intCurrentPage) accesses key 2

g_strKeys(3,g_intCurrentPage) accesses key 3

g_strKeys(4,g_intCurrentPage) accesses key 4

g_strKeys(5,g_intCurrentPage) accesses key 5

g_strPictureFile(g_intCurrentPage)

g_strTextFile(g_intCurrentPage)

g_strSoundFile(g_intCurrentPage)

The three file references are straightforward, single-dimensional arrays, whereas the key array is two-dimensional because each page has five elements.

Basic Routines for Index Handling

At this detailed level of design, we could identify at least one common routine that we needed to design. We required a function in both Page Index and Title Index input that could extract data from a string read from disk.

Function: ExtractFieldData

This function would be a field extraction function. We needed a function that, if it was provided with a string, could be used to extract delimited data fields from the string. For example, the string was **strTarget**, and it contained all eight data fields of the Page Index record. We could call the function as follows:

```
booResult = Extract(strTarget,strFields(),8)
```

strTarget is the content of the full line read in by the input module. **StrFields** is a string array, which would be set up by the extraction routine to contain the eight fields, minus the delimiters. So, **strFields(1)** would contain the first field's data, **strFields(2)** the second field's data, and so on. If no data were found between delimiters, a blank string would result. The final parameter indicates how many fields to extract from.

The routine would become generic because we could define how many fields to extract. We could use the routine in the Title Index input module as well. The only difference would be the value of the last argument. We also decided to let the routine check for the end-of-data marker in the Page Index, which would consist of all fields being set to **[END]**. This function would be redundant for Title Index processing because the terminator would be found only in a Page Index.

The routine would always return a function set to **TRUE**, unless it had found the **[END]** marker. If the routine couldn't find the number of fields the operator asked for, it would return the ones not present as blank, but it would still indicate **TRUE**.

We specified a simple design as follows:

FUNCTION: **ExtractDataFields(StrToSearch, StrFields( ),intFields) as Boolean**
DESCRIPTION: Scans a string and returns requested number of delimited fields' data.

ARGUMENTS: StrToSearch   Name of string array from which to extract.

              StrFields( )   Array to receive the data.

              IntFields   Number of fields to extract.

              Function result = True for all conditions except when **END** of **DATA** found.

                                   = False if all fields contain "END".

NOTES:

If any field is not found, then all subsequent **StrFields** elements will be blank on return.

If all fields extracted are found to contain **END** then the result of the function is **FALSE**.

In all other cases, it is **TRUE**.

ACTION:

If **intFields<0**, then **EXIT**, setting function **TRUE**.

Check **intFields<=number** of elements in **StrFields( )**.

If not, then set **intFields** to actual number found.

Clear output array.

Loop from 1 to number of data fields requested.

        Find location of next "["; if not found, then go to **NO DELIMITER**.

        Find location of next "]"; if not found, then go to **NO DELIMITER**.

        Extract data from between [and] and place in output array.

End Loop.

Loop from 1 to number of data fields requested.

If **output field<>"END"** then **EXIT**, setting function **TRUE**.

End Loop.

EXIT, setting function **FALSE** (that is, **END** marker found).

ERROR CONDITIONS:

NO DELIMITER.

EXIT, setting function **TRUE**.

This design had now created the need for us to define a function to locate the delimiter.

Function: LocateDelimiter

We designed a function that first searched a given string from a predefined character position, looking for a target character code, and then returned the value of the position as the result of the function. If the function couldn't find the required character, it returned the value of 0.

FUNCTION: **LocateDelimiter(StrToSearch,StrChar,intStartPosition) as Integer**

DESCRIPTION: Return position of first occurrence of target character in string from start position as result of function.

ARGUMENTS: StrToSearch   String to search.

StrChar   Character to search for.

IntStartPosition Position in string to start searching from.

Function result = 0 if StrChar not found, else=position of **StrChar**.

ACTION:

Loop from start position to end of target string.

　　　If current character=Character to search for, then **EXIT** setting function to position of character.

End Loop.

EXIT, setting function to 0.

We'd now specified enough for someone to go away and develop all the modules associated with reading and writing the Index files.

Display Page

As we determined in the previous chapter, the display page development was dependent on the modules to load and display the various multimedia files and text. So, we'd look at all these modules together. The work we'd performed in the various feasibility studies would be a great help as we developed these modules.

We designed the modules using pseudocode and referred to the feasibility studies for guidance. What follows are the design specifications for the **DisplayPage**, **DisplayImage**, **ShowVideoClip**, and **PlaySound** modules and a text handling module. You should find the specifications straightforward and meaningful.

DisplayPage Subroutine

We decided that this routine would be a subroutine with no calling arguments. The subroutine would act only on the contents of the in-Memory Page Index. Our first attempt at a design came out like this:

SUBROUTINE: DisplayPage( )
DESCRIPTION: According to format, display all the contents of a given page.

ACTION:

Set up key panel text fields with keys for current page.

If Text Book format, then

       LoadAndDisplayText.

End if.

If Album format, then

     If image, then **LoadAndDisplayImage.**

     If video, then **LoadAndPlayVideo.**

End if.

     If Reference format, then

     If image, then **LoadAndDisplayImage.**

     If video, then **LoadAndPlayVideo.**

LoadAndDisplayText.

End if.

If sound is present, then **LoadAndPlaySound.**

End:

This routine needed to know about screen objects on the viewer so that it could call the library modules with the screen objects' names. For this reason, we would implement it as a viewer, private, infrastructure routine.

Initially, we decided that **DisplayPage** would use the page record arrays to set up the data for the calls to the image, video, text, and sound routines and to set up the keys on screen. That approach was fine until, later on, we started looking at the design for the file selection form in the Page Index Editor.

Influence from the Page Index Editor

If you recall, the file selection form in the Page Index Editor must allow a user to select a video, image, text, or sound file from the file store and load it onto the screen to edit or create a page's content. When we started to design the routines required in the file-selection form, it became obvious to us that the routines would have to make decisions based on book format, image container area, and so on; their design started to become quite complex. While trying to design the code, it became apparent that most of the data and routines needed were already established in the viewer's design.

Then, Archie had the idea of making **DisplayPage** more generic. He argued that **DisplayPage** could be called in one of two ways. The first type of call required **DisplayPage** to use the in-Index arrays to populate the screen objects, which satisfied the requirement to load a page from a Page Index record (much as the first attempt at the design had indicated). The second type of call required the module to use the content of the three file-reference, text-box objects in the viewer and leave the keys on screen untouched. This second call would then furnish the requirement for creating and/or editing a page's contents. The file selection form's code would then need only to set up the correct screen text object at the bottom of the viewer with the appropriate file reference, and directly call **DisplayPage** in the viewer form using the second type of call. Leaving the keys untouched meant that they would exhibit whatever condition the user had manually set.

This design made enormous sense. **DisplayPage** would inherently know how to set up the screen according to format. It could either get its data from the in-Memory Page Index to display a page from a book, or it could get its file data from the file-reference text boxes— **txtPictureFileName.Text**, **txtTextFileName.Text**, and **txtSoundFileName.Text**—to redraw the page when the user wished to use the Page Editor to edit one of the multimedia objects.

Put another way, this alternative use of **DisplayPage** would allow the routine to be used to reconstruct the screen in the page editor **Alert 1 Changed State**, when the user was editing page records. The routines in the file selection form needed only to take the file reference specified by the user, place the reference in the appropriate text box inside the viewer form, set the alert state, and call **DisplayPage** using its alternative entry.

This approach changed the design of **DisplayPage**. If we had been designing only for the viewer, we would have lost this possibility, but, because we were designing the complete system now, our original thinking for **DisplayPage** was influenced. If you don't design with the complete system in mind, as this example demonstrates, you can easily compromise the later stages of the design.

Final Design for DisplayPage

The new design for **DisplayPage**, to accommodate both the viewer and the Page Index Editor requirements, became the following:

SUBROUTINE: DisplayPage(intDisplayType)
DESCRIPTION: Option 1: According to format, display all the contents of a given page.

Option 2: According to format, update image/video, text, sound according to contents of:

txtPictureFileName.Text for image or video

txtTextFileName.Text for text

txtSoundFileName.Text for sound track

ARGUMENT:

intDisplayType optional argument:

If absent, set up from Page Index record.

If present, set up from text objects and leave keys.

Action:

If **intDisplayType** is not present, then:

Set up key panel text fields with keys for current page from memory arrays.

PictureToLoad=g_strPictureFile(g_intCurrentPage)

TextToLoad=g_strTextFile(g_intCurrentPage)

SoundToLoad=g_strSound(g_intCurrentPage)

Else

Leave keys alone

PictureToLoad=txtPitureFileName.Text

TextToLoad=txtTextFileName.Text

SoundToLoad=txtSoundFileName.Text

End if

If Text Book format, then:

LoadAndDisplayText using TextToLoad.

End if

If Album format, then:

If image, then LoadAndDisplayImage using PictureToLoad.

If video, then LoadAndPlayVideo using PictureToLoad.

End if

If Reference Book format, then:

If image, then LoadAndDisplayImage using PictureToLoad.

If video, then LoadAndPlayVideo using PictureToLoad.

LoadAndDisplayText using TextToLoad.

End if

If sound present, then LoadAndPlaySound using SoundToLoad.

End

Testing Considerations

Testing for **DisplayPage** will consist of setting up some file references in an in-Memory Index structure and calling the routine with a page number set. We could simulate this situation quite easily, just by setting the first element of the arrays and setting **g_intCurrentPage** to **1**. As we have already established, we couldn't test **DisplayPage** until we had developed all the other multimedia and text-load modules.

We could test **DisplayPage**'s second mode by setting up dummy versions of the text labels and providing an alternative initialization of the test. The result of this test would be to load the page using the text box references rather than the Page Index record.

Design for LoadAndDisplayImage

We covered image handling in the feasibility study that we did early in the project. Fundamentally, we needed to make this routine completely generic. We needed to call the routine in such a way that we had defined all the information it needed to operate, regardless of page format.

First, the routine would load the image into an image control. If you recall, we could put a GUI routine into a library, provided that we defined the identity of the screen object at runtime in the calling sequence. The routine would have to scale the image to fit into the image container area, which was a function of the book format. Again, we didn't want the routine to have to be format "aware," so we needed to supply details via the calling arguments concerning the area into which we wanted the image sized and then placed. These details would consist of the width, height, left, and top values of the container area. With these details, the routine had everything it needed to scale and position the image correctly. We were placing the onus on the calling routine to make sure that the container area was fully defined.

If you recall from the prototypes, we needed to load the image into an image control with its **stretch** property set **FALSE**. The control then would automatically expand to the full size of the image. This ability allowed us to get the image's true dimensions, which we used to scale the image into the container area. We then set the image control's **stretch** property to **TRUE** and resized the control to the values we had calculated that allowed it to fit within the area. We then positioned the image control so that it was neatly fitted into the center of the area and made it visible.

NOTE: *If you have any trouble with the above description, go back to the feasibility study we did in Chapter 2 before you continue.*

Here's the specification that we came up with:

**FUNCTION: LoadAndDisplayImage(StrFileRef,imgObject,intMaxW,intMaxH,intLeft,intTop)_
As Boolean**
DESCRIPTION: To load, scale, and position an image into the available image area on screen

ARGUMENTS:

StrFileRef	Image file reference.
ImgObject	Name of image control to hold picture.
IntMaxW	Maximum permitted width of image.
IntrMaxH	Maximum permitted height of image.
IntLeft	Left coordinate of container area for image.
IntTop	Top coordinate of container area for image.
Function result	=True if image loaded OK.
	=False if image not loaded.

ACTION:

On any error, **Goto LoadFail**.

Set **imgObject.Visible** to **FALSE**.

Set **imgObject.Stretch** to **FALSE**.

Load image into **imgObject**.

     Call **SizePicture**.

Resize **imgObject** according to **SizePicture** results.

Position **imgObject** in center of available area.

Set **imgObject.Stretch** to **TRUE**.

Set **imgObject.Visible** to **TRUE**.

EXIT, setting function **TRUE**.

ERROR HANDLING:

LoadFail:

     EXIT, setting function **FALSE**.

The important thing about this specification was that it was totally generic. We could use it for either the Picture Album or Reference Book formats. In fact, as long as the container area was defined appropriately before the routine was called, we could use the code to scale and place an image into any image container in any program.

SizePicture

We did, of course, need to specify **SizePicture**. But, then, we did have some assistance from the feasibility study. We produced the specification directly from that work:

SUBROUTINE: SizePicture(intCW,intCH,intActualW,intActualH)
DESCRIPTION: Calculate actual size of image required to fit into defined container area.

ARGUMENTS:

IntCW	Maximum possible width allowed in container area.
IntCH	Maximum possible height allowed in container area.
IntActualW	On entry—Holds image's full-sized width.
	On exit—Set to hold scaled width.
IntActualH	On entry—Holds images full-sized height.
	On exit—Set to hold scaled height.

ACTION:

Aspect Ratio=intActualW/intActualH

If **intActualW>intCW**, then

   intActualW=intCW

   Calculate new **intActualH**

End if

If **intActualH>intCH**, then

   intActualH=intCH

   Calculate new **intActualW**

End if

END:

LoadAndPlayVideo

Once again, we could specify the design for this function based on the work we had done in the feasibility study. Don't forget that, to play a video, we needed to have a video form and a multimedia control on hand, both of which we could declare in the arguments.

FUNCTION: LoadAndPlayVideo(StrFileName,frmForm,mmcObject,intMaxW,intMaxH, intLeft,intTop) as Boolean
DESCRIPTION: To load and run a video clip on screen.

ARGUMENTS:

StrFileName	File reference to video clip.

FrmForm	Name of form in which to play video.
MmcObject	Name of multimedia control for video.
IntMaxW	Maximum width of playing area.
IntMaxH	Maximum height of playing area.
IntLeft	Position of top LHS of playing area.
IntTop	Position of top LHS of playing areas.
Function result	= True if video loaded OK.
	= False if video not loaded OK.

ACTION:

If any error, then go to **VIDEO ERROR**.

Close **mmcObject**.

Set **mmcObject.devicetype** to **AVIVIDEO**.

Load file name into **mmcObject**.

Define video form's window handle.

Open **mmcObject**.

Force **mmcObject** to play video.

Position **frmForm** in center of container area.

EXIT, setting function **TRUE**.

VIDEO ERROR

EXIT, setting function **FALSE**.

Design for LoadAndPlaySound

In analysis, we had defined two requirements for this function—one to play a WAV file and one to play a MID file. When we looked at the feasibility work in preparation for designing the functions, we decided that we had to design only a single function to load and play the sound file, regardless of the file type. We could do that because the multimedia control could automatically determine the type of sound file. So, the design for a single function became the following:

FUNCTION: **LoadAndPlaySound(StrFileName,mmcObject) as Boolean**
DESCRIPTION: Load a file and play as a WAV or MID as appropriate.

ARGUMENTS: StrFileName   File reference to WAV or MID file.

	mmcObject	Name of multimedia control for playing sound.
	Function result	=True if sound loaded OK.
		= False if sound not loaded OK.

ACTION:

If any error, then go to **SOUND ERROR**.

Close **mmcObject**.

Load file name into **mmcObject**.

Open **mmcObject**.

Force **mmcObject** to play sound.

EXIT, setting function **TRUE**.

SOUND ERROR

EXIT, setting function **FALSE**.

At this stage, Archie pointed out that nothing could beat good preparation for design. He was referring to the feasibility work we had done, which had clearly made a positive impact on the work we had to do to design the necessary modules.

Design for Text Handling

To load and display text, we defined the following:

FUNCTION: **LoadAndDisplayText(StrFileName,txtObject) as Boolean**
DESCRIPTION: To read in and display text in a text display area, with correct font characteristics.

ARGUMENTS:	**StrFileName**	Name of text file to load.
	TxtObject	Name of screen object to receive text.
	Function result	= True if file loaded OK.
		= False if file not loaded OK.

ACTION:

Call **OpenAndReadTextIntoMemory**.

If text read OK, then

set function to **TRUE**.

Load **txtObject** from string.

Else

      set function to **FALSE**.

End if

Exit function

We decided to use a function called **OpenAndReadTextIntoMemory**, a new generic, pure function to handle the actual opening and reading in of the text file.

OpenAndReadTextIntoMemory Function

We had to think a bit about text files before we produced the required design. The way in which we had defined input from the Index files was for the program to read in a complete line on every read. We could have the program do the same here, but that action would return all the characters up to the first carriage return/line feed pair, which we were used as line delimiters by the operating system. The first line read after the file was opened would be input from Byte 1 of the file up to the first terminator pair. The next line read would then input from the first character of the new line to the next terminator pair. So, if we read the file one line at a time and built up a string for output to the text control, we would lose all the line-feed carriage returns because the VB line-read function would not transfer these to the input string. This meant that when we put the resultant string into the text box, the string would not be structured the same as data in the text file. Any carriage returns forced by the person who created the file would be lost—in other words, the paragraph structure would disappear.

So the design indicated that we needed to add the carriage return and line-feed terminators back to the string before it was concatonated with the lines already read in.

FUNCTION: **OpenAndReadTextIntoMemory(StrFileName,StrText) as Boolean**
DESCRIPTION: Open a text file, read line by line, and build up a string containing the complete content of the file, including carriage-return, line-feed terminators.

ARGUMENTS: StrFileName   Name of file to read in.

            Strtext   Name of string into which text is placed.

        Function result =True if file read OK.

                  = False if file not read OK.

ACTION:

On any error, go to **TEXT FAIL**.

Open file **StrFileName** for input.

Blank **StrText**.

```
LOOP while not END OF FILE.
      Read next line into StrTemp.
         Strtext=Strtext+StrTemp+vbCr+vbLf
End loop.
Close file.
EXIT, setting function TRUE.
ERROR HANDLING:
TEXT FAIL:
Close file.
EXIT, setting function FALSE.
```

vbCr and **vbLf** are VB system constants that represent the carriage return and line-feed ASCII codes.

The Rest of the Design

It had taken us the whole day to get this far, which was not bad progress. At a rough estimate, we believed we had completed about 20 percent to 30 percent of the total design. We had three days allocated for design, so, by that reckoning, we were on target. In fact, we finished the bulk of the design a good half-day ahead of schedule.

By now, you should have a good idea about pseudocode. The pseudo language is quite intuitive, and the structure adopted is simple to comprehend. All the examples we have looked at consist of simple sequential code with minor loop requirements. This format lends itself well to description by pseudocode.

You've seen the process of creating the specifications at work. You should be able to read the definitions in Appendix G easily. We haven't looked in detail at any flow diagrams; we'll leave that until we start to develop the relevant code. You can then look at design from a programmer's, rather than a designer's, perspective.

Module Testing

After you have completed the design for your project, it's time to consider the testing requirements you will place on the programmers who will convert the design into code. To recap, we are considering two principal types of testing—module testing in development and formal acceptance testing.

The formal acceptance testing consists of performing a series of predetermined, documented tests and checking a "Pass" or a "Fail" on the documentation. You could conduct development testing in the same way, but that can be very restricting for the programmers. Moreover, programmers are not good, objective testers. So we'll leave the more formal aspects of testing to both system and acceptance testing when we have the integrated software environment to check out.

When we started the case study, we said we would relax the formal aspect of module testing—it just wasn't necessary on a project of this size and would merely hamper development. But whatever the size of your project, you must produce some guidelines for what the programmers should test—what they should look for and what they must report. Remember, the better the testing in development, the less hassle later. You have to come up with a testing strategy that each programmer can understand and employ consistently.

Testing for Expected Conditions

So, what sort of things should a programmer be told to test for? The answer to that question clearly depends on the nature of the module itself. You can consider the module as a black box. It has inputs with which it performs a given function, and then it produces outputs. Clearly, the first step should be to determine what output is expected from a given set of inputs, and the second step should be to determine whether the result is as expected. The programmer will then have to assess the number of variations and determine how many are different enough to merit an individual test. You want the programmer to check as much of the functionality as possible. Consequently, a key theme is to establish the possible variations between input and corresponding output, and then to devise a single test to accommodate each major variation you identify. For each such variation, you need a defined input and predicted output that can be verified.

Let's look at an example from the case study. The **LoadAndDisplayImage** module takes a file reference, loads the file into the image control, and sizes the image. A simple test would be to give the module the name of an image and see whether it loads that image, centered in the image container area. But look at the possible variations:

♦ Image width and height fit into container area without modification.

♦ Image width is too big for container; height is OK.

♦ Image width is OK, but height is too big for container.

♦ Both height and width are too big for container.

Each of these possible input conditions will lead to a different path through the code. We have, therefore, four individual tests to perform on the module for a given image type.

To be precise, the programmer ought to repeat the four tests for each single file type; that's certainly something the acceptance testing will specify. However, if time is running out, the programmer can relax this requirement because nothing in the code he or she writes is image type-specific (that is, there are no alternative routes through the code according to image type).

NOTE: *This is the type and level of detail to which we want the programmers to go to determine what tests to apply.*

Of course, these tests apply only to the code doing what it's supposed to do. What happens if the program meets an exception condition?

Testing for Exception Conditions

The other aspect of testing is to get the programmer to define all the exception conditions and devise a single test to ensure that the code works for each possible error condition. Most programmers fail to thoroughly check a given module's error-handling capability. The design specification has, hopefully, identified the possible error conditions, and the programmer needs to check each one.

Again, let's look a specific example from the case study. We'll look at navigation of the Page Index and the **Go To Page** function, in which the user defines the page number to display. You've not yet seen the design specification for this, so here it is:

SUBROUTINE: GoToPage( )
DESCRIPTION: Gets the page number required from the user and displays that page.

ARGUMENTS: None

ACTION:

Solicit the page number from the user.

If page number not integer value, then go to **FAILED FORMAT**.

If **page number<1**, then set page number to **1**.

If **page number>max page**, then set page number to **max**.

Set global page number variable to new value.

Display page.

EXIT

ERROR HANDLING:

FAILED FORMAT

Provide suitable error message.

EXIT

The obvious test is to type in a page number and verify that that page comes onto the screen. But we have two exception conditions and one error condition to check. The first two conditions are to check that any integers less than 1 or greater than the maximum page number are trapped correctly to either the first or the last page, as appropriate. The error test is to check that the module handles garbage input (that is, the user types in a string of alpha characters instead of a number).

From the design, we can identify the following tests for this module:

- ◆ Correct page is retrieved when integer lies between first and last page.

- ◆ First page is displayed for a **page number<1** entered.

- ◆ Last page is displayed for a **page number>max** page number.

- ◆ Error condition: non-integer is input—error handling invoked.

Now, we have three possible normal conditions that need to be checked, and one exception condition that results in the module being unable to fulfill its objective.

We identified all these conditions from the design specification. Consequently, someone other than the programmer who produced the module could establish the module tests. We will, however, ask the programmer to define the tests. Our reasoning is that, after the programmer has developed the code, other conditions might manifest themselves that the design overlooked. In that case, the programmer would be expected to identify such occurrences.

Quality Assurance

Setting up the test definitions and conducting the tests is a lot of work. That's why I made a big point earlier about trying to establish estimates for module development that included testing. But why bother? The answer is *quality assurance (Q/A)*. Many programmers will become quite offended if you intimate that they don't automatically produce quality software. (In my experience, however, the worst programmers seem to be most upset by the implication.) The point is this: The goal is to establish a system that *assures* that quality is part of the development process. To do that, we need to *prove* that quality is assessed at every stage of the process. And we provide that proof with reviews, reports, and test results.

Traceability

As I've said earlier in this book, software is finding its way into literally every walk of life, from washing machines to communications devices, from aircraft control systems to elevators. Software is the heart of many systems, and a system is only as good as the program that runs it.

Suppose you build a software-controlled device that is to be sold to and used by the general public. Suppose that the software has an obscure bug in it, which doesn't manifest itself in manufacturing or system testing. Let's say the device is also deemed "safety critical." In other words, the system might result in damage to property or persons if it goes wrong. But because of a certain combination of events, the bug causes some sort of a failure when a customer is using the device.

Clearly, such software must be rigorously tested. But—in all but the smallest applications—it's impossible to test modern software, particularly event-driven applications, such that every single combination of code execution can be tested. Consequently, what you must prove is that you took every reasonable precaution to make sure that the system was designed, developed, and tested to the highest standards. All the specifications and testing are vital to prove to whomever needs proof—be that a customer or a judge—that you constructed your software to the best of your ability, with quality assurance embedded in the process.

Saying to a lawyer "But we tested it over and over again" does no good. The lawyer needs documented evidence that the testing actually took place, and evidence of what the testing comprised. In some industries, such evidence must be shown as part of the acceptance process. This is particularly so if you are involved in any projects associated with the pharmaceutical industry. Pharmaceutical manufacturers must meet stringent national and international regulations concerning their manufacturing and testing processes. And those regulations include any software these manufacturers purchase from suppliers that contributes to their manufacturing process.

Not only do such clients insist on going over your code with a fine-toothed comb, they frequently do the same with your project documentation, particularly that related to testing and results. But, what happens if you don't have any traceable audit data? Before you get the contract to develop this sort of critical system, you will be told what type of quality criteria you must meet. One such criterion is likely to be that you have the correct systems and procedures in place to provide suitable traceability throughout your SDLC. So, you won't get the order to begin with unless you meet the specified criteria. (That's how critical quality assurance is becoming in the software industry—if you can't prove you have a quality system in place, don't bother applying for the work.)

Some organizations probe deeply when they do an external audit, often to the extent of talking directly to the programmers. But these organizations are not on a witch-hunt. They are trying to establish that you took all necessary precautions to produce a good product and that you can back up your claims with paperwork—that's the heart of quality assurance. Unfortunately, most people in the software industry regard Q/A as testing, but testing is only a part of it. Proper Q/A pervades every aspect of the process of turning concept into code.

Module Testing Guidelines

Let's get back to guidelines for module testing and define a suitable set to give to a programmer, together with a set of module design specifications. Together, these guidelines and specifications will require significant documented testing from each programmer. The trick is to define the guidelines so they do not become an excessive burden that outweighs their value. (When a contract mandates requirements for exhaustive testing, ensure that you cost the extra work required into the module development expenses.)

Each project is different, and so are its testing requirements. Consequently, the best approach is to address each project individually and define a set of standards or guidelines that are most applicable to the project. Hopefully, you will be able to address the testing requirements for each project by making minor modifications to a set of standard guidelines.

For example, in the case study, we didn't need the massive amount of auditability that a project for the pharmaceutical industry would require, so we'd use standard guidelines. Where necessary, we'd apply project-specific modifications to the guidelines. The trick, as always, would be to find the right balance. Here are the module testing guidelines we produced for the E-MagBook project programmers:

Guidelines for Module Testing

1. Assess the variation of likely inputs.

2. Go through the design and/or code and list possible pathways for normal processing of defined inputs.

3. Go through the design and/or code and list possible exception pathways.

4. Establish a list of input conditions, pathways, and expected output for all normal module behavior.

5. Establish a list of input conditions, pathways, and expected output for all exception handling.

6. Make sure that you test each defined condition and get the expected result. Record the event.

7. If your test fails, record the fact and indicate the action you took.

8. When you have completed the module and all tests have passed, have the project manager authorize the record and store the authorization in the project file.

You might think all this formality is excessive, but addressing accountability at this level is becoming an increasingly common requirement for software houses. We didn't need to go overboard on our testing guidelines for the E-MagBook project. But formal testing is a discipline and frame of mind you must get into as an integral part of the SDLC.

Objective Design Review

When you develop a design, code a module, or are involved in any creative processes on a project, you tend to develop a subjective view of the work. Consequently, you need to have such work reviewed by other people who are knowledgeable about the project but who did not work directly on the area that requires reviewing. This principle applies to everything you do as a software developer. (For example, when Archie had written some code and tested it, Julie could review it.) Someone who has not been involved in a job can often look at the work and see all sorts of things you can't see because you are too close to it. (You can't see the forest for the trees, so to speak.)

If you work in a team-driven environment, you need to get used to the idea of someone else examining your code. At first, that process can be a bit daunting, and you can become very protective when your work is first exposed to reviews. But consider the review as a positive exercise—and remember, you will be asked to review other peoples' work, too.

An employer views a good programmer not only as someone who has a flair for writing programs, but also as someone who can work in a team environment—someone who doesn't mind having his or her work reviewed, and who can willingly and constructively review other people's work. As an essential part of guaranteeing quality, reviewing and being reviewed must become second nature to you. And the quality assurance comes from being able to audit written reviews. (As in most cases, evidence that you have done something is crucial.)

If you work in a well-established environment, systems and procedures will be in place to tell you how to go about a review. You will have lists of things to look for, and, if you spot anything that isn't on the list, you'll be expected to speak out. That is all part of quality assurance.

Return to the Case Study:
Reviewing the Design

It was now Thursday of Week 4. The work had become quite technical. We had produced design specifications based on pseudocode and a handful of flow diagrams to describe the more complex areas. As with all the work we had produced so far, we left time for review. We'd asked Charlie to review the design to check for compliance to standards and also to provide a technical review. I was there to help him with any questions he might have.

The complete design is presented in Appendix G. If you want to review it, use the following criteria to judge it from the point of view of a programmer:

♦ Do you think you could code from the design specification?

♦ Are all the pathways clear?

♦ Is all the exception handling clear and complete?

♦ Could you establish module test criteria from the design alone?

Monitoring Progress in Development

After you have produced a development plan, you need to monitor the plan while it's in progress. (In the case study, we'd been monitoring our plan daily in a simplistic manner so far. But we were about to start running parallel activities with critical paths that would affect other individuals if the work was delayed, so we would need to monitor our progress more formally.)

Waiting until the end of a project to compare "planned time" against "actual time spent" provides you with a brilliant indicator of how good or bad your estimating was, but that approach doesn't stop you from overrunning your estimates. The purpose of progress monitoring is to prevent you from missing deadlines, because you never want to deliver late. More than anything else, customers hate being told, just before a scheduled delivery is due, that you will not make the delivery date. (They hate being told you'll be late any time, but to learn a few days before delivery that the product isn't ready is guaranteed to cause major aggravation.)

As a consultant, I've been to project meetings where we've been told, week after week, that the software development is "on schedule." Then, suddenly, just before delivery, we learn the software is actually going to take another three months to complete. I've never come across a situation where the delay announced at the eleventh hour wasn't known about for a considerable amount of time beforehand. Those involved often have a tendency to hope the problem will go away and right itself—wishful thinking, I'm afraid. Good project management involves assessing the plans constantly: How are we performing? Are we on target? What are the risks? How can we measure progress?

Allocated Time vs. Actual Time

A project plan has *allocated time*—that is, an amount of time allocated to perform a given task or activity. The process of completing the project itself involves *actual time*—that is, the time the given task or activity in reality required to complete. When you compare the number of days allocated to the number of days actually spent to complete the task, you have a measure of performance. For example, you planned that a given task would take 10 days, and you did the job in 8 days, or 12 days, or whatever time. The point is, by comparing these numbers you have an absolute measure of performance—two days under target, or two days over, or whatever. But you do this measurement retrospectively. You need a method to do a similar measurement with activities that are still in progress. We will refer to that measurement as *work achieved*.

Work Achieved

At the end of each week (five-day working week), you can see what progress has been made on the project. Make sure that, in each week, you have a measurable goal, even if it's only something such as *Have test harness completed and installed, ready for use*. At the end of each week, see how many of the designated tasks have been met. Then, use your judgment to determine how much you have *achieved* against the plan.

For example, let's assume that you have broken Task X down into a series of sub-tasks. You will work full-time on this project for five weeks. You need to fulfill 20 person-days of effort in a total of 25 available days. Assume, therefore, that you have four days allocated and one contingency day each week (the 80 percent availability factor again). At the end of each week, determine what you have completed, what is still outstanding but you should have completed, and so on. Then, provide your third figure: your estimated *achieved* time against the plan.

Let's see how this method works with the example. You have to complete Task X, which you've broken down into sub-tasks A, B, C, and D. You've planned these tasks as shown in Figure 6.14.

The figure shows the project week number in the first column. Column 2 shows when each sub-task is due to start, and Column 3 shows when each sub-task is due to end. "Planned time" is our estimate of how long the task will take. In Week 1, you expect to complete the whole of Task A

Week	Tasks Started	Tasks Completed	Planned Time
1	a	a	2 days
1	b		2 days
2		b	3 days
2	c		1 day
3		c	3 days
3	d	d	1 day

Figure 6.14
Planned time for development Task X.

in two days. You expect to start Task B and achieve two days out of a total of five—that is, two-fifths of the work. In Week 2, you expect to complete Task B in an additional three days. Then, you expect to start Task C and achieve one day, or one-fourth, of the total required for Task C. In the final week, you expect to complete Task C, and start and complete Task D. At the end of the first week, let's say the situation looks like what you see in Figure 6.15.

You had a very good first week. You set out to complete Task A, which you did, in one day instead of two. So you spent one day (actual time), but achieved the two days against the plan and completed the sub-task. Task B was even better. You originally planned to start it and achieve two days' progress in Week 1 and a further three days' progress in Week 2, at which point you would complete the sub-task. In fact, you started and completed Task B in just two days of Week 1—the equivalent of achieving five days against two actually spent. This was very good progress in the first week. You are now well ahead of schedule. You have three extra days of contingency time.

What happened next? The next week was not so good, as you can see in Figure 6.16.

You had nothing to do on Task B because you finished that in the previous week, ahead of schedule. But you got bogged down in a sub-task (Task C) that was supposed to take a total of four days, starting in Week 2 and ending in Week 3. You spent the whole week on Task C and

Week	Tasks Started	Tasks Completed	Planned Time	Status	Actual Time	Achieved
1	a	a	2 days	Done	1 day	2 days
1	b		2 days	Done	2 days	5 days
2		b	3 days			
2	c		1 day			
3		c	3 days			
3	d	d	1 day			

Figure 6.15
Planned and actual time spent for development Task X after the first week.

Week	Tasks Started	Tasks Completed	Planned Time	Status	Actual Time	Achieved
1	a	a	2 days	Done	1 day	2 days
1	b		2 days	Done	2 days	5 days
2		b	3 days	Done		
2	c		1 day	WIP	5 days	0 days
3		c	3 days			
3	d	d	1 day			

Figure 6.16
Task X after Week 2.

got nowhere. You lost all your hard-earned extra contingency time, and, what's worse, you have only three planned days left for this sub-task, in which to complete four days of planned effort. It's time to call in the cavalry because something is clearly very wrong. Our built-in, early-warning system has triggered. Help arrives. What happens next?

What do you have to do? You have to complete a total of four person-days' estimated effort in three actual days to get back on schedule. You've already put five days of effort into Task C, and you've gotten nowhere. With help from the cavalry, you get back on track, as Figure 6.17 shows.

You put two people on Task C, and they took a further combined six person-days of effort to complete the task. Therefore, the project required a grand total of 11 person-days to produce Task C, counting the work you did the week before. You managed to finish Task D in the one day planned.

Swings and Roundabouts

The preceding example is software development for you—swings and roundabouts. Early warning of issues, together with built-in contingency time, are essential to be able to meet those all-important time schedules. Being able to bring in the cavalry also helped. But re-member—never deliver late.

Week	Tasks Started	Tasks Completed	Planned Time	Status	Actual Time	Achieved
1	a	a	2 days	Done	1 day	2 days
1	b		2 days	Done	2 days	5 days
2		b	3 days	Done		
2	c		1 day		5 days	0 days
3		c	3 days	Done	6 days	4 days
3	d	d	1 day	Done	1 day	1 day

Figure 6.17
Week 3 for Project X.

Estimating is not always easy. Planning is not always easy. Gauging performance is not always easy. Perhaps that's why so many software projects are late. (But all engineering disciplines face the same problems, yet only the software industry seems to have such an outstandingly poor reputation.)

Basic Rules to Help Monitor Progress

To achieve a development on time by successfully monitoring progress, we can establish these rules:

- *Split up the job*—into reasonably well-defined tasks, none of which requires more than 5 to 10 days' effort.

- *Split tasks into sub-tasks*—if you can.

- *Think "early warning"*—which could mean the difference between delivering on time and overrunning.

- *Plan the tasks with plenty of contingency*—so that when the early warning system kicks in, you have some maneuverability.

- *Monitor all the time*—the only way to get early warning.

- *Look for trends*—which should give you a good indication of where problems lie and, possibly, why.

- *When in trouble*—call for help early.

Control the Ego

Some programmers make it a matter of honor to sort out an issue, regardless of the time it takes. That might be self-edifying, but if such behavior is affecting the schedule, the programmer will not be very popular. In fact, he or she becomes a project liability, and a good manager will do everything possible to get rid of such a liability if the behavior becomes an identifiable trend with any individual.

Keep it Small

Small is beautiful in the world of software. Small teams work far more efficiently than big teams. The bigger the team, the more time you'll spend communicating and managing. If you have a query and the person who can answer it is sitting a few feet away from you, you have access to the answer more readily than if that person were in a different room, building, town, state, or country.

Efficiency can also be accomplished on big projects by selecting small teams to work on self-contained aspects of the total project. This is another very strong argument for good modular design. Each self-contained development can be run as a mini-project, and, provided the interfaces between the self-contained entities are well defined, integration of the modules will not be a major issue.

It's rarely true that you can't split up big projects into smaller sub-projects, but where this is not possible, then really good communications across the team is vital. Email provides an extremely efficient way of disseminating information across a large group. The drawback tends to be the volume of redundant information you are exposed to, all of which must be read to verify whether the content is applicable to your particular circumstances within the project.

Early Warning

Good planning and constant monitoring will ensure that you have early warning of problems. Then, when you learn of a problem, take whatever action is needed to ensure that you can meet the delivery date. If your action still does not sort out the problem, then functionality must be shed to avoid missing a contractual delivery date, albeit with reduced functionality. See what you can move to another phase so that you have a product to deliver on time. Then, you can set about recovering the situation in that later phase. Almost without exception, it is better to deliver *something* that the customer can use rather than *nothing*.

NOTE: *I can't stress enough how important it is for programmers to meet time schedules. The software development industry has not only a bad name—it has an appalling one in this context. As developers, we can rectify that situation, but doing so requires an educational process. I cannot teach you in this book (or any other book for that matter) how to estimate accurately, and plan with precision. That skill comes only with experience. In this book, you get a feel for what's required, but, at the end of the day, it's up to you. Don't forget that many engineering disciplines face the same sort of issues that you will face, and they have a much better reputation than the software industry. Don't get into the habit of thinking that because you are writing software, overrunning your schedule is acceptable. It isn't.*

The Next Step

You've chosen your platform, the design is complete, and independent reviewers have thoroughly reviewed the design. You have a testing strategy for the programmers. You are ready for coding to start.

In the case study, we were now as prepared as we could be for the development of the viewer. If, for any reason, Archie or Julie suddenly disappeared, we had enough documentation to get someone up to speed quickly to take over. Although the viewer was not a particularly big project, we would need to do a detailed progress assessment at the end of each week and call in the cavalry if the assessment indicated we had a problem. If that would happen, we might again start assessing progress daily.

Chapter 7
Start of Development

The time has, at last, arrived for coding to start. We will begin by looking at a strategy for parallel development. In the case study, we were ready to start developing the viewer program's development modules (subroutines, functions, and data structures), testing and recording the results for each one as we went along. We had drawn up a plan, and both programmers knew what they had to do and how—the design specification had seen to that. Archie and Julie had guidance notes on how to test, and they were all ready to start developing version 1 of the E-MagBook viewer program.

You can follow the work in the case study in one of two ways: You can build the routines and test them exactly as the book shows, or you can read about the work and use the code provided on this book's companion CD-ROM. In either case, you will experience modular development and the testing that goes hand in hand with the development.

NOTE: *There are two types of "module" referred to in this chapter. There is the development module which is a piece of self-contained code consisting of one or more subroutines, functions, and/or data structures and then there is the VB module file which contains one or more development modules. In the case study, we used the VB module files as libraries to house the development modules that we created.*

Setting Up the Development Strategy

The first thing a development team must establish is just who will do what, by when, and using what rules or strategy. In the case study, we had a programming team of two—Archie and Julie—who'd been involved in the project since Day 1. But if they had been newcomers, the first thing on the agenda would have been for them to read the requirements specification. With that background knowledge, the models from analysis and the designs would make sense.

The first thing Archie and Julie did was to hold a brief, startup meeting. They went through what each would do that week, carefully noting the dependency—Julie's work had to be ready on time for Archie to complete his work. Their schedule was based on the plan we had produced and that I showed you in Chapter 5 (you can see the plan in Figure 5.3). They set up two directory areas on the network—one for Archie and one for Julie. Then, they created two copies of a VB module file called **ViewerLib**. This would be the main library that would hold the common functions and subroutines, and the data structures they would develop. Each would work from his or her individual copy of the library. When it came time to "hand over" code, they would reconcile the two copies of the libraries so the copies were identical.

After the two libraries were back in phase, in terms of content, Archie and Julie would commence their next tasks and reconcile the work again whenever one needed code that the other had produced. That way, they could develop the code, test it, confirm that it had passed the tests, and then make it available to the team as a whole.

After a programmer has completed a code module (meaning a subroutine or function in this case), the module must be *frozen*. In other words, the programmer can make no more changes to the module, except to fix a problem encountered in the course of its use. In such circumstances, the person responsible for the module would make the modification, test it, "pass" it, and then release the module to the other person's copy in a controlled manner, so everyone was totally aware of what was taking place. Changing a completed module requires good communications and coordination across the team.

Version Control

As you can imagine, such communications and coordination across a large team can be a potential nightmare. A programmer needs to be sure that a completed routine he or she will use is the latest, frozen version.

Development aids, such as version-control packages, are available that allow automatic control of the version numbers and release status of routines. Using one of these packages involves checking out a frozen routine from the library to modify the routine. The process of checking out the routine locks it against anyone else attempting to change it until you have checked it back into the library. To modify, change, and test a routine, everyone on the team must follow the protocol required to check out the routine, and then check it back into the library. In the case study, Julie and Archie didn't have the luxury of such a package; they would have to manage themselves and their code production very carefully.

Rules for **ViewerLib**

Archie and Julie produced a list that contained the names of the routines they were developing that would go into **ViewerLib**; the list included the person responsible for creating each routine. They decided that, during development, they would put into the library all routines and data structures (including general GUI and non-GUI routines) that the viewer or editors would use, although the library was predominately for the viewer.

The criteria for the inclusion of functions and subroutines into **ViewerLib** was that the code would use only the public data structures, which would also be part of the library and/or arguments passed to and from the routine. No library routine could access a screen object unless the name of the object was one of the calling parameters, which would make the routine generic. So a *general GUI routine* is a routine that uses screen objects whose identities are dynamically declared to the routine at runtime.

They would place none of the test-harness code in the library—that is, any code they wrote for testing the routine(s) they were developing. They would place any routines that the viewer needed and that accessed screen objects directly in the test harness's main form; they would have to copy that code to the final version of the viewer, in which it would become infrastructure code. The same applied to any infrastructure data.

NOTE: *Establishing the described rules is important for successful team code development. As long as everyone understands and adheres to the rules, parallel code production and its subsequent sharing by other team members can be successful.*

Avoid Duplicate Development

In the course of converting the design specifications to code, a programmer might quite possibly decide to create more routines to house some of the code. These will be routines that were not considered in the design as single entities, but that might result from attempting to produce VB code from the high-level, pseudocode statements. In the case study, if additional, common routines should come into being as a result of the development, Julie and Archie would add those routines to **ViewerLib** as appropriate and reconcile the routines between their two libraries when necessary. However, it would be absolutely essential that each inform the other about such additions before reconciliation. Doing so would prevent the possibility of their creating similar routines and thereby duplicating effort.

Duplicate development can happen all too easily on a busy project that involves many programmers. A situation can evolve in which each programmer is developing a variant of a routine to handle a common function—a good reason to keep teams small and working in proximity. The possibility of duplicate development is also another good reason to have another programmer review your completed code. Making other programmers aware of the routines being created avoids duplication of effort and can save valuable time.

Initial Status of Development Library

In the case study, we had defined the data structures **Viewer Screen Definitions**, **Title Index**, and **Page Index** in the design. Consequently, these data structures were the first items to go into both libraries in the frozen, or final, state. If we had to make any changes to one of these data structures, careful coordination and reconciliation would be necessary.

Archie and Julie created two libraries, each containing the data structures I just mentioned. They then set up the status conditions of each library (one for Julie and one for Archie), describing the state of the routines or data structures that they were to develop. In the library, they gave any routine or data structure that had been completed a status of *FINAL*, a version number of *1.0*, and an indication of the development module's type—*Data*, *Gen GUI* (for general GUI), or *GEN*, (for a general routine that is completely independent of the GUI). For routines being worked on, the status was shown as *DEV*. For all routines undergoing development, they assigned an *Owner*—the person to go to in the event of a query. Figure 7.1 shows the initial status of both programmers' versions of **ViewerLib**.

The version number is filled in only for final, or completed, routines and data structures. The developer can use VB's automatic version incrementing to track changes made in the program during development. As I explained earlier, to change a frozen routine or data structure for any reason, the item must be checked out of everyone's library by marking its status as *DEV* until the fix or change has been implemented. After the change has been completed, the unit's version number is changed and the status reverts once again to *FINAL*.

Because of the need to update each person's status table, this crude method of checking out and checking in routines works only with a very small team. Clearly, after a team expands beyond a handful of people, you would need an automatic check-in/check-out, version-control system.

In the case study, Julie and Archie would coordinate all their work, and neither would do or start anything without informing the other person. As you can imagine, if communications between programmers fail, the potential exists for considerable confusion.

Status of Archie's ViewerLib at Day 1

Module (sub/function/data structure)	Type	Status	Version	Owner
Viewer Screen Definitions Data	Data	FINAL	1.0	
Title Index Data Structure	Data	FINAL	1.0	
Page Index Data Structure	Data	FINAL	1.0	
LoadAndDisplayImage	GEN GUI	DEV		Archie
Size Picture	GEN	DEV		Archie
LoadAndPlayVideo	GEN GUI	DEV		Archie

Status of Julie's ViewerLib at Day 1

Module (sub/function/data structure)	Type	Status	Version	Owner
Viewer Screen Definitions Data	Data	FINAL	1.0	
Title Index Data Structure	Data	FINAL	1.0	
Page Index Data Structure	Data	FINAL	1.0	
OpenAndReadTextIntoMemory	GEN	DEV		Julie
LoadAndDisplayText	GEN GUI	DEV		Julie
LoadAndPlaySound	GEN GUI	DEV		Julie

Figure 7.1
Status of both versions of **ViewerLib** at start of development.

Test Programs

In the development stage, each development module (subroutine, function, or data structure) or group of modules will be developed and then tested. It's worth my pointing out that the test programs don't have to be polished works of art. In other words they do not have to be robust and well-written. Provided the test programs check out the functionality of the developed modules under test, the test programs themselves can be quite basic. For example, imagine a test program in which the user manually defines the number of data fields contained in a string, from which text will then be extracted. Suppose further that the program is limited internally to a maximum of 10 such data fields; that the test program can't cope with an input of 11 data fields and produces a fatal subscript error in that situation really doesn't matter. What's important is that the program works correctly within its operational range. (Of course, this criterion would not apply to a routine in the final version of the viewer. Such a production routine must be able to cope with its operational range of values and adequately handle boundary conditions.)

We want to avoid the test harness becoming a major piece of development in its own right. If that happens, its value to us as a development tool might be compromised. For example, because test programs are quite basic, you might find that some of the test programs on this book's supplemental CD crash quite easily. Before you use any of these programs, make sure you understand from the text in the book what the test program is supposed to do, and that you follow the procedures in the correct order.

Remember, at this point, we are relaxing the quality aspects of the test programs so we can develop test harnesses swiftly. This is the only time we allow such relaxation of quality assurance. If a particular bug in a test program becomes irksome—for example, frequently encountering it is a great nuisance—spending time to remove the bug might be justifiable. The criterion must be that, in fixing a bug, the time you spend is not at the expense of the routines being tested, whose quality must be of the highest order.

The Logbook

Now, we come to one of the most valuable possessions of the developer—the programmer's logbook. Our company issues a logbook as part of the new-employee orientation process, and Julie and Archie each had one. The programmer's logbook serves many functions—it's a diary, journal, logbook, notebook, and lots of other things. The programmer enters into the logbook (and captures for posterity) anything and everything that is, or might be, useful in his or her work. Using a logbook must become a habit.

Your logbook will have two main types of entry. You'll make a note of *transient information* for use in your immediate activity and never use it again. You'll keep referring to *reference information* in the course of your work. Let's look at some of the many ways to use this valuable tool.

Designing and developing software is a complex business. As you've already seen from the E-MagBook project, which is small, a huge amount of information has resulted from the work we've done so far. If you work on a big project with many programmers, the quantity of material becomes even more demanding—you cannot possibly remember everything you are told or everything you come across. Your logbook becomes an extension to your memory.

For example, you might need to use a version-control program to check in and check out the source code on a big project. You receive a manual, and you might even be given some training. Then, you must start using the program in earnest. If you jot down the basics in your logbook throughout this process, each time you come to something you are not sure of, you can just look it up in your logbook notes.

Jot down people's names, so you know both their surname and first name if you have to call them. When you make a support call to a component supplier, create a log: Whom did you talk to? What did they recommend? Will they get back to you? Did they supply you with a reference number to use if you call them back about the same problem later? If someone rings up and wants to leave a message for a colleague, jot the message down in your logbook (which should always be at hand—believe me, it's far better than using lots of little bits of paper).

Your logbook can become something of a knowledge base. You may have trouble finding a reference, but the effort of searching through your notes pays off time and time again. Using keywords as headers makes life much easier—you can find things as you scan the pages.

All good programmers use some form of logbook. The amount of information you are exposed to in the IT industry is colossal, and the quantity is constantly increasing. Think of the number of times you've said to yourself, "I'm sure I've done that before; now, just how did I do it?" or "I'm sure I fixed that once." In the long run, a logbook can save you a lot of time and heartache.

Ready for Development

What you've experienced in this section is an example of setting up a development methodology. The team has agreed to do things a certain way and also to keep each other well-informed— vital for a successful project. Specifically, each programmer has a set of development tasks to undertake against a plan. In the case study, two versions of **ViewerLib** had been created—one for Archie and one for Julie. Julie's work included a dependency, in that Archie would not be able to start the next phase of his work until Julie had completed her current tasks. Each programmer knew what he or she had to do and—just as importantly— each knew what the other had to do. The team was ready to start development.

The Case Study:
Viewer Development Startup

According to the plan for viewer development (see Figure 5.3 in Chapter 5), Archie and Julie were going to start with the development of the **Display Page** routines. Both programmers would work on the routines simultaneously, and the routines were scheduled for completion in the first week. As soon as Julie had completed her tasks (development of **Display Text** and **Play Sound**), she would move on to develop the **Title Handling** development module. She must have her components of the **Display Page** development task completed by Day 4, or she would start to hold Archie up.

Archie would work on the **Display Image** and **Play Video** development modules, which he would finish at the same time as Julie finished her first two modules. He would then take all the bits and pieces and complete the **Display Page** module in Day 4. If all went according to plan, he would then start work on the **Read Page Index** module, hoping to achieve 50 percent of its completion by the end of Friday.

Julie had 1.5 days to complete the **Title Handling** module. We didn't have much extra contingency time in Week 1. In fact, Archie had none, apart from what was built into the time estimates of the modules themselves; Julie had an extra half-day. We had put most of the contingency time into the second week of the viewer development (Archie had only one day, which was a possible risk factor). Don't forget, they would have to test the routines, produce a log of tests performed, and actually produce code.

Creation of ViewerLib

As I've already stated, both Archie and Julie started with libraries that, from the outset, contained three data structures defined in the design. If you want to follow their development on your own PC, exactly as it happened, you should create two versions of **ViewerLib** in separate directories to reconstruct the starting point.

Before you continue, on your C: drive, create a directory called *DEV_JULIE* and one called *DEV_ARCHIE*. If you intend to follow the development on your PC, you will also experience firsthand the sort of issues that reconciliation brings up.

Alternatively, you will find each library (**ViewerLib_At_StartUp**) in the same two development directories (DEV_ARCHIE and DEV_JULIE) on the CD. Copy one of the versions of **ViewerLib_At_Startup** to your development areas and peruse that file while you read the following steps about how to construct the routine.

Step 1

Start a new VB EXE project. On the VB option menu, select Project. From the drop-down menu, select Add Module. You are going to create a VB file module, which we will use as our **ViewerLib** to contain the public subroutines, functions, and data structures of the viewer.

Step 2

After Step 1, a sub-window appears with two tabs: NEW and EXISTING. Select NEW and click the OPEN button at the bottom of the sub-window. Figure 7.2 shows this screen.

Step 3

Click the VB menu option View. Then, click the VB drop-down menu option Project Explorer. This will show a new main form (Form1) and a new VB module (Module1). Highlight the module name, and press F4 to bring up the properties form. Change the VB module name to *ViewerLib*.

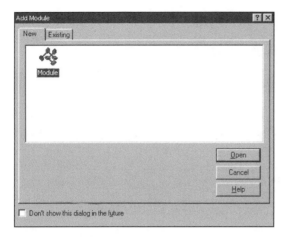

Figure 7.2
VB "module" creation.

Step 4

Double-click ViewerLib in the project window to bring up the code window. Enter **Option Explicit** as the first line of the general declarations. If you recall, one of our coding standards for VB is that you always declare **Option Explicit**. This declaration instructs VB to allow only variable names that have been declared; it helps reduce finger trouble and the effects of bad spelling of variable names. Without the **Option Explicit**, any variable spelling is allowed, and each time the program encounters a new spelling, VB automatically creates a new variable. Such behavior can lead to great confusion while you are creating code; hence, the standard.

Step 5

Set up the following code in the declarations section:

```
Option Explicit
' -----------------------------------
' DATA STRUCTURE: Viewer screen definitions, V1.0
' Created: <Date>
' used to construct text, album & ref book screen layouts.
' Values are captured on program load from the design time setup.
'
Public g_intOrigin1_Left As Integer    ' Book and Album origin
Public g_intOrigin1_Top As Integer     '

Public g_intOrigin2_Left As Integer    ' Image Container for Ref Book
Public g_intOrigin2_Top As Integer     '

Public g_intOrigin3_Left As Integer    ' small text box in ref origin
Public g_intOrigin3_Top As Integer
```

```
Public g_intOrigin4_Left As Integer      ' large text box in ref origin
Public g_intOrigin4_Top As Integer

Public g_intHeight1 As Integer           ' Book height, Album height
Public g_intHeight2 As Integer           ' Ref image max height
Public g_intHeight3 As Integer           ' ref small text height

Public g_intWidth1 As Integer            ' Book width, Album width
Public g_intWidth2 As Integer            ' Ref image max width
Public g_intWidth3 As Integer            ' ref text box width
```

This is the data structure for setting up the various screen objects on the viewer according to format type. If you can't remember what the formats are all about, look at the associated viewer-format-design diagram in Chapter 6, Figure 6.13. The diagram shows the position of all the origins and where to find the dimensions to use when setting up a given format.

Step 6

Now, set up the definitions for the Title Index data structure and also the Page Index data structure. Add the following two data structures immediately after the viewer screen definitions:

```
' -----------------------------------
' DATA STRUCTURE: Title Index Global, Dynamic arrays, V1.0
' Created: <date>
'
Public g_intCurrentTitle As Integer        ' Pointer to title record

Public g_strTitleTitle() As String         ' Free format title
Public g_strTitleDescription() As String ' Free format description
Public g_strTitleFileName() As String      ' Page Index file ref
' -----------------------------------
' DATA STRUCTURE: Page Index Global, Dynamic arrays, V1.0
' Created: <date>

Public g_intFormatType As Integer          ' 1=Book, 2=Album, 3=Ref book
Public g_strFontType As String             ' for all pages
Public g_intFontSize As Integer            ' for all pages

Public g_intCurrentPage As Integer         ' Pointer to page record

Public g_strKeys() As String               ' two-dimensional array
Public g_strPictureFile() As String        ' one-dimensional array
Public g_strTextFile() As String           ' one-dimensional array
Public g_strSoundFile() As String          ' one-dimensional array
```

All these parameters are described in the previous chapter in the sections concerning Title Index and Page Index handling.

Store the VB module as **ViewerLib.bas**—once in Archie's directory, and then once in Julie's directory. You now have the main Index structures onboard. Please check spelling and so on for accuracy.

Programming Standards

Programming consists of translating a design into actual code. If you give the same design to 10 programmers, the result will be 10 different programs. Programming is a creative business, and, like most such activities and most things in life, some people are very good at it, some are mediocre, and some are poor.

A software development project is likely to have a number of programmers of different abilities taking part. As in the case study, simultaneous program development will be occurring. From a project management perspective, we would like to be in a position from which we can swap programmers in and out of the project with relative ease. For example, suppose a key programmer becomes sick in the middle of developing a critical routine that at least three other programmers need before they can move on to their next assignments. We need to be able to move in a spare programmer to take over the key programmer's work as quickly as possible.

We have heaps of good project documentation to get the new programmer up to speed, but then he or she must wade into the code that the absent programmer has left behind. This experience can range from uplifting and quite enjoyable to what I can only describe as sheer hell.

In such situations, the new programmer can experience an overwhelming temptation to start all over again. So, how do we go about preventing such a waste of time and effort? The answer, which should come as no shock, is bound up in quality assurance.

A key component of quality assurance is the programming standards we have established. Each development language might have a set of standards. Programming standards are designed to provide a consistent approach to programming without too seriously hampering a programmer's flair.

The secret to avoiding programmers having to start all over again when they are faced with someone else's code is *consistency*. So, let's look at a set of standards and see how they help. What follows is an extract of VB programming standards, presented in no particular order, which we set up for the case study (I will introduce other standards as the code is revealed):

- Always use meaningful names for subroutines, functions, and variables.

- Always use Hungarian notation for variables; declare global, public variables with a prefix of **g_**; and declare private infrastructure routines with a prefix of **i_**.

- All routines must have a header that contains any relevant details about the code, including its function (if that is not obvious from the routine's name).

♦ If a routine contains arguments, the header must define the purpose of each argument.

♦ The routine's date of creation must appear in the header.

♦ The name of the programmer who created the code must appear in the header.

♦ Ideally, each program routine should be approximately one to two screens' worth of code.

♦ If a routine is greater than one screen's worth of data, the routine must be split into clearly defined, self-contained sections, each of which can be viewed in a single screen.

♦ Do not use unnecessary comments (for example, **intP=intP +1**   'increment intP).

♦ Comment complex sections of code with newcomers in mind.

♦ Where functions are used, set a default return condition at the start of the code.

♦ Always use **Option Explicit**.

♦ All variables must have their types declared.

♦ Where data conversions are performed, the program must use explicit conversion functions.

♦ Try not to rely on VB default behavior; always be explicit.

♦ Use **Go To** statements only for error handling, to divert processing to error traps, and use **Go To** statements only to transfer control forward—never backward—in the code.

♦ Place all error-handling code at the bottom of the routine.

♦ Where possible, always start arrays from element 1, not element 0.

Comments and Meaningful Names

As mentioned, unnecessary comments should not appear in the code. For example, if a line of code reads

```
intPointer  = intPointer + 1
```

adding the comment **increment pointer by one** is pointless. What the code is doing is obvious because the programmer has chosen a sensible name—**intPointer**—which indicates the variable's use, and the **+ 1** is a real giveaway to what the program is doing. Another good reason to keep comments to a minimum is that when a programmer makes changes to routines, he or she often does not update the comments in the code.

The standards also require that programmers use Hungarian notation. Doing so ensures that the type of each variable is obvious wherever you encounter the variable in the program. For example, **intTemp** is a temporary integer, **strTemp** is a temporary string, and so on. The first three characters represent the variable type, and, of course, **Temp** is another giveaway to functionality.

We've also specified a means to easily identify infrastructure variables (prefixed with **i_**) and public, or global, variables (prefixed with **g_**). This standard ensures that you can easily identify each type of variable at a glance. If the variable has no prefix, the variable is either local to the routine or a defined argument variable.

Subroutine or Function Header

You must make a routine's function obvious, either from the name you give the routine (for example, **LoadAndDisplayImage**) or from a comment that appears in the header. This header will also supply details about the code if the details are not obvious from the routine's name. For example, if you call the routine **ReadFileFromDisk**, you don't need a comment that repeats this information.

Defining each argument in the call in the header is vitally important. An example shows how important this standard is:

```
Subroutine ConvertString(strInput as string, strFrom as string, strTo as_
    string)
```

On its own, this subroutine is obviously some sort of conversion routine. As a guess, one would say that **strInput** is the string that is to be converted, but from what to what? What this routine does is not clear from the preceding line. Look at the difference a standard header makes:

```
Subroutine ConvertString(strInput as string, strFrom as string, strTo as_
    string)
' GENERAL ROUTINE: for string handling. V1.0
' Date Created: 20-SEP-2000
' Created by:   Julie
' Routine to convert all occurrences of a defined string to another string.
' Arguments.    strInput    input string to be processed
'               strFrom     Look for all occurrences of this string in
'                           strInput
'                           and convert to strTo
'               strTo       See above
```

The function of this routine is now clear. Imagine that you must take over someone else's code, and consider just how grateful you would be to see clear definitions of functionality and argument use in the headers of all routines you encounter. Another important aspect of the header is the *change log*, which we will discuss in detail later on.

Type Declarations and Conversion

Insisting that all variables have their type declared is good practice. VB is a very tolerant language, and declaring type is not actually necessary. In fact, VB will do its utmost to help you convert from one type to another. Unfortunately, this characteristic can yield unpredictable results. Consequently, we insist that you fully define every variable in terms of type, and, when you convert from one type to another, you must use the relevant conversion function.

For example, VB is quite happy for you to write **intTemp=strTemp**, and it will actually do the conversion for you. The result will be fine 99.9 percent of the time, but a time will come when the automatic conversion leads to an unpredictable result. Consequently, our standards demand that you program this line as **intTemp=Cint(strTemp)**. You can trap any error condition with an **On Error Go To** statement, confident in the fact that, if the function fails, the string does not contain a number.

This discussion might sound somewhat pedantic, but we need to be able to look at a line of code and predict exactly how it will behave. If you let VB do the thinking for you, you might not be able to predict exactly what the outcome will be without trying out every combination of possible input. For example, how would VB convert the string **A1243** in the preceding example? If we use explicit conversion statements, we can guarantee that the program will force an error, which is a predictable and sensible thing to happen.

For the same reason, insisting that type declarations are made in the calling sequences of subroutines and functions is also good practice. If a call is made with incorrect types, the compiler will trap the error. This action is infinitely preferable to VB being "clever" and sorting it all for you. Under that condition, you would have to consider that you couldn't predict 0.1 percent of occurrences when VB does something.

Size of Routines

The ideal size of a routine is a single screen's worth of code. That is, you can see the entire routine on your PC's screen without having to scroll. A single screen's worth of code isn't really practical all the time, so we set a limit of about two screens. If the routine must go beyond this limit, you need to structure the code so you can identify blocks of it you can examine on screen as meaningful entities.

This size limitation is particularly relevant to routines with lots of nested loops. More than two pages of nested loops becomes difficult to follow. If you move the code in loops out to subroutines or functions, the loop structure becomes far easier to understand.

The **Go To** Statement

You should use **Go To** statements only for error handling. Under no conditions should you ever use a **Go To** statement to transfer control backward. Doing so leads to spaghetti-code structures, which are impossible to follow. We applied these standards we've looked at in the preceding sections to the case study. Let's go back to the case study now.

Return to the Case Study:
The **Display Image** Development Module

Developing the **Display Image** module was Archie's first task. If you recall, the design was straightforward, consisting of the **LoadAndDisplayImage** function and a support routine called **SizePicture**. (Before you go any further, study the design specifications for these two routines, either in the previous chapter or in Appendix G. And, if you need to, revisit the feasibility study in Chapter 2, because the code here is based on that work.)

One possible approach for the development of these two routines would have been for Archie to develop the subroutine **SizePicture** first, check it thoroughly, and then develop the main function, testing it with a version of **SizePicture** that he knew worked. In this instance, however, the subroutine had already been created in the feasibility study, so Archie developed the code together and built a single test harness.

Test Harness Requirements

The requirements for the test harness for the **Display Image** routine were that it had to allow Archie to select a file name from the file store and feed it to the main function under test, **LoadAndDisplayImage**, and then observe the result. Archie decided he would need a command button that allowed him to load files (using the file dialog box) and see the result, in the same way we had done for the feasibility study (using an image control). He also wanted to be able to define a container area's dimensions to be used in the call to **LoadAndDisplayImage** as the design demands. He decided he would do this by setting up the image control at design time and then use the **form_ load** event to capture the container area details from the settings of the image control at the moment of loading.

Container Data Structure

At this stage, Archie realized that a data structure was needed that the viewer could use to define the *current container area*, which would depend on book format type. We already had a set of global variables to catch the various combinations, but what we didn't have was a set of variables to define the current values according to what format was in use. So, in starting up his program, Archie introduced into his library a new data structure, which he would have to reconcile with Julie's library. However, because Julie was not currently working on anything that required image handling, he could leave reconciliation until later.

If you recall, the feasibility study used two controls—the picture control and the image control. Archie had already decided to use just one image control for the viewer, as described at the end of the feasibility study. Sensibly, he used the same name that would be employed in the viewer program, **imgImageIt**.

Creation of LoadAndDisplayImage

To reproduce Archie's efforts to build a test program, the **LoadAndDisplayImage** routine, and the subroutine **SizePicture**, you can follow these steps. Alternatively, you can load the project **ImageTest1** from Archie's development area (DEV_ARCHIE) on the CD and then read about its construction in the following steps.

Step 1

Open a new VB EXE project in Archie's development directory. Add Archie's version of **ViewerLib** to it. This project will be called **ImageTest1**.

Step 2

Set up the form as Figure 7.3 shows.

The form contains four screen controls. Create and name them as follows:

- *Image control*—**imgImageIt**, used to display the selected image.
- *Text box*—**txtImageFile**, used to display the name of the selected image file.
- *File dialog control*—**dlgDialog1**, used to provide the VB file dialog box for file selection.
- *Command button*—**cmdLoadFile**, used to perform a test.

You can also set up a label, as shown in Figure 7.3 to indicate the function of **txtImageFile**. The name of this label is unimportant, and you can use the VB default names if required.

Step 3

Add the following data structure to **ViewerLib** and place it directly under the viewer screen definitions, immediately before the Title Index definitions:

```
' -----------------------------------
' DATA STRUCTURE: Runtime Image container position and dimensions, V1.0
' Created: <date>
' Depends on book format and is set up from Viewer Screen Definitions.

Public g_intImageContainer_Left As Integer   ' Position for image area
Public g_intImageContainer_Top As Integer
Public g_intImageContainer_Width As Integer ' dimensions
Public g_intImageContainer_Height As Integer
```

Before any image can be displayed, the running program must have set up this data structure. The data can then be used in the call to the routine to load and display an image to define the container area. Because this data constituted a new, global data structure, both Archie and Julie approved it together. In this way, even though she didn't yet need it, Julie was aware of the data structure's existence and purpose.

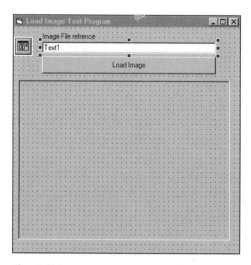

Figure 7.3
The form for test program **ImageTest1**.

Step 4

Archie set up the following code for the test program's **Form_ Load** event. The code provides initial values for the container area global data structure:

```
Private Sub Form_Load()
' TEST CODE:
' Capture image container area for Testing from
' design time setting for image control.
g_intImageContainer_Left = imgImageIt.Left
g_intImageContainer_Top = imgImageIt.Top
q intImageContainer_Width = imgImageIt.Width
g_intImageContainer_Height = imgImageIt.Height
End Sub
```

The code simply sets the global image container parameters in **ViewerLib** to those of the image control as Archie had set them at design time, thus capturing the image container values for position and dimensions, ready for testing. To change the parameters, all he would have to do would be to stop the program, modify the layout of **imgImageIt**, and rerun the program, which provided a perfectly adequate test arrangement.

NOTE: *Note how test code is being clearly identified as such (* **TEST CODE***: appears immediately after the first line), to avoid its being confused with any infrastructure code. This structure will be useful when we have to extract the developed infrastructure elements from the test programs for insertion into the actual viewer program at system integration time.*

Step 5

Now, install the code in the Load Image button, which will allow you to invoke the file dialog box to select an image file for loading. Place the following code in the Load Image button's click event:

```
Private Sub cmdLoadFile_Click()
' TEST CODE:
' Load and display image Test Program
Dim booResult As Boolean
Dim strTemp as string

' Get name of file to load, load and display image
dlgDialog1.Action = 1
txtImageFile.Text = dlgDialog1.FileName
strTemp = txtImageFile.Text

booResult = LoadAndDisplayImage(strTemp, imgImageIt,_
        g_intImageContainer_Width, g_intImageContainer_Height,_
        g_intImageContainer_Left, g_intImageContainer_Top)

MsgBox "Result of Load = " & booResult
End Sub
```

This code is pretty much the same code we used in the feasibility study. It uses the dialog box to let Archie select a file name, which is placed in **txtImageFile.Text**. Then, **LoadAndDisplayImage** is called with all the parameters as defined by the design specification to indicate the screen object for holding the image and its container area.

Step 6

Now, add the **LoadAndDisplayImage** code into Archie's **ViewerLib**:

```
Public Function LoadAndDisplayImage(strFileName As String,_
            imgObject As Control,_
            intMaxWidth As Integer, intMaxHeight As Integer,_
            intLeft As Integer, intTop As Integer)
' GENERAL GUI ROUTINE: V1.0
' Handles loading of an image.
' Arguments;
'    strFileName    Image File Ref of bitmap to load
'    imgObject      Screen image control to place image into
'    intMaxWidth    Max width available for image
'    intMaxHeight   Max height available for image
'    intLeft        Left position of container area
```

```
'   intTop           Top position of container area
'   Function    =    True if file loaded OK
'               =    False if file not loaded OK
' ----------------------------------
Dim intActualWidth As Integer
Dim intActualHeight As Integer

' Load image into control with stretch switched off so that control will
' expand to full size of bitmap.
LoadAndDisplayImage = False              ' Default return value
imgObject.Visible = False
imgObject.Stretch = False

On Error GoTo LoadFail
imgObject = LoadPicture(strFileName)     ' Trap error enabled
On Error GoTo 0                          ' switch off error trap

' call routine to check out that width and height fit into container
intActualWidth = imgObject.Width
intActualHeight = imgObject.Height

Call SizePicture(intMaxWidth, intMaxHeight, intActualWidth, intActualHeight)

' resize image control, set to stretch, position and make visible
imgObject.Stretch = True
imgObject.Width = intActualWidth
imgObject.Height = intActualHeight
imgObject.Left = intLeft + (intMaxWidth - intActualWidth) / 2
imgObject.Top = intTop + (intMaxHeight - intActualHeight) / 2
imgObject.Visible = True

LoadAndDisplayImage = True
Exit Function
'
=============================================================================
' Error has occurred
LoadFail:
MsgBox "Failed to Load an Image"
Exit Function

End Function
```

According to company standards, Archie and Julie added descriptions of the calling parameters at the top of every routine they produced. Once again, the code is based on the feasibility study. Note that **LoadAndDisplayImage** has been set to **False** at the start of the code, another standard to declare explicitly the default condition. This is not necessary, because VB defaults the value to **False** in any case. However, as Julie pointed out, not all programmers know the VB defaults by heart, and being explicit about default values is much better practice.

Initially, the image control is set **invisible** with its **stretch** property set **False**. When the image is loaded into the control, the image expands to its exact size, if you recall from the feasibility study. The actual dimensions are then set in **intActualWidth** and **intActualHeight**, then **SizePicture** is called as specified in the design. The routine returns a scaled set of values if either or both failed to fit inside the container area. These new values are then used to set the image control's size, this time with the **stretch** property set to **True**. Again, this process is exactly as we saw it done in the feasibility study and according to the design.

Next, the position of the image is set. This is new. The total margin width is that of the container minus that of the scaled image. The left margin will, therefore, be half this value. If we add this margin width to the container's **left** parameter, we have the **left** attribute for the image control. The same applies for height; the margin width being half the difference between container height and image height and this value can then be added to the container **top** attribute to get the top of the required location at which to place the image control. Having set up both dimensions and position, the operator can make the image control visible once more.

If a file fails to load, the routine produces an error message and exits with **LoadAndDisplayImage** set to **False**, per the requirements specification.

Step 7

Finally, add this code as a new routine to **ViewerLib**:

```
Public Sub SizePicture(intContainerW As Integer, intContainerH As Integer,_
        intActualW As Integer, intActualH As Integer)
' GENERAL ROUTINE: Size an image into a container area on screen V1.0
' Arguments:
'    intContainerW    Max allowed width
'    intContainerH    Max allowed height
'    intActualW       Actual width on entry, modified width on return
'    intActualH       Actual height on entry, modified height on return
' Ensure image dimensions, intActualW & H, fall inside the container area
' intContainerW & H.
' --------------------------------------------
Dim sngAspectRatio As Single

sngAspectRatio = CSng(intActualW) / CSng(intActualH)

' 1. Check width lies inside container
If intActualW > intContainerW Then
        intActualW = intContainerW  ' clamp to container width
        intActualH = CInt(CSng(intActualW) / sngAspectRatio)
End If
```

```
' 2. Check out height lies inside container
If intActualH > intContainerH Then
        intActualH = intContainerH  ' clamp to container height
        intActualW = CInt(CSng(intActualH) * sngAspectRatio)

End If

' H and W must now lie inside container
Exit Sub

End Sub
```

This code also is similar to the code we developed in the feasibility study. First, the code calculates the aspect ratio of the image. Then, it takes each dimension in turn and determines whether the dimension is greater than the allowed value. If a dimension is too large, it is reset to the largest value allowed. The other dimension is recalculated using the aspect ratio. If a dimension is not greater than the maximum allowed, it remains unchanged. Each dimension is checked in turn, so that on exit, **intActualH** and **intActualW** are guaranteed to fit inside the container area.

One difference exists between this code and the feasibility code, in which mixed-mode arithmetic (integer and single precision real values are mixed together) was used. When Julie reviewed the code Archie produced on his first attempt, she pointed out that the program was dividing two integers to produce a single precision real value (**sngAspectRatio=intActualW/intActualH**). She quite correctly pointed out that dividing two integers in a computer might result in a loss of resolution because, if the dividend is not an integer, the result must be rounded up or down to become an integer value. We had no idea whether VB converts each value to type **Single** before it performs the division or whether it converts the dividend. To be precise and avoid possible loss in accuracy, both integers must first be converted to type **Single**. Furthermore, Archie then had to check each arithmetic statement and ensure that the same degree of precision existed throughout the line. If he did not do this, the end result would contain small discrepancies. To be quite frank, such discrepancies would not be evident in the E-MagBook program. But, we were trying to establish standards so that, when the precise resolution *was* significant, the program automatically accommodated the precision requirement through best practice.

Testing LoadAndDisplayImage

Running the program was exactly the same as in the feasibility study. When you clicked the command button, you could select a file name. The program then would attempt to load the file as a bitmapped image. The program, with an image loaded, looked like what you can see in Figure 7.4.

You can see an additional screen object in Figure 7.4. To assist in determining whether the image was being centered correctly, Archie set up a rectangle shape control called

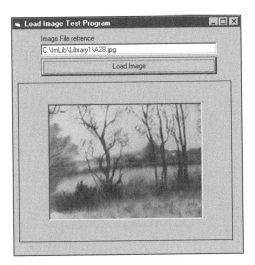

Figure 7.4
Image test program 1 in use.

shpRectangle, which indicated the size and location of the container area. To set this up, Archie set the size and position of the rectangle to coincide with that of **imgImageIt** in the VB integrated design environment (IDE). From then on, he had a reference point to check the program's functioning.

Archie examined the code and designs, and established the key pathways that needed to be tested. He came up with the following test definitions:

NOTE: H *and* **W** *are actual height and width of test image* **CH**, *and* **CW** *are the dimensions of the container area.*

- *Test 1*—Load an image where **H=<CH** and **W=<CW**, and check that the image is loaded, sized, and positioned correctly. Check that the image lies in the middle of container area.

- *Test 2*—Repeat Test 1 with **H<CH** and **W=>CW**.

- *Test 3*—Repeat Test 1 with **H=>CH** and **W<CW**.

- *Test 4*—Repeat Test 1 with **H>CH** and **W>CW**.

- *Test 5*—Repeat Test 1 through Test 4 for at least one other supported file type.

- *Test 6*—Attempt to load a file that is not a supported, bitmapped file, and check error handling.

- *Test 7*—Attempt to load a nonexistent file, and check error handling.

Where the condition being tested involves two possible situations, that is, =< (is equal to or less than)—both possibilities should be checked. However, because identical code is involved in each case (that is, only one pathway exists for = and <), it is not absolutely necessary to check the two conditions at this level of testing. If different pathways were clearly identified, one test would be necessary for each possibility. If in doubt, and time permitting, performing all the tests does no harm. Certainly, for formal acceptance testing, which has no knowledge of code pathways, both types of test would be mandatory.

Note that Test 5 requires Tests 1 through 4 to be rerun with one other file type. We've discussed this before, but, primarily, the pathways through the code are not dependent on file type. In other words, a BMP file will be handled in exactly the same way as a JPEG file in terms of sizing and positioning. To be safe, Archie decided to include one other file type to verify VB image file handling.

Archie conducted Test 6 by typing in the name of a text file. For Test 7, he typed the name of a nonexistent file into the dialog box. Thanks to the code in the feasibility study, he completed the test program and testing in one day. This time also included Julie's review of Archie's work, which resulted in changes to the code to maintain arithmetic precision where originally the program was performing mixed, integer, and single-precision calculations, as I explained earlier. It's also worth pointing out that, during the day, Archie's laptop was accidentally powered off, and he lost a great deal of his work, which he had to re-create.

NOTE: *The moral to this story is back up your work frequently during development.*

Even Archie had to admit that producing code had never before been quite so easy, particularly after he had lost all his work and had to reenter it. Archie's updated **ViewerLib** status table now looked like what you can see in Figure 7.5.

The LoadAndPlayVideo Development Module

The code for this general GUI routine, **LoadAndPlayVideo**, is based on the feasibility study we conducted and that I presented in Chapter 2. Make sure you understand the design specification, and, if you need to, revisit the feasibility study before you proceed.

There is one fundamental difference between this routine and what we did in the feasibility study. In the study, we let the multimedia service load the movie into a window that it opened automatically; we had no say in the matter in terms of the video's position on screen. In the final version to be used in the viewer, we changed the code to supply the window identity, or handle, of our very own **frmVideo**. By specifying our own window for the video to run in, we could place the video form wherever we wanted to put it. When the service created its own window, we didn't know the window's identity and had no control over where it was loaded.

Creation of LoadAndPlayVideo

We developed the video test program along the same lines as we had the image test program. Once again, you can create the test program by following the instructions, or you can simply read about how to do it and use the completed test program from directory **VideoTest1** in Archie's development area from the CD.

Status of Archie's ViewerLib at end of Day 1				
Module (sub/function/data structure)	Type	Status	Version	Owner
Viewer Screen Definitions Data	Data	FINAL	1.0	
Title Index Data Structure	Data	FINAL	1.0	
Page Index Data Structure	Data	FINAL	1.0	
Runtime Container Dimensions and Position	Data	FINAL	1.0	
LoadAndDisplayImage	GEN GUI	FINAL	1.0	
Size Picture	GEN	FINAL	1.0	
LoadAndPlayVideo	GEN GUI	DEV		Archie

Figure 7.5
Archie's version of **ViewerLib** showing current status.

Step 1

Start a new VB EXE project, call it **VideoTest1**, and add Archie's **ViewerLib** VB module (the one you have set up for the **ImageTest1** program) to it. The main form consists of controls similar to those you used in the previous test program. Add a second form, and call it **frmVideo**. Place a multimedia control in **frmVideo**, as Figure 7.6 shows. Screen controls to set up are the following:

♦ *Shape rectangle*—**shpRectangle**, defines container area for test.

♦ *Text box*—**txtVideoFile**, used to display name of video file loaded.

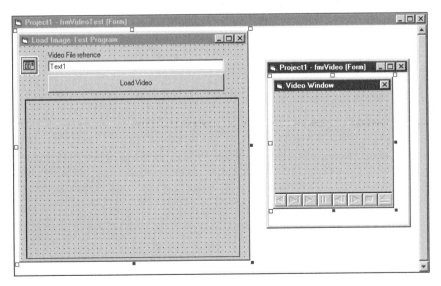

Figure 7.6
The video test program, showing the main and video forms.

♦ *File dialog control*—**dlgDialog1**, used to allow file selection for test video clip.

♦ *Command button*—**cmdLoadVideo**, the button that invokes a test.

♦ *Video window*—**frmVideo**, the window in which the video will be played.

♦ *Multimedia control*—**mmcVideoPlayer**, loaded into the video window.

Once again, set up a label to indicate the content of **txtVideoFile** as shown in Figure 7.6.

Step 2

This time, set the test program's **Form_Load** event as follows:

```
Private Sub Form_Load()
' TEST CODE:
' Video Test Program 1
' Capture image container area
g_intImageContainer_Left = shpRectangle.Left
g_intImageContainer_Top = shpRectangle.Top
g_intImageContainer_Width = shpRectangle.Width
g_intImageContainer_Height = shpRectangle.Height
End Sub
```

Archie set up the image container dimensions and positions from the shape rectangle this time. Again, he could modify the container by stopping the program, changing the rectangle, and rerunning the program to see the effect when a new video was loaded.

Step 3

Now, place the following code into the command button's click event:

```
Private Sub cmdLoadVideo_Click()
' TEST CODE:
' Video Test Program
Dim booResult As Boolean
Dim strTemp as String

' Set up image file reference and display
dlgDialog1.Action = 1
txtVideoFile.Text = dlgDialog1.FileName
strTemp = txtVideoFile.Text

booResult = LoadAndPlayVideo(strTemp, frmVideo,frmVideo.mmcVideoPlayer,_
            g_intImageContainer_Width, g_intImageContainer_Height,_
            g_intImageContainer_Left, g_intImageContainer_Top)
MsgBox "Result of Load = " & booResult

End Sub
```

This code is identical to that used for the image test, with the exception that this code calls **LoadAndPlayVideo**. Note, too, that the identity of the video form is passed to the routine, as is the full multimedia control reference—as **frmVideo.mmcVideoPlayer**. All this should be familiar from the feasibility study and the design specifications.

Step 4

Now, set up the **LoadAndPlayVideo** function itself in Archie's version of **ViewerLib**:

```
Public Function LoadAndPlayVideo(strFileName As String, frmForm As Form,_
                mmcObject As Control,_
                intMaxWidth, intMaxHeight, intLeft, intTop) As Boolean
' GENERAL GUI FUNCTION: Handle AVI video clips, V1.0
' Arguments:   strFileName   Video clip file ref
'              frmForm       Name of Video Form
'              mmcObject     Multimedia Control to play video
'              intMaxWidth   Dimensions of container area
'              intMaxheight      "
'              intLeft       Position of container area
'              intTop            "
'              Function   =  True if video load OK
'                         =  False if video not loaded
'   Loads fixed-sized video and centers form in container area
' ----------------------------------
LoadAndPlayVideo = False
On Error GoTo VideoError

    mmcObject.Command = "Close"
    mmcObject.Notify = False
    mmcObject.Wait = True
    mmcObject.Shareable = False
    mmcObject.Silent = False
    mmcObject.DeviceType = "AVIVIDEO"
    mmcObject.FileName = strFileName
    mmcObject.hWndDisplay = frmForm.hWnd     ' define window to be used
    mmcObject.Command = "Open"
    mmcObject.Command = "PLAY"
    If mmcObject.ErrorMessage <> "" Then GoTo VideoError


' Position the video window.

    frmForm.Left = intLeft
    If intMaxWidth > frmForm.Width Then
        frmForm.Left = intLeft + (intMaxWidth - frmForm.Width) / 2
    End If
    frmForm.Top = intTop
```

```
        If intMaxHeight > frmForm.Height Then
            frmForm.Top = intTop + (intMaxHeight - frmForm.Height) / 2
        End If

        frmForm.Show

LoadAndPlayVideo = True
Exit Function
' =====================================================================
' Error loading Video
VideoError:
    mmcObject.Wait = True
    mmcObject.Command = "Close"
    MsgBox " Error attempting to play Video file"
Exit Function
End Function
```

The code is based on the feasibility version, with the addition that we used **frmForm.hWnd**, the form's window handle, to define the window or form in which to play the clip.

Initially, an error trap is set up, and the multimedia channel is closed, in case it was playing something. The notification event is disabled, **shareable** and **silent** are set **False**, and then **AVIVIDEO** is declared. The file name is loaded, the window handle to **frmVideo** is provided, and the control is requested to play the video.

Apart from supplying the window handle, all the preceding code, down to where it sets up the position of the video window, should be quite familiar from the feasibility exercise. Note how, once again, Archie had explicitly set the default value of the return parameter to **False**. Error trapping results in the channel being closed down, and an exit occurs after an error message has been produced. If you have any trouble understanding this code, a quick, return visit to the feasibility study and an examination of the design spec should help you.

The big difference between the final version of the routine and the feasibility code is that we could now position the video form. First, the program makes a check to ensure that the width and height of the form are less than the values of the container. If the width of the container is greater than that of the form, the margin's total width is the difference between the container width and the form's width. In this case, the left position of the video form is set to start at the container's left-hand side, and half the total margin width is then added. (If you recall, something similar was also done for the image.) The same process applies to height. If the video form's dimensions, which are fixed at design time, are bigger than those of the container, then left and top values are clamped to the values of the left and top of the container itself. However, when Archie ran the program, it didn't behave quite as he wished.

Testing LoadAndPlayVideo

Archie discovered that positioning the video window wasn't as straightforward as he first thought. He wanted the video centered inside the image container area. First, if the main form of the test program was placed with its top, left-hand side at the origin of the screen, he could get the video centered only with respect to the X-axis. This was because the **.left** value of the video form defines its position relative to the screen origin, and not to the origin of the main form from which the calculations are made. Provided the main form was positioned correctly, the **.left** measurement was okay. This was acceptable, because the E-MagBook would always run with the viewer maximized. But, try as he might, Archie could not get the **.Top** measurement to come close to a sensible position, and he eventually called me in to have a look.

The problem was that the calculated value was measured from the origin of the main form, which was actually below the window title bar. The height of this bar was causing the **.Top** value to be too small. We had to introduce a "fiddle factor" (a fixed correction factor), which we achieved by trial and error. Eventually, we settled on a value of 300 twips. So you will need to add the following line to the **LoadAndDisplayVideo** general function, just before the **Show form** command:

```
frmForm.Top = frmForm.Top + 300   ' compensate for height of main form title
frmForm.Show
LoadAndPlayVideo = True
Exit Function
```

Figure 7.7 shows what to expect when the main form is positioned correctly.

The testing regime that Archie defined to check out all paths was as follows:

NOTE: H *and* **W** *are height and width of* **frmVideo. CH** *and* **CW** *are height and width of container area.*

♦ *Test 1*—Set up **frmVideo** with **H<CH** and **W<CW**, Load an AVI file, and check that it runs and is positioned correctly.

♦ *Test 2*—Repeat Test 1 with **H<CH** and **W>CW**.

♦ *Test 3*—Repeat Test 1 with **H>CH** and **W<CW**.

♦ *Test 4*—Repeat Test 1 with **H>CH** and **W>CW**.

♦ *Test 5*—Load a video, and check that all multimedia controls work OK.

♦ *Test 6*—Pick a file that is not a video. Check that error handling is correct.

♦ *Test 7*—Attempt to load a nonexistent file, and check error handling.

After we had worked out the fiddle factor for positioning the video window, to get the **.Top** attribute to compensate for the main form's title bar, we executed and logged Test 1. We

Figure 7.7
Video Test 1 program running.

conducted Test 2 immediately afterward, and so on. To accommodate the tests that required dimension changes, we stopped the program, changed the video form or container dimensions in the VB design environment, and reran the program with the new settings. To perform Test 6, Archie attempted to load a text file.

Note that, when you exit from the video test program, the video form remains on screen. This results because no code has been written to unload the form. To remove the video form as part of the test program's unload event is quite simple. The point is this: The facility is unnecessary to the testing of the **LoadAndPlayVideo** development module. You don't have to construct the test programs to the same quality level that you require for the production routines.

Archie finished development and testing of this sub-module by the end of Day 2. Some of the time had been wasted because his laptop had been acting up again—although, thanks to his backup procedure, he didn't lose any files this time. However, he had to transfer all his files onto another machine while his own was being repaired. He also had Julie review the code. This time, she found no problems with it. Archie could now mark **LoadAndPlayVideo** as *FINAL* in his version of the library. He had taken two days instead of three to complete the first two routines, and part of that time included wasted time caused by the problems with his laptop. He could start working on the **DisplayPage** development module a day early. The question was, When would Julie have the two text and sound modules ready that he needed? Let's see how she got on.

The DisplayText Development Module

Julie's initial development task was to produce **LoadAndDisplayText**, for which she also needed to develop a routine, **OpenAndReadTextIntoMemory**. As usual, make sure you understand the design specifications before you proceed.

Whereas Archie had decided to develop **DisplayImage** and **SizePicture** together, and check their combined functioning in a single test program, Julie opted to develop her functions from the bottom up (this was one alternative to Archie's approach). She intended to develop the low-level routine, **OpenAndReadTextIntoMemory**, first. She would then thoroughly test the routine on its own before she froze it. She would then develop and test the higher-level routine, **LoadAndDisplayText**, confident that the low-level routine was solid.

Creation of OpenAndReadTextIntoMemory

The **OpenAndReadTextIntoMemory** function would be totally independent of the GUI. Julie decided to set up a test routine, which allowed her to select a text file using the dialog box, call the function with the name of the selected file, and then use the **Debug.Print** method to print the text string read-in into the immediate window. To create the program, follow these steps; alternatively, follow the development using the project available in directory **TextTest1** of Julie's development directory on the CD.

Step 1

Create a new VB EXE project, and create a form containing a command button called **cmdLoadText** and a text box named **txtTextFile**. Include a dialog box, and call it **dlgDialog1**. Load Julie's version of **ViewerLib**. Save the program and form as **TextTest1**.

Step 2

Place the following code in the command button's click event:

```
Private Sub cmdLoadText_Click()
' TEST CODE:
' Text Test
Dim strText As String
Dim booResult As Boolean
Dim strTemp as String

dlgDialog1.Action = 1
txtTextFile.Text = dlgDialog1 FileName
strTemp = txtTextFile.Text

booResult = OpenAndReadTextIntoMemory(strTemp, strText)

MsgBox "Result of text read " & booResult
Debug.Print strText

End Sub
```

In a manner that should now be very familiar, the program obtains the file name from the file dialog control and places it in **txtTextFile**. The function is then called, using the string obtained from the text box as the file-name argument. The routine loads the text into the second argument, **strText**. Then, Julie used the **Debug.Print** method to output the result of the read into the immediate window for comparison with the original test file.

The following code constitutes the **OpenAndReadTextIntoMemory** function, which you should place in Julie's version of **ViewerLib**:

```
Public Function OpenAndReadTextIntoMemory(strFileName As String,_
                strText As String) As Boolean
' GENERAL ROUTINE: Text handling, V1.0
' Arguments:   strFileName   Full name of text file to read
'              strText       Name of string to place text into
'              Function  = True if file input OK
'                        = False if file not input
' -----------------------------------
Dim strTemp As String

OpenAndReadTextIntoMemory = False        ' Default Setting
On Error GoTo NOTEXT

    Open strFileName For Input As #1
        strText = ""

        Do While Not EOF(1)
            Line Input #1, strTemp                 ' Input a single line
            strText = strText + strTemp + vbCr + vbLf  ' replace CR/LF
        Loop                                       ' continue till EOF

    Close #1

OpenAndReadTextIntoMemory = True
Exit Function
' ==========================================================================
NOTEXT:
Close #1
strText = ""
MsgBox "Failed to read in Text File"
Exit Function

End Function
```

The routine follows the design quite precisely. To begin with, the program sets the function to **False**, explicitly as a default value. Then, an error trap is set up before the file is opened for input. The text will be read in, line by line, using the **Line Input** command. This command reads an entire text line into the variable **strTemp**, which is then appended to **strText**, as is a carriage return, line-feed pair. (We discussed this in detail in the previous chapter when we were designing this development module.) Because **strText** is defined as a calling parameter, it is initially blanked off (set to contain no characters), just to be on the safe side. The **Do While** loop continues reading in from the file until the program encounters an "end of file," as dictated by the construct **Do While Not EOF(1)**. Once it reads an "end of file" mark, the program closes the file, sets the return function parameter to **True**, and executes an exit. Should an error occur, the file is closed, and an error message is output before the function exits, with the return parameter set to **False** by default.

Testing OpenAndReadTextIntoMemory

The test situations Julie intended to log were the following:

♦ *Test 1*—Genuine text file read and printed successfully with correct paragraphing.

♦ *Test 2*—Nontext file read in and handled in error.

♦ *Test 3*—Attempt to read a nonexistent file; check error handling.

To test the function, Julie first produced a text test file using the Windows Notepad editor. You can see the content of this test file in Figure 7.8.

No wraparound is enabled in this test file, so each paragraph appears as a single line. A new line starts only when a carriage return is manually entered into the text. The file has been structured with some very long lines (paragraphs) to begin with, and each line ends with a

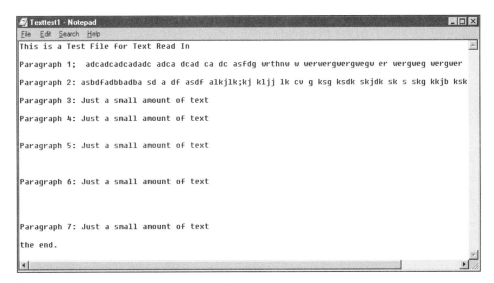

Figure 7.8
Julie's test text file created using the Windows Notepad editor.

forced carriage return and line feed. Julie wants to make sure that the text that appears in the immediate window matches the content of the test file in terms of layout, to prove that the paragraph structure is preserved. (Don't forget that a text box can be set up to wrap the text as the width of the control dictates.)

Julie then ran the program, read in the file, and compared the result in the immediate window with the original file content. Figure 7.9 shows what the immediate window looked like. As you can see, the paragraph (or line) structure has been maintained, proving that the function is handling the file correctly.

Test 2: No Failures

Then, Julie received a bit of a surprise. Try as she might, she could not get the program to fail in Test 2. She opened and read video files, image files, programs—all manner of files. Each time, the program loaded the contents and printed out strange characters on the immediate window. As she soon realized, the **Open** statement would open absolutely any DOS file, and the **Line input** command would read all the bytes—initially, from the first byte up to a couple of bytes that contained the terminator pair, if they existed. If the program couldn't find a terminator pair, it would read the entire file in one read. Eventually, she decided to read a file on the removable disk and remove the disk while the read was taking place. Unfortunately— or fortunately, depending on how you look at it—Windows trapped all the error conditions before the program got a chance to react to the error. Julie couldn't get Test 2 to fail, and she came to me with the problem.

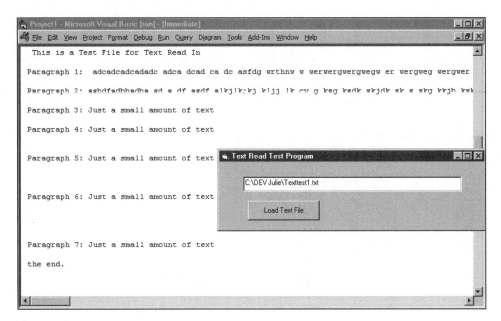

Figure 7.9
Result of text read, using test program **TextTest1**, shown in immediate window.

We decided that she would place a comment against the test, indicating that a failure could not be emulated. We decided that we would, nevertheless, pass the test. She had more joy with Test 3, which handled a nonexistent file correctly.

Creating LoadAndDisplayText

Creating this module proved to be a simple task. (You first need to understand the design specification for **LoadAndDisplayText**.) Julie decided to build on the test program she had already produced. First, she created an instance of a text box on the form. Then, she created a second button control, which would read in the file and display it in the text box. Follow these steps to create the modified program. If you don't want to construct the test code from scratch, you'll find **TextTest2** in the directory of that name in Julie's development directory on the CD.

Step 1

In the test program used to check out **OpenAndReadTextIntoMemory**, create a text box called **txtText**. Set the **MultiLine** property to **True**, and set up a vertical scrollbar.

Step 2

Create a second command button called **cmdLoadAndDisplayText**, and add the following code to the click event:

```
Private Sub cmdLoadAndDisplayText_Click()
' TEST CODE:
' Test Text Loading

Dim booResult As Boolean
Dim strTemp as String

dlgDialog1.Action = 1
txtTextFile.Text = dlgDialog1.FileName
strTemp = txtTextFile.Text

booResult = LoadAndDisplayText(strTemp, txtText)

MsgBox "Result of text read " & booResult
End Sub
```

This code is similar to the test code we used to check **OpenAndReadTextIntoMemory**, with the exception that we are now calling the **LoadAndDisplayText** function.

Finally, add the **LoadAndDisplayText** code to Julie's version of **ViewerLib**:

```
Public Function LoadAndDisplayText(strFileName As String,_
                txtObject As Control) As Boolean
' GENERAL GUI FUNCTION: Load and place text in text box, V1.0
' Arguments:    strFileName    name of file to open and read in
'               txtObject      name of text box to populate with file content
'               Function     = True if file opened and read OK
'                            = False if file not read OK
' ----------------------------------
' Local variables:
Dim strText As String

LoadAndDisplayText = OpenAndReadTextIntoMemory(strFileName, strText)

If LoadAndDisplayText = True Then
    txtObject.Text = strText
Else
    txtObject.Text = ""
End If

txtObject.Visible = True

End Function
```

The code starts by calling **OpenAndReadTextIntoMemory**. The Boolean result of the function is transferred to **LoadAndDisplayText**. The code then sets up the screen control, whose identity has been passed as a calling parameter, with the resultant string from **strText**. Should the routine that opened and read the text file indicate a failure, the text box content is set to contain no characters. Of course, we hadn't been able to make that routine fail, except with a nonexistent file name. Nevertheless, the code is in place. Note that Julie had cleared the text box in the event the program failed to read in any text. We had missed the need to clear the text box in the design.

Testing LoadAndDisplayText

Figure 7.10 shows the results of running the program and using the second command button.

Julie tried a variety of different-sized text boxes to make sure that the paragraphing came out correctly. In all cases, it did. Her logged tests amounted to the following:

♦ *Test 1*—Read in a known text file, and verify that it formats as required in text box.

♦ *Test 2*—Read in text file to at least three differently dimensioned text boxes (large, medium, and small), and verify formatting.

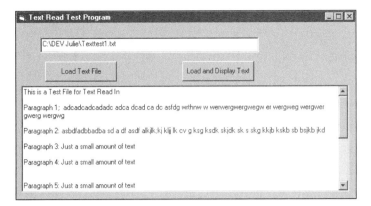

Figure 7.10
The modified test program showing the result of a **LoadAndDisplayText** operation.

◆ *Test 3*—Read in a very large text file containing several thousand characters.

◆ *Test 4*—Failure code verified by inspection.

◆ *Test 5*—Error handling of reading a nonexistent file verified.

Checking formatting simply amounted to making sure that the number of lines between paragraphs on the original text file was preserved. To create a large text file using the editor, Julie created a block of text and then used Copy and Paste to double the text block. She then used Copy and Paste to double the text block again, and so on. Quite quickly, this procedure leads to a huge volume of text.

Test 4 consisted of verifying that the failure code was correct because she couldn't simulate a failure. To back up the validation, she asked Archie to validate the code in his review, which he did. In just the first day, Julie had completed all the text-handling requirements that were scheduled for two days. On Day 2, a whole day ahead of schedule, she immediately went on to sound-file handling.

Handling Bugs in Development

When you test the code for the first time, you get bugs (normally), and you fix them. But what happens if you can't fix the bugs? The first thing you need to do is call for help. If you spend ridiculous amounts of time trying to sort out a single bug, no one will thank you for doing so if you have messed up the project schedules. So, the first thing to do is discuss the problem with someone. Quite often, just talking through how your code works suddenly lets you realize what the problem is.

Also, quite often, the questions that another person might ask in trying to understand your problem might trigger something in your mind, even if the questions were not directly relevant. If you still have a problem that you can't resolve, it's time to call in the supervisor or whoever is your immediate superior on the project.

Prioritize

If a supervisor can't shed any light on a potential solution, the first thing he or she will do is assess how serious the issue is by asking the following questions:

◆ Can the problem be fixed?

◆ Can a workaround be found?

◆ Does the problem make the code unusable?

◆ Will rectification jeopardize the project timetable?

Is There a Solution?

Clearly, if the problem can be rectified, and the solution does not put the project schedule at risk, no more needs to be said. However, the project manager must keep a close eye on things so that, if the fix proves to be more of a problem than expected, he or she can take action before the problem has an impact on the project.

Is There a Workaround?

If no one can see a simple solution, the next thing to consider is a possible workaround. With a workaround, you write code to bypass whatever is causing the issue, if that's possible. The project manager will need to see how the workaround will affect the schedule and whether the impact is severe. If a risk to the schedule exists, clearly, everyone will need to reconsider the options.

Can a Fix Wait?

Assuming you can see a fix or a workaround, but it is likely to take a while, you have to prioritize the bug. Is it a showstopper? If the answer is "Yes," and you have no option but to fix the bug, you need to reassess the project timetable. If the problem is really serious, don't hide the issue from the customer. Get the situation out into the open and, depending on the nature of the issue, the client might even be able to help.

If the fix can wait, you have a situation in which the code is obviously usable within some limitations and can, therefore, be released. You can explain the situation to the client. If waiting to sort out the underlying issue until later is unacceptable to the client, you can explain that doing otherwise will place the schedule in jeopardy. With most reasonable customers, this information has quite a sobering effect. You'll usually find that the client will live with the restrictions you might have to impose initially rather than let the problem affect the delivery date.

Keep the Fix in View

When a fix has to wait, it can easily become lost in the project. The project manager is responsible for ensuring that issues are logged and not lost. At some stage, the problem must be resolved. A useful procedure for ensuring that these issues don't get lost is to document them when the decision is made to defer a solution. Then, at regular intervals, review the project's issue list. Ideally, if you do this once a week, you won't lose site of any of the things that you must schedule into the project later.

We are talking about *issue management*. Without issue management, a project can rumble on toward disaster. As issue after issue is shelved, everyone happily continues with the development, conveniently forgetting that a lot of extra work is building up.

The other reason to regularly review the issue log is that some issues might actually go away as work on the project continues and more code is developed. The programmer might suddenly stumble on a convenient solution or workaround based on his or her new understanding as a result of subsequent work. Without the review process, the issue might not be closed. Because issue management is clearly an important aspect of a software development's management, we will return to the topic later in the book.

Return to the Case Study:
The LoadAndPlaySound Development Module

Julie's next task was to develop and test the sound-playing facility. The design we had produced and that we discussed in the previous chapter was for the **LoadAndPlaySound** function. Make sure you understand both the design and the relevant feasibility study in Chapter 2 before you continue.

Creation of LoadAndPlaySound

Julie was able to use code from the multimedia feasibility study that we had performed way back at the beginning of the project. To set up your test program, either read on, using the **SoundTest1** project located in Julie's directory on the CD, or follow these steps directly.

Step1

Start a new VB EXE project, and call it **SoundTest1**. Create an instance of a multimedia control, a file dialog box, a text box, and a command control, as Figure 7.11 shows. Note which button controls to enable for the multimedia control (these are as the control buttons that the viewer will require).

The controls are named as follows:

◆ *File dialog control*—**dlgDialog1**, allows test files to be selected.

◆ *Text box*—**txtSoundFile**, allows name of selected test file to be viewed.

◆ *Command button*—**cmdLoadAndPlaySound**, allows test to be performed.

◆ *Multimedia control*—**mmcSoundPlayer**, services sound-playing requirements.

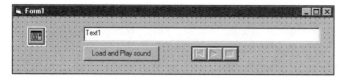

Figure 7.11
The form layout for test program **SoundTest**.

Step 2

Insert the following code into **cmdLoadAndPlaySound**'s click event:

```
Private Sub cmdLoadAndPlaySound_Click()
' TEST CODE:
' Sound Play Test

Dim booResult As Boolean
Dim strTemp As string

dlgDialog1.Action = 1
txtSoundFile.Text = dlgDialog1.FileName
strTemp = txtSoundFile.Text

booResult = LoadAndPlaySound(strTemp, mmcSoundPlayer)

MsgBox "result of sound load " & booResult

End Sub
```

The above code follows the same lines as all the test programs completed so far.

Step 3

Next, insert the following code into Julie's version of **ViewerLib**:

```
Public Function LoadAndPlaySound(strFileName As String,_
              mmcObject As Control) As Boolean
' GENERAL GUI FUNCTION: Load and start WAV and MID files, V1.0
' Arguments: StrFileName    File ref of WAV or MID file to play
'            mmcObject       Multimedia control to play sound through
'            Function   =  True if sound loaded OK
'                        =  False if sound not loaded
' -----------------------------------
LoadAndPlaySound = False                    ' Default return code
On Error GoTo NoSound
    mmcObject.Wait = True
    mmcObject.Visible = True
```

```
    mmcObject.Command = "CLOSE"        ' ensure previous session closed
    mmcObject.Wait = True              ' down (if any)
    mmcObject.FileName = strFileName
    mmcObject.Command = "OPEN"         ' Open for a new file
    mmcObject.Command = "PLAY"         ' and play it
    If mmcObject.ErrorMessage <> "" Then GoTo NoSound
LoadAndPlaySound = True
Exit Function
' ======================================================================
' error handling
NoSound:
    mmcObject.Wait = True
    mmcObject.Command = "CLOSE"
    MsgBox " Error attempting to play sound file."
Exit Function
End Function
```

The code is based on the feasibility study and follows the design exactly.

Testing LoadAndPlaySound

The program allowed Julie to select any file name and attempt to play it as a sound file. She had to test three types of file: WAV, MID, and a file type that was neither of these types. The tests Julie logged were as follows:

♦ *Test 1*—Load a WAV file, and verify that it plays and that multimedia control buttons function OK.

♦ *Test 2*—Repeat Test 1 for a MID file.

♦ *Test 3*—Load any file except WAV and MID, and check error handling.

♦ *Test 4*—Check error handling of nonexistent file request.

An Issue Surfaces

Then, we found our first real problem. No matter how she tried, Julie could not get a MID file to rewind by clicking the Previous button. She tried the Back button as well. She could not get the file to rewind, whether or not it was playing. With a WAV file, the multimedia control worked perfectly. According to instruction, Julie spent the minimum of time trying to sort the problem herself, and then she came to see me.

The first thing we did was to classify the seriousness of the problem; it was not a showstopper. Even if the prototype went out with this bug, Monty's team still could display the concept. As long as they were aware of the problem, they could keep away from that bit of functionality.

We looked at Julie's workload and her current progress. Fixing this problem could take quite a while because it would involve a workaround. So, we decided to postpone any further work on the problem, log the failure in the test logs, and classify it as a nuisance to be dealt with at an appropriate time. This was our first issue for which we did not have a resolution. Consequently, we created a project issue file and logged the following information:

E-MagBook Development Project Issue Log: Issue 01.

LoadAndDisplaySound MID Rewind Failure: Priority Not Urgent.

MID files cannot be rewound using the multimedia control, whether or not the sound track is playing. Workaround, for viewer, is currently to use the reload button, but this does not work when a sound is still playing after its page has been replaced by another. Proper solution will be required in code associated with rewind button's click handler. WAV files function OK.

We'd also added some extra information that resulted from our initial thoughts on the matter. Classifying bugs in this way is absolutely essential to avoid going off on a tangent and spending a lot of time fixing what is not a serious problem. You can easily be sucked into resolving an issue and using up all your contingency time until the problem starts to affect the schedule. So, we'd shelved the issue for the time being. However, we needed to make sure we didn't forget it. We assigned it a priority of *not urgent*, and we would review the issue log once a week.

Completion of LoadAndPlaySound Testing

Apart from this minor hiccup, Julie had now finished her initial tasks in two days, as opposed to a scheduled three days. I was totally against using this extra time to solve the rewind issue, so she moved on to the **TitleHandling** module.

The Reconciliation Process

We'd had two programmers working on simultaneous developments in the case study. Archie had created a brand-new data structure and completed his development tasks. Both the data structure and the developed routines were locked away in his version of **ViewerLib**.

Julie had completed her two development tasks, and the resultant routines were now locked away in her version of **ViewerLib**. In the case study, reconciliation was simply a matter of creating a single library that contained all the elements of Archie's and Julie's individual libraries. The end result was that the two libraries contained identical content at the end of the reconciliation process, and both programmers could then continue with their next development tasks. (This reconciliation needs to be performed only when one programmer needs access to routines the other programmer has created. In the case study, Archie needed the routines that Julie had developed to create and test the **DisplayPage** development module.)

Everything was being controlled manually. At the end of the development we'd been through to this point, the two versions of **ViewerLib** were reconciled and were represented by the status description you can see in Figure 7.12.

Status of ViewerLib after First Reconciliation				
Module (sub/function/data structure)	Type	Status	Version	Owner
Viewer Screen Definitions Data	Data	FINAL	1.0	
Title Index Data Structure	Data	FINAL	1.0	
Page Index Data Structure	Data	FINAL	1.0	
Runtime Container Dimensions and Position	Data	FINAL	1.0	
LoadAndDisplayImage	GEN GUI	FINAL	1.0	
Size Picture	GEN	FINAL	1.0	
LoadAndPlayVideo	GEN GUI	FINAL	1.0	
OpenAndReadTextIntoMemory	GEN	FINAL	1.0	
LoadAndDisplayText	GEN GUI	FINAL	1.0	
LoadAndPlaySound	GEN GUI	FINAL*	1.0	

*See issue log; issue 01 for outstanding, nonurgent problem with LoadAndPlaySound.

Figure 7.12
Status of **ViewerLib** after first reconciliation of the two versions.

Note that the **LoadAndPlaySound** routine had been singled out as *FINAL*, but with a nonurgent issue outstanding that needed to be resolved. You can find the library as it existed after this first reconciliation in either Julie's or Archie's development area on the CD, in a file called **ViewerLib_After_Recon1.bas**.

The Equivalent Software Version-Control Procedure

If we had been using a version-control package, the situation would have been different. Each programmer would have created a new routine through the version-control package itself. The software would create a routine that was automatically checked out and, therefore, unavailable to any other programmers. The others could see the routine and possibly even view its latest content, but they couldn't use any checked-out routines in their current project.

After a routine was completed, fully tested, and had passed the tests, it could be checked back into the system via the version-control facility. The routine would have a version number and could now be used by anyone. However, if anyone wanted to modify it, it would have to be checked out again.

The real power of such a control package is that it maintains all the previous versions of a routine. One programmer can be developing a suite based on Version 1 of a routine while another programmer is creating Version 2 of the same routine. The system ensures that the two versions remain completely independent of each other, allowing Version 1 to be included in any programmer's development as a read-only unit, and stopping all programmers except the one who had checked it out from accessing Version 2.

This capability to segregate different versions also allows the control system to put together earlier versions of a program release. For example, suppose we have a program that consists of routines A, B, and C. We might construct Version 1 of the program from Version 1 of routine A, Version 2 of routine B, and Version 1 of routine C. After a period of development, routine A moves up to Version 2 and routine B to Version 3; routine C remains at Version 1. We can construct two programs using the correct version numbers of applicable routines. We construct Program 1 from routine A (v1.0), routine B (v2.0), and routine C (v1.0). We construct the later program, Program 2, from routine A (v2.0), routine B (v3.0), and routine C (v1.0). In this way, we can separately maintain different manifestations of the same program.

We'll see later that such a capability is essential to maintain a released version of software, together with new software you're testing, and even newer software you're developing—all for the same program suite. Using a good version-control package lets you manage the development and support of different generations of the same product.

Management of Module Testing

The project manager, or whoever is given the task, can do plenty to monitor and manage the development module-testing process. Because the programmers are producing test records, the manager can examine these records. By inspecting the records, the project manager can see the definition of the tests, their status, and what's left to do, to get a good indication of progress.

As the project manager, you can ask to see the result of a given test by having the programmer repeat the test, so you can verify the recorded result. The management of module testing is best left to someone who understands programs and, in particular, the concept of testing different pathways according to variations of input and so on. If you understand these concepts, you can better assess a programmer's real progress—you can ask more pertinent questions and are more likely to understand the answers you receive. (Programmers are notorious for speaking in jargon—indeed, some programmers do it quite deliberately just to get rid of the questioner.)

As a rule, programmers, particularly inexperienced ones, don't volunteer information; typically, you have to pry it out of them. Individuals who understand programming, programmers, and the concepts surrounding code construction and analysis of pathways can best get such information from them. That's not to say that managers without programming backgrounds can't manage module testing, but programmers can much more easily mislead them, whether accidentally or intentionally.

Return to the Case Study:
The DisplayPage Module

Archie was a good day ahead of schedule when he started working on the **DisplayPage** subroutine. This routine had a dependency on Julie's work, but she had finished early, too, so they were able to reconcile their libraries at the end of Day 2.

Go back to the previous chapter (or to Appendix G) and study the design we came up with for this subroutine before you proceed. For the first time, the Page Index global data entities would be called into play. When the routine was called without the optional argument, **g_intCurrentPage** would be pointing to an Index entry or a page number, and the display routines must use the following file references:

- *g_strPictureFile(intCurrentPage)*—for the image or video clip.

- *g_strTextFile(intCurrentPage)*—for the text file.

- *g_strSoundFile(intCurrentPage)*—for the sound file.

- *g_strKeys(1,intCurrentPage)* to *g_str(5,intCurrentPage)*—for keys 1 through 5.

The container area for the image or video needed to have been set up according to format type—or, to be more specific, **g_intFormatType**. Finally, the text box must be set up with the font characteristics defined in **g_strFontType** and **g_intFontSize**. If you recall, the font characteristics of the display-text object would be inherited from the Page Index.

It was clear to Archie that the test program needed to let him set up file references and keys for the first entry of a single-entry index. He would then need to be able to set up the format type—Text Book, Picture Album, or Reference Book—and only then call **DisplayPage** to display Page 1 for testing.

In the previous chapter, we introduced the need for three routines to set up the image and text-box dimensions, and the position for each of the three format types. These routines use the values in the **Viewer Screen Definitions** data structure to obtain the necessary values for setting up the principal screen objects. Specifically, Archie needed to develop **SetFormat1**, **SetFormat2**, **SetFormat3**, and the routine to capture the design-time data into the **Viewer Screen Definitions** data structure. He would call this routine **CaptureViewerDesignParameters**. You can find the design for all four routines in Appendix G. As usual, have a look at them before you proceed.

Creation of DisplayPage Test Program—Part 1

To build the first part of Archie's test program to check out the format-layout setup, follow these steps; alternatively, read on and load the project in directory **DisplayPage_Part1** from Archie's development directory on the CD.

Step 1

Start a new VB EXE project, and load your copy of Archie's version of **ViewerLib** (i.e., the one you have been building in your copy of Archie's development area). (This is also available on the CD as **ViewerLib_At_Recon1** in Archie's development area.) Be sure to load Archie's version, because we are going to update it. Figure 7.13 depicts the screen layout for the project.

The following steps let you set up the form for the **DisplayPage** test program, which contains two sections. You will use the upper part of the screen to set up page data manually. That is,

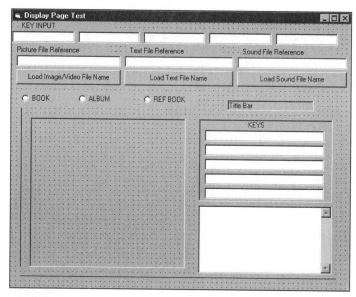

Figure 7.13
The form for the **DisplayPage** test program.

you can insert the keys and file-reference strings directly into the text boxes. The lower portion of the screen contains the page display, showing keys, text, and image in any of the three formats, as defined by the BOOK, ALBUM, or REF BOOK radio buttons. This screen is, by far, the most sophisticated test screen you've developed yet.

Step 2

Create an array of five text fields called **txtKeyData**, and place the fields at the very top of the form, as Figure 7.13 shows. Archie would use these fields to set up the keys that required manual entry for a test. In the screenshot, these fields are labeled "KEY INPUT."

Step 3

Just below the keys, create three text boxes—**txtPictureFileName**, **txtTextFileName**, and **txtSoundFileName**—with appropriate labels, as Figure 7.13 shows. Underneath each text box, create a button control, as shown, naming the controls from left to right **cmdLoadImage**, **cmdLoadText**, and **cmdLoadSound**.

The three text boxes in the second row of screen objects will also be available on the viewer in its final form. If you recall, the design stipulates that the viewer must place the names of the reference files into three text boxes so they will be visible when the viewer runs as a child form of the Page Index Editor. Under normal conditions, when the viewer is running standalone, these text boxes will be hidden. In the test program, we can make double use of them. First, we can use them to set up file names manually for feeding into the Index arrays. The test program can also use them to verify what it is setting up in terms of a picture, text, and sound.

We will run two tests of the **Display Page** subroutine: one in which the routine is requested to load a page from the Index and a second in which the routine is required to load the files from the three file-name text boxes, leaving the keys untouched. The second option will be required when the viewer form is available in the Page Index Editor program.

Step 4

Create a vertical line called LINE1 and a horizontal line called LINE2, as the lower half of the form in Figure 7.13 shows. These lines will delimit the edges of the simulated text and album container areas, much as we will do in the final version of the viewer.

Step 5

Create the main image control—**imgImageIt**—and the text control—**txtText**—as Figure 7.13 shows. Set the text control to be **multiline**, and set it up with a vertical scroll bar.

Step 6

Create a panel from a picture control and call the panel **PicKeyPanel**. Using the panel as a container, create an array of five text boxes, from element 1 through element 5, called **txtKeyView**, and positioned as the screenshot in Figure 7.13 shows, just above the text box. You will have to create element 0 first, but as soon as you have created elements 0 through 5, you can delete **txtKeyView(0)**.

Step7

Create three radio buttons—**rdoOption1**, **rdoOption2**, and **rdoOption3**—and label them according to the screenshot in Figure 7.13. Also create a label—**lblTitleBar**—which will indicate what type of book format has been selected. You can see the label on Figure 7.13 next to the third radio button. Note that the label is a screen object that will be present on the viewer itself.

Step 8

Create the **CaptureViewerDesignParameters** subroutine in the general area of the main form (this subroutine refers directly to screen objects by name, so it cannot be classed as GEN GUI and, therefore, according to our standards, cannot be placed in **ViewerLib**. In fact, the subroutine is what we are referring to as a private GUI, infrastructure routine for the viewer program:

```
Private Sub CaptureViewerDesignParameters()
' VIEWER INFRASTRUCTURE GUI ROUTINE:  V1.0
' Defines the position and/or dimensions of key screen objects by
' picking up their properties as they were defined at design time.
' --------------------------------
g_intOrigin1_Left = Line1.X1          ' Book and album origin
g_intOrigin1_Top = Line1.Y1
```

```
g_intOrigin2_Left = imgImageIt.Left          ' Ref image origin
      g_intOrigin2_Top = imgImageIt.Top

      g_intOrigin3_Left = txtText.Left         ' Small text origin (Ref)
      g_intOrigin3_Top = txtText.Top

      g_intOrigin4_Left = picKeyPanel.Left     ' Large text (ref) origin
      g_intOrigin4_Top = picKeyPanel.Top

      g_intHeight1 = Line1.Y2 - Line1.Y1       ' Heights for Book and Album
      g_intHeight2 = imgImageIt.Height         ' Image height (ref)
      g_intHeight3 = txtText.Height            ' small text for ref

      g_intWidth1 = Line2.X2 - Line2.X1        ' width for book text, album pic
      g_intWidth2 = imgImageIt.Width           ' width for pic in ref format
      g_intWidth3 = txtText.Width              ' width for text in ref format

   End Sub
```

This code is a very straightforward translation from the design statement. Note, however, that Line1 must be the vertical line with **Y1** at the top and **Y2** at the bottom. Likewise, Line2 must be the horizontal line with **X1** on the left and **X2** on the right. This routine will capture all the information needed to set up the screen for any of the three formats.

Step 9

Now, set up code for the three radio "option" buttons as follows:

```
Private Sub rdoOption1_Click()
' TEST CODE:
' Set text format
 g_intFormatType = 1   ' text Book
 Call SetUpFormat1
End Sub

Private Sub rdoOption2_Click()
' TEST CODE:
' set album format
 g_intFormatType = 2
 Call SetUpFormat2
 ' set up the image control so you can see size of container
 imgImageIt.Top = g_intImageContainer_Top
 imgImageIt.Left = g_intImageContainer_Left
 imgImageIt.Width = g_intImageContainer_Width
 imgImageIt.Height = g_intImageContainer_Height
End Sub
```

```
Private Sub rdoOption3_Click()
' TEST CODE:
' set reference format
 g_intFormatType = 3
 Call SetUpFormat3
' set up the image control so you can see size of container
 imgImageIt.Top = g_intImageContainer_Top
 imgImageIt.Left = g_intImageContainer_Left
 imgImageIt.Width = g_intImageContainer_Width
 imgImageIt.Height = g_intImageContainer_Height
End Sub
```

Setting up the book format consists of setting **g_intFormatType** to **1** and then calling **SetUpFormat1**. The other two radio buttons are similar, but after each call to the appropriate **SetUpFormat** routine, the image control is set up with the image container parameters. These radio buttons will allow testing of the formatting routines. When a radio button is clicked, the observed effect will be to set up the image control, if there is one, to the dimensions of the image container. This action will allow us to check out the behavior of the setup routines.

Step 10

Now, set up the three format routines in the general section of the main form. The code is simple in each case, following the design:

```
Private Sub SetUpFormat1()
' VIEWER INFRASTRUCTURE GUI ROUTINE:  V1.0
' set up for BOOK format. Text box on screen only
' ----------------------
lblTitleBar.Caption = "E-Book"

' remove main Picture control
imgImageIt.Visible = False
g_intImageContainer_Left = 0
g_intImageContainer_Top = 0
g_intImageContainer_Height = 0
g_intImageContainer_Width = 0

' maximize text control and set font
txtText.Left = g_intOrigin1_Left
txtText.Top = g_intOrigin1_Top
txtText.Width = g_intWidth1
txtText.Height = g_intHeight1
txtText.Font = g_strFontType
txtText.FontSize = g_intFontSize
txtText.Text=""
```

```
        txtText.Visible = True

End Sub

Private Sub SetUpFormat2()
' VIEWER INFRASTRUCTURE GUI ROUTINE: V1.0
' set up for ALBUM format.
' -------------------------
lblTitleBar.Caption = "E-Album"
txtText.Visible = False

' set up Picture container
g_intImageContainer_Left = g_intOrigin1_Left
g_intImageContainer_Top = g_intOrigin1_Top
g_intImageContainer_Height = g_intHeight1
g_intImageContainer_Width = g_intWidth1
imgImageIt = LoadPicture("")  ' Clear any previous image
imgImageIt.Visible = True

End Sub

Private Sub SetUpFormat3()
' VIEWER INFRASTRUCTURE GUI ROUTINE: V1.0
' set up for reference format.
' -------------------------
lblTitleBar.Caption = "E-Reference"

' set up Picture container
g_intImageContainer_Left = g_intOrigin2_Left
g_intImageContainer_Top = g_intOrigin2_Top
g_intImageContainer_Height = g_intHeight2
g_intImageContainer_Width = g_intWidth2
imgImageIt = LoadPicture("")  ' Clear any previous image
imgImageIt.Visible = True

' maximize text control
txtText.Left = g_intOrigin3_Left
txtText.Top = g_intOrigin3_Top
txtText.Width = g_intWidth3
txtText.Height = g_intHeight3
txtText.Font = g_strFontType
txtText.FontSize = g_intFontSize
txtText.Text=""
txtText.Visible = True

End Sub
```

In each of the three routines, the text box and the image container area are set up according to the design details. To understand the code fully, you might need to consult the viewer-format-design diagram. See Figure 6.13 and refer to the design specifications.

Step 11

Place this code in the test program's **Form_Load** event:

```
Private Sub Form_Load()
' TEST CODE:
' force a font type and size
g_strFontType = "Ariel"
g_intFontSize = 12
' capture parameters from screen objects
Call CaptureViewerDesignParameters
End Sub
```

This code captures the design parameters and makes sure that some values are placed into the font globals.

Testing DisplayPage—Part 1

When Archie had reached this point, he decided to test the format-setting functionality, which would test the following:

♦ *Test 1*—Check Format 1 (Book) layout configured OK for different design setups.

♦ *Test 2*—Check Format 2 (Album) layout configured OK for different design setups.

♦ *Test 3*—Check Format 3 (Ref Book) layout configured OK for different design setups.

The three radio buttons allowed Archie to switch to one of the three formats on demand. When he ran the program, he could check each format in turn by clicking the appropriate radio button. He could then stop the program; modify **Line1**, **Line2**, **imgImageIT**, and **txtText** in the design environment; run the program; and check that the three formats were correctly accommodated with the new settings. Figures 7.14, 7.15, and 7.16 show what each layout looked like.

Creation of the DisplayPage Function—Part 2

All that remains now is to set up the page display routine itself and some command buttons to allow testing. Once again, you can construct the test program by following the steps, or you can read about the code and use the test project available in **DisplayPage_Part2**, located in Archie's development directory on the CD.

Step 1

Add a new button control, **cmdLoadPageFromIndex**, to the form. Add another command button called **cmdLoadPageFromFileNames**. You will use these buttons to test loading from

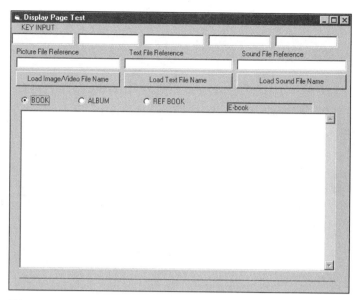

Figure 7.14

Display Page Test program 1 after the BOOK radio button had been clicked.

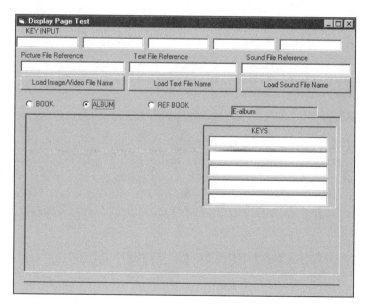

Figure 7.15

Display Page Test program 1 after the ALBUM radio button had been clicked.

the simulated Page Index entry, or directly from the file-name text boxes, per the design specification. Add a multimedia control named **mmcSoundPlayer**, and set up its buttons as Julie did for Sound Test 1. Also, load the video form—**frmVideo**—used in the video test program. Finally, add the dialog control, **dlgDialog1**. The layout then becomes as Figure 7.17 shows. Store the project in a new directory.

Step 2

Add the following code to the control buttons used to set up the picture, text, and sound file references:

```
Private Sub cmdLoadImage_Click()
' TEST CODE:
  dlgDialog1.Action = 1
  txtPictureFileName.Text = dlgDialog1.FileName
End

 Private Sub cmdLoadText_Click()
' TEST CODE:
  dlgDialog1.Action = 1
  txtTextFileName.Text = dlgDialog1.FileName
End

 Private Sub cmdLoadSound_Click()
' TEST CODE:
  dlgDialog1.Action = 1
  txtSoundFileName.Text = dlgDialog1.FileName
End Sub
```

All this code does is allow the user to select a file name and then load it into the relevant text box. The facility enabled Archie to set up three file references manually from the file store. He could also set up the five keys manually, using the key fields, by placing the cursor on the selected field and typing straight into the field. These combined facilities enabled Archie to set up a complete test entry in the upper section of the screen. The Load From Index button would then use this data to set up the internal Index entry before calling the **DisplayPage** module to populate the objects in the lower portion of the screen, which simulated the viewer's Page View mode of operation. The alternative button, Load From Files, tests the alternative call to **DisplayPage**.

Step 3

Add the following code to the Load From Index button control's click event:

```
Private Sub cmdLoadPageFromIndex_Click()
```

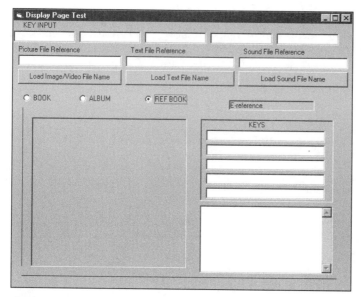

Figure 7.16
Display Page Test program 1 after the REF BOOK radio button had been clicked.

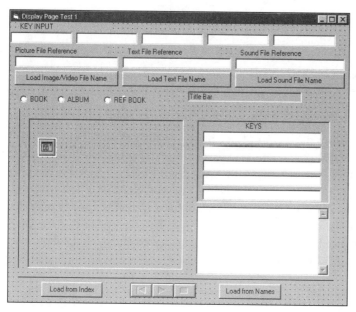

Figure 7.17
Display Page Test program 2 form with the rest of the screen objects added.

```
' TEST CODE:
' set up page entry array
' and call with no argument.
Dim intLoopCounter As Integer

' Clear screen
txtText.Text = ""
imgImageIt = LoadPicture("")

' Create a single page index
ReDim g_strKeys(5, 1)
ReDim g_strPictureFile(1)
ReDim g_strTextFile(1)
ReDim g_strSoundFile(1)

' populate page 1 from screen
For intLoopCounter = 1 To 5
     g_strKeys(intLoopCounter, 1) = txtKeyData(intLoopCounter).Text
Next intLoopCounter

g_strPictureFile(1) = txtPictureFileName.Text
g_strTextFile(1) = txtTextFileName.Text
g_strSoundFile(1) = txtSoundFileName.Text

' DISPLAY PAGE
g_intCurrentPage = 1
Call DisplayPage

End Sub
```

The code first clears the image and text screen objects, and then creates element 1 of the Page Index arrays, using the **ReDim** statement. The design specifies that the internal Page Index is a dynamic array and that it will grow and shrink according to demand. In the above code, we want to create only a single element of the array (forgetting element 0), and then populate the element with data from the screen objects. The code sets up the five, memory key strings of the first entry and the file-reference text strings from the relevant screen objects.

After the entry is complete, **DisplayPage** can be called with **g_intCurrentPage** set to **1**, exactly emulating the situation where the viewer is required to display Page 1 of a book. Note that the code populates all the elements of the Page Index, regardless of the format type that will be specified. This is quite in order, because the code will simply ignore any of the component strings that are not applicable for a given format setting. For example, if the format is Picture Album, the code in **DisplayPage** will ignore the text reference; if the format is Text Book, the code will simply ignore any picture reference.

Step 4

Add this code to the Load From Names button control:

```
Private Sub cmdLoadPageFromNames_Click()
' TEST CODE:
' Call DisplayPage with alternate
' argument setting to load from file name text boxes.

' Clear screen
txtText.Text = ""
imgImageIt = LoadPicture("")

' Clear Index to ensure it cannot be used for this test
ReDim g_strKeys(0, 0)
ReDim g_strPictureFile(0)
ReDim g_strTextFile(0)
ReDim g_strSoundFile(0)

' populate page 1 from file names
g_intCurrentPage = 0     ' cannot be used
Call DisplayPage(1)      ' alternate call

End Sub
```

The above code forces the alternate call to **DisplayPage**, first ensuring that the Index has been cleared out so that, should the code try to use an Index entry, the tester will be alerted by a program failure.

Step 5

Now, we're ready for the **DisplayPage** routine itself, which you should insert into the general section of the test program, because it will be an infrastructure routine of the final viewer program. The code is split into self-contained blocks; after each such block is a description of the code within it.

Step 5—Section 1

```
Public Sub DisplayPage(Optional intAlternateDisplay As Integer = 0)
' VIEWER INFRASTRUCTURE GUI ROUTINE:  V1.0
' Arguments:
'    intAlternateDisplay  if present, use file references to create display
```

```
'   if not present, create display from Index entry
' --------------------------------------
Dim intLoopCounter As Integer
Dim intVidorPic As Integer
Dim booResult As Boolean
Dim strThePictureRef As String
Dim strTheTextRef As String
Dim strTheSoundRef As String
Dim strTheKeys(5) As String

Call SetUpTheData(intAlternateDisplay, strThePictureRef, strTheTextRef,_
                                       strTheSoundRef, strTheKeys())

' Set up keys
If intAlternateDisplay = 0 Then
    For intLoopCounter = 1 To 5
            txtKeyView(intLoopCounter).Text = strTheKeys(intLoopCounter)
    Next intLoopCounter
End If
'..............................................................
```

Section 1 Notes: The above code calls a subroutine to set up **DisplayPage** for whichever parameters will provide its data. For **intAlternateDisplay** set to 0, the data is obtained from the Index record addressed by **g_intCurrentPage**, which, in the case of the test program, is **1**. The routine will set up the three string references appropriately. If the argument is not 0, the code sets up the three strings from the text boxes on screen that contain the file references.

Upon return from the routine, the code in **DisplayPage** then transfers the keys from the local array that has been set up by the subroutine **SetUpTheData** and transfers the strings into the screen objects used to hold the page's keys.

Step 5—Section 2
```
'..............................................................
' Display Text Book Format
If g_intFormatType = 1 Then
    booResult = LoadAndDisplayText(strTheTextRef, txtText)
 End If
'..............................................................
```

Section 2 Notes: This code is calling Julie's function, used for Format 1, to load and display the text of a Text Book.

Step 5—Section 3
```
'..............................................................
' Display Album Format
```

```
If g_intFormatType = 2 Then
    intVidorPic = VideoOrPicture(strThePictureRef)
    If intVidorPic = 1 Then
        booResult = LoadAndDisplayImage(strThePictureRef, imgImageIt,_
                g_intImageContainer_Width, g_intImageContainer_Height,_
                g_intImageContainer_Left, g_intImageContainer_Top)
    Else
        booResult = LoadAndPlayVideo(strThePictureRef, frmVideo,_
                frmVideo.mmcVideoPlayer,_
                g_intImageContainer_Width, g_intImageContainer_Height,_
                g_intImageContainer_Left, g_intImageContainer_Top)
    End If
End If
'......................................................................
```

Section 3 Notes: First, Archie had to set up a function to check the file name and determine whether the file was a video file (AVI extension). This function was **VideoOrPicture**, which you'll see later. Then, depending on which file it was, he called the appropriate routine to display an image or show a video. (Don't forget, **LoadAndDisplayImage** and **LoadAndPLayVideo** have already been produced and tested, and are in **ViewerLib**.)

Step 5—Section 4

```
'......................................................................
' Display Reference Format
If g_intFormatType = 3 Then
    intVidorPic = VideoOrPicture(strThePictureRef)
    If intVidorPic = 1 Then
        booResult = LoadAndDisplayImage(strThePictureRef, imgImageIt,_
                g_intImageContainer_Width, g_intImageContainer_Height,_
                g_intImageContainer_Left, g_intImageContainer_Top)
    Else
        booResult = LoadAndPlayVideo(strThePictureRef, frmVideo,_
                frmVideo.mmcVideoPlayer,_
                g_intImageContainer_Width, g_intImageContainer_Height,_
                g_intImageContainer_Left, g_intImageContainer_Top)
    End If

    booResult = LoadAndDisplayText(strTheTextRef, txtText)

End If
'......................................................................
```

Section 4 Notes: The above code is the same as the Picture Album code for the image, but the above code uses the Reference Book's container settings. The **LoadAndDisplayText** function gets the text of the reference page onto the screen.

Step 5—Section 5

```
'............................................................
' Now check for a sound file - all formats
If strTheSoundRef <> "" Then
    booResult = LoadAndPlaySound(strTheSoundRef, mmcSoundPlayer)
End If
'
'............................................................
```

Section 5 Note: For all formats, a sound file is played, if there is one.

Step 5—Section 6

```
'............................................................
' DIAGNOSTIC AID also required by PAGE EDITOR
' Indicate the file references for this page
If intAlternateDisplay <> 1 Then
    txtPictureFileName.Text = strThePictureRef
    txtTextFileName.Text = strTheTextRef
    txtSoundFileName.Text = strTheSoundRef
End If
End Sub
```

Section 6 Notes: The final act of **DisplayPage** is to show the file references that have been used when the routine has been called to display from a Page Index record. Note that the **DisplayPage** subroutine places all three references in the text boxes, regardless of the format being displayed. This approach will allow the operator to see the full situation in the Page Index Editor program. It also provides an extremely useful debugging aid. In the test program, if anything goes wrong, we'll see the text boxes change value.

This functionality is actually required functionality that was not specified in the design. Consequently, Archie updated the design accordingly. If you look at the design specifications in Appendix G for **DisplayPage**, you will see a change log defining the update. You can also see which part of the specification has changed as a result of the update.

Step 6

Archie had decided to create a general subroutine to handle the setup of the file reference strings, which would be determined by the type of call being made (that is, use the Index, or use the file-reference text boxes). Here is the code you can place in the general section of the test program:

```
Private Sub SetUpTheData(intAlternativeDisplay As Integer,_
               strThePictureRef As String, strTheTextRef As String,_
strTheSoundRef As String, strTheKeys() As String)
' VIEWER INFRASTRUCTURE ROUTINE:  Page handling V1.0
```

```
' ARGUMENTS:
'    intAlternativeDisplay  = 0 if display from page index
'                           = 1 if display from file ref text boxes
'          strThePictureRef = will contain required picture file ref on exit
'             strTheTextRef = will contain required text file ref on exit
'            strTheSoundRef = will contain required sound file ref on exit
'
' ------------------------------
Dim intLoopCounter As Integer

If intAlternativeDisplay = 0 Then     ' display from Index
   ' Set up the keys
   For intLoopCounter = 1 To 5
      strTheKeys(intLoopCounter) = g_strKeys(intLoopCounter,
                 g_intCurrentPage)
   Next intLoopCounter
   ' Set up the file references
   strThePictureRef = g_strPictureFile(g_intCurrentPage)
   strTheTextRef = g_strTextFile(g_intCurrentPage)
   strTheSoundRef = g_strSoundFile(g_intCurrentPage)
Else
   ' Keys not needed
   ' Set up the file references
   strThePictureRef = txtPictureFileName.Text
   strTheTextRef = txtTextFileName.Text
   strTheSoundRef = txtSoundFileName.Text
End If

End Sub
```

Archie modified the design of **PageDisplay** to reflect the preceding code, and then he created a design specification for **SetUpTheData** before he started to program.

Step 7

We have the brand-new routine Archie created to determine whether a file is an AVI file. We can transfer this routine into **ViewerLib** because it is totally independent of the program infrastructure and screen objects in which it runs:

```
Public Function VideoOrPicture(strFileName as string) As Integer
' GENERAL ROUTINE: Determine if file is video or not. V1.0
' Arguments:
'        strFileName    name of file to determine type
'            Function   = -1  no string
'                       = 0   is AVI
'                       = 1   Not AVI
```

```
' -------------------------
Dim intLength As Integer
Dim strExtension As String

' extract extension code from file name
VideoOrPicture = -1                          ' start with error code
intLength = Len(strFileName)
If intLength = 0 Then Exit Function

strExtension = Mid(strFileName, intLength - 2, 3)_
                    ' extract last 3 characters

VideoOrPicture = 1      ' assume NOT AVI
If UCase(strExtension) = "AVI" Then VideoOrPicture = 0  '  AVI CONFIRMED

End Function
```

To ensure that he kept the design documentation up to date, and to assist him in creating the routine in the first place, Archie first created a simple design specification. You can see this design specification in Appendix G.

Testing DisplayPage—Part 2

At this stage, Archie was in a position to check page handling in total. He had already tested the format-setting code, so his testing now consisted of the following:

♦ *Test 1*—Set up a Text Book page, and check layout for a number of files with varying amounts of text. For each test page, perform test for Load From Index and again for Load From Files. Include sound present and not present.

♦ *Test 2*—Set up a number of Picture Album pages, and check for correct layout. For each test page, perform test for Load From Index and again for Load From Files. Include sound present and not present. Check both static image and video.

♦ *Test 3*—Set up a number of Reference Book pages, and check for correct layout. For each test page, perform test for Load from Fndex and again for Load From Files. Include sound present and not present. Check both static image and video.

♦ *Test 4*—Verify text error handling in all modes.

♦ *Test 5*—Check image error handling in all modes.

♦ *Test 6*—Check sound error handling in all modes.

♦ *Test 7*—Change design layout and repeat Tests 1 through 6.

♦ *Test 8*—Change text font parameters in test program's load handler, and check that text pages are formatted correctly.

♦ *Test 9*—Ensure that keys are transferred from Index record for Load From Index mode.

♦ *Test 10*—Ensure that keys are undisturbed for Load From Files mode.

This list represents quite a complex test regime. However, with the capability to set up keys and file references manually, coupled with the capability to select format mode from the radio buttons, Archie performed the testing surprisingly quickly. That speed illustrates the key difference between formal testing and this less rigid approach. To give you an idea of how to go about Test 1, here's a possible sequence:

♦ *Input Fields*— Clear all keys and file-reference text boxes.

♦ *Test Text File 1*—Place the name of the text file into the text-file reference box using the Load Text File Name button control.

♦ *Set Text Format*—Click the BOOK radio button.

♦ *Load From Index*—Click Load From Index, and verify tha tthe text loads into the text box OK.

♦ *Clear Text Box Manually*—Place the cursor in the text box, highlight the entire contents, and delete.

♦ *Load From File Ref*—Click Load From Files, and verify that the text loads into the text box OK.

And so on.

You can also use these instructions to set up testing for a Picture Album if you substitute *album* for *text* in the list.

Because you have access to all the text input fields throughout the test program, you can very simply perform tests to verify the behavior of **DisplayPage**. For example, to verify that a Load From Files leaves the keys on display unchanged, simply set them up with something manually, and then check that they are untouched by clicking the Load From Files button. If you then load from the Index, the keys will be overwritten by whatever is in the key fields at the top of the test screen.

Archie took two days to develop and fully test the **DisplayPage** routine—twice as long as was planned. This type of development module testing requires a logical and methodical approach, a little ingenuity, and some hard work. But, then, no one said it was going to be easy.

Title Handling

With title handling, we switch back to Julie. When she had completed her **Display Page** components, she moved straight to her next development task, **Title Handling**. This task was to develop two development modules—**Read A Specified Title Index Into Program** and **Title Selection** (displays list of titles and allows user to select a single item).

Together, these two modules would allow Julie to build the code for the viewer's Title Selection mode of operation. The following design specifications are relevant to the development of title handling:

♦ *File Structure*—Title Index file format

♦ *Data Structure*—Title Index in-memory data structure

♦ *Function*—**ReadInTitleIndex**

♦ *Function*—**LoadTitleComboBox**

If you recall, after we had designed the main routines for Title Index and Page Index handling, we identified two common, low-level, handling functions. One function was to extract the data from between a given number of delimiter pairs in a string, and the other function was to find a given character in a string. All input Index-handling code would require these functions. The routines are as follows:

♦ *Function*—**ExtractDataFields**

♦ *Function*—**LocateDelimiter**

Before you go any further, you need to study the design specifications for these modules. In fact, we covered all of them except **LoadTitleComboBox** in the previous chapter. Alternatively, you can find all the specifications in Appendix G.

Creating the LocateDelimiter Test Program

Sensibly, Julie wanted to develop the two low-level functions—**ExtractDataFields** and **LocateDelimiter**—first—again, developing from the bottom upward, as she had done for the text-handling routines. She could then test the basic functions in isolation and include them as *reliable* functions in the test program for reading in a Title Index.

As I've already indicated, building software this way, from the bottom up, lets you construct solid foundations—clearly, good development practice. You can see the form Julie developed for testing the **LocateDelimiter** routine in Figure 7.18.

Follow these steps to create the form and required code, or simply read about the procedure and use the project contained in **TitleTest1** in Julie's development directory on the CD.

Step 1

Create a new VB EXE project, and call it **TitleTest1**. Load Julie's **ViewerLib** library, either the one you have been creating, or **ViewerLib_At_Recon1** from Julie's development area on the CD. As on the form layout in Figure 7.18, create a text field to hold the target string to be searched, and call the field **txtTarget**. Next, create a command button (which will be used to load a default string from memory), and call this button **cmdLoadString**. Create two text boxes called **txtCharactertoLocate** and **txtStartPosition**, as shown, with a **Search** command button called **cmdSearch** just below the two text boxes. Finally, create a label called **lblPositionFound** to show at what position a requested character has been located.

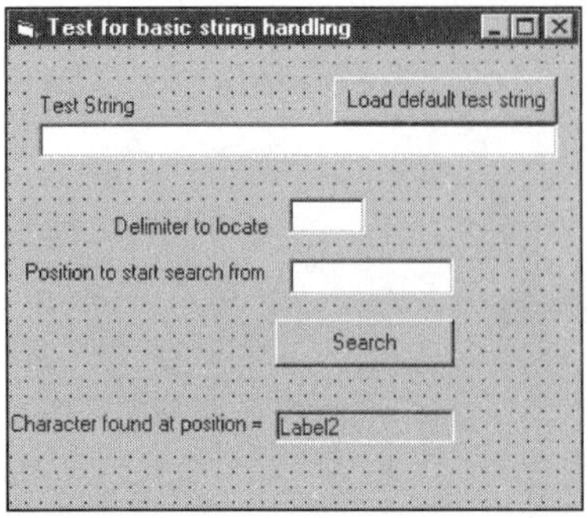

Figure 7.18
Test program form for development of **LocateDelimiter** routine.

Step 2
Place the following code in the **cmdLoadString** click event handler:

```
Private Sub cmdLoadString_Click()
' TEST CODE:
txtTarget.Text = "[Field 1][Two]    [Third field][4th]         [fifth]_

                [sixth][7th][8th]"
End Sub
```

This code loads a default, test target string with many fields (hard coded) into the target text box.

Step 3
Place this code in the **cmdSearch** click handler:

```
Private Sub cmdSearch_Click()
' TEST CODE:
Dim strChar As String
Dim intStartPos As Integer

strChar = Mid(txtCharacterToLocate, 1, 1)
intStartPos = CInt(txtStartPosition.text)
lblPositionFound = CStr(LocateDelimiter(txtTarget, strChar,_
                        intStartPos))

End Sub
```

Because **txtCharacterToLocate** is a text box, Julie has (very sensibly) used the VB **Mid** function to extract only the first character in case more than one character has been entered. She has also used the **CInt** (Convert to Integer) function to convert the input string in

txtStartPosition to a number. As we've already discussed, using this function is good practice to avoid unexpected results that can come from VB attempting to perform automatic conversions.

No error-handling code has been installed, but that doesn't matter for a test program. If a test program fails with a fatal error, you just start the program up again and carry on. Having no error-handling code *would* matter, however, if the code were a production routine.

Finally, the **LocateDelimiter** function is called, and its result (an integer) is converted to a string and placed in the text label.

Step 4

The following code is placed into Julie's version of **ViewerLib**:

```
Public Function LocateDelimiter(strSearch As String, strCharacter As_
         String,_
              intStartPosition As Integer) As Integer
' GENERAL ROUTINE: String Handling, V1.0
' Scans the input string from the designated start position looking for the
' target character and reports back the location as result of the function.
' Arguments:
'   strSearch          The string to be scanned
'   strCharacter       The character to search for (the target)
'   intStartPosition   Start search char position.
'           Function  = 0 - failed to find target character
'                     > 0 the position of the target found
' -----------------------------------
' Local variables:
Dim intPointer As Integer

LocateDelimiter = 0            ' default is failed to find
If Len(strSearch) = 0 Then Exit Function

For intPointer = intStartPosition To Len(strSearch)

    If Mid(strSearch, intPointer, 1) = strCharacter Then
        LocateDelimiter = intPointer
        Exit Function
    End If

Next intPointer

End Function
```

The code starts by setting the return parameter to 0, indicating "Not Found," and executing a return if the length of the target string is 0. It then scans the target string from the start position, checking to see whether each character matches the target character. If the program finds a match, the routine exits, with the function set to the value of the character position. Otherwise, if it finds no match, the return parameter has already been set to 0.

Testing LocateDelimiter

Julie ran the program to check the following:

◆ *Test 1*—For a given delimiter and start position, check that the routine locates the next occurrence of the delimiter.

◆ *Test 2*—If start position contains the delimiter, check that the position returned correctly.

◆ *Test 3*—If string contains no delimiter at or after start position, check that 0 returned.

◆ *Test 4*—If string is blank, check that 0 returned.

Figure 7.19 shows what the test program's form looked like after she had conducted a test.

Julie had set the target string to the default, hard-coded string; she requested the program to find the first right bracket (]) at or after position 12. The result indicated that the character was found at position 14. To check the result, she placed the cursor on the string in the text box, clicked the mouse button, and then moved the mouse from the first character, counting as she went. In this simple way, she was able to verify all the tests. We now had a reliable **LocateDelimiter** function.

Creating ExtractDataFields

Julie then added to the form that we'd already produced to increase its capability to check not just **LocateDelimiter**, but also **ExtractDataFields**. Figure 7.20 shows the completed form layout.

To create the form and code, follow these steps, or load the project **TitleTest2** from Julie's development directory on the CD, and follow the text for explanation of the code.

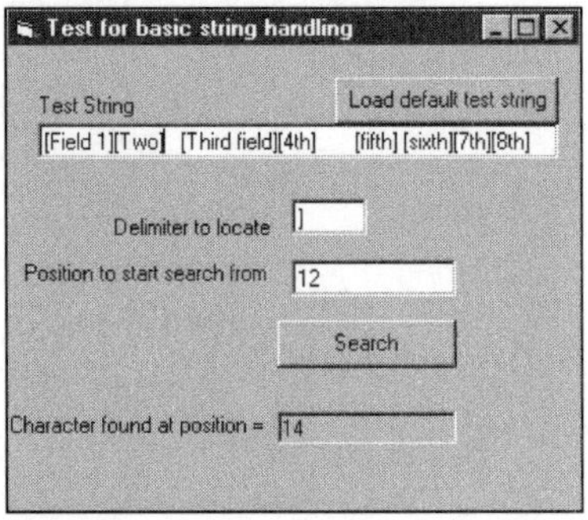

Figure 7.19
LocateDelimiter test program after a test has been conducted.

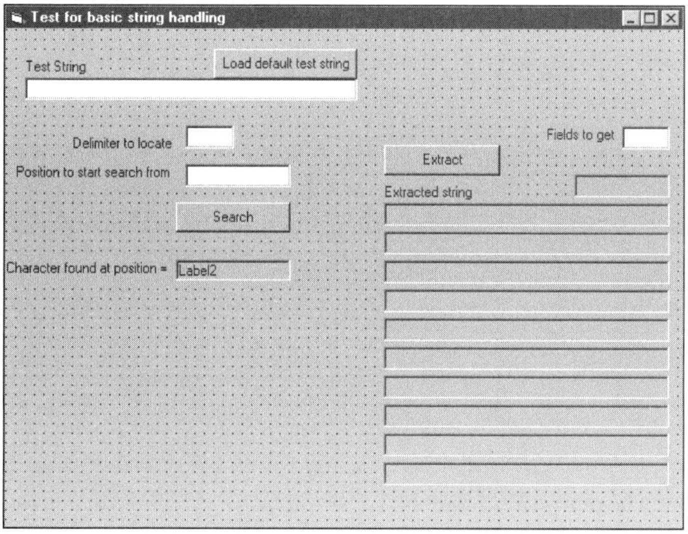

Figure 7.20
Final version of the test program to check both **LocateDelimiter** and **ExtractDataFields**.

Step1

Create a text field called **txtFields** (shown next to the "Fields To Get" label in Figure 7.20). This text field will be used to define how many data fields to extract from the test string. Create an array of 10 text fields called **txtField(1)** through **txtField(10)**; remember, according to our programming standards, we don't start arrays from 0. These text boxes have been set up as nonaccessible to the user—that is, the **Lock** property is set to **True**. (Just in case you are wondering, the text boxes could equally have been made from labels as we are only using the data field in a read-only manner.) Also, create a text field called **txtResult** (located above and to the right of the first **txtField** text box) to show the result of the function as **True** or **False**. Finally, create a command button called **cmdExtract**.

Step 2

Place the following code in the **Extract** button's click event:

```
Private Sub cmdExtract_Click()
' TEST CODE:
Dim intNumberOfFields As Integer
Dim strTemp As String
Dim booResult As Boolean
Dim strFields(10) As String
Dim intLoopCounter As Integer

For intLoopCounter = 1 To 10
    strFields(intLoopCounter) = "******************"
```

```
Next intLoopCounter

intNumberOfFields = CInt(txtFields.Text)

booResult = ExtractFieldData(txtTarget.Text, strFields(), intNumberOfFields)
txtResult.Text = booResult

For intLoopCounter = 1 To 10
   txtField(intLoopCounter).Text = strFields(intLoopCounter)
Next intLoopCounter

Exit Sub

End Sub
```

This code is the primary test code. The code begins by placing a default string of asterisk (*) characters into each element of the array that the extraction program will be asked to populate. This format allows Julie to check that the extract program clears the correct number of fields designated before it populates the array with its findings. The program then sets the number of fields to extract from **txtFields**, using the **CInt** function. It calls the **Extract** function and then loads the results into the text boxes on screen.

Step 3

The code to perform the extraction, although lengthy, is straightforward and follows the design closely. Make sure you review the design before you go through the code. Add the following routine to Julie's version of **ViewerLib**:

```
Public Function ExtractFieldData(strTarget As String,_
               strFields() As String, intNumberOfFields As Integer)_
               As Boolean
' GENERAL ROUTINE: Extract data from [  ] delimiters,  V1.0
' Arguments:
'        strTarget       String to be searched
'        strFields()     External string array to receive extracted data
'  intNumberOfFields     Number of fields to extract
'            Function     True in all cases except where all fields
'                         extracted contain 'END'
' Function = True is only relevant to Page Index handling, where
' it signifies 'END OF DATA.'
' -------------------------------------
' Local variables:
Dim intStartPos As Integer
Dim intEndPos As Integer
Dim intLoopCounter As Integer
Dim intLeftBracketPos As Integer
```

```
Dim intRightBracketPos As Integer
Dim intTemp As Integer

ExtractFieldData = True        ' Default return value

' Check number of fields does exist - then clear out array
intTemp = UBound(strFields)
If intTemp < intNumberOfFields Then intNumberOfFields = intTemp

For intLoopCounter = 1 To intNumberOfFields
    strFields(intLoopCounter) = ""
Next intLoopCounter
' Find fields and extract data
intStartPos = 1
For intLoopCounter = 1 To intNumberOfFields
    intLeftBracketPos = LocateDelimiter(strTarget, "[", intStartPos)
    If intLeftBracketPos = 0 Then GoTo error1

    intRightBracketPos = LocateDelimiter(strTarget, "]",_
                                    intLeftBracketPos + 1)
    If intRightBracketPos = 0 Then GoTo error1

    strFields(intLoopCounter) = Mid(strTarget, intLeftBracketPos + 1,_
                        (intRightBracketPos - intLeftBracketPos - 1))

    intStartPos = intRightBracketPos + 1
Next intLoopCounter

' Check for END terminator record
If strFields(1) = "END" Then
    ExtractFieldData = False            ' False means END OF FILE
    If intLoopCounter > 1 Then
        For intLoopCounter = 2 To intNumberOfFields
            If strFields(intLoopCounter) <> "END" Then
                ExtractFieldData = True    ' True means NOT END OF FILE
                Exit Function
            End If
        Next intLoopCounter
    End If
End If

Exit Function
'=========================================================================
error1:
ExtractFieldData = True
Exit Function
End Function
```

Chapter 7

The routine starts by making sure that the array contains the required number of elements. If it does not, **intNumberOfFields** is modified to be the correct number. Next, the array that the caller has supplied to hold the results is cleared. Starting from the first byte position of the string, the routine then scans for the first occurrence of a left bracket ([). Having located one, the routine then scans from the next character position looking for the first occurrence of a right bracket (]). If both characters have been found, the code uses the positions to do an extract from the target string and populate element 1 of the output array. This process is repeated until the required number of fields has been extracted, or until the code fails to detect a pair of delimiters, in which case, an error trap occurs. Finally, the code checks to see whether all extracted fields are set to **END**. The routine returns a result of **True** in all cases except where all the extracted fields indicate an end terminator.

Testing ExtractDataFields

Figure 7.21 shows how the form looked after Julie had conducted a test. Note that the two test functions—**Search** and **Extract**—are totally independent.

In Figure 7.21, Julie had performed two tests. She had tested what happened if she entered a number (600) larger than the string to call **LocateDelimiter**, and she had also set up a test to extract the first seven data fields from the target string. The only common aspect is that both tests worked on the text string loaded into the text box designated **Test String**; otherwise, the tests were totally independent.

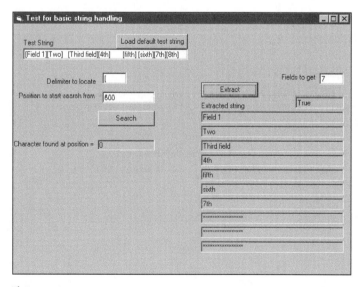

Figure 7.21
Test program's form after an extraction test has been performed to check out **ExtractDataFields**.

On her test log, Julie classified the tests that she had performed on the **ExtractDataFields** as follows:

♦ *Test 1*—The first field alone can be successfully located.

♦ *Test 2*—Up to 10 fields can be successfully extracted in the right order.

♦ *Test 3*—Successful operation results even if no delimiters are present.

♦ *Test 4*—Successful operation results if fewer fields than requested are present.

♦ *Test 5*—Only the requested number of results are returned.

♦ *Test 6*—If the number of elements created to receive the data fields is smaller than the requested number of data fields, the program continues to operate, filling only those elements available to it.

At the end of all this testing, Julie had two routines to reconcile with Archie. He would need the routines when he moved on to building the **Page Index Handling** development module. So, they stopped work and reconciled their libraries once more at a suitable juncture. The current state of both libraries was now as Figure 7.22 shows.

Figure 7.22 does not show the routines Archie was working on (that is, the routines with a DEV status). Note that Archie had a contribution to make as well, because **VideoOrPicture**,

Status of ViewerLib after Second Reconciliation

Module (sub/function/data structure)	Type	Status	Version	Owner
Viewer Screen Definitions Data	Data	FINAL	1.0	
Title Index Data Structure	Data	FINAL	1.0	
Page Index Data Structure	Data	FINAL	1.0	
Runtime Container Dimensions and Position	Data	FINAL	1.0	
LoadAndDisplayImage	GEN GUI	FINAL	1.0	
Size Picture	GEN	FINAL	1.0	
LoadAndPlayVideo	GEN GUI	FINAL	1.0	
OpenAndReadTextIntoMemory	GEN	FINAL	1.0	
LoadAndDisplayText	GEN GUI	FINAL	1.0	
LoadAndPlaySound	GEN GUI	FINAL*	1.0	
VideoOrPicture	GEN	FINAL	1.0	
LocateDelimiter	GEN	FINAL	1.0	
ExtractDataFields	GEN	FINAL	1.0	

*See issue log; issue 01 for outstanding, nonurgent problem with LoadAndDisplaySound.

Figure 7.22
ViewerLib status after the second reconciliation.

Status of Viewer Infrastructure Modules			
Infrastructure Routine	**Source**	**Status**	**Version**
SetUpFormat1	PageDisplay Test 2	FINAL	1.0
SetUpFormat2	PageDisplay Test 2	FINAL	1.0
SetUpFormat3	PageDisplay Test 2	FINAL	1.0
CaptureViewerDesignParameters	PageDisplay Test 2	FINAL	1.0
DisplayPage	PageDisplay Test 2	FINAL	1.0
SetUpTheData	PageDisplay Test 2	FINAL	1.0

Figure 7.23
Status of viewer infrastructure routines completed at time of **ViewerLib**'s second reconciliation.

a routine created for **DisplayPage**, was also ready to be merged into the common library. This reconciliation was vital to Archie so he could continue with the next task, which involved Page Index handling. In addition to **ViewerLib**, we had some viewer infrastructure routines. Figure 7.23 lists these routines.

Creation of ReadInTitleIndex

Julie had completed the low-level routines—**LocateDelimiter** and **ExtractDataFields**—and each had passed its testing. She must now complete the **ReadInTitleIndex** development module. She had decided to test both this routine and the next one that she had to develop, **LoadTitleComboBox**—together. **ReadInTitleIndex** could be used to populate the in-memory Index, and then **LoadTitleComboBox** could be used to transfer the titles into the combo box. When a title was selected from the combo box, Julie could verify that it was the correct one, simply by examining the contents as strings in text boxes.

In the previous chapter, we looked at basic Title Index handling for input and output. The viewer would always load the same file—E:\E-MagBook\Title.idx—whereas the Title Index Editor would allow the user to select a file for loading from a dialog box.

Study the design for **ReadInTitleIndex** before you proceed. (We discussed **ReadInTitleIndex** in the previous chapter, and it is also available in Appendix G.) In preparation for her next routine, Julie produced a single form to do the testing for both loading from disk and populating the combo box. She also produced a single Title Index test file. Follow these steps to set up the test program and its code, or look for **TitleTest3** on Julie's development area of the CD.

Step 1

Create a new VB EXE project and form layout, as Figure 7.24 shows.

Create and label the objects as follows:

♦ *Command Button*—**cmdLoadIndex**, to load the default Title Index.

♦ *Command Button*—**cmdPopulateComboBox**, to populate the combo box.

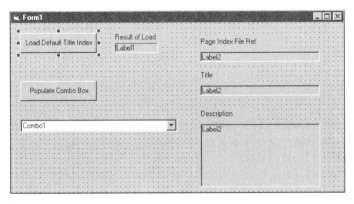

Figure 7.24
Form layout for program to test title loading and combo box population.

♦ *Label*—**lblResultOfLoad,** to show True or False after Index load.

♦ *Combo Box*—**comCombo,** the combo box to hold the Title Index titles.

♦ *Label*—**lblFileRef,** used to contain the Title Index file reference.

♦ *Label*—**lblTitle,** used to hold the title selected from the combo box.

♦ *Label*—**lblDescription,** used to hold the description of the title selected from the combo box.

Step 2

Create a test file called **Title.idx** to contain the following or, alternatively, use file **Title.idx** in the directory **TitleTest3** in Julie's development area on the CD:

```
[E-BOOK TITLE INDEX]xxxxxxx
[File Ref 1]xx
[Title 1]xxxxxxxxxxxxxxxx
[description 1 description 1 description 1 description 1 description 1]xx
[END OF RECORD]
[File Ref 2]
[Title 2]xxxxxxx
[description 2 description 2 description 2 description 2]xx
garbage
garbage
[END OF RECORD]
[File Ref 3]xx
[Title 3]xxxxxxxxxxxxxxxx
[description 3 description 3]xx
[END OF RECORD]
[File Ref 4]xx
[Title 4]xxxxxxxxxxxxxxxx
[description 4 description 4 description 4 description 4 description 4]xx
[END OF RECORD]
```

```
[File Ref 5]xx
[Title 5]xxxxxxxxxxxxxxxx
[description 5 description 5 description 5]xx
[END OF RECORD]
```

Place the test file in C:\E-MagBook\Title.idx.

I've shown only five entries (Julie actually tested with 50). Note that the entry number is embedded into the record layout to assist in testing. Lots of spurious characters have been added after the data fields to ensure that the program ignores them as required. The file also contains an extended record, with more than three lines before the end-of-record indicator.

Step 3

Place this code into the click event for the Load Index command button:

```
Private Sub cmdLoadIndex_Click()
' TEST CODE:
' INDEX HANDLING
Dim booResult As Boolean
Dim strFileName As String
Dim intLoop As Integer

' Attempt to load from removable E:
Do
    strFileName = "E:\TITLE.IDX"
    booResult = ReadInTitleIndex(strFileName)

    If booResult = True Then
        lblResultOfLoad = "E: LOAD OK"
        Exit Do
    End if

    strFileName = "C:\E-MAGBOOK\TITLE.IDX"
    booResult = ReadInTitleIndex(strFileName)

    If booResult = True Then
        lblResultOfLoad = "C: LOAD OK"
        Exit Do
    End if

    lblResultOfLoad = "FAILED"
Exit Sub

Loop
```

```
For intLoop = 1 To UBound(g_strTitleTitle())
Debug.Print "   File Ref " & g_strTitleFileName(intLoop)
Debug.Print "      Title " & g_strTitleTitle(intLoop)
Debug.Print "Description " & g_strTitleDescription(intLoop)
Debug.Print "----------------------"
Next intLoop

End Sub
```

The code first tries to load a hard-coded file name (**Title.idx**) from the removable disk drive, E:. If this works, an exit is executed from the loop. If the read failed, a second attempt is made, searching on C:\E-MAGBOOK. If this works, an exit from the loop occurs. If the second attempt was not successful, an error message results.

If you don't have an E:drive, remove the code associated with setting up for a read on drive E: and use drive C:. Make sure you put the test file into C:\E-MagBook. The preceding code allows testing from a genuine E-MagBook on the removable disk drive, or from drive C:.

Step 4

Enter this code into Julie's version of **ViewerLib**:

```
Public Function ReadInTitleIndex(strFileName As String) As Boolean
' GENERAL ROUTINE: Title Index Handling, V1.0
' Arguments:
'        strFileName    full path and name of Title Index file
'             Function = True - File read OK
'                      = False - file not read OK
' -----------------------------
' Local variables:
Dim strTemp As String
Dim strFields(3) As String
Dim booResult As Boolean

ReadInTitleIndex = False        ' default setting

Call ClearTitleIndexMemory

' open Title Index file
On Error GoTo NoFileFound
Open strFileName For Input As #1

' Extract and verify header
On Error GoTo EndOfFile
Line Input #1, strTemp        ' read Header Line
booResult = ExtractFieldData(strTemp, strFields(), 1)
If strFields(1) <> "E-BOOK TITLE INDEX" Then GoTo Err1
```

```
    ' LOOP to read records
    Do
        Line Input #1, strTemp
        booResult = ExtractFieldData(strTemp, strFields(), 1)
        g_intCurrentTitle = UBound(g_strTitleFileName()) + 1
        ReDim Preserve g_strTitleFileName(g_intCurrentTitle)
        ReDim Preserve g_strTitleTitle(g_intCurrentTitle)
        ReDim Preserve g_strTitleDescription(g_intCurrentTitle)

        g_strTitleFileName(g_intCurrentTitle) = strFields(1)

        Line Input #1, strTemp
        booResult = ExtractFieldData(strTemp, strFields(), 1)
        g_strTitleTitle(g_intCurrentTitle) = strFields(1)

        Line Input #1, strTemp
        booResult = ExtractFieldData(strTemp, strFields(), 1)
        g_strTitleDescription(g_intCurrentTitle) = strFields(1)

        Do
            Line Input #1, strTemp
            If strTemp = "[END OF RECORD]" Then Exit Do
        Loop

    Loop

    Close #1
    ReadInTitleIndex = True
    Exit Function
    ' ===============================================================
    ' Error handling
    NoFileFound:
    Close #1
    'MsgBox "Error: No File Found: " & strFileName    ' diagnostic purposes only
    Exit Function
    ' ..............................................................
    Err1:
    Close #1
    MsgBox "ERROR: File is not a Title Index: " & strFileName
    Exit Function
    ' ..............................................................
    EndOfFile:
    ReadInTitleIndex = True
    Exit Function

    End Function
```

Although this code is quite lengthy, it is structured so that relevant blocks can be examined in single screen sections; therefore, according to our standards, the code is suitable.

The code starts by opening the file, reading Line 1, extracting the header, and verifying it. If the content is not the expected header, we have an error trap to **Err1**. If the code can't open the file, it traps to **NoFileFound**. If the file has opened and is of the right type, the routine starts the main loop. Here, it reads three lines at a time, in the following order: file reference, title, and description. The one and only field extracted from each line is placed in the corresponding arrays of the Memory Index. Note that, if the first line is read OK, all three arrays are expanded together, even though the other two lines have not been read in. Julie realized that if a record contained only one or two lines, followed by an end-of-file marker, the third entry would never be set up. She decided to create all three empty array elements after Line 1 had been read in, so that the correct number of elements of each array would always exist for all entries in a Title Index. She wanted to avoid the program producing partially created last Index entries, which would lead to failure when any code tried to access all three arrays in the last element. This is a good example of considering boundary condition handling.

After the code has read in all three lines, exactly as the design specified, it reads lines until it finds the end-of-record marker, at which point it goes on to read in Line 1 of the next record, and so on.

Step 5
Finally, add this routine to clear the Title Index to **ViewerLib**:

```
Public Sub ClearTitleIndexMemory()
' GENERAL ROUTINE: Title Index Handling, V1.0
' ----------------------
g_intCurrentTitle = 0
ReDim g_strTitleFileName(0)
ReDim g_strTitleTitle(0)
ReDim g_strTitleDescription(0)
Exit Sub
End Sub
```

Testing ReadInTitleIndex
You can see an example of the test program in action in Figure 7.25.

In Figure 7.25, the Load Default Title Index command button has been clicked. You can see the result in the immediate window. Note that Julie set up many interesting combinations for the Title Index records. Some records had more then three lines, and some included all sorts of strange characters between the fields, all of which the program ignored, as intended.

Julie logged the following tests:

♦ *Test 1*—Check ability to open a file on E: and read in.

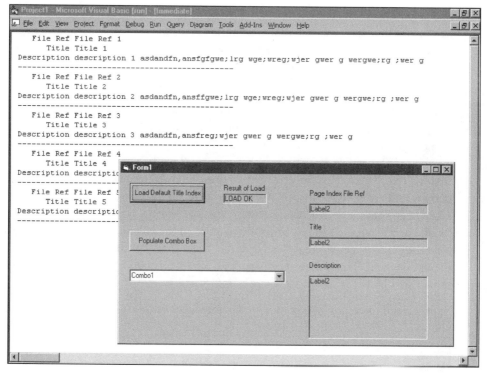

Figure 7.25
The **ReadInTitleIndex** test program in use.

- ◆ *Test 2*—Check ability to open a file on C: and read in.

- ◆ *Test 3*—Check for correct handling of a non Index file.

- ◆ *Test 4*—Check detailed handling of a correctly structured file.

- ◆ *Test 5*—Check handling of short (3 lines) and long (>3 lines) records.

- ◆ *Test 6*—Check premature end-of-file handling.

A Major Fault

Julie discovered a major fault while she was running the tests. When she ran the program, she could successfully read a file on E: for the first request. All subsequent requests, however, failed to read in from E: and defaulted to the Title Index on C:, which opened every time.

The fault turned out to be that Julie was not closing the file channel in the end-of-file handling routine. If the program executed the end-of-file trap, it left the channel open; the next open request failed, but then closed the channel. So, defaulting to the second directory on C: always worked. To rectify the problem, change the end-of-file handling in **ReadInTitleIndex** to the following:

```
EndOfFile:
Close #1
ReadInTitleIndex = True
Exit Function
```

Tip

Forgetting to close files in error handlers can cause obscure problems such as this. Whenever your code terminates file handling, ensure that you close the channel; otherwise, the next open statement will fail and might be treated as a nonexistent file error.

Creating the PopulateCombo Test Program

All Julie had left to do was to use the content of the in-Memory Index to populate the combo box. We didn't look at this particular section of the design in the previous chapter. Primarily, she had to specify a single routine called **PopulateCombo**. Look at the design in Appendix G before you start creating the code, so you know what to expect.

Follow these steps to add to the test program produced in the last section, or continue to examine **TitleTest3** on the CD while you read these notes.

Step 1

Place the following code in the Populate button's click event:

```
Private Sub cmdPopulate_Click()
'  TEST CODE
Call PopulateCombo(comCombo)
End Sub
```

The **PopulateCombo** routine is called with the name of the screen object to populate as an argument.

Step 2

Place this routine into Julie's version of **ViewerLib**:

```
Public Sub PopulateCombo(comTitleIndex As Control)
' GENERAL GUI ROUTINE: V1.0
' Arguments:
'         comTitleIndex Name of combo box to populate
' --------------------------
' Local variables:
Dim intLoopCounter As Integer

comTitleIndex.Clear
```

```
For intLoopCounter = 1 To UBound(g_strTitleTitle())
    comTitleIndex.AddItem g_strTitleTitle(intLoopCounter)
Next intLoopCounter

comTitleIndex.ListIndex = 0

Exit Sub
End Sub
```

The code simply clears the combo box and then adds each title from the in-memory Index array to the combo box, using a loop specified from **1** to the upper bound of the title array. Finally, the routine sets the list Index to **0**, which displays the first entry of the combo box. Although our standards are clear that we should avoid starting arrays at element 0, we don't have much choice here, because this is the way the VB control has been programmed by Microsoft; unfortunately, we are stuck with a 0 here.

Step 3

Create the following code in the click event of the combo box:

```
Private Sub comCombo_Click()
' TEST CODE:
lblFileRef.Caption = g_strTitleFileName(comCombo.ListIndex + 1)
lblTitle.Caption = g_strTitleTitle(comCombo.ListIndex + 1)
lblDescription.Caption = g_strTitleDescription(comCombo.ListIndex + 1)

End Sub
```

The click event simply uses **comCombo.ListIndex** to extract the data from the in-memory Index. But, remember, the combo box's list starts at element 0, so we have to add one to **comCombo.List** to access the Title Index arrays to extract the correct data associated with the requested title. Also, double-check that you have placed the code in the click event and not the change event, as Julie did. Realizing what she had done took her a while.

Testing PopulateCombo

Testing involved first loading the file into the Memory Index, then populating the combo box and, finally, selecting an entry from the box. Figure 7.26 shows a screenshot of the test program after Julie had run a successful test.

In Figure 7.26, behind the test program form, you can see the immediate window that contains the result of the **Load Default Title Index** action.

The test conditions Julie was able to log were the following:

♦ *Test 1*—Check that the combo box is properly populated from in-Memory Index.

♦ *Test 2*—Check that the selected entry results in correct data on view.

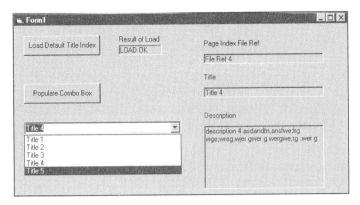

Figure 7.26
The **TitleTest3** program after an Index has been read using the Load Default Title Index button and then the Populate Combo Box button.

Julie completed all the title-handling routines and their testing in just 1 day, against the planned 1.5 days. She had now spent 3 days on the project and achieved 4.5 days of progress.

Her next task was to develop the Workbench capability, which she could begin ahead of schedule—she wasn't supposed to start work on it until the following week. We'll leave her to that and see how Archie was getting on.

Read Page Index Development Module

After the second **ViewerLib** reconciliation, Archie had the collection of routines that he needed to begin the **Read Page Index** development task. All the **ViewerLib** routines Julie had created had been tested and were, consequently, reliable. **ViewerLib_At_Recon2** in Archie's development area on the CD contains the routines after this second reconciliation.

To complete the **Read Page Index** development task, you need to be familiar with the following design specifications:

◆ *File Format*—Page Index file format.

◆ *Data Structure*—Page Index Memory structure.

◆ *Function*—**ReadInPageIndex**.

◆ *Function*—**ExtractDataFields** (already completed by Julie).

◆ *Function*—**LocateDelimiter** (already completed by Julie).

Archie decided to test the routines using the same sort of test program Julie had invented for the Title Index, with the exception that he would let the user select the file name rather than hard-code it, as in Julie's version.

When Archie looked at the specifications for **ReadInPageIndex**, he realized the routine was doing quite a lot. Consequently, he decided to create a routine just to handle the file open and header line processing. The header line had to be checked to verify that the file was, indeed, a Page Index and font characteristics had to be extracted as well. To this end, he created a new routine called **ReadPageIndexHeader**. He classified this routine as a general routine, so it could be placed in **ViewerLib**. He updated the specification for **ReadInPageIndex** accordingly with a note indicating which code he had made into a subroutine.

Creation of the ReadInPageIndex Test Program

Figure 7.27 shows the form Archie produced for the test program.

The Get Name button that you see in Figure 7.27 allowed Archie to select a file from the file store and place its name in the Page Index File Name field. The Load File button would then attempt to load the file as a Page Index, printing the result in the immediate window. To create the test program, follow these steps, or load the test program **PageTest1**, located in directory **PageTest1** of Archie's development directory on the CD.

Step 1

Create a new VB EXE project called **PageTest1**. Add Archie's version of the library after the second reconciliation. If you have any doubts about any version you are creating, use **ViewerLib_At_Rcon2** from Archie's development area on the CD.

To the main form, add the controls you see in Figure 7.27 as follows:

♦ *Label*—**lblIndexFileName**, holds the name of the selected file.

♦ *Command Button*—**cmdGetName**, used to load a name into the label.

♦ *Command Button*—**cmdLoadFile**, used to instigate the loading.

♦ *File Dialog Control*—**dlgDialog1**, standard file-selection dialog box.

Step 2

Place the following code in the Get Name command button's click event:

```
Private Sub cmdGetName_Click()
'  TEST CODE:
dlgDialog1.Action = 1
lblIndexFileName.Caption = dlgDialog1.FileName
End Sub
```

By now, the code you see above should seem very familiar.

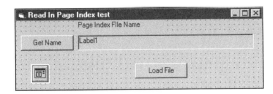

Figure 7.27
Form of the test program used to check loading of a selected Page Index.

Step 3
Place this code into the Load File button's click event:

```
Private Sub cmdLoadFile_Click()
' TEST CODE:
Dim booResult As Boolean
Dim intLoopCounter

booResult = ReadInPageIndex(dlgDialog1.FileName)
MsgBox "Result of reading in Index file = " & booResult

' RESULTS
Debug.Print "Format Type = " & g_intFormatType
Debug.Print "  Font Size = " & g_intFontSize

For intLoopCounter = 1 To UBound(g_strPictureFile())

    Debug.Print "Keys are; " & g_strKeys(1, intLoopCounter) &_
                          g_strKeys(2, intLoopCounter) &_
                          g_strKeys(3, intLoopCounter) &_
                          g_strKeys(4, intLoopCounter) &_
                          g_strKeys(5, intLoopCounter)
    Debug.Print "Picture File Name = " & g_strPictureFile(intLoopCounter)
    Debug.Print "   Text File Name = " & g_strTextFile(intLoopCounter)
    Debug.Print "  Sound File Name = " & g_strSoundFile(intLoopCounter)

Next intLoopCounter

End Sub
```

At the beginning of the routine, **ReadInPageIndex** is called to read in the file named in the dialog box property. The result is published in a message box. Then, Archie used a loop to print the keys, picture name, text name, and sound name for every single entry in the Index from Entry 1 to the maximum, as determined by the **Ubound(g_strPicture( ))** function.

Step 4

Now, enter the following code into **ViewerLib**. Although there is a lot of code, it is simple:

```
Public Function ReadInPageIndex(strFileName As String) As Boolean
'GENERAL ROUTINE: Page Index Handling V1.0
' Arguments:
'     strFilename      Full Index file path and name
'     Function    =    False if failed to load
'                 =    True if loaded OK
'     loads the in-memory arrays
' -------------------------------
' Local variables
Dim strField As String
Dim strSource As String
Dim intTemp As Integer
Dim intLoopCounter As Integer
Dim intEntry As Integer
Dim booResult As Boolean
Dim strFields(8) As String

ReadInPageIndex = False

booResult = ReadPageIndexHeader(strFileName)
If booResult = False Then Exit Function
g_intCurrentPage = 0

On Error GoTo FatalError
Do
    Line Input #1, strSource                 ' read in full line

    booResult = ExtractFieldData(strSource, strFields(), 8)
    If booResult = False Then Exit Do        ' Terminator [END] found

    g_intCurrentPage = g_intCurrentPage + 1

    'Keys 1 to 5
    ReDim Preserve g_strKeys(5, g_intCurrentPage)
    For intLoopCounter = 1 To 5
        g_strKeys(intLoopCounter, g_intCurrentPage)_
            =strFields(intLoopCounter)
    Next intLoopCounter

    'Picture File reference
    ReDim Preserve g_strPictureFile(g_intCurrentPage)
    g_strPictureFile(g_intCurrentPage) = strFields(6)
```

```
            'Text File reference
            ReDim Preserve g_strTextFile(g_intCurrentPage)
            g_strTextFile(g_intCurrentPage) = strFields(7)

            'Sound File reference
            ReDim Preserve g_strSoundFile(g_intCurrentPage)
            g_strSoundFile(g_intCurrentPage) = strFields(8)

Loop

Close #1
g_intCurrentPage = 1
ReadInPageIndex = True
Exit Function
' ===================================================================
' error handling
Errhandler:
MsgBox "Failed to find requested E-MagBook" & vbCrLf &_
        "Please contact your supplier"
Close #1
Call ClearPageIndexMemory
ReadInPageIndex = False
Exit Function

FatalError:
MsgBox "Unexpected end of file read."
Close #1
ReadInPageIndex = True
Exit Function

End Function
```

Initially, function **ReadPageIndexHeader** is used to open the file on Channel 1, read in the header, and verify it. If this operation passes the status check, the next line is read in using a **DO** loop, and eight data fields are extracted into the **strFields** array. The keys are then transferred into the next entry number as dictated by **g_intCurrentPage**. Then, the picture, text, and sound references are set up. Note how a **ReDim** statement is used to increase the size of each array before the relevant item is added.

Step 5

Add this routine, which functions to open the file and extract the header, to Archie's version of **ViewerLib**:

```
Function ReadPageIndexHeader(strFileName As String) As Boolean
' GENERAL ROUTINE: Page Index handling, V1.0
```

```
' Arguments:
'               strFileName      name of Index file to open
'                    Function = True if file read OK
'                             = False if file not read OK
' Open file and Read in header and verify correct file type
' --------------------------------
' Local variables
Dim strSource As String
Dim strTemp As String
Dim strFields(4) As String
Dim booResult As Boolean

ReadPageIndexHeader = False
' Open File and verify file type
On Error GoTo Errhandler          ' trap any file access errors

Open strFileName For Input As #1

Line Input #1, strSource          ' read Header Line
booResult = ExtractFieldData(strSource, strFields(), 3)

g_intFormatType = 0
If strFields(1) = "IMAGE DATA BASE INDEX" Then g_intFormatType - 3
If strFields(1) = "IMAGE DATA BASE ALBUM" Then g_intFormatType = 2
If strFields(1) = "IMAGE DATA BASE BOOKS" Then g_intFormatType = 1

If g_intFormatType = 0 Then
    MsgBox "File is not a valid Library" & vbCrLf & "Clearing Index"
    Close #1
    Call ClearPageIndexMemory
    Exit Function
End If

' Pick up font type and size
g_strFontType = "MS Sans Serif"       ' set default in case there
g_intFontSize = 10                            ' are no values in file

If strFields(2) <> "" Then g_strFontType = strFields(2)
If strFields(3) <> "" Then g_intFontSize = strFields(3)

ReadPageIndexHeader = True

Exit Function
'
```

===

```
' Error handling
Errhandler:
MsgBox "Failed to read in header"
Close #1
End Function
```

First, the code opens the file and reads in Line 1. It extracts three fields and checks that the first field is one of the three allowed formats. From this determination, it can set the **g_inFormatType** parameter. Next, the code sets up a default font and size, and then it overwrites the default only if it has found values in the second and third data fields.

Step 6

And, finally, add this routine to **ViewerLib**:

```
Public Sub ClearPageIndexMemory()
' GENERAL ROUTINE: Page Index Handling, V1.0
' --------------------
g_intCurrentPage = 0
ReDim g_strKeys(5, 0)
ReDim g_strPictureFile(0)
ReDim g_strTextFile(0)
ReDim g_strSoundFile(0)
Exit Sub
End Sub
```

The arrays are cleared by re-dimensioning them to nothing, (element 0, to be precise; but, then, 0 means nothing, doesn't it?). Setting **g_intCurrentPage=0**, indicates that no Index is loaded.

Testing ReadInPageIndex

The testing consisted of loading a file name to the label and then clicking the Load File button. As a first attempt at a test file, Archie used the following data, which he entered by hand, using an editor:

```
[IMAGE DATA BASE INDEX][MS Sans Serif][10]
[1/Key1][1/Key 2][1/3][1/Key 4][1/FIVE][1/Picref][1/TextRef][1/Soundref]
[2/Key1][2/Key 2][2/3][2/Key 4][2/FIVE][2/Picref][2/TextRef][2/Soundref]
[3/Key1][3/Key 2][3/3][3/Key 4][3/FIVE][3/Picref][3/TextRef][3/Soundref]
[END][END][END][END][END][END][END][END]
```

Archie had set up all the fields with meaningful test data so he could track how they were processed. The test program after it had read in the above file appears in Figure 7.28.

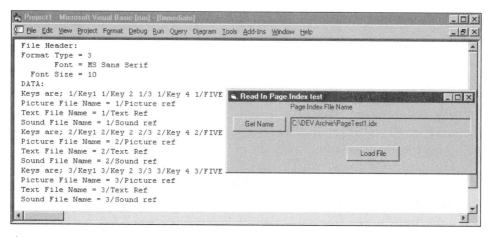

Figure 7.28
Test program after a Page Index has been selected and loaded.

The collection of tests that Archie was able to log were as follows:

♦ *Test 1*—Ensure all three Page Index header types (Text, Album, and Ref) produce correct format specifier.

♦ *Test 2*—Ensure rejection of an incorrect header.

♦ *Test 3*—Check that font size and type are picked up correctly.

♦ *Test 4*—Check whether default font data picked up if the font not present in the file header.

♦ *Test 5*—Check for the correct processing of a data line.

♦ *Test 6*—Check for correct handling of a short data line (that is, less than eight fields).

♦ *Test 7*—Check for correct handling of a long data line (that is, more than eight fields).

♦ *Test 8*—Check handling when there are characters between data fields.

♦ *Test 9*—Check **END** handling.

♦ *Test 10*—Check whether handling is OK without an **END**.

The End of Week 1

We were now at the end of Week 1 in the development of the viewer, and things seemed to have gone well. Up to this point, the code apparently had been written and tested, and each test had been logged as a pass. Of course, all that's not what really happened. Here are notes from the week.

Option Explicit

One of Archie's problems was that he kept forgetting to put **Option Explicit** in the general declaration of the test program when he created one. The end result was that he typed many incorrectly spelled variable names—and VB let him do that, because it didn't know any better. Sometimes, the errors were to the result of "finger trouble" and, sometimes, the result of poor spelling; sometimes, he just got the name wrong. Regardless of the errors, the omission of **Option Explicit** wasted time. As soon as Archie set **Option Explicit**, the compiler showed him all his mistakes, because it couldn't reconcile an incorrect name with the public declarations in **ViewerLib**.

Help Checking Names

Julie used quite a neat procedure to make sure she was getting names right as she typed them in. She typed a variable name in lowercase characters—always. If the variable had been defined in a data statement somewhere, when she went on to the next line of code, VB did a quick check to see whether any of the variables existed. If they did, it changed the case of the characters according to how they were set up in the definitive data statement.

You'll find this method to be a very useful, on-the-fly check that you are entering the names correctly. For example, suppose the variable is defined in a data declaration statement as **g_intFormatType**. Whenever Julie had to type in that name, she used **g_intformattype**. When she moved on to the next line, VB changed her entry to **g_intFormatType** to match the way in which it had been set up. Otherwise, if she had spelled the variable **g_intfromattype** by mistake, as she moved on to the next line, the name would have remained in lowercase. When she explained her technique to Archie, he stopped wasting a lot of time simply by watching for automatic uppercase conversions after he typed a variable name.

Progress Monitoring

The big question was, How ahead of schedule were we? In line with our discussion about planning, we set up a simple table to see how the week had gone. Into the table, each person put his or her assessment of progress. Figure 7.29 shows this table. Let's now recap what took place in Week 1 according to Figure 7.29.

Programmer 1's progress

Archie started by developing the **LoadAndDisplayImage** routine, and he completed this routine in just one day, although it had been planned for two days. In one day, therefore, he had achieved two days' progress, and the routine was now complete. Next, he worked on the **LoadAndPlayVideo** routine, spending one day, as planned, to complete the routine.

He started his third task, the development and testing of the **DisplayPage** routine, a day early (because Julie was also ahead of schedule and had supplied him with the required routines to load and display text and sound files). According to the plan, Archie had one day to complete development and testing of this routine. The job proved to be much bigger than we had anticipated, and he spent two days on it. So, in two days' actual time spent, he achieved one day's progress and completed the **DisplayPage** routine.

Progress Report at End of Week 1 in the Viewer					
Resource	**Module**	**Planned**	**Actual**	**Achieved**	**O/S**
Archie	Display Image (Week 1)	2.0	1.0	2.0	0
Archie	Play Video (Week 1)	1.0	1.0	1.0	0
Archie	Display Page (Week 1)	1.0	2.0	1.0	0
Archie	Read Page Index (Weeks 1 and 2)	2.0	1.0	2.0	0
Archie	Manual Navigation (Week 2)	1.0			1.0
Archie	Search (Week 2)	2.0			2.0
Julie	Display Text (Week 1)	2.0	1.0	2.0	0
Julie	Play Sound (Week 1)	1.0	1.0	1.0	0
Julie	Title Handling (Week 1)	1.5	1.0	1.5	0
Julie	Workbench (Week 2)	2.5	0.5	0.5	2.0

Figure 7.29

Progress statistics for end of Week 1 of viewer program development.

Archie started on the routine to read in a Page Index on Friday morning. This routine was planned as a 2-day activity, spanning Weeks 1 and 2. Archie managed to complete the whole job in just one day, although he stayed quite late. One day of actual time achieved two days' progress to complete the routine.

At the end of the week, Archie had achieved six days' progress in five actual days. His remaining tasks were to complete navigation and searching, a total of three days' planned effort, in the following week. Archie was confident that he could complete his side of the development plan by the end of Week 2.

Programmer 2's Progress

Julie's progress also started off well. She completed the **LoadAndDisplayText** development in just one day, achieving two days of progress against the plan and completing the task.

Next, she spent one day on the sound routine and completed it according to the planned estimate of one day. She then managed to complete **Title Handling** in 1 day as opposed to 1.5 planned days, therefore achieving 1.5 days' progress in 1 actual day spent.

So, after 3 days in Week 1, she had achieved 4.5 days' progress and was able to start the Workbench development module. However, we had a little crisis in the testing department on Thursday and Friday, and when I saw that Julie had completed her entire week's work in three days, I transferred her to the testing department to help out for most of Thursday and all day Friday. She had, however, managed to put in half a day on Workbench and felt that she had two days of work still outstanding. She would have the whole of Week 2 to complete 2 days' outstanding development.

The Next Step

We were very pleased with progress at the end of Week 1 of development. We were halfway through the period we had scheduled for viewer development. We were ahead of schedule, and we had logged only one issue, that of the MID-file-rewind problem.

In the following week, we would complete all the viewer development modules. If we managed to maintain the excellent progress and stay ahead of schedule, we would start system integration early. We went home on Friday evening confident that we would complete the viewer development at least on time and, hopefully, a day or two early. If only we had known what would happen to Archie over the weekend, we would not have been so complacent.

Chapter 8
Completion of the Viewer

I n this chapter, we're going to look at completion of a development, system integration, and preparation for system testing. At the end of all this work, we will have a completed, fully assembled, and tested software product ready to be handed over from development to the testing department for rigorous, objective, independent testing before we pass the software on to our client.

In the case study, it was now the second week of the viewer's development phase. At the end of Week 1, according to our progress monitoring, both Archie and Julie were ahead of schedule. They had completed the **DisplayPage** development module, and the **Title Handling** and **Read Page Index** modules. Julie had started work on the Workbench functionality and at the end of the first week had estimated that component to be one-fifth complete. Julie would complete the Workbench in Week 2 and possibly would be ahead of schedule. Archie would move straight on to the **Navigation** and **Search** modules, and, if he completed them in the allotted three days, he also would be ahead of schedule. Then, disaster struck.

In this chapter, we'll see how Archie and Julie completed the development of the viewer. We'll then look at how they assembled the viewer in a system-integration exercise (in which all the modules produced in the development phase are bolted together and made to work as a complete system for the first time). We'll look at what we needed to consider to prepare for system testing of the viewer.

The Case Study:
Disaster Strikes

As measured on the Friday night of the previous week, our progress was excellent, and we were forecasting early completion of development. Unfortunately, Archie's decision to go away with some friends for the weekend changed that forecast.

Archie's mother rang me Monday morning with the bad news. On the group's bike ride in a forest, Archie had lost control and gone over the handlebars. His injuries weren't serious, but he was sufficiently hurt to necessitate a night's stay in a hospital for observation. He would probably be off work for two or three days. Archie called later in the day to give us the details and apologize for "letting us down" on the project. I assured him that, with all the contingency time we had because of his and Julie's sterling efforts in the previous week, I didn't think his absence should be a problem.

Re-Planning

So, Julie and I had a bit of re-planning to do. As a "worst-case" situation, we decided to assume that Archie would be off for the whole week. Julie had an estimated two days of effort left on the Workbench, and I asked her to review the design specifications for the **Navigation** and **Search** modules, which Archie would have tackled next. Julie said she felt confident she could do both tasks in the three days allocated and also complete the Workbench, which would take two days—a grand total of five days' required effort. We now had no contingency time left.

Risks

The fundamental risk was whether Julie would be available for all five days to complete the viewer. The week's goals required 100 percent availability from Julie. Julie felt quite confident that she was technically up to handling the work. Thanks to the drag-and-drop feasibility work, she considered the Workbench was well in hand. The **Search** module was possibly the most complex part remaining. I would do all the code reviews, so, all in all, we felt that we had the risk factors down to a minimum. Nevertheless, with only one, full-time employee on the project at 100 percent availability, we were vulnerable. As a result, we again decided to monitor progress daily. The earlier warning we had of a problem, the better—if necessary, I would step in to assist with some programming.

Another Buy-in

Julie's acceptance to take on the extra work is another example of the buy-in principle we discussed earlier. In theory, even with Julie working on her own, we should still be able to finish the project on time. However, doing so was dependent on Julie taking full responsibility for software completion. If she ran into any trouble, she must ask for help immediately to avoid putting the plan into jeopardy.

Tip

By now, you should appreciate the need for planning with built-in contingency time. If things go well, and you build up even more contingency time because of early completion of modules, treat that extra contingency time preciously. You never know what's around the corner. Whenever you are planning software development projects, always remember that they involve people. People can get sick; they can have accidents. Guard your contingency time preciously. Always resist the temptation to quote a tight time schedule to impress. Gaining a reputation for quoting time schedules that people have confidence in, based on a good track record, is far more impressive.

Julie had just five days to complete the Workbench, and the **Navigation** and **Search** functionalities. Much of this functionality was *event driven*.

Event-Driven Programming

All the code that we've developed up to now for the viewer has consisted of general subroutines and functions, which we have placed in **ViewerLib**. We've also developed a handful of GUI-bound routines and placed them in the infrastructure of the code that we set up in the various test programs to check out the general routines.

In the test programs, we wrote code that is activated when a user clicks the appropriate button. For example, to test the module that loads and displays an image, we used a button control's click event to perform the test.

VB screen objects all react to various types of events pertinent to the nature of the object itself. The simplest example is a button control, which has a defined set of events to which it will react. When you create an instance of a button control on a form, you can place code into the button's click event. Whenever VB encounters a user placing the mouse cursor on the screen button and clicking the left mouse button, VB will execute any code present in the screen control's click-event handler.

This event is an interaction between the user and your code, brought about by the operating system's runtime environment. If we think of Windows and VB as the operating system environment, the environment receives a multitude of external events. In the case of the viewer, these events will be predominately mouse-move events (as the user moves the cursor across the viewer) and click events (when the user clicks a button). The operating environment looks to see what objects have events registered for a mouse move; each movement of the mouse over such an object invokes the object's event handler.

Event Queues

Imagine the cursor being moved across the image control in the Workbench. For each new position, the system registers a mouse-move event. If so many movement events exist that the event-handling code can't keep pace, a queue develops. For each event, the code is executed from the first line to the exit. The code might then be rerun because of a second event, and so on. The number of events might even be so great that the code simply can't respond to them all, and some events will be lost.

Because of this potential for queued and lost events, keeping event handlers short is sensible. For example, you clearly don't want a complex algorithm to be executed each time the mouse-move event on an object is triggered.

Informing the User

If the event you need to handle will require a considerable amount of time to complete its code, the last thing you want is for the user to continue generating many more events that will queue up. For example, suppose the user requests a search by clicking the viewer's Search button. While the search is being conducted, we don't want the user clicking away on other buttons—possibly even trying to start other searches. The result would be total confusion, because all the queued events would be processed after the first search was completed.

You need to indicate to the user that something is happening so "please wait." The ideal way to let the user know is to change the cursor from a pointer to an hourglass, which users recognize as a universal indicator to wait while the current function completes.

Modal and Non-Modal Functions

An even more important issue arises when you want to solicit information or a response from the user. Suppose you want the user to decide whether a given function should be continued or aborted. You are likely to place a message box on the screen with an OK option and a Cancel option. This message box is an example of a *modal* function, in which all other event handling in the program is disabled until the message box receives a response. Just imagine the chaos that might ensue if this were not the case.

Non-modal functionality means that any event can occur at any time. If another event is triggered while the system is handling a previous event, the system queues the triggered event. Using a modal message box ensures that all event handling is suspended, allowing you to control the situation until you get a response from the user.

Screen Updates

You need to get used to the fact that, if your event-handling code changes something on screen, the screen object isn't updated at the time you make the change. The screen object is updated after the event in which the change was instigated has been released. For example, suppose that, in the course of handling the viewer's **Search** function, you wanted to put a sign on the screen that states, "Search In Progress." If you did this by setting the caption of the comment label as soon as the **Search** button's click handler was invoked, the message would not appear on screen until after the search had been completed, and the Search button's click event had been released.

One way to cause a screen update to occur in the preceding example is to set up the screen comment, and then invoke a modal message box to ask the user whether the search should be continued. This method actually enables VB to update the screen, even though your handler has not completed the search. When the user clicks the message box's OK button, the program continues handling the search. If the user clicks the Cancel button, the program aborts the search.

Under normal conditions, any screen changes created by an event handler will not be instigated until the event handler has completed. This fact also implies that a screen object's change event will not be triggered until after the code that caused the change has been completed. For example, if a button's click event causes a text box's contents to be changed, the text box's change event will not be triggered until the code in the button's click handler has completed. As a result, you should never expect a screen object's content to have changed or its events to have been triggered in the event handler that caused the change. This information might seem irrelevant at this moment, but it will have bearing on the development of the editors.

Case Study Events

Completion of the viewer involved setting up Workbench, **Navigation**, and **Search** event handling, which involved button-click events, mouse-move events, and drag-and-drop events. We would also make use of the form's load event to initialize the program.

Return to the Case Study:
Completion of the Viewer

For Julie, it was business as usual. Let's start by seeing how she tackled the Workbench functionality, remembering that she had started the work in the previous week.

Reconciliation of Versions

Julie's first task was to take the routines that Archie had created in his version of **ViewerLib** for the Page-Index testing and reconcile those routines with her own version of the library. Doing this produced a definitive version of **ViewerLib**. If you are performing all the steps involved in the development, you will need to do the same. Run two versions of the VB design-time environment. Into one version, load the **PageTest1** project; into the other version, load the **TitleTest3** project. Copy and paste any routines that you don't have from Archie's library into Julie's library. (These routines should be **ReadInPageIndex**, **ReadPageIndexHeader**, and **ClearPageIndexMemory**.) Figure 8.1 shows the resultant state of **ViewerLib**. Alternatively, you can make use of **VierwerLib_At_Recon3**, which you will find in Julie's development area on the CD.

Preparing for the Workbench

The two objects that constitute the Workbench are **imgImage2**, which holds a copy of the image from the page, and **txtText2**, which holds a copy of the text. Before you look at the code Julie developed, take time to study the designs in Appendix G. I did not introduce these particular designs in Chapter 6, so you will be looking at them for the first time. The development consists of three modules: **Manually Position WB Objects**, **Manually Size WB Objects**, and **Print WB Objects**. We had used a mixture of flow diagrams and pseudocode to define the designs for the Workbench routines.

To augment the design, you can also review the feasibility study that we did in "Move Feasibility—Drag-and-Drop," (Appendix D) a fundamental part of the Workbench functionality. Armed with knowledge of the design and the code developed in the feasibility

Status of ViewerLib after Third Reconciliation

Module (sub/function/data structure)	Type	Status	Version	Owner
Viewer Screen Definitions Data	Data	FINAL	1.0	
Title Index Data Structure	Data	FINAL	1.0	
Page Index Data Structure	Data	FINAL	1.0	
Runtime Container Dimensions and Position	Data	FINAL	1.0	
LoadAndDisplayImage	GEN GUI	FINAL	1.0	
Size Picture	GEN	FINAL	1.0	
LoadAndPlayVideo	GEN GUI	FINAL	1.0	
OpenAndReadTextIntoMemory	GEN	FINAL	1.0	
LoadAndDisplayText	GEN GUI	FINAL	1.0	
LoadAndPlaySound	GEN GUI	FINAL*	1.0	
VideoOrPicture	GEN	FINAL	1.0	
LocateDelimiter	GEN	FINAL	1.0	
ExtractFieldData	GEN	FINAL	1.0	
ReadInPageIndex	GEN	FINAL	1.0	
ReadPageIndexHeader	GEN	FINAL	1.0	
ClearPageIndexMemory	GEN	FINAL	1.0	
ReadInTitleIndex	GEN	FINAL	1.0	
ClearTitleIndexMemory	GEN	FINAL	1.0	
PopulateCombo	GEN GUI	FINAL	1.0	

*See issue log; issue 01 for outstanding, nonurgent problem with LoadAndDisplaySound.

Figure 8.1
State of **ViewerLib** after the third reconciliation.

study, you will find the next sections easy to follow. We'll start with the drag-and-drop-handling code for the **Manually Position WB Objects** module.

Creation of WB Drag-and-Drop

Drag-and-drop is defined in the flow diagrams (Design Specification 18 in Appendix G) that show what must happen for the following event list:

♦ *imgImage2_Mouse Move Event*—Tracks the position of the mouse cursor as it moves over the **Image** control. The coordinates registered are copied into **i_sngXPos** and **i_sngYPos**, and the identity of the object is stored in **i_strTagit** as "IMAGE." (The **i_** prefix indicates that these are infrastructure data items.)

- *imgImage2_DragDrop Event*—Triggered when the text box is dragged over the **Image** control and released, or when the **Image** control is dragged and dropped over itself.

- *txtText2_MouseMove Event*—Tracks the position of the mouse cursor as it moves over the **Text Box** control. The coordinates registered are copied into **i_sngXPos** and **I_sngYPos**. The identity "TEXT" is stored in **i_strTagit**.

- *txtText2_DragDrop Event*—Triggered when the image is dragged over the **Text Box** control and released, or when the **Text Box** control is dragged and dropped over itself.

- *Form_DragDrop Event*—Triggered when either the **Image** control or **Text Box** control is dropped onto the form.

From the design flow diagrams, you get a very precise picture of the event-driven nature of the preceding functions. To create the necessary code, follow these steps, or make use of the **WBTest1** project available in Julie's development area on the CD:

Step 1

First, create a new EXE project called **WBtest1**. Just as you did for the feasibility study, create two objects on the form—**imgImage2**, the image control, and **txtText2**, the text box. Preload **imgImage2** with an image, and place some text into **txtText2** at design time.

Step 2

Place the following code into the main form's **DragDrop** event handler:

```
Private Sub Form_DragDrop(Source As Control, X As Single, Y As Single)
' VIEWER INFRASTRUCTURE EVENT HANDLER: WB Handling, v1.0
' ----------------------------------
' Image control or text box has been dropped onto form,
' reposition accordingly, taking account of pickup offset

    Source.Move X - i_sngXPos, Y - i_sngYPos

End Sub
```

Source is either the **Image** control or the **Text Box** control. Whichever one was dragged, its pickup point was recorded by the last **MouseMove** event on that object and recorded in **i_sngXPos** and **i_sngYPos**.

Remember that X and Y are the point on the form at which the source object was released. If you have any trouble understanding this code, read the feasibility study in Appendix D and all will be revealed. This code, when completed, will form part of the viewer's infrastructure code and the data items are part of the viewer's infrastructure data, which is why we've used the prefix **i_**.

Place the following definitions in the general declarations of the test program:

```
' VIEWER INFRASTRUCTURE DATA:
' WB DragDrop Data structure, V1.0
' pickup points, tracked by MouseMove events
Private i_sngXPos As Single    ' X  of drag pickup position
Private i_sngYPos As Single    ' Y  of drag pickup position
Private i_strTagit As String   ' .tag of object being dragged
```

These three parameters are used to track the mouse across a given object. When the user clicks the mouse to drag the object, the most recent mouse-move event has recorded the pickup position and object identity in these variables, as described in detail in the feasibility study. The complete data structure will have to be copied into the viewer form at the time of system integration.

When Julie first set up the code for **WBTest1**, she used integers for the pickup point variables. During system testing of **WBTest2**, when she was checking the toolbar functions, Julie discovered that the program crashed when she dragged and dropped very large images. The problem was caused by integer overflows, as I describe later. To overcome the fault, Julie had to convert all pickup variables to single-precision, real values, as opposed to integers. Rather than inflict on you the need to change many variable names, all the subsequent code has been changed already. Later, in the description about testing the toolbar functions, you'll find more detail about the error Julie encountered.

Place the following code into the **MouseMove** event handler of **imgImage2**:

```
Private Sub imgImage2_MouseMove(Button As Integer, Shift As Integer, X As_
                              Single, Y As Single)
' VIEWER INFRASTRUCTURE EVENT HANDLER: WB Handling, V1.0
' --------------------------------
' record X and Y position of cursor and object type
i_sngXPos = X
i_sngYPos = Y
i_strTagit = "IMAGE"

End Sub
```

This event handler is triggered every time the mouse position is moved across the image control. The event handler is running almost continuously as you move across the object. Each time the event handler is triggered, it captures the position of the cursor and the object's identity.

Place the following code into the **MouseMove** event handler of **txtText2**:

```
Private Sub txtText2_MouseMove(Button As Integer, Shift As Integer, X As_
                              Single, Y As Single)
' VIEWER INFRASTRUCTURE EVENT HANDLER: WB handling, V1.0
' --------------------------
' record X and Y position of cursor and object type
i_sngXPos = X
i_sngYPos = Y
i_strTagit = "TEXT"

End Sub
```

The above code is similar to the **Image** control's code.

Add this code to the **DragDrop** event handler of **imgImage2**:

```
Private Sub imgImage2_DragDrop(Source As Control, X As Single, Y As Single)
' VIEWER INFRASTRUCTURE EVENT HANDLER: WB Handling, V1.0
' --------------------------
If i_strTagit = "IMAGE" Then
   ' imgImage2 moved onto itself
   Source.Move Source.Left + X - i_sngXPos, Source.Top + Y - i_sngYPos
Else
   ' Text block is being dropped onto picture
   Source.Move imgImage2.Left + X - i_sngXPos, imgImage2.Top + Y -
   i_sngYPos
End If

End Sub
```

The code calculates the new position for the dropped object according to which object is dropped. For more details, consult the feasibility study on drag-and-drop handling in Appendix D.

If you really understand the above code, you should realize that it could be reduced to a single line. However, if you reduce the code to one line, make sure you comment the code well. Julie was aware that the code could be only one line, but she said that a single line would be "obscure in the extreme," to quote her directly. She regarded drag-and-drop handling as complex and felt that someone else reviewing the code would be better able to understand it as it related directly to the design.

The alternative approach (to create a single line of code) is to reduce the section to

```
Source.Move imgImage2.Left+X-i_sngXPos, imgImage2.Top+Y-i_sngYPos
```

and make the identity of the parameters redundant—clever, but obscure. Again, when you're developing your code, try to think about the programmers who will succeed you, and write the code so it is accessible to them.

Step 7

Add this code to the text box's **DragDrop** event:

```
Private Sub txtText2_DragDrop(Source As Control, X As Single, Y As Single)
' VIEWER INFRASTRUCTURE EVENT HANDLER: WB Handling, V1.0
' --------------------------
If i_strTagit = "TEXT" Then
    ' Text2 moved onto itself
    Source.Move Source.Left + X - i_sngXPos, Source.Top + Y - i_sngYPos
Else
    ' Image is being dragged onto text
    Source.Move txtText2.Left + X - i_sngXPos, txtText2.Top + Y- i_sngYPos
End If

End Sub
```

This code is similar to that of **imgImage2**'s **DragDrop** event handler (and it can also be reduced to a single line).

Step 8

Set the **DragMode** property of both **imgImage2** and **txtText2** to automatic.

Testing Drag-and-Drop

You should be able to run the drag-and-drop test program similarly to what we did in the feasibility study. Julie logged the following tests:

♦ *Test 1*—Image can be picked up and dropped onto the form correctly.

♦ *Test 2*—Text box can be picked up and dropped onto the form correctly.

♦ *Test 3*—Image can be picked up and dropped onto itself correctly.

♦ *Test 4*—Text can be picked up and dropped onto itself correctly.

♦ *Test 5*—Image can be picked up and dropped onto the Text Box control correctly.

♦ *Test 6*—Text can be picked up and dropped onto the Image control correctly.

♦ *Test 7*—In all cases, the text overlays the image where both overlap.

Thanks to the feasibility study, Julie managed to get this functionality up and running swiftly. Note that—unusually—no error conditions existed to check out.

The only problem that Julie did experience resulted because she inadvertently placed the code for the text box's **MouseMove** event handler into the **MouseDown** event. She took almost half an hour to realize what had gone wrong because the image box behaved impeccably, but the behavior of the text box was erratic, to say the least.

Creation of WB Sizing Functionality

The design for the Workbench sizing functions again shows them as a series of events that are triggered when the user clicks the appropriate button control. Make sure you study the design before you proceed. To create this functionality, follow these steps, or load the **WBTest2** project from the CD:

Step 1

On **WBTest1**'s form, create a toolbar by creating an instance of a picture control. Onto the toolbar, place button controls, as you see in Figure 8.2.

Name the tool bar **picPictureToolBar** and the button controls, from left to right, as follows:

♦ **cmdIm2ExpandDown**

♦ **cmdIm2ExpandUp**

♦ **cmdIm2ExpandDownH**

♦ **cmdIm2ExpandUpH**

♦ **cmdIm2ExpandDownW**

♦ **cmdIm2ExpandUpW**

♦ **cmdToolEnd**

♦ **cmdText2ExpandDownH**

♦ **cmdText2ExpandUpH**

♦ **cmdText2ExpandDownW**

♦ **cmdText2ExpandUpW**

♦ **cmdTextButtonOnOff**

♦ **cmdPrint**

Step 2

Create the code for the image manipulation controls as follows:

```
Private Sub cmdIm2ExpandDown_Click()
' VIEWER INFRASTRUCTURE EVENT HANDLER: WB Handling, V1.0
' --------------------------------
```

```
Dim sngAspect As Single

picPictureToolBar.Visible = False
  If imgImage2.Height > conImageMinHeight And_
    imgImage2.Width > conImageMinWidth Then
        sngAspect = imgImage2.Width / imgImage2.Height
        imgImage2.Width = imgImage2.Width - conImageMinWidth
        imgImage2.Height = imgImage2.Width / sngAspect
  End If
picPictureToolBar.Visible = True
picPictureToolBar.ZOrder
End Sub
```

According to the design, the code checks to see whether both width and height are above minimum values. If they are, the aspect ratio is calculated. The value defined by the minimum width is then subtracted from the width, and the height is calculated using the aspect ratio and the new width. Julie had introduced a number of constants here that would be set up shortly.

In the course of testing, Julie discovered that, if the image became very large and overlaid the toolbar, she lost the buttons. To prevent that from happening, she adopted the policy of first switching off the toolbar, then manipulating the dimensions of the **Image** control, and, finally, switching the toolbar back on. For good measure, she also brought the toolbar to the front using the **Zorder** method, which forces the object on which it is executed to be shown on top of all other screen objects that occupy the same screen area as the object itself. You will see the **Zorder** statement throughout the next set of code definitions.

The need to remove the toolbar and then redraw it came about because of unforeseen issues that arose from manipulating large images across the toolbar. This situation is a prime example of testing code to its operational limits. If Julie had not tried to test very large images, the problem might not have manifested. The constants defined in this routine are for minimum height and width allowed on the image. These constants are defined in the last step of the code sections.

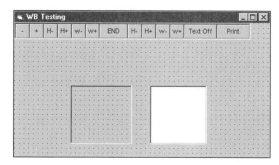

Figure 8.2
Workbench Test Program 2's form showing the toolbar containing image and text-box-resizing button controls.

Step 3

Add this code to **cmdIm2ExpandUp**'s click event:

```
Private Sub cmdIm2ExpandUp_Click()
' VIEWER INFRASTRUCTURE EVENT HANDLER: WB Handling, V1.0
' ---------------------------
Dim sngAspect As Single

picPictureToolBar.Visible = False
    If imgImage2.Width < conImageMaxWidth And_
                    ImgImage2.Height < conImageMaxHeight Then
        sngAspect = imgImage2.Width / imgImage2.Height
        imgImage2.Width = imgImage2.Width + conImageMinWidth
        imgImage2.Height = imgImage2.Width / sngAspect
    End If
picPictureToolBar.Visible = True
picPictureToolBar.ZOrder

End Sub
```

This code follows precisely the structure of the **ExpandDown** version of code. Note the introduction of the constant **conImageMaxWidth**.

Step 4

Add this code to the **cmdIm2ExpandDownH** click event:

```
Private Sub cmdIm2ExpandDownH_Click()
' VIEWER INFRASTRUCTURE EVENT HANDLER: WB Handling, V1.0
' ---------------------------
picPictureToolBar.Visible = False
    If imgImage2.Height > conImageMinHeight Then
            imgImage2.Height = imgImage2.Height - conImageMinHeight
    End If
picPictureToolBar.Visible = True
picPictureToolBar.ZOrder

End Sub
```

This code includes no attempt to preserve the aspect ratio.

Step 5

Place this code in the **cmdIm2ExpandUpH** click-event handler:

```
Private Sub cmdIm2ExpandUpH_Click()
```

```
' VIEWER INFRASTRUCTURE EVENT HANDLER: WB Handling, V1.0
' ---------------------------
picPictureToolBar.Visible = False
    If imgImage2.Height < conImageMaxHeight Then
        imgImage2.Height = imgImage2.Height + conImageMinHeight
    End If
picPictureToolBar.Visible = True
picPictureToolBar.ZOrder

End Sub
```

This code is pretty much like the **ExpandUpW** version, except that this code works exclusively on the height of the **Image** control.

Step 6

Place this code into the **cmdIm2ExpandDownW** click-event handler:

```
Private Sub cmdIm2ExpandDownW_Click()
' VIEWER INFRASTRUCTURE EVENT HANDLER: WB Handling, V1.0
' ---------------------------
picPictureToolBar.Visible = False
    If imgImage2.Width > conImageMinWidth Then
            imgImage2.Width = imgImage2.Width - conImageMinWidth
    End If
picPictureToolBar.Visible = True
picPictureToolBar.ZOrder

End Sub
```

Strangely enough, this code is similar to **cmdIm2ExpandDownH**.

Step 7

To complete the handling of the image manipulation, place the following code into **cmdIm2ExpandUpW**'s click-event handler:

```
Private Sub cmdIm2ExpandUpW_Click()
' VIEWER INFRASTRUCTURE EVENT HANDLER: WB Handling, V1.0
' ---------------------------
picPictureToolBar.Visible = False
    If imgImage2.Width < conImageMaxWidth Then
            imgImage2.Width = imgImage2.Width + conImageMinWidth
    End If
picPictureToolBar.Visible = True
picPictureToolBar.ZOrder

End Sub
```

With these routines, you can now expand and contract the image control, preserving aspect ratio or altering dimensions independently once the constants have been defined.

Step 8

Leave the **cmdToolEnd** button for the moment. Ultimately, this button will let the user return the viewer to the Page View mode from the Workbench mode of operation.

Step 9

In the same way that we set up routines to handle expansion and contraction of the **Image** control, Julie set up controls to expand and contract the text box. (Remember that the project has no requirement for expansion or contraction of both dimensions together.)

Add the following code to the **cmdText2ExpandDownH** click-event handler:

```
Private Sub cmdText2ExpandDownH_Click()
' VIEWER INFRASTRUCTURE EVENT HANDLER:
' WB functionality, Contract text box's Height only, V1.0
' --------------------------
picPictureToolBar.Visible = False
    If txtText2.Height > conTextMinHeight Then
        txtText2.Height = txtText2.Height - conTextMinHeight
    End If
picPictureToolBar.Visible = True
picPictureToolBar.ZOrder

End Sub
```

This code is the same as the corresponding routine already set up for the **Image** control.

Step 10

Now, add this code to the **cmdText2ExpandUpH** click-event handler:

```
Private Sub cmdText2ExpandUpH_Click()
' VIEWER INFRASTRUCTURE EVENT HANDLER:
' WB functionality, Expand text box's Height only, V1.0
' --------------------------
picPictureToolBar.Visible = False
    If txtText2.Height < conTextMaxHeight Then
        txtText2.Height = txtText2.Height + conTextMinHeight
    End If
picPictureToolBar.Visible = True
picPictureToolBar.ZOrder

End Sub
```

This routine is the same as the corresponding **imgImage2** routine.

Step 11

And, now, here's the code for the **cmdText2ExpandDownW** click-event handler:

```
Private Sub cmdText2ExpandDownW_Click()
' VIEWER INFRASTRUCTURE EVENT HANDLER: WB Handling, V1.0
' --------------------------
picPictureToolBar.Visible = False
    If txtText2.Width > conTextMinWidth Then
        txtText2.Width = txtText2.Width - conTextMinWidth
    End If
picPictureToolBar.Visible = True
picPictureToolBar.ZOrder

End Sub
```

The above code is the same as corresponding code for **imgImage2**.

Step 12

Finally, for **txtText2** manipulation, you need to place this code into the **cmdText2ExpandUpW** click-event handler:

```
Private Sub cmdText2ExpandUpW_Click()
' VIEWER INFRASTRUCTURE EVENT HANDLER: WB Handling, V1.0
' --------------------------
picPictureToolBar.Visible = False
    If txtText2.Width < conTextMaxWidth Then
        txtText2.Width = txtText2.Width + conTextMinWidth
    End If
picPictureToolBar.Visible = True
picPictureToolBar.ZOrder

End Sub
```

The above code is the last of the routines to alter the dimensions of the text box.

Step 13

Now, we have the code for a button control that switches **txtText2** on and off:

```
Private Sub cmdTextButtonOnOff_Click()
' VIEWER INFRASTRUCTURE EVENT HANDLER: WB Handling, V1.0
' --------------------------
If txtText2.Visible = True Then
    txtText2.Visible = False
    cmdTextButtonOnOff.Caption = "Text On"
Else
    txtText2.Visible = True
```

```
        cmdTextButtonOnOff.Caption = "Text Off"
End If

End Sub
```

This code simply looks to see what state the text box is in and switches it to the opposite. This routine also changes the caption to an appropriate title. Julie understood that in Picture Album mode the Workbench would not have a text box. She decided that the infrastructure routine she and Archie would develop at system integration time to switch from viewer Page View mode to Workbench mode would have to disable all the text controls on the toolbar. Likewise, for Text Book formats, she would need the code that invoked the Workbench to disable all the image-manipulation buttons.

Step 14

Finally, load the following constants into the data-declaration section of the test program:

```
' VIEWER INFRASTRUCTURE DATA:
' Workbench max and min values, V1.0
'
Private Const conImageMinHeight = 500          ' min/max dimensions for Image2
Private Const conImageMinWidth = 500
Private Const conImageMaxHeight = 50000
Private Const conImageMaxWidth = 50000

Private Const conTextMinHeight = 500           ' min/max dimensions for Text2
Private Const conTextMinWidth = 500
Private Const conTextMaxHeight = 50000
Private Const conTextMaxWidth = 50000
```

The operational limits are being defined here. We don't want images to shrink to silly sizes, and we don't want them to grow to huge dimensions.

NOTE: *The settings for these constants were chosen arbitrarily, and they actually caused a problem with Julie's first attempt to code the Workbench functions. The problem was associated with the fact that she initially used integers to store the data captured in the mouse-move events. I have provided the full details concerning this problem later in this section.*

Testing WB Sizing Functionality

The testing that Julie was able to log with this program was as follows:

♦ *Test 1*—Check that the image can be expanded up to maximum size, preserving aspect ratio.

♦ *Test 2*—Check that the image can be contracted down to minimum size, preserving aspect ratio.

♦ *Test 3*—Check that the image width can be expanded to max width, independent of height.

- *Test 4*—Check that the image height can be expanded to max height, independent of width.

- *Test 5*—Check image width can be contracted to min width, independent of height.

- *Test 6*—Check image height can be contracted to min height, independent of width.

- *Test 7*—Check text box can be switched off and on.

- *Test 8*—Check text width can be expanded to max, and text reformats correctly.

- *Test 9*—Check text height can be expanded to max, and text reformats correctly.

- *Test 10*—Check text width can be contracted to min, and text reformats correctly.

- *Test 11*—Check text height can be contracted to min, and text reformats correctly.

- *Test 12*—Drag-and-drop handling continues to work okay during Tests 1 through 11.

This represents quite a combination of tests. Clearly, reaching the maximum size of images and text boxes would require many clicks on the button controls, because the expansion constants were set to 500 twips. To help speed up the testing of image- and text-expansion capability, Julie changed the increments defined in the constants from 500 twips to 5,000 twips, which allowed her to reach maximum dimensions quite quickly. This kind of modification is perfectly valid, and it allowed Julie to quickly reach the operational limits of the program.

Program Crash

The importance of regression testing and testing to program limits is emphasized in what happened to Julie when she ran Test 12. You must remember that, initially (as in the feasibility study), the two parameters used to track the cursor position across a screen object were integers—**i_intXPos** and **i_intYPos**.

In the course of dragging and dropping an image expanded to a very large size, Julie caused the program to crash with an "Overflow" error. This crash was somewhat unexpected, because the drag-and-drop handling had passed all its tests in **WBTest1**. The crash occurred when Julie was dragging and dropping a huge image, resulting from manual expansion in an attempt to place the bottom, right-hand corner of the image on the screen. Before she could accomplish this, she received the error message. The testing of drag-and-drop handling had not produced any problems. The difference in this situation was the size of the image. VB error trapping highlighted the line that causing the problem as the first line in the mouse move event of **imgImage2**: **i_intXPos=X**.

Julie realized what the problem was as soon as she saw the line. **i_intXPos** was a single-precision, signed integer, which has a valid range of −32,768 to +32,767. When the image is 50,000 twips in size, **X** or **Y** can be far bigger than the integer limit. To overcome the problem, all Julie had to do was change all **i_intXPos** references to **i_sngXPos** and redefine the variable as a "single." She had to do the same for **i_intYPos**. You've been spared this problem because we started by defining the variables as "single" in **WBTest1**.

NOTE: *Julie's experience with the program crash is yet another good example of the need to test code to its operational limits. Her experience also demonstrates the need for regression testing. Good testing requires ingenuity and thoroughness—but, above all, testing at the operational limits.*

The only other problem Julie encountered was that, sometimes the image disappeared when it was expanded to a very large value. However, decreasing the dimensions brought the image back again. She showed me the problem, and I suspected that finding a way to avoid it might take a while, because we couldn't always predict when the image would disappear. However, a full recovery of the image was always possible by decreasing the dimensions, so we decided to log the problem as a nonurgent issue, together with the other issue of not being able to rewind MID files.

Creation of WB Print Functionality

According to the design, the code to print out the content of the Workbench clears the screen and makes it white, then issues a print, having first removed the toolbar. When the print is over, the toolbar is re-enabled, and the background color of the form is reinstated. To construct the required code, follow these steps, using the test program developed so far, or load **WBTest3** from Julie's development directory on the CD:

Step 1

Continue to use the test program we developed in the last section. The code to place in the **cmdPrint** button control's click-event handler is as follows:

```
Private Sub cmdPrint_Click()
' VIEWER INFRASTRUCTURE EVENT HANDLER: WB Handling, V1.0
' ---------------------------
Dim strTemp As String
Dim intResponse As Integer

picPictureToolBar.Visible = False
frmEViewer.BackColor = shpWhite.BackColor
txtText2.BackColor = shpWhite.BackColor
txtText2.BorderStyle = 0
' ..............................................
strTemp = "Continue with print?"
intResponse = MsgBox(strTemp, 33, "Print Format")
If intResponse = 1 Then
        picPictureToolBar.Visible = False
        frmEViewer.PrintForm       ' PRINT IT
End If
' ..............................................
frmEViewer.BackColor = shpGray.BackColor
txtText2.BackColor = shpGray.BackColor

txtText2.BorderStyle = 1
```

```
picPictureToolBar.Visible = True

End Sub
```

According to the design specification, the preceding routine switches off the toolbar and sets the background color of the form to white; the code then switches the text box's background color to white, and switches off the text border. The code then asks the user if it is okay to proceed with the print. If proceeding is not okay, the code continues without issuing the print command. If the user confirms the print, a print is issued, and the routine then switches the toolbar back on, switches on the text outline, and switches colors back to gray.

Step 2

Add two shape controls to the project—**shpWhite** and **shpGray**. Set the background colors appropriately, and set each object's **visible** property to **False**. You must also change the name of the form to **frmEViewer**, because the print code contains a reference to the viewer form.

Testing WB Print Functionality

Julie logged the following tests at this stage:

♦ *Test 1*—Check that a print occurs as seen on screen—that is, WYSIWYG.

♦ *Test 2*—Check that the program functions correctly if a printer is not present.

♦ *Test 3*—Check that printing can be rejected correctly.

Completion of Workbench

Julie had started the modules in the previous week, and she had managed to complete all the code and test it by the end of Monday, although she did stay late. The result was 1.5 days actual effort (0.5 days from the previous week) to accomplish 2.5 days planned effort—good progress, but, without Archie, we needed it.

Julie now had a full four days to complete the **Navigation** and **Search** modules. We had originally planned these two developments at three days' effort. Even without Archie, the schedule should be okay, provided Julie remained available for the whole period.

WB Infrastructure Code

The handling code that we had developed so far for the Workbench was locked up in the test programs. After we started the viewer's system integration, we'd carry all the private, infrastructure code and data we had developed from these test programs across to the relevant locations in the viewer.

Navigation

The **Navigation** module would be the easiest development of all. Quite sensibly, Julie decided to expand the **PageTest1** program that Archie had developed, because doing so would allow her to read in a Test Index. She could then set up the button controls and develop what would become viewer infrastructure code to handle navigation.

According to the design specifications, the function of each button involved calling **DisplayPage**. (Note that we had made the design specifications for navigation generic, and the specs actually refer to navigation through either a title or a Page Index.) Julie had contemplated setting up the whole **Navigation** module to use the code that Archie had already produced to display a page, but she recognized that doing so wouldn't gain her very much after a lot of extra work. So, she decided to add some buttons to the **PageTest1** and create her own private version of **DisplayPage** to simply populate some screen labels with the entry's string contents. She knew that, if this worked correctly, when they bolted in the **Display Page** for the real viewer, it also would work; going through all the trouble to integrate it now was pointless.

Creation of the Navigation Test Program

You can see the modified layout of the **PageTest1** test program in Figure 8.3. This program became **NavTest1**.

To create the form and its contents, follow these steps; alternatively, load **NavTest1** from Julie's development directory on the CD:

Step 1

Load the **PageTest1** project, and set up the extra controls as shown in the screenshot in Figure 8.3. These controls are as follows:

♦ *Control array*—**lblKeys(1)** through **(5)**, to hold the keys for a page.

♦ *Page number label*—**lblPageNumber**, to hold a displayed page's number.

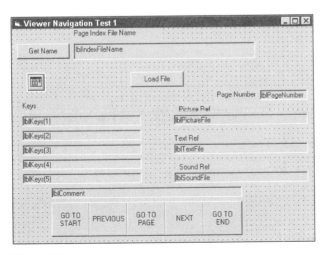

Figure 8.3
The **Read In Page Index** test program's form, modified to accommodate navigation testing, which resulted in **NavTest1**.

- *Data record label*—**lblPictureFile**, to hold the image-file reference string.

- *Data record label*—**lblTextFile**, to hold the text-file reference string.

- *Data record label*—**lblSoundFile**, to hold the sound-file reference string.

- *Comments*—**lblCommentLine**, to hold any comments the test program might produce.

- *Go to page 1*—**cmdGoStart**, command button.

- *Previous*—**cmdPrevious**, command button.

- *Go to*—**cmdGoToPage**, command button.

- *Next*—**cmdNext**, command button.

- *Go to last page*—**cmdGoEnd**, command button.

Step 2

Insert the following code into the **Go To Start** command button's click-event handler:

```
Private Sub cmdGoStart_Click()
' VIEWER INFRASTRUCTURE EVENT HANDLER:
' Navigation Functionality, V1.0
' --------------------
If g_intCurrentPage < 1 Then
    MsgBox "Index is empty"
    Exit Sub
End If

g_intCurrentPage = 1
LblCommentLine.caption = "At Start of Index"
Call DisplayPage

End Sub
```

If **g_intCurrentPage** is less than 1, no Index is loaded. Otherwise, the code sets the page to 1 and displays with a comment. Note that **lblCommentLine** will be one of the viewer's screen objects.

Step 3

This code is for the **PREVIOUS** button control:

```
Private Sub cmdPrevious_Click()
' VIEWER INFRASTRUCTURE EVENT HANDLER:
' Navigation Functionality, V1.0
' --------------------
If g_intCurrentPage < 1 Then
    MsgBox "Index is empty"
    Exit Sub
```

```
End If

If g_intCurrentPage = 1 Then
    MsgBox "Already at Start of Index"
    Exit Sub
End If

g_intCurrentPage = g_intCurrentPage - 1
Call DisplayPage

End Sub
```

The Index might be empty, or it might already be at Page 1. If neither is true, the page number is decremented and its contents then displayed.

Step 4

This code goes into the **NEXT** button control's click-event handler:

```
Private Sub cmdNext_Click()
' VIEWER INFRASTRUCTURE EVENT HANDLER:
' Navigation Functionality, V1.0
' --------------------
If g_intCurrentPage < 1 Then
    MsgBox "Index is empty"
    Exit Sub
End If

If g_intCurrentPage = UBound(g_strPictureFile()) Then
        MsgBox "Already at End of Index"
        Exit Sub
End If

g_intCurrentPage = g_intCurrentPage + 1
Call DisplayPage

End Sub
```

Again, note how the code checks for an empty Index or for whether the file is already at the end of the Index. If neither is true, the code increments the page number and displays the contents.

Step 5

Now, for the **GO TO END** button, place this code into the click-event handler:

```
Private Sub cmdGoEnd_Click()
' VIEWER INFRASTRUCTURE EVENT HANDLER:
' Navigation Functionality, V1.0
```

```
'  --------------------
If g_intCurrentPage < 1 Then
    MsgBox "Index is empty"
    Exit Sub
End If


g_intCurrentPage = UBound(g_strPictureFile())
Call DisplayPage
lblCommentLine.Caption = " At End of Index"

End Sub
```

If the Index is not empty, the code simply sets the page number to the last page and displays the contents.

Step 6

Last, but not least, here is the code to go to a specified page:

```
Private Sub cmdGoToPage_Click()
' VIEWER INFRASTRUCTURE EVENT HANDLER:
' Navigation Functionality, V1.0
'  --------------------
Dim strTemp1 As String
Dim strTemp2 As String

If g_intCurrentPage < 1 Then
    MsgBox "Index is empty"
    Exit Sub
End If


strTemp1 = "Type in Number of Page Required"
strTemp2 = InputBox(strTemp1, "Go to Page...")
If strTemp2 = "" Then Exit Sub

On Error GoTo ErrHandler
g_intCurrentPage = CInt(strTemp2)
If g_intCurrentPage < 1 Then
        g_intCurrentPage = 1
        Call DisplayPage
        lblCommentLine.Caption = "At start of Index"
        Exit Sub
End If
If g_intCurrentPage > UBound(g_strPictureFile()) Then
        g_intCurrentPage = UBound(g_strPictureFile())
```

```
            Call DisplayPage
            lblCommentLine.Caption = "At end of Index"
            Exit Sub
End If
Call DisplayPage
Exit Sub
=================================================================
ErrHandler:
MsgBox "Sorry; Not a valid Page number."
End Sub
```

This code uses **InputBox** to get a response to "Type in Number Of Page Required." The result is taken as a string and converted to an integer. If an error results in the conversion, the program exits with a suitable error message. Otherwise, the code checks for boundary conditions and displays the first or last page as appropriate, setting the comment line with a suitable message.

Step 7

Finally, Julie developed a simple module to display the string of a page in the screen objects. Add this code to the general section of the main form:

```
Sub DisplayPage()
' TEST CODE:
' Test routine for Navigation checkout
Dim intLoopCounter As Integer
For intLoopCounter = 1 To 5
   lblKeys(intLoopCounter) = g_strKeys(intLoopCounter, g_intCurrentPage)
Next intLoopCounter

lblPictureFile.Caption = g_strPictureFile(g_intCurrentPage)
lblTextFile.Caption = g_strTextFile(g_intCurrentPage)
lblSoundFile.Caption = g_strSoundFile(g_intCurrentPage)

lblEntryNumber.Caption = CStr(g_intCurrentPage)
End Sub
```

The keys are set up from the entry's **strKeys** array, and the file-reference strings are copied from the appropriate arrays. Finally, the current page number is placed in the appropriate label.

Testing Navigation Functionality

After an Index was loaded, Julie used the buttons to move backward and forward through the Index, and to select pages at random using the **GO TO PAGE** button. You can see the test program's form when it's in use in Figure 8.4.

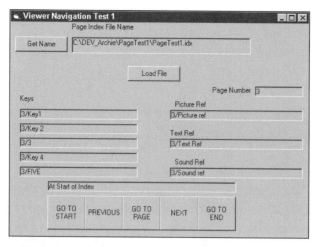

Figure 8.4
The **Read In Page Index** test program's form when used to check the **Navigation** functionality.

Julie was able to log the following tests using this test program:

♦ *Test 1*—Ensure that the navigation handles blank Index okay.

♦ *Test 2*—Ensure that the navigation cannot go outside onboard Index.

♦ *Test 3*—Ensure that the boundary checking provides correct messaging for **Start** and **End**.

♦ *Test 4*—Ensure that the **Go to page** handles noninteger input okay.

♦ *Test 5*—Ensure that the **Go to page** handles **page > end** or **page < start**.

♦ *Test 6*—Check that the correct sequencing: forward, reverse, start, end.

Although the tests look relatively simple and short, Julie took this opportunity to build a range of Indexes, and she gave the modules under test a really good hammering. Testing consisted of performing the test and checking that what showed in the labels matched what was on the printed version of the Index file. This test verified that the program had located the correct record. To make life easier, Julie set up all the keys and file references to indicate which record number they came from. You can see this file on the CD in the **NavTest1** directory in Julie's development directory. All the infrastructure code that the viewer will require for navigation handling is now available in the navigation test program.

Search Functionality

Julie's next task was to set up the **Search** facility and test it. Let's review what searching was all about. We had five possible selection words—that is, five keys the user could request the program to find—and each page had a maximum of five possible keys. The user could type in any number of selection items and then "tell" the program that those items must all be present on a page for a match to occur. Alternatively, the user could request that, if any one of the selection words was present in any of the page's keys, a match was deemed **True**.

Interpreting the Flow Diagram

In the design specification for the **Search** module, flow diagrams were employed to define the search engine. Two diagrams were used to show how the three requests would be handled at the top level.

Forward Searching

The first diagram, shown in Figure 8.5, specifies how to process a request to search from Page 1 and how to process a request to search forward from the next entry.

The flow diagram in Figure 8.5 shows two events that "enter" the algorithm at different points. To **Search Forwards From Page 1**, the algorithm first sets **CP** to 0. **CP** is the current page number and equivalent to **g_intCurrentPage**. If the user requests **Search From Next Page**, the program bypasses **CP=0** and therefore, **CP** is set to whatever page is currently on display.

First, the algorithm checks to see whether **CP** is already on the last page number. If it is, an appropriate message is produced, and the algorithm is terminated. Otherwise, the program conducts a search of the Index from **CP**. This search results either in a match or in no match

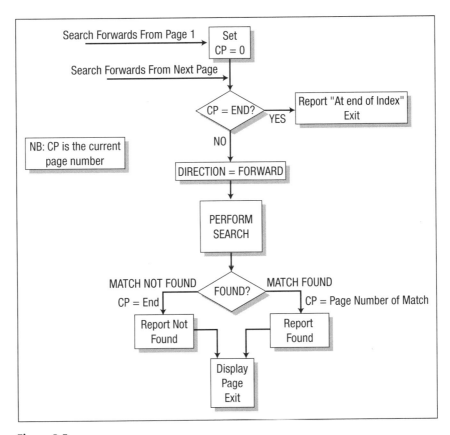

Figure 8.5

Top-level flow diagram to indicate how forward searching in the viewer is to be implemented.

being found by the end of the Index. Consequently, **CP** is set either to the last page number or to the page number at which a match was found (which, don't forget, might well be the last page number). The program makes a report concerning the outcome of the search.

Reverse Searching

Figure 8.6 shows the **Search Backward From Previous Page** algorithm, and the diagram is very similar to Figure 8.5.

In the algorithm for reverse searching, a check is made to see if **CP** is already set to **1**. If so, the appropriate message is produced and an exit executed. Otherwise, the search is performed and, according to the result, appropriate messages produced.

Messages can be produced in two ways. One method is to use the message-box facility, which prevents the user from doing anything else until the message has been acknowledged (modal operation), and the second way is to place a text message in the comment label (non-modal operation). The user can ignore a non-modal message, whereas he or she must act upon a modal message. A modal message gives some reassurance that the user will read the message first.

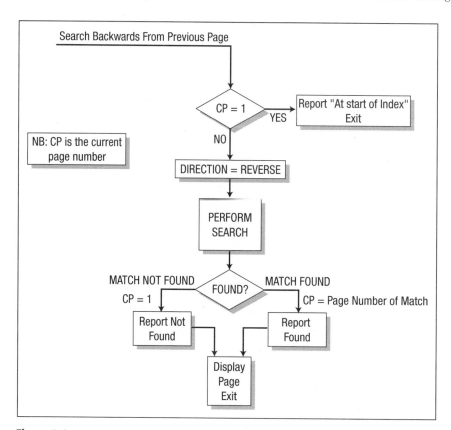

Figure 8.6

Top-level, flow diagram to indicate how reverse searching in the viewer is to be implemented.

Top-Down Approach

When Julie developed the **Title Index** modules, she first developed the low-level routines to extract data fields and find delimiters. After she had tested these basic routines and found them to be robust, she developed the top-level routines that employed them. Developing the low-level modules first is an example of the bottom-up approach.

To handle searching, Julie decided to first produce the infrastructure code required to accommodate the two, top-level, flow diagrams. The routine to perform the actual search was called **SearchIt**. Julie produced a simple, dummy version of **SearchIt** that forced a **False** or **True** return so she could check the basic handling of the infrastructure code at the top level. This was an alternative approach to the bottom-up approach she had used for title handling.

Creation of Top-Level Search Handling

Julie decided that because she needed a Page Index on board to test searching, adding the **Search** functionality to the already extended **Read In Page Index** test program that had now become **NavTest1** would be sensible. Follow these steps to implement top-level searching; alternatively, load the **SearchTest1** project from the appropriate directory in Julie's development area on the CD:

Step 1

Open the **NavTest1** project, and add the three buttons, as shown in Figure 8.7. Save the form and project as **SearchTest1**.

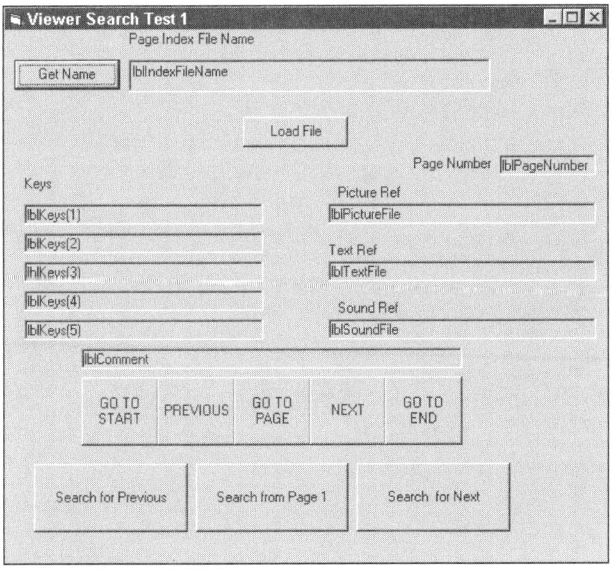

Figure 8.7

SearchTest1 form, created from **NavTest1**, showing the addition of the test buttons required to check searching.

The buttons from left to right are as follows:

♦ **cmdSearchPrevious**—Search from current Page backward to page 1

♦ **cmdSearch**—Search from Page 1 to end of Index

♦ **cmdSearchNext**—Search from next page to end of Index

Step 2

Place the following code into the **cmdSearch** click-event handler:

```
Private Sub cmdSearch_Click()
' VIEWER INFRASTRUCTURE EVENT HANDLER:
' Search Functionality, Search from Page 1, V1.0
' -------------------------
g_intCurrentPage = 0
Call cmdSearchNext_Click
End Sub
```

From the flow diagrams, Julie realized that the only difference between **Search From Page 1** and **Search From Next Page** was a line to set the page number to 0. Consequently, the **SEARCH NEXT** button's click-event handler could be called by **cmdSearch**—after all, **cmdSearch** is just a private subroutine accessible from any infrastructure code.

Step 3

Add this code to the **cmdSearchNext** click-event handler:

```
Private Sub cmdSearchNext_Click()
' VIEWER INFRASTRUCTURE EVENT HANDLER:
' Search Functionality, Search forwards from current page, V1.0
' -------------------------
Dim booSearchResult As Boolean
Dim booLoadResult As Boolean
Dim booForwardSearch As Boolean

If g_intCurrentPage >= UBound(g_strPictureFile()) Then
    MsgBox "You are already on Last Page"
    lblCommentLine.Caption = "Already on Last Page"
    Exit Sub
End If

    booForwardSearch = True

    booSearchResult = SearchForIt(booForwardSearch)

    If booSearchResult = True Then
        Call DisplayPage
```

```
            lblCommentLine.Caption = "Result of successful search"
            Exit Sub
        Else
            Call DisplayPage
            MsgBox "Failed to find entry searching forward"
            lblCommentLine.Caption = "At End of Index"
        End If

End Sub
```

The code follows the flow diagram reasonably precisely. Note that modal messages are being given to indicate boundary conditions, and the comment line is being set up. When a search results in a successful match to an entry, only the comment line is set.

Step 4

Finally, here is the code for the reverse search, which needs to be placed in the click-event handler of the **cmdSearchPrevious** button control:

```
Private Sub cmdSearchPrevious_Click()
' VIEWER INFRASTRUCTURE EVENT HANDLER:
' Search Functionality, backward search from current page, V1.0
' ------------------------
Dim booSearchResult As Boolean
Dim booLoadResult As Boolean
Dim booForwardSearch As Boolean

If g_intCurrentPage <= 0 Then
        MsgBox "You are already at Start of Index"
        LblcommentLine.caption = "At Start of Index"
        Exit Sub
End If

booForwardSearch = False
booSearchResult = SearchForIt(booForwardSearch)

If booSearchResult = True Then
    Call DisplayPage
    lblCommentLine.Caption = "Search was successful"
  Else
    Call DisplayPage
    MsgBox "Failed to find entry searching in reverse"
    lblCommentLine.Caption = "Last Search Failed"

End If

End Sub
```

Again, this code follows the flow diagram precisely.

Finally, place the following temporary test code into the general declaration section of the main form:

```
Private Function SearchForIt(booDirection As Boolean) As Boolean
' TEST CODE:
' Search Engine TEST 1 indicate NOT FOUND
If booDirection = True Then
        g_intCurrentPage = UBound(g_strPictureFile())
Else
        g_intCurrentPage = 1
End If
SearchForIt = False
Exit Function
' ------------------------
' TEST 2 indicate FOUND
If booDirection = True Then
        g_intCurrentPage = UBound(g_strPictureFile()) / 2 ' halfway
Else
        g_intCurrentPage = 1
End If
SearchForIt = True

End Function
```

Julie could set up two simple tests, which are shown above. In the first test, if the direction of the search was set to **True**, the test routine would set the current page to be the end of the book and set **SearchForIt False**. If the direction were reverse, the routine would set the page number to **1**. This structure allowed **Failed To Find A Match** handling to be checked out. The second test was invoked by cutting the code for Test 2 and pasting it above the code for Test 1 (crude, but effective). This second test set the current page to halfway through the Index if the search direction was forward and to **1** if the search direction was backward. **SearchForIt** was then set **True** to check **Match Found** handling.

Testing Top-Level Search Routines

Julie was able to perform the following tests of the infrastructure **Search** routines using the dummy search engine:

♦ *Test 1*—Search-fail handling is okay for forward searching.

♦ *Test 2*—Search-fail handling is okay for reverse searching.

♦ *Test 3*—Successful search forward handled okay.

♦ *Test 4*—Successful search reverse handled okay.

♦ *Test 5*—If already on last page, forward search is not performed; message produced okay.

♦ *Test 6*—If already on first page, reverse search is not performed; message produced okay.

You can use the Test Index available in directory **SearchTest1** in Julie's development area on the CD. The testing requires a combination of navigation and Search-button use.

Development of Basic Search Routines

The basic routines for searching consist of **SearchForIt**, which is the GUI-bound infrastructure function that sets up the call to the main library-search utility, called **ExamineIndex**, which is a pure function. Before this pure function can be called, the screen-selection criteria must be extracted from the screen objects and placed in memory variables, as must the settings of the two radio buttons. This procedure ensures that **ExamineIndex** then can be written independently from the screen objects, for insertion into **ViewerLib**.

To create the proper version of **SearchForIt** and set up ready for **ExamineIndex**, follow these steps; alternatively, load project **SearchTest2** from the CD:

Step 1

Add five text boxes to the form in **SearchTest1**. The resulting additions to the form are shown in Figure 8.8.

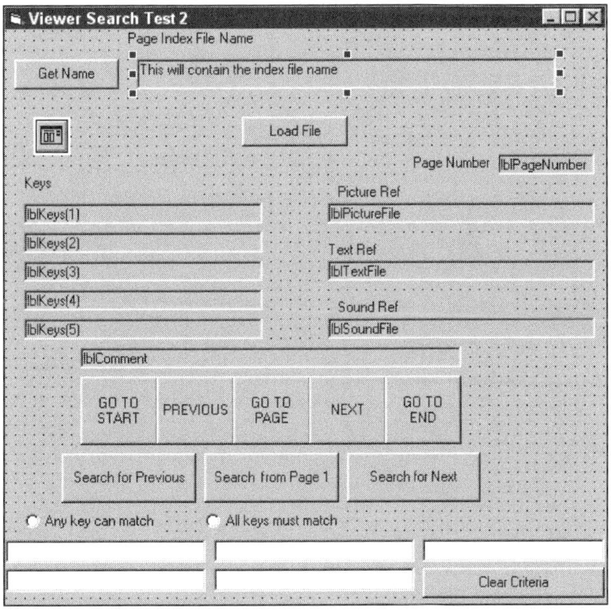

Figure 8.8
The top-level search, **Navigation** and **Page Index** test form, showing the addition of search-selection objects.

The objects to add, as Figure 8.8 shows, are as follows:

- *Selection text boxes*—**txtSelect(1)** through **txtSelect(5)**, used to input search criteria.

- *Search-type indicator*—**rdoAll**, radio button, which, when set to **True**, indicates that all keys entered in selection criteria must be present in a page's set of keys for a match to be declared.

- *Search-type indicator*—**rdoAny**, radio button, which, when set to **True**, indicates that any one of the selection keys can be present in a page's keys for a match to be declared.

- *Clear-selection criteria*—**cmdClearCriteria**, button used to clear **txtSelect** array.

Step 2

Set up this routine in the general declarations of the main form, overwriting the simple test harness that we used in the previous section:

```
Private Function SearchForIt(booDirection As Boolean) As Boolean
' VIEWER INFRASTRUCTURE GUI ROUTINE:
' Search Functionality, prime for search, setting up variables from
' screen objects to call search engine,  V1.0
' Argument:   booDirection = True  - search forwards from current page
'                          = False - search in reverse
'          Function result = True if match found
'                          = False if search failed
' ----------------------------------
Dim intLoopCounter As Integer
Dim booResult As Boolean
Dim booAllWord As Boolean
Dim strSelection(5) As String

SearchForIt = False              ' Default setting is 'search failed'

booAllWord = rdoAll.Value     ' (Note: If false, then rdoAny must be True)
For intLoopCounter = 1 To 5
   strSelection(intLoopCounter) = txtSelect(intLoopCounter).Text
Next intLoopCounter

SearchForIt = ExamineIndex(booDirection, booAllWord, strSelection())

End Function
```

This routine places into variables the contents of the screen objects that contain the selection criteria and the radio buttons. These variables are then transmitted to the general search function as arguments in the call. Only one of the radio button's values needs to be transferred because, whatever its state, the other radio button must be the opposite.

Creation of the Main Search Routine

Let's start by looking at the flow for the main search routine, which is a pure function—that is, no direct or indirect (link made at runtime) access exists to screen objects. Figure 8.9 depicts the logic of the routine.

We'll begin on the top, left-hand side of the flow diagram. A variable we've called **INC** is set to –1; if the search is to be conducted in the "forward" direction, the variable is changed to +1. We then start the main loop of the algorithm. At this stage, **CP** (the current page number, better known as **g_intCurrentPage**), is set to 0 for a call from the Search button, or **CP** is set to the page number of that on view if the call came via the NEXT or PREVIOUS buttons.

In the main loop first add 1 to or subtract 1 from the current page number. Remember, **INC** is –1 or +1, according to the search direction requested. This procedure now gives us the page number of the next page to check. We then make sure that we haven't reached the start or the end of the Index. If we have, appropriate action is taken, and the algorithm terminates with the return parameter set to show that a match was not found.

Starting at **L=1**, the next step is to execute a loop that will check all five possible selection criteria, which, in the flow diagram, are represented as **Select(1)** through **Select(5)**. So **Select(L)** is checked to see whether it is blank. If it is, the algorithm continues from the end of the loop where **L** is incremented. If the selection is not blank, it is checked against each of the five possible keys of page **CP** in a function that returns a result of **True** or **False**, depending on whether a match was found. What happens next depends on whether the user requires that all selection criteria or only one criterion must be honored.

If all criteria must be met, and if the result of the check against the keys for **Select(L)** was **False**, the program can exit the loop because it can't declare the page a match if one of the selection words has failed. If, however, the word did match, the program can continue to check the rest.

If "any word" can match, as soon as the routine finds one word that does, the routine can declare the result of the search a success. Otherwise, for **All Must Match**, the program must wait until after the loop has been completed and then determine whether it still has a success code, meaning that all the words were found. To convert the flow diagram to code, you can either work directly from the diagram, as Julie did, or you can develop pseudocode as an interim stage. You can see the end result of Julie's endeavors next.

Installation of Basic Search Routines

Follow these steps to complete the **Search** functionality:

Step 1

Add this routine to Julie's version of **ViewerLib** in program **SearchTest1**:

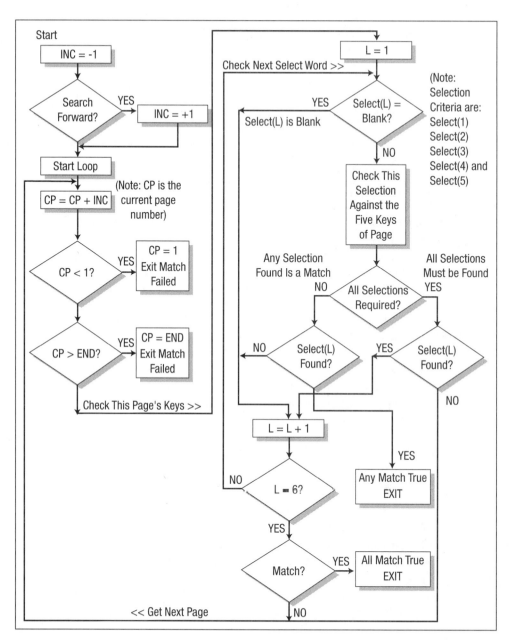

Figure 8.9

Logic for the main search routine, **ExamineIt**.

Step1—Section 1

```
Public Function ExamineIndex(booSearchForward As Boolean, booAllWord As_
               Boolean, strSelections() As String) As Boolean
' GENERAL ROUTINE: Searching,  V1.0
' Arguments;
'       booSearchForward - forward = true, reverse = false
'            booAllWord - All selection must be found = true, else any one
'                         selection found constitutes a match.
'          strSelections - 5 element string array containing selections
'         Function result - True - match found
'                          - False - search failed
' NB: g_intCurrentPage points to first entry to search
' -----------------------------------Dim intLoopCounter As Integer
Dim intIncrement As Integer
Dim booResult As Boolean

ExamineIndex = False
intIncrement = -1
If booSearchForward = True Then intIncrement = 1
' -------------------------------------
```

Notes on Section 1: The code constitutes the first part of the flow diagram, setting **INC**. What follows next is the start of the main loop.

Step 1—Section 2

```
Do
    g_intCurrentPage = g_intCurrentPage + intIncrement    ' on to next page
    If g_intCurrentPage < 1 Then
        g_intCurrentPage = 1
        Exit Function
    End If

    If g_intCurrentPage = UBound(g_strPictureFile()) + 1 Then
        g_intCurrentPage = UBound(g_strPictureFile())
        Exit Function
    End If
```

Notes on Section 2: The code performs the checks to see whether the boundaries are still inside the Index. If the program has gone out of bounds, the search has failed to locate a match.

```
' search each selection criteria entry in turn
For intLoopCounter = 1 To 5

If strSelections(intLoopCounter) <> "" Then
ExamineIndex = CheckAgainstKeys(strSelections(intLoopCounter))

If booAllWord = True Then
If ExamineIndex = False Then Exit For        ' All must match
Else
If ExamineIndex = True Then Exit Function    ' Any can match
End If
End If

Next intLoopCounter
```

Notes on Section 3: In the code, we check each of the selection words in turn. If **booAllWord** indicates that all words must match, and the search indicates a failure, we can end the search on this page. If **booAllWord** is **False**, and the program finds a match, we can exit the function with a match having been registered (because only one of the selection criteria needs be present in the page's keys).

```
If ExamineIndex = True Then Exit Function
```

Notes on Section 4: If the routine gets to this stage, all the selection criteria have been checked. If **ExamineIndex** is still **True**, we have a match.

```
Loop

Exit Function        ' failed to find a match
End Function
```

Notes on Section 5: This section is the end of the loop, and the code continues from the top of the loop once more. In fact, the routine should never get to the **Exit Function** shown here, because all the termination traps in the loop result in an **Exit Function** being executed.

Finally, add this routine to **ViewerLib**:

```
Public Function CheckAgainstKeys(strSelect As String) As Boolean
' GENERAL ROUTINE: Searching, V1.0
' Arguments:
'                  strSelect - one of the selection strings
'      Function result True - match found
'                       False - no match found
' check this string against all five keys of current page
' -----------------------------------
Dim intLoopCounter As Integer
Dim strTemp As String

CheckAgainstKeys = True
strTemp = UCase(strSelect)

For intLoopCounter = 1 To 5
  If strTemp = UCase(g_strKeys(intLoopCounter, g_intCurrentPage)) Then Exit_
     Function
Next intLoopCounter

CheckAgainstKeys = False

End Function
```

The code simply takes the string supplied and checks it against each key in turn. We are not bothered about the difference between uppercase and lowercase letters in the keys, so both entities are converted to uppercase before the check is performed.

Step 3

Add the following code to the **cmdClearCriteria** button's click-event handler:

```
Private Sub cmdClearCriteria_Click()
' VIEWER INFRASTRUCTURE EVENT HANDLER:
' Clear down search selection text boxes, V1.0
' -----------------------
Dim intLoopCounter As Integer

For intLoopCounter = 1 To 5
    txtSelect(intLoopCounter).Text = ""
Next intLoopCounter

End Sub
```

The selection array, which will ultimately be located on **picSelectionPanel** of the viewer, is cleared out. With completion of the clear-down handler, Julie was ready to start testing.

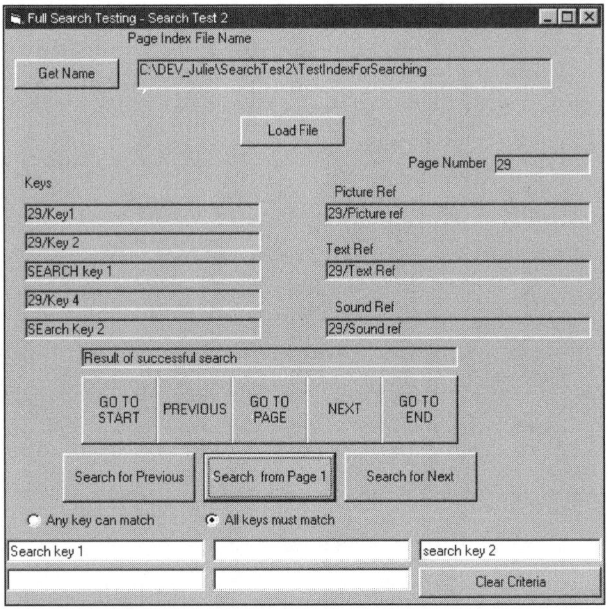

Figure 8.10
The **Search** test screen during testing.

Testing Search Functionality

Figure 8.10 shows what the test program's form looked like during testing.

As you can see in Figure 8.10, Julie has loaded a Test Index. The Test Index is available in **SearchTest2** of Julie's development area on the CD. The Test Index contains various keys set up as **Search Key n**, where *n* is an integer from one through five. This arrangement allows various combinations of key searches to be performed. In Figure 8.10, the form has been set up to search for **Search Key 1** and **Search Key 2**.

The testing Julie was able to log consisted of the following:

♦ *Test 1*—Check that a single key can be located with **ANY** or **ALL** settings.

♦ *Test 2*—Check that two keys can be located with **ANY** or **ALL** settings.

♦ *Test 3*—Check that three keys can be located with **ANY** or **ALL** settings.

♦ *Test 4*—Check that four keys can be located with **ANY** or **ALL** settings.

♦ *Test 5*—Check that five keys can be located with **ANY** or **ALL** settings.

♦ *Test 6*—Check that multiple matches function OK, forward and reverse.

♦ *Test 7*—Check case independence.

♦ *Test 8*—Check that all selection words can be cleared using the Clear button.

Obviously, many possible combinations can be defined for searching. The preceding set is a suitable minimum to indicate that Julie checked many of the code's pathways. System testing will be more rigorous.

Searching Without an Index Present in Memory

The first thing Julie discovered was that the search buttons all failed if no Index was in memory—that is, **g_intCurrentPage =0**. She missed this when she was checking out the top-level **Search** functions. To overcome the problem, she had to insert the following lines at the start of each Search button's click event, to perform the same check all the **Navigation** controls executed:

```
If g_intCurrentPage < 1 Then
    MsgBox "Index is empty"
    Exit Sub
End If
```

What didn't help a great deal was that the **Search** button actually set **g_intCurrentPage** to 0 before calling **SearchNext_Click**. With the new code installed, any click on the Search button caused the Index to become empty. All subsequent calls to Search and Navigation buttons then failed.

Dual Purpose Leads to Cross Purposes

The problem lay in the fact that Julie was trying to use the variable **g_intCurrentPage** for two different purposes. The variable was being used as a page indicator, which, if it was set to 0, indicated that the Index was empty; it was also being used to prime **cmdSearchNext_Click** when it was called as a routine from **cmdSearch**. Unfortunately, these uses caused a clash and led to some very strange test program behavior, which wasted a lot of Julie's time.

When she discovered what was causing the problem, Julie decided to use a private, infrastructure variable called **i_booCalledFromSearch** which, if **True**, indicated to **cmdSearchNext_Click** that it was being called from **cmdSearch**. As long as **cmdSearchNext_Click** reset the variable to **False** before it had completed its function, **i_booCalledfromSearch** would be **True** only when the Search button was invoked and called **cmdSearchNext_Click**.

To sort out the clash, follow these steps:

Step 1

Create an infrastructure variable in the general section of the test program called **i_booCalledFromSearch**, as follows:

```
' VIEWER INFRASTRUCTURE DATA: Search control, V1.0
Private i_booCalledFromSearch As Boolean
```

Change **cmdSearch_Click**, as follows:

```
Private Sub cmdSearch_Click()
' VIEWER INFRASTRUCTURE EVENT HANDLER:
' Search Functionality, Search from Page 1, V1.0
' -----------------------
If g_intCurrentPage < 1 Then
    MsgBox "Index is empty"
    Exit Sub
End If

i_booCalledFromSearch = True
Call cmdSearchNext_Click

End Sub
```

Add the following, highlighted code to **cmdSearchNext_Click**:

```
If g_intCurrentPage < 1 Then
    MsgBox "Index is empty"
    Exit Sub
End If

If i_booCalledFromSearch = True Then
    g_intCurrentPage = 0
    i_booCalledFromSearch = False
End If
```

The rest of the code continues without change.

Viewer Module Development Completed

By the end of the week, Julie had completed the tasks she had "signed on for." As we had anticipated, Archie had taken a bit longer to get over the knocks and bruises than he had first expected, and he was unable to get into the office at all that week.

Julie was convinced that the design specifications had made coding much simpler because much of the logic had already been worked out, albeit at a high level. She was quite sure that, without the specifications, she would not have been able to complete all the work that she ended up having to take on.

We were now ready for system integration—and on time, thanks to the amount of contingency time that we had built into the plan to accommodate 50 percent of the programming staff suddenly not being available.

System Integration

At this stage in a project, all the pieces of the jigsaw puzzle have been constructed, and it's time to put them together.

General Routines

First, you need to make a list of all the general routines you have created. These routines are held in libraries, so integration will simply be a question of adding the library module to the project. In the case study, we had only one library for the viewer. When we came to integration of the editors, more than one library would be available, so we needed to determine which libraries would be required for the system (program) we would be integrating.

Remember, all the general routines are independent of the program into which they will be integrated. Some routines are pure functions, and the rest are GUI related. When a function is GUI related, the association with the program's actual screen objects will be made via the calling arguments at runtime.

Integrating the Forms

From the requirements capture, you have the forms. You can now integrate all the form layouts to create the required panels with their embedded screen controls. In the case study, for the viewer, we have a Title Selection panel and a Viewer Mode panel. We need to organize the forms so that we have three layers of screens, as the case study will define.

The Definitive Event List

You can now create a definitive list of all the infrastructure event handlers that the system requires. Much of the code will have been developed in the test programs, so you can identify which events you can integrate immediately, and which will require development of additional code to complete integration.

For example, in the case study, we can identify events required to switch the key and search selection panels on and off. Archie and Julie did not create this code at module-development time, so they will have to create it at system-integration time.

Setting Up the State Transitions

You can now set up sufficient infrastructure code and data to allow the program to run, and to let you switch from one program state to another. In the case of the viewer, we will set up sufficient button click-event handlers so that we can switch among the Title Selection mode, Page View mode, and Workbench mode in a manner consistent with the state-transition diagrams we developed during analysis. The result is that we now have an *operational shell*.

Adding the Infrastructure Code and Data

After you have constructed the program shell, you can start integrating the infrastructure modules and data that you created during development. This integration will be a matter of copying the infrastructure event handler, the infrastructure GUI routine, or the infrastructure data structure from the appropriate test program to the target program. The result gives you substantial functionality, but elements of infrastructure code will still be missing. From the list of required event handlers, you can determine what is missing and fill in the gaps.

Preliminary Testing

After everything has been integrated, the programmers can perform their first pass at system testing. This testing can consist of rerunning module tests, suitably modified to accommodate the fact that the system is now integrated. The ultimate test is to run the acceptance test scripts, although having sufficient time to do this thoroughly is unlikely. Nevertheless, running as much of the test scripts as possible is highly advisable.

Hand Over to Testing Department

After the programmers and any project-management resource involved deem the system ready for full-scale, formal, system testing, they hand over the system to the testing department. At this stage, all the code is frozen and marked at Level 1. From now on, any modifications to a module, general routine, public data, or infrastructure routine or data must be made using the full change-control procedure for updating code. We'll discuss this standard in more detail in the next chapter.

Techniques for Copying Code

You can extract the infrastructure routines and data created in the test programs for integration into the final program in all sorts of ways. I describe a simple technique here that involves two instances of VB running on the PC.

First, load the VB development environment, and load the main program that is being integrated. In the case study, this program will be the E-MagViewer. Minimize this version of VB. Next, load a second instance of the VB environment, and load the test program that contains the required infrastructure modules. You now have two versions of the VB design environment, and you can switch between the two.

Copying Infrastructure GUI Routines

Find the required infrastructure GUI routine in the test program, and highlight all the code, including the subroutine or function declaration and everything up to and including the **END** statement. Place the code lines in the paste buffer by using Ctrl+C.

Now, maximize the first instance of VB, which contains the main program. Place the cursor beneath the **END** statement of any routine in the form in which you want to place the code from the test program. Use Ctrl+V to copy the code in the paste buffer into the target form. The general GUI routine has now been integrated into the final program.

Copying Infrastructure Data

You copy infrastructure data in exactly the same way as you copy an infrastructure GUI routine. Move the data structure into the paste buffer, and then integrate it into the final program.

Copying Infrastructure Event Handlers

Copying infrastructure event handlers is slightly different from copying infrastructure GUI routines. After you place the required screen control onto the final program's form, the event handler is created, even though it is empty. To populate the event handler, all you have to do is go to the instance of VB that contains the test program, locate the event handler, and highlight all the lines from beneath the first subroutine declaration through the last line immediately before the **END** statement. **NB** do not include the **END** statement in the selected code.

Next, invoke the instance of VB that contains the final program, and locate the empty event handler. You can now populate the event handler from the paste buffer by placing the cursor just beneath the subroutine declaration and pressing Ctrl+V.

Return to the Case Study:
Viewer System Integration

On Monday of Week 3, in the development phase, the start of the seventh project week, we were back to full strength. Archie's bruises and sprains had subsided, and his doctor had given him a clean bill of health. We were all relieved to see him back at work.

Thanks to all our contingency time, we had still managed to come in on time with the development of all the viewer modules. The first thing to do now was to check the inventory. We had all the general modules developed in **ViewerLib**, and a variety of infrastructure code and data currently embedded in the test programs.

Figure 8.11 shows the final state of **ViewerLib**. Julie had taken over **ViewerLib** after the previous reconciliation, and this version represented the sum of both programmers' work.

The state of the infrastructure elements, still embedded in their test programs, was as shown in Figure 8.12.

Next, we looked at the viewer layout to see what event handlers we still needed. To determine this, we used the screen layouts that we had developed for the viewer, back in analysis, to determine what we needed. Figure 8.13 shows the result.

A code review also revealed that the **Search** event handlers were not setting the hourglass on and off to indicate that the function might take some time in a lengthy book.

Status of ViewerLib

Module (sub/function/data structure)	Type	Status	Version	Owner
Viewer Screen Definitions Data	Data	FINAL	1.0	
Title Index Data Structure	Data	FINAL	1.0	
Page Index Data Structure	Data	FINAL	1.0	
Runtime Container Dimensions and Position	Data	FINAL	1.0	
LoadAndDisplayImage	GEN GUI	FINAL	1.0	
Size Picture	GEN	FINAL	1.0	
LoadAndPlayVideo	GEN GUI	FINAL	1.0	
OpenAndReadTextIntoMemory	GEN	FINAL	1.0	
LoadAndDisplayText	GEN GUI	FINAL	1.0	
LoadAndPlaySound	GEN GUI	FINAL*	1.0	
VideoOrPicture	GEN	FINAL	1.0	
LocateDelimiter	GEN	FINAL	1.0	
CheckAgainstKeys	GEN	FINAL	1.0	
ClearPageIndexMemory	GEN	FINAL	1.0	
ClearTitleIndexMemory	GEN	FINAL	1.0	
ExamineIndex	GEN	FINAL	1.0	
ExtractFieldData	GEN	FINAL	1.0	
PopulateCombo	GEN GUI	FINAL	1.0	
ReadInPageIndex	GEN	FINAL	1.0	
ReadInTitleIndex	GEN	FINAL	1.0	
ReadPageIndexHeader	GEN	FINAL	1.0	

*See issue log; issue 01 for outstanding, nonurgent problem with LoadAndDisplaySound.

Figure 8.11
Final state of **ViewerLib**.

Installation of Viewer Forms

In this section, you can see how Archie and Julie started integrating the forms we developed back in analysis to make up the viewer program. They took all the forms and created a single program that contained the two picture controls—**picTitleSelectionPanel** (which housed all the Title-Selection screen objects) and **picFrontPanel** (which housed all the View mode screen objects). They set up the toolbar for the Workbench mode on the form itself, plus the text and image controls to be used in that mode.

To save you from all this work, complete the following steps to create the blank viewer, once again using the CD:

Step 1

Create a directory on drive C: and call the directory DEV_EViewer. Open a new VB EXE project.

Status of Viewer Infrastructure Modules

Infrastructure Routine	Source	Status	Version
SetUpFormat1	PageDisplay Test 2	FINAL	1.0
SetUpFormat2	PageDisplay Test 2	FINAL	1.0
SetUpFormat3	PageDisplay Test 2	FINAL	1.0
CaptureViewerDesignParameters	PageDisplay Test 2	FINAL	1.0
DisplayPage	PageDisplay Test 2	FINAL	1.0
SetUpTheData	PageDisplay Test 2	FINAL	1.0
WB DragDrop Event Handlers	WB Test 3	FINAL	1.0
WB Toolbar Button Event Handlers	WB Test 3	FINAL	1.0
WB Print Page Event Handler	WB Test 3	FINAL	1.0
Navigation Button Event Handlers	Nav Test 1	FINAL	1.0
Search Button Event Handlers	Search Test 2	FINAL	1.0
SearchForIt	Search Test 2	FINAL	1.0
i_booCalledFromSearch	Search Test 2	FINAL	1.0

Figure 8.12
Final state of viewer infrastructure elements developed.

List of Event Handlers Still to be Developed for the Viewer

Event Handler	Notes
Form_Unload	Will Contain All Code Required to Shut Down Viewer.
Form_Load	Will Contain All Required Initialization Code; Invokes Title Selection Mode.
New Disk Button	Set up and Call ReadTitleIndex for E:\E-MagBook\Title.idx.
Open E-MagBook Button	Set up and Call ReadInPageIndex with Selected Index File Reference, Switch to Viewer Mode.
WBN Button	Set Image and Text Defaults, Switch to WB Mode.
WBO Button	Switch to WB Mode.
Titles Button	Switch to Title Selection Mode.
Text Button	Switch off Keys and Select Panels, Set Big Text for Ref.
Select Button	Switch off Keys, Switch on Select Panel, Set Small Text for Ref.
Keys Button	Switch off Select, Switch on Keys Panel, Set Small Text for Ref.
Reload Button	Call Display Page to Reload All Elements.
WB Toolbar End Button	Switch to Viewer Mode.

Figure 8.13
List of event handlers the viewer program required.

Step 2

Load the form **DEV_BankEViewer\frmEViewer.frm** from the CD into your new project, using the Project drop-down menu option Add Form.

Step 3

Using the Project drop-down menu option, click Remove Form1. Now, run the program. When you do this, VB will tell you in an error message that no main routine exists:

"Must have startup form or a sub Main( )"

Click OK, and a form comes up, as shown in Figure 8.14. Click the Startup Object combo box, and you will get a list of two items (as shown in Figure 8.14), one of which is **EViewer**. Select **EViewer**, and click the OK button. The program will now start up. Because the program contains no code, it can't do a lot.

Step 4

Save the form and project, calling them both **EViewer**, and place them in C:\DEV_EViewer. You can remove the red label used to identify the form.

Form EViewer

The GUI consists of three layers, which correspond to Title Selection mode, Page View mode, and Workbench mode. In addition, a panel located on the form contains the four text boxes that will be used in the Page Index Editor. Have a good look around the form, and familiarize yourself with the objects, all of which should be familiar from the requirements document and the form prototypes. Move the two, main, picture-container controls by picking them up at their top, left-hand corners. If you try to pick them up from anywhere else, you might click

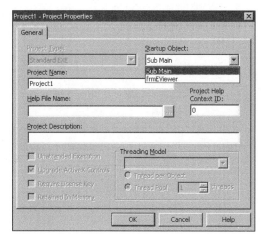

Figure 8.14
VB Project Properties form for selecting the startup object in a newly loaded form.

one of the controls within the container, which will let you move only that object and not the picture container as a whole.

Layer 1—Title Selection Mode

The first layer is contained within **picTitleSelectionPanel**, which houses all the screen objects for the Title Selection mode of operation. You can see the screen in Figure 8.15. You can switch **picTitleSelectionPanel** on and off simply by setting its **visible** property; this action allows Title Selection mode to be enabled or disabled.

Layer 2—Page View Mode

The picture control **picFrontPanel** contains the second layer, which consists of all the objects to make up the Page View mode of operation, as Figure 8.16 shows. Note that the key panel is on view in the top right of Figure 8.16. The search selection criteria panel is located immediately underneath the key panel in this figure and therefore not visible. All these objects should be familiar to you from the screen prototyping and design.

Note also the two red lines on **picFrontPanel**. These lines are the two-shape controls set up to indicate the maximum height and width of the Text Book or Picture Album viewing areas. I defined these objects in Chapter 6.

Layer 3—Workbench Mode

The final layer consists of the form itself, when **picFrontPanel** and **picTitleSelectionPanel** are both invisible (or moved out of the way in the design environment). Figure 8.17 depicts this layer and shows the Workbench toolbar, the image control, and text box.

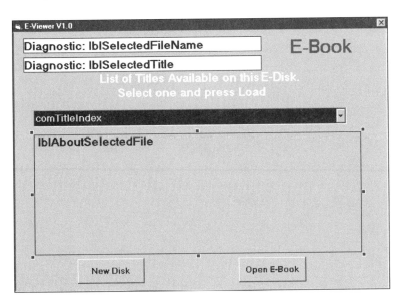

Figure 8.15
Layer 1 of the viewer program, which consists of the Title-Selection container and associated screen objects.

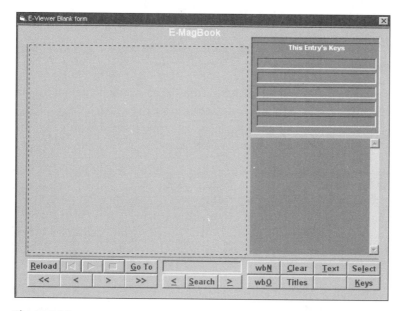

Figure 8.16

Layer 2 of the viewer program, which consists of **picFrontPanel** acting as a container for all the Page View mode screen objects. Note that the selection criteria panel is underneath the key panel and therefore masked.

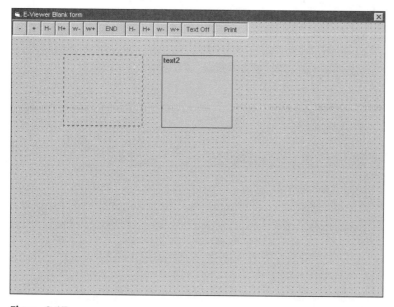

Figure 8.17

Layer 3 of the viewer, which consists of the form and the Workbench objects.

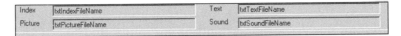

| Index | txtIndexFileName | | Text | txtTextFileName |
| Picture | txtPictureFileName | | Sound | txtSoundFileName |

Figure 8.18
The diagnostic panel located on the main form.

Diagnostic Aids

Figure 8.18 shows the diagnostic panel, which is situated on the main form, but below the 480-pixel level. The panel contains four text boxes to house the Index file name and the names of the multimedia files loaded on a given page. If you recall, this part of the GUI is required only for the page editor. However, Archie and Julie set up the diagnostic panel right from the start because it would be a useful debug facility while we were integrating the viewer components.

Viewer Mode Switching

Next, Archie and Julie installed the infrastructure code that allows the program to switch between the three modes of operation, as defined in the state transition diagram we created during analysis. Complete the following steps to install the required code:

NOTE: *Be careful when moving the two main panels around the form. Make sure you pick them up at their top, left-hand corners for dragging and dropping. If you try to pick them up elsewhere, you might instead move one of the embedded controls.*

Step 1

Add the following code to the Titles button on **picFrontPanel**:

```
Private Sub cmdLoadNewTitles_Click()
' VIEWER INFRASTRUCTURE EVENT HANDLER:
' Select Title mode, V1.0
' -----------------------
' Disable WB objects
   picPictureToolBar.Visible = False
   imgImage2.Visible = False
   txtText2.Visible = False

'Disable Page View Mode
   picFrontPanel.Visible = False

'Enable Title Selection
   picTitleSelectionPanel.Visible = True

End Sub
```

The code switches the program from Page View mode to Title Selection mode simply by making the appropriate screen objects visible or invisible.

Step 2

Load this code into the **wbO** button on **picFrontPanel**:

```
Private Sub cmdOldWorkBench_Click()
' VIEWER INFRASTRUCTURE EVENT HANDLER:
' Select WB mode, V1.0
' Image and text box set to previous dimensions
' ------------------------
' SWITCH ON WB MODE (OLD SETTINGS)
    picPictureToolBar.Visible = True
    imgImage2.Visible = True
    txtText2.Visible = True

' Hide Page View Mode
    picFrontPanel.Visible = False

' Hide Title Selection
    picTitleSelectionPanel.Visible = False

End Sub
```

This code switches the program from Page View mode to WB mode simply by switching off the two main picture containers and switching on the WB screen objects.

Step 3

Load this code into the wbN Button on **picFrontPanel**:

```
Private Sub cmdWorkbench_Click()
' VIEWER INFRASTRUCTURE EVENT HANDLER:
' Select WB mode, V1.0
' ------------------------
' SWITCH ON WB MODE (NEW SETTINGS)
    picPictureToolBar.Visible = True
    imgImage2.Visible = True
    txtText2.Visible = True

'Hide Page View Mode
    picFrontPanel.Visible = False

' Hide Title Selection
    picTitleSelectionPanel.Visible = False

End Sub
```

This code switches the program from Page View mode to WB mode with default settings for the image and text controls, which are yet to be defined.

Step 4

Load this code into the Open E-Book button on **picTitleSelectionPanel**:

```
Private Sub cmdLoadIndex_Click()
' VIEWER INFRASTRUCTURE EVENT HANDLER:
' Open an E-MagBook, V1.0
' ------------------------
' Disable WB objects
   picPictureToolBar.Visible = False
   imgImage2.Visible = False
   txtText2.Visible = False

'Enable Page View Mode
   picFrontPanel.Visible = True

' Hide Title Selection
   picTitleSelectionPanel.Visible = False

End Sub
```

Opening an E-MagBook consists of disabling the Workbench objects (they are almost certainly already disabled, but making sure they are does no harm), enabling the Page View mode panel, and disabling the Title Selection mode panel.

Step 5

Place this code into the **picPictureToolBar** button **END**:

```
Private Sub cmdToolEnd_Click()
' VIEWER INFRASRUCTURE EVENT HANDLER:
' End Wb mode, V1.0
' ------------------------
' Disable WB objects
   picPictureToolBar.Visible = False
   imgImage2.Visible = False
   txtText2.Visible = False

'Enable Page View Mode
   picFrontPanel.Visible = True

' Hide Title Selection
   picTitleSelectionPanel.Visible = False

End Sub
```

The code switches the program from WB mode back to Page View mode. Note that this code is currently the same as the code for **cmdLoadIndex**.

Step 6

And this code goes into the main form's load event:

```
Private Sub Form_Load()
' VIEWER INFRASTRUCTURE EVENT HANDLER:
' Start up, V1.0
' ---------------------------
' Set Form dimensions to 640 by 480 and position in
' top left of screen for screens > 640 by 480
frmEViewer.Width = 9660
frmEViewer.Height = 7260
frmEViewer.Top = 0
frmEViewer.Left = 0
' .......................................................
' Set WB objects
picPictureToolBar.Left = 0          ' make sure toolbar at top left
picPictureToolBar.Top = 0
picPictureToolBar.Visible = False
imgImage2.Visible = False
txtText2.Visible = False
' .......................................................
' Set Title Selection
picTitleSelectionPanel.Width = 9580     ' Fits 640 by 480
picTitleSelectionPanel.Height = 6880
picTitleSelectionPanel.Left = 0          ' container at top left
picTitleSelectionPanel.Top = 0
picTitleSelectionPanel.Visible = True  ' start up mode
' .......................................................
' Set Page View to same as title selection panel
picFrontPanel.Width = picTitleSelectionPanel.Width
picFrontPanel.Height = picTitleSelectionPanel.Height
picFrontPanel.Left = picTitleSelectionPanel.Left
picFrontPanel.Top = picTitleSelectionPanel.Top
picFrontPanel.Visible = False
' .......................................................
' position file reference diagnosic panel
picDiagnosticPanel.Top = picFrontPanel.Height
End Sub
```

This section of code will be the very first code executed when the form loads. The code ensures that the panels are in their correct positions, regardless of what was done to them at design time, and that WB and Page View objects are switched off and the title selection panel switched on. This code will expand as we start to integrate more functionality into the program and startup requirements become obvious. We had to obtain many of the widths and heights by trial and error, setting the screen to 640×480 pixels and trying out the program.

Testing Mode Switching

If you now run the program, the startup code will invoke Title Index mode. Sufficient infra-structure code is now installed to ensure that the containers are positioned correctly, and that, if you click Open E-MagBook, Page View mode will be selected. From here, you can invoke the Workbench, either by clicking wbN or wbO—currently, there is no difference between them. You can also return to Title Selection mode by clicking the Titles button in Page View mode.

Developing and testing mode switching were the fist things Archie and Julie did. They were able to log the following tests:

◆ *Test 1*—Program can switch between all three modes of operation as indicated by the state-transition diagrams for the viewer program.

◆ *Test 2*—Regardless of where **picTitleSelectionPanel**, **picFrontPanel**, and **picWBToolBar** are placed at design time, they are all locked to the top, left-hand corner of the form when they are visible.

◆ *Test 3*—Ensure program works satisfactorily on 640×480-pixel and 800×600-pixel screens.

Note that both image controls have been set up with no borders; consequently, during mode-switch testing, you won't see the image containers at all.

Backdrop Images

Finally, you will find two images called **BackDrop.bmp** and **BackDrop2.bmp** on the CD in directory **DEV_BlankEViewer**. Using the properties window of **picFrontPanel**, load **BackDrop** into the container. (Click the picture property, and then click the little button control that appears on the end of the line.)

Next, select the properties of **picTitleSelectionPanel**, and load **BackDrop2**. These are the images Samantha set up for the prototype. Now, run the program and see the difference the images make.

Installation of Title Selection Mode of Operation

The next thing Archie and Julie did was to install the final version of **ViewerLib** and get the Title-Index-load button to work. Clicking this button invokes the program to read in the Title Index file and populate the combo box with the titles. All the code is based on what we set up for Title Index testing. Follow these steps to install the facility:

Step 1

If you have been constructing the project from scratch, use the VB project menu's Add Mod-ule function to load your final version of **ViewerLib** into the project (this will be the version used with **SearchTest2**). Alternatively, add **ViewerLib_For_Integration.bas** from Julie's de-velopment area on the CD. If you do decide to use this version of the library, rename it **ViewerLib** after you have loaded it.

In the directory C:\DEV_EViewer, save the main form as **EViewer**, save the library as **ViewerLib**, and save the project as **EViewer**. Run the program to make sure the introduction of the library modules causes no errors.

Step 2

Add the following code to the New Disk button control on the Title Selection panel:

```
Private Sub cmdLoadNewIndex_Click()
' VIEWER INFRASTRUCTURE EVENT HANDLER:
' Get new Title Index,  V1.0
' ------------------------
Dim booResult As Boolean
Dim strFileName As String
Dim intLoop As Integer

Do
      ' Attempt to load from E:
 strFileName = "E:\E-MAGBOOK\TITLE.IDX"
 booResult = ReadInTitleIndex(strFileName)
 If booResult = True Then  Exit Do

 MsgBox "Cannot find a Title Index. Please load an E-MagBook disk"
 Exit sub
Loop

Call PopulateCombo(comTitleIndex)

End Sub
```

This code is taken, with slight modifications, from the Title Index Test 2 program. In Julie's and Archie's version of the **cmdLoadNewIndex_Click**, shown above, the default load device is drive E:, the removable disk. You're not likely to have a removable drive on drive E:. Consequently, I suggest that you change the "E:" reference in the above code to "C:" so the program won't fail to run.

Step 3

To get the program to read in the default Index on startup, we can place a call to the "New Disk" click-event handler in the form's startup event. Simply add this code to end of the **Form_load** event handler, just before the **END** statement:

```
' Load the default Index in the current removable
Call cmdLoadNewIndex_Click
End Sub
```

The new code simply calls the event handler of the button, and the program loads the Title Index file.

Add this code to the click-event handler of the combo box:

```
Private Sub comTitleIndex_Click()
' VIEWER INFRASTRUCTURE EVENT HANDLER:
' Title Selected - show it. V1.0
' -----------------------------
' Populate screen objects with selection
lblSelectedFileName.Caption = g_strTitleFileName(comTitleIndex.ListIndex +
1)
lblSelectedTitle.Caption = g_strTitleTitle(comTitleIndex.ListIndex + 1)
lblAboutSelectedTitle.Caption =
g_strTitleDescription(comTitleIndex.ListIndex_
            + 1)
End Sub
```

This code is based on what Julie did in the title test program. However, the field names are not quite the same—a minor detail. Both **lblSelectedTitle** and **lblSelectedFileName** are diagnostic aids and are set invisible under normal conditions.

Tip

Be careful to make sure you set the preceding code in the click-event handler and not the change-event handler by mistake. If you insert the code into the change-event handler, nothing happens when you try to select a title.

Copy the whole of the E-MagBook directory from the CD onto your hard disk.

Testing Title Selection Mode

We can now run the program, and it will attempt to load an Index from the form's startup code. The program will read in the Title Index supplied with the CD, which you have copied onto your C: drive.

One thing Julie spotted was that, if the program failed to find an Index, the combo box was still set up with the content of the previous Index. This behavior was clearly wrong. She looked up her test logs at development and realized that she had not actually tested that combination of events. To rectify the shortcoming, she and Archie added this line to the top of the **cmdLoadNewIndex_Click** handler, before the start of the **Do** statement:

```
comTitleIndex.Clear
```

Installation of Viewer Page Index Handling

Now, we're going to see some real progress as we complete the installation of the viewer's **Page Index Handling**:

Step 1

Add the following line to the form's load event, just before it calls **cmdNewIndex_Click**:

```
Call CaptureViewerDesignParameters
```

If you recall, this routine, created for the **DisplayPage** test program, sets up the design-time parameter defaults for the height, width, and position of the image container and text box for the three formats.

Step 2

Add the following new code to the Open E-MagBook button's click-event handler (new code is highlighted):

```
Public Sub cmdLoadIndex_Click()
' VIEWER INFRASTRUCTURE EVENT HANDLER:
' Open an E-MagBook, V1.0
' --------------------
Dim strTemp As String
Dim booResult As Boolean

strTemp = lblSelectedFileName.Caption
booResult = ReadInPageIndex(strTemp)
If booResult = False Then GoTo Errhandler

Select Case g_intFormatType
    Case 1
            Call SetUpFormat1
    Case 2
            Call SetUpFormat2
    Case 3
            Call SetUpFormat3
End Select

txtIndexFileName.Text = strTemp

' Disable WB objects
    picPictureToolBar.Visible = False
    imgImage2.Visible = False
    txtText2.Visible = False
```

```
'Enable Page View Mode
   picFrontPanel.Visible = True

'Disable Title Selection
   picTitleSelectionPanel.Visible = False

' Display page 1
g_intCurrentPage = 1
Call DisplayPage

Exit Sub
' ======================================================================
' come here if error encountered
Errhandler:
Call cmdLoadNewTitles_Click  ' re-invoke Title Selection
Exit Sub

End Sub
```

The code calls the appropriate format routine according to the setting in **g_intFormatType**. Note that, if an error occurs when reading the file, the code re-invokes the title selection mode via the Titles command button.

Step 3

Load another version of VB and load the **PageDisplay2** test project. Using copy and paste, extract the following GUI routines from the main form's general area, and place them into the general area of **frmEViewer**:

- **CaptureViewerDesignParameters**
- **SetFormat1**
- **SetFormat2**
- **SetFormat3**
- **DisplayPage**
- **SetUpTheData**

Because these routines are infrastructure, they were created directly in the test program's code area and not in **ViewerLib**.

Step 4

Load the video form created in testing the video play facility into the project using the AddModule option from the VB Project drop-down menu. You can also find the video form in **DEV_BlankEViewer** on the CD. Make sure that you save the video form as a file, *frmVideo*, in directory C:\DEV_EViewer.

If you haven't already done so, copy the whole of the E-MagBook directory from the CD to your hard disk. This action creates a complete set of E-MagBooks on your hard drive. You can now run the E-MagBook viewer program and see the first page of each title.

Testing Page Index Read

For some reason, both Julie and Archie were astonished to see the first page of each Page Index they tried display on screen when they ran the program. Of course, the code had already been thoroughly tested before they placed it in the viewer. Their success, however, was a clear testament to modular development. If you make your modules as self-contained as possible, and if you can test them in isolation and then install them into the final system, you know they will all be solid routines you can rely upon.

The two programmers tried different indexes of each type—Text Book, Picture Album, and Reference Book. The only issue that arose centered on the key panel. The key panel was always there, underneath the text box in Text Book format, on top of the album in Picture Album mode, and as required for the Reference Book format. We decided we would sort out the Text, Keys, and Select button controls next because they would resolve the issue, which was really an infrastructure-handling problem.

Installation of Text, Keys, and Select Button Handling

This procedure consists of installing code to handle the Text, Keys, and Select button controls in Page View mode. The code does, however, depend on the format in use. You can install the code Archie and Julie produced by following these steps:

Step 1

Add the following code to the Keys button click-event handler:

```
Private Sub cmdShowKeys_Click()
' VIEWER INFRASTRUCTURE EVENT HANDLER:
' Show key panel, V1.0
' --------------------
picSelectionPanel.Visible = False
picKeyPanel.Visible = True
If g_intFormatType = 3 Then
        txtText.Height = g_intHeight3
        txtText.Left = g_intOrigin3_Left
        txtText.Top = g_intOrigin3_Top
End If
picKeyPanel.ZOrder

End Sub
```

Whenever the user clicks the Keys button, this code switches off the selection panel (whether or not it was on screen) and switches on the key panel (even if it was already on screen). If Format 3 (Reference Book format) is in use, the code resizes the text box to fit under the key panel, as defined in the design specifications.

Step 2
This code goes into the Select button's click-event handler:

```
Private Sub cmdShowCriteria_Click()
' VIEWER INFRASTRUCTURE EVENT HANDLER:
' Show Select panel, 1.0
' ---------------------
picSelectionPanel.Visible = True
picKeyPanel.Visible = False
If g_intFormatType = 3 Then
        txtText.Height = g_intHeight3
        txtText.Left = g_intOrigin3_Left
        txtText.Top = g_intOrigin3_Top
End If
picSelectionPanel.ZOrder

End Sub
```

This code is the same as that for key-panel selection, except that, in this case, the selection panel is being set up.

Step 3
Finally, place this code into the Text button's click-event handler:

```
Private Sub cmdSizeText_Click()
' VIEWER INFRASTRUCTURE EVENT HANDLER: V1.0
' -----------------
picSelectionPanel.Visible = False
picKeyPanel.Visible = False
If g_intFormatType = 3 Then
        txtText.Height = g_intHeight2
        txtText.Left = g_intOrigin4_Left
        txtText.Top = g_intOrigin4_Top
End If

End Sub
```

Both panels are switched off, regardless of their actual states, and, if the format is 3, the text box's height is increased according to the design specifications.

Testing Text, Keys, and Select Button Handling

The program now allowed Archie and Julie to experiment with the three buttons. The program showed them that they needed to force a call to **cmdSizeText_Click** to clear both panels before opening a book—unless it was a Reference Book, in which case, a call to **cmdShowKeys** was required. To add this piece, place the following code

```
If g_intFormatType = 3 then
        Call cmdShowKeys_Click
Else
    cmdSizeText_Click
End If
```

in the click handler of the Open E-Book button control (**cmdLoadNewIndex_Click**) on the title selection panel, just before the following line:

```
picFrontPanel.Visible = True.
```

Julie and Archie were now able to load the first page of a Page Index file, switch the keys and/or the selection panel on and off, or remove both the keys and selections.

Installation of the Navigation and Search Functionality

Follow these steps to install the **Navigation** and **Search** modules:

Step 1

Set up a second copy of VB, and load the search test program, **SearchTest2**, into that copy.

Step 2

Copy the click-event-handler code of all the navigation and search buttons into the relevant button controls on the final version of the viewer.

Step 3

Copy the general routine **SearchForIt** from the search program into the general area of the viewer.

Testing Navigation and Search Functionality

If you have run the program using E-MagBook copied from the CD, you are testing against quite a sophisticated set of Page Indexes in E-MagBook. When Julie and Archie tested, they used a much more basic set of Test Indexes. As a consequence, you might notice problems with the program developed so far—problems that Julie and Archie missed when they did their preliminary testing.

For Julie and Archie, three minor problems surfaced. First, no sign of a page number appeared on the page-number label. Second, the messages placed in the comment label were not cleared when the next page was displayed. Finally, there was still no sign of an hourglass to indicate that a search was in progress. To rectify the problems, follow these steps:

Step 1
Add this line to the start of the **DisplayPage** routine:

```
lbCcommentLine.Caption = ""
```

Step 2
Add this line to the bottom of the **DisplayPage** routine:

```
lblCurrent.Caption = CStr(g_intCurrentPage)
```

Step 3
Create the following two infrastructure routines in **frmEViewer**'s general area:

```
Sub SwitchOnHourGlass()
' VIEWER INFRASTRUCTURE ROUTINE:
' Switch on the hourglass mouse pointer
frmEViewer.MousePointer = 11
End Sub
Sub SwitchOffHourGlass()
' VIEWER INFRASTRUCTURE ROUTINE:
' Switch off the hourglass mouse pointer
frmEViewer.MousePointer = 0
End Sub
```

Step 4
Place calls to **SwitchOnHourGlass** before any calls to **SearchForIt**. Place calls to **SwitchOffHourGlass** at the end of the Search buttons' event handlers. If in doubt, study **frmEViewer**'s search button event handlers from the CD.

Final Note
Inevitably, something will be missed in module development, but, as you can see, not many issues are surfacing in the case study. If you have noticed other errors or issues in your testing, be patient. Hopefully, when full-system testing gets under way, we will encounter the same issues and handle them systematically.

Installing the Workbench Facility
All the code to handle the Workbench is available in the Workbench test program, **WBTest3**, as infrastructure code. Follow these steps to install the complete facility in the viewer:

Load the Workbench test program into the second copy of VB. Copy the drag-and-drop related infrastructure data across to the general section of the viewer. Also, transfer the list of constants declared for image and text manipulation. Copy the **Form_DragDrop** event code from the test program to the **DragDrop** event handler of the viewer form.

Repeat Step 1 for the **DragDrop** code of the image control, **imgImage2**, and the text control, **txtText2**.

Now, repeat Step 1 for the **MouseMove** events in both image and text controls.

Now, copy all the infrastructure data structures from **WBTest3** to the viewer—including the drag-and-drop data structures and the constants used in the toolbar.

Replace all the code in the wbN command button's click-event handler with the following code:

```
Private Sub cmdWorkBench_Click()
' VIEWER INFRASTRUCTURE EVENT HANDLER:
' WB, V1.0
' ----------------
If g_intFormatType = 1 Then     ' Book format
        txtText2.Text = txtText.Text
        txtText2.Left = txtText.Left
        txtText2.Top = txtText.Top
        txtText2.Width = txtText.Width
        txtText2.Height = txtText.Height
        txtText2.Visible = True
        imgImage2.Visible = False
End If
```

In the section of code shown above, the page's text is copied from **txtText** to **txtText2** for Text Book formats. The position and dimensions are set up according to **txtText**. The control is then made visible, and the image control is made invisible.

In the next code snippet

```
If g_intFormatType = 2 Then     ' Album format
        imgImage2.Left = 200
        imgImage2.Top = 500
        imgImage2.Stretch = False
        imgImage2 = imgImageIt
```

```
        imgImage2.Stretch = True
        imgImage2.Visible = True
        txtText2.Visible = False
End If
```

the image is copied from **imgImageIt** into **imgImage2**, while the control's **Stretch** property is disabled. The control expands to the full size, and then the **Stretch** property is set to **False**. The text box is set invisible.

```
If g_intFormatType = 3 Then       ' Ref Book
        imgImage2.Left = 200
        imgImage2.Top = 500
        imgImage2.Stretch = False
        imgImage2 = imgImageIt
        imgImage2.Stretch = True
        imgImage2.Visible = True

        txtText2.Text = txtText.Text
        txtText2.Left = 1200
        txtText2.Top = 1200
        txtText2.Width = txtText.Width
        txtText2.Height = txtText.Height
        txtText2.Visible = True
End If
```

The above code sets the image as required in Picture Album mode and sets a small version of the text box.

```
' SWITCH ON WB MODE (NEW SETTINGS)
' Enable WB objects
    picPictureToolBar.Visible = True

'Hide Page View Mode
    picFrontPanel.Visible = False

' Hide Title Selection
    picTitleSelectionPanel.Visible = False

End Sub
```

Although this code is lengthy, it is very straightforward and structured in clearly self-contained blocks, so it's easy to view.

Step 6

Now, for the easier Workbench button, replace the original code with the following code:

```
Private Sub cmdOldWorkBench_Click()
' VIEWER INFRASTRUCTURE EVENT HANDLER:
' WB, V1.0
' ------------------
If g_intFormatType = 1 Then      ' Book format
        txtText2.Text = txtText.Text
        txtText2.Visible = True
        imgImage2.Visible = False
End If

If g_intFormatType = 2 Then       ' Album format
        imgImage2.Stretch = True
        imgImage2 = imgImageIt
        imgImage2.Visible = True
        txtText2.Visible = False
End If
```

If the image is to be loaded into whatever dimension was previously set up for it, the **Stretch** property obviously must be set to **True**, because the control must not automatically resize to the original image in this instance.

In the next code snippet

```
If g_intFormatType = 3 Then      ' Ref Book
        imgImage2.Stretch = true
        imgImage2 = imgImageIt
        imgImage2.Visible = True

        txtText2.Text = txtText.Text
        txtText2.Visible = True
End If

' SWITCH ON WB MODE (OLD SETTINGS)
' Enable WB objects
    picPictureToolBar.Visible = True

'Hide Page View Mode
    picFrontPanel.Visible = False

' Hide Title Selection
    picTitleSelectionPanel.Visible = False

End Sub
```

as a whole, the above code section follows that of the wbN control, with the exception that, in the above code, no changes are made to the position or dimensions of the objects.

Step 7

From the **WBTest3** program, copy all the code from the toolbar's click-event handlers to those of the viewer program, with the exception of **END**, which we have already set up. Make sure that the **DragMode** property of both the **Image** and the **Text Box** controls is set to **True**.

Archie and Julie had now completed the first drop of the image viewer. They took the whole day to achieve this because, quite sensibly, they insisted on performing tests to make sure that each phase of integration had gone correctly. After they were satisfied they had bolted the basic components together successfully, they declared that the program was ready for system testing.

Preparation for System Testing

System testing is exactly what it says: You check the completed system as if you were a user. In the development phase, module testing should have provided solid, robust modules, tested in isolation. Now, we were using the program for the first time.

While the programmers usually perform module testing, as I've said before, the person who wrote a given piece of software is usually the worst possible person to test that software. You really need someone totally objective who doesn't understand the code—in fact, the person doesn't need to understand programming at all. Testers require only knowledge of the application. They must understand what the application is all about from a user's point of view. Clearly, testers need to be computer literate, and proficient with mouse and keyboard, but that's it. The more they know about the underlying code, the less use they are.

Consequently, Julie and Archie didn't do the system testing. They observed the process so they could fix any problems and assist with clarification of functional definitions where there were issues. We used one of our best testers, known in the company as "the Application Killer." Her real name is Anne, and you could not imagine a milder individual—until you put her in front of a monitor and tell her to break the program. She follows the prescribed tests, but she does more than that. She takes any testing job on as a challenge to find a program's weakness. If the test script instructs her to enter a number into a data field, the first thing she does is enter a string of alpha characters. She is very good at doing what the programmer doesn't expect a user to do—and that's the difference between good and mediocre testing.

The Test Scripts

In Chapter 3, we defined a template for a test specification. This template consisted of a meaningful title, a reference to what functionality was being tested, a set of preconditions that must be met before starting the test, the steps to be executed, and the results. The specification then culminated in a conclusion.

Together with the test specification, we also defined a test sheet, which would contain the formal result, which indicated when the test was conducted, who conducted the test, and the test results. A member of the testing department—Anne, in fact—had created the test scripts in parallel with the design. She had spent a day reading the requirements specification to get up to speed with the application domain detail, and then she had used the scenarios to form test specifications.

The Function of Test Scripts

The primary function of formal, acceptance test scripts is to prove to the customer that you have supplied what the customer required. In other words, you have produced software that fulfills the needs defined in the requirements specification.

You will use the test scripts to test the system and find any bugs, although the test scripts won't be the only tool you use. When you hand over the system to the client, you don't want the test specifications to locate bugs; you want the specifications to verify functionality and, through their successful use, demonstrate robustness.

Hand-Over of the Software

The next step in the project is for the software department to hand over the system to the testing department. All the code is frozen and marked as Version 1.0, as is the released system. From now on, the only changes that can be made to the code in the software will be under strict change-control procedures. In the case study, the E-MagBook viewer is now ready for system testing.

Chapter 9
Testing and Support

In this chapter, we will look at system testing and acceptance testing, and how to manage both activities, which are quite different in nature. We'll then discuss how to set up support for an application that you have out in the field, whether the application is with one or many customers.

In the case study, we were starting the seventh week of the project. Archie and Julie had put together a completed viewer, which worked. Despite Archie's accident, we were on schedule. In this chapter, we will look at the system testing of the viewer by our own staff, followed by Monty's acceptance testing.

The case study will help you appreciate how the issues arising from system and acceptance testing differ; system testing is concerned more with bugs, and acceptance testing deals more with expectations and interpretation of requirements. Both types of testing are dependent on the acceptance test scripts that we started to develop from the scenarios, which we discussed earlier in the book. Finally, we'll use the case study to help illustrate aspects of support.

System Testing

The testing department will use the acceptance tests only as a guideline for any system testing they must perform. In fact, testers will be far more rigorous than the formal specifications require. They will hunt for bugs at every available opportunity. They may deviate from the formal test specifications if they spot something during testing that needs further examination. The system testing process is thus far less regimented than the acceptance testing in the respect that a tester can deviate from the scripts in the pursuit of bugs. After the developers hand over the system to the testing department, the testers take complete control over the software; from that point on, they will document all the software's failings.

Test Management

The testers can quickly produce lists of things they regard as bugs. The big question is how will the activity be managed to avoid swamping the developers. Someone must closely monitor the issues that accumulate and assess the issue type and its severity. The problems need to be fed to the developers in batches, concentrating on the serious errors first.

When the developers have had to address a batch of issues, they will need to put out a new software release. The software will then need to be retested. Initially, testing can concentrate on the issues that caused the rework, but it doesn't end there. They might need to retest the whole system to ensure that the fixes introduced into the system haven't adversely affected functionality that previously worked.

Someone needs to take charge of system testing. Taking charge involves monitoring the issues that arise, categorizing the issues, calling a halt to testing at a suitable time, and ensuring that the developers do any necessary rework. After the fixes are released, this person must manage testing of the fixes and system retesting as a whole. To do all this successfully requires a liaison and cooperation between the head of the testing team and the head of the development team.

A Model for System Testing

Figure 9.1 shows a model for system testing. Notice how this model—like most of the situations we have encountered—is heavily based on iteration.

The model's purpose is to provide a manageable environment in which to test and fix problems. The alternative is a "free for all" in which a tester yells, "I've got a problem," a developer fixes the problem, another tester yells, "I've got a problem I didn't have before," a developer fixes it, and so on. Total chaos. No one knows what's being fixed and which fixes are causing new problems. Let's look at key steps of the model in detail.

Development Creates a New Release

At some point, after the software has initially been developed, the head of development must release the software for system testing. This release occurs when the developers are satisfied that they have completed testing their modules and successfully integrated those modules, and that any additional system testing was also successful. The first release of software to the testers is Development Release, Version 1.0.

System Testing

In system testing, the testers will log every issue they encounter. An issue can be a genuine bug, which causes the software to "fall over," or crash; a nonconformity with the requirement specifications; or an aspect of the GUI that the tester regards as unfriendly—issues can be all sorts of things. The tester simply logs the detail of anything that he or she thinks is a problem.

At some point, any further testing might not be possible until the issue log is resolved. Alternatively, some errors might be so serious that they need immediate sorting, even though testing on the failed software can continue in other unrelated areas of functionality. Testers must document, and management must assess and prioritize, each issue. How serious is the fault—is it a showstopper? How easily can the fault be fixed? Will the problem have an

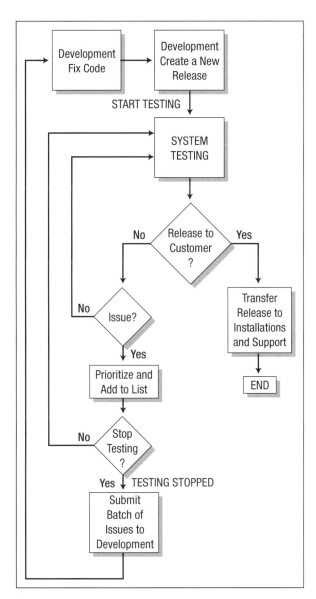

Figure 9.1
A simple model for system testing.

impact on the release schedule? Eventually, an issue list is frozen, and testing is stopped and not restarted until the software has been fixed and rereleased.

Issue Assessment

As frequently as necessary, management assesses the growing issues log. Each issue is assigned a category (for example, minor or major), or given a numerical value that represents its seriousness on a scale from 1 through 5, for example. Minor issues are not showstoppers and might well be cosmetic. For example, the tester might not like the way in which an error condition is presented to the user. Driving that back into development as a major issue is pointless when the system is perfectly usable. Such an issue does not prevent the system from being used according to the requirements specification; it doesn't cause the program to crash. Testing can, therefore, continue.

Alternatively, a breech of the requirements specification or a bug that causes the program to crash is a major issue. Clearly, such faults need to be rectified as soon as possible. Whether continuing testing is sensible depends on the nature of the fault discovered. Everyone must remember that the software is being used for the first time. For the first time, people who had no part in the software development are trying out the programs. These testers will do things to the software that the developers didn't try or didn't think would be done. Testing involves doing both the expected and the unexpected. For example, let's say a tester is presented with a data field into which he or she is expected to enter a number. The first thing the tester will do is enter a series of alpha characters, and then click the OK button.

Unfortunately, what is an issue is not always apparent. When an issue centers on the meaning of terms used in the document, having a domain expert available to discuss matters of functionality or to interpret the requirements specification is vital. The issue might also have nothing to do with the released software, but might be the result of the testing system's hardware or software environment. For example, the testers might be using an older version of the proprietary database system than the programmers used in development, and, consequently, incompatibility issues manifest as bugs. The developers might be the best people to assess such a fault, or your support staff might be better placed to determine the nature of the problem. Assessing such issues might involve liaison among developers, testers, and the support team—and all this liaison effort needs to be managed.

NOTE: *System testing is a busy time. Many things are being tried out for the first time. Everything about the system is new to everyone—testers, coders, support staff, and managers. As a result, a methodical approach is very important at this stage—without such support, chaos reigns supreme.*

The prompt and accurate assessment of issues is a vital aspect to managing a software development's system-testing phase.

Release to Customer?

If all issues have been resolved, the testers are happy, and the developers are happy, you can release the software to the client. Unfortunately, the process is rarely quite that simple. You might need to make a business decision to release even though a host of minor issues still need to be resolved. For example, a spelling mistake in a message is not a showstopper, but it is something you must eventually rectify. A batch of spelling mistakes is no reason to hold up acceptance testing.

A number of stakeholders need to be involved in making the final decision to release the software to the client. The development manager, the testing manager, and the project manager, respectively, represent the software, quality assurance, and commercial aspects of a project. The software must be evaluated from all these perspectives before the final decision is made—Are we ready to release this software to the customer for acceptance testing? After the decision to release has been made, the release code is transferred to the installations/support department to handle the actual process.

Stop Testing

The other key decision point in the testing model we've been looking at is when to send the software back to development with an issue list to be addressed. Usually, the testing and development managers together can assess when to call a halt, but a good project manager will get into that decision-making process as well.

A planned period of time exists in which testing must be completed. Clearly, the schedule is vital to the project and must not be disrupted. Decisions must be made that involve a mixture of business reality, accepted levels of quality, and seriousness of issues. Let's now look at the testing model in use in the case study.

The Case Study:

System Testing

The first thing that Anne, the head of testing, did was to reread all the test scripts, making particular note of the preconditions. She had already read up on the project by looking at the requirements documentation and the application scenarios when she undertook production of the test scripts. She was, therefore, quite knowledgeable about the viewer already, even though she had never seen the program working. (Anne's familiarity with the software at this stage was another tribute to the nature of the documentation we had produced in Phases 1 and 2 of the System Development Life Cycle (SDLC).)

Test Title and Page Indexes

Anne asked Archie and Julie to help her prepare some Title and Page Indexes. She got the hang of the format quite quickly, thanks to the design documentation definitions. In no time, she was developing some comprehensive Indexes using the Windows Notepad editor. Samantha had already supplied a number of images and text pages that varied in length, so, armed with all these, Anne was able to put together a sizeable cross-section of page content for each format type.

For example, she selected images that were much bigger than the Picture Album container area, and she selected images that were tiny, so she had one extreme to the other. Using the Windows Paint package, she also created some images that had only one dimension bigger than the container area, and so on. Anne was very good at providing variations that would stretch the system. She made careful notes of which Index was best suited for which test—and all this was before she had even started testing. In Anne's words, "Preparation for testing is everything."

Test Hardware

The PC Anne was testing on contained a removable drive E: and supported an 800×600-pixel monitor, which could be switched to 640×480 pixels. We would not be able to test on a genuine E-MagBook until acceptance testing. We had already agreed with Monty that, if the viewer worked on a PC, we had a basis for delivering the completed program. If we had problems with the viewer on a genuine E-MagBook, Monty would still accept the software demonstrated on a standard PC and sort out the issues later on the actual E-MagBook.

The First Pass of System Testing

Archie and Julie handed over Development Version 1.0 of the viewer program to Anne on the Wednesday of project Week 7. Anne started familiarizing herself with the software that day and then began testing in earnest. Anne treated the test specifications that she was given as absolute minimum. In addition to doing each test, she performed a large number of variations on each step, which provided a much more comprehensive degree of testing than the specifications alone achieved. At the end of her first session, Anne had a series of issues she wanted to discuss so that we could classify them and take appropriate action. On Thursday morning, we discussed the issue list that Anne had compiled.

The First Issue List

We all—Archie, Julie, Anne, and myself—assembled to discuss Anne's issues. We would classify each problem as a Level 1 (minor) through Level 3 (to be fixed ASAP) issue. Our strategy would be to clear up all Level 3 issues and as many Level 2 issues as practical before we handed the software back to Anne. We would then tackle the Level 1 issues, although these could wait if the schedule demanded.

Overall, Anne believed that the program was quite solid, because she had not had any occurrences of lockups or total failures in almost a day of solid testing. The issues she did have ranged from cosmetic improvements to genuine bugs.

Although Archie and Julie looked a little apprehensive, they clearly had developed a good professional relationship with Anne and did not see her as a threat. This comment might sound odd, but, as a rule, developers don't like being shown bugs of their own making. To get the best out of both disciplines, a good working relationship between developers and testers is important.

NOTE: *An important point to remember is that respect must be earned.*

Issue: Go Start/Go End Inconsistency

The first issue Anne had logged was inconsistency in how the software handled **Go To Start** and **Go To End** pages, compared with how it handled the **Next** and **Previous** functions. Continuing to use the Next button eventually would get her to the last page in a book. If she clicked Next again—that is, she was already at the end of the book—the program would tell her, "Already at End of Index." The same principle applied to the Previous button when she was already on the first page. Anne felt that the Go To Start and Go To End buttons should do the same. As the code was currently written, when she was already at the start or the end, and she tried to go to Page 1 or the last page, she received no notification that she was already there.

The inconsistency was not a major issue, but a user would expect consistency, so we had to consider the issue seriously. We could easily reproduce the reported software behavior, and we could fix it quite simply, but, because the issue was not of major consequence, we classified it as a Level 2 issue. (Incidentally, we could trace the fault back to the design.)

Tip

Consistency of software behavior is very important, particularly in Windows applications. Users become quite cross if similar functions work in different ways. This attention to detail helps to make the difference between good and poor products.

Issue: Sound and Video Continue When User Returns to Title Selection

Next, Anne reported that if she had a sound playing on the currently selected page and then she returned to the Title Index Selection mode, the sound continued playing. Furthermore, if she then went to another book that didn't have a soundtrack on Page 1, the sound from the previous book would still be playing. If the sound involved was a narration, it would be totally out of context in the second book.

The same problem also occurred with a video. Although the video window was hidden when she returned to Title Selection mode, Anne could still hear sound if the video had an embedded sound track, and the video would also pop up every time a message appeared in Title Selection mode. Anne recommended that all sounds and videos be stopped when the user returned to the Title Selection mode. No one disputed this, and we classified the issue as Level 3 because it was quite a serious fault. This issue led to the introduction of two new functions—**CloseDownVideo** and **CloseDownSound**—as you will see. Each routine would contain the code to shut down the appropriate multimedia channel and, in the case of the video, to unload the form as well.

Issue: Manual Rewind Failure of MID files

Anne then mentioned the rewind problem with MID files, which we already knew about. We logged this as a Level 1 problem on the grounds that using the Reload button as a temporary solution allowed a rewind to occur.

Issue: The Text Button

Anne then had something to say about the Text button control in Page View mode. This issue was cosmetic, but Anne thought that the word *Text* on the button was confusing. Her argument was that when you were looking at a Picture Album, the **Text** switch doesn't switch in any text; it just removes either the selection panel or the keys. She thought the Text button needed to be called something else. Although she was right, we classified this issue as Level 1 because it was not a showstopper from a management perspective.

Issue: Video Window Not Shut Down

When a video clip was being played, a problem occurred when Anne moved to the next page, which contained an image. The video window didn't shut down; it was still there behind the main form, and it kept popping up when a message box appeared on the screen—for example, when a warning appeared that the user had reached the end of Index. Anne also could hear a video's sound track still playing when she'd moved off to another page that didn't have a video. The video form needed to be closed down after the user had left the page on which the video had been invoked. We assigned a Level 3 to this issue.

Issue: Image Not Cleared

In fact, the video clip problem was worse than I have described. If the previous page to the one containing a video contained an image, the previous image remained on the screen when the user viewed the video clip, and the video clip ran on top of the old image. From the notes she had made when she encountered the fault, Anne was able to demonstrate this problem for us quite easily.

Both Archie and Julie were astonished that they had not encountered such an obvious fault when they did their initial system testing. The truth is, they had their hands full integrating the newly developed modules—on its own, a substantial task to perform. Expecting them to test out the system as thoroughly as Anne could do—and to also put together a brand new system—would have been unreasonable.

Issue: Radio Buttons

Anne's next issue concerned bringing up the selection criteria panel for the first time. When she did this, neither of the two radio buttons was selected. This problem was an oversight, but it could lead to potential confusion for the user the first time he or she had the system perform a search.

We could have accomplished the fix by setting one of the radio buttons to **True** at design time, but we decided to execute the setting via code instead. Inserting a line of code somewhere at initialization time that set the appropriate button's **value** property to **True** would be better. If we inserted the code, it would be independent of the design status. We classified this issue as Level 3.

Issue: Workbench Context-Sensitive Toolbar

Anne tactfully pointed out that someone had forgotten about the Workbench toolbar's context-sensitive capability. When the program was in Picture Album mode, only the picture buttons were supposed to be enabled; when it was in Text Book mode, only the text buttons should be enabled. As Anne pointed out, having all the buttons available all the time was confusing. No one argued; the problem was functionality that had been missed. The fix was simple, and we classed the problem as Level 2. The fix involved creating three subroutines: one to disable all the buttons, one to enable the text-only buttons, and one to enable the picture buttons.

Issue: Inconsistency with Forward/Reverse Search Messages

The messages that appeared on screen concerning the results of forward and reverse searching were inconsistent. The forward search placed "Result of Successful Search" in the comment label when an entry was found, but the reverse search produced nothing. We classed this as a Level 2 issue; we determined that, in the reverse search code, the line that set up the comment line appeared before the call to **DisplayPage**. Because the **DisplayPage** function automatically clears the comment line, the message never appeared in the reverse-search function. We also discovered that the messages the forward and reverse searches produced were not identical.

Issue: Header Failures Are Okay

Anne pointed out to us that if the user read in a Page Index file that had an incorrect font type or an illegal value for the font size, he or she would get a "Failed To Read Header" error message. She pointed out this detail because, although it was not a fault as such, she wasn't sure we were aware of it. She thought the error message might be quite misleading to a user. This was, once more, Anne demonstrating her thoroughness—one of the reasons she was our best tester.

We decided that, once an E-MagBook was set up, the user should never see this error message. However, in case the message did ever appear, we decided to change it to "Unable To Load Requested Title." And we classified the problem as a Level 1 issue.

Issue: Disappearing Images

The next error Anne reported was a real bug, and she admitted that it was the only serious one she'd managed to find. The bug involved the Workbench and images that had been positioned in such a way that only the bottom or right side of the image was on the screen. For example, if the user moved the image so that the bottom, right-hand corner was on view and then shrank the image further, the user could lose the image if the bottom, right-hand corner's coordinates became negative. The whole image would then be somewhere to the left of the screen, or above it, or both. Anne demonstrated this to us, again using her notes to re-create the problem. This error was a definite Level 3. She also suspected the same would happen with the text box, but she hadn't checked that out. Nevertheless, Archie and Julie made a note in their logbooks to sort out text position as well as image position.

The solution was to check whether the right side, X-coordinate or the bottom, Y-coordinate of the object was negative after a size reduction had been executed. Having the program check **Object.Left+Object.Width** and **Object.Top+Object.Height** could determine the situation.

If either of these was (or both were) negative, **Object.Left** and/or **Object.Top** could be reset to 0 to bring the control back onto the screen. Once again, with such meticulous attention to detail, Anne had demonstrated her superior testing skills.

Issue: Hot Keys and Tab Stops

Anne had found that we had missed some GUI functionality that, in her opinion, nearly all the programmers she had come in contact with paid only lip service to. This functionality centered on hot keys and tab order. I had completely forgotten to warn Archie and Julie about these issues, and, far worse, we had totally neglected either facility in the design.

Anne was forever pointing out to our developers (and to me) that some people prefer to use hot keys, or to tab across the buttons, rather than use mouse clicks to activate common functions. Then, Anne produced her chart and showed us what the hot-key character assignments were for the button controls we had defined. You can see her summary of the situation in Figure 9.2.

We could easily implement hot keys for New Disk, Open E-MagBook, and Titles. For the Workbench toolbar, we decided to implement hot keys only for the End, Print, and Text On/Off buttons. We were unable to implement hot keys for the navigation buttons because they used chevrons (< and >) in their button captions, and the chevrons were already being used as hot keys for the search buttons. Consequently, tab ordering was essential to ensure that any button or text field that could not be reached with a hot key was available by tabbing to the button or text field.

We classed this omission as a Level 3 issue. Setting up the hot keys would be easy, but getting the tab order correct would be quite demanding. First, we would need to set the **TabStop** attribute to **False** for items that we didn't want included in the tab order—such as the two text boxes **txtText** and **txtText2**, the keys, and the diagnostic text boxes that contained the file-reference strings. Then, we had to make sure that any panels serving as containers that were not visible because they were overlaid by another container were marked invisible. Otherwise, even though the user couldn't see them, all the controls contained within would become part of the tab order. You can see how tabbing and hot keys were set up for the final version of the viewer by looking at project **EViewer** in the directory **DEV_EViewer** on the CD.

Finally, Anne gave us her hot-key and tabbing test scripts to include when we had completed the fixes. (As I said, all three of us had completely neglected a major user issue—that is, providing an alternative to using the mouse to navigate around the controls of a VB form.)

Issue: wbO First-Time Use

Anne had an issue with the **wbO** function. She reported that some odd dimensions resulted if she used the **wbO** button before she'd used the **wbN** button. The screen object's dimensions that resulted were the design-time settings of **imgImage2** and **txtText2**. We decided to set up something more suitable in the **Form_Load** event, and we classed the issue as Level 3.

Hot Keys Allocated	Hot Keys Not Allocated
A	Title Selection Mode: New Disk (suggest D)
B	Title Selection Mode: Open E-Book (suggest B)
C Clear Selection Criteria	
D	Page View Mode: << Go To Start Page
E	Page View Mode: < Go To Previous
F	Page View Mode: > Go To Next
G Go To	Page View Mode: >> Go To End
H	
I	Workbench Mode: All toolbar buttons
J	
K KEYS	Titles (suggest I)
L SELECT	
M	
N WB with New Setting	
O WB with Old Settings	
P	
Q	
R RELOAD	
S SEARCH	
T TEXT	
U	
V	
W	
X	
Y	
Z	
> SEARCH NEXT	
< SEARCH PREVIOUS	

Figure 9.2
Hot-key assignments for the viewer.

Issue: Program Closedown

According to Anne, when she shut down the program, the most recent video clip continued to play on its own. This situation made us realize we had not set up a **Form_Unload** handler to correctly close down the video and sound channels. All this fix would require would be calls to **CloseDownSound** and **CloseDownVideo**. We classed the issue as Level 3.

Issue: Index or Book?

Anne informed us that we kept using the word *Index* in error messages and reports. She pointed out that the reader is reading a *book*. She thought displaying messages such as "At End Of Book" rather than "At End Of Index" would be better. No one could dispute that she was right again. We classified the issue at Level 3.

Issue: No Videos in Workbench Mode

Anne reported that videos were not being handled in Workbench mode at all. This was a Level 3 omission of functionality. This omission led to many code additions to ensure that the video form remained on screen whenever the focus was switched to one of the text-manipulation buttons.

Issue: Reload Button

Finally, Anne showed us that the **Reload** button on her test version did nothing. In fact, it contained no code at all—a Level 3 issue. And this issue concluded Anne's report.

The Issue, or Bug, List

Figure 9.3 shows the classified list of bugs or issues we needed to remedy.

This list contains a reference identity, all Anne's findings, and a category classification of seriousness. This list represents accountability at work. We had logged everything and represented the total of our findings after the first session of system testing. Note that the classification of issues was achieved by group consensus, but, as project manager, I had the final say. Ultimately, categorization and prioritization of issues is a management function that must take into account both quality of end product as well as commercial constraints.

Ref No.	System Testing Issues for Viewer	Category
V00001	Sound and video continue to play after returning to Title Selection mode	3
V00002	Video not closed down after moving from the page	3
V00003	Previous image not cleared when page loaded with video clip	3
V00004	Reload button required	3
V00005	Radio buttons in Selection Criteria both off on startup	3
V00006	Images/text can disappear off WB screen when moving objects	3
V00007	imgImage? and txtText? require sensible dimensions for default use	3
V00008	Hot keys and tab ordering	3
V00009	Program closedown not implemented	3
V00010	Change messages from "Index" to "Book"	3
V00017	Videos not available in WB	3
V00011	Go Start/Go End message handling is inconsistent	2
V00012	WB toolbar needs to be format sensitive	2
V00013	Inconsistencies in search messages	2
V00014	MID rewind problem	1
V00015	Text button caption not appropriate	1
V00016	"Failed To Read Header" message inadequate	1

Figure 9.3

Issue list from first run of system testing the viewer.

Changing "Frozen" Code

As I've mentioned several times previously, after the developers hand the code over to the testers, the code becomes "frozen." The developers give each code module (data structure, infrastructure GUI routine, event handler, or library routine) its own version number. For example, we had classified all the code you've seen in the case study at Version 1.0. Any changes we made from now on would need to be recorded. We would change the version number in the code being modified, and we would produce an audit log in the header of the code itself.

Change Logs

If we look at one of the fixes required in the case study, you will be able to see how we built up a change log. Let's sort out issue V00011, the Go To Start/Go To End inconsistency. We can also implement the requirement to change the term *Index* to *Book*, which was issue V00010, for any code units we encounter along the way. Here is the fix in **cmdGoToStart:**

Example 1

```
Private Sub cmdGoStart_Click()
' VIEWER INFRASTRUCTURE EVENT HANDLER:
' Navigation Functionality, V1.2
' -------------------
' CHANGE LOG:
' <DATE> V00011  Go Start/Go End message handling is inconsistent
' <DATE> V00010  Change messages from 'Index' to 'Book'
' ---------------------------------
If g_intCurrentPage < 1 Then
    MsgBox "Book is empty"                    ' V00010
    Exit Sub
End If

If g_intCurrentPage = 1 Then                  ' V00011
      MsgBox "Already at Start of Book "      ' V00011 & V00010
      Exit Sub                                ' V00011
End If                                        ' V00011

g_intCurrentPage = 1
Call DisplayPage
lblCommentLine.Caption = "At Start of Book" ' V00010

Call SwitchOnHourGlass
End Sub
```

First, we've incremented the version number of the code from 1.0 to 1.2, immediately indicating that we have made two changes since development was completed. We have introduced a change log that shows all the modifications that have taken place to this subroutine since it was first produced and "frozen." The reference number is the one we assigned to the issue, and you can find that reference number in the issue table. All the lines of code that we have added or modified, which constitute the changes, have the corresponding issue number appended to them as a comment. This way, a programmer can track a bug fix through the code by doing global searches for, in this example, V00011 and V00010.

When a programmer performs a search on an issue number in the VB IDE, the first thing he or she finds will be the change log in a given module, followed by all the lines that were changed. Clearly, this approach is fine for small changes. But if the code is changed beyond all recognition, a comment to the effect that this is a rewrite should also be included in the change log.

Although this process may seem painstaking, it provides good traceability when you or another programmer is attempting to work out what was done to solve a given issue. This standard also encourages a methodical and disciplined approach to fixing bugs, which can be very important, particularly if a fix needs to be "unwound," or undone. When a line of code is modified, commenting out the original lines so that a programmer can see the "before" and "after" effects is even a good idea. Alternatively, keep the previous versions of the routines so the routines can always be reclaimed. We'll return to this subject when we look at support. The key point about the change log is that you should be able to see the complete history of the module.

Example 2

Now we'll do the fixes that involve **DisplayPage** and see the end result. These fixes relate to the video not being closed down before the program moves to the next page that does not contain a video, and the fact that the previous image is not removed when a video is set up. These are issues V00002 and V00003.

First, we created a routine—**CloseDownVideo**—to remove the video clip and made **imgImageIt** invisible. Take a look at how we altered **DisplayVideo**, providing a complete audit of the change:

```
Public Sub DisplayPage(Optional intAlternateDisplay As Integer = 0)
' VIEWER INFRASTRUCTURE GUI ROUTINE:  V1.2
' Arguments:
'    intAlternateDisplay  if present, use file references to create display
'                         if not present, create display from Index entry
' -----------------------------------------
' <Date> V00002  Video not closed down after moving from the page
' <Date> V00003  Previous image not cleared when page loaded with video clip
' -----------------------------------------
```

```
Dim intLoopCounter As Integer
Dim intVidorPic As Integer
Dim booResult As Boolean
Dim strThePictureRef As String
Dim strTheTextRef As String
Dim strTheSoundRef As String
Dim strTheKeys(5) As String


lblCommentLine.Caption = ""


Call CloseDownVideo(frmVideo, frmVideo.mmcVideoPlayer)  ' V00002


Call SetUpTheData(intAlternateDisplay, strThePictureRef, strTheTextRef,_
        strTheSoundRef, strTheKeys())


' Set up keys
If intAlternateDisplay = 0 Then
    For intLoopCounter = 1 To 5
            txtKeyView(intLoopCounter).Text = strTheKeys(intLoopCounter)
    Next intLoopCounter
End If
'..................................................................
' Display Text Book Format
If g_intFormatType = 1 Then
    booResult = LoadAndDisplayText(strTheTextRef, txtText)
 End If
'..................................................................
' Display Album Format
If g_intFormatType = 2 Then
    intVidorPic = VideoOrPicture(strThePictureRef)
    If intVidorPic = 1 Then
        booResult = LoadAndDisplayImage(strThePictureRef, imgImageIt,_
            g_intImageContainer_Width, g_intImageContainer_Height,_
            g_intImageContainer_Left, g_intImageContainer_Top)
    Else
        imgImageIt.Visible = False  ' V00003
        booResult = LoadAndPlayVideo(strThePictureRef, frmVideo,_
            frmVideo.mmcVideoPlayer, g_intImageContainer_Width,_
            g_intImageContainer_Height, g_intImageContainer_Left,_
            g_intImageContainer_Top)
    End If
End If
'..................................................................
' Display Reference Format
If g_intFormatType = 3 Then
    intVidorPic = VideoOrPicture(strThePictureRef)
```

```
    If intVidorPic = 1 Then
        booResult = LoadAndDisplayImage(strThePictureRef, imgImageIt,_
                g_intImageContainer_Width, g_intImageContainer_Height,_
                g_intImageContainer_Left, g_intImageContainer_Top)
    Else
        imgImageIt.Visible = False   ' VO0003
        booResult = LoadAndPlayVideo(strThePictureRef, frmVideo,_
                frmVideo.mmcVideoPlayer, g_intImageContainer_Width,_
                g_intImageContainer_Height, g_intImageContainer_Left,_
                g_intImageContainer_Top)
    End If

    booResult = LoadAndDisplayText(strTheTextRef, txtText)

End If
'............................................................
' Now check for a sound file - all formats
If strTheSoundRef <> "" Then
    booResult = LoadAndPlaySound(strTheSoundRef, mmcSoundPlayer)
End If
'............................................................
' DIAGNOSTIC AID also required by PAGE EDITOR
' Indicate the file references for this page
If intAlternateDisplay <> 1 Then
    txtPictureFileName.Text = strThePictureRef
    txtTextFileName.Text = strTheTextRef
    txtSoundFileName.Text = strTheSoundRef
End If

lblCurrent.Caption = CStr(g_intCurrentPage)

End Sub
```

I have highlighted the changes. As you can see, even in a big body of code, you can use VB's search facility by searching on the change-log number to easily home in on changes and see the complete history of a single issue.

Example 3

In this example, we'll look at code that must be replaced or code that must be created from scratch. How you log a big change depends on how much code is to be replaced. If you will be doing a virtual rewrite of the code, a single log entry stating that everything is being rewritten is sufficient. If a section of, say, five or six lines needs to be changed, comment out the section to be rewritten so that a programmer coming after you can see what the code used to be and can compare the original code with the rewritten code.

In the case of a new subroutine or function that comes into being as a result of fixing a bug or an issue, set the version number initially to V1.0, and provide a comment indicating that the code has been created to fix a specified issue.

Here are the two routines that closed down the sound and video channels in the case study. You can see that the routines start off as Version 1.0. They include a change log indicating that they were created to resolve an issue:

```
Public Sub CloseDownSound(mmcSoundPlayer As Control)
' GENERAL GUI ROUTINE: Stop sound V1.0
' Arguments:
'       mmcSoundPlayer  name of multimedia control to close
' ------------------------------
' <date>  Code created to fix bug report;
' V00001: close down sound
' ------------------------------
mmcSoundPlayer.Command = "Close"
End Sub

Public Sub CloseDownVideo(frmVideo As Form, mmcVideoPlayer As Control)
' GENERAL GUI ROUTINE: Stop video V1.0
' Arguments:
'       frmVideo - name of video form to remove
'       mmcVideoPlayer  name of multimedia control to close
' ------------------------------
' <date>  Code created to fix bug report;
' V00001: close down video
' --------------------
frmVideo.mmcVideoPlayer.Command = "Close"
Unload frmVideo
End Sub
```

Note that we've not only closed the video channel, but also unloaded the video form. In either case—video or sound shutdown—whether or not the multimedia channel is being used doesn't matter. We can still issue the commands; if the channel is not being used, nothing happens.

In the above cases, when you search for fixes to V00001, the comments make it immediately apparent that these two routines have been created in response to an issue or bug log. We have written these two routines as general, GUI subroutines, and we need to place them in **ViewerLib**.

Change Management

As I've mentioned previously, managing changes to the code in a software development is critical. In the case study, we established all the infrastructure elements to facilitate the management and tracing of changes to code. Julie and Archie worked on the fixes, documenting and commenting them appropriately. You can see the end result by looking at the final version of code in the DEV_EViewer directory on the CD. Load the **EViewer** project, and use the search facility in the VB design environment to trace each change, using its issue number to see what modules were changed or created and how. One advantage of using a five-digit issue number is that you can also search for *all* issue fixes by hunting for V000.

The release of the newly fixed software must be managed so that testers switch to the new release cleanly. You might need to target your testing to the areas of functionality that have been fixed. The big issue is how much of the old software you will need to test to ensure that software has not been broken by the fixes introduced. My advice is if in doubt, test every-thing—which neatly brings us to automated testing.

Automated Testing

When Julie and Archie had completed all their changes and had performed sufficient testing to satisfy themselves that they had fixed the problems, they released EViewer Version 1.1 to Anne for retesting. In addition to checking the specific fixes, Anne retested the whole sys-tem from scratch before she passed it. However, we had decided not to implement V00014 (MID rewind) and V00015 (Text button). I was still reluctant to spend any time on V00014. Anne agreed that it was not a showstopper—and, provided we informed Monty about it, we could tackle it at our leisure. As for V00015, I wanted to get some feedback from Monty and Samantha first.

By Friday of project Week 7, Anne was confident enough to release the program for accep-tance testing. Note that this decision was Anne's (objective testing department), not ours (subjective development department).

Regression Testing

One of the most important features of testing is the capability to test a complete system after any changes have been made. This capability ensures that a fix has not affected previously working functionality, and that old bugs previously fixed don't creep back into the system. (The recurrence of old bugs can easily happen if you have no automated version-control system.) To briefly review a concept from Chapter 3, testing a complete system that used to work to ensure that it still does work is known as *regression testing*.

Automation of Test Scripts

As I mentioned in an earlier chapter, you can buy some sophisticated software packages that let you set up automatic testing of Windows applications. These packages work a bit like digital tape recorders.

First, the tester sits down and performs the test manually, but with both the test software package and the application under test running. The test system captures all the tester's key presses and mouse movements as a type of digital tape recording using a scripting language. When the tester is finished with the tests, he or she can examine the scripts and put simple checks into them to make sure that they obtain the desired result when they are run against the application under test.

If you recall, I earlier described the process as being like a digital tape recording of external events. By reading the script files to see what events were performed, and then re-creating those events for the application, the test software lets you automatically play back the events you created into the application under test. If the scripts also contain checking statements, the testing software can automatically check the result after each operation has been completed. The result is like having an automatic tester working on the application. The test package performs a test on the application and verifies the result. The scripting code drives the process.

For example, consider the E-MagBook. We can manually set up a situation to select Page 24 in a Reference Book and use a suitable testing package to capture the events necessary to do this into a scripting file. We can then modify the resulting script the test package produced. For example, we can have the software check that the file references brought up in the diagnostic labels of the viewer are correct (that is, the contents of **txtPictureFileName** can be read and compared with a hard-coded string that is expected). When we then run the test via the test software, it will automatically select Page 24, but then our extra scripting code will check the values in the diagnostic labels against the hard-coded, expected values. If the values are as expected, the test is complete and passed. If the values are different than expected, the test fails. In either case, we can set up the script to act accordingly and report a pass or fail. Here's a very simplistic version of what the scripting code might look like:

```
Invoke cmdGoToPage_Click
Set focus on input box
Enter 24 into input box
Invoke OK button of dialog box
Check content of screen object txtPictureFileName = E:\Images\Image342.bmp
If check failed then Stop
Check content of screen object txtTextFileName = E:\Text\TextPage24.txt
If check failed then Stop
Check content of screen object txtSoundFileName = E:\Sound\Nararation24.wav
If check failed then Stop
```

The test software needs to have intimate knowledge of the screen objects the application uses. The code above first activates the button click event **Go To Page**. This action results in the application producing the dialog box to receive the page number. The testing software is then instructed to make Windows place the focus on the input field and enter "24" into it. The script then instructs the testing package to activate the OK button on the dialog box. This action results in the application fetching and loading Page 24. This action by the application results in the three text boxes—**txtPictureFileName**, **txtTextFileName**, and

txtSoundFileName—being set up with the appropriate text strings. The test script then gets the testing software to check the contents of each of the application's screen objects against the hard-coded, expected strings. If any check fails to find a match, the test script stops. The test software will move on to the next tests in the sequence only if all three text boxes contain the required strings.

The testing software actually drives the application via the operating system, simulating the events that would occur if a user were running the application directly. All the information about what events to fire comes from the script file, which was captured when a tester performed the actual sequences when he or she was running the application. Obviously, setting up all the required tests and modifying the scripts to perform the appropriate tests is quite a painstaking process, but, once you've done it, all you have to do is run the test scripts and sit back. And you can do this time after time without making any changes to the script files.

Quality Assurance

Automated testing really comes into its own when code comes back after bugs are fixed. You can check all the functionality to make sure that, in fixing a bug, you have not broken something else. This retesting is vital for good quality assurance. A good, automated package will even provide the paperwork to show the tests you have done and their results, which offers a high level of auditable information.

Unless you can automate testing, painstaking though it is to set up, you will never be able to check code properly every time it comes back from the development team, because the process of going through the test scripts is so labor intensive. For example, with automation, you can set up a batch of tests and run them overnight—you will come in the next morning and the results will be available in a file.

Robot Clients

As an example of how sophisticated automated testing can be, you can even use the type of technology we have been looking at for automated testing to set up "robot" clients to execute performance testing on servers. You can achieve this level of sophistication by getting each robot client to "hit" the server with data requests as if the client were one or more users. You can set up such a scenario by developing testing scripts that invoke the application on the client to make requests on the server. By controlling the number of requests per second from each robot, and by introducing a degree of random behavior, you can simulate heavy traffic on a network and use automated testing tools to record response times under these conditions.

You can make the applications running in the robot clients write data as well as issue queries to the servers. Consequently, you can set up quite sophisticated simulations of user types on a given server, testing the application in a "busy" environment.

Know What's Available

Get to know about automated testing tools—they are essential to modern software development. As hardware and software improve in capability, more and more testing innovations come onto the market, and you need to keep up with them. As I've said before, testing GUI-based software manually is difficult because of the many possible combinations of execution pathways in an event-driven environment. You might be able to set up the testing and perform it manually once. But, in the course of a project, you may well be called upon to repeat the level of testing many times. Without automation, this repetition quickly becomes impossible.

Acceptance Testing

In an ideal software-development world, you will clear every issue and release the software with a clean bill of health. But, life's never quite that straightforward. As you've seen in the case study, we had quite a thorny problem with MID file handling that still needed to be resolved. Similarly, releasing completely "issue-free" software is unlikely. You will need to make pragmatic business decisions about the known problems. Clearly, if you have any showstoppers, you must address those issues.

Code reviews, automated testing, and manual testing are all essential, together with records of the tests done and their results, to verify that the software system has been adequately tested. In the case study, Anne's testing of the viewer was successful, and, by the end of the week, she had passed the viewer for delivery to the customer, despite the MID problem. But, as Anne herself put it, "This doesn't mean that the software is 'bug free'—it merely indicates that the testing hasn't revealed any more issues." And that comment accurately summarizes system testing.

After you are satisfied that the software is ready, you can install it on the customer's site, in preparation for acceptance testing using the formal test scripts you prepared as part of the development project. Because these are the same test scripts that were used in system testing, you should be confident that acceptance testing will reveal no bugs.

Ground Rules

In terms of acceptance testing, the last thing you want to do is take source code to the customer's site and make uncontrolled changes to the code being tested. You need to execute acceptance testing in the same way you ran system testing. You list, and then assess, the issues. You should expect to resolve many issues by examining the requirements document and clarifying aspects of that document that you might have forgotten or didn't fully appreciate earlier. In the case study, we had a huge arsenal of documentation to rely on, signed off by the customer as a definitive statement of required functionality.

If we did find any genuine software bugs, we would log them and deal with them back at our office, where we could create fixes, test the system, and issue a new release of the software to take back to the customer site, confident that we had implemented full quality assurance.

I gave instructions to both Archie and Julie that they were only to log issues and make no attempt to change code on-site. They would take source code on laptops only for reference purposes, to help address any issues that arose, but, under no circumstances, were they to change one line of code on the test system.

Failure to Install

Suppose the program you are trying to install on-site won't run at all, but, with a simple tweak, you can make it operational. With the immense variation in PC hardware and software environments that exists nowadays, an installation failure is a common scenario. In such situations, you can attempt to make the code work on-site, but you must bring back documented details about the problem and what you had to do. You must then analyze the situation before you introduce the changes into the master source set. In other words, the site fix is not official, and you must reintroduce the fix on-site at a later date, after you have gone through the correct channels to produce a fix.

The Quick Fix

Changing code on-site is a potential management nightmare. You can be under enormous pressure to fix problems on-site, and you must avoid doing so unless you have no other way out. On a big project, with a properly installed version-control system, producing quick, on-site fixes might even be impossible—which, in this case, would be no bad thing.

Programmers are, by nature, eager to please. They take great pride in their skill and in the speed at which they implement fixes. So, whenever I hear a fellow programmer say, "It's only a one-line fix," fear grips me. Over the years, I have experienced my own and other people's one-line fixes that have unleashed a catalog of disaster. The problem with the quick fix is that it is rarely thought through properly. This problem can be compounded by the fact that, when a programmer starts producing the fix, he or she realizes that the fix is much more complex than was first thought.

In reality, the quick fix is seldom quick. For the sake of quality assurance, *avoid attempting quick fixes.* The only proper way to approach code modification of any sort, whether the modification is for further development or to fix an issue, is to go through the full, development cycle or the full, change-control procedure.

The Fix Cycle

When you are presented with an issue, you must assess the issue and determine the impact, if any, a fix will have on the system as a whole. Create the fix, test it, and then get the fix into the next release scheduled for system testing. No other way provides the correct level of accountability, audit trace, and testing.

As we've discussed, regression testing will ensure that nothing you have done has affected other elements of the functionality that you did not modify. One of the most common pitfalls of the quick fix is breaking something that used to work. After system testing passes the software, you can make your fix official.

Acceptance Testing

I called Monty's office on Friday afternoon to confirm arrangements for acceptance testing for the following Monday. Monty was stranded in the Far East. I asked to speak to Samantha, but she was flying back from the East Coast and wouldn't be in until Monday. No one had any idea when Monty was due to return—something about an air-traffic-controllers' strike in Europe.

Rather than having them just turn up at Montasana Systems on Monday, I told Archie and Julie to come into our office first thing. I then called Monty's office at 9.00 A.M. According to his ever-efficient secretary, who had been busy all weekend making the arrangements, Monty was due to fly back that morning, but he probably would not be in the office until Wednesday at the earliest. The secretary located Samantha, who was most apologetic when she answered her phone.

She explained that Monty was supposed to have been back on Friday night. They were scheduled to have an early-morning meeting on Monday to prepare for acceptance testing. She had the target PC set up, loaded with a full VB environment, so she suggested that we come over and get started.

I was concerned that Monty wouldn't be there, but Samantha said she had been in touch with him over the weekend, and he was happy for her to start the testing. After he returned to the office, Samantha would go over all the details with him. The situation wasn't ideal, but it was better than nothing. Not that I didn't trust Samantha to do a good job—the question was about who had the last word, and that was Monty. He was the person we needed to ensure was satisfied with the product we had produced. I suspected that Samantha would have slightly different ideas from Monty in terms of what she expected to see, for example. No matter how good your requirements specification is, clients will still have expectations. Also, quite a long period of time had passed between the completion of the specifications and this moment. Monty or Samantha might have forgotten details, or their ideas might have become clouded by other aspects that had cropped up since they had approved the project. And, of course, we had to remember that they also had been working on aspects of the product's future functionality.

Monty and Samantha had been demonstrating the static forms that we helped to produce, and they were no doubt discussing such things as Web browsing and composite pages, which might cloud their understanding of what was presently required of them for acceptance testing of the Mark 1 viewer—the first delivered version of the viewer. We would have to go through the exercise of "managing" Samantha's expectations, and then start all over again with Monty. Still, we had planned a week for these activities, and, provided Monty was able to start on Thursday at the latest, we should be okay.

Installation

Samantha welcomed Archie and Julie late that Monday morning and showed them where the test PC was located. The two programmers installed the viewer, but VB failed to find a multimedia control. They hunted for the control using the Components option on the project menu, but there was still no sign of it.

♦ *Installation Issue 1*—No multimedia component available.

This issue is one that component technology brings with it. You need access to a correctly licensed component. Just copying across from the component on your laptop to a customer's machine is not a bright idea if that causes a license breach. Fortunately, Samantha and Julie were sufficiently "aware," from a commercial point of view; so, Samantha went off to find a legal copy of a VB kit that contained the multimedia component.

Back in the early negotiations, Monty had declared that we would not need to supply any components associated with the operating system or VB because he had fully licensed versions of everything that was required. Within a short space of time, Samantha had located a copy of the required component, which she had moved onto the test PC.

Software Licenses

The missing multimedia component was the only hitch Julie and Archie encountered in the on-site installation, but that hitch does bring up an important issue. When you are negotiating a contract with a customer for software/hardware supply, make sure you cover all licensing aspects. (After all, how would you feel if software you had developed was being pirated all over the place?)

Protocol for Issues Raised

The brief I had given to Archie and Julie was quite simple—witness performance of the acceptance tests, assist where necessary, and document all issues that arise. Julie and Archie spent the whole day with Samantha and came back into the office the following morning—at which time, we had a debriefing session.

The first thing I asked Archie and Julie was whether they had found any genuine bugs. They told me not one had manifested, although Samantha thought she had found a couple of bugs until Archie pointed out she had placed a completely empty disk in drive E:. This example demonstrates why having a representative of the supplier on-site to assist in acceptance testing is so important—he or she can step in where there is clearly "finger trouble" and guide the tester.

Many of Samantha's issues were actually requests for extra functionality. In your own software developments, when you are recording such issues on-site, it is vital that you make no commitments to the client. No matter how forceful the client is, the line is very clear: You must assess all issues in the context of the project as a whole, both technical and contractual. You need to inform the client that you will make an official response in due course. Let's look at the type of issues that arose in the case study.

Issue: Text Color

Samantha realized that text color was not part of the requirement that we worked to, but she wanted to be able to set up the color of the text on the Title Selection page and also of the text on each page when the program was in Page View mode. We created a "wish list." This list would consist of things that both Samantha and Monty wanted that were items over and above what we had agreed to in the requirements specification.

We would be able to produce a written response to all their issues, quoting for any extra work and agreeing to take on certain things without cost (only if we had a business justification for doing so). We needed to be flexible here, to keep the good relationship intact.

Tip

Customers need careful management. You need to know when to be firm and when to give a little. This management is quite a delicate balancing act. Of course, this is where the requirements specification comes into its own. If you can point out that the requirement was to do A and the customer is demanding that the system do A plus B, you have a good position from which to be firm. Unless the customer is totally unreasonable, this approach usually works. However, to give a little is good practice, to avoid straining the relationship. It's just a matter of human nature that people are far more willing to accept defeat if you throw them a little something to sweeten the bitter taste of defeat.

We logged our first wish-list items as follows:

♦ *Wish list Item 1*—Title Selection mode: Text color setting required.

♦ *Wish list Item 2*—Page View mode: Text color setting required.

Trivial though these sound, the above items beg all sorts of questions: Should the color be set for each different page, or for all pages (that is, is text color an attribute of the book, or should it be an attribute of each page)? What happens if the color is set to the same color as the text box's background color? And so on.

After we'd established the complete wish list, we could produce a requirements specification for all the additions and quote them as extras. Also, we didn't want the demand for extra functionality to interfere with the development plan for the editors, unless Monty decided the new requirements were more important. Never forget: If you agree to do anything over and above what you set out to accomplish, doing so will affect your plan, and possibly your ability to deliver software on time and within budget.

Tip

You must study the potential impact on your plan of any change and act accordingly, because you always want to deliver on time. Adding extra burden to the development without considering resource and other issues is bad business practice.

Issue: Go To Page Box

Samantha wasn't terribly keen on the message box we used to get the page number from the user for the **Go To Page** function. She said the message box didn't look very good. We went back through the requirements specification, and it included no detail about how this box would look. It performed the function as stated, but we had a cosmetic issue about how the GUI looked in a given set of circumstances. We logged this issue as another wish-list item. Clearly, we needed to get some idea of a design from Samantha for how she wanted the message box to look. The other possibility was that Monty might say it was perfectly adequate as it stood.

We could not do much with the VB message box, but we could set up our own panel—even use a picture panel with a text box and a label or two—and get the input that way. We did, however, need to make the operation modal, because we didn't want the user moving off onto another page or using the navigation controls while we're still trying to get the input for page number. So a new facility would need some thought. We logged the issue.

Issue: Text, Keys, and Select Buttons

We had already logged a development issue that the Text button had a misleading caption. We had decided to wait and see what happened at acceptance. Samantha suggested that we do away with the Text button and have only the Keys and Select buttons, each of which acted like a toggle switch. For example, if keys were on screen and the Keys button was clicked again, the key panel would be removed. If the button was clicked again, the key panel would appear, and so on. That way, we would need only the two keys. This suggestion seemed sensible, and we marked it down as a solution to the Text button issue that we had already noted in the bug log (from development), and which we still hadn't closed.

Issue: Workbench Sizing Increments

Samantha also thought that the increments we used for expanding and contracting the image and text boxes in the Workbench were too small. She would like them to be user definable. This issue was clearly a wish-list item.

Issue: Page Number

Samantha wanted to see the page number presented as *Page 4* instead of just the numeral. That modification would be easy—we could add that on our next drop of the software, when we delivered the editors.

Issue: Searching—First Characters Only

Samantha had a valid point concerning searching. Sometimes, Samantha and her staff might want to use a fairly lengthy key, so that it would serve as a mini-description as well as a key, particularly in Picture Album mode. The problem was that, for searching, the user would have to type in the whole key with 100 percent accuracy—which, in the case of a lengthy key, might present difficulties. For example, in a Reference Book, a key might be "Night Watch, by Rembrandt." The user might want to have a look at "Night Watch" and type in only those two words as the selection criterion. The viewer, as it stood, wouldn't register a hit, because the whole key did not match the lengthier "Night Watch, by Rembrandt."

Samantha wanted to let the search check only the number of characters the user typed in. In our example, that would be the characters "Night Watch", so "Night Watch, by Rembrandt" would register as a hit. When we looked at it, we decided this was a valid complaint about the software. However, the specification was clear: The search involved checking that the selection was present in its entirety. So, the complaint was not about the software; it was about the requirements specification. We were, therefore, perfectly in our rights to say that we had met what was required of the development, and that to implement the required functionality would be an extra service.

We needed to log the requirement as an issue, assess the size of the change, and then make a business decision about whether we should charge for the change. We could implement the facility for free if doing so would be good public relations. We would not, however, be bullied into making the change for free, because the requirements specification was clearly inadequate for this additional functionality. This example demonstrates why making the customer sign off on the requirements specification and take ownership of it is so important.

We added the item in question to the wish list. Clearly, we needed to assess the size of the job before we made any decisions about whether the item was chargeable. A temporary solution for the example was to have two keys: "Night Watch, by Rembrandt" and "Night Watch". Although that approach would be wasteful of keys, it did indicate that we already had a potential solution. But, as Samantha pointed out, five keys are not a lot to play with.

Issue: Text Search

Samantha also wanted as an option the ability to search the text of a Text Book or a Reference Book. She appreciated that this request was for an extra capability, and she wanted a cost for the development. We would define the requirement fully in a requirements specification (which might well consist of no more than a single page or two) and quote for it. We also needed to schedule the work without interfering with the current development plan, unless Montasana wanted the effort to be included now—in which case, we would have to modify the plan. Such factors would influence both price and delivery date.

NOTE: *Julie, in particular, approved of the approach we were taking with Samantha—that is, of defining the requirement for a change and quoting a cost, instead of just agreeing to make the change. At her previous company, Julie's managers had taken on too many requested "extras" without a murmur. They usually had done so to appease an already-angry customer who had been let down with a late delivery. To placate the irate client, Julie's bosses had agreed to do all sorts of extras without specifying them fully. The result was that the company was late with the next target date as well. And to placate the customer further, management agreed to add more functionality, and subsequently failed to meet the next quoted delivery date, and so on. The process becomes a truly vicious circle, exacerbated by the fact that they did not fully assess some of the changes before they undertook them. Some tasks proved to be much bigger than the programmer had anticipated when he or she had been put on the spot on-site and been asked to quote how long a given job would take. Julie had examples of programmers making statements such as "Oh, that's half an hour's work." What they* *had neglected was the effort required to assess the change, implement it, test it, and then release it for system testing. In some cases, that "half hour" had led to a solid week's effort, because, when the change was implemented, it had prevented previously working software from functioning correctly with the changed code.*

Issue: Phonetic Searching

Samantha's next point was really interesting. She wanted to sell the product in both Europe and the Americas, and spelling was an issue. Although Montasana might well have certain titles in both American English and European English, they would like a user to be able to execute a search that was independent of the two spellings.

The solution this situation required was an algorithm that worked on the sound rather than the spelling of a word. We needed a routine that could convert a word to something that represented its phonetic structure. A well-known algorithm existed that we could adopt and that would convert a word into a number pattern, in which the numbers represented the sounds of letters that remained in the word after the vowels were removed. So the word *color* would reduce to a number that represented the sounds made by *c*, *l*, and *r*; and that number would find a match with *colour* or *color*. We had used this algorithm before. In fact, I couldn't think why we hadn't mentioned it earlier for inclusion in the requirements specification.

Phonetic searching would clearly be extra functionality, and we needed to specify the functionality in detail to answer questions such as, Is this function an option for the user, or will it be invoked for every search? Does this function include the capability to use only the first few letters? And so on.

Issue: "Failed to Find" Handling

Although Samantha agreed that how the system reported "End of Book Encountered" when a search failed was okay, she didn't like the way in which it showed the last entry, even though it indicated "End of Book" on the comment line. She would prefer that the screen go blank. She wanted the same result for "Previous" searching that failed. We definitely needed to define this issue in detail as a wish-list item. However, as you will note in the examples supplied in the E-MagBook directory on the CD, the special first-page and last-page images proved to be a simple way to sort out this issue without any changes to the code.

Issue: Videos

Samantha was quite happy about how the videos had been implemented as fixed-size windows because all of Montasana's videos would conform to that size. But, when Monty had shown the static screen prototypes to one of the project's backers, he had shown them another system unrelated to electronic books, which allowed the videos to be any size; furthermore, the user could expand video clips to the full screen. Samantha wanted something similar.

From a technical viewpoint, we could put the video into a window that was user adjustable, and the image would expand to fit into the newly sized window. However, one drawback to doing this was that the function worked only via the multimedia control if the control itself defined the window. As a result, we could not program the form's position because we did not know the form handle, that is, its identity within the operating system. We decided the best way to implement the required facility would be as a Workbench capability. The multimedia control could automatically position the video window, but we would set it up such that the user could position the video form, and stretch or contract it, exactly like the functionality available in the Workbench for images.

We needed to define and cost all this functionality in a specification. We needed to assess the impact of the additional functionality on the development program, and so on. We could achieve this requirement only as an addition in a properly controlled change request.

Acceptance Issue List

Just as we had done for bugs, we now produced an "issue list" for acceptance, which included all the things Samantha had come up with in the first run through the acceptance tests. We were happy to see that she had not come up with any bugs.

NOTE: *If you recall, system testing is when you want to see bugs—you don't want to see them at acceptance testing.*

You can see the acceptance issue list in Figure 9.4.

Figure 9.4 shows a simple list in which each entry has a reference number, a date on which the entry was logged (not shown), a category, and status. For "Category," we have classified the majority of entries as "Wish List." One entry is marked as a fix for bug log V00015, and its status is marked as "Transferred." For all the others, the status is "Open" and will remain so until we have produced a requirements specification and a quote—or until the issue goes away. When we write the requirements specification, we can refer to the requirement number, which gives a good level of accountability (that is, Why is this requirements specification being produced? Answer: It's a result of a requirement logged at acceptance on a wish list. Or, alternatively, What happened to issue W00005? Answer: A requirements specification resulted.)

The list provides a tool for the controlled and methodical management of issues brought up in acceptance testing—and prevents issues being lost. Had we encountered any bugs in acceptance testing, we would have logged them on the bug list.

Completion of Acceptance Testing

Monty was back in his office on Thursday morning, and Archie, Julie, and I went to assist in the second run of the acceptance testing. We spent much of the time going over things Samantha had already been through—searching, the variable video size, and so on. On the whole, Monty was very pleased. He would have the first E-MagBook available the following day, Friday.

Acceptance Issues		Category	Status
W00001	Title Selection Mode: Text Color Setting Required	Wish List	Open
W00002	Page View Mode: Text Color Setting Required	Wish List	Open
W00003	Go To Page Cosmetic Improvements	Wish List	Open
W00004	Text, Keys, and Select Buttons	Fix for V00015	Transferred
W00005	WB Variable Sizing Increments	Wish List	Open
W00006	"Page Number" Added To Number	Wish List	Accepted
W00007	Searching, First Characters Only	Wish List	Open
W00008	Text Search	Wish List	Open
W00009	Phonetic Searching Option	Wish List	Open
W00010	Failed To Find Handling	Wish List	Open
W00011	Variable Sized Videos	Wish List	Open

Figure 9.4
The acceptance issue list produced after acceptance testing of the viewer program.

All three of us arrived at Monty's offices Friday morning. We were in the meeting room where the concept had first been put to us. Monty and Samantha arrived with a real E-MagBook, which they placed on the table even though it was in pieces. The E-MagBook was loaded with Version 1.1 of the viewer. Monty then took out an E-MagBook removable disk from his pocket, placed it into the E-MagBook drive, and switched on the PC. The E-MagBook came to life for the very first time and worked flawlessly. (Incidentally, you can see a photograph of the hardware components used in this testing in Chapter 12, Figures 12.1 and 12.2).

Wrapping Up Acceptance

Finally, we presented Monty with the user guide for the viewer that our author had produced. This guide was a preliminary document that the three of us—Julie, Archie, and I—had approved. For the final version of the E-MagBook, Montasana would produce its own user guide that encompassed aspects of the hardware in addition to the viewer program. What we had produced would be sufficient to get Montasana's sales staff and anyone else up to speed with the program.

Monty formally accepted the software via a signed document, and we were free to start the next phase of the project—development of the editors. Monty accepted that the wish list would remain such until we had delivered the editors. At that point, we would address all the wish-list items. Monty felt that a delay in handling the issues was not a bad thing, because he would probably get more feedback from sales staff and clients in the coming weeks, which would lead to more modifications to the new requirements—or even demands for more new facilities. Waiting to see what was going to happen before addressing the wish list in earnest seemed a sensible strategy. He was also keen to start detailed specifications for Web browsing and composite displays in the near future. His parting words as we left the building were, "Presumably, we start the warranty period on the viewer from today?" "That's right," I said. "Any problems, just give us a ring."

We all shook hands. We were quite elated—a job well done. Monty's team would be setting up E-MagBooks all weekend and shipping them out to salesmen all over the country. At last, the prototype was ready for full demonstration. And we had delivered *on time* and *within budget*.

More about Testing

Formal acceptance testing is a contractual necessity, but the testing can be very artificial. For example, consider an airport baggage-handling facility. Acceptance testing can be performed using dummy suitcases, numbered and clearly identifiable. You can project the suitcases onto the conveyors from the check-in desks at a controlled rate. If you are testing automatic bar code reading and sorting, you can track what happens to a suitcase as the computer identifies it, decides what to do with it, and activates the machinery to transport it to the proper loading bay. But the client's real interest is whether the software will work during normal operation of a busy airport—not with phony suitcases going nowhere. In many situations, the ultimate test will be when the system goes live. So, even after acceptance testing, testing might still have a long way to go.

Alpha Testing

Our whole methodology has been based on trying to get things right. We test at module level, inspect the code, test at system level, and then let the client test. In theory, if all this testing has gone satisfactorily, when we put the software live, chances are good that it will work.

Unfortunately, the success of going live depends on how well we have simulated the live environment in our testing. Going live is always a risk. We try to minimize the risk with all our preparation and testing, but the risk still exists. If the system we have designed and developed is controlling expensive plant equipment, the risk might be colossal. So, we introduce the software to the live environment incrementally—in other words, where that's possible, in stages where each stage is as self-contained as possible. We introduce the software to the live environment on a weekend, or very late at night, or during a shutdown period, when production or demand on the system is minimal and when we have a degree of control.

We can perform *alpha testing*—that is, we test the system live for the very first time in as controlled a situation as we can manage. During this period, we *must* have a mechanism that will let us fall back to the old system (the way the business used to be handled before the new software came along) if things go wrong.

If problems arise in testing, we analyze them, we fix them, and we issue new releases for further alpha testing (having first done module and system testing to the best of our ability). Slowly, as the software becomes more stable, people start to become more confident in it, and we can begin to increase the load on the system until it reaches the desired operational level.

A time comes when alpha testing has proved that the software is stable in a genuine, live environment, with no holds barred. The customer can then sign off on alpha testing, and we move into *beta testing*.

Beta Testing

Our software has now proved itself in the rigorous, live environment. The software is still, however, "new," and it might not have been exposed to every combination of circumstances that the live environment is capable of throwing at it. There might be peak loading situations that occur only once a month, for example.

The next stage—*beta testing*—is to put the software into the live environment to experience the full range of operational conditions (that is, no special conditions are imposed). This may involve releasing the software to many different locations and seeing how each location reacts. Beta testing is still a time of risk, although the risk is not as great as in alpha testing. Still important is that we can switch in the old system to take over if something major goes wrong wherever we are testing the software.

An Incremental Approach

Software can be extremely complex, particularly if it is responding to a multitude of external events that require fast responses by the system. Wherever and whenever possible, install and test bits of the final system at a time. Gain confidence at each stage that the code you are testing is robust and works well. Incrementally build up the functionality that is going live. Solving problems that pop up in live testing is so much easier if you "ramp up" the complexity of the system incrementally. The alternative is the "big-bang" approach.

The Big-Bang Approach

The big-bang approach to software development is possibly the major cause of stress in the computer industry. The *big-bang approach* is to write the system, test it, and, when you are happy with its performance, let it go live all at once in the full environment. No matter how much testing you do, no matter how much you think about and analyze a situation, there will always be something the customer forgot to tell you or something no one knew about. My own personal feeling about the big-bang approach to software installation is that it presents far too great a risk in most instances. The more complex the live environment is, the more combinations of code pathways will exist, and, consequently, the more difficult assessing all the risks will be.

Unfortunately, if projects are delayed, the pressure to go live before you are ready can become enormous—usually resulting in a big-bang approach as an attempt to recover lost time. And that's another good reason for always delivering on time. If you are put in a situation in which you are forced to adopt the big-bang, go-live scenario, my best advice is to spend a great deal of time doing risk assessment and working out contingency plans. Above all, make sure you always have a fallback plan for going to a working system with minimum delay if things go wrong.

Software Support

So, what's software support all about? Software support is a big topic, but I'll try to give you a crash course to complete the picture of how you take a concept, turn it into code, and then support your software in the field. When software comes out of development and passes both system testing and acceptance testing, it goes *live*. Remember, our goal is to introduce *controlled live testing* as part of the acceptance scenario. But, after software has truly gone live, the developers initially need to support it. Let's start by looking at the types of problems a customer might call you with:

◆ *Finger Trouble*—These problems are the ones reported by inexperienced users who don't fully understand how to work the system.

◆ *Genuine Bugs*—These problems require technical solutions by support or development staff.

◆ *Environmental Problems*—These issues are associated with modern, PC-hardware and operating-software environments.

◆ *Wish List*—These issues are clearly requests for additional functionality beyond what was contractually agreed upon.

These definitions are fundamental to how we set up support of a software product. I will expand the definitions as we move on.

Setting Up Support

As you can see, the reasons for a user requiring support vary. You want to avoid having developers tied up answering support calls that non-programmers can handle. Programmers should spend their time programming—that's what they are good at, and that's what they are paid to do.

If we look at the case study, Monty was distributing E-MagBooks, with our software loaded, to his sales staff, potential distributors, and even some of his special customers. Consequently, for *warranty support* (support immediately after acceptance), any issues that arose had to be reported to Monty's project manager—in this case, Samantha—and she would contact us. We needed her to coordinate all the calls from Monty's user base, whatever that might consist of. (The last thing we wanted was for anyone who now had an E-MagBook to be pestering us for support, particularly concerning problems which had nothing to do with us.)

The Single Channel

We needed a single channel of communications between us—K&C Consultants and Montasana Systems—for support issues. Samantha and her team could initially assess all the issues. Any issues that Samantha could deal with would then be shielded from us. We would be disturbed only when a problem arose that Samantha's team could not address.

An interesting question had to do with what would happen when Monty started selling to the public. Montasana systems, or one of its agents, would set up a Help desk. The designated group would handle any support calls from the public. Only if they couldn't handle something would it come back to us—but, once again, only via Samantha.

I'm emphasizing here the need for a single communications channel into the software supplier and into the developers. This communications channel must be designed such that all the trivial issues never get to the developers, and so that they are bothered only with problems that cannot be solved anywhere else.

Figure 9.5 illustrates the type of support channel we required in the case study. In Monty's case, "users" were a mixture of his sales staff, distributors, selected clients, and anyone else he had given an E-MagBook to for evaluation.

Non-Software Problems

In the case study, having only one official channel into Montasana for support was important to us. Issues would come up with the disks that Samantha's department would create, some people wouldn't understand how the Workbench worked because they hadn't read the manual, people would want to know what certain messages meant, and so on. We didn't want to become involved with queries we couldn't address or with the simple ones someone else could handle.

We'd told Monty in our contractual documentation that warranty issues must be reported via a named person or persons in his company, such as Samantha. We could not accommodate calls from anyone else, except by prior arrangement. We also stipulated that issues passed on to us must concern only clear nonconformity (that is, the software failed to do something that was clearly specified in the requirements document). Finally, any wish-list items must come through a separate channel.

Education

You can't guarantee that that the type of support channel we have discussed will function the way you want it to. On the whole, as time goes on, customers become better at understanding the difference between a support issue and a requirement for further development, and when they can deal with something themselves. To a large extent, the process is one of education. Initially, customers ring up with anything they can't handle. After a while, when it has been pointed out to them for the umpteenth time that they are talking about a future requirement and they need to contact sales, they start to get the message about new requirements. Customers soon start understanding what environmental issues are all about after it has been explained to them a number of times that the PC must be running Windows 98 and not Windows 95 before the software will load correctly—as the user guide indicates.

Standby

During warranty support, the software is still very new, and the developers need to be on standby. And this standby status should be reflected in their commitments for the period of the warranty. In other words, their availability to work on other projects should be reduced accordingly. For example, normal availability is considered to be 80 percent. This availability can drop to 40 percent during a warranty period so the developers are available just two days a week for new work. Ideally, you want this support channel directly into development to last for as short a time as possible.

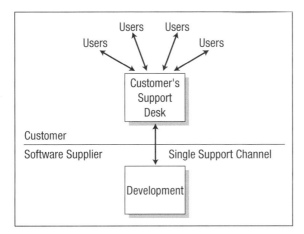

Figure 9.5
Typical support channel between a software house and its client.

Support after Warranty

After the software has been bedded in, and the warranty period has expired—and depending on the size of the product and its level of sales—a software house might need to have trained its own support-desk personnel in the product. This training allows you to shift the burden of support from the developers to trained support specialists. Typically, a mixture of application specialists, support specialists, and programmers run the support desk. Given this approach, the structure we would likely see between K&C Consultants and Montasana would develop into something like what you see in Figure 9.6.

We still had only a single channel to Montasana's support desk, but, this time, that channel ran between Montasana's support desk and ours. We would have to train application staff for our support desk. Application staff includes people who understand the application, like Anne did. Our people would take the calls from Monty's support staff, categorize each call, and try to provide a remedy. Monty's central support desk would be assisting all the sales staff, selected clients, and genuine internal users. They would also take calls from any regional support desks that Monty might set up, depending on how sales to the public went. Distributors of the final product might even set up these regional desks. Once again, in the case study, everything was being channeled back to the central support desk at Montasana, and then passed back to us only if Montasana staff couldn't handle the issue. Our own support desk then had a channel into the development department for assistance. This structure completely shielded the development department from unsolicited contact with the software users, but the department would still be available to the frontline support desk as a last resort.

As always, wish-list items must come through a separate channel so that we could (at the risk of sounding very boring), produce a requirements specification, cost the job, and prepare a quote. At the time of warranty, the software house usually has very few domain experts, and the burden of support tends to fall on those few. In the case study, Anne would start training

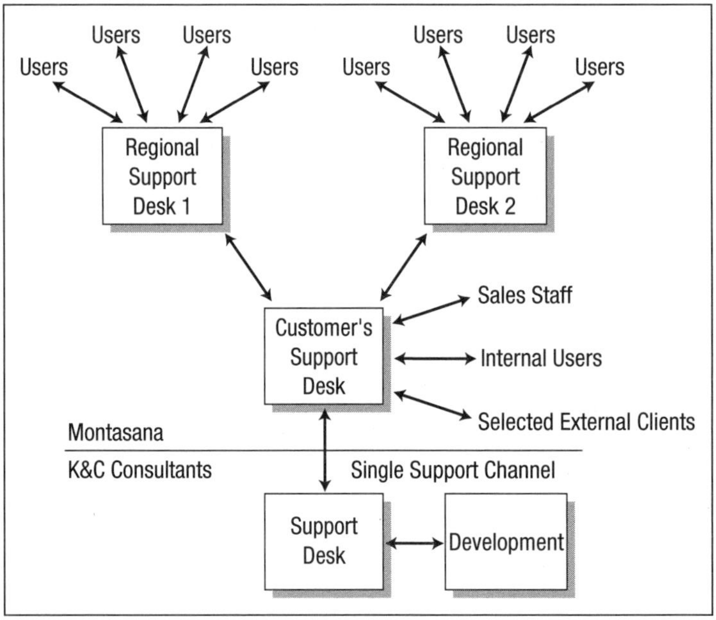

Figure 9.6
After-warranty support set-up.

one other application person fairly soon, with the intention of gearing up our support desk for when warranty ended. (Some of our support staff also serve as testers, because testing was where our main application-level expertise lies.)

After the warranty period, programmers who were involved in the development might find themselves on the support desk at various times. Clearly, you must maintain application-support coverage during normal working hours, at a minimum. And to cover holidays, sickness, and so on, you sometimes might have to send people from development to the support desk. Doing this is actually quite healthy because it helps to keep programmers in touch with real-world use of the software they develop. As a developer, being exposed to support issues actually makes you think hard from the user's point of view about the software you develop in the future.

If the customer wants extended coverage—weekends, or even, in some cases, 24-hour coverage—the customer pays accordingly for that privilege. (Appreciate that the customer is receiving *application support*, *environment support*, and *software support*.)

Revenue from Support

Handled properly, support can provide a software house with a good revenue stream. You can offer varying levels of support, even 24-hour coverage, for which a client pays a substantial premium. But, after the software is established, it shouldn't go wrong. Let's look at an example to illustrate what support is really all about.

A system was put into an automated warehouse for which the client demanded 24-hour support during the week. The customer did maintenance on the plant equipment on the weekend, which was the only time the computer-control software was free. The client was paying for the expertise to diagnose system problems at any time of the day or night.

Initially, the software that was supplied was supported for nonconformity to specification, but, over the years, the support team had become very knowledgeable about the whole system—the conveyors, the cranes, the automated weighing and measuring gear, and so on. When a fault occurred anywhere in the plant, the computer often indicated an error condition that the support staff could sometimes interpret better than the warehouse shift staff could. For example, if a crane stopped communicating with the computer, the message that came up was "Crane XYZ not communicating." The message usually meant that a cable had snapped, a plug had come out, or something fairly trivial had happened. Being far better problem solvers than the customers for the system involved, the support staff could often guide the shift operators to a hardware failure far more quickly than the customers could find the problem on their own.

Over the years, more and more software was added to the system, software that told the site operators what to look for when a fault message came up, and the calls to the support desk diminished considerably. But the client's management team felt much happier paying for software support to be available as necessary. Such support was an insurance policy. In our example, when the automatic systems failed, product could no longer be placed in storage, and it started to back up from the production lines, which ran 24 hours, around the clock, five days a week. Running production without the automated warehouse could be accommodated only for about three hours, then space became a problem, and the shift staff had to contemplate shutting the lines down. Shutting down would cost "huge bucks" in loss of production time. Getting an application specialist out of bed to see if he or she could analyze the problem and guide them to a solution was cheaper for them. (Of course, the possibility of a genuine software bug always exists as well. I've certainly come across a bug that remained dormant in a system for more than 12 years, even though the software was used almost every day. Only a certain, unusual, combination of external events caused the program to fail.)

Call Handling

So how do you handle a support call? Figure 9.7 shows a flow diagram that describes the sort of analysis and decision flow you will need.

A call comes in, and someone on the support desk takes the initial message. The person who takes the call might know a lot about the application, or he or she might be able to pass the call to someone else at the desk who can help. In such cases, logging the call details and providing a solution there and then, on the phone, might be possible. If that's the case, you can close the call.

The two types of call are *open* and *closed*. Your aim will be to close the call as quickly as you can. If you can close on the same call in which you logged the issue, that's great. Regardless of

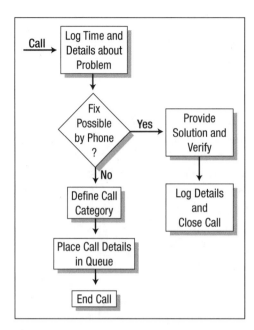

Figure 9.7
Simple model for support-call handling.

the time it takes to solve a problem, you will always log both the details and the solution, usually via a call-logging system. Such a system allows anyone to see what open calls are outstanding, and, more importantly, it allows database searches for issues, to determine whether a call being reported has already been dealt with, for example. If the issue has been resolved elsewhere, a solution might already be recorded.

If the person answering the call can't help, he or she takes down as much detail as possible from the caller. The goal is to gather enough information to be able to reproduce the fault on the support facility's own computers. If that can't be done, further information might be required, or the support facility might need to dial in to the client's machine to see the fault in action.

As far as the first contact between client and support facility is concerned, at best, the fault is recorded and cleared by a solution provided over the phone. At worst, the details of the problem are recorded, a category is defined, and the issue report is placed in a queue for an application specialist to look at. Again, a call-logging system usually does all this.

De-Queuing a Call from the Pending Queue

Typically, when application experts take a shift on the support desk, the first thing they do is to look at the pending queue to see what faults are logged and whether they can do anything about them. This process is called *de-queuing* the pending queue. When support

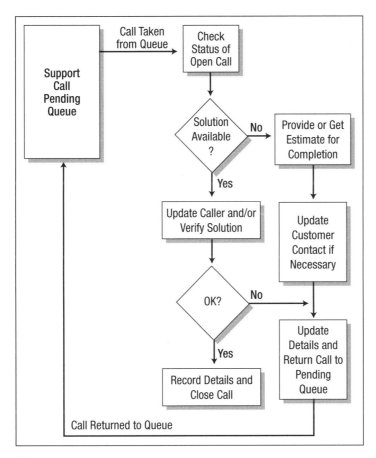

Figure 9.8.
De-queuing the support queue.

specialists are not answering calls, they work on what they have assembled from the queue that their individual expertise allows them to solve. This process of de-queuing is shown in Figure 9.8.

If a specialist has already processed a call taken from the queue, a solution might have been logged, but not yet passed on to the customer. If that is the case, the client can be contacted and given the relevant information. It's then necessary to verify that the solution worked. If all is well, the call can be closed down. Of course, this may not all happen at the same time—the process might require a number of iterations around the steps listed in the flow diagram in Figure 9.8 to get client verification that the solution worked and then close the call.

Alternatively, the call might require work. In that case, the support specialist either does the work or gets an estimate from someone who can do it. Someone then will inform the customer and place the call back in the pending queue until a solution is found, or until the client requests another status report. It might well be that the person tasked with sorting out the problem is a developer. Using a developer to sort out the problem must, of course, be a last-case scenario—that is, the support staff has first considered all other avenues.

Initial Assessment

When a support specialist looks at a call's details, he or she does an *initial assessment* to determine whether the issue can be resolved over the phone. If resolution is possible that way, the support specialist calls the contact, imparts the information, and, if the result is successful, closes the call. If the assessment of the detail indicates that the problem cannot be fixed over the phone, the support person must try to reproduce the fault to analyze the problem further.

Reproducing the Fault

Being able to reproduce the fault is one of the most important aspects of support, and doing so can be a nightmare. Being able to duplicate a reported failure depends on the quality of information recorded from the initial call, which varies enormously, depending on how much the client could explain and how much the support person who took the initial call could understand. More often than not, someone will need to call the client to get more information or clarification. That way, two people are talking to each other who both understand the application from a user's point of view—the customer with a problem and the support specialist with a potential solution. The goal is to get sufficient information to be able to reproduce the fault. If the support person can get to that stage, he or she can analyze the situation, experiment, and (hopefully) come up with a solution, assuming the issue does not require a software modification. When such a solution is possible, the support specialist can simply ring the client, explain the solution, and close the call.

Available Expertise

Ideally, application domain experts are available on the support desk to handle any aspect of the software intricacies from a user's point of view. Support desks usually have a number of "experts" with differing experience available to assist in finding solutions to customers' problems, including those who understand servers and PC environments (that is, "environmental" specialists). Some of these people might also have specific application expertise. But, primarily, they have deep knowledge of things such as PC hardware, networks, servers, operating systems, system management, and other related areas. Only if the support staff can see no possible solution to the problem should they pass the problem back to development. As always, the goal is to let the developers get on with development unless their involvement is vital.

Ownership

Ownership is a term we've used before. In support, because so many people can be involved in solving an issue at any given time, always having one person take ownership of a support call at each stage of the process is vital. Taking ownership of a call is an important concept from a management point of view. When you take a call, you own it until you close the call, place it in the queue, or pass it to someone else who agrees to take ownership. The person who takes the call out of the queue and decides to run with it then takes ownership until the call is closed or handed over to someone else, and so on.

The support manager is constantly scanning the queue to see the status of all open calls. If the manager is not happy about the status of a specific call, he or she can contact the owner of the problem to determine what should be done next.

Is It a Software Bug?

Software bugs are by no means obvious, even though the symptoms of the problem might appear to indicate that the fault is in the code. Remember, only when no one on the support team can find a solution does the problem go back to developers—not before the support team has explored every avenue. You might think a software bug ought to be obvious, but I can assure you that whether software has a bug is often far from clear.

For example, a user calls and states that the program ran okay yesterday but doesn't run okay today. As soon as the system is run, it crashes with a GPF (General Protection Fault) error. The support person must ask the right questions to establish why the program worked yesterday and not today. Software doesn't suddenly stop working unless something has changed. With the right questions, the details start to emerge. For example, the client's maintenance department was "playing" with the system last night. Further investigation reveals that the maintenance person "borrowed" some RAM from the PC. This action leads to an application failure with a GPF, because the application is not structured to determine whether the system has sufficient memory for the application to run. In many ways, a support person needs to be like a detective, analyzing the situation and questioning the witnesses.

Support people must be methodical and resourceful, calling on development only as a last resort. My belief is that you stop developing to support software only when your support people fail to support. Obviously, how your company implements support depends a lot on the size of the company, the products, and the customer base. But, in all cases, you want to minimize the impact support has on development.

Support from Development Staff

So, how do you involve development staff in support? One way is to involve them on a rotational basis: Each programmer can spend some time providing support from within the development department, supplying bug fixes on various projects. This developer's time is then dedicated to support activities. For example, each programmer might be seconded to do support work for one week out of every two months. The goal is to maintain a reasonable level of support coverage within the development department for support-desk access when necessary.

Because the demand for programmers to support code is likely to fluctuate, you need to be able to anticipate when peaks are likely. Clearly, after a major upgrade to the operating system or to the hardware on a large system, the possibility is greater that some difficult issues will arise that might require the involvement of someone who has a good understanding of old application software.

At any given time, the development department must have a contact person who support personnel can get in touch with. The nominated person must then take ownership of the problem, and the original call will be transferred into development. From the call details, the support manager can see when the problem was transferred and to whom, and can follow up on the problem's progress as and when necessary. When the developer has assessed the situation, he or she can update the original call log in the support system (to which development must have access).

Solutions developers produce might be issued in the form of patches to distributed software, or in the form of fixes contained within a new release. We'll discuss all these subjects later. Whatever the outcome, the support manager must be kept informed concerning the nature of the work development has undertaken and how they will deliver a solution to the customer.

Response Times

Customers expect support desks to react to problems in a certain time. The time actually depends on the type of contract the customers have purchased. Let's consider a three-level support facility. Level 1 is the minimum support offering, in which a client is guaranteed that an application specialist will get back to the caller in, for example, five hours from the first call. At that stage, the customers are guaranteed that they will be talking to someone who has a deep knowledge of the application domain. However, the support department must make sure it has the relevant number of specialists available to meet its contract commitments. Level 1 support might be available from 9:00 A.M. to 5:00 P.M.; so, if someone calls at 4:30 P.M., the five hours starts, stops at 5:00 P.M., and then commences again at 9:00 A.M. the next day.

With Level 1 support, the number of faults closed in the five-hour response time is likely to be low, because a customer who takes out this level of support usually has been using the system for some time. The customer is, therefore, probably quite familiar with the programs, and the calls you tend to get are few and far between. But, if you do receive a call, it can be for quite an obscure problem that often requires dialing in to the customer's computer to gather more data. This likelihood is especially true on realtime, process-control systems, to which you dial in and monitor the plant activity, trying to gather as much information as you can about what's happening on the system.

After the warranty period for an application has expired, but when things are still very new, starting a client at Level 2 or Level 3 support is sensible. Level 2 support might offer a three-hour response time, and Level 3 a one-hour response time for access to an application expert. And, of course, the cost of each support level is dependent on the guaranteed response time and whether coverage is extended to out-of-office hours.

The response time quoted for a given level of support is the time in which the customer is guaranteed that an application domain expert will contact him or her. Response time is *not* the time in which a problem fix is guaranteed—providing such a figure is simply not possible.

Call Priority

You can also use the three levels of response time to define the processing priority of calls. For example, Level 3 calls might be handled in priority over Level 2, and Level 2 over Level 1. Level-1 users might wait quite a while for a solution if the support desk is very busy. But, then, that delay will be reflected in the lower-cost service in the pricing structure for the three-tiered support package.

After a call has been assessed, the problem is solved on what is termed a "best-endeavors basis," driven at a priority level dictated by the support level the client has purchased. Sometimes, upgrading a call's priority from one level to the next higher level might be necessary, depending on a wealth of factors. For example, if the problem affects a large number of users and is holding up their operation, upgrading its priority is a sensible way to proceed. However, you might want to write into a support contract that, if a reported problem involves a solution that turns out to have nothing to do with the supported software, a fee might be charged. This addition to the contract lets you recoup any additional expense, which may be incurred in doing your utmost, above and beyond the call of duty, to solve a client's problem.

One-Stop Shop

Although small software houses usually can't do this, offering customers a single telephone number for hardware, operating system, and application support is a big commercial advantage. Quite often, even though the customer calls for software support, you end up being involved as well with operating system and sometimes hardware support. A customer usually first consults the application specialists, regardless of the nature of the problem. Consequently, having a good relationship with a hardware support team to whom you can pass on hardware issues is quite useful.

With the backing of a hardware support group, you can front-end all the calls and contact the necessary support facility if you need to. Now that hardware is so much more reliable and compact than it used to be, you can even consider taking on a basic hardware-support role, in which you simply replace complete systems to get the customer back up and running. Provided backup procedures are adequate, and you have a transportable medium that lets you set up a blank system with all the backup files, you can offer a comprehensive service. Customers will pay well for the luxury of calling a single number to get all their support issues solved.

When you do not offer a one-stop-shop support capability, your customer must understand the repercussions of this limitation and be adequately covered for hardware support when that is necessary. Before you enter into a software-development contract, ask yourself what will happen if any of the hardware becomes faulty. Does the contract include a clear demarcation of responsibility? If it does not, make sure you clarify those roles of responsibility for the customer.

Backups

When the application involves the management of data, establishing good backup procedures for the customer is essential. Contractually, you need to indicate that the ultimate responsibility for backups belongs to the client. You can set up the systems and procedures that provide the backup capability, but, unless you are specifically given responsibility for the customer's backup requirements (another potential revenue stream), you must ensure that the customer is aware of his or her responsibilities.

A good support facility will constantly check that its supported clients are executing regular backups and will also check that full system recovery is possible. Doing backups religiously every day is of no value if, on the one occasion a backup is required, reconstructing the system fails.

Disaster recovery (restoring a user's system—getting it up and running after a catastrophic failure) is yet another potential revenue stream that your support desk can offer. Doing disaster recovery, of course, depends on the frequency and reliability of the backup mechanisms both you and your customers have in place.

Backups and their production are not usually the responsibility of the software supplier's support desk. But I strongly recommend keeping a wary eye on your customer and making sure the customer understands both the importance of doing system backups and ensuring the quality of those backups.

Software for Support Desks

You can find a lot of really good software to help run your support facilities. You can buy software to track calls from when they come in to your support desk to when the calls are closed. Most of these facilities provide a comprehensive knowledge base that builds up over time from data the support people enter in the normal course of their work. Such information can help with speedy diagnosis of common problems and possible identification of obscure issues if they have happened before.

Support-Call Categories

We defined support-call categories earlier:

♦ Finger trouble

♦ Environmental problems

♦ Genuine software bugs

♦ Wish-list items

Finger Trouble

Finger trouble is normally expressed as an RTM issue, where RTM indicates that the solution is to "read the manual." Finger trouble is basically an issue that would not have been an issue if the customer had bothered to read the manual, been trained correctly, had more operational experience, and so on. A software supplier can offer training—sometimes you might be able to train two or three operators, sometimes a whole department, depending on how serious the customer's commitment to training is.

Finger trouble can be a difficult area for support. If the person calling with the problem has been trained in the use of the application software, you can usually get to the bottom of a problem and resolve an RTM issue swiftly. If the person hasn't received any training in the application, the process can be a long haul because you have to do a lot of explaining, ask a lot of questions, and, above all, be very patient.

RTM calls can range from things such as, "How do I get the data from your system into an Excel spreadsheet?" to "Why is it that, at midnight, I can't log on to the system?" The Excel issue might be easy to respond to—for example, no one mentioned Excel in the requirements specification, consequently, the facility was not developed. The midnight login issue might best be solved if the customer would read the user's manual, which would tell him or her that, at midnight, the system performs backup and maintenance procedures that require all users to be logged out. And logging in is suspended until 1:00 A.M.

Another Example RTM Problem

Let's look at a more detailed example of the type of RTM call you might experience. A voice-recognition system was installed in a baggage-handling hall at an airport. Using the system, sorters were to direct baggage to particular flights by saying the flight number into a mike set. This particular voice-recognition system required about half an hour's voice training for each user before that person could be allowed to operate the system. Each new user was trained without fail.

People would call in saying that the system had stopped working. The system was okay for most of the morning and then it suddenly stopped working. Operators couldn't divert bags, and they had to resort to manual handling. To the customer, this was a serious breakdown, because the throughput of the bags onto the sorters dropped dramatically if the handlers had to manually key in the location of each bag.

After a few pertinent questions to the customer, determination was made that this problem always happened after a shift change. Eventually, the problem was traced. Whenever the operator going off shift forgot to log off the system, and the new operator forgot to log on as a new user, the new user's voice input was checked against the previous user's voice patterns. Because some individuals seemed to have very similar voice patterns, they got away without logging off or on, but others did not. You might think the users would instinctively understand the need to initially identify themselves to the computer so it knew who they were and got the right voice characteristics loaded. But making such assumptions is unwise. Just because a solution to a problem is obvious to you, as a programmer don't assume the solution should be obvious to a user who does not possess your detailed understanding of the software.

Environmental Issues

Environmental issues have come into their own since the advent of PCs and PC networks—and, in particular, the client/server setup. The demand for Windows-type software is enormous. This demand has led to lots of software written for PCs to access data on networked databases. The PC has replaced the old-fashioned terminal. The problem is that users don't want to run only their primary business applications from the PC—they also want to run word processors, spreadsheets, screen-savers, games, and so on. In terms of support, the client/server setup can be a complete nightmare.

Single Servers with Dumb Terminals

In the days of single servers and distributed dumb terminals, life was simple. You installed the software on the server, and you supported the software on the server. If anything went wrong, you fixed the problem on the server, and everyone was happy once again because, as soon as they logged onto the fixed server, they were running the latest software. Handling the environment didn't require any discipline on the part of the user. Life was simple.

This environment was also very frustrating for the users. Often, they wanted to take data from the server and manipulate it in a certain way, which was not an option in terms of the server's functionality. Then, along came the PC—and, in particular, the spreadsheet. At last, users could manipulate data. They could use a simple concept, the spreadsheet, to do anything they wanted to the data. Users just needed to get the mainframe to supply them with data. Once they had that data, they could use it however they wanted. But extracting the data from the mainframe usually proved to be the problem.

Client/Server

Client/server changed the limited environment for users. With client/server, users could obtain data from the central database and output the information onto the PC's disks. This capability integrated the PC directly into the data flow, but, in terms of support, the capability brought with it horrendous logistical issues.

For example, let's suppose you've developed a client/server system. Software is running on one or more servers, and software is running on each PC. The client connects to the database, and you run the application. Now, suppose a bug surfaces. The bug might require a fix on the server—all well and good. You fix the server, and the clients are happy again. But, suppose the problem lies on the client. You must provide a fix for every single client, and there might be hundreds of them. Until you have transferred the fix to all clients, not every user has access to the latest version of the software.

You can set up the client to download its software every time a user logs on. Then, all a user must do to get the latest version is log off and log on again. Great, except loading the software onto the client might take so long that the user starts complaining. So, you put in proxy servers that allow high-speed loading compared to the server, and then you only have to update the proxy servers.

The nightmare doesn't stop there. A PC breaks down, so the user grabs another and plugs it in. The application stops dead. A support person might take a while to realize that the PC the user plugged in is actually an old PC, with a totally different graphics card that causes problems with the application. Or possibly, the customer's original PC has an older version of a DLL that the application requires. Or, the replacement PC might have a network card that's not set up correctly. Or, the replacement PC might have a hard drive without sufficient capacity for the application. Or, the PC might have a faulty CD drive that keeps crashing the system. Or, the application might not be compatible with the version of the operating system on the PC. And so on.

Internet/Intranet Applications

Support of applications that are executed via browsers is much easier than with the client/server arrangement I previously defined, because the browser tends to execute only code that is downloaded from the server when the code is first invoked, in the form of Java applets, for example. This setup is an example of the *thin client*, in which the only software on the PC is the browser. All application-related code resides on the server and is transferred to the PC's memory only when it's required. The code is not present on the PC's disks.

In many ways, the thin client has moved us back to the dumb-terminal-connected-to-a-server scenario, because all a user has to do is log out and log back on again to know that the latest application software is now available. This scenario makes support of such systems so much simpler: Fix the code on the server, and everyone will automatically be using the latest code. The penalty is, of course, the time it takes to load the code when it is first required.

What's Changed?

If you listen to a support person on the phone with a customer, he or she will ask such things as, "What's changed on the system since you last used it successfully? Has there been any maintenance on the network? Is this the same PC you used yesterday? Have you moved the PC to a different part of the network? Is it still connected to the same hub in your room?" The earlier comparison to the detective seeking clues becomes more appropriate.

In a great number of support calls that indicate a problem with software that used to work and now doesn't, the answer lies in what has changed—hardware and/or software—between the time when the application worked and when it stopped.

Real Software Bugs

At times, you do encounter real software bugs in a client's systems. After you've established that a problem's not an RTM and not an environmental problem, you're left with a genuine software bug—possibly. You still never know until you've fixed exactly what was causing the problem. You could still be dealing with a really obscure environmental issue. The one thing that a developer should demand when taking ownership of a support issue is that the support desk has been able to reproduce the fault. If that has not been possible, the developer's job becomes much harder.

Reproducing the Fault

As you troubleshoot problems with clients' computer systems, the ideal is that your support staff can duplicate the conditions that bring on the fault on your own in-house systems. The report the support desk passes on to development will provide details on how to reproduce the fault. Then, the designated person has the responsibility to fix the problem. To do this, the developer might need to sit down with an application support person to reproduce the fault or, possibly, dial in to the customer's machine.

This is a real problem-solving scenario. We diligently try to discourage a programmer's natural desire to wade into the code and start tampering on the off chance he or she might solve a problem. Those involved must fully analyze and determine a solution to the problem before they modify any code.

Supported Code Ownership

The code the developer will be looking at and modifying is frozen code that is out in the field being used by genuine customers. The code is, therefore, owned by support and not by development. This principle is fundamental to the support operation. A given system might be in a number of different states. It might be operational on-site as Version 1. The code might be in development for an upgrade to Version 2, and you might even be writing the requirements specification for Version 3.

Your support and/or installations team should always look after the code for the stable, operational version of a software system. When the warranty period has expired, the developers will hand over a copy of the frozen source code to the application support people. The support/installations team will then use this code as the source for their distribution kits, which they send to customers. The support department "owns" this software, in the respect that no changes are made to it without their authorization.

In large organizations, the support staff might even be able to support the code directly with a team of support programmers whose job is to "fix" code problems and do no development. In this instance, the difference between a development programmer and a support programmer is that a development programmer is more akin to a car designer, whereas the support programmer is more akin to the car mechanic. Both activities demand different skills; finding a developer who makes a good support programmer is rare, and vice versa.

You need to appreciate that, if, as a developer, you are engaged in support at any time, you are required to use a different skill set. This skill set involves problem solving and providing a solution that involves minimal change to the code. A developer's natural tendency is to start modifying code before the problem is fully analyzed. The professional support programmer will not modify code until he or she fully understands the nature of the fault and is convinced of a solution that has minimal impact on the system.

Modifying Distributed Code

To modify distributed code, a programmer checks out the relevant code modules from the support distribution sources, fixes the fault, and tests it thoroughly. The programmer then passes this code to the support group, who will conduct their own testing, if necessary, through the testing department. After a modification is passed, support will make a patch distribution, a new release, or whatever they deem necessary to get the fix to the customer's site, where they install the fixed software and control the proceedings from then on.

Support must test the fix on-site, and the customer must pass the fix before it is allowed to go live. This must all occur as a very controlled and carefully managed operation, with a great deal of accountability, auditability, and traceability—in other words, all the fundamental components of quality assurance. The programmer has done his or her part and hands over control to the support department to complete the operation. If support needs further assistance from the developers, those involved will ask for it. Remember, developers develop systems, and support personnel support systems. In this case, I'm including installation and distribution as part of the support activity, although that arrangement is not always the case.

Getting Fixes into Development

As programmers fix bugs, they must make sure they get the fix into both the latest version of software being developed and the distribution systems. Doing this requires coordination on the part of the programmer making the fix, the support distribution system, and the software manager in development. The manager needs to know about any bug fixes to the current distribution so that he or she can schedule the fixes into the development system (assuming those fixes are relevant to both old and new source code). If this reconciliation with new software is not done correctly, old bugs can be reintroduced in the next upgrade. And reintroducing old bugs in a new release can have one of the most damaging effects possible to a software house's reputation.

One other thing to note is that, at all stages of the proceedings, the development team must be able to reconstruct any particular release number of a given application. This reconstruction is feasible provided that a version control system manages the source code. If, for any reason, you need to drop back to a previous release level, the version control system can automatically generate the earlier version of the application from the collection of source code. Consequently, you must store all previous versions of code. This requirement is another reason why checking source code in and out is so fundamental—it is possible to have a number of development threads existing at the same time across more than one version of an application. You've seen some of the issues involved in reconciling source code in a development that was being run by only two people. Just imagine trying to control a development with teams of programmers on a large development if you weren't able to lock other programmers out of a given source module that required a change.

Dial-in Support

A vital aspect of support is being able to dial in to the customer's machine to see a problem firsthand. Sometimes, because of the complexity of the system, reproducing the fault might be impossible, particularly where plant equipment, such as conveyor belts and cranes, is involved.

Dialing in to a server is no problem. The modem can be directly connected to the server, and your PC can then act as a terminal, or a client to the server. But how do you ensure that the server can support remote PC software? Some superb PC products exist that let you connect to a PC on its site, and either take control over the PC, or monitor a customer using it. Figure 9.9 illustrates this setup.

The customer's site is in the top portion of Figure 9.9, and the software supplier's support desk is at the bottom of the figure. The support desk uses one of its PCs, which is running the special connection software, to dial in to the modem connected to one of the customer's PCs, which is designated as a support PC and is also running the special connection software.

When the connection has been made, the client's PC display appears on the support PC. Anything that the customer does on the PC at the customer site can be see on the support PC—keyboard input, mouse cursor movements, everything. The support PC mirrors the customer's screen exactly, albeit slowly, because of the limited speed of the link. Remember, GUI applications produce a lot of screen traffic that needs to come down the line to tell the support PC how the customer's screen now looks. After you have established the link, you can ask the customer to show you the fault. You obviously need a data connection from PC to PC and a voice connection, so the support person can talk to the customer as they are using their respective PCs.

If the support person wants to intervene, he or she can ask the customer to stand back, and then the support PC's keyboard and mouse controls the customer's PC. The support person can upload and download files as well, and, of course, if the support PC on the client's site is networked, the support person can access servers and other PCs at the client's site. The re-

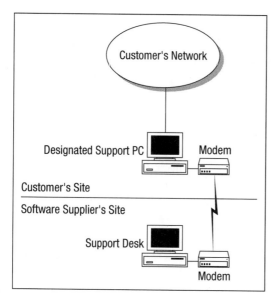

Figure 9.9
PC-to-PC support via modem connection.

mote PC, of course, is limited to the speed of the modem connection. Consequently, downloads or uploads can be slow. However, with this type of technology, your company can successfully support remote systems, even across states or countries. Dial-in support is worth its weight in gold as a support tool.

Your support staff can also communicate via the support software itself, by opening up a little messaging window in which they can send and receive text messages. However, my experience is that having a secondary voice connection opened at the same time as the PC-to-PC link works better. Because the support PC is connected to the main server on the customer's network, you can control the entire system, if you need to, and, provided you have the authorization, you can implement changes on the server or on the client's PC. Without this PC-to-PC communications software, supporting client/server systems at all satisfactorily would be extremely difficult. In addition to monitoring and controlling, you can send patches—and even full distributions—using the technology described.

Automatic Monitoring

You can also develop monitoring software that uses remote-access technology. For example, you can have a monitoring PC that dials into a number of critical systems every night, either via a PC on-site, or directly into a modem on the server. The dial-in PC connection then activates a server task that performs a variety of checks on the state of data files, databases, and so on, and reports back. When the support staff comes in the next morning, they look at the reports to determine whether anything needs attention. A good use of this sort of technology is monitoring database file sizes. Some databases cannot increase their file allocations after they have filled their predesignated entitlement. Using automatic monitoring, you can be informed when the size of the database has reached a point at which the disk allocation needs to be extended.

Hardware-support companies use this type of capability to call their various sites and interrogate the error-log reports that the operating-system device drivers produce automatically. For example, if they monitor the number of retry errors on a server's disks over a period of time, and if they see the number start to increase and become excessive, they know that such an increase is often an early warning of an imminent disk failure. Quite often, the client learns about such a problem only when a support engineer rings up to schedule a disk replacement.

Security

Not all customers welcome suppliers or support desks freely logging on to their systems. Some customers are paranoid (and with reason) about letting anyone have remote access to their servers. One neat way round this problem is to get the customer to agree to a dial-back facility.

The Dial-Back Facility

With a dial-back facility, to make a connection from the support desk to the customer's site, the support PC dials up the client's computer and then "talks" to a piece of software to establish who the call is coming from. Then, the support PC dials off and breaks the link. The software at the customer's end authenticates the call and then dials the support PC back on a number it *knows* belongs to the support organization. That way, the customer can greatly narrow hackers' ability to dial in. The customer's computer has a guaranteed number that belongs to the support organization, and, if a request to connect comes in, such a connection will be made, by a dial-back call, only to the number that connects to a known physical location.

Email

In addition to allowing customers to send email support issues to a support desk and receive responses via email, you can also use automatic email to inform customers of issues, public holiday arrangements, restricted coverage if your systems are down, and so on. In fact, you can use automatic email for all sorts of purposes. Application software can set up alerts, in which it can automatically transmit to registered email addresses. For example, if an application program detects certain error conditions, it can send an email to the system manager, the supplier's support desk, the managing director, and anyone else on the action list. Such software can also automatically set off beepers, activate telephone warnings, and so on.

Security Issues

Always take customer's security seriously. You should never, under any circumstances, put a client's system at risk by being careless or stupid in your endeavor to solve a support issue. As a developer or a support person, you have a professional duty to safeguard your clients' and your employer's interests. You should never treat security lightly.

Patches

A big system comprises many independent binary modules or executables. On some systems, you can fix a bug in perhaps one software module—in other words, by using a *patch*. All you might need to do is send an upgraded executable or binary file to fix the fault. You need to record the exact content of each site. Again, you can find a wealth of good support packages that are designed to help you keep track of what's where. However, patching also requires that you have good systems and procedures to follow.

In the event you create a patch, you need a procedure that everyone involved must follow before the patch goes to site, to ensure that the support database is up-to-date. This procedure can be automated to a large degree, whereby the same software that updates the support database also controls the transmission of patches. However, at some stage, you are dependent on a person doing something correctly, and that's where adherence to procedures becomes vital—another essential aspect of quality assurance—this time, in the support of software-distribution patching.

Making a Patch Live

Sometimes, a single patch might be critical to a number of other sites. In that case, you can schedule transmission of the patch to all sites that need it, but the patch must not go live.

First, you will transmit a patch into a holding area on the customer's system. To make any patch go live on a given site, you must first contact the system manager on-site and get his or her authorization to proceed. Then, the patch is installed, either by your support desk or by customer's staff, for the system manager or representative to check in a test environment. If the site representative approves the patch, then—and only then—does a patch go live.

If the patch needs to be distributed to all the clients on a client/server network, you will first transfer the patch into a holding area on each client. Only when all the clients have been updated do you then "order" the PCs to switch over to the new software. You must make patches go live in as controlled and accountable a way as possible. You must never let patches go live without telling the site's system manager first. If anything goes wrong, the site manager is the person who will have to react.

Patches are a necessary evil. As a rule, send patches to a site only if they are absolutely necessary. One big problem with patches is releasing patches that have dependencies on other patches. Before such a patch can go live, all the other patches on which it is dependent must also be installed. This complexity is another very good reason for using a support system that keeps track both of patches and their dependencies, and of the status of patches on each customer site.

All the things I've mentioned about auditability and accountability in software development extend into support as well. These criteria are just as essential in support as they are in development, if not more so.

Scheduled Releases

You don't want to continue to add patches to your sites, patch after patch after patch. If you adopt the policy of using patches only when they're absolutely necessary, not all sites will have the same patch level.

Every now and then, you can issue a maintenance release of the software. This release will contain all the bug fixes you have made since the previous major release, and you can install the new release on all supported sites. This release then brings all sites up to the same revision level. Alternatively, you can place patches in the next version update to the software—that is, the next new release. A maintenance release tends to contain just fixes to known problems, but no new functionality. Typically, a major product might have as many as 2 maintenance releases a year and 1 new release every 18 months to 2 years.

How Long to Support?

The product life cycle is geared toward developing a product to meet a demand. After you've designed and developed the product, you release and start to sell it. Further developments keep the product in demand. You support the product until no one wants it any more.

While all this is going on, you need to find out what the future requirements are that the next generation of product needs to meet. Because of the time it takes to get a concept to market, you may need to be capturing requirements for the next generation of software product while you're starting to sell the previous version.

The goal is to be in a position to start selling the new product as sales of the old one-drop off. This relationship implies that you will eventually be in a position of supporting two generations of product. However, you can provide incentives to your customer base to drop the old and take on the new. Figure 9.10 illustrates the product life cycle, including the life and death of two generations of a system.

In the first of the two diagrams in Figure 9.10, you see the birth of the product, the requirements capture, analysis, design, development, and testing. When the product is ready, it starts to sell, and you receive revenue. This revenue consists of sales and support income. Eventually, the income levels out, and then it starts to drop; the product is dying. No more new sales occur; all the revenue is coming from renewal of support contracts. Eventually, no one is using the product any more, and it dies.

The second diagram shows what a software house tries to do to keep the revenue from its products at a suitable level. During the life of the first generation of product, the company starts to invest in preparing for the next generation. Development of this new product starts

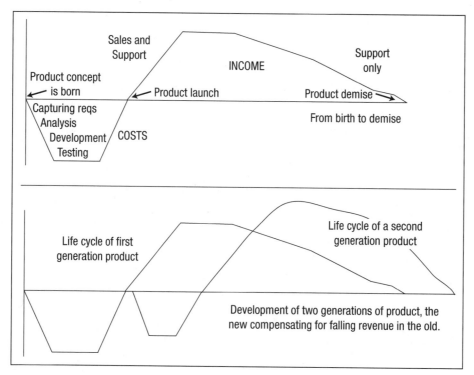

Figure 9.10
Product development life cycle.

while sales of the first generation are still going up. If the calculations are done correctly, and the market is assessed accurately, the rising income of the new generation compensates for the falling income of the first. That's the theory.

Return to the Case Study:
The End of Testing

The end of acceptance testing is always a good time for celebration. One thing is more satisfying than producing a robust, well-designed, software product that does what the customer wants—and that's doing all this within budget and on time.

The weekend after acceptance testing, Montasana loaded up 50 prototype E-MagBooks with the viewer and shipped them out to salesmen all over the country. Each package was sent with two removable disks that contained examples of Text Books, Picture Albums, and Reference Books that Samantha and her team had painstakingly made using the Notepad editor.

The Next Step

We were now ready to start the final phase of the project—the development of the Title Index Editor and the Page Index Editor, which would make the generation of titles and Page Indexes much easier.

Chapter 10
Development of the Title Index Editor

In this chapter, you will see how we started a new project phase and completed the Title Index Editor development in the case study. A key theme in the development of both editors was software reusability, which I discuss in this chapter, and which is demonstrated throughout the case study.

During the development of the Title Index Editor, the customer tried to shift the goalposts on us by asking for early delivery, and you will see how we handled that request without compromising our contractual situation. Having the goalposts move while a project is in progress is a common problem, and we will look at how to handle this eventuality.

The prototype viewer was now fully operational. So far, we'd had no support calls. We suspected Samantha was getting calls, but she was clearly handling them without having to contact us.

Starting a New Project Phase

Whenever a new project phase starts, you should hold a brief start-up meeting. Invite all the people who are relevant to the work that must be conducted. A phase start-up meeting needs to accomplish three things:

♦ *Review what needs to be done*—from both a technical and a project viewpoint.

♦ *Modify your approach according to what's happened in previous phases*—if necessary.

♦ *Reassess the risks*—in light of your experiences.

Phase Review

Reviewing what has to be done in a new phase is always essential. New people might be coming into the project for the first time; if they have no prior knowledge of what has been done on the project, someone will need to bring them up to speed. People who were present at the project start-up meeting might be getting involved only now. Because a considerable time might have elapsed since the project began, getting these people back up to speed is important. As the project has progressed, its nature might also have changed, and you will need to convey any differences in project context to the team.

We've discussed reviewing in all sorts of contexts in this book. Reviewing helps to keep things fresh in people's minds. Reviewing reinforces aspects of a project that you have forgotten completely and prepares you for what you have to do next.

Experience-Based Modifications

When you start a project, you produce plans, and you make assumptions about a whole variety of things that must be accomplished. After you start work on the project, many of your original assumptions may prove to be inadequate or even wrong.

Reviewing helps you to reassess all the previous assumptions you made concerning the new phase. When you find assumptions that are clearly inappropriate, misguided, or simply incorrect, the review is an ideal opportunity to rectify the situation before you start work on the new phase.

Throughout a project, you are learning; your understanding of all the complexities of the project grows. For example, you might have discovered in an earlier phase that one of the software components you had decided to use has a serious problem. If you will also require this component in a later phase, when you get to that phase, you can review the situation with the knowledge that you have a problem, which may mean your original approach wasn't practical. Review time is when you can decide what to do next, based on your previous experiences.

Reassessment of the Risks

From start-up time, as the project gathers momentum, risks come and go. As you gain experience, what you thought were risks might turn out not to be. New risks might materialize. Projects are dynamic entities in which things can change rapidly.

During the course of a long project, the underlying technology that you chose back in the "mists of time" might have gone through a radical overhaul, and new developments are now available that might change the nature of some of your earlier project considerations. When such changes remove risks that you originally regarded as potential threats, you might now be able to neutralize the threats. For example, suppose that one of the requirements you have to meet in a development is that you must make the end product multilingual. The application development environment you chose, most suitable to the majority of the requirements, does not support the multilingual capability. You will have to develop the functionality as part of the development. Because of the complexities of making software switch between languages on the fly, you have assessed this part of the development as of being of high technical risk. When you come to the phase in which the facility is to be developed, you discover that the supplier of the language that you are using has managed to develop language ability in the latest release of the product. This has the potential to neutralize the risk of having to develop that capability in-house.

The start of a new phase is always a good opportunity to reassess how the project is going. The really important thing to remember is that the project is the product of your learning experience so far. You must put all your experience with previous project phases to good use at this time, so you can maximize the project's likelihood for success in the new phase.

The Case Study:
Start of Project Phase 3

We had completed and delivered the viewer, and Phase 2 of the project had reached a satisfactory conclusion. We were now about to start Phase 3—the development of the Title Index Editor and the Page Index Editor. Just as we had done for each of the previous phases, we began with a start-up meeting to review the situation. In a nutshell, we now had three weeks in which to develop the E-MagBook's remaining software.

Reviewing the Plan

We started by reviewing the original plan for the development of the two editors. You can find all the plans for Phase 3 in the following figures:

- *Figure 5.6*—Project Weeks 9, 10, and 11, development of the editors.

- *Figure 5.7*—Project Week 12, integration and system testing of both editors, plus start of Week 1 of documentation production.

- *Figure 5.8*—Project Week 13, acceptance testing of editors and completion of editor documentation.

In Week 1 of Phase 3 (project Week 9), we had to develop all the modules for the Title Index Editor. In Weeks 2 and 3 of Phase 3, we had to produce all the modules associated with the Page Index Editor. We had our all-important contingency time built into the time we had allocated to each module, and a bit of contingency time was floating around on the plan as well. For example, Archie has a day of contingency time in Week 1, a day in Week 3, as well as the contingency time inherently built into the timetable. Julie had two days of contingency time in Week 1, and just more than a day in Week 3. Hopefully, no accidents would happen this time.

Another Buy-In

After we had reviewed the plan, the next thing on the agenda of the phase start-up meeting was to determine whether we had a buy-in to this plan from the two programmers. I asked Archie and Julie if, after all they had learned in the past few weeks of designing the system and developing the viewer, they both still felt this plan for editor development was realistic and one they could guarantee.

Having seen contingency time at work first-hand, Julie felt quite confident. Remember, she had managed to complete the viewer development after Archie's accident, thanks to the fact that both programmers had made good progress in the first week, which had allowed them to build up even more contingency time than planned. This extra contingency time, together with the time inherent in the original plan, allowed one programmer to complete the work of two people in the latter part of the phase. Archie concurred that the plan was achievable, and both programmers committed to deliver on time.

Much of Julie's apprehension and worry about fixed-price work seemed to have dissipated, thanks to the methodical approach we had fostered in the entire project. Both programmers were also elated that they had delivered the viewer on time. Meeting a delivery deadline has only a positive effect on a project team.

Review of Work to Be Done

Next, we took a look at the top-level design diagrams we had produced for each editor during the design phase:

♦ *Figure 6.6*—The Title Index Editor top-level design.

♦ *Figure 6.7*—The Page Index Editor top-level design.

We followed this review with a look at each individual development task.

Archie's Title Index Editor Tasks

As you can see from the plan (as shown in Figure 5.6 in Chapter 5), Archie would start work on the **Load Index** module, which involved manual selection and loading of Title Index files. Archie was convinced that this task would be simple, because the main module— **ReadInTitleIndex**—and the **Title Index** data structure were both already available in **ViewerLib**. We had a lot of reusability here.

Archie's next task was to develop **Navigation**, which consisted of the **Go To Start**, **Go To End**, **Next**, and **Previous** functions. Based on what they had done in the viewer, Archie was convinced that this task was also simple, even though it included no direct reusability of previously developed modules. He would model his solution on what Julie had done for the viewer's **Navigation** function.

Archie's final task for Title Index Editor development was to build the **Save Index** functionality. This functionality was the only aspect of his work that was brand new, but he was satisfied that he had good design specifications to follow.

All in all, based on past experience and what he now knew about the project, Archie was expecting early delivery of his components for the Title Index Editor because he had no dependency on any of Julie's work, and vice versa.

Julie's Title Index Editor Tasks

Julie was going to set up **Change Handling** functionality associated with state transitions within the Title Index Editor. The state-transition changes in the editors were more complex than those of the viewer; nevertheless, she felt comfortable that she could achieve the functionality required and have it tested in the one day allocated.

Her next task would be to implement the **Index Manipulation** functions—**Add**, **Insert**, **Overwrite**, and **Delete**. All this work was new, and Julie would have only the design to go on. But, then, she had two whole days of contingency time, which made her feel much more comfortable. She had already reviewed the design specifications involved in her proposed work, and she didn't see any major issues. With the degree of contingency time she had been given, Julie felt confident she could meet the deadline for completion by project Week 10.

Archie's Page Index Editor Tasks

Archie's first task for the Page Index Editor was to set up the viewer functionality. He would accomplish this by setting up the viewer form as an MDI (Multiple Document Interface) child window in the Page Index Editor. He admitted he wasn't too sure about how to go about the task, but he felt that the three days allocated for the job gave him sufficient contingency time.

Archie's second task—**Index Manipulation**—would be very similar to the Title Index Editor's version of the same functionality. The ability to model what Julie would do for the Title Index Editor, coupled with a good design specification, gave him confidence that he could complete the task in the three days allocated.

Archie's final task was to develop **File Selection**. He felt very confident about this task because of the work he and Julie had performed creating the File Selection form prototype, during which they had written code to link the file-selection boxes. (This work is available in Appendix E.)

Archie had a total of three tasks to complete, each within three days, over a two-week period. Although the Page Index Editor plan showed one day of contingency time, he felt that the nine days allocated to the three tasks contained ample (inherent) contingency time. With all this contingency time, he felt confident he could deliver the modules according to plan. He identified integrating the viewer functionality into the Page Index Editor as his major area of risk.

Julie's Page Index Editor Tasks

Julie would start her work on the Page Index Editor by developing the **Load Index** and **Save Index** functionalities as her first two tasks. In addition to using the design specifications, she could look at how Archie accomplished the same functionality for the Title Index Editor and possibly use his code as a model (although no direct usability was obvious). Julie felt that, because she could embed the viewer code in **ViewerLib** into the Page Index Editor, she would be able to read in a page index file immediately. All she needed to do was set up the infrastructure to let a user call the **Read In** routine with a selected file name. She felt she would develop **Load Index** in less than one day and, possibly, **Save Index** in a single day. She was, therefore, quite confident about early delivery for the first two tasks.

Her next two tasks were **Text Save** and **Text Font** handling. Because she had developed the **Text Read** function in the viewer, she felt confident about handling text output. Julie admitted that the **Copy** and **Paste** functionality was currently a complete mystery to her; therefore, she classified the development of that task as her major risk. However, because she was anticipating good progress in the earlier tasks required, she felt confident she would have extra contingency time available if she ran into trouble with paste buffer handling.

Julie's final task was **Change Handling**. This area represented another risk, because change handling seemed to be a lot more complex in the Page Index Editor; however, Julie hoped that her work in change handling in the Title Index Editor would let her determine how to go about the same functionality in the Page Index Editor.

All in all, Julie felt she could meet the required completion date. She was confident she could build up extra contingency time to counterbalance any complexity she might encounter in what she regarded as the more onerous development tasks.

Confirmation of Buy-In

Having weighed the risks and the contingency-time factors, both programmers felt confident they could develop both editors within the agreed-upon schedule. They both took on the responsibility of meeting the deadlines.

Tip

To reiterate, from a project management point of view, the buy-in is an extremely important concept in software development. Making programmers feel comfortable about meeting deadlines is vital. You don't want them working long days, six or seven days a week; in the end, their doing so would be counterproductive. At all costs, you must try to avoid programmers' feeling bullied into taking on schedules they know they cannot—or they have absolutely no idea whether they can or cannot—meet. This conflict happens a great deal in the industry. Plans are often drawn up without consulting the people who will be carrying out the work, and a time frame is imposed on them.

If you are asked to give an opinion concerning a schedule you are supposed to meet, be honest. Don't agree to something you don't understand or don't have faith in. In the long run, if you continually give estimates that never come true, you'll automatically be blamed for late delivery.

Assessing schedules represents a difficult balancing act. You don't want to make too many waves by screaming that the task is impossible in the time given, and you don't want to be bullied into accepting impossible timetables you know you can't meet. But, again, no one said this work was going to be easy. As you develop your programming skills, you also must develop your estimating skills. Professional programmers must be as good at estimating schedules as they are at programming.

Reviewing Functionality

With the aid of the form layouts we had produced for the requirements specification, we did a quick review of the functionality the editors required.

Title Index Editor Key Aspects

The following figures define the relevant form layouts:

- *Figure O in Chapter 5*—The Title Index form in **Alert 1 Normal State**.

- *Figure P in Chapter 5*—The Title Index form in **Alert 1 Changed State**.

The form layouts included a single GUI form with a file drop-down menu that contained New, Open, Save, and Save As commands to handle a Title Index. Each Title Index contained three data fields per entry: the Page-Index file reference, the title, and the description. Both of the first two items would be handled in text boxes with scrolling available. When the program was running, the Title Index form would show a single entry from the Index. The user could change the content of any of the three fields, in which case the program would go into the **Alert 1 Changed State**, in which the navigation controls and file menu were inhibited. This state forced the user to add, insert, or overwrite the content of the Index with what was on screen, as appropriate, or it forced the user to abort the changes. When the program was in the **Alert 1 Changed State**, the **Delete** function would be disabled and replaced by a **Release** option that would let the changes be aborted, if required.

All changes made to the in-Memory Index would not be transferred to disk until the user performed a **Save** or **Save As** function. When a discrepancy existed between Memory and Disk Index content, the Title Index form text box would indicate an **Alert 2 Changed State**.

Page Index Editor Key Aspects

The following figures show the two forms that define the Page Index Editor:

- *Figure Q in Chapter 5*—The Page Index form in **Normal State**.

- *Figure R in Chapter 5*—The Page Index form in **Level 1 Change State**.

- *Figures T, U, and V in Chapter 5*—The Page Index Editor with the File Selection form set up for picture, text, and sound selection, respectively.

We had a program with four forms: the Editor form (set up as the main project form), the Viewer form (set up as an MDI child form), the Video form, and the File Selection form. Each form would be a completely independent entity, but, using object dot notation (which we discussed in Chapter 6), we could access and manipulate code and variables between forms if we needed to. (If you recall, this process simply involves upgrading a form's infrastructure routine or data structure from private to public status. The only restriction is that the upgraded infrastructure entity is still not accessible to any library routines.)

The viewer would have to undergo some modifications to enable **Change Handling** so that the keys and text field would become accessible to the user, but only when the Viewer form was running in the Page Index Editor environment. Apart from **Change Handling**, the viewer would function exactly as it did when it was executing as a standalone program.

The key editing functions of the Page Index Editor would be set up in a button control bar at the top of the screen and also in drop-down menus. Page Indexes could be loaded, modified, and saved, so, too, could text files. These capabilities for text files would serve as alternatives to keyboard entry directly into the text box of the embedded viewer.

The Add, Delete, Insert, and Overwrite options would behave in exactly the same way that their counterparts in the Title Index Editor would function. The capability for a user to select a multimedia file would be available via the File Selection form. Selection of a file would consist of defining the drive, directory, and file, using linked controls to construct a full file reference for a specific type of multimedia object—that is, an image or video clip, a sound file, or a text-block file. Selected files would have their reference strings placed in the relevant file-name text boxes at the bottom of the Viewer form. The Viewer form's infrastructure module—**DisplayPage**—would then be called and requested to load a page using the text-box strings rather than the in-memory's current entry. (If you recall, making a call to **DisplayPage** with the argument **intAlternateDisplay** set to **1** performs the required function.) Users can copy and paste page entries using the clipboard, and they can clear the file-reference text boxes individually or en masse.

Result of Review

The general consensus after our review of Phase 3 of the project was that we did not need to modify the current plan, and Julie and Archie had confidence they would complete the development of the required modules on time and, possibly, earlier than scheduled. Both programmers knew what they had to do and by when. One significant aspect was that no dependencies existed between code one programmer produced and the work the other programmer was doing.

We also decided that general modules developed for the Title Index Editor would go into a library called **TitleLib**, and any general modules for the Page Index Editor would go into **PageLib**. We were all set to begin development of the Title Index Editor.

Software Reusability

One main management problem in a software development is trying to stop programmers from reinventing wheels. If, as a programmer, you need to write code to handle a piece of well-defined functionality, the first thing you must ask is whether someone has already programmed something similar. If the functionality has not been coded, has any element of it been coded in some reusable form? If someone has programmed the functionality, use that module, and save yourself the effort.

In the case study, we paid great attention to reusability in the analysis and design, where we deliberately hunted for common functions according to the requirements specifications. And this focus was very successful. For example, we identified the need to develop a single module to read in a Title Index and another module to read in a Page Index. The viewer would use both modules, the Title Index Editor would use one of them, and the Page Index Editor would use both.

Independent Development Modules

When you can develop an independent module (subroutine or function) for reuse, you can set the module up so that it can be driven in many different ways, with the calling arguments dictating the chosen method. This flexibility is demonstrated in the case study. For Index input, the calling code set up the name of the file to be loaded in the call to the routine to execute the load. Whether the calling code would load a hard-coded file name, such as E:\E-MagBook\index.idx, or would let the user define the name through a file-selection process didn't matter. The same routine would read in the file, regardless of how it obtained the file name. As we've seen, we could test such self-contained, independent, modules as standalone entities, and then integrate them into the final system as verified, robust software components.

Infrastructure Event Handlers

I've used the term *infrastructure* to indicate that a given routine or data structure is part of the program's makeup and is totally specific to it—the data structure or routine usually accesses screen objects directly. The event handlers comprise the code that executes when an event is triggered. This functioning makes the code very specific, not just to the program, but also to the screen object for which it is an event handler.

To gain reusability from an event handler, you can put the code that is not specific into a library. If you recall, we can even put code that accesses screen objects into libraries by using the call to make the link between actual screen-object identity and a generic reference inside the routine. To do this, we must declare the object as a screen control in the argument. Even so, the routine is quite general and becomes specifically tied to a given screen object only for a single instance of its execution. Subsequent instances of its execution might be to manipulate a completely different screen object, the only criterion being that the object is of the same type (that is, a text box or a picture control).

In the case study, we had generic designs for many of the event handlers the two editors would use. Where we couldn't use general routines in libraries to handle common functions, we could use one set of code as a model for the next use. As an example, consider the **cmdAdd** event handler required to add an entry to an Index. If you look at the design, you can see that the function is the same in both programs. The user is asked to confirm whether the function should be executed. If the user indicates the function should be aborted, the code exits. If the function is to proceed, the code must increase the size of the Index by one and then copy the data from the current screen objects to the newly created final entry. Finally, the code must update the screen display to show the final entry of the Index, which now becomes the current entry. **Alert 1 Normal State** and **Alert 2 Changed State** are set. All this functionality is evident from the design and is a completely generic definition. The fundamental difference between the programs for the two editors was that, when we would write the code, the screen objects and the structure of the two Memory Indexes would be different.

To gain a somewhat crude level of reusability, we would write the code once for the Title Index Editor and then use the same code for the Page Index Editor, modifying only screen and Index references as required. We would still have two sets of code to maintain—one event handler in the Title Index Editor and one in the Page Index Editor—but, at least, they would look similar.

Infrastructure Routines

Finally, in terms of software reusability, you also can use any routines that are specific to a program (usually because of a direct association with the screen objects used in the program) to create a similar function in a different program where only the screen objects differ.

In the case study, to assist in one of her testing requirements, Julie missed an opportunity to make use of code Archie had previously written. Her oversight was not a big deal, but she had to write some code in a test program to perform a crude level of navigation around a Title Index. Archie had already completed the **Navigation** capability for the Title Index Editor proper, but, because he'd completed early, Julie missed the implication. Admittedly, in this instance, the situation didn't lead to massive duplication of effort—in fact, Julie created a minimal facility quite swiftly. But the situation serves to illustrate the point that failing to spot reusable software entities can cause you unnecessary effort.

Return to the Case Study:

Title Index Editor—Part 1

We would base the development of the Title Index Editor on the design specifications you will find in Appendix G. We discussed some of these designs in detail in Chapter 6; others will be quite new to you. To understand how Julie and Archie developed the code for the Title Index Editor, you need to study the relevant design specifications, as the steps that follow advise.

The process of creating a development module, building a test program, and checking the developed routine is the same as the process we employed for the viewer. By now, module development and testing should be second nature to you. Here, in Part 1 of the Title Index Editor development, we will look at how Archie accomplished his developments in the week assigned for all three of his tasks. Specifically, he would tackle the following:

♦ *Load Title Index*—selection and loading of a Title Index.

♦ *Navigation*—navigation functionality for the in-Memory Title Index.

♦ *Save Index*—saving the in-Memory Title Index to a disk file.

Load Title Index Module

Archie's first task was to establish the routines for manual loading of a Title Index. According to our development-task descriptions, **Load Title Index** consisted of developing the **Select Title Index For Input** routine. The development task could then use **ReadInTitleIndexFile**, already developed for the viewer, to use the file name specified to load a genuine Title Index. These combined functions—**Select** and **Load**—provide a self-contained development module that emulates the software that the Title Index Editor program's menu option Open would require.

Design for Select Title Index For Input Module

Here is the relevant design required to assist in the construction of the **Select Title Index For Input** module:

DESIGN SPEC: GetIndexFileNameForInput
FUNCTION: GetIndexFileNameForInput(dlgDialog as control, strFileName as string)as_Boolean

DESCRIPTION: This function solicits the name of a file required for input from the user.

> **ARGUMENTS: dlgDialog**—Name of dialog box to activate.

> **StrFileName**—Function that will place the name of file selected in this variable.

> Result of function=False—No file selected.

> > =True—File name provided.

ACTION:

If any error, then go to error handler.

> Clear **strFileName**.

> Set file filter to Index file types only (***.idx**).

> Action **dlgDialog** for an OPEN function.

> Set **strFileName** from dialog box result.

> If **strFileName** is blank, then EXIT setting function FALSE.

> EXIT setting function TRUE.

ERROR HANDLER:

> EXIT setting function FALSE.

END:

GetIndexFileNameForInput was, in fact, a completely generic, general routine, which could be used to get the name of any Index file (Title Index or Page Index) for input to either of the editor programs. Although the routine was GUI bound, it had been structured so that the identity of the file dialog box was passed at runtime. As a consequence, we could place the module in **TitleLib**.

The design was very simple: **strFileName**, the string that would contain the name of the file selected, was first cleared. The filter Index would then be set up for Index type files, using ***.idx**. The dialog box was activated by setting its **Action** property, for an **Open** function. When the user had completed file selection, the program would place the file name chosen into **strFileName**. If the value placed in the string was blank, or an error occurred along the way, the result of the **GetIndexFileName** would be set to **False**.

The File Menu's Open Option

Archie's intention was to set up a test program that would let him check out both the file-selection module and the code to handle the Open file menu option. The **Open, Save**, and **Save As** functions for the two editors were identical, so, at design time, we had also produced designs to indicate how each event handler should be constructed. We defined the design specification for handling the **Open** event for either editor as follows:

DESIGN SPEC: Edit Menu Option Open
GENERIC EVENT HANDLER: Edit Menu Option OPEN

DESCRIPTION: The menu drop-down function OPEN for both Title and Page editors. Allows the user to select the name of an Index file and then load it into the in-memory Index arrays.

NOTES: The OPEN menu option must be disabled when the editor is in the **Level 1 Alert State**.

ACTION:

Call function **GetIndexFileNameForInput**.

If function failed, then report condition and EXIT leaving currently loaded Index intact.

Call function **IndexLoad** with specified file name.

If function failed, then

      Clear screen objects

      Clear Memory Index

      Clear **Index Alert** status if it was on

      EXIT

End if

Update name of Index file on screen.

Display contents of entry 1 on screen.

Clear **Level 2 Alert State** if it was on.

For Page Index Editor Only: switch viewer into Page View mode.

END:

This specification applied to both editors, with a single line at the bottom that was Page-editor specific. The first thing to happen when a user clicked the drop-down menu option Open would be that **GetIndexFileNameForInput** would be called. If the call to the function was successful, the Title Index file selected could be read in using routine **ReadInTitleIndex** with the file name supplied by **GetIndexFileNameForInput**.

Archie would be able to develop the code to handle the Title Index Editor **Open** event handler as well as the routine to get a file name. To set up the test program, Archie very sensibly decided to reuse Julie's test program **TitleTest3**. If you recall, Julie developed this program to read in the Index file from E:\E-MagBook\title.idx. Archie would modify the program to allow any file name to be selected and then read into memory, provided the file was a genuine Title Index.

Archie modified the form layout of **TitleTest3** by removing the **Load Default Title Index** button. (Julie had used this button to force the program to load E:\E-MagBook\title.idx.) He then set up a file drop-down menu to handle **Open**, **Save**, and **Save As** functions in preparation for his next two development tasks. You can see the final result in Figure 10.1.

Reusing the test program **TitleTest3** saved Archie considerable time. If you want to reproduce what he did, follow these steps. Alternatively, load **TitleTester1** from the directory of that name located in Archie's development area on the CD.

Step 1

Load Julie's completed project, **TitleTest3**. Remove the version of **ViewerLib** that is attached to the project.

Step 2

Add Module **ViewerLib** from directory **DEV_EViewer** on the CD. (The version of **ViewerLib** in this directory is the final version produced in the viewer development, the version that you will require for editor development.)

Step 3

Create a directory called **TitleTester1** in your version of Archie's development area on your hard drive. Save the modified form as **frmTitleTester1** in the newly created directory of the same name.

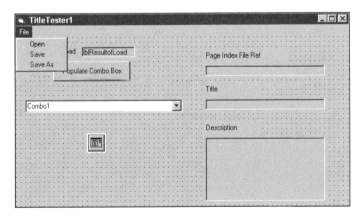

Figure 10.1
Julie's **TitleTest3** form, modified to accommodate a drop-down menu comprising **Open**, **Save**, and **Save As** test functions.

Add a new module using the Project drop-down menu in VB and call this new module **TitleLib**. This is the library associated with the Title Index Editor's modules.

Remove the button marked **Load Default Title Index** from the form. Save **ViewerLib** in the **TitleTester1** directory. (Having initially loaded **ViewerLib** from the CD, if you don't save **ViewerLib** to your new working directory, VB will require the CD to be present every time you want to work with this project.)

Save the newly created **TitleLib** in directory **TitleTester1**, even though the library is currently empty. Also, save the project in your version of directory **TitleTester1**, and give the project the name **TitleTester1** as well.

The directory **TitleTester1** should now contain a form, a copy of **ViewerLib.bas**, the newly created **TitleLib.bas**, and the project file.

Create a drop-down menu structure for the test program's main form as follows:

File	**mnuFileDummy**
Open	**mnuOpenTitleIndex**
Save	**mnuSaveTitleIndex**
Save As	**mnuSaveTitleIndexAs**

The form should now look like the form in Figure 10.1.

Add the following test code to **mnuOpenTitleIndex_Click**:

```
Private Sub mnuOpenTitleIndex_Click()
' TITLE EDITOR INFRASTRUCTURE EVENT HANDLER: V1.0
' Menu drop-down option OPEN
' --------------------------
Dim booResult As Boolean
Dim strFileName As String

booResult = GetIndexFileNameForInput(dlgDialog, strFileName)
If booResult = False Then
     MsgBox "Failed to get file name."
     lblResultOfLoad = "Load Failed"      ' DIAGNOSTIC
     Exit Sub
End If
```

```
booResult = ReadInTitleIndex(strFileName)

If booResult = False Then
      MsgBox "Load Failed"
      lblResultOfLoad = "Load Failed"     ' DIAGNOSTIC
      txtFileRef.Text = ""
      txtTitle.Text = ""
      txtDescription.Text = ""
      Call ClearTitleIndexMemory
      Exit Sub
End If

txtIndexFileName.Text = strFileName

g_intCurrentTitle = 1
txtFileRef.Text = g_strTitleFileName(g_intCurrentTitle)
txtTitle.Text = g_strTitleTitle(g_intCurrentTitle)
txtDescription.Text = g_strTitleDescription(g_intCurrentTitle)

lblResultOfLoad = "Load OK"     ' DIAGNOSTIC

Exit Sub

End Sub
```

Although the preceding code might not be exactly like the **Open** event handler will be in the final version of the Title Index Editor (note that diagnostic lines are present, for one thing), it is very close to the required version. Consequently, the code will serve as an excellent starting point when we come to integration, and to the point at which we need to set up the Title Index Editor's Open drop-down-menu option.

At the start of the code, the program obtains the file name and then tries to read in the file using the standard load routine we developed for the viewer. Note that, after a successful load of the Title Index, the program sets the current entry number to 1 and loads the first entry via a call to **DisplayEntry**. After a bad load, the program sets the value of the current entry pointer to 0 (in the call to **ClearTitleIndexMemory**), indicating that the Index is empty. If you recall, we also developed the **ClearTitleIndexMemory** subroutine for the viewer, and this subroutine is available in **ViewerLib1**.

Step 8

Make sure you set **Option Explicit** in the general definition section of **TitleLib**. Enter the following code into **TitleLib**:

```
Public Function GetIndexFileNameForInput(dlgObject As Control, strFileName_
        As_String) As Boolean
```

```
' GENERAL FUNCTION: V1.0
' Code to get an Index file name for input (Title or Page Index)
' Arguments:
'          dlgObject - Common dialog control
'        strFileName - On return contains name of file opened
'  Function result - False - failed to get a file name
'                  - True - File name present in strFileName
' ----------------------------------
GetIndexFileNameForInput = False          ' default is failure
strFileName = ""


' Select File name to open
On Error GoTo Errhandler
dlgObject.FileName = strFileName
dlgObject.Filter = "Index Files (*.idx)|*.idx|All files (*.*)|*.*"
dlgObject.FilterIndex = 1                 ' OPEN
dlgObject.Action = 1
strFileName = dlgObject.FileName
If strFileName = "" Then Exit Function
GetIndexFileNameForInput = True
Exit Function
' ===================================================
Errhandler:
Exit Function
End Function
```

The dialog box, the identity of which is defined in the calling parameters, is used to solicit a file name from the user. If the result is blank, or an error occurs, the routine exits. If a file name is present, that name is transferred back to the calling code via the calling argument. Note that the dialog box is called with no default file name set, because **strFileName** is blank.

Step 9

Add a text box to the form, and call it **txtIndexFileName**. This text box emulates the text box that will appear in the final version of the Title Index Editor, and it will hold the name of the Title Index file loaded.

Step 10

Convert the three labels **lblFileRef**, **lblTitle**, and **lblDescription** to text boxes: **txtFileRef**, **txtTitle**, and **txtDescription**. Do this by deleting the three labels and creating three text boxes to take their position. You will need to change all label references to text references in the test program. (This change concerns only the combo box, click-event-handler code.)

Remember, this test program was originally used to check out loading the Title Index file in the viewer. Julie chose arbitrary label names for that purpose. Now, Archie was setting up code for the Title Editor proper, so he started to use screen objects in the test program that related to the final program, as specified in the screen-object definitions we had produced at design time.

Step 11

Create an instance of the common dialog box on the test program's form, and call the dialog box **dlgDialog**. Make sure that the **CancelError** property is set to **True**. Setting the **CancelError** property to **True** ensures that a **Cancel** request is trapped as an error and forces the function to exit set to **False**. (If you don't set **CancelError** to **True**, when a user requests a **Cancel**, the dialog box's file setting is still set up with the contents from the previous time that an **Open** was requested. When the return is executed, the calling code receives the previous **Open**'s file name and promptly reopens the file, which is clearly not what the user expects.)

Testing Load Title Index

Archie quickly had the test program up and running. To test, he simply invoked the Open menu option and clicked on a Test Index file. The message boxes told him what happened if anything went wrong. He could also see from the **ResultOfTheLoad** caption whether an **Open** had been successful. For a successful load, Entry 1 would be shown in the text boxes, and he could click the Populate Combo Box option to see a list of entries. From the list, he could then select any entry and view the result in the text boxes. In this way, he could verify that the program had read in the file he had selected. Archie was able to log the following tests:

♦ *Test 1*—Successful load of a selected Title Index.

♦ *Test 2*—Error handling when trying to open a non-Title Index file.

♦ *Test 3*—The Cancel option works, leaving the previous file open.

If you recall from the viewer's development, at this stage, the programmer looks at the various pathways through the code and makes a list of exceptions and completion conditions. From this list, the programmer logs the tests that were performed and their outcome, to verify each identified pathway.

We had further reusability in this development task (anticipated at design time), in that Julie could use the function **GetIndexFileName** to read in a Page Index when she started work on the Page Index Editor. Before Archie and Julie began their separate jobs, and after they had together reviewed the designs, they had discussed what functions would be developed. They had agreed on how to proceed so that reconciliation of **TitleLib** would allow one programmer to make use of what the other had developed. All through the project, they keep each other informed about what they were doing, with particular reference to any general routines each was developing, in case the other could use them and avoid duplication of effort wherever possible.

Creating Navigation Functionality

Archie had completed **Load Title Index** development and testing by lunchtime, so, after a sandwich, he went straight to the **Navigation** functionality. We had generic design specifications for **Navigation** through either a Title or a Page Index, which you should review in Appendix G before you proceed. In fact, we'd already used the specification to develop the event handlers for the viewer. The Title Index Editor required only the **GoStart**, **GoEnd**, **Next**, and **Previous** functions, and, like the viewer's controls, we could code these directly into the click handlers of the navigation buttons.

To set up for testing, Archie modified the test program he had developed to test the loading of Index files. He modified the program as defined in the following steps, which you can repeat to create the **Navigation** functionality. Alternatively, you can load the **TitleTester2** project from Archie's development area on the CD. Figure 10.2 depicts the form he created.

Step 1

Load the VB project **TitleTester1** that you developed in the last section, and add navigation controls, as shown in Figure 10.2. From left to right, these controls are **cmdGoStart**, **cmdPrevious**, **cmdNext**, and **cmdGoEnd**.

Step 2

Place the following code in the **cmdGoStart** click-event handler:

```
Private Sub cmdGoStart_Click()
' TITLE EDITOR INFRASTRUCTURE EVENT HANDLER:
' Navigation Functionality, V1.0
' --------------------
If g_intCurrentTitle < 1 Then
    MsgBox "Index is empty"
    Exit Sub
End If

If g_intCurrentTitle = 1 Then
        MsgBox "Already at Start of Index "
        Exit Sub
End If

g_intCurrentTitle = 1
Call DisplayEntry

End Sub
```

Because the design for the navigation functions was generic, Archie realized that he could copy the viewer's **cmdGoStart_Click** and paste it into the test program's equivalent button handler. Then, all he would have to do would be to convert viewer references to title refer-

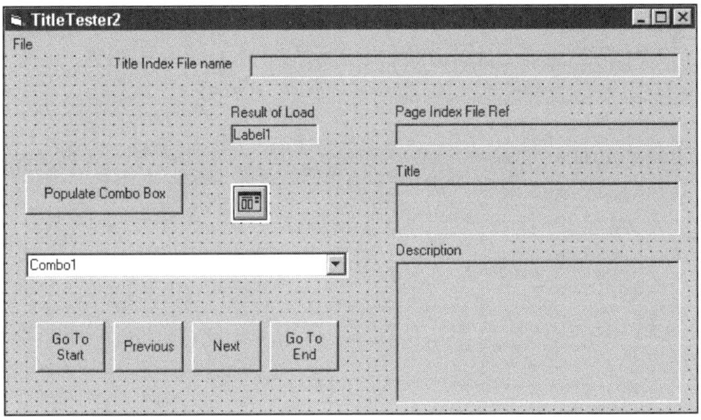

Figure 10.2
TitleTester2's main form, created from **TitleTester1**. The additional controls consist of the navigation buttons Go To Start, Previous, Next, and Go To End.

ences. Although Copy and Paste followed by manual modification was a crude form of reusability, it did save Archie time. And he knew that the basic functionality worked in the viewer, so it was likely to work the first time in the test program.

<table><tr><td>**Step 3**</td></tr></table>

Place this modified copy of the viewer's **cmdPrevious** click-event handler into the test program:

```
Private Sub cmdPrevious_Click()
' TITLE EDITOR INFRASTRUCTURE EVENT HANDLER:
' Navigation Functionality, V1.0
' ------------------
If g_intCurrentTitle < 1 Then
    MsgBox "Index is empty"
    Exit Sub
End If

If g_intCurrentTitle = 1 Then
    MsgBox "Already at Start of Index"
    Exit Sub
End If

g_intCurrentTitle = g_intCurrentTitle - 1
Call DisplayEntry

End Sub
```

Again, the code represents good, if crude, reusability.

Step 4

Place this modified copy of the viewer's **cmdNext** click-event handler into the test program:

```
Private Sub cmdNext_Click()
' TITLE EDITOR INFRASTRUCTURE EVENT HANDLER:
' Navigation Functionality, V1.0
' -------------------
If g_intCurrentTitle < 1 Then
    MsgBox "Index is empty"
    Exit Sub
End If

If g_intCurrentEntry = UBound(g_strTitleTitle()) Then
        MsgBox "Already at End of Index"
        Exit Sub
End If

g_intCurrentTitle = g_intCurrentTitle + 1
Call DisplayEntry

End Sub
```

This code is based on the viewer's **cmdNext_Click** handler.

Step 5

Place this modified copy of the viewer's **cmdGoEnd** click-event handler into the test program:

```
Private Sub cmdGoEnd_Click()
' TITLE EDITOR INFRASTRUCTURE EVENT HANDLER:
' Navigation Functionality, V1.0
' -------------------
If g_intCurrentTitle < 1 Then
    MsgBox "Index is empty"
    Exit Sub
End If

If g_intCurrentEntry= UBound(g_strTitleTitle()) Then
        MsgBox "Already at End of Index "
        Exit Sub
End If

g_intCurrentTitle = UBound(g_strTitleTitle())
Call DisplayEntry

End Sub
```

Step 6

Add this routine to the general section of the test program:

```
Private Sub DisplayEntry()
' TITLE EDITOR INFRASTRUCTURE GUI ROUTINE:
' Set up screen objects from current Index entry, V1.0
' ------------------------
txtFileRef.Text = g_strTitleFileName(g_intCurrentTitle)
txtTitle.Text = g_strTitleTitle(g_intCurrentTitle)
txtDescription.Text = g_strTitleDescription(g_intCurrentTitle)

End Sub
```

This code simply takes the contents of the current entry and places the strings in the relevant screen objects. The code is using the names that will be used in the final version of the Title Index Editor, so the code can be copied directly into **EtitleEditor** at system-integration time.

Step 7

Set up the following routine in the general section of the test program:

```
Private Sub ClearScreenData()
' TITLE EDITOR INFRASTRUCTURE GUI ROUTINE:
' Clear screen objects, V1.0
' ------------------------
txtFileRef.Text = ""
txtTitle.Text = ""
txtDescription.Text = ""

End Sub
```

Step 8

Replace the designated code lines in **mnuOpenTitleIndex_Click** as follows. Replace all occurrences of

```
txtFileRef.Text = g_strTitleFileName(g_intCurrentTitle)
txtTitle.Text = g_strTitleTitle(g_intCurrentTitle)
txtDescription.Text = g_strTitleDescription(g_intCurrentTitle)
```

with

```
Call DisplayEntry
```

Replace all occurrences of

```
txtFileRef.Text = ""
```

```
txtTitle.Text = ""
txtDescription.Text = ""
```

with

```
Call ClearScreenData
```

Archie had extracted code from **mnuOpenTitleIndex_Click** and created two useful infrastructure GUI routines from the extracted code.

Testing Title Index Editor Navigation

The program allowed Archie to check out moving around a Title Index. He first tested the code with no Index onboard, and then he loaded an Index and checked that he could move backward and forward through it. He also checked out start and end handling to ensure they were consistent with the way in which viewer navigation worked.

The tests Archie conducted were the following:

♦ *Test 1*—Check that empty Index handling works correctly with all navigation buttons.

♦ *Test 2*—Check correct navigation of a genuine Index, <<, <, >, >>.

♦ *Test 3*—Check that start and end limit handling is OK.

The only hitch in his tests was that the Index number was not being displayed. Archie corrected this by creating a label (**lblIndexNumber**, according to the screen variable list for the Title Editor) to hold the entry number, and placing the following line into the **DisplayEntry** routine:

```
lblIndexNumber.Caption = CStr(g_intCurrentTitle)
```

Archie completed the first two tasks—**Load Index** and **Navigation**—and their testing in Day 1, putting him a whole day ahead of schedule. But, as we have seen previously, we might need this day later.

Creating the Save Module

Archie now had to create the module to output a Title Index file. In Chapter 6, we looked at the design for the routine to output an Index file. Part of that design consisted of checking to see whether the required file already existed, informing the user of the results, and asking whether overwriting an existing file or creating a new one was okay, depending upon what the program had found.

Later, when Julie and Archie began to design the Save and Save As menu options, they realized that the output module was not the right place to put the code that would check file status and solicit authorization to proceed. Their reasoning was that they wanted both the **Save** and **Save As** functions to call **WriteOutTitleIndex**.

However, a typical Windows Save menu option doesn't ask the user whether it is okay to output—the program just goes ahead and executes the function regardless, unless the file does not already exist. When the file does not exist, the program executes the **Save As** function. Consequently, they had to modify the design for **WriteOutTitleIndex** to align it with how the **Save** and **Save As** functions behaved.

This example demonstrates well the value of iteration, in which an earlier design has had to be modified as a result of other design aspects discovered later. Archie and Julie implemented the change to **WriteOutTitleIndex** using a change log, so you can see how they modified the design from the version you saw in Chapter 6. Such change is perfectly normal and further indicates how important it is to design for all known functionality—and not only for the components to be developed in the immediate future.

In summary, study the design specifications in Appendix G for the following functions before you start building the code:

♦ *Function*—**WriteOutTitleIndex**

♦ *Function*—**OKToProceed**

♦ *Event Handler*—**Save_Click( )** (used by editors)

♦ *Event Handler*—**SaveAs_Click( )** (used by editors)

♦ *Function*—**GetIndexFileNameForOutput**

The Save As option used a function to determine whether the output file selected already existed. This function was made up from code that was originally designed to be in the output function itself. The program would use the result obtained from its check of whether the file existed to ask the user whether to proceed. If the user authorized proceeding, the program would, as appropriate, either overwrite an existing file or create a new file. The user was thus given the capability to abort the function. This capability was created in a routine called **OKToProceed**, and, because it has been designed as a general module, the routine could also be used for the **Save As** function in the Page Index Editor—all of which made this function very useful. Remember, this functionality was originally designed into **WriteOutTitleIndex**, but we had taken it out of that module to avoid a clash of use between the **Save** and **Save As** functions.

Follow these steps to create the output functions for testing after you are familiar with the design specifications. Alternatively, load the **TitleTester3** project from Archie's development area on the CD. All the following steps relate to additions to the test program we created in the previous section.

Step 1

Place this code into the **mnuSaveTitleIndex_Click** event handler of the test program:

```
Private Sub mnuSaveTitleIndex_Click()
```

```
' TITLE EDITOR INFRASTRUCTURE EVENT HANDLER: V1.0
' Menu drop-down option SAVE
' -------------------------
Dim booResult As Boolean
Dim strTemp As String

If g_intCurrentTitle < 1 Then
    MsgBox "Index is empty"
    Exit Sub
End If
' .................................................
strTemp = txtIndexFileName.Text

If txtIndexFileName.Text <> "" Then
    booResult = WriteOutTitleIndex(strTemp)
    If booResult = False Then
        MsgBox "Failed to save file"
        Exit Sub
    End If
Else
    Call mnuSaveTitleIndexAs_Click
End If

Exit Sub
End Sub
```

As the design for this module indicates, this code simply checks that the Index is not empty, and that an Index file name exists to use. If an Index file name exists, the program calls **WriteOutTitleIndex** with the name of the file to receive the data. If no file name is present in the screen object that houses the file reference for the Title Index, a call is made to the **Save As** function to ask the user for a name. (Windows users expect a Save menu option to work that way if no file name is specified.)

Step 2

Place this code in the **mnuSaveTitleIndexAs_Click** event handler:

```
Private Sub mnuSaveTitleIndexAs_Click()
' TITLE EDITOR INFRASTRUCTURE EVENT HANDLER: V1.0
' Menu drop-down option SAVE AS
' -------------------------
Dim booResult As Boolean
Dim strFileName As String

If g_intCurrentTitle < 1 Then
    MsgBox "Index is empty"
```

```
      Exit Sub
End If
' ...............................................
strFileName = txtIndexFileName.Text
booResult = GetIndexFileNameForOutput(dlgDialog, strFileName)
If booResult = False Then
        MsgBox "Failed to output File"
        Exit Sub
End If

' request authorization to proceed
booResult = OKToProceed(strFileName)
If booResult = False Then Exit Sub
' .....................................................
' OK to proceed

booResult = WriteOutTitleIndex(strFileName)
If booResult = False Then
        MsgBox "Failed to output File"
        Exit Sub
End If

txtIndexFileName.Text = strFileName
MsgBox "File output successfully"
Exit Sub

End Sub
```

The code uses a routine called **GetIndexFileNameForOutput**, similar to **GetIndexFileName ForInput**. From the user's response, **GetIndexFileNameForOutput** supplies an existing name, or a name that does not yet exist. If a file name is returned by this call, the user is asked whether overwriting an existing file is okay, or whether to create a new file, as appropriate (this is done in **OKToProceed**). The code goes ahead and calls **WriteOutTitleIndex** only if the user approves. Depending on the success of the operation, the code reports the result as evident in the code.

Step 3

Create the generic function **GetIndexFileNameForOutput** as follows, which you should insert into **TitleLib**:

```
Public Function GetIndexFileNameForOutput(dlgObject As Control,_
                                    strFileName As String) As Boolean
' GENERAL ROUTINE: V1.0
' Get name of output file
' Arguments:
```

```
'      dlgObject - Common dialog control
'    strFileName - On entry, contains default file name in use
'                  On return contains actual name of file output to
'    Function Result - True - File name supplied
'                    - False - no name supplied
' --------------------------------
GetIndexFileNameForOutput = False              ' default is failure

' Select File name to output
On Error GoTo Errhandler
dlgObject.FileName = strFileName
dlgObject.Filter = "Index Files (*.idx)|*.idx|All files (*.*)|*.*"
dlgObject.FilterIndex = 1
dlgObject.Action = 2
strFileName = dlgObject.FileName
If strFileName = "" Then Exit Function

GetIndexFileNameForOutput = True
Exit Function
' =======================================================
Errhandler:
MsgBox "Failed to output " & strFileName & "Index File."
Exit Function

End Function
```

This code corresponds closely to the **GetIndexFileNameForInput** routine, except that the **Action** property of the dialog box is set to **2**, and **strFileName** is initially used to set up the dialog box.

Step 4

Add this code to **TitleLib**:

```
Public Function WriteOutTitleIndex(strFileName As String) As Boolean
' GENERAL ROUTINE: V1.0
' Arguments:
'   strFileName -   File name currently in use on entry
'                   Name of file output to on return
'     Result of Function - True - file output OK
'                        - False - unable to output file
' --------------------------------
Dim intLoopCounter As Integer
Dim booResult As Boolean

WriteOutTitleIndex = False
If strFileName = "" Then Exit Function
```

```
On Error GoTo FailedToOutput

Open strFileName For Output As #1

Print #1, "[E-BOOK TITLE INDEX]"

For intLoopCounter = 1 To UBound(g_strTitleTitle())
    Print #1, "[" & g_strTitleFileName(intLoopCounter) & "]"
    Print #1, "[" & g_strTitleTitle(intLoopCounter) & "]"
    Print #1, "[" & g_strTitleDescription(intLoopCounter) & "]"
    Print #1, "[END OF RECORD]"
Next intLoopCounter

Close #1

WriteOutTitleIndex = True
Exit Function
' ========================================================
' Error handling
FailedToOutput:
MsgBox "Title Index Output failed"
Close #1
Exit Function

End Function
```

In the preceding code, the contents of the Title Index are output, line-by-line, according to the specification for the Title Index data file.

Step 5

Add this routine to **TitleLib**:

```
Public Function OKToProceed(strFileName As String) As Boolean
' GENERAL ROUTINE: V1.0
' ----------------------------
' Arguments:
'     strFileName  - Name of file to check
' Takes a file name and attempts to open that file.
' Based on result (exists, does not exist) asks for authority
' to proceed.
' ----------------------------
Dim intStatus As Integer
Dim strTemp As String
Dim intTemp As Integer


' check status of file and request authorization to proceed
```

```
OKToProceed = False
intStatus = 0

On Error GoTo 1000:
  Open strFileName For Input As #1
  intStatus = 1                      ' File exists
1000:
intStatus = intStatus + 1            ' = 2 if file exists and 1 if not
Close #1

' If File exists - see if it is to be overwritten
If intStatus = 2 Then
  strTemp = "This file already exists. Are you sure want to overwrite it?"
  intTemp = MsgBox(strTemp, vbQuestion + vbOKCancel, "OVERWRITE EXISTING_
          FILE"
  If intTemp = 1 Then OKToProceed = True
End If

' If File does not exist - see if it is to be created
If intStatus = 1 Then
  strTemp = "This file does not exist. Do you wish to create a new file"
  intTemp = MsgBox(strTemp, vbQuestion + vbOKCancel, "CREATE NEW FILE")
  If intTemp = 1 Then OKToProceed = True
End If
Exit Function

End Function
```

This routine attempts to open the file. The error trap is set up such that **intStatus** will be **2** if the file opened and therefore exists, or **intStatus** will be 1 if the file did not open. Based on this result, an appropriate message is given, and the user is asked whether the program should proceed.

This level of attention to detail—checking whether a file exists and informing the user—is essential to make the Save As option safe in terms of avoiding inadvertent overwriting of files. This approach is contrary to the Save option, which will indiscriminately overwrite the current disk file.

Testing the Save Modules

Archie ran the test program and loaded a Title Index. He used the Save As option to output the file to another file name. He then inspected the two files using an editor. After he proved the module's basic functionality, he set about testing a variety of load and save combinations, as follows:

♦ *Test 1*—Read in a Title Index and Save As a different name. Check that files are the same.

♦ *Test 2*—Read in a Title Index and Save. Reread Title Index and make sure it is unchanged.

♦ *Test 3*—Read in an Index, manually blank out the Index file name on screen, and try to save. Check that "Save As" is invoked.

♦ *Test 4*—Read in a Title Index and output as a new name. Check that authorization to create a file is requested and check that file content is correct.

♦ *Test 5*—Read in a Title Index and overwrite an existing file. Check that authorization to overwrite a file is requested and check that file content is correct.

♦ *Test 6*—Check that Save and Save As are inhibited if Index is empty.

Altogether, Archie took only two days to complete and test all the functionality he was scheduled to do in four days—in other words, two days spent, four days achieved. Let's see how Julie fared with her tasks.

The Case Study:
Title Index Editor—Part 2

Julie's tasks for the first week of Project Phase 3 consisted of the following:

♦ *Change Handling*—handling of changes that set and clear the **Alert 1 State** and the **Alert 2 State**.

♦ *Index Manipulation*—consisting of modules to handle adding, inserting, overwriting, and deleting Title Index entries.

Creation of the Change Handling Module

Julie's first job was to set up the **Change Handling** module.

Alert Handling

On the Title Index Editor form were three data fields: **txtFileRef**, **txtTitle**, and **txtDetails**. If the user changed the content of any of these text boxes, the corresponding change event needed to trigger the program into setting what we defined as the **Alert Level 1 Changed State**. (This state is an alert condition that indicates to the user that the content of the text boxes on screen is no longer the same as the in-Memory Index entry.) The Index entry consisted of **g_strTitleFileName(g_intCurrentTitle)**, **g_strTitleTitle(g_intCurrentTitle)**, and **g_strTitleDescription(g_intCurrentTitle)**.

In a second alert condition, the in-Memory Index did not contain the same data as the Index disk file. You can review the state transitions of the editors by looking at Figure 4.20, located in Chapter 4.

Design Specifications

The design specifications for setting and releasing the alert states are as follows:

DESIGN SPEC: Alert State Handling for the Editors
SUBROUTINE: SwitchOnAlert1

DESCRIPTION: Sets the editor into the **Alert 1 State**, which indicates that screen data is not the same as memory.

ACTION:

Set alert color on main form.

Disable all navigation button controls.

Replace Delete Index-manipulation button control with Release button.

Disable menu options New, Open, Save, Save As.

END:

SUB: SwitchOffAlert1

FUNCTION: Clear the editor from the **Alert 1 State**, now indicating screen data is the same as memory.

ACTION:

Clear alert color on main form

Clear alert color on all data fields subject to change handling

Enable all navigation button controls

Replace Release button with Delete Index-manipulation button

Enable menu options New, Open, Save, Save As.

END:

SUB: SwitchOnAlert2

FUNCTION: Sets the editor into the **Alert 2 State**, indicating memory is not the same as the disk data.

ACTION:

Set alert color on the text box showing Index file name

END:

SUB: SwitchOffAlert2

FUNCTION: Clear the editor from **Alert 2 State**, now indicating memory data is the same as disk file.

ACTION:

Clear alert color on the text box showing Index file name.

END:

These specifications define four GUI infrastructure subroutines: two to switch on the appropriate alert state and two to switch off the alert state.

Change Events

According to the design, the next thing we had to do was to specify what events triggered a change of state. We produced a list of all the events that changed data on screen, in memory, or on disk, for which the alert status must be changed. You can see the list in Figure 10.3.

Constructing the ChangeHandling1 Form

Julie decided that the easiest way to set up change handling would be to take the prototype form developed for the requirements specification and install the required code directly into the form. Remember that the prototype form was a shell, which contained no code whatsoever. She set up all the screen-object names correctly according to the screen-object list we had defined at design time.

To prevent your having to go through this procedure, you can simply add the form **frmETitleEditor** from directory DEV_BlankETitleEditor on the CD to a new VB EXE project.

Event List for Triggering and Clearing Alert State in Both Editors		
EVENT	**Special Conditions**	**ACTION**
txtFileRef_change	Title Editor only, Manual change only	Set Alert State 1
txtTitle_change	Title Editor only, Manual change only	Set Alert State 1
txtDescription_Change	Title Editor only, Manual change only	Set Alert State 1
txtKeyView(1) to (5) array	Page Editor only, Manual change only	Set Alert State 1
txtText	Page Editor only, Manual change only	Set Alert State 1
cmdAdd_Click	Do at end	Clear Alert State 1 + Set Alert State 2
cmdInsert_Click	Do at end	Clear Alert State 1 + Set Alert State 2
cmdOverWrite_Click	Do at end	Clear Alert State 1 + Set Alert State 2
cmdDelete_Click	Alert 1 Normal State only, Do at end	Set Alert State 2
cmdRelease_Click	Alert 1 Changed State only, Do at end	Clear Alert State 1
cmdPaste_Click	Page Editor only, Do at end	Set Alert State 1
cmdClearTextBox_Click	Page Editor only, Do at end	Set Alert State 1 and txtText to alert color
cmdClearKeys_Click	Page Editor only, Do at end	Set Alert State 1 and key to alert color
cmdRemove/Picture/Sound/Text/All	Page Editor only, Do at end	Set Alert State 1
cmdSaveTextFile_Click	Page Editor only, Do at end	Clear txtText's background alert color
mnuNew_Click	Alert 1 Normal State only, Do at end	Clear Alert State 2
mnuOpen_Click	Alert 1 Normal State only, Do at end	Clear Alert State 2
mnuSave_Click	Alert 1 Normal State only, Do at end	Clear Alert State 2
mnuSaveAs_Click	Alert 1 Normal State only, Do at end	Clear Alert State 2
mnuTextSave_Click	Page Editor only, Do at end	Clear txtText's background alert color
mnuTextSaveAs_Click	Page Editor only, Do at end	Clear txtText's background alert color
mnuSetFont Click	Page Editor only, Do at end	Set Alert State 2

Figure 10.3

List of events that cause setting or clearing of **Alert State 1** and **Alert State 2** in the editors.

Remember to remove the default Form1, run the program, and, when VB complains that there is no **main()**, designate **ETitleEditor** as the main form. If you recall, this was a procedure we also had to adopt with the viewer. Figure 10.4 shows the resulting form for the test program.

To install the **Change Handling** module, you can either follow these steps or, alternatively, load the **ChangeHandling1** project from the directory of the same name on the CD.

Step 1

Make sure that the test program's form looks like the one you see in Figure 10.4. Note that another button labeled Delete is immediately underneath the Release button. Note the three shape controls on the test program's form. These shapes will hold colors. The controls are required for change handling so we can switch colors easily, much as we did in the multimedia evaluation exercise back in Chapter 1.

Step 2

Insert the following variable in the general data declaration of the main form:

```
Option Explicit
' TITLE EDITOR INFRASTRUCTURE DATA STRUCTURE: V1.0
' Parameter which indicates when a screen object has focus
Private i_booFocus As Boolean
```

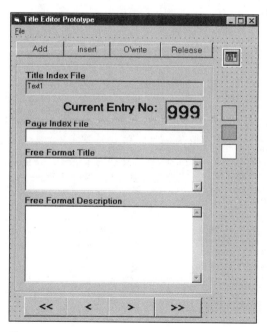

Figure 10.4

Test program **ChangeHandling1**, created from the prototype form developed to illustrate the Title Index Editor in the requirements specification.

The design information (see Figure 10.3—in particular, the event list) made evident that the data-field change event must set the alert status only when the user caused that status, as indicated by the comment "manual change only." If the content of a data field changed because a new entry was being displayed (an automatic change), we didn't want the **Alert** status to be invoked. To achieve this functionality, Julie came up with the idea of using the **GotFocus** and **LostFocus** events of the text objects to set and clear a variable called **i_booGotFocus**. If the change-event code was triggered, and **i_booFocus** was **True**, the user must be changing the field. If **i_booFocus** was not set when the change event was triggered, the user was not causing the event, and the program itself must be performing an automatic update of the data field. (This is a very good example of the need to understand your events.)

Step 3

Insert the following code into the **GotFocus** and **ReleaseFocus** events for **txtFileRef**, **txtTitle**, and **txtDescription**. For the **GotFocus** handler of each text box mentioned, add the following:

```
' TITLE EDITOR INFRASTRUCTURE EVENT HANDLER: V1.0
' User has focus on this screen object
' ---------------------
i_booFocus = True
End Sub
```

For the **LostFocus** handler of each text box mentioned, add the following:

```
' TITLE EDITOR INFRASTRUCTURE EVENT HANDLER: V1.0
' User has removed focus on this screen object
' ---------------------
i_booFocus = False
End Sub
```

You must install these two sets of code in each text box that the user can change. As I stated earlier, when the user places focus on the screen object, **i_booFocus** is set, indicating that the user has focus on the object. When the user releases the focus, **i_booFocus** is cleared, indicating that the object is now free.

Step 4

Insert the following code into the relevant text-box change-event handlers:

```
Private Sub txtFileRef_Change()
' TITLE EDITOR INFRASTRUCTURE EVENT HANDLER: V1.0
' Screen object's content has changed
' -------------------------
If i_booFocus = False then exit sub
If txtFileRef.BackColor = shpRed.BackColor Then Exit Sub
```

```
txtFileRef.BackColor = shpRed.BackColor
Call SetAlert1Status
End Sub

Private Sub txtTitle_Change()
' TITLE EDITOR INFRASTRUCTURE EVENT HANDLER: V1.0
' Screen object's content has changed
' ---------------------------
If i_booFocus = False then exit sub
If txtTitle.BackColor = shpRed.BackColor Then Exit Sub
txtTitle.BackColor = shpRed.BackColor
Call SetAlert1Status
End Sub

Private Sub txtDescription_Change()
' TITLE EDITOR INFRASTRUCTURE EVENT HANDLER: V1.0
' Screen object's content has changed
' ---------------------------
If i_booFocus = False then exit sub
If txtDescription.BackColor = shpRed.BackColor Then Exit Sub
txtDescription.BackColor = shpRed.BackColor
Call SetAlert1Status
End Sub
```

In each of the preceding cases, the change-event handler executes the code only if **i_booFocus** is **True**. This action can happen only when the **GotFocus** event has fired for the text box in question. The remaining code then looks to see whether the text box is already in the **Alert State**. If the background color is set to the alert color, the code exits the handler. If the text box is not set up with the alert color, the code sets the background to the alert color and then calls the routine to switch on the **Alert 1 Changed State**, at which point the entire form will be changed to the alert color.

Step 5

Insert the following code sections at the end of each of the click-event handlers, as defined after the code:

```
' ------------------
' CHANGE HANDLING FOR INDEX FUNCTIONS
Call ClearAlert1Status
Call SetAlert2Status
End Sub
```

Place the above code at the end of the following event handlers:

```
a) Private Sub cmdADD_Click()
```

```
b) Private Sub cmdDelete_Click()
c) Private Sub cmdInsert_Click()
d) Private Sub cmdOverWrite_Click()
```

At the end of each of the preceding event handlers, the call to **SwitchOffAlert1Status** resets the screen to the **Normal State**, and the call to **SetAlert2Status** sets the Index file-name text box to the alert color, to indicate that the content of the memory (which has just been modified, for example, by an **Add**, **Delete**, **Insert**, or **Overwrite** function) is no longer the same as the disk file.

Step 6

Place the following code section at the end of the menu functions, as listed after the code:

```
' ---------------------
' CHANGE HANDLING FOR MENU OPTIONS
Call ClearAlert2Status
End Sub
```

Place the above code at the end of the following event handlers:

```
a) Private Sub mnuNewTitleIndex_Click()
b) Private Sub mnuOpenTitleIndex_Click()
c) Private Sub mnuSaveTitleIndex_Click()
d) Private Sub mnuSaveTitleIndexAs_Click()
```

When each of the above-named event handlers has completed its code, the last thing the event handler will do is switch off **Alert State 2**, indicating that the memory is now the same as the disk file.

Step 7

Here is the code that you need to insert in the general section of the form, to switch on the **Alert 1 Changed** state:

```
Public Sub SetAlert1Status()
' TITLE EDITOR INFRASTRUCTURE GUI ROUTINE: V1.0
' ---------------------
' form background to red
frmTitleEditor.BackColor = shpRed.BackColor

' Disable navigation
cmdGoStart.Enabled = False
cmdGoEnd.Enabled = False
cmdNext.Enabled = False
cmdPrevious.Enabled = False
```

```
' Disable File menu options
mnuFile.Enabled = False

' remove delete and show release
cmdRelease.Visible = True
cmdDelete.Visible = False

Exit Sub
End Sub
```

Step 8

Insert this code into the general section of the form to switch off the **Alert State**:

```
Public Sub ClearAlert1Status()
' TITLE EDITOR INFRASTRUCTURE GUI ROUTINE: V1.0
' ----------------------
' form back to grey
frmTitleEditor.BackColor = shpGrey.BackColor

' Data fields back to white
txtFileRef.BackColor = shpWhite.BackColor
txtTitle.BackColor = shpWhite.BackColor
txtDescription.BackColor = shpWhite.BackColor

' Enable navigation
cmdGoStart.Enabled = True
cmdGoEnd.Enabled = True
cmdNext.Enabled = True
cmdPrevious.Enabled = True

' Enabled File menu options
mnuFile.Enabled = True

' remove Release and bring back Delete
cmdRelease.Visible = False
cmdDelete.Visible = True

Exit Sub
End Sub
```

Step 9

Finally, you need to insert the two routines to switch on and off the **Alert 2 State** into the general section of the main form:

```
Private Sub SetAlert2Status()
```

```
' TITLE EDITOR INFRASTRUCTURE GUI ROUTINE: V1.0
' - - - - - - - - - - - - - - - - - - - - - - - - - - - - - - -
If txtIndexFileName.BackColor = shpRed.BackColor Then Exit Sub
txtIndexFileName.BackColor = shpRed.BackColor
Exit Sub
End Sub

Private Sub ClearAlert2Status()
' TITLE EDITOR INFRASTRUCTURE GUI ROUTINE: V1.0
' - - - - - - - - - - - - - - - - - - - - - - - - - - - - - - -
txtIndexFileName.BackColor = shpGrey.BackColor
Exit Sub

End Sub
```

Step 10

Add this code to the **Release** button's click-event handler:

```
' CHANGE HANDLING
Call ClearAlert1Status
End Sub
```

Running and Testing Title Index Editor Change Handling

Interpreting the design and setting up the code took Julie longer than she expected, even though the set of functionality was really quite simple. Testing consisted of the following:

♦ *Test 1*—Check that any changes to the three data fields cause **Alert 1 Change State** to be set.

♦ *Test 2*—Check that Delete button is removed and Release button appears when **Alert 1 Changed State** is set.

♦ *Test 3*—Check that Release button clears Alert 1 Changed State, Release button disappears, and Delete button reappears.

♦ *Test 4*—Check that Release button does not alter the condition of **Alert 2 State**.

♦ *Test 5*—Check that navigation controls are disabled when **Alert1 Changed State** is set.

♦ *Test 6*—Check that file menu options New, Open, Save, and Save As are disabled when **Alert 1 Changed State** is set.

♦ *Test 7*—Check that navigation is re-enabled when **Alert 1 Normal State** is set.

♦ *Test 8*—Check that file menu options are re-enabled when **Alert 1 Normal State** is set.

♦ *Test 9*—Check that **Alert 1 Changed State** is cleared, if it's on, when Add, Insert, and Overwrite are invoked.

- *Test 10*—Check that **Alert 2 Changed State** is enabled when Add, Insert, Delete, and Overwrite are invoked.

- *Test 11*—Check that **Alert 2 Normal State** is set when New, Open, Save, or Save As is invoked.

The technique of building the change-handling code into a shell of the Title Index Editor was actually a very neat way to test state-transition handling before we had installed the rest of the program. After we had put the rest of the program's code in place, change handling would become very obscure. The way Julie went about testing change handling meant she had concentrated on nothing *but* **Change Handling**, and she had not been side-tracked by other functionality that might cloud the issues of testing and checking.

At system-integration time, with the change-handling code already installed, Julie and Archie would only have to add code to the shell that they had produced. Julie took a whole day to implement and test **Change Handling** in detail, and the time required surprised her quite a lot. She made a number of simple mistakes, such as getting the colors mixed up, or confusing "change" and "click" events, and putting code for one into the other. These were all simple mistakes, but they slowed her down. Although not a lot of code was involved in the **Change Handling** module, Julie needed to understand and test in detail a fair number of logical combinations. Julie certainly found the state-transition diagram and the event list useful. However, for one actual day spent, Julie had achieved the one-day's progress required to complete the task as planned.

Preparing for Development of the Index Manipulation Functions

On Julie's second day of project Week 9, she made a start on the four **Index Manipulation** functions. These functions were **Add**, **Insert**, **Overwrite**, and **Delete**. She needed a test program that let her read in a Title Index and manipulate its contents by adding to the Index by inserting an entry here and there, overwriting the contents of a given entry, and deleting selected entries. To achieve this level of functionality, she would require some simple navigation capability to let her check entries and move to locations where she could then modify the content, insert an entry, and so on. She decided to take a copy of the form she had developed for the viewer in test program **TitleTest3** and use that as the basis for her Index testing program.

In the design presented in Appendix G, the **Add**, **Insert**, **Overwrite**, and **Delete** functions are specified as generic definitions for both editors. Study these design specifications in detail before you proceed, because we did not discuss them in Chapter 6. You will find the specifications straightforward. In Figure 10.5, you can see the form for the first Index test program Julie created.

To prepare for **Index Manipulation** development and testing, you can follow these steps. Alternatively, you can load **TitleIndexTest1** from Julie's development area on the CD.

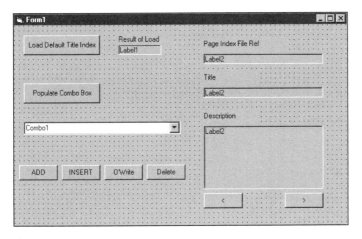

Figure 10.5
The form for Julie's first Index test program, **TitleIndexTest1**.

Step 1

Create a new directory in Julie's work area on your hard disk, and call the directory **TitleIndexTest1**. Create a new VB EXE project, and load the form **TitleTest3** from Julie's work area. Remove the redundant **Form1**, and add module **ViewerLib** from **DEV_Eviewer**, either from your work area or from the CD. Remember, this version of **ViewerLib** that you are loading is the version from the completed viewer development.

Step 2

Run the test program you have just created and, when VB complains that there is no main form, select **TitleTest3** from the drop-down menu. (You've had to do this each time we've created a new project and loaded an existing form as the basis of a new development.)

Step 3

Store the main form and project as **TitleIndexTest1**.

Step 4

Add four button controls, which will be used to perform the manipulation functions, and two more button controls, which will perform simple **Next** and **Previous** navigation functions on the form. The buttons are as follows: **CmdAdd**, **cmdInsert**, **cmdOverWrite**, and **cmdDelete** for Index manipulation, and **cmdPrevious** and **cmdNext** for navigation. The form should now resemble what you can see in Figure 10.5.

Step 5

Convert the three data labels **lblFileRef**, **lblTitle**, and **lblDescription** to text boxes with the same names, but prefixed by **txt** rather than **lbl**. Also, change appropriately all references to these labels that appear in the code. Set the **Multiline** property of the title and description text boxes to be **True**.

Step 6

Place the following code in the **cmdPrevious_Click** event handler:

```
Private Sub cmdPrevious_Click()
' TEST CODE:
' --------------
If g_intCurrentTitle = 1 Then Exit Sub
g_intCurrentTitle = g_intCurrentTitle - 1
Call DisplayEntry
End Sub
```

Step 7

Place the following code in the **cmdNext_Click** event handler:

```
Private Sub cmdNext_Click()
' TEST CODE
' --------------
If g_intCurrentTitle = UBound(g_strTitleTitle()) Then Exit Sub
g_intCurrentTitle = g_intCurrentTitle + 1
Call DisplayEntry
End Sub
```

Step 8

Place the following code in the general section of the test program:

```
Private Sub DisplayEntry()
' TEST CODE
' --------------
txtFileRef.Text = g_strTitleFileName(g_intCurrentTitle)
txtTitle.Text = g_strTitleTitle(g_intCurrentTitle)
txtDescription.Text = g_strTitleDescription(g_intCurrentTitle)
lblEntryNumber.caption = Cstr(g_intCurrentTitle)
End Sub
```

Step 9

Add the following code to the end of **cmdLoadIndex_Click**:

```
' ---------------------
' THIS CODE IS REQUIRED BY THE TITLE EDITOR
' AFTER A TITLE INDEX FILE HAS BEEN LOADED
g_intCurrentTitle = 1
```

```
Call DisplayEntry
End Sub
```

Step 10

Create a label called **lblEntryNumber** just above the Index buttons. This label will let you see what entry is being displayed at any given time during testing. The code you have entered provides a basic level of navigation, a **Next** and a **Previous** function (with no frills), together with a routine to output the current entry to the screen objects. At this stage, Julie tested the program just to make sure she could load the Test Index and navigate through it. Remember, she was using the Load Default Title Index button to load an Index into the Index memory.

Creating the Add to Index Function

After Julie could load an Index and manipulate around it, she then developed the **Add to Index** function according to the design specifications. To simplify things, she created a couple subroutines along the way, one to increase the size of the Index by one (the **Insert** function would also need this subroutine) and one to copy screen data to the current entry.

Step 1

Insert this code into the click-event handler for the Add button:

```
Private Sub cmdAdd_Click()
' TITLE EDITOR INFRASTRUCTURE EVENT HANDLER: V1.0
' ADD on-screen data to end of Index
' --------------------
Dim strTemp As String
Dim intResponse As Integer
Dim booResult As Boolean

strTemp = "Add this to current Index"
intResponse = MsgBox(strTemp, vbQuestion + vbOKCancel, "ADD to Index")
If intResponse <> 1 Then Exit Sub
' ....................................................................
' update in-Memory Index
Call IncreaseTitleIndexByOne
Call TransferFromScreenToEntry
Call DisplayEntry
' Place CHANGE HANDLING code here
Exit Sub
End Sub
```

According to the design, the code first checks that the user wants to perform an **Add**. This check serves as an escape clause for the user, should the Add button have been clicked by error. (Users like escape clauses.) If the user gives approval for an **Add**, the code increases the size of the Title Index by one, transfers the data from screen to the last entry, and then sets up the display according to **g_intCurrentTitle** (which will have been set by the call to increase the Index by one entry).

Note how Julie placed a comment at the end, reminding whoever integrates this code into the final Title Index Editor program that he or she must add the change-handling code.

Step 2

Add a new module called **TitleLib** to the project. (This module would be Julie's version of the library for any general routines she would create.) Place this code into Julie's version of **TitleLib**:

```
Public Sub IncreaseTitleIndexByOne()
' GENERAL ROUTINE: V1.0
' Increase size of Title Index by one
' -----------------
g_intCurrentTitle = UBound(g_strTitleFileName()) + 1
ReDim Preserve g_strTitleFileName(g_intCurrentTitle)
ReDim Preserve g_strTitleTitle(g_intCurrentTitle)
ReDim Preserve g_strTitleDescription(g_intCurrentTitle)

End Sub
```

This routine can be called regardless of what **g_intCurrentTitle** is set to on entry, because the entry is immediately set to the last entry plus one. The program then resizes the dimensions on all three elements in the array, preserving the settings already loaded. On exit, **g_intCurrentTitle** automatically points to the newly created last entry. (By the way, don't forget to add **Option Explicit** to the general section of the **TitleLib** module.)

Step 3

Create this routine in the general section of the test program's main form:

```
Private Sub TransferFromScreenToEntry()
' TITLE EDITOR INFRASTRUCTURE GUI ROUTINE: V1.0
' move content of screen data text boxes to current Index elements
' --------------------------------
g_strTitleFileName(g_intCurrentTitle) = txtFileRef.Text
g_strTitleTitle(g_intCurrentTitle) = txtTitle.Text
g_strTitleDescription(g_intCurrentTitle) = txtDescription.Text

End Sub
```

Testing the Add to Index Function

At this stage, Julie ran the program and loaded the default Title Index. She checked that all the entries were correct by using the Next and Previous buttons. She then selected Entry 1 and manually modified the three data fields. She then clicked Add. This action placed the screen content into a newly created, final entry. She then verified the entry was final by stepping backward. She also verified that the entries up to this new one were still intact—in particular, Entry 1, which was on view when she made the modifications.

Using this simple technique, Julie was able to verify the following:

◆ *Test 1*—The **Add** function will take what is on screen and add it to the end of the Index.

◆ *Test 2*—The **Add** function can be aborted, and doing so has no impact on data already in the Index.

◆ *Test 3*—Adding to an empty Index creates the first entry.

◆ *Test 4*—**Add** works when the current entry is Entry 1 and when the current entry is the last entry.

The program failed on Test 3 with an "Array Out of Bounds" subscript failure. Any ideas why?

The routine that increases the size of the array first determines the array's initial size by using the **Unbound** function. This function fails when no Index exists, because the dynamic array does not exist after initial program load. This problem can be overcome quite simply by creating the array with element 0 (which we will never use because we always start arrays from element 1) in the **Form Load** event:

```
' Clear out the Index
Call ClearTitleIndexMemory
```

Julie then started to test the functionality in earnest and moved on to the next function only when she was satisfied that **Add** worked correctly. Remember, all her testing was based on observing what happened to the in-memory Index. To assist, Julie used meaningful strings to insert into entries, such as "Addition number 1" as the title for her first added entry, and so on. As she scanned through the entries, such comments made it easy for her to determine where they had come from and thereby helped her to assess whether the software was functioning correctly.

Creating the Overwrite Index Function

As you can see from the design specifications, this function is the simplest of the **Index Manipulation** functions.

Step 1

Place this code in the **OverWrite_Click** event handler:

```
Private Sub cmdOverWrite_Click()
' TITLE EDITOR INFRASTRUCTURE EVENT HANDLER: V1.0
```

```
' Overwrite memory entry with on-screen data
' ----------------------
Dim strTemp As String
Dim intResponse As Integer
Dim booResult As Boolean

If g_intCurrentTitle < 1 Then
    MsgBox "Title Index is empty"
    Exit Sub
End If

strTemp = "Overwrite current Index entry?"
intResponse = MsgBox(strTemp, vbQuestion + vbOKCancel, "OVERWRITE to Index")
If intResponse <> 1 Then Exit Sub
' .............................................................
' update in-Memory Index
Call TransferFromScreenToEntry
Call DisplayEntry
' Place CHANGE HANDLING code here
Exit Sub
End Sub
```

This code is very similar to that of the **Add** function, but without any call to increase the size of the Index. Also, this code checks that the Index is not empty on entry because, if no Index exists, the code cannot overwrite anything. The **Add** function, on the other hand, can add to an empty Index—it is the only **Index Manipulation** function that can be performed on an empty Index.

The **Overwrite Index** function operates on the entry defined by **g_intCurrentTitle** and places the screen content into this entry, which is then displayed. Note that Julie put a reminder here with reference to adding the change handling code, for the integration stage later.

Testing the Overwrite Index Function

Julie could now add to and overwrite the contents of an Index. In addition to the **Add** tests, this new code allowed the following tests:

- *Test 1*—Any changes made on screen can be moved into the current entry, overwriting the previous contents.

- *Test 2*—If the Index is empty, the function is aborted.

- *Test 3*—The user can abort the function.

- *Test 4*—Insert occurs okay when positioned at Entry 1 and at last entry.

Once again, Julie tested until she was satisfied that **Overwrite** functioned correctly. And, just to be on the safe side, she repeated the **Add** tests again.

Creating the Insert Index Function

As specified in the design, **Insert Index** involves creating a new entry at the end of the Index, then increasing by one all the entry numbers from the current entry number to the end. The on-screen data can then be used to overwrite the current entry, which has been changed to the current entry number plus one.

Step 1

Insert this code into the **Insert** click-event handler:

```
Private Sub cmdInsert_Click()
' TITLE EDITOR INFRASTRUCTURE EVENT HANDLER: V1.0
' Insert screen content between
' g_intCurrentTitle-1 and g_intCurrentEntry
' ----------------------
Dim strTemp As String
Dim intResponse As Integer
Dim intLoop As Integer

If g_intCurrentTitle < 1 Then
    MsgBox "Title Index is empty"
    Exit Sub
End If

strTemp = "Insert into Index?"
intResponse = MsgBox(strTemp, vbQuestion + vbOKCancel, "INSERT into Index")
If intResponse <> 1 Then Exit Sub
' ..............................................................
' update in-memory Index
intResponse = g_intCurrentTitle        ' save current position value
Call IncreaseTitleIndexByOne

' shuffle entries
For intLoop = UBound(g_strTitleTitle()) To intResponse + 1 Step -1

  g_strTitleFileName(intLoop) = g_strTitleFileName(intLoop - 1)
  g_strTitleTitle(intLoop) = g_strTitleTitle(intLoop - 1)
  g_strTitleDescription(intLoop) = g_strTitleDescription(intLoop - 1)

Next intLoop

g_intCurrentTitle = intResponse
Call TransferFromScreenToEntry
Call DisplayEntry
' Place CHANGE HANDLING code here
End Sub
```

The preceding code behaves like the other Index functions until we get to **Update in-Memory Index**. At this point, the current entry number is preserved in **intResponse**, a conveniently free integer that is no longer required. Then, the Index size is increased by one. In the **For** loop that follows, each entry is moved forward one place. The loop starts at the end of the Index and works its way back to the original current entry number. If you have trouble understanding this code, draw an Index of five locations on paper. If the current entry is in Location 4, work through the code to see what happens. In this example, the routine will extend the size of the Index to six entries. The **For** loop starts by moving Entry 5 to the position of Entry 6; it then moves Entry 4 to Position 5. This means that the new Entries 4 and 5 are identical. At the end of the loop, the code will transfer the contents of the screen into Location 4, completing the insert function.

At the end of the code, the current pointer, **g_intCurrentTitle**, is then reset to the value it originally had when the routine was entered, thereby making the newly inserted data the current entry.

Testing the Insert Index Function

Testing the **Insert Index** function pretty much followed the way in which Julie had tested the other functions, which involved setting the current pointer somewhere in the Index, modifying the screen data, and then requesting an **Insert Index**. Using the navigation controls, she could then check whether the Index now looked like she expected it to.

Julie was able to perform these tests:

♦ *Test 1*—**Insert Index** increases the size of the Index by one and shuffles all previous entries forward one place.

♦ *Test 2*—**Insert Index** correctly places the screen content at the current location.

♦ *Test 3*—User can abort the function.

♦ *Test 4*—If the Index is empty, the function is aborted.

♦ *Test 5*—**Insert Index** occurs without error when located at the last entry or at the first entry.

After Julie had tested **Insert Index** to her satisfaction, she started to mix in the **Add** and **Overwrite** operations as well.

Creating the Delete Index Function

According to the design, **Delete Index** simply involved moving all the entries beyond the current location back one position and then reducing the size of the Index by one. To accomplish this functionality, Julie created both a routine to decrease the Index size by one and the code to perform the actual **Delete Index** function.

Step 1

Insert this code into the Delete button's click-event handler:

```
Private Sub cmdDelete_Click()
' TITLE EDITOR INFRASTRUCTURE EVENT HANDLER: V1.0
' Delete current location
' ----------------------
Dim strTemp As String
Dim intResponse As Integer
Dim booResult As Boolean
Dim intLoop As Integer

If g_intCurrentTitle < 1 Then
    MsgBox "Title Index is empty"
    Exit Sub
End If

strTemp = "Delete this entry?"
intResponse = MsgBox(strTemp, vbQuestion + vbOKCancel, "DELETE entry")
If intResponse <> 1 Then Exit Sub
' ....................................................................
' If Index only consists of one entry, clear it and exit
If UBound(g_strTitleTitle()) = 0 Then
    Call ClearTitleIndexMemory
    Exit Sub
End If

' Otherwise delete current entry from Memory Index
intResponse = g_intCurrentTitle        ' save current position value

For intLoop = intResponse To (UBound(g_strTitleTitle()) - 1)

  g_strTitleFileName(intLoop) = g_strTitleFileName(intLoop + 1)
  g_strTitleTitle(intLoop) = g_strTitleTitle(intLoop + 1)
  g_strTitleDescription(intLoop) = g_strTitleDescription(intLoop + 1)

Next intLoop

Call ReduceTitleIndexByOne
g_intCurrentTitle = intResponse
Call DisplayEntry
' Place CHANGE HANDLING code here
Exit Sub
End Sub
```

After the user has authorized the program to proceed with a **Delete Index** action, the code checks to see whether the Index contains only one entry. If it does, the Index is cleared, and the routine exits. If the Index contains more than one entry, the current position, as indicated by **g_intCurrentTitle**, is preserved. Next, all the entries from the beginning of the

Index to the entry just preceding the current one are moved one place forward. This action overwrites the current entry with the contents of the entry just preceding it. The Index size is then reduced by one, and the new current entry, located at **g_intCurrentTitle**, is displayed.

To illustrate the function of the code, consider the example we used in the previous section, which consisted of an Index containing five items. Suppose the current entry is Number 3 when we enter the previous routine; in the preceding **For** loop, Entry 4 will be moved to Entry 3, thereby overwriting the current entry; Entry 5 will move to Entry 4, and the Index will then be reduced to four elements.

Step 2

Place this routine in Julie's version of **TitleLib**:

```
Public Sub ReduceTitleIndexByOne()
' GENERAL ROUTINE: V1.0
' reduce size of Title Index by one
' ------------------
g_intCurrentTitle = UBound(g_strTitleFileName()) - 1
ReDim Preserve g_strTitleFileName(g_intCurrentTitle)
ReDim Preserve g_strTitleTitle(g_intCurrentTitle)
ReDim Preserve g_strTitleDescription(g_intCurrentTitle)

End Sub
```

The arrays in the above code are re-dimensioned with a value one less than their original size.

Testing the Delete Index Function

To test the **Delete Index** functionality, Julie only had to load an Index and then delete each entry in turn, checking that the rest of the Index was still intact after each deletion.

She tested this function as follows:

♦ *Test 1*—**Delete Index** removes only the current entry.

♦ *Test 2*—**Abort** works without affecting the Index.

♦ *Test 3*—If the Index is empty, the function is aborted.

♦ *Test 4*—**Delete Index** works on the first and last entry of the Index.

♦ *Test 5*—**Delete Index** works on an Index with only one entry.

Test 4 failed when Julie tried to delete the last entry of an Index. Any ideas why?

When the routine is entered, **g_intCurrentTitle** is pointing to the current entry. If this entry happens to be the last one, **g_intCurrentTitle** is no longer valid after the deletion has taken place, because the Index has been shrunk by one. **intResponse** holds the original value of the pointer, and this value is now one too many. When the test version of **DisplayTitle** tries to set up the screen from entry **g_intCurrentTitle**, it finds that the element of the arrays does not exist—hence, the error.

To resolve the issue, Julie put in a final check after the program reset **g_intCurrentTitle** from **intResponse**, as follows:

```
g_intCurrentTitle = intResponse
If g_intCurrentTitle > UBound(g_strTitleTitle()) Then_
                g_intCurrentTitle = UBound(g_strTitleTitle())
```

The detection of this error illustrates the importance of checking the boundaries of the extreme operational limits of any piece of code. In fact, the error made Julie think about an Index containing only one entry—which she checked out in Test 5. The code involves shuffling entries forward from the beginning entry to the current entry. In this special case—of a one-entry Index—shuffling was meaningless. So, although the function appeared to work, Julie realized that the algorithm was suspect for handling an Index where the current entry number was 1 and the size of the entry was also 1. She decided to add some specific code for handling a single-entry situation, to ensure that the situation would always be handled as she required. She placed the following code immediately after the point at which the user is asked to verify that the **Delete Index** function is to proceed:

```
' If Index consists of one only entry, clear it and exit
If UBound(g_strTitleTitle()) = 0 Then
    Call ClearTitleIndexMemory
    Exit Sub
End If
```

All the Index functions were now available, and Julie started to check combinations of **Add**, **Insert**, **Delete**, and **Overwrite**. Julie took just one day to develop and test all the **Index Manipulation** functionality—one day actually spent to achieve two days' progress and complete the development task.

Making Good Progress

At the end of Day 2 of the Title Index Editor development, both programmers had finished their allotted tasks. Archie had achieved four days' progress in two days actually spent on the project. Julie had spent two days and made three days' progress. Events then took a turn that let us capitalize on this excellent progress.

Handling Complications

In general, projects rarely run perfectly smoothly. In the case study, we'd done very well up to this point. Let's look at some things that can help you handle complications that are likely to arise.

Contingency Time

We'd had no major hiccups on the case study, thanks to a reasonable degree of contingency time built into the plan. When Archie was off sick for a whole week, the level of contingency time that we had planned allowed Julie to complete her own and Archie's tasks, and we still completed both sets of activities on schedule.

Contingency time provides the slack that lets you handle complications—up to a certain point. If you build up contingency time because of early completion, store it; don't waste it. Contingency time is one of the main weapons in the project manager's armory to handle complications.

Resources

For a software-development project, the principal resources are the programmers. We've already discussed keeping programmers happy and making sure that they get to program as often as possible, and that they see plenty of variation in their work experience.

In the natural course of events, some people turn out to be better programmers than others. Some people turn out to be good teachers; some are good at finding bugs; some are good at developing complex algorithms. Looking at your resources to see what each person is best at is quite important.

Identifying someone who is very good at explaining complex things might well come in handy if you are faced with getting new programmers up to speed. Always be mindful of people's strengths—and, of course, also be mindful of their weaknesses. Then, when a complication arises, you can instantly determine who is the best resource to react to the problem.

Small Teams

The case study has given some idea of how much easier working in small teams is, compared to working in larger groups. In small teams, each team member can review other team members' code. That way, everyone gets to know a little about what the team as a whole is doing.

If the project has fostered a good team spirit, you'll find that, as complications arise, team members will be willing to cooperate to solve problems. This attribute is less obvious in large development teams, where each member has less of an identity. Another attribute of small teams is that they react much faster to complications than a big team will.

Leading a Team

To say that a team is only as good as its leader is not an exaggeration. In this context, it's important that a programmer lead—i.e., have primary management control—over each development team. Most problems a team leader will address will be technical issues; consequently, he or she must have a good knowledge of both the tools in use on the project and the project details.

Team leaders might well be your most important project resource when it comes to handling complications. When a programmer has a problem associated with the project, he or she will go to the team leader for advice, so the team leader might spend a great deal of time handling the complications that arise in the life of a project. Consequently, you can't plan a team leader's time in quite the same way you plan a programmer's time.

If the team leader will be involved in programming and in supervising the team, you need to determine the split for the leader's time. You might want to start by designating 50 percent of the leader's time for programming and 50 percent for management responsibilities.

Escalation

Every project needs a means by which problems can be moved, or *escalated*, through a series of levels, with each level involving more senior project members. A problem usually surfaces when a programmer runs into a problem on the shop floor. Remember that one of our prime rules for projects is that people ask for help before a problem jeopardizes schedules. If the programmer can't solve whatever issue he or she has encountered, the team leader/supervisor is the next stop. But what happens if the supervisor can't provide a way forward? If you have an issue the supervisor can't deal with, his or her next action will likely be to inform the development manager. If the development manager requires assistance, it might be time to bring in the development director, and so on.

The principle of escalation is that, if you're unable to resolve the problem, the next person up in the chain is likely to have more experience and influence than you. That person may not be able to solve your problem directly, but he or she might be able to point you in the right direction in one of a variety of ways. Indeed, some of these ways might never occur to you in a million years. For example, you might have a problem with an aspect of the operating system that no one seems to understand. Your development director might well know the development director of the company that supplied the operating system. If, for one reason or another, all the normal channels of communication into that supplier have failed, your development director might be able to put direct pressure on the supplier to help you sort out the problem. Another scenario might be that your company owes the supplier money for goods received and, if you feel the level of support you have been receiving is poor, you might withhold payment as a last resort to improve that level of support. I am not recommending this approach—I'm merely pointing out that the process of escalation through levels of people with different levels of experience and influence might offer you solutions you could not have thought about without others' involvement.

As you can see, having the right knowledge does not solve all problems. Projects are complex entities that involve interlinked activities across a wide range of disciplines. A clear pathway up which to escalate (that is, move) issues ensures that you have backup support and allows you to draw upon your company's combined experience and expertise.

Replanning

Certain complications in your project might require that you replan part, or even all, of the project. Replanning a project in progress is very difficult. You might face a situation in which many activities have already started, some are finished, and some are almost finished. Some of the resources who were working on the project might have left and moved on to other projects.

Replanning a project is analogous to hitting a moving target. In the case study, just after Archie and Julie had completed development of the Title Index Editor ahead of schedule, a number of complications arose that demanded some replanning.

Return to the Case Study:
A Spanner in the Works

On the Tuesday afternoon of project Week 9, just as Archie and Julie were completing development of the Title Index Editor modules early, Monty called me. He wanted to step up momentum quite dramatically on the project. He'd had our static prototype forms out in the sales field for a couple of weeks, and the salesmen now also had working E-MagBooks. Together, the prototype forms and the working E-MagBook had already generated considerable interest. Monty had shipped working E-MagBooks out to two potential distributors on the weekend, and they were back in touch with him by Monday evening. Apparently, a big exhibition was coming up in Europe, and both distributors wanted to have an E-MagBook present at this important event.

When I told Archie and Julie, they both thought this news about the exhibition was wonderful. I explained that, on the one hand, it meant we were involved with what would likely be a successful product if the early indications were any indication, but, on the other hand, fulfilling Monty's request would disrupt our current plans.

The two distributors were promising Monty that, together, they would commit to 2,000 E-MagBooks as an initial sale, provided they could have fully operational, demonstration units with a good selection of titles in a variety of European languages on the exhibition stand. Both my programmers were quite startled by such an early commitment to 2,000 E-MagBooks running the viewer they had both developed. The problem was that the exhibition was only seven weeks away from the coming weekend, which gave Monty little time to compile a good selection of titles in different languages. He wanted the editor programs as soon as possible.

Reassessing

We needed to look at our planning in detail against this new demand to have editors ready sooner than scheduled. We started by making the assumption that the current plan to complete the editors remained in place, as you can see in the top section of Figure 10.6 (shown later in the "Summary" section), which shows the original, guaranteed plan.

We were now in project Week 9, development of both editors should be completed at the end of Week 11, system testing of both editors would be complete at the end of Week 12, and acceptance testing would be complete at the end of Week 13. That would make the editors available to Monty by the beginning of project Week 14. The exhibition would start at the end of project Week 16—at that weekend, to be precise—and run for two weeks. If we delivered the fully accepted programs according to this original schedule, Monty would have just three weeks to build and test a range of books using the editors. We were still happy to guarantee this schedule, which represented Monty's worst-case scenario. This plan would give him three weeks of preparation time for the exhibition.

We had actually developed the Title Index Editor's modules ahead of schedule. If we decided the idea was a good one, Archie and Julie could start integrating the Title Index Editor the next day. With that plan, they estimated that, at the latest, they would have the completed Title Index Editor up and running by Friday evening of the current week. We could then start system testing the Title Index Editor at the beginning of Week 10 rather than waiting for completion of the Page Index Editor, as we had originally planned. We could start the Page Index Editor development as originally scheduled and run its development simultaneously with fixing any problems from Title Index Editor system testing—although assigning these parallel activities to only Archie and Julie *did* present a substantial risk.

However, both Julie and Archie were convinced that the Page Index Editor development was much simpler than we had originally estimated. They could model much of the Index handling code and change-handling functionality on what they had done in the Title Index Editor because the designs were generic, to accommodate the requirements of both editors. The same commonality applied to Index output. The only real difference between the common functions of the two programs lay in the structure of the Index entry and the associated screen objects for displaying an entry. Consequently, both programmers felt that the risk of coping with development of the Page Index Editor at the same time they were handling any issues that might arise from testing the Title Index Editor were minor.

They also felt they could achieve integration of the Page Index Editor in the two weeks we had allocated to module development; at the same time, they could handle any Title Index Editor issues that arose out of either system or acceptance testing. They were confident that at the end of project Week 11, the Title Index Editor would be available for Monty's use, and the Page Index Editor would be available for system testing.

At the time we held this discussion, Archie and Julie had completed the Title Index Editor module development, fully three days ahead of schedule, which indicated they were correct in their assumptions about how quickly they could develop an editor. With the Title Index Editor out of the way, we believed we could system test the Page Index Editor, and Monty could accept it, in one week. We would require that Monty was ready to accept the Page Index Editor sometime in Week 12. If we could achieve all this, the completed, fully tested, and accepted Page Index Editor would be available to Monty one week ahead of schedule.

This whole new strategy had increased the risk factors considerably. Remember, the Page Index Editor was more complex than the Title Index Editor, and, despite much similarity with the Title Index Editor, the Page Index Editor did have extra functionality. However, based on our experience of the project so far, we were confident we could give Monty a month instead of three weeks to set up his E-Books for the demonstration.

Best Endeavors

I called Monty and told him that we could guarantee only the current plan to complete both editors—including his acceptance—by the end of Week 13. That was our contractual commitment, which we were still guaranteeing to meet. This schedule would give him three weeks in which to use the two editors to set up all the books his customers required for the exhibition. I explained to Monty that this schedule was his "worst-case" scenario.

I told him that, on a *best-endeavors* basis, we would try to make delivery of the Title Index Editor within two weeks, so he would have it for use by the beginning of Week 12, and not Week 14 as originally planned. We would also try to advance availability of the Page Index Editor by at least one week, so it would be available for use by the start of Week 13 rather than Week 14. This change would give Monty five weeks to prepare the Title Indexes and four weeks to prepare the Page Indexes concurrently with the Title Indexes.

We were dependent on Monty (or his staff) to be available for acceptance testing of the Title Index Editor in Week 11 and the Page Index Editor in Week 12. Monty's real concern was for access to the Page Index Editor. He felt that, if we really could do so, bringing in the Page Index Editor a week ahead of schedule would help enormously—and sooner would be even better.

Summary

We'd not actually altered our contractual agreement in terms of the guaranteed commitments we had made to Montasana. We were still guaranteeing to meet the original schedule, but we would attempt to have both programs available earlier on a *best-endeavors* basis. This meant *"We can't guarantee early delivery, but we will do our best."* As long as we met what we had guaranteed, Montasana would not come back to us with any contractual issues.

Figure 10.6 summarizes the old and new plans. Of course, Monty wouldn't be happy if all we could do was deliver as we had originally guaranteed to do, at the start of Week 14, but to *guarantee* early delivery was simply too much of a risk for us as a company, even though we were confident we *could* deliver early.

Julie was impressed with this cautious approach and approved very much of the term *best endeavors*. Faced with a similar situation, she was convinced that her previous company would simply have asked Monty when he needed the software, and then it would have agreed to the date without too much thought about replanning, or about the contractual consequences of not meeting a newly accepted deadline. (She believed that would have been the case because the general ethos within that company centered on the premise that delivery dates were always a work of fiction in the software business.)

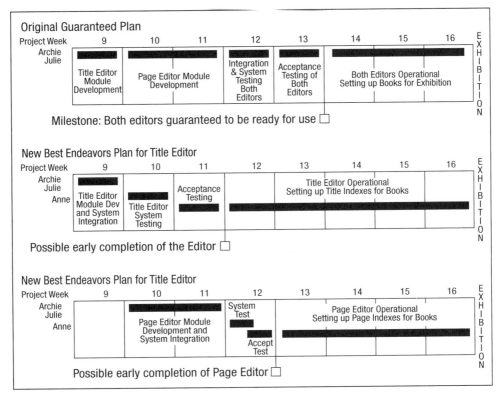

Figure 10.6
Summary of original Project 1 plan and new best-endeavors plan.

The Buy-In

Once more, in line with our normal way of doing things, I asked Archie and Julie to take full responsibility for attempting to bring in the project early. They were both extremely confident. Successful completion of the viewer and early completion of the Title Index Editor had given them enormous confidence and self-esteem.

I made it clear to them that I was not asking them to guarantee early delivery, but to guarantee that they would make every effort—which was quite different. I was, however, expecting a guarantee that they could still deliver according to the original plan, which was our bottom line.

Changing Goalposts

A criticism that many software companies have of their clients is that customers frequently change the goalposts in a project. By this, I mean the customer in some way changes the basic definition of the project. Changing the project's context can have a devastating effect on timetables if the change is not handled correctly.

By now, you have had a good grounding in what software development entails. Following the SDLC, we have requirements-capture, analysis, design, development, integration, system-testing, and acceptance-testing phases. If the customer starts changing the project's goals, the impact this will have on the project depends on where in the life cycle the change is demanded.

Changing the Requirements

The time to change the requirements is when they are being documented or immediately after that point and before a design is started. The basic problem with this principle is that a customer might not fully appreciate what the requirements are until the system materializes and the customer starts using it. If that happens, someone failed to capture the requirements in a way that highlighted the customer's true needs. (That possibility is why we spent a lot of time on form layouts and application scenarios in the case study.) If, at the end of the day, the customer still wants changes (and few don't), you must make any change to the requirements in a controlled way with a high degree of audit documentation directly back to the requirements document itself.

As we've already discussed, finding out what the customer's future requirements will be—back when you're capturing the requirements—is extremely important. If you understand where the customer ultimately wants to go with a system that you are ready to develop, chances are good that the goalposts will shake, but not move, as the project progresses.

Changing the Schedule

When the customer demands changes to the schedule, you must appreciate that you have only a certain number of resources and a limited capability. Demands to change the schedule usually come about as a result of late deliveries in the first place. When the ethos that failing to meet delivery dates is okay infiltrates a software house, you'll find the customer will frequently change milestones and the length of phases in the vain hope that something will turn up on time.

Extras

Extras form the biggest problem. If you handle requirements for extras properly, they can be financially quite rewarding. If you find yourself in a situation in which the customer is demanding extras on the grounds that you've failed to meet delivery dates, and the extras serve as compensation—well, you know exactly where you went wrong, don't you?

Managing the Customer

In addition to managing the project, you must manage the client. You've seen this principle is action in the case study, when we went through customer acceptance of the viewer. Provided you have a strong contractual platform from which to conduct negotiations, you can manage the customer's expectations, demands, and concerns.

Your tools are the contractual agreement between customer and supplier, the requirements document, the test specifications, and the plan. Your ability to handle the customer will be only as good as the tools available to you. Sometimes, you have to give, and, sometimes, you have to take. Being tough is sometimes necessary to manage a customer who might have unrealistic expectations. At the same time, if you give a little here and there and have a reputation for being flexible, when *you* need some help in return from the customer, you'll find the people at the other end of the phone much more amenable.

Return to the Case Study:
Further Complications

On Wednesday morning, before Julie and Archie started to integrate the Title Index Editor modules, we had to meet again. This time, Monty wanted us to start work on the Extended Reference and HTML/Web additions. He also wanted a specification change so that any page in any book type could switch to the Web.

New Requirement

First, we had to assess this new requirement. We had a conference call with Monty and Samantha, and we ascertained the following: All pages in Version 1 of the viewer (the program we had just completed) had to be one of three types—a Text Book, a Picture Album, or a simple Reference Book format. Monty wanted to extend this specification so that, optionally, a given page in a given format could be either in the designated format or a Web page reference.

From a technical point of view, this requirement did not compromise the current design. The Page Index data record consisted of eight fields. The design would let us extend this record to any number of fields. We could add a ninth field that would be the URL. The Version 1 viewer would ignore the extra field and would expect to see the eight fields of a standard page, whereas if a Version 2 viewer found Field 9, it could switch to the browser and load the URL. A book could be set up so that it could be viewed on old viewers according to the book's format, and the same Index could be used on a Mark 2 viewer to invoke the browser wherever the program encountered a ninth data field. This arrangement gave us backward compatibility to E-MagBooks running the old viewer. E-MagBooks running the new version of software could use the alternative, Web-page URL to access a Web site through the mobile telephone that Monty was going to install. So, although we would have to expand the design, we had not compromised it.

Composites and HTML/Web Pages

Monty wanted us to start work on the capability to display composites and HTML/Web pages as soon as possible. Fortunately, we had considered both functions during the design phase, and we were quite confident that we could expand the current design to accommodate both requirements. Monty's backers were so impressed with the preliminary customer feedback from the form prototypes and the result of the first E-MagBook prototypes that they were offering to increase funds to take the next development step early.

Assessment

Monty clearly wanted us to start a new project to develop the Mark 2 viewer now, rather than at some time in the future after we had completed the current project (as we originally believed would be the case). We would include the capability to handle composites and HTML/ Web pages as new book formats in this new project. We would also include the requirement to provide optional capability to handle a Web page instead of the designated page format. In other words, we would tie Monty's new requirements into the new project rather than disrupt the current one. Our goal would be to start a second project while the first was still in progress, with as minimal an impact on the current plan as possible.

Further Replanning

Capturing the requirements of the next generation of software while the first generation is still being developed is not uncommon. The reason stems from the fact that it takes such a long time to get a software product off the drawing board and out into the field. If you recall, we looked at product development life cycles in Chapter 9, where we discussed this delay and its implications in terms of revenue streams.

To start a second project, we proposed that I start work on the requirements document for the new functionality at the beginning of the next week (project Week 10). I would also continue to manage the first project, which was proving to be very little effort on my part. I could then do the analysis and any necessary iteration through the requirements document for Version 2 of the viewer in the following week. That plan gave me two weeks to complete Phases 1 and 2 of the SDLC for the second E-MagBook project. We would then let Monty read and accept the new requirements document in project Week 12, which looked like a busy time for Montasana, because acceptance of the Page Index Editor was due then as well.

While Monty was reviewing the requirements specification, I would plan (with Archie and Julie's help) the development in full and provide a fixed price for completion. Fortunately, Monty was not pressing us to produce a fixed-price quote at this stage. All he wanted was a price for the development of the requirements specification. Design would commence once we had acceptance of the requirements and an order for development, probably in Week 13 of the current schedule. Subject to detailed planning, the earliest we would be starting module development would be Week 14 or Week 15.

Julie and Archie would be involved in a number of activities over the next few weeks. These activities would consist of completing the software for Project 1, assisting in system and acceptance testing, helping me with any queries I had concerning the new requirements, supporting the viewer and editors while customers were using them in earnest out in the field, and training the support-desk staff. We decided getting a new programmer up to speed to assist them in the weeks to come would be prudent. Therefore, we also had to include in the

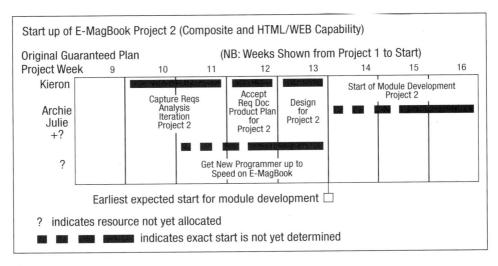

Figure 10.7
Preliminary plan for starting Project 2.

schedule a new programmer coming up to speed. We now had a preliminary plan to add to the Project 1 plan. You can see this preliminary plan for the start of Project 2 in Figure 10.7.

Assessment of the Risks

We now knew a lot about the software for the E-MagBook, because we had finished much of it. We knew a lot about the technology involved (multimedia). The fundamental risk that we now faced was that everyone was becoming involved in more than one activity, but not on a full-time basis. For example, while Julie and Archie were developing the Page Index Editor modules, they would also be on call to sort out any viewer issues Samantha reported. In addition to this support role, they must respond to any issues that Anne might come up with as she system-tested the Title Index Editor. Then, they needed to be involved in the Title Index Editor's acceptance testing.

To minimize the risks, we would have to monitor how much the different demands being put on them interrupted their work. We would have to monitor progress daily to determine whether the interruptions were becoming a nuisance and having an impact on early delivery of the Page Index Editor. The E-MagBook project was starting to take off in a big way.

Completion of the Title Index Editor

At this stage in the project, enthusiasm for the E-MagBook was running high. What had started its life all those weeks ago on the drawing board as a series of rough sketches was turning into a major project. I still hadn't told Archie or Julie about another of Monty's ideas to turn the viewer into a learning aid with question-and-answer quizzes. He was also talking about adding the capability to allow users to take notes by typing them into the viewer, and of being able to record voice. He was generating, on average, one new requirement every couple days.

Archie and Julie got back to work without fuss after our replanning session. Let's see how they got on to complete the work by integrating the modules developed into a working Title Index Editor. If you recall, Julie had created a Title Index Editor shell that contained all the code elements to manage change handling. This shell was the basis of the final system.

Module Integration

Similarly to how they had performed integration for the viewer program, Julie and Archie would copy the test programs' infrastructure modules into the Title Index Editor. First, the two programmers made lists of the three sets of modules they needed to integrate. They split the lists into infrastructure event handlers, infrastructure GUI routines, and **TitleLib** routines. For each module listed, they defined the source test program. The list will be evident in the steps that follow. Follow these steps to install the Index **Load**, **Save**, and **Navigation** functions. Alternatively, load the final version of the Title Index Editor from **DEV_ETitle Editor** on the CD.

Step 1

Launch a copy of the VB development environment (**IDE**) and load Julie's **Change Handling** test program. No other modules are loaded. Save the form and program as **ETitleEditor** in a new directory, which will hold the final version of the program. Call this directory DEV_ETitleEditor.

Step 2

Add the VB module file **ViewerLib.bas** from the viewer's final version directory, DEV_EViewer. Because this library module contains code routines that primarily the viewer uses, and that the editors might also use, we will continue to store the module in the viewer's final directory.

Step 3

Load Archie's version of **TitleLib** from his directory **TitleTester3** (you can also find it on the CD). Restore the library in **DEV_ETitleEditor** as **TitleLib**. This version of the title library contains only the routines Archie developed in the course of his development and testing of the Title Index Editor. These are as follows:

♦ *TitleLib routine*—**GetIndexFileNameForInput**

♦ *TitleLib routine*—**GetIndexFileNameForOutput**

♦ *TitleLib routine*—**OKToProceed**

♦ *TitleLib routine*—**WriteOutTitleIndex**

Step 4

Launch a second copy of the VB design environment and load Archie's title test program, **TitleTester3**, which contains the loading, output, and navigation routines for the Title Index Editor.

Search through all the code in **TitleTester3**, and copy all the infrastructure elements required for the Title Index Editor. These are as follows:

- *Button event-handler code*—**cmdGoEnd_Click**

- *Button event-handler code*—**cmdGoStart_Click**

- *Button event-handler code*—**cmdNext_Click**

- *Button event-handler code*—**cmdPrevious_Click**

- *Menu event-handler code*—**mnuOpenTitleIndex_Click**

- *Menu event-handler code*—**mnuSaveTitleIndex_Click**

- *Menu event-handler code*—**mnuSaveTitleIndexAs_Click**

- *Infrastructure general GUI routine*—**DisplayEntry**

- *Infrastructure general GUI routine*—**ClearScreenData**

Step 5

Select the file menu Open option, and remove the lines that referred to the diagnostic label **lblResultOfLoad**, which was used in **TitleTester3**. Each such line is commented as **DIAGNOSTIC**. Also remove the following line:

```
MsgBox "file name obtained OK"
```

The above line is a useful diagnostic but would get on a user's nerves in the final product so it is no longer required.

Step 6

Set up the following code in the **form_load** event:

```
Private Sub Form_Load()
' TITLE EDITOR INFRASTRUCTURE EVENT HANDLER: V1.0
' -----------------------
' Clear out the Index and screen data fields
Call ClearScreenData
Call ClearTitleIndexMemory
'
' Make sure DELETE button is not hidden
cmdRelease.Visible = False
cmdDelete.Visible = True

' Initialize the entry indicator and set normal state
Call ClearAlert1Status
Call ClearAlert2Status
```

```
lblIndexNumber.Caption = ""

End Sub
```

The preceding code ensures that both the screen and Index are cleared, the Delete button is on view, the Release button is hidden, and the program is put into **Alert 1 Normal State** and **Alert 2 Normal State**.

Testing Open, Write, and Navigation Functionality

When they had integrated all the modules from Archie's work, the two programmers performed some testing based on the tests Archie had set up to check out his three development tasks. Two problems surfaced immediately. The first problem was an error in the file-selection dialog box name. The code referenced **dlgDialog1**, and the control had been named **dlgDialog**. Archie changed the control name accordingly to **dlgDialog1**.

The second issue was that the entry-number label was not being updated—they couldn't tell what entry number was on screen. Julie had already encountered this problem in her Index-manipulation testing. The solution was to add the following line to **DisplayEntry**:

```
lblIndexNumber.Caption = CStr(g_intCurrentTitle)
```

With the above fix, you should now be able to load a Title Index navigate backward and forward through it, and output the Index using the Save and Save As menu options.

The New Option

Archie had identified that he and Julie had not addressed the New menu option, which they did as follows.

Step 1

Set up **mnuNewTitleIndex_Click** with the following code, remembering to leave in place the change-handling code that Julie had already implemented:

```
Private Sub mnuNewTitleIndex_Click()
' TITLE EDITOR INFRASTRUCTURE EVENT HANDLER: V1.0
' Menu drop-down option NEW
' ------------------------
Dim strTemp As String
Dim intResponse As Integer

strTemp = "Are you sure you want to create a new Index?"
intResponse = MsgBox(strTemp, vbQuestion + vbOKCancel, "CREATE new Index")
If intResponse <> 1 Then Exit Sub
'........................................................................
' indicate Index 'empty'
```

```
Call ClearScreenData
Call ClearTitleIndexMemory
' --------------------
' CHANGE HANDLING FOR MENU OPTIONS
Call ClearAlert2Status
End Sub
```

After they had inserted the preceding code, Julie and Archie checked out its functionality and moved on to integrating Julie's code.

Integrating Index-Manipulation Code

Integrate Julie's code by following these steps.

Step 1

Into the second copy of the VB design environment, load Julie's test project, **TitleTest3**. Copy the following routines from **TitleTest3** into the Title Index Editor:

♦ *Button event-handler code*—**cmdAdd_Click**

♦ *Button event-handler code*—**cmdDelete_Click**

♦ *Button event-handler code*—**cmdInsert_Click**

♦ *Button event-handler code*—**cmdOverwrite_Click**

♦ *Infrastructure general GUI routine*—**TransferFromScreenToEntry**

Step 2

Now, copy the following routines from Julie's version of **TitleLib** into the final version of the library module:

♦ **TitleLib** *routine*—**IncreaseTitleIndexByOne**

♦ **TitleLib** *routine*—**ReduceTitleIndexByOne**

Step 3

Finally, add this code to the Release button handler:

```
Private Sub cmdRelease_Click():' TITLE EDITOR INFRASTRUCTURE EVENT HANDLER:
V1.0
' Release a screen change
' ---------------------
Call ClearAlert1Status
Call DisplayEntry
' CHANGE HANDLING
Call ClearAlert1Status

End Sub
```

The preceding code clears the **Alert 1 State** condition, clears the display, and issues a reload of the current page from memory.

Tabs and Hot Keys

At this point, Julie and Archie also decided to sort out tabs and hot keys, a relatively simple job in the case of the Title Index Editor. They also thoroughly tested these functions. You can see the results in the completed version of the Title Index Editor on the CD.

First System Test of the Title Index Editor

Archie and Julie were ready to do some serious testing on Thursday afternoon. They also reviewed the code from top to bottom. During the course of this preliminary system testing, a major fault showed up. When the system performed Index functions on an in-Memory Index, and then output the Index to disk and read it back as a new Index, data sometimes disappeared. Program faults don't get much more serious than losing data.

Have you discovered the bug? If you've been testing adequately, you must have seen it. This is how Julie and Archie described the symptoms:

Bug Report:

If you create or modify the title or description fields in a Title Index and if doing so involves manually inserting carriage returns, the data is entered correctly into the Memory Index. When you Save or Save As, the file is written out to disk. If you then read back this file into memory, some or all of the text might be missing from the title and description. This error is totally reproducible as long as you force carriage returns into the text.

I'm going to such lengths to show you how to report a bug because, as a software developer, you now must determine what's wrong. If the description of a bug is rubbish, you can't expect to find the bug in a hurry. You need to make sure you are supplied with good descriptions, so that, first, you can reproduce the fault, and, second, you can track down the bug.

So, what's wrong in terms of the case-study problem? The answer lies in the carriage returns because, according to the report, the problem manifests itself only when carriage returns have been entered into the text field. I ought to point out that we had to do a lot of experimentation to discover this fact, so don't feel too bad if you missed it. You have a fault description, so see if you can fix the problem. Alternatively, you can track change log T000002 in the final version of the Title Index Editor from \DEV_ETitleEditor on the CD. (If you discovered the major fault in any system testing you did, I'm impressed—your discovery shows a methodical nature. If you realized a problem existed when you were reviewing the designs or setting up the code, I'm *very* impressed.)

The Next Step

We've seen Archie and Julie complete the Title Index Editor to the point where they could hand over the product for full-scale system testing by the testing department, using the acceptance test scripts. We've seen a smooth development, interrupted by the need to reschedule as a result of client demands. We handled these demands in a controlled manner, taking into account resource and financial implications. The end result was that we had now restructured the project to bring in more people and start some parallel activities. In terms of planning and monitoring, the project was becoming more complex, but we had ensured that the changes would have no impact on the original plan for the editors. We were endeavoring to bring in the editors early, and we had succeeded in getting the Title Index Editor to system testing well in advance of the original plan.

The project was growing, things were changing, but we were still well in control. The most significant fault so far had been the missing data in the Title Index Editor. We urgently needed to address that problem, and then we would be ready to start development of the Page Index Editor. All that remained was to start the Page Index Editor development, using as much of the Title Index Editor as possible as a model, to help speed up the process of turning the Page Index Editor designs into working code.

Chapter 11
Project Completion

In this penultimate chapter, we will take a brief look at software ownership. We will also look at handling multiple versions of source code. I have devoted the majority of the chapter to the case study, in which the project had expanded, and we had more people working on it. We were now classifying the development of the Mark 1 Viewer and editors as Project Stage 1. We were calling development of the Mark 2 Viewer and associated updates to both editors Project Stage 2. We'll look at how we completed the Mark 1 Page Index Editor. The completion of this program marked the end of Stage 1, but we'll also look at how Stage 2 was faring.

If you recall, despite the upheaval we'd gone through in terms of the overall project, we'd managed to avoid disrupting the plan for Stage 1. We'd succeeded in producing the Title Index Editor ahead of schedule, and we were endeavoring to bring in the Page Index Editor early as well. However, we had new risks, because much more parallel activity was going on, which might have an impact on Archie and Julie's time and, therefore, affect their development schedules. Everything needed careful monitoring. At this stage, I had started the requirements specification for Web-enabling the viewer. Rob, a programmer coming into the project, had started to study all the project documentation we had produced so far. Anne had assigned Paulo, a tester from her department, to test the completed Title Index Editor. What had been a three-person project (or, strictly speaking, two-and-a-fraction-person project) was expanding to a six-person project by the end of the week. Before we begin to close the case study, let's take a brief look at software ownership.

Software Ownership

Who owns the software you write? Do you own it? Does the customer own it? These issues can be thorny, and spending some time discussing software ownership is worthwhile as we approach the end of the E-MagBook project—or, at least, the end of the first part of an expanding project.

When the Customer Pays for Development

As you sort out the issue of software ownership, the simplest situation is one in which the customer pays you as a software developer to create software to fulfill the customer's requirements. In some cases, the contract between you and the client specifically states that the client will retain ownership of the source code you develop. In principle, this arrangement is fair enough. If you, as a company or as an individual, have been paid to develop a product, you can't claim the product is yours. But, within that context, you need to protect yourself in a number of ways.

Retaining Rights to Common Functions

One goal of the analysis stage, if you recall, is to hunt out common functionality, which you can then design into modules, so you can develop and test each module in isolation. When you create general modules, you have a vested interest in being able to reuse those modules in other projects.

For example, suppose you are asked to develop a system that requires you to write a graphics package to produce very specific types of graphs. As a developer, the routines in your graphics library could be very useful to you in other projects. Consequently, you need to ensure that, in the contract you sign with your customer, you retain the right to reuse, in other projects, individual code modules you used your skills and ability to develop on this project. Most customers will agree to this sort of request, provided that you agree, in turn, not to use the reusable elements in any project that directly competes with the business area in which the client's contracted work will be used. This arrangement gives you the degree of freedom you need to be able to reuse general modules. Don't forget—we are talking only about situations in which the customer is paying for the complete development and intends to own the source code.

Externally Funded Products

If you are putting up all the money to design and develop a software product, clearly, you own the source code. But, if funding is coming from somewhere else, you need to understand the terms under which you can reuse any software you develop. For example, if a consortium of food-manufacturing companies assists you financially to develop products specifically for the food industry, you need to make sure you understand the extent of the agreement. Within the agreement that binds you all together, you must understand the repercussions if you use any of that software outside the food industry. Does the consortium get a share? Are you prohibited from using any elements of the developed software outside the food industry? If you can't find the answers to these questions, seeking some legal advice would be wise. If you ignore the situation and assume that you are free to use the software elsewhere, you might be in for a big shock at a future date. Getting such issues out in the open at the start of a contract is in everyone's best interests.

Importing Preexisting General Components

In addition to considering the implications of using general-purpose code you have developed as part of a funded project outside that context, you need to think about the repercussions of *importing* general components from your own development library. If you will be supplying a number of general-purpose routines you have already written, then, effectively, you are not being paid to write those routines within the context of the current project. As a result, you do not need to include source code when you hand the system over to the client. The client is not funding that particular source code. If the client insists that you must supply the source code, you can legitimately charge for it. At the same time, you need to protect your rights to reuse your own code, unless the client makes you an offer—which you accept—for the client's exclusive ownership of the source code. When you intend to import your own predeveloped components, you need to clearly identify these components in the pre- or post-sales phase so the customers do not assume they are getting the rights to the code.

Joint Collaborations

If you become involved in a collaborative effort, make sure the benefit is not one-sided. Make sure that you, as a developer or a company, have access to other developments resulting from the collaboration. After all, even if your contribution is only your time, it's still quite important. You also need to know what will happen if the joint collaboration breaks up. What will you, as a member, get out of the break-up, and what are your liabilities, if any? Make sure your interests are protected.

Legal Contracts

Much though you may detest the idea, and expensive though it might be, seeking legal advice is necessary to protect your rights in the software industry. When you become involved with partners in a business venture, common sense says to make sure you have an agreement that benefits you as much as it does your partner. Partnerships don't last forever and, more often than not, the circumstances in the process of a partnership breaking up are acrimonious rather than good-natured. That is, sadly, when the legalities of the agreement you signed at the beginning of the relationship become very important.

You don't want to discover when a partnership is being dissolved that the agreement is very much against your interests. You're far better off discovering that fact when the partnership is being formed, because you can do something about the agreement at that stage. When you reach a point where breakup is inevitable, you're too late to do anything about the terms under which the breakup will occur.

The Software for the E-MagBook

As a genuine example of software ownership, the software for the case study in this book, *Project Management for Programmers*, actually belongs to K&C Consultants who hold the copyright. The code is distributed freely together with the book, and the only restriction is that the code is not to be used for any commercial purpose. In other words, you cannot make any money from any use you make of the distributed code. Its sole purpose is as a learning aid in conjunction with the content of this book.

Handling Source Code

In this section, we will look at how to handle source code in situations in which more than one version of the program exists. We'll use the case study as an example. In the case study, we had no version-control system. We were about to start developing the Page Index Editor, which would require changes to the viewer to introduce **Change Handling** functionality. Because we needed to change the viewer code, we would have to create a new version of the Viewer form. For the first time, we were going to have more than one version of code present in a project.

Code Segregation

Management of the code in the case study would now become more complex. Until now, we had one version of the Viewer form. After we produced a second version, we must keep the new version totally separate from the first. This separation was vital because we were supporting Version 1.1 out in the field. Version 2.0 would be a new-development version of the viewer, even though the only difference from the first version would be associated with its use in the Page Index Editor environment. If we had problems with Version 1.1, we would need to rectify the problem inside the Version 1.1 code, test the viewer, and release it to Monty, confident that the 1.1 viewer had a fix to the reported problem. If the fix was also pertinent to Version 2.0, we would need to get the fix into the Version 2.0 code set as well, so when Version 2.0 was released, it would not reintroduce the fault that we had fixed in Version 1.1. We needed to achieve total segregation between the two sets of code, so, if we did something to one set, the change would have no effect on the other set.

Project Source Code

To help us segregate the versions of code, we could load forms into projects from specific directories. Let's consider an example in which we have a number of forms. We'll look at how the form locations change according to which version of the program we wish to create.

Let's assume we have developed a program called ALPHA. This program consists of Form A and Library A. These two entities are housed in Directory 1. After initial completion of program ALPHA, we have the following:

Program ALPHA Version 1.0

Composed of: Form A (Version 1) located in Directory 1

Library 1 (Version 1) located in Directory 1

To create Version 1 of ALPHA, both Form A and Library 1 are loaded from Directory 1. The program is compiled and built from the sources contained in Directory 1.

Then, we start on a second development of program ALPHA—program ALPHA Version 2.0. We create a new directory—Directory 2. We modify Form A, and we place the modified version in Directory 2. Library 1 remains unchanged, but we create a second, new library—Library 2—in Directory 2. We can generate Program ALPHA Version 2 as follows:

Program ALPHA Version 2.0

Composed of: Form A (Version 2) located in Directory 2

Library 1 (Version 1) located in Directory 1

Library 2 (Version 1) located in Directory 2

As you can see, all the new elements are created in Directory 2. Because Library 1 has not changed, it is still loaded from Directory 1.

Next, we create a program BETA, which is made up as follows:

Program BETA Version 1.0

Composed of: Form B (Version 1) located in Directory 3

Library 1 (Version 1) located in Directory 1

Library 2 (Version 1) located in Directory 2

Library 3 (Version 1) located in Directory 3

As should be apparent, Form B and Library 3 are new entities, presently required only by program BETA. Library 1 is unchanged and now used in three programs. Library 2 is unchanged and used in two programs.

Finally, we develop a third program that requires modifications to Libraries 1 and 2. This third program—program GAMMA—is generated as follows:

Program GAMMA Version 1.0

Composed of: Form C (Version 1) located in Directory 4

Library 1 (Version 2) located in Directory 4

Library 2 (Version 2) located in Directory 4

Without a proper version-control system, we must be able to generate any version of any program in a manner that ensures the program has all the correct components. Program GAMMA has a new version of Library 1. Rather than make the changes to Library 1 in Directory 1, we have created a new instance of Library 1 in Directory 4 and modified the resulting file. This approach ensures that any changes we make to Library 1 are completely segregated from program ALPHA, either Version 1 or Version 2. This segregation is essential to ensure that we can continue to build both ALPHA and BETA without introducing problems that might result from a later development of either of the two libraries involving changes that are unrelated to programs ALPHA and BETA.

As you can imagine, trying to keep source code in line is not easy, but doing so is essential to manage the code so that you can use the code in whatever context you need it without future developments compromising it. A good version-control system will let you perform all the described functions and automatically guarantee segregation among various versions of the same program.

The Case Study:
The Page Index Editor

As was now their custom, Julie and Archie began with a brief start-up meeting to get the Page Index Editor development under way. They reviewed the designs together and decided they could model a large proportion of the Page Index Editor on the Title Index Editor code. According to the original plan (which you can see in Figure 5.6 in Chapter 5), the tasks they had to complete in the first three days were for Archie to set up viewer functions within the Page Index Editor and for Julie to handle loading and saving the Page Index.

They were now looking at a development from a position of real strength: What they had learned from the Title Index Editor would be invaluable over the next few days. As a result of that experience, they had already decided to amalgamate **Change Handling** into Archie's task of getting the viewer set up within the Page Index Editor. So, Archie's three-day task was now "Set up viewer functions and **Change Handling**." Julie and Archie were convinced that, in theory, this combined task would take less than three days. And even if Archie did take three days to complete, he would still save the time originally allocated for Julie to implement **Change Handling**.

Their completed plan was a reasonable assessment of what needed to be done, by whom, and when. The programmers were replanning based on experience, and also based on the goal to come in early so that we could give Monty more preparation time before the exhibition. Let's start by following what Archie did to complete implementation of the viewer functionality and **Change Handling**.

Setting Up the Viewer and Change Handling

The main task facing Archie was to build the shell of the final editor program and implement the viewer within that shell. Similar to how Julie had implemented **Change Handling** in the Title Index Editor, Archie would set up **Change Handling** for the Page Index Editor.

Recap

The E-MagBook project now included six major software components, as follows:

♦ Viewer form

♦ Video form

♦ Title Editor form

♦ Page Editor form

♦ **ViewerLib**

♦ **TitleLib**

As we've discussed, we had no version-control system, so we had to exercise the utmost care to ensure Archie and Julie didn't tread on each other's toes. They must continue to work closely together and keep each other well-informed about what each was doing.

Modifications to the Viewer

To construct the Page Index Editor, Archie realized he needed to make modifications to the viewer, mainly for **Change Handling**. To accommodate changes to a working program, he created a new version of the viewer's code and labeled the new code Version 2.0. (Remember, the viewer's Version 1.1 code was frozen and in operational use in the field.)

We now had a second copy of the viewer's code that we were free to change, because it was classed as "in development." If Version 1.1 developed any problems, we would fix them in the frozen code and release a new version of the executable code from that code set. We also needed to ensure that the modification would be propagated into the development code as well. (If you recall, we discussed all this in Chapter 9, under "Support.") Three generations of the viewer now existed—the first generation was in the field, the second generation was in development, and the third generation was still on the drawing board (requirements specification and analysis in progress)—all adding to the project's rich tapestry.

Creating the Basic Shell with the Viewer

If you want to follow these steps, you will be able to emulate Archie's work. However, from now on, I'll be providing slightly less help. If you have problems, you have design specifications to look at; you have the experience gained from the construction of the Title Index Editor, and you have the actual code from the Title Index Editor. As a last resort, you can always look at the final version of the viewer and Page Index Editor on the CD in the DEV_EViewerV2 and DEV_EPageEditor directories.

Follow these steps to set up the development version of the viewer and amalgamate the viewer into the editor. Alternatively, copy the DEV_EViewerV2 and DEV_EPageEditor directories to your hard disk and load the appropriate project.

Step 1

Create a new VB EXE project, and load the blank **EPageEditor** form from the DEV_BlankEPageEditor directory on the CD. Just as you did for the Title Index Editor, remove **Form1** of the new project, and attempt to run the program. When VB complains it can't find a **main ( )**, select **EPageEditor** as the main form from the options available on the VB panel presented. (If you can't remember what this procedure is all about, go back and look at how the viewer was created, as described in "Installation of Viewer Forms" under the main heading of "System

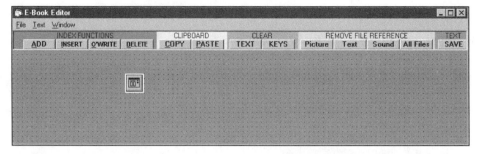

Figure 11.1
The blank Page Index Editor form.

Integration" in Chapter 8.) Now, return to the VB design environment. The Page Index Editor form should look like it does in Figure 11.1.

A picture control is used as the container for the buttons you see at the top of the Page Index Editor form. The colored backgrounds are created from labels, which are first placed on the toolbar, and then the buttons are created on top of the labels. The background coloring has been set up to categorize the functions. The toolbar has its alignment property set to **Top**. This designation forces the toolbar to line up with the top of the form. Also, notice the common dialog box. All the names for the controls come from the screen-object definitions set up for the Page Index Editor.

Step 2

Use the project Add Form drop-down option from the Project menu to load the Viewer 1.1 form from its directory, DEV_EViewer. Then, load the Video form from the same directory. Set the **MDIChild** property of the Viewer form to **True**, and change the version number of the form's caption to "E-Viewer DEV Version 2.0".

Now, create a new directory to hold Version 2.0 of the viewer. Call the directory DEV_EviewerV2, and save the Viewer form as **EViewer2** into it. This is the development code Version 2 of the Viewer form. You do not need to save the Video form here because we don't anticipate any changes to it. If we need to change the Video form, we'll move it *then*.

NOTE: *From now on, if we make any changes to the viewer code, we must remember that two versions of the code exist—Version 1.1, in use in the field, and Version 2.0, the development version. We can use Version 2.0 of the Viewer form either to generate a Version 2 viewer program or as part of the Page Index Editor program. Consequently, we must ensure that any changes we make to Version 2 of the viewer do not stop it from being run on its own as a Version 2 viewer. So far, the only change that affects the viewer's dual nature is the **MDIChild** property setting. To allow the viewer to function as a standalone executable, we must reset this property to **False** before we create the executable viewer. Remember, our main objective is to have one version of the viewer Version 2.0 source code that we can use to generate either the viewer program itself or the form that runs inside the Page Index Editor.*

Step 3

Using the Project menu option Add Module, load **ViewerLib** from DEV_EViewer.

NOTE: *We currently anticipate no changes to **ViewerLib**, so it can remain in Viewer 1.1's directory. If we make any changes to **ViewerLib**, it becomes a new development version and must be stored in the viewer Version 2.0's directory.*

Step 4

Create a new VB file module, and call it **PageLib**. You will place any new general code for the Page Index Editor in this new library. You can store this module as **PageLib.bas** in DEV_EpageEditor.

Step 5

Place this code in the Page Index Editor's **Form_Load** event handler:

```
Private Sub MDIForm_Load()
' PAGE EDITOR INFRASTRUCTURE EVENT HANDLER: V1.0
' Initialization.
' ------------
' Load the Viewer and make visible
frmEViewer.Height = 8000
frmEViewer.Show

End Sub
```

When the Page Index Editor runs, both the Video and Viewer forms are unloaded. You must first get the viewer on screen. You do this via the **.Show** method, which loads and shows in one command. The viewer also needs to expose the four, file-name text boxes, which are located at the bottom of the form. If you recall, these text boxes are not needed in the E-MagBook, and the screen has no room for them anyway, because its capacity is only 640×480 pixels. On the editor, the minimum screen size is 800×600 pixels, so we can extend the height of the viewer to expose the text boxes that tell us what the Index and file references are.

Testing the Basic Shell

If you run the program now, the Page Index Editor loads with the Viewer form on display. Because the viewer has been set up as a child window of the editor, if you click one of the empty Page Editor buttons, you don't loose the Viewer form, even though focus is not on the viewer.

Archie now spent some time making sure that all the viewer's functionality was still available in this new environment. Specifically, he tested the following:

◆ *Test 1*—Loading Title Indexes.

◆ *Test 2*—Selecting books of each type.

♦ *Test 3*—Checking that text, image, video, and sound were okay.

♦ *Test 4*—Checking Workbench mode.

All the functionality of the viewer was available. You can see the viewer in use within the editor in Figure 11.2.

The only problem to surface was that the Video form was not neatly centered in the image-container area for Picture Albums or for Reference Books. If you recall, the **.Left** and **.Top** attributes of a form were set up relative to the start of the coordinate system on the screen, in the top, left-hand side. The viewer was no longer positioned at the top left of the screen. Instead, it was below the Page Index Editor's toolbar (forced by the fact that the toolbar had its **alignment** property set to **Top**); hence, the video window no longer overlaid the viewer's container as originally intended. Archie had a quick word with me about the situation, and we decided it wasn't a problem, so we left it as it was.

NOTE: *The fix, if you want to be precise, involved using the Viewer form's **.Left** and **.Top** attributes as part of the calculation for the Video form's final destination. However, that fix required the form identity to be passed to the **LoadAndPlayVideo** routine, which was also a **ViewerLib** entity, and which we were reluctant to change at that point.*

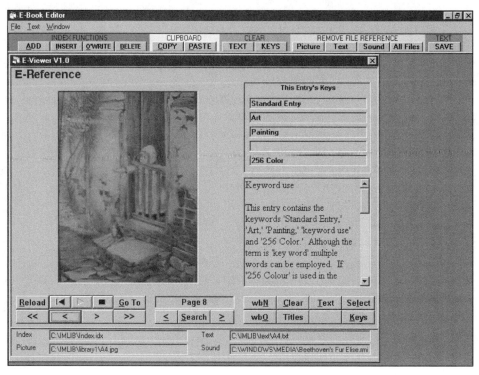

Figure 11.2
The Page Index Editor program running with the Viewer form in operation.

When Archie had finished checking the viewer functions within the editor, he closed the project and created a new one. He loaded the Viewer form (Version 2.0), the original version of the Video form, and **ViewerLib**. He removed the default **Form1** created by VB. He then changed the viewer's **MDIchild** property to **False** and ran the program to verify standalone operation. This process allowed him to complete testing by logging the following additional test:

◆ *Test 5*—Ensure that viewer can still be set up as a standalone program.

Development Environments

Worth recapping here are the state of the software versions and the source of respective projects' code. The following descriptions of directory content and project makeup indicate how we were managing the E-MagBook project in terms of component files.

Directories

The following sections identify the directories that were currently in use and their contents.

Viewer Version 1.1 Directory (DEV_EViewer)

The DEV_EViewer directory contained the viewer that was currently operational and at Version 1.1. This version could be run only as a standalone executable. The directory consisted of the following:

◆ *The main viewer form*—**frmEViewer**.

◆ *The video form*—**frmVideo**.

◆ A *library of program-independent modules*—**ViewerLib**.

◆ *The VB project files*—To generate the standalone viewer.

Viewer Version 2.0 Directory (DEV_EViewerV2)

The DEV_EViewerV2 directory contained the viewer that was being modified to run either as a standalone executable or as part of the Page Index Editor. The directory consisted of the following:

◆ *The main viewer form, Version 2*—**frmEViewer**.

◆ *The VB project files*—To generate the standalone viewer Version 2.0.

Title Index Editor Version 1.0 Directory (DEV_ETitleEditor)

The DEV_ETitleEditor directory contained the Title Index Editor currently undergoing final system testing. It consisted of the following:

◆ *Title Editor form*—**frmTitleEditor**.

◆ *Library of general, program-independent modules*—**TitleLib**.

◆ *The VB project files*—To generate the Title Index Editor executable code.

Page Index Editor Version 1.0 Directory (DEV_EPageEditor)

The DEV_EPageEditor directory contained the development version of the Page Index Editor:

◆ *Page Editor form*—**frmPageEditor**.

◆ *Library that would contain general program independent modules*—**PageLib**.

◆ *The VB project files*—To generate the Page Index Editor executable code.

Projects and Source Files

From the directories listed in the previous section, we could generate a viewer using Version 1.1 code or Version 2.0 code, a Title Index Editor, or a Page Index Editor. The relationship between projects and files was as follows.

Viewer Version 1.1

Version 1.1 of the viewer consisted of the following:

◆ C:*DEV_EViewer**frmEViewer*—The Viewer form and all its code.

◆ C:*DEV_EViewer**frmVideo*—The form for playing videos.

◆ C:*DEV_EViewer**ViewerLib*—The library containing program-independent modules.

Viewer Version 2.0

Version 2.0 of the viewer consisted of the following:

◆ C:*DEV_EViewer2**frmEViewer*—The Viewer form and all its code.

◆ C:*DEV_EViewer**frmVideo*—The form for playing videos.

◆ C:*DEV_EViewer**ViewerLib*—The library containing program-independent modules.

Title Index Editor Version 1.0 Project

Version 1.0 of the Title Index Editor consisted of the following:

◆ C:*DEV_ETitleEditor**frmTitleEditor*—The Title Editor form and all its code.

◆ C:*DEV_ETitleEditor**TitleLib*—The library containing program-independent modules.

◆ C:*DEV_EViewer**ViewerLib*—The library containing program-independent modules created for the viewer.

Page Index Editor Version 1.0 Project

Version 1.0 of the Page Index Editor consisted of the following:

◆ C:*DEV_EPageEditor**frmEPageEditor*—The Page Editor form and all its code.

◆ C:*DEV_EPageEditor**PageLib*—The library containing program-independent modules created for Page Index Editor development.

◆ C:\DEV_EViewer\ViewerLib—The library containing program-independent modules created for the viewer.

◆ C:\DEV_EViewer\frmVideo—The form used for playing back video clips.

◆ C:\DEV_EViewer2\frmEViewer—The Version 2.0 Viewer form and its associated code.

First-Level Change Handling

The project now started to become quite interesting. The objects that initiated change events that caused the program to go into the **Alert 1 State** were the viewer's keys and main text box, but those objects were located in the Viewer form. When the viewer ran standalone, all those text boxes were locked—the user couldn't modify their contents. Archie appreciated that he would have to place code in the viewer to handle change events. This requirement in itself was not a problem. However, when the viewer was in standalone mode, Archie didn't want the viewer to start up with the text boxes unlocked. So, whatever he did with the viewer for use in the Page Index Editor must not affect how the viewer behaved when it ran as an independent program.

We had anticipated all this in the design for **Change Handling** in the Page Index Editor. If you look at the design in Appendix G, you will see that Archie had to place some code in the viewer's **Form_Load** event that locked the keys and text box. The Page Index Editor then contained code to unlock the boxes after the viewer had loaded.

Change Handling should be familiar from the development of the Title Index Editor, so I have defined the steps here in very broad terms. In this section, we look at how Archie implemented the required code in the viewer. Use the design and the Title Index Editor code as models to help you. As a last resort, look at the CD version of the code.

Step 1

You will add code to set the **Lock** property of the keys and main text box in the viewer's **Form_Load** event handler. First, add the lines highlighted below to the change log of the **Form_Load** event handler:

```
Private Sub Form_Load()
' VIEWER INFRASTRUCTURE EVENT HANDLER:
' Start up, V1.3
' -----------------------------
' Set Form dimensions to 640 by 480 and position in
' top left of screen for screens > 640 by 480
' CHANGE LOG:
' <date>V00005 Radio buttons in Selection Criteria both off on startup
' <date>V00007 imgImage2 & txtText2 require sensible dimensions for
    default use
' -----------------------------'
' <date> DEV 2.0 Lock user out of keys and text blocks
' -----------------------------
```

The preceding code section (the code that makes up the **Form_Load** event handler) is now Version 1.3. This version number indicates that three modifications/additions have been made to the code. The first two changes were to accommodate bug fixes, as shown. The third change was a development addition for Version 2.0 of the viewer. The change log would provide a complete audit trail of what had happened to the event handler since Version 1.0 of the code was released. Throughout the project, all changes and additions caused by the Version 2.0 development could be traced using "DEV 2.0" as a search key in the VB environment.

Now, add the code required to lock the text box and keys into the **Form_Load** event handler, and tag each line added with "DEV 2.0." Test that the editor program runs and that the user is locked out of the keys and text blocks.

Step 2

You can now insert code in the Page Index Editor's **Form_Load** event handler to unlock the fields after the viewer has loaded. Remember to use object dot notation to allow the editor to access viewer screen controls. You can now run the program, and you should be able to modify the text box or the keys on the viewer. The Page Index Editor has influenced the behavior of the viewer.

Step 3

Add a shape control to the viewer, and call the control **shpRed**. This is the third shape control, because we have already used two—**shpGray** and **shpWhite**—to set up the Workbench screen for printing. Set **shpRed**'s background color to **Red**, as the name indicates. **ShpGray** and **shpRed** are equivalent to the shapes that were used in the Title Index Editor to handle **Alert 1 State** and **Alert 2 State** changes from **Normal** to **Change** state and vice versa. Make sure that the visible properties of all shape controls are set to **False**.

Step 4

Set up the **Change** event in the keys as follows:

```
Private Sub txtKeyView_Change(Index As Integer)
' VIEWER INFRASTRUCTURE EVENT HANDLER:
' Key may have been changed by the user, V1.0
' ---------------------------
' <date> DEV 2.0: Created for change handling in Page Editor
' ---------------------------
If i_booFocus = False Then Exit Sub
If txtKeyView(Index).BackColor = shpRed.BackColor Then Exit Sub
txtKeyView(Index).BackColor = shpRed.BackColor
picFrontPanel.BackColor = shpRed.BackColor

End Sub
```

According to the event table that you studied for the editor's **Change Handling** (see Figure 10.3 in Chapter 10), the keys and text enter the alert state only if the user has changed the content by placing focus on the field and typing something into it. So, if the content changes because of a new page being read in, the alert state must not be switched on. If you recall, we achieved this state in the Title Index Editor by using a variable called **i_booFocus** to indicate that the control does or does not have focus. **i_booFocus** is set by the **GotFocus** event on the keys and main text box whenever focus is received. The variable must be cleared when focus is lost. This action serves as an **AND** gate for the preceding code, which means if the text box has focus *and* a change event has occurred to set the alert state.

Step 5

Now, add appropriate code to set or clear **i_booFocus**, as required, in the **GotFocus** and **LostFocus** event handlers of the keys. (Use the Title Index Editor as a model if you are unsure what to do.)

Step 6

Add this definition to the general declaration section of the viewer:

```
' VIEWER INFRASTRUCTURE DATA: V1.0
Private i_booFocus As Boolean      ' DEV 2.0 indicates when user has focus
                                   ' of keys or text box
```

Step 7

Set up the **Change**, **GotFocus**, and **LostFocus** event handlers for **txtText**.

Running and Testing First-Level Change Handling

When Archie ran the program, he checked that normal use of the viewer within the Page Index Editor was not impaired—that is, using the navigation buttons didn't set off the alert state. To see the Page View mode panel turn to the alert state, removing the backdrop was necessary. Archie set up an instruction to remove the viewer's image in the **Load** event of the Page Index Editor. The line is as follows:

```
frmEViewer.picFrontPanel.Picture = LoadPicture("")
```

When Archie changed the contents of the viewer's text box, the alert state came on. He checked to be sure that the same happened with each of the key fields.

His testing amounted to the following:

♦ *Test 1*—No alerts are set off by normal viewer usage.

♦ *Test 2*—Manually changing the text box creates alert state. All other changes do not.

♦ *Test 3*—Manually changing each key creates alert state. All other changes do not.

♦ *Test 4*—Each key is handled independently of the others.

So far, so good—all four tests resulted in no problems.

Second-Level Change Handling

The next aspect of **Change Handling** was for the Page Index Editor to pick up the fact that the **Alert 1 Change State** had been set in the Viewer form and to take the next level of action, which was to perform the following:

♦ Disable all the button controls on the Viewer form.

♦ Disable all the file-menu controls on the Page Index Editor form.

♦ Disable the **Delete** control and enable the Release button on the Page Index Editor form.

We could consider these functions as **Alert State Propagation**. None of the above actions were difficult to implement, but the question at design time was How does the editor get to know that the viewer has gone into the **Alert 1 Change State**?

We needed an event handler that was triggered regularly in the Page Index Editor, and, each time the event handler ran, it would look to see whether the viewer's **picFrontPanel**'s background color had been set to the alert color. If the panel's color had been set, the code could check to see whether the Release key was visible. If the Release key was on screen, the editor would know that the viewer must be in the alert state because the Release key was visible only in the **Alert 1 Change State**. If the Release key was not visible, this would be the first time the editor was aware of the new alert state. The viewer's button controls would then be disabled, together with the menu options, and the editor's Delete button could be removed and the Release button enabled. In this way, propagation of the **Alert 1 Change State** would occur from viewer to editor.

To make propagation work, we could make use of the VB timer control. The timer would provide an event that would execute after a preset time period had expired. VB and the operating system would handle the detail. From a programmer's point of view, if we started a timer, the timer's completion event would be triggered each time the period expired. We could then restart the timer or exit without reinitiating the event. This arrangement is known as a *watchdog timer*—watching out for something to happen regularly and taking action when that event happens. The flow diagram in Figure 11.3 illustrates the design of **Alert 1** propagation between viewer and editor.

To implement a watchdog timer in the editor, follow these steps.

Step 1

Set up a timer control on the Page Editor form and call the timer **tmrWatchDog**. Next, add this code to the end of the editor's **Form_Load** event handler:

```
' Start up the watchdog timer
tmrWatchDog.Interval = 500
tmrWatchDog.Enabled = True
```

The above code causes the timer to go off as soon as the program loads. When half a second has elapsed, the operating system will schedule the timer's event handler to execute.

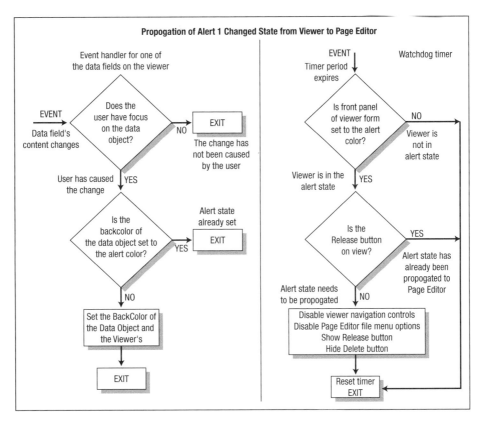

Figure 11.3
Watchdog timer in the Page Index Editor.

Step 2

Place this code in the timer's **Completion** event handler:

```
Private Sub tmrWatchDog_Timer()
' PAGE EDITOR INFRASTRUCTURE EVENT HANDLER: V1.0
' Watchdog timer event.
' ----------------
If frmEViewer.picFrontPanel.BackColor = frmEViewer.shpRed.BackColor Then
    If cmdRelease.Visible = False Then
        ' viewer has gone into alert state since last run of this code
        Call CompleteAlert1Status
    End If
End If
tmrWatchDog.Enabled = True              ' and off again
End Sub
```

If the viewer's picture panel—**picFrontPanel**—had gone red and the release button was not yet on view on the Page Editor form, a call would be made to complete the alert state in the preceding routine. Whether or not the alert state had to be completed, the timer would then reset to execute the code again in half a second. In this way, the alert state, first detected in the viewer because the user had changed a data field on screen, would be propagated through to the editor, as outlined in the design specification.

Step 3

Set up an infrastructure routine called **CompleteAlert1Status** in the general section of the Page Index Editor to disable the viewer's command buttons and the Page Index Editor's menu options, remove the Delete button, and bring on the Release switch. You can use the Title Index Editor's **SetAlert1State** routine as a model, although you will have to disable the following extra button controls: all search buttons, and the Reload, GoTo Page, wbN, wbO, and Titles buttons, all of which are located on the viewer. (Remember, when you are referring to any screen object on the Viewer form, your reference must use full, object dot notation; therefore, you would reference **cmdGoStart**, for example, as **frmEViewer.cmdGoStart**.)

Step 4

Now, set up the Release button's click-event handler with a single call to **ClearAlert1Status**, and then a call to **frmEViewer.cmdReLoad_Click**, which will cause the current page to be reloaded as it was before the change was made. Once again, produce a general subroutine in the Page Index Editor called **ClearAlert1State**, modeled from the version in the Title Index Editor. This time, the routine performs exactly the same function as in the Title Index Editor's equivalent, except that, in this case, the data fields are the keys and text box on the Viewer form. You also need to release all search buttons and the Reload, Go To Page, wbN, wbO, and Titles buttons. Remember to use object dot notation for viewer screen objects.

Testing Second-Level Change Handling

When Archie first ran the program, he received a compiler error telling him that for the **Call frmEViewer.cmdReLoad_Click** line, the method or data member was not found. This somewhat misleading message actually indicated that the routine Archie was calling was private. Archie set the subroutine public and commented the routines as follows:

```
Public Sub cmdReLoad_Click()
' PAGE EDITOR INFRASTRUCTURE EVENT HANDLER: V 1.0
' -----------------------
' Routine created to fix issue;
' <date>  V00004  Reload button required
' <date>  DEV 2.0 Routine made public so callable from Page Editor.
' --------------------------------
```

Setting a form's infrastructure routine to public was quite acceptable according to our design architecture, provided that we called the routine only from other infrastructure code—that is, the routine must not be called from a library module.

Archie now had most of the **Change Handling** environment set up. He could load a book via the viewer's inherent functionality, thumb through the book, and select a page for modification. If he then changed the main text content (assuming he was not looking at a Picture Album), the viewer would go into the **Alert 1 Change State**, followed (at the most) half a second later, by the editor doing the same. He could then switch off the alert status by clicking the Release button.

The level of **Change Handling** now available allowed Archie to test the following:

♦ *Test 1*—**Alert 1 Change State** is correctly propagated from viewer to Page Index Editor.

♦ *Test 2*—**Alert 1 Change State** in both forms can be fully cancelled using the Release button.

Archie noticed that the editor picked up the fact that the **Change** events had occurred in the viewer at variable times, depending on where in the timer's half-second cycle the change was fired. Sometimes, if the event occurred at the start of the timer's cycle, quite a delay was noticeable between when the viewer and the editor turned red. We decided to reduce the time period to a quarter of a second, or 250 milliseconds. I wouldn't recommend going below that time frame. Remember, at an interval of 250 milliseconds, the event is firing four times a second, which is not a burden by any means. But always keep this type of asynchronous event handler as short as possible, and let it run at a frequency that doesn't have an impact on system performance.

Completion of Change Handling in the Page Index Editor

In a process similar to how Julie set up **Change Handling** in the Title Index Editor, follow these steps to complete **Change Handling** for the Page Index Editor. Alternatively, study the text and the completed editor located in DEV_EPageEditor on the CD.

Step 1

Set up the empty Index Manipulation button event handlers for **cmdAdd**, **cmdInsert**, and **cmdOverWrite** with a call to **ClearAlert1Status** and a call to **SetAlert2Status**. Set the event handler for **cmdDelete** with a single call to **SetAlert2Status**. (This procedure is identical to what Julie did with the controls in the Title Index Editor.)

Step 2

Create subroutine **SetAlert2Status** and subroutine **ClearAlert2Status** similarly to what we did in the Title Index Editor. Remember, in this instance, you are accessing a text box in the viewer, so you will need to use full, object dot referencing on **txtIndexFileName**.

Step 3

Set up menu options New, Open , Save , and Save As to call **ClearAlert2Status**.

Create a routine called **SetAlert1Status**, which allows the Page Index Editor to set the Viewer form's **picFrontPanel** to the alert color. After it has done that, make it call **CompleteAlert1Status**.

Use the Event-Action table (see Figure 10.3 in Chapter 10) set-up in the design for editor **Change Handling** to determine which other button controls and menu options need calls to switch on and off the alert status and implement the necessary code. Note that some functions require the text block or keys to have their background color changed.

When a button control changes the state of the three file-reference text boxes, you can call **frmEViewer.DisplayPage**, with the argument set to 1, to indicate that you want the page redrawn using the file references and not the Index.

Running and Testing Change Handling

Change Handling in the Page Index Editor is quite extensive. Archie could now check out full scenarios:

◆ *Test 1*—Check that Add To Index clears **Alert 1 Change State** and sets **Alert 2 Change State**.

◆ *Test 2*—Check that Insert Into Index clears **Alert 1 Change State** and sets **Alert 2 Change State**.

◆ *Test 3*—Check that Overwrite Index clears **Alert 1 Change State** and sets **Alert 2 Change State**.

◆ *Test 4*—Ensure Delete is not available in **Alert 1 Change State** and is replaced by the Release button.

◆ *Test 5*—Check that Delete From Index sets **Alert 2 Change State**.

◆ *Test 6*—Check that all file menu options are disabled in **Alert 1 Change State**.

◆ *Test 7*—Check that viewer's navigation, Search, Reload, Go To Page, wbO, wbN, and **Titles** buttons are not available in **Alert 1 Change State**.

◆ *Test 8*—Check that menu option New clears **Alert 2 Change State**.

◆ *Test 9*—Check that menu option Open clears **Alert 2 Change State**.

◆ *Test 10*—Check that menu option Save clears **Alert 2 Change State**.

◆ *Test 11*—Check that menu option Save As clears **Alert 2 Change State**.

◆ *Test 12*—Check that Paste switches on **Alert 1 Change State** and that all data fields in viewer go to the alert color.

- *Test 13*—Check that the Clear Text button switches on **Alert 1 Change State** and colors the text block with the alert color.

- *Test 14*—Check that the Clear Keys button switches on **Alert 1 Change State** and colors all keys with the alert color.

- *Test 15*—Check that Remove Picture File Ref switches on **Alert 1 Change State** and colors picture file reference.

- *Test 16*—Check that Remove Text File Ref switches on **Alert 1 Change State** and colors text file reference.

- *Test 17*—Check that Remove Sound File Ref switches on **Alert 1 Change State** and colors sound file reference.

- *Test 18*—Check that Save Text File (button and menu) clears text alert color.

- *Test 19*—Check that the Set Font menu option sets **Alert 2 Change State**.

- *Test 20*—Check that the Save Text As menu option sets **Alert 2 Change State** and clears text box color.

And, of course, being conscientious and knowing that Anne would do the same, Archie loaded the standalone Viewer Project Version 2.0 and tested that it still functioned as before.

Review of Change Handling

Archie had Julie review the code he had implemented, to check that it was in line with the way in which they had set up the Title Index Editor, and she was happy with the results. What was important about how **Change Handling** for the Page Index Editor was designed was that the modifications required in the viewer to enable **Change Handling** were absolutely minor. The changes constituted a minimal invasion of the viewer's functionality, but they also had been implemented in a well-protected way, so the standalone viewer was totally protected from the changes. When the viewer was loaded to run within the editor's environment, the editor overrode the locks on the keys and text box after the viewer had been loaded. Subsequent user changes then triggered the **Change** event, but only in the Page Index Editor environment. This functionality could not be invoked when the viewer ran standalone because of the locks that the viewer's **Form_load** event would place on the screen text boxes.

When the editor was running, the **Change** status was propagated through to the editor via the watchdog timer, so the viewer had absolutely no interaction with the editor to achieve full **Change Handling** functionality. We went to all this trouble so we would have just a single version of the Version 2 viewer code, which we could use to generate the viewer *program* or the Page Index Editor Viewer *form*. We had only one set of Version 2 code to maintain, regardless of whether it was for standalone use or for use within the editor.

Hopefully, you can appreciate how much easier this design made the project. The thought of having to implement the viewer's functionality as a second version inside the editor would mean two sets of code to maintain. Differences would exist due to **Change Handling**, and, of course, these differences would lead to the viewer functionality merging with that of the editor, increasing the support burden. By the design, however, the editor was allowed to manipulate the controls within the viewer directly, and even call its functions and subroutines. But the vital point is that it could do all this without compromising the viewer's integrity.

Progress Check

If you recall, the new plan allowed two weeks for us to develop and integrate all the Page Index Editor modules. In the original plan, the two weeks were allocated for module development only. Originally, Archie was to integrate the viewer into the editor within a three-day period. Julie was to implement **Change Handling** in 1.5 days. Archie had completed integration of the viewer and all the **Change Handling** required in only two days. Some **File Selection** work would be necessary on **Change Handling**, but that was all. We summed up Archie's progress as follows:

♦ Planned Progress for Viewer Integration and Change Handling=4.5 days

♦ Actual time spent=2 days

♦ Progress=4.0 days

♦ Still Outstanding=0.5 days

For two days spent working, Archie had achieved four days' progress. The 0.5 days outstanding was Archie's estimate of work required to complete the **File Selection** work on **Change Handling**. At the start of Day 3, Archie began work on **Index Manipulation**, a day ahead of schedule. Now, let's see how Julie got on in those first few days.

Handling of the Page Index

Julie's tasks for the first three days were to set up **Load Index** and **Save Index** for a Page Index Editor file. If you recall, Archie did the equivalent for the Title Index Editor. Julie set up an independent test program to verify the Index functions, much as Archie had done for the Title Index Editor. You've seen the process at work in the development of the Title Index Editor, with the idea being to generate a totally independent testing facility. When Julie had completed all the **Load Index** and **Save Index** functionality, she and Archie could integrate it into the final version of the Page Index Editor.

Creation of New and Open Functions

The designs for these functions were defined as generic specifications for both Title Index Editor and Page Index Editor handling, so you're already quite familiar with them. The only difference between the two lay in the data fields that would be manipulated. Julie developed the code along the lines they had employed for the Title Index Editor. She built a test program and added the functions one by one.

As an alternative, and because you are not actually working in a team environment, you can build the functionality directly into the editor shell you produced in the previous section. Remember that Julie and Archie worked in parallel, and, once they had finished, they integrated all the code into the final version of the viewer.

NOTE: *The steps that follow assume you will add the functionality directly to the editor shell you produced in the last section. If you want to create an independent test facility, feel free, making the appropriate modifications to the steps that follow.*

Step 1

Use the Title Index Editor event handler **mnuNewTitleIndex_Click** as a model to create **nmuNewPageIndex_Click**. Remember to leave the change-handling code in the **New** function. Also, remember to change any "Title" references to "Page"; for example, **Call ClearTitleIndexMemory** becomes **Call ClearPageIndexMemory**.

Step 2

After you've set up the basic function, add the following code to the event handler, just before the change-handling section:

```
Call GetBookType

' Switch viewer into Page View mode
frmEViewer.picTitleSelectionPanel.Visible = False
frmEViewer.picFrontPanel.Visible = True
```

The **Call** in the above code invokes a general routine to solicit and then set the format type required by the user for the new Index. The next two lines of code make sure that the Viewer form is set up in Page View mode. Julie realized that the New menu function could be invoked while the Viewer form was in the Title Selection mode. Consequently, she put the above code at the end of the New menu option to ensure that the viewer switched to view mode.

Step 3

Add the following subroutine to the general section of the Page Index Editor:

```
Private Sub GetBookType()
' PAGE EDITOR INFRASTRUCTURE ROUTINE: V1.0
' Get Book type from user
' -----------------------
Dim intResponse As Integer
Dim strTemp As String
Dim strTemp2 As String

intResponse = 0
While intResponse < 1 Or intResponse > 3
```

```
        strTemp = "Define Index type to be created; 1=E-BOOK, 2=E-ALBUM,_
        3=E-REFBOOK
         BOOK """
        strTemp2 = InputBox(strTemp, "E-MagBook Type")
        If strTemp2 = "" Then Exit Sub
        If strTemp2 = "1" Then intResponse = 1
        If strTemp2 = "2" Then intResponse = 2
        If strTemp2 = "3" Then intResponse = 3
Wend

g_intFormatType = intResponse
Call SetUpBookType
End Sub
```

The preceding code simply asks the user to specify the book type that is to be created and then sets up the appropriate parameters by calling **SetUpBookType**.

Step 4

Add the following routine to the general section of the Page Index Editor:

```
Private Sub SetUpBookType()
' PAGE EDITOR INFRASTRUCTURE ROUTINE: V1.0
' set up screen etc for the selected E-Book type
' ------------------------
g_strFontType = "MS Sans Serif"    ' default settings
g_intFontSize = 10

Select Case g_intFormatType
        Case 1
            Call frmEViewer.SetUpFormat1
        Case 2
            Call frmEViewer.SetUpFormat2
        Case 3
            Call frmEViewer.SetUpFormat3
End Select
End Sub
```

After you've entered the above code, you will need to promote infrastructure routines **SetUpFormat1**, **SetUpFormat2**, and **SetUpFormat3** in the viewer from **Private** to **Public**. When you do this, make sure you include a change log to indicate why you are promoting the infrastructure routines.

Step 5

Add the following to the general section of the Page Index Editor:

```
Sub ClearScreenData()
' PAGE EDITOR INFRASTRUCTURE GUI ROUTINE: V1.0
' ------------------------
Dim intLoopCounter As Integer

For intLoopCounter = 1 To 5
    frmEViewer.txtKeyView(intLoopCounter) = ""
Next intLoopCounter
frmEViewer.txtText.Text = ""
frmEViewer.imgImageIt = LoadPicture("")

frmEViewer.txtIndexFileName.Text = ""
frmEViewer.txtPictureFileName.Text = ""
frmEViewer.txtTextFileName.Text = ""
frmEViewer.txtSoundFileName.Text = ""

frmEViewer.lblCurrent.Caption = ""
frmEViewer.lblCommentLine.Caption = ""
End Sub
```

All the above references are to screen objects "owned" by the Viewer form.

Step 6
Check the function by running the program and clicking New.

Step 7
You can model the **Open** function after that of the Title Index Editor. Note that the Page Index Editor code will make use of module **TitleLib**, which contains **GetIndexFileName**. Consequently, you will need to add module **TitleLib** to the project. Remember also that some of the references in the Title Index Editor version are now found in **frmEViewer**, and you will need to change "Entry" to "Page". After the file has been selected in the code, the only extra things you need to do are enter a call to **SetUpBookType** to ensure the book format is set correctly and enable "Page View mode", as you did for the New menu option. If you are in any doubt about the code created up to this point, consult the final version of the editor in DEV_EPageEditor on the CD.

Testing New and Open Functions
The **New** and **Open** functions are now fully functional and can be selected when the viewer is in any of its three modes—Title Selection, Page View, and Workbench—because the last thing each function does is select "View Mode" in the Viewer form. The Page Index Editor **Open** function is totally consistent with the way in which the viewer opens a Page Index because the editor uses the same routine the viewer employs to load the file.

The tests that Julie was able to log were the following:

♦ *Test 1*—New sets Page View mode and selects format correctly from user definition.

♦ *Test 2*—New works from Title Selection mode okay.

♦ *Test 3*—New works from Page View mode okay.

♦ *Test 4*—New works from Workbench mode okay.

♦ *Test 5*—Open sets Page View mode and selects format correctly.

♦ *Test 6*—Open Works from Title Selection mode okay.

♦ *Test 7*—Open works from Page View mode okay.

♦ *Test 8*—Open works from Workbench mode okay.

♦ *Test 9*—Failure to Open is handled correctly from Title Selection mode.

♦ *Test 10*—Failure to Open is handled correctly from Page View mode.

♦ *Test 11*—Failure to Open is handled correctly from Workbench mode.

Remember that Julie has developed a test program to check out the above, whereas, if you follow the steps, you will be integrating directly into the Page Index Editor.

Creation of Save and Save As Functions

The Title Index Editor provides you with a template for developing the **Save** and **Save As** functions.

Step 1

Create the **Save** function. Note from the design that **Save** will function correctly only from Page View mode. You can easily determine whether the program is in Page View mode by seeing whether **picFrontPanel** is visible. Use the Title Index Editor version of **Save** as your template. If you are in doubt about anything relative to this function, check the final version of code on the CD.

Step 2

Set up the **Save As** function in the same way as you did the **Save** function, again using the version in the Title Index Editor as the template.

Step 3

Now, using **WriteOutTitleIndex** and those all-important design specifications, create an equivalent routine for output of the Page Index Editor. Place the code in **PageLib**. This routine is the first one to be placed in the new library. If you need help, have a look at the final version of the Page Index Editor on the CD.

Testing New, Open, Save, and Save As Functions

We've already identified some of the tests. Clearly, two of the more important tests are to prove that an Index can be read in and then output to a new file name, and that the two files, old and new, are identical. You should also prove that you can't output a blank Index file.

Julie conducted her testing more or less along the same lines that Archie had used for the Title Index Editor's menu functions. Julie set her test program up with a copy of the viewer loaded as an MDI form, so she had access to a copy of the unmodified viewer (that is, no **Change Handling** installed), **ViewerLib**, and her own private version of **PageLib**. (As you can see, working alone and working in a team—where you need to consider what the other people are doing, and how you are going to merge it all together—have big differences between them.)

End of Day 2

Julie also took two days to complete the **Load Index** and **Save Index** functions for the Page Index Editor files, which put her one day ahead of the original schedule. Archie's next task was to develop **Index Manipulation**. Using the Title Index Editor as a template, he estimated he would be early. To give them an even bigger edge, the two programmers decided that Archie would continue to work on the shell editor that he had just produced (with a fully integrated viewer and **Change Handling** implemented). Such a strategy would obviate the need to integrate **Index Manipulation** in the final version.

Julie's next task was to complete **Text Save** and **Text Font**, which she would develop in isolation to Archie. The separate development would require integration at a later date, together with her **Load Index** and **Save Index** functions. Julie was also confident she would complete the two functions early.

Up to this point, Julie and Archie had both been subjected to interruptions by Anne's testing of the Title Index Editor, although the issues were minor, and I had had to talk with each of them to discuss issues concerning the new developments of HTML and composite handling. I reiterated to them that, if they felt external requests for help from the other project team members started to become a burden, they must let me know, so that such interruptions did not become too much of a burden and start to affect their development progress. At the end of Day 2, both programmers stated that the impact of interruptions so far had been minimal.

Currently, the risks posed by multiple activities occurring on the project were manageable. Nevertheless, we must continue to monitor progress carefully in our attempt to complete early development of the Page Index Editor.

Page Index Manipulation

Archie implemented **Page Index Manipulation** directly into the version of the Page Index Editor he had developed, which contained the integrated viewer and **Change Handling**. By following the steps in the next sections, you can add this functionality directly into the program that you developed in the last section. Alternatively, compare the following steps with the code you will find in DEV_EPageEditor on the CD.

Creation of Add, Insert, Delete, and Overwrite

Look at each of the **Add**, **Insert**, **Delete**, and **Overwrite** functions in turn; study the design notes; and use the equivalent code from the Title Index Editor to create the code for the Page Index Editor. If you have any problems, consult the final version in DEV_EPageEditor on the CD.

Note that you will need to create general routines: **IncreasePageIndexByOne** and **ReducePageIndexByOne** in **PageLib**, and the GUI function **TransferFromScreenToPage** in the general section of the main form. Finally, you will need to call **DisplayPage** with the argument absent. The Title Index Editor development provides you with our model; all you need is a methodical approach.

Testing Add, Insert, Delete, and Overwrite

You now have a lot of testing to do. Clearly, you need to check each function and **Change Handling**. Be methodical. Log the tests, and think of variations as you go along. Because he was using the shell, Archie was unable to **Load** and **Save** indexes (Julie had developed that functionality independently in a test program). However, Archie could **Load** an Index through the standard viewer functionality and then **Add**, **Insert**, **Overwrite**, and **Delete**, but he conducted all his testing on the in-memory data because he had no way to save his changes. You, however, can add the new functionality to the Page Index Editor you've developed so far, which gives you the capability to load and save Index files at will. You can appreciate that sequentially adding the functionality to the project as you go along gives you a bigger testing headache. Developing each piece of functionality in isolation lets you check code in a much more focused manner.

Archie paid particular attention to checking out what happened at the operational extremes, where most bugs lurk. For example:

♦ *Test 1*—Check Add when at start and end of Index.

♦ *Test 2*—Check Insert when at start and end of Index.

♦ *Test 3*—Check Overwrite when at start and end of Index.

♦ *Test 4*—Check Delete when at start and end of Index.

Archie managed to develop all the functionality and complete a comprehensive set of testing by Friday afternoon. He took the full three days planned to complete the functionality. For three days' actual effort, he made three days' progress against the plan. In fact, his progress was slightly better than that, because he had also completed integration of the **Index Manipulation** functions into what would become the final version of the Page Index Editor. He had been subject to a number of interruptions, but, overall, we were very pleased with his progress by the end of the first week. He had only **File Selection**, which was scheduled for three days, left to develop and implement. Even if he took the full three days—which he was confident he would not need—he would still have two days to integrate all of Julie's developments and perform a first pass of system testing before they handed over the software to Anne's department for full system testing. Archie managed to leave the office early on Friday afternoon for a well-earned weekend (amid some parting comments about the need for cautious bike riding).

Text Save and Font Handling

Julie's tasks, originally scheduled for two days, were to handle a request to save the content of the text box into a file using Save and Save As menu options, and to allow the font to be set. Again, in an attempt to save time, she developed the code in the copy of the editor she was working on, integrating it into the functionality she had already created. Remember, she didn't have full **Change Handling** functionality, she had no **Index Manipulation** functionality, and all her software would have to be integrated into Archie's version of the Page Index Editor.

Once again, you can simply add the code directly into the editor you have developed so far, or look at the final version of the Page Index Editor from the CD.

Creating Save Text Handling

As the design indicates, the **Save Text** functions were similar to those of the Index, for which Julie had a model in the Title Index Editor. Follow these steps to set up text, saving in the version of the Page Index Editor you have created so far.

Step 1

Create the Save menu function using the logic in the Save Title Index Editor option as your model. Change the checkbox for an empty Index to a checkbox for an empty text box. Make sure all the Index references are changed to text box references, and so on. The call to **WriteOutPageIndex(strTemp)** becomes a call to a new routine called **WriteOut TextFile(strTemp, strTemp2)**. Note the extra argument (more about this later) will require a **DIM** statement.

Step 2

Create the Save As menu option using the logic in the Save As Title Index Editor option. Make all the modifications required to make the code pertinent to text handling only. Change the call from **GetIndexFileNameForOutput** to **GetTextFileNameForOutput**. You will also need to modify the call to **WriteOutPageIndex(strTemp)**, as specified in Step 1. You can use the call to **OkToProceed** without modification (reusability rules).

Step 3

You can create a routine called **GetTextFileNameForOutput**, which, with appropriate modifications, is directly equivalent to **GetIndexFileNameForOuput**, and place it in **PageLib**. The only difference between the routines is that in **GetTextFileNameForOutput** the applied filter is set to ***.TXT** rather than ***.IDX**. You can copy **GetIndexFileNameForOutput** and then change the name and filter settings as required.

As you are building the final version of the Page Index Editor, make sure that the **Change Handling** code you created earlier has been preserved. Remember, the Save As option needs to set the **Alert 2 Change State** because the name of the text file might have changed. Setting the **Alert 2 Change State** ensures that the user will employ one of the Index manipulation buttons to bring the Index disk file and Memory Index back in line.

Now, we come to the only bit of unique code. The routine to output the text file is as follows:

```
Public Function WriteOutTextFile(strFileName As String, strText As String)-
As Boolean
' GENERAL ROUTINE: V1.0
' Low level output of text file
' Arguments:
'   strFileName -   File name to output to
'        strtext -   Text to output
' -----------------------------------
Dim intLoopCounter As Integer
Dim booResult As Boolean

WriteOutTextFile = False
On Error GoTo FailedToOutput

If strFileName = "" Then GoTo FailedToOutput
Open strFileName For Output As #1

    Print #1, strText

Close #1

WriteOutTextFile = True
Exit Function
' ===================================================
' Error handling
FailedToOutput:
MsgBox "Text Ouput failed"
Close #1
Exit Function

End Function
```

The code really couldn't be much simpler. Note that, unlike the equivalent Index output functions, this code contains a second argument—the text string to output. This argument is necessary to make the routine independent of the GUI.

Step 6

Place a call to **mnuSaveText_Click** in the **cmdSaveText_Click** handler.

Creating Font Handling Code

For the **Font Handling** code, place the following code into the **cmdSetFont_Click** handler:

```
Private Sub mnuSetFont_Click()
' PAGE EDITOR INFRASTRUCTURE EVENT HANDLER: V1.0
' Set font for all page in current book
' --------------------------------

If frmEViewer.picFrontPanel.Visible = False Then
    MsgBox "Cannot set font unless Viewer is in Page View Mode"
    Exit Sub
End If

' set font type on entry to reflect current state
dlgDialog.FontName = frmEViewer.txtText.Font
dlgDialog.FontSize = frmEViewer.txtText.FontSize
dlgDialog.FontBold = frmEViewer.txtText.FontBold
dlgDialog.FontItalic = frmEViewer.txtText.FontItalic

' Get requested font
dlgDialog.Flags = &H1&     ' List only screen fonts supported by system
dlgDialog.Action = 4       ' Display font dialog box
If dlgDialog.FontName = "" Then Exit Sub

' set up as requested
frmEViewer.txtText.Font = dlgDialog.FontName
g_strFontType = frmEViewer.txtText.Font
frmEViewer.txtText.FontSize = dlgDialog.FontSize
g_intFontSize = frmEViewer.txtText.FontSize

' CHANGE HANDLING - status of book has changed
Call SetAlert2Status
End Sub
```

This code operates only if the viewer is in the Page View mode—that is, the front panel is visible. The dialog box is set up with all the current font characteristics of the text box. The action property is then set to 4, which, the manual tells us, switches on the font-selection dialog box. If the resultant selection is blank, the program exits. If it is not blank, the text box and memory variables are set up with the new values. Note that, although bold and italic are being handled initially, they are not being stored on return because this was not a requirement. You determine the **.Flags** setting by reading the VB manual. This setting ensures that only screen fonts supported by the system are listed. This setting was not featured in the design, but is a result of translating design to code and of knowing from the manual how the dialog box works. So, the motto is this: Know your components.

Testing Text Handling and Font Control

Julie checked **Text Handling** by entering text into the text box and then saving it. She checked the content of the resulting output file using the Notepad editor. She checked **Font Handling** by setting a new font, saving the Index, and reloading the Index to make sure that all pages switched to the new font. The following tests Julie did show the kinds of things she checked:

♦ *Test 1*—Check that a modified text box can be saved to file and the alert condition on text box is cleared.

♦ *Test 2*—Check that a modified text box can be saved to a new file and the alert condition on the text box is cleared; **Alert 2 Change State** switched on.

♦ *Test 3*—Change text to an entry in a genuine book. Save text, and check that it comes back correctly modified when the book is reloaded.

♦ *Test 4*—Check that Save Text updates a file as expected.

♦ *Test 5*—Check that Save Text As allows new files to be created.

♦ *Test 6*—Check that Save Text As allows old files to be overwritten.

♦ *Test 7*—Check that font can be changed in any page, and that the change affects all pages of the Index.

♦ *Test 8*—Check that font change is stored with the Index and maintained when the Index is reloaded.

Notice how Julie had chosen all the tests so she could conduct them on the test program she was developing, which contained no **Index Manipulation** functions.

Julie managed to complete the two functions and their testing in just one day. She had now completed three actual days of effort and achieved five days' progress. She could start the **Copy** and **Paste** development early—excellent progress.

Yet Another Request from Monty

On Wednesday, Monty rang up and said he would be having a brainstorming session with one of his main European dealers early the next week. He wanted to know whether we could supply some assistance in getting the program itself set up to work in French and German. This process would involve translation of all the text strings in the code and captions on screen. As usual, he was willing to pay for the privilege.

We assessed progress on Wednesday evening, and Julie had only **Copy** and **Paste** left. We therefore agreed that she could go to Monty's the next day with copies of the source code to set up French and German prototypes of the Version 1.1 viewer. This process would involve getting the right font into all the appropriate controls so that the buttons, messages, and so on all came up with the correct font type. She would modify the program twice—once for French and once for German, producing two sets of source code. Depending on how time went, she might try a Spanish version as well. Samantha had painstakingly gone through every single message and caption and had translations for all of them. Julie needed only to set up the program.

She would not try to make the program multilingual—such a capability was a long way off. The exercise Monty was asking for would produce one version of the code for each language. We made it clear to Monty that we would not maintain these prototypes and that they were special, one-off prototypes. Monty accepted the terms and agreed he would not require further development of the prototypes until we had decided on a strategy for handling multilingual functionality as a later development.

This new plan meant that Julie was out of the game for at least a day. We told Monty that, if he wanted us to complete the Page Index Editor early, Julie would have to be back with us on Monday at the very latest. Both Julie and Archie were confident they could still complete development and integration of the Page Index Editor by the end of the following week.

Tip

Once again, we were exhibiting a degree of flexibility essential to a small software house. As a company, we needed to respond to potential business demands as quickly and as efficiently as we were able. The contingency that we built into our plans for software developments covered not only problems on the project, but also our need to continue looking for new work. Helping Monty to prove the versatility of the viewer would do us only good in the long run, because Monty had now agreed that we would automatically receive all the future work for the E-MagBook. Things were racing ahead at a much faster pace than Monty had anticipated, and he wanted to cement us into the E-MagBook project. We were also starting to negotiate a percentage of sales, for which Monty would expect reduced development rates.

How's Progress?

On Friday afternoon, we monitored progress in Julie's absence. Archie had completed viewer integration, **Change Handling**, and **Index Manipulation**, all of which were integrated into what would become the final editor. He was a day ahead of schedule and could start on **File Selection** on Monday. Julie had completed **Load Index** and **Save Index** functions, and the **Text Save** and **Text Font** functions. Although she was two days ahead of schedule, that time was now gone because she was still working on translated prototypes. She would start on **Copy** and **Paste**, and also implement the required **Clear** functions, on Monday, according to the original plan. Archie was scheduled to spend three days on **File Selection**, and Julie was scheduled to spend two days on **Copy** and **Paste**. Assuming they were both finished by Thursday, they would have two days for integration, generally tidying up the code, and some preliminary testing. We would require 100 percent availability from both programmers, which was the main risk factor.

Testing the Title Index Editor had raised a couple of issues, which Archie handled, and I had made good progress with the requirements document for the Web browser and composites. Archie had agreed to review these requirements over the weekend. This was the first time in the project that anyone would have to work on the weekend. However, the work would involve only a couple hours of reading, which Archie could do in the comfort of his own home.

I had started on the design for HTML, Web, and composite handling, even though the requirements specification had not been reviewed. I had spent time discussing issues with Archie, so he knew what I was doing. This discussion was vital while our work overlapped, so that we didn't start contradicting each other. Rob, our new programmer on the project, had made excellent progress coming up to speed, and, by Friday, he was starting to look through the viewer code in detail.

Monty kept Julie working on language conversions both Thursday and Friday. Things were going so well he wanted to see whether they could do some more languages. Thanks to the Internet and contacts in various countries, he had genuine translations and font sets arriving throughout the two days. I spoke to Monty and made it clear that Julie had to be back on Monday; otherwise, he would jeopardize early delivery of the Page Index Editor. That sobering thought had the desired effect, and he agreed to release her from translations on Friday evening.

File Selection Functions

I discussed **File Selection** at great length in Chapter 5 after I reviewed the functional requirements. Julie and Archie had actually put some very basic code together to make the VB file controls function as a unit for producing the Page Index Editor form-layout screen shots. Revisit the section if you cannot recall how **File Selection** works, and then study the design specifications in Appendix G and the **File Selection** work Archie and Julie did that's contained in Appendix E.

Reviewing the Technical Requirements

Archie began, as always, by reviewing the design. The key element of **File Selection** was the file-list-box click-event handler. This event handler was where the code determined what to do with the file selected. First, the code must determine which type of file it was dealing with—picture, text, or sound. Then, the code must load the appropriate text box on the Viewer form that held the file reference. Next, based on file type, the code needed to load the image or video clip, load the text into the text box, or play the sound. That functionality was what the design notes stated.

At this stage, the **File Selection** code needed to display the new situation on screen and set **Alert 1 Change State**. Displaying the screen involved the alternative call to **DisplayPage** and using an argument, which forced **DisplayPage** to load the image, text, and sound from the file references rather than the in-Memory Index. The keys shown on screen would remain unchanged.

The File Selection form could be used in three modes. It could be used to select a picture file, text file, or sound file. First, the user would have to define which mode the form was to enter. The user would do this by clicking one of the three labels, which would be located at the top of the form. This action would cause the background colors of the objects on the form to be set up—red for picture/image selection, green for text, and blue for sounds—as we had shown in the requirements specification.

The Creation of File Selection Functionality

The code to select a file would be the same in each of the three cases—picture, text, or sound selection. What would be done with the final, derived file string would depend on which of the three possible modes the user had enabled. The code to handle a file load could determine the mode by checking the color of the panels at the top of the form.

We decided we would allow a user to set up any of the three file references, regardless of which format type was current. So, for a Text Book, the user would be able to set up a picture file, but it would never be displayed as long as the Index remained a Text Book. Allowing this flexibility would enable a user to set up references that might be used in a future format, but that were not currently supported.

To implement the modified version of the **File Selection** functionality directly into your version of the Page Index Editor, follow these steps.

Step 1

Load the blank form **frmFileSelect** from DEV_BlankEPageEditor on the CD.

Step 2

Add the following line to the Page Index Editor's **Form_Load** event, just after the viewer has been loaded:

```
' Load the File Selection Panel
frmFileSelect.Show
```

Step 3

Place the following code in the File Selection panel's **Load** event:

```
Private Sub Form_Load()
' PAGE EDITOR(File Selection) INFRASTRUCTURE EVENT HANDLER: V1.0
' File Selection Form - set dimensions and locations
' -------------------------------
frmFileSelect.Height = 7245
frmFileSelect.Width = 3810
frmFileSelect.Left = 9700
frmFileSelect.Top = 0
```

```
strPictureFilter = "*.BMP;*.JPG;*.TIF"
strTextFilter = "*.TXT"
strSoundFilter = "*.WAV;*.MID"

End Sub
```

We worked out the preceding dimensions through trial and error.

Step 4

Place the following declarations in the general section of the Title Selection form:

```
Option Explicit
' PAGE EDITOR(File Selection) INFRASTRUCTURE DATA: V1.0
' File Selection type context variables
Dim strPictureFilter As String
Dim strPictureDrive1 As String
Dim strPictureDir1 As String

Dim strTextFilter As String
Dim strTextDrive1 As String
Dim strTextDir1 As String

Dim strSoundFilter As String
Dim strSoundDrive1 As String
Dim strSoundDir1 As String
```

These variables would let us save the context of a given file type when the user switched to another type. When the original file type was reselected at a later date, the appropriate variables from above could be used to reset the drive, directory, file, and filter boxes to their previous setting for the file type being reselected. For example, when the user switched from picture selection to text selection, all the picture settings for drive, directory, file, and filter controls would be saved, and the previous set of text settings would be reinstated. If, at a later time, the user were to switch back to picture mode, all the settings from its previous time of use would be reset.

Step 5

Insert the following code into the Drive box's change-event handler:

```
Private Sub filDrive1_Change()
' PAGE EDITOR(File Selection) INFRASTRUCTURE EVENT HANDLER: V1.0
' Drive has changed.
' -------------------------------
filDir1.Path = filDrive1.Drive
End Sub
```

If you followed the work in Appendix E, this code will be obvious. The **Drive** change event is fired each time the drive shown in the box is changed. The preceding code sets up the path attribute of the Directory selection box. So, if you click C:, **filDir1.Path** becomes C:\. This, in turn, causes a change event in the Directory selection box.

Step 6

Enter the following code into the Directory box's change-event handler:

```
Private Sub filDir1_Change()
' PAGE EDITOR(File Selection) INFRASTRUCTURE EVENT HANDLER: V1.0
' Directory has changed.
' ------------------------------
filFile1.Path = filDir1.Path

End Sub
```

A change in the Directory box causes the **filFile1.Path** to be set to **filDir1.Path**. So, if the directory \E-MAGBOOK\IMAGES is selected, and the drive is already set to C:, **filFile1.Path** becomes C:\E-MAGBOOK\IMAGES. A change to the Drive box percolates through to both the other boxes via their change events. If you need further explanation of this sequence of events, consult Appendix E.

Step 7

The volume of code for handling a click on a file name in the File Selection box looks formidable. However, the code is very straightforward, as determined by the design, which you must study initially. Insert this code into the change-event handler of **filFile1**:

```
Private Sub filFile1_Click()
' PAGE EDITOR(File Selection) INFRASTRUCTURE EVENT HANDLER: V1.0
' A file is selected by user
' ------------------------------
Dim intTemp As Integer
Dim strTemp As String
Dim booResult As Boolean
Dim intSelected As Boolean

' This code only works in 'Page View mode'
If frmEViewer.picFrontPanel.Visible = False Then
    MsgBox "Viewer must be in Page View Mode for File Selection to work."
    Exit Sub
End If
' .....................................................................
' construct the file name and path
intTemp = Len(filFile1.Path)
```

```
    If Mid(filFile1.Path, intTemp, 1) = "\" Then    ' Does last char contain '\'?
        strTemp = filFile1.Path & filFile1.FileName ' Add file name if it does
Else
        strTemp = filFile1.Path & "\" & filFile1.FileName  ' Else; Add '\' and
                                                           ' then file name
End If
intSelected = 0                  ' No file has been selected
'
.............................................................................
' Process according to what has been selected, Picture/Video, Text or Sound
' selection, determined by color of the three panels at top of form.
'
' 1. PROCESS PICTURE/VIDEO SECLECTION
If lblPicture.BackColor <> frmEViewer.shpGray.BackColor Then
    frmEViewer.txtPictureFileName.Text = strTemp
    frmEViewer.picFrontPanel.BackColor = frmEViewer.shpRed.BackColor
    frmEViewer.txtPictureFileName.BackColor = frmEViewer.shpRed.BackColor

    If g_intFormatType = 1 Then
        MsgBox "WARNING: an image/video will not show on a text book."
        Exit Sub
    End If
    intSelected = 1         ' Picture has been selected
End If
' ...........................................................................
' 2. PROCESS TEXT BLOCK
If lblText.BackColor <> frmEViewer.shpGray.BackColor Then
    frmEViewer.txtTextFileName.Text = strTemp
    frmEViewer.txtTextFileName.BackColor = frmEViewer.shpRed.BackColor
    frmEViewer.picFrontPanel.BackColor = frmEViewer.shpRed.BackColor  '
Alert

    If g_intFormatType = 2 Then
        MsgBox "WARNING: Text will not appear in an album."
        Exit Sub
    End If
    intSelected = 1             ' Text has been selected
End If
' ...........................................................................
' 3. PROCESS SOUND
If lblSound.BackColor <> frmEViewer.shpGray.BackColor Then
    frmEViewer.txtSoundFileName.Text = strTemp
    frmEViewer.txtSoundFileName.BackColor = frmEViewer.shpRed.BackColor
    frmEViewer.picFrontPanel.BackColor = frmEViewer.shpRed.BackColor   '
```

```
Alert
    intSelected = 1          ' Sound has been selected
End If
'........................................................................
If intSelected = 0 Then
    ' No file type selected
    MsgBox "File type not selected, please try again."
    Exit Sub
End If
'........................................................................
' display the page
Call frmEViewer.DisplayPage(1)
End Sub
```

intSelected is used in the preceding code to determine whether a file type has been selected. When the program first loads, no default type is selected. For the code to work correctly when the program is first run, the background colors of all the type selection labels (**Picture**, **Text**, and **Sound**) must be exactly the same as that of **shpGray**. Because the code is well-structured and clearly set up in sections, it is simple to follow.

Step 8

Set up the click-event handler of the **Picture** label at the top of the screen as follows:

```
Private Sub lblPicture_Click()
' PAGE EDITOR(File Selection) INFRASTRUCTURE EVENT HANDLER: V1.0
' Switch on PICTURE selection Mode
' --------------------------------
Call SaveCurrentFilter

lblPicture.BackColor = shpForPicture.BackColor

filDrive1.Drive = strPictureDrive1
filDrive1.BackColor = shpForPicture.BackColor

filDir1.Path = strPictureDir1
filDir1.BackColor = shpForPicture.BackColor

filFile1.BackColor = shpForPicture.BackColor

txtFileFilter.BackColor = shpForPicture.BackColor
txtFileFilter.Text = strPictureFilter

lblSound.BackColor = shpGray.BackColor
lblText.BackColor = shpGray.BackColor

End Sub
```

For whichever selection mode is enabled, the filter currently in use is stored, so that it can be reinstated next time that mode is switched on. Then, the program sets all the screen controls with the picture color. Finally, the color of the other two mode buttons is neutralized.

Step 9

Using the code in Step 7 as a template, set up the code for text and sound **File Handling**.

Step 10

Add this routine to the general section of the File Selection form:

```
Sub SaveCurrentFilter()
' PAGE EDITOR(File Selection) INFRASTRUCTURE GUI ROUTINE: V1.0
' -------------------------------
If lblPicture.BackColor = shpForPicture.BackColor Then
   strPictureFilter = txtFileFilter.Text
   strPictureDrive1 = filDrive1.Drive
   strPictureDir1 = filDir1.Path
End If

If lblText.BackColor = shpForText.BackColor Then
   strTextFilter = txtFileFilter.Text
   strTextDrive1 = filDrive1.Drive
   strTextDir1 = filDir1.Path
End If

If lblSound.BackColor = shpForSound.BackColor Then
   strSoundFilter = txtFileFilter.Text
   strSoundDrive1 = filDrive1.Drive
   strSoundDir1 = filDir1.Path
End If

End Sub
```

This code allows filters to be preserved for a given file selection type. When the requested mode is next selected, the previously set up filter is pulled out and made applicable once again. Each file type can, therefore, concentrate on its own file type for filtering.

Step 11

Place this code in the change-event handler of the Filter Selection text box:

```
Private Sub txtFileFilter_Change()
' PAGE EDITOR(File Selection) INFRASTRUCTURE EVENT HANDLER: V1.0
' -------------------------------
On Error GoTo 1000:
```

```
filFile1.Pattern = txtFileFilter.Text
1000:
Exit Sub

End Sub
```

This code is activated each time the slightest change to the Filter Selection text box occurs. Because the event is being fired off when each character is typed in, a good chance exists that the file selection is incomplete; this condition results in an error being generated when the pattern is set in **filFile1**. Archie neatly handled this situation with an error trap.

Testing the File Selection Functions

The first time Archie clicked any of the **File Selection** labels, the program crashed with "invalid property value" at the **filDrive1.Drive=strPictureDrive1** line in the **lblPicture_Click** handler. Type selection involves reinstating the type's most recent drive, directory, and filter settings. When the program first loads, the variables in which these items are stored are all blank; hence, the error. Archie went back to the design and found that this situation had not been accommodated. To rectify the situation, he inserted the following code in the file selection form's **Load** event:

```
' Set up default values for selection file selection controls
strPictureDrive1 = filDrive1.Drive
strPictureDir1 = filDir1.Path

strTextDrive1 = filDrive1.Drive
strTextDir1 = filDir1.Path

strSoundDrive1 = filDrive1.Drive
strSoundDir1 = filDir1.Path
```

This code guarantees that some settings exist for these parameters. It highlights quite a significant area of error in software development. Initial conditions of variables and the like need to be determined, so that the code never has to operate on something that is not set up sensibly. Initial conditions and operational limits are two big areas for testing, as Anne will tell you.

At this stage, you can completely check out the **File Selection** functionality. Archie logged the following tests:

♦ *Test 1*—Check that code functions only in viewer Page View mode.

♦ *Test 2*—Check that an error message is provided if no file type is selected.

♦ *Test 3*—Check that text can be selected—that is, that the File Ref text box is updated and **Alert State** is set.

- ◆ *Test 4*—Check that a text warning is provided if Picture Album is the current format.

- ◆ *Test 5*—Check that an image can be selected—that is, that the File Ref text box is updated and **Alert 1 Change State** is set.

- ◆ *Test 6*—Check that video can be selected—that is, that the File Ref text box is updated and **Alert 1 Change State** is set.

- ◆ *Test 7*—Check that an image warning is provided if aText Book is opened.

- ◆ *Test 8*—Check that sound can be selected—that is, that the File Ref text box is updated and **Alert 1 Changed State** is set.

- ◆ *Test 9*—Check that pages are made up correctly for all file types and book formats.

- ◆ *Test 10*—Check that Release still works correctly, restoring the screen as it was.

Archie spent the two days developing the code and testing it for **File Selection** functionality. Because he also had full Index functionality available in his semi-integrated final version of the editor, his testing was quite extensive.

Completion of Page Index Editor

Julie rejoined us on Monday. The work she had done to set up the viewer in different languages had gone well. She had translated all the captions, all the text messages, and, of course, the page content. The problems Julie had faced were those of getting the longest translations to fit into the available space on button controls. This challenge required a lot of effort. (If you design a system from scratch to be multilingual, you need to design the screen layouts around the language that uses the longest strings.) Some of the button-control captions had presented considerable difficulty. Nevertheless, Monty now had E-MagBooks demonstrating English, French, German, Dutch, Spanish, and Italian. He was very happy, and we had earned some extra revenue.

The first thing on the agenda was to reconcile Julie's development environment with the latest versions from Archie's work, so that Julie had the up-to-date version of both the viewer and **Change Handling**. Only then would she be in a position to start coding. However, you can continue to update the final version of your program directly.

Creation of Copy and Paste

The design for **Copy** and **Paste** is straightforward. At design time, we had decided that we would create a delimited string to hold the data fields (keys and picture, text, and sound file names), and then place the whole string on the clipboard using the **SetText** method of the VB **Clipboard** object. To copy the data, all we needed to do was construct the string and then invoke the **SetText** method. To retrieve the string from the **Paste** buffer, we could use the **ClipBoard.GetText** method. This method would transfer the string from **Paste** buffer to a variable in the code. Because the data fields were delimited using square brackets, we could use the **ViewerLib** function **ExtractFieldData** to reclaim the data and place the appropriate screen objects. Study the design specifications before you proceed.

Step 1

Place this code in the Copy button's click-event handler:

```
Private Sub cmdCopy_Click()
' PAGE EDITOR INFRASTRUCTURE EVENT HANDLER: V1.0
' Copy screen data field contents to clipboard
' ----------------------
Dim strTemp As String
Dim booResult As Boolean

If frmEViewer.picFrontPanel.Visible <> True Then
    MsgBox "This option only functions in Page View Mode."
    Exit Sub
End If

strTemp = "[E-MAGBOOK CLIPBOARD PACKET]"
strTemp = strTemp & " [" & frmEViewer.txtKeyView(1).Text & "]"
strTemp = strTemp & " [" & frmEViewer.txtKeyView(2).Text & "]"
strTemp = strTemp & " [" & frmEViewer.txtKeyView(3).Text & "]"
strTemp = strTemp & " [" & frmEViewer.txtKeyView(4).Text & "]"
strTemp = strTemp & " [" & frmEViewer.txtKeyView(5).Text & "]"
strTemp = strTemp & " [" & frmEViewer.txtPictureFileName.Text & "]"
strTemp = strTemp & " [" & frmEViewer.txtTextFileName.Text & "]"
strTemp = strTemp & " [" & frmEViewer.txtSoundFileName.Text & "]"

Clipboard.SetText strTemp

MsgBox "On-screen data has been transferred to ClipBoard."

End Sub
```

The data fields required are packed into the field delimiters in the same order that they appear in the Page Index Editor data file, but one field higher, because the header appears in Field 1. After the string has been assembled, it is transferred to the clipboard.

Step 2

Insert this code into the Paste button's click-event handler:

```
Private Sub cmdPaste_Click()
' PAGE EDITOR INFRASTRUCTURE EVENT HANDLER: V1.0
' Extract screen data from clipboard
' ----------------------
```

```
Dim strTemp As String
Dim strField(9) As String
Dim strHeader As String
Dim intTemp As Integer
Dim booResult As Boolean
Dim intLoopCounter As Integer

If frmEViewer.picFrontPanel.Visible <> True Then
    MsgBox "This option only functions in Page View Mode."
    Exit Sub
End If

strTemp = Clipboard.GetText

booResult = ExtractFieldData(strTemp, strField(), 9)
If strField(1) <> "E-MAGBOOK CLIPBOARD PACKET" Then GoTo Errorhandler

On Error GoTo Errorhandler
For intTemp = 1 To 5
    frmEViewer.txtKeyView(intTemp).Text = strField(intTemp + 1)
Next intTemp

frmEViewer.txtPictureFileName.Text = strField(7)
frmEViewer.txtTextFileName.Text = strField(8)
frmEViewer.txtSoundFileName.Text = strField(9)

Call frmEViewer.DisplayPage(1)   ' display page using alternative data

' Alert handling goes here
Exit Sub
' =================================================================
' Error handler
Errorhandler:
MsgBox "ClipBoard does not contain recognizable data."

End Sub
```

Note the comment in the code about alert handling, which has already been set up. Because the first field in the **Paste** buffer contains a coded header, the routine can tell whether the **Paste** buffer contains a correctly formatted E-MagBook packet. If it does, the data is unpacked and transferred onto screen. The **DisplayPage** routine is called and requested to load from the file references rather than from the Index entry.

Testing Copy and Paste

Copy and **Paste** functionality is an extremely useful addition to the editor, and one Samantha couldn't wait for, because she was still manipulating Page Indexes using the Notepad editor.

Julie tested **Copy** and **Paste** by loading an Index, modifying an entry, copying the modified entry to the **Paste** buffer, moving elsewhere in the Index, and pasting the modified entry back onto the screen. She could then add, insert at current point, or overwrite the current entry with the screen's pasted contents. I'm sure you can imagine the tests that were performed; no doubt, they are similar to the ones you came up with.

Creation of the Clear Functions

The **Clear** functions are classified as the following:

- *Clear text key*—**cmdClearTextBox**

- *Clear keys*—**cmdClearKeys**

- *Remove picture*—**cmdRemovePicture**

- *Remove text*—**cmdRemoveText**

- *Remove sound*—**cmdRemoveSound**

Each function involves clearing a viewer screen object. In the case of the **Remove** functions, the **Alert State** must be invoked and the screen redrawn with the new settings.

Follow these steps to install **Clear** handling.

Step 1

Insert the following line at the start of the **cmdClearTextBox_Click** handler:

```
frmEViewer.txtText.Text = ""
```

If you recall, **Change Handling** code has already been inserted into this module. All that is needed now is for the line that actually clears the text box.

Step 2

Add the code to **cmdClearKeys_Click** to clear the keys.

Step 3

For all three **Remove** functions, add a line that clears the relevant viewer screen object and, at the end of the code, add a line to call **DisplayPage(1)** in the Viewer form. The **Display Page** call ensures that the page is updated and removes the multimedia object associated with the file reference that has been blanked.

Step 4

You can set up the command button to remove all three file references with a call to each of the individual click events to clear picture, text, and sound. This sequence redraws the page three times. If doing so is a nuisance, you can easily alter the code so it performs three clears, then the appropriate alert handling, and then ends with a single call to **DisplayPage(1)**.

Testing Clear Functions

This testing proved to be a simple task. By now, you should be more than able to set up the required tests. Julie completed **Copy** and **Paste**, and all the **Clear** functions, in one day of effort.

System Integration, Testing, and Acceptance

On Tuesday, Julie was ready for integration, but Archie was not available until Wednesday. For the first time in the project, we had a programmer with nothing to do. We made use of the time by having Julie assist Rob in his study of the project. She also had time to review my requirements specification for HTML, Web, and composite handling, so she used the time well.

Final integration, which began on Wednesday of the second week, involved putting all Julie's developments into Archie's version of the Page Index Editor. Julie and Archie worked closely together to get this right. Because they had started integrating at an earlier stage, the process went quite smoothly. As a final bit of infrastructure development, they put in the **Windows** functions, which let the user reload either the Viewer form or the File Selection form if either was closed down. The functions also provided an alternative way to set focus on the relevant form.

Step 1

Set up the menu option to select the viewer, as follows:

```
Private Sub mnuEViewerSelect_Click()
' PAGE EDITOR INFRASTRUCTURE EVENT HANDLER: V1.0
' ----------------------
frmEViewer.Show
frmEViewer.ZOrder
End Sub
```

The above code uses a **.Show** to bring the form back if it is removed and a **.ZOrder** to give the form focus.

Step 2

Add this code to the file-selection **Window** option:

```
Private Sub mnuFileSelectionSelect_Click()
' PAGE EDITOR INFRASTRUCTURE EVENT HANDLER: V1.0
' ----------------------
frmFileSelect.Show
frmFileSelect.ZOrder

End Sub
```

Step 3

Set up the exit function as follows:

```
Private Sub mnuExit_Click()
' PAGE EDITOR INFRASTRUCTURE EVENT HANDLER: V1.0
' ----------------
Unload Me
End Sub
```

And use the **MDIForm_QueryUnload** event to see what the user wants to do:

```
Private Sub MDIForm_QueryUnload(Cancel As Integer, UnloadMode As Integer)
' PAGE EDITOR INFRASTRUCTURE EVENT HANDLER: Close Down V1.0
' ---------------------------
Dim strTemp As String
Dim intResponse As Integer

strTemp = "Are you sure you want to exit the E-MagBook Page editor?"
intResponse = MsgBox(strTemp, vbQuestion + vbOKCancel, "EXIT EDITOR")
If intResponse <> 1 Then
     Cancel = 1     ' abort the exit
     Exit Sub
End If

Cancel = 0     ' Close down
Call CloseDownVideo(frmVideo, frmVideo.mmcVideoPlayer)
Call CloseDownSound(frmEViewer.mmcSoundPlayer)

End Sub
```

The above code lets us see whether the user really wants to shut down and, if so, ensures that the multimedia channels are closed.

Preliminary System Testing

Archie and Julie started serious system testing on Thursday, which culminated in their going through the acceptance scripts. By Friday evening, they were confident they would be handing over a truly robust product to Anne's department for independent, in-house, system testing. They had achieved their goal of having the Page Index Editor ready, fully integrated to start proper system testing, one week early.

The main problem the programmers encountered in their preliminary testing concerned **Index Manipulation** functions performed when the user was at the end of the Index. Check this situation out. Document any errors so you can reproduce and then fix them.

System Testing

Anne's department had already started testing the Title Index Editor, and they had also found some problems with **Index Manipulation** when they were at the end of the index. However, they found very little wrong with the Page Index Editor, because of the level of testing Archie and Julie had conducted.

If you load the final versions of the Page Index Editor or the Title Index Editor from the CD, you can track the bug fixes and so on that we made to the program as a result of Anne's findings. Each code section has its own version number, indicating how many times the code had been modified from when it had originally been frozen. For each change, you will see a "P" reference for the Page Index Editor code and a "T" reference for the Title Index Editor code (if you recall, we used "V" references for the viewer). We can use these change-log numbers to track all the associated changes, as you have seen earlier in this book. Full accountability and auditability are built into the source code from the point at which it was frozen.

Acceptance

Monty accepted the editors at the start of Week 13, having put people onto testing them over the weekend—such was his demand to get both programs operational. One issue that occurred during acceptance testing is worth mentioning. The requirements specification was quite clear about how sounds should be handled. When a page was encountered that contained a sound track, the sound file was loaded and played. The sound was to continue playing even when the reader moved on to another page, provided the page didn't have its own sound track. The result was that, under some conditions, an inappropriate sound track might be playing over a page. For example, Page 12 might have a narration that applied only to the image on Page 12. If the narration was still playing when Page 13 was in view, then the narration might well be totally misleading. Both Monty and Samantha agreed that we had developed the software according to the requirements they had signed off on. However, they regarded the issue as quite serious, and they wanted us to take some remedial action as swiftly as possible, for which they would pay.

With a little bit of lateral thinking, we came up with a solution that didn't involve any code changes. We created a completely blank WAV file, which could be allocated to any page where the creator of the book wanted to cancel any soundtrack that might still be playing from a previous page. You can see this technique in action on the examples from the CD. Monty was prepared to accept this solution in the prototype, but we agreed to schedule a proper solution in the development of the Mark 2 editor.

The sound problem and its solution is a prime example of how, with a bit of lateral thinking, you can sometimes come up with a solution that doesn't involve any code changes. Such a solution is quick and avoids disrupting schedules. The moral is this: Before you contemplate code changes, be sure there is no other way forward.

The Page Index Editor went live a week ahead of schedule, as we had promised to try to achieve. Julie and Archie went to Montasana's site and assisted the five people Samantha had set up to start creating the E-MagBooks for the exhibition. When the time of the exhibition arrived, Monty had a considerable array of book types to demonstrate in a variety of languages. The exhibition was heralded as a great success. I completed the requirements specification for the Mark 2 Viewer on time, and Rob started development on time. But that's another story....

Chapter 12
Overview for Success

In this book, we've explored software development—from the first contact with a customer who wants us to take a concept and turn it into software, right up to setting up a desk to support the developed product in the field. In the case study, we turned the idea of an electronic book using multimedia technology into reality.

In this chapter, we'll summarize the requirements for you to win a contract, manage a project, and deliver a quality software product, on time and within budget.

In the Beginning...

Someone, somewhere has a need, which software can meet. The first stage is for that "someone" to look for and find a suitable supplier—a company capable of taking a concept and turning it into computer programs.

As a software supplier, you need to scan appropriate journals and magazines looking for prospective customers who require software development in areas in which you have expertise. After you have found a prospective client, the next stage is to have a preliminary meeting with that client to determine the potential project's top-level requirements. Your aim is to understand enough of the project to make decisions based on the following:

♦ Can we do the job?

♦ Do we want to do the job?

If the answer to both questions is "Yes," the next step is to win the business—unless the client is handing that to you on a silver plate.

A Methodology for Software Development

You can't just sit down and write software without having a working methodology behind your approach. All projects are different, and the methodology is designed to help you approach a project consistently, regardless of the nature of the work, to manage the processes involved and solve complex problems in a structured and coordinated manner.

SDLC

In this book, we have modeled a development methodology on the System Development Life Cycle (SDLC). We used a seven-phase model as the basis for our methodology:

♦ *Phase 1*—Capture the customer's requirements in the requirements specification.

♦ *Phase 2*—Analyze the requirements to gain a deeper, more technical understanding of them.

♦ *Phase 3*—Design a solution based on modular components.

♦ *Phase 4*—Develop each software module as an independent entity that can be tested in isolation, to allow verification of its functionality.

♦ *Phase 5*—Integrate all the developed modules, and test the completed system as a whole.

♦ *Phase 6*—Implement the completed, fully tested system for the customer, and allow the customer to perform formal acceptance testing.

♦ *Phase 7*—Set up a support and maintenance capability for the completed product.

During these seven phases, you will determine *what* a customer requires the software to do, and *how* you, as a supplier, will achieve a solution and define a clear path for the development and testing of a quality product.

A Phased Approach

Splitting projects into well-defined phases is essential for planning and management. The following are key attributes for a phased approach:

♦ At the end of a phase (whether a project phase or an SDLC phase), which must include a tangible deliverable, that deliverable must be verified and found consistent with and across any deliverables from earlier phases.

♦ Iteration is the key to ensuring consistency across phases.

Using SDLC as a model, you will split your project into a series of manageable project phases, each of which might encompass one or more of the SDLC phases. As you come to the end of each SDLC phase, you will have a planned deliverable. You must verify this deliverable before you can proceed to the next SDLC phase.

In some cases, verification of the output from one SDLC phase might indicate discrepancies in the output from an earlier phase. In that case, you return to the earlier phase, eliminate the discrepancy, and then continue with the current SDLC phase.

Keys to Quality

Quality is not just about testing. Quality must invade every aspect of the project. The keys to quality are the following:

- The presence and implementation of systems and procedures that ensure a high degree of consistency across all the difference facets of your business.

- A set of written standards that determine how you, as a company, develop software and control all the resultant processes.

- The ability to audit projects to indicate adherence to standards, and to prove that adherence to external auditors.

- A high degree of accountability that includes recording what happens at key decision points within a project.

- The ability to determine, from the written records, where a project went wrong, and to ensure that the errors and mistakes of previous projects are not repeated in future projects.

- For each project, a tailor-made, quality plan exists that defines what standards will be applied to the project and how those standards will be policed.

Planning

To make the methodology work for you, you need a project plan for each project you undertake. This plan must be capable of providing the following:

- Clear indications of personnel requirements across the life of the project.

- Built-in contingency time to allow you to manage problems without affecting the key delivery dates.

- A series of well-defined milestones, which represent key dates by which you must produce certain deliverables. Milestones are vital for monitoring progress.

- With respect to milestones, clear indication of the demarcation of responsibilities between customer and supplier.

Identifying Your Customer

Know who your customer is. Your customer might be an external client or an internal department. The identified customer will be the owner of the requirements specification that is produced as part of the project. Part of your job will be to keep the customer informed about the project, and to manage the customer's expectations and aspirations. As well as identifying whom the customer is, it is also important to assess the customer's level of understanding of the software development process. This understanding is necessary to avoid situations where the customer makes unrealistic technical demands. If you identify such a customer, then it will be necessary to provide a degree of education to that client with respect to your development methodology to ensure that any demands made by that client are tempered by a better understanding of the complexities involved in software development.

Armed with a suitable methodology and a knowledgeable client, you are now ready to develop professional software. Your motto should be the following: We deliver software on time and within budget.

The Pre-Sales Project Phase

Before you can start a project, you must win an order. Someone needs to give you a mandate to commit the resources to develop software. To obtain an order, you might have to execute a preliminary project phase to size the job.

Whether you are being asked to quote a cost, a timetable, or both, you need to go about the process methodically, so that, each time you commit to a cost and timetable, you arrive at consistent results. Whether or not the project will be for a fixed price, any customer will demand estimates and timetables. To establish how much a development will cost and how long it will take, you need to do a number of things, which we'll discuss next.

Preliminary Concept Meeting

In the first meeting between you and the customer, the customer will present you with an overview of the requirements. This overview can take many forms. At one end of the spectrum, you might be presented with a huge document that defines the client's requirements in detail. At the other end of the spectrum, you might attend a meeting, as in the case study, in which a hurried and ill-prepared presentation is provided, complete with hand-written diagrams. Whatever the situation, you need to absorb as much information as possible from this meeting and develop a top-level view, or understanding, of the prospective project.

Preliminary Requirements and Analysis

From the information you receive at the concept meeting, you need to perform a preliminary execution of SDLC Phases 1 and 2. Do sufficient work to achieve the following:

♦ Produce a list of key functional requirements.

♦ Define each major area of functionality from a top-level viewpoint.

♦ Get a feel for the complexity of the project.

♦ Establish a list of functional components that will service the key functional requirements; your focus should be on developing each component as an independent software entity.

♦ Identify areas of risk.

Project Activities

From your development and analysis of a preliminary set of requirements, determine a list of activities that must be executed to complete the project, as you understand it. These activities must include the following:

♦ The detailed capture of requirements into a requirements specification.

♦ The detailed analysis of the requirements.

♦ The design of a modular solution to fulfill all requirements, both immediate and future.

♦ Individual module development and testing.

♦ System integration and testing.

♦ Installation on customer site.

♦ Assistance and management of customer acceptance.

♦ Review of all SDLC phase outputs.

♦ Iteration of all SDLC phases.

♦ Development of formal test specifications.

♦ Development of user documentation and Help-text facilities.

♦ Management.

Estimates

For each of the activities you have listed, you now need to develop an estimate. Estimates consist of the following:

♦ The minimum time in which you believe the activity can be completed.

♦ The maximum time in which you believe the activity can be completed.

♦ The range, max-min, which indicates the level of uncertainty in the estimate.

♦ The type of resources required—for example, programmer, analyst, tester, and so on.

The idea behind the min-max approach is that you provide a range of effort you believe a particular activity will require; this range indicates your degree of uncertainty in the estimate. Whether you quote a fixed price or a ballpark figure, always use the min-max approach.

Your breakdown of the software's required functionality into self-contained, functional entities will allow you to estimate for the design and development activities with a reasonable level of precision. You can supply a max-min figure for each individual module and summarize the figures to establish numbers for the complete activity.

Risk Identification

From the estimates and your better understanding of the top-level requirements the preliminary analysis produces, you can identify the potential risks associated with the project. Risks take many forms, from financial risks to technical risks.

Risk Reduction

For areas of technical risk, you can conduct or propose feasibility studies to minimize such risks. For other forms of risks, you will need either to take suitable action to minimize the risk, or to take those risks into account in your project estimates and costing.

Costing Strategy

If you are lucky, the customer will pay for the time you take to complete the project. This arrangement places the risk clearly on the customer and, consequently, tends to be a rare situation. You will find most such agreements in projects that deal with the unknown, on the leading edge of technology, where a "research" philosophy is required. Nevertheless, plans and estimates are still relevant—even when the customer is paying for time.

In most cases, the customer wants a fixed price or a ballpark price (that is, a reasonable estimate). In either case, you can do all your estimating on the min-max principal. Provide fixed prices only when you are confident you can deliver. Otherwise, provide a min-max, and indicate that after you have a better understanding of the requirements, you will quote a fixed price that you guarantee will lie somewhere within the min-max range. When a customer demands a fixed price, despite your reservation, quote a price with which you are comfortable based on all the information available to you, and using a commercial judgment based on how much you want the work, and whether or not it will lead to further work.

The Proposal, Plan, and Quotation

The culmination of the pre-sales project phase is the production of a proposal, plan, and quotation. The proposal is used to:

♦ Indicate the top-level requirements, which define the extent of supply (what is to be delivered in terms of functionality) for the project.

♦ Indicate any limitations to the extent of supply.

The plan is used to:

♦ Indicate when things will happen, and facilitate accurate progress monitoring.

♦ Indicate how long each activity will take.

♦ Indicate required resource levels.

♦ Indicate milestone events.

♦ Indicate key responsibilities between supplier and customer for meeting milestones.

The quotation is used to:

◆ Indicate a fixed price for completion of the project, where applicable.

◆ Indicate a min-max price range for project completion.

◆ Indicate the conditions under which a min-max pricing strategy is applicable.

◆ Indicate payment timetable and terms.

Management of Pre-Sales Phase

You can have many activities to manage in the pre-sales phase. Much coordination will also likely be needed between the pre-sales team and the customer. On a large project, the pre-sales phase might be a mini-project all its own.

Typically, when a short time is allocated to perform the necessary work to develop a proposal, a plan, and a quote, you will break down the activities into tasks and plan for completion of one or more tasks within a day, if possible. You can then monitor progress simply by determining whether or not a given day's tasks have been completed.

The quote you provide is based on your understanding of the requirements. You must reflect this understanding in the proposal. A potential problem is that the customer changes the goal posts in terms of requirements, but still expects you, as a supplier, to meet your quoted timetable and costs. You need to manage such a situation so that you can modify the contractual context of the project to take into account the shifting goal posts. This management might involve iteration of part or all of the pre-sales phases.

An Unsuccessful Bid

If your proposal, plan, and quote fail to get you the business, you need to find out why, so that you can modify your approach for the next time. Most customers are quite willing to discuss why you failed to get an order; quite often, the reason is something completely outside your control.

Because whether or not you will be successful in a bid is uncertain, make sure you do only enough work to produce a realistic quote. Don't get bogged down in masses of detail. Record the result of the bid and the reasons why you failed, so that others can learn from the experience.

The Successful Bid

Even if you are successful, finding out why the opposition was rejected is worthwhile. You never know, but you might pick up invaluable information that you can use to good advantage in your next encounter with the rivals.

If your bid is successful, don't start work until you have a clear commitment from the customer in the form of an order. If you do start work early, make sure that you are not putting yourselves at risk. Taking the word of your contact in the customer's company is one thing, but, until you have that company's written commitment in the form of an official order, you put yourself and your own organization at risk. After you receive the order, you are ready to start the project, which you will deliver on time and within budget.

NOTE: *I've highlighted in Chapters 1 and 2 much of what we've reviewed to this point. In the pre-sales phase of winning the order for the E-MagBook software development, the case study also illustrates the processes required.*

Project Start-Up

Project start-up is the point at which you can gather together all the key stakeholders who will be involved in the project and explain the project to them. Your explanation will be only at a high level. The fundamental attributes of a project start up are:

♦ To introduce all the principal stakeholders to the project's terms of reference, based on the proposal and plan you produced in the pre-sales phase, and on the detail of the received order.

♦ To introduce each stakeholder on the project and indicate each person's function and the chain of command.

♦ To indicate when in the project's life-cycle stakeholders will be required.

♦ To introduce the quality plan and quality audit program.

♦ To set up a more detailed plan for getting the project started in a way that you can monitor progress.

You should keep start-up meetings—indeed, all meetings—short. You should attempt to discover what the key issues are before you hold a meeting, so that those involved have already discussed the nature of the issue and determined a way forward by the time you hold the meeting. That way, meetings become productive points in the project where information can be disseminated and informed decisions made without going over all the underlying detail, which everyone has already addressed outside the meeting. After the start-up meeting has occurred, Phase 1 of the project can commence.

Capturing the Requirements

The first phase of the project usually includes the capture and detailed analysis of the requirements. Thus, the first project phase tends to consist of the first two phases of the SDLC, together with iteration between the phases to produce two consistent sets of SDLC outputs—that is, the requirements document and the results of analysis.

The Requirements Specification

The requirements specification is the most important project document of all. The major characteristics of the requirements document are as follows:

♦ Regardless who the author is, the customer owns the document.

♦ The document is written in plain English; domain experts and software engineers alike must be able to understand it.

- The document must be devoid of any computer jargon. Where jargon of any form is used (including application-domain terminology), terms and acronyms must be fully explained.

- The document defines the extent of supply of the software to be developed and can, therefore, be used as a contractual document.

- When disputes arise concerning the delivered functionality, the requirements specification is the sole arbiter.

- The document can be used to temper the customer's expectations by defining limitations and restrictions, as well as required functionality.

- If possible, the document should contain application scenarios, which describe how a user would employ the software.

- If possible, the document should contain form prototypes to show how the functionality is required using the Graphical User Interface (GUI).

- The document can be used to bring anyone—manager, programmer, tester, and so on—up to speed in terms of the required software's functionality.

- The document possesses a version number and contains a "change log" in which every change is defined in full. Changes include modifications, additions, and deletions to the original requirements specification.

- Future requirements that are likely to influence the design of the current project must be outlined in the requirements specification to avoid compromising the design.

The requirements specification defines the extent of supply in that it specifies all the functionality that the customer wants from the software. The document defines this functionality in the language of the application domain. For example, in the case study, the application domain was that of electronic books.

Earlier in the book, I introduced the concept of application scenarios, based on OOP use cases, which serve as alternative descriptions to augment the requirements specifications. Together, the requirements specifications and application scenarios present a solid foundation on which to build software. I have also advocated the use of form prototypes in the requirements specification, because the prototypes focus the customer's attention on the functionality in a way that relates to the actual software solution (as the case study highlighted).

Challenging and Evolving the Requirements

You should be constantly challenging your understanding of the requirements. You discover most about the requirements in the analysis phase. When you discover discrepancies or omissions, you must update the requirements specification. If the document has been frozen, then you can change it only in a controlled way that involves your change-control procedures. The content of the requirements document evolves from your initial understanding of the project in the pre-sales phase to the final version, when you have completed the analysis. The document continues to evolve as you learn more about the nature of the project.

Managing the Capturing Process

The capturing process can be quite haphazard, as the case study demonstrated. The more work you do, the more you might need to modify your original premise. Consequently, management of this process can be quite difficult. The key aspects of capturing the requirements are to ensure that you have sufficient time to review the completed document, and time to make changes. Review and change time need to be available after your first pass through the requirements document, and then again after your analysis.

In the case study, the analysis had a profound impact on the requirements document and required considerable time for modifications to the document to accommodate aspects of the analysis. If you are unable to assess progress yourself, you will have to put pressure on the people performing the work to keep you informed, which can be a delicate situation. The more effort you put into understanding the requirements, the more respect you will earn. If you can contribute to the process, that's even better. But, as a manager, you must avoid becoming a hindrance. If that happens, you will find that controlling the project's participants becomes difficult.

Analyzing the Requirements

Analyzing is all about breaking something down and splitting it into its component parts. In the case of a software project, you are putting the requirements under the microscope.

The analysis techniques we used in this book involved the following:

♦ Analyzing the key data entities and their relationships.

♦ Analyzing the required programs' input and output requirements.

♦ Analyzing the key states in which a program could operate, and the events that caused the program to change from one state to another.

♦ Breaking down the requirements into generic, self-contained components.

♦ Developing prototype forms to analyze how the GUI was to be used.

The result of analysis is a set of alternative descriptions that show the requirements from different viewpoints.

During the analysis process, your understanding of the requirements is likely to evolve quite dramatically. Consequently, using the outputs from analysis to assess the correctness of the requirements documentation is essential. When you encounter discrepancies and anomalies, you must rectify them.

Management of Analysis Phase

Management of the analysis phase is similar to what you needed to do to manage the capturing of requirements. You must ensure sufficient time to review the requirements and analysis documents together, so that both sets of output are consistent. The more you can contribute to the actual analysis process without becoming a hindrance, the easier you will find the process is to manage. To reiterate, you must not move on to design until you have total consistency between the requirements document and the result of analysis.

Designing the Solution

When you have verified the requirements documentation and the output from analysis, you can move on to the design phase. Following are the key elements for design:

♦ The design considers the complete system, including future functionality that is not required in the current project, but that will be developed later.

♦ Each of the self-contained, functional entities identified in analysis is designed as a single, self-contained module.

Design with the intention of specifying building blocks, each of which is an independent entity that you can develop and test in isolation from the rest of the system. Design must, therefore, encompass how the various components interface with each other; that way, programmers can develop a given module with full understanding of how it must interact with the rest of the system. Without this knowledge, a programmer cannot be expected to develop a module so that it will integrate correctly into the completed system environment.

Management of the Design Phase

Because the project design works from a list of functional entities established in analysis, you have a reasonable yardstick with which to measure progress. You can check to see which items have been completed, and at what time. You can obtain estimates for completion of each module, and you can revise the estimates, if necessary, as the design phase moves forward, fine-tuning the new estimates from your experience gained.

If you treat each design specification as a deliverable, you have a shopping list you can check off as the phase progresses. However, don't forget to plan for a degree of iteration. Keep a constant eye on consistency between design specifications and requirements, and the results of analysis. If you can't do this yourself, solicit opinions from those who are qualified to make such assessments.

Developing and Testing the Modules

Development centers on a list of development tasks. A given task will consist of developing one or more modules, and a test harness that lets the programmer check the functionality of each individual module. This testing must be recorded to provide accountability and quality audit information.

Typically, the development task is one a single programmer can undertake. The programmer's job consists of the following:

♦ To convert the design specification for a given module into code.

♦ To analyze the code pathways and devise a series of tests to test each possible pathway.

♦ To write sufficient code to test the developed module(s) according to the tests devised.

♦ To record the result of the tests for the development task.

Management of Development

Because the development tasks are standalone tasks, and their completion is contingent upon the programmer recording tests and results, you can verify the status of each module by asking to see the test record. For each development task, a clear deliverable can be demonstrated. As a result, you can, at least, assess whether or not a module is complete. The capability to assess individual components of the development lets you run many parallel tasks provided you keep an eye on the critical paths.

Providing the programmers with clear instructions of what you expect from them—that is, determining the tests to be conducted, and what you want them to record—is paramount. Programmers can be difficult to manage. People who are or were programmers and have good people-management skills are the best programmer managers. Nothing on earth irritates a programmer more than having a nontechnical manager asking questions the programmer regards as irrelevant. Programmers view such questions as interference, and an irritation to be removed as quickly as possible. As a defense mechanism, programmers will typically reply to questions using as much jargon and being as obscure as possible (in the hope that the manager will become so frustrated that he or she will give up and go away). Consequently, in my opinion, managing programmers is the most complex task a project manager has to perform. Even in situations in which the project manager interfaces only with a software manager or supervisor, the same problems seem to surface.

Programmers respect managers who understand their world and can talk the same language. If that doesn't describe you, find someone who is more acceptable to manage the programmers directly, and then work with that person as a buffer. Your main weapon is the "buy-in": If you can't get programmers to accept responsibility for meeting deadlines, you are doomed. Neither carrot nor stick will help if you don't have their buy-in. Never attempt to force timetables on programmers without their commitment to the timetables; in the long run, that approach just doesn't work.

As a project manager, your goal is to foster an ethos of success and avoid the downward spiral into acceptance of late delivery as the normal state of affairs. At times, you might need to "sell" the project to the programmers, generate enthusiasm, and *create* that ethos for success.

System Integration and Testing

When you've completed the development and testing of the respective modules, the next step is to slot together all the modules and provide any code that is needed to glue the modules into the program. You're now ready to start system integration and testing.

The following are key aspects of system integration and testing:

♦ Thanks to the modular nature of the development, the integration phase should be straightforward.

♦ Programmers should not perform system testing.

♦ Testing must be based on the acceptance test scripts as a minimum.

♦ Testing should be rigorous and uncover as many "bugs" as possible.

Never let the programmers perform system testing. You need objective, domain experts who know nothing about the underlying code. As an absolute minimum, ensure that testing is based on the acceptance testing that the customer will employ; this minimum requirement ensures that each aspect of functionality has at least one defined test. Encourage testers to use their ingenuity to "break" the system at every possible opportunity. Be sure to allow time for re-work. In essence, system testing is the time when you want your team to find as many bugs as they possibly can.

Management of Integration and Testing

If the module testing in development was successful, and the design specifications were accurate, integration should be a relatively straightforward operation. You can judge progress by the number of bugs the testers are finding each day (or hour, as applicable). You should expect the rate at which the testers discover bugs to be high initially, and then to start dropping off. Monitor this trend frequently. In particular, make note of the rate after the development team has released a new, corrected version of the software for testing.

Build a list of bugs until continued testing is no longer possible. Halt testing and give the bug list to development. After the new release is ready, in addition to testing specific fixes, make sure that testers perform regression testing to ensure that the application of fixes has not damaged previously working functionality.

One particular thing to look out for is the reappearance of apparently "fixed bugs" in later releases. Finding such bugs is an indication that version control is breaking down. Ideally, the product is ready when no more bugs appear; practically, at some stage, you might have to decide that you can release the product for customer acceptance with certain acceptable constraints. Where you must release an imperfect product, solicit opinions and assessments from your key stakeholders, with a commitment to making a pragmatic, balanced judgment. Keep the customer informed.

Customer Acceptance

With your help, the customer now has the opportunity to test the software. The key aspects of acceptance testing are the following:

♦ The software is tested against an accepted test plan and test scripts.

♦ The customer performs the testing.

♦ The testing should reveal no bugs.

♦ The supplier manages any issues that arise.

♦ The requirements specification is the sole arbiter of issues concerning delivered functionality.

Management of Acceptance

When you manage the client's acceptance of the product, you are managing the client's expectations. If issues with the software exist that you already know about, come clean, and define the context in which the testing is to take place. If the project has gone according to plan, the only issues you should be dealing with are those of functionality. This is where the requirements specification and the testing specifications are your main weapons. Record all issues, even if they are resolved on-site. Respond to all issues formally as soon as you can, so a written record of the outcome exists.

Your fundamental aim in acceptance testing is to get the client to a position where he or she will sign off on the delivery. You can achieve this goal with or without reservation by the client. In situations in which the client has reservations, be sure you have documented those reservations.

Project Documentation

From start to end, projects generate lots of documentation. Here's a typical list of the sort of documentation you might find:

♦ *Project Terms of Reference*—This is the top-level documentation that tells you what the project is all about. Typically, you can create the Project Terms of Reference from the proposal, the quotation, and the preliminary plan, as well as the order detail.

♦ *Contractual Correspondence File*—This file contains all correspondence of a contractual nature between customer and supplier (and any other parties involved).

♦ *Non-Contractual Correspondence File*—This file contains all non-contractual, usually technical, correspondence between customer and supplier.

♦ *Project Plans*—These are the detailed project plans for all phases. These plans can be altered only through a change-control procedure.

♦ *Quality Plan*—This plan includes the details concerning the standards to apply to aspects of the project, and details about when audits will occur to check for adherence to the designated standards. This plan can be changed only through a change-control procedure.

♦ *Requirements Specification*—This is the document that defines the functionality the customer requires. The corresponding file can also hold the results of the analysis and scenarios. You can modify this documentation only through a change-control procedure.

♦ *Design Specifications*—These are the documents that define the structure of the system. This documentation can be modified only through a change-control procedure.

♦ *Test Scripts and Results*— All tests that are executed must be recorded. Test scripts can be modified only through a change-control procedure.

♦ *Risk Assessment and Analysis Reports*—This group of documentation includes all aspects of risk handling.

♦ *Issue Log*—This log contains a documented account of each project issue, the issue "owner," its status, and its resolution.

♦ *Change Log*—This is a documented log of all changes requested for any project aspect.

♦ *Reviews*—These include reports and so on that detail the result of reviews conducted on any aspect of the project, from the state of the requirements specification to a performance review of testing.

♦ *Audit Reports*—These reports are the results of the audits. When recommendations are made because of breaches of standards and the like, such recommendations must be monitored.

And most projects will have other, miscellaneous documentation as well.

A lot of documentation accompanies software projects. The bug logs and issue logs that we created in the case study are just specific instances of issue logs. The change logs we recorded in the software are specific instances of change logs. How the documentation is arranged is a matter for the project managers to determine, but a key aspect of project documentation is that it is accessible to the project team as a whole. And tying all the documentation together can be quite a challenge.

The first "port of call" for anyone interested in a project is the Project Terms of Reference. This file provides the project background, and a reader should be able to determine from the file where to look next in the project documentation for a specific area of interest.

Issue Management and Change Control

Projects are not static entities. They change their nature and their course throughout their life cycle. Issue management and change control are the formal methods by which you can control the meandering of a software project. Your aim is to leave behind a documented trail of what issues arose and how they were dealt with. All projects should maintain an issue log and a change log. These logs recount the birth, life, and demise of every issue and change that affected the project, and they afford good accountability. The issue log and change log are key aspects of project documentation.

Issue Management

All issues that arise in a project must be managed. Key aspects of issue management are the following:

♦ All issues are recorded in the project issue log.

♦ Each issue has an identifiable owner.

♦ The issue log is monitored regularly, and each issue is periodically reassessed in terms of its impact on the project.

♦ The priority of an issue, in terms of its resolution, can be altered according to circumstances.

♦ All relevant stakeholders must be kept informed of issues and their status.

First, you must record issues in the project's issue log. You must periodically review issues to determine whether they have been addressed. When issues have not been dealt with, you must frequently reassess their urgency so that you can alter their priority as appropriate. Ensure that someone owns the issue. This ownership provides you with a contact so you can monitor the issue's progress.

Never assume an issue is being resolved satisfactorily without periodically checking on its progress. Good project management involves constantly checking the state of issues and reassessing their impact on the project. You can get early warning of impending catastrophe only if you ask the right questions frequently. Don't expect people to volunteer information that things are going wrong well in advance.

When you're reviewing the progress of issues, always record your findings in the project files. The issue log tells the project's history. As I've already indicated, this log is one of the most important aspects of project management in terms of controlling the project and learning from experience gained.

Change Control

When changes are required to any aspect of a project, make sure that a written change request exists that defines who is asking for the change and what the change consists of. The request must be available in a project change log. Change requests are frequently the outcome of an issue logged in the issue log. Key aspects for change control are the following:

♦ All changes are initiated with a formal change request recorded in the project's change log.

♦ All change requests are assessed and prioritized.

♦ Changes that are to be implemented are authorized by the relevant stakeholders, and then properly planned into the project.

♦ Changes are implemented and completed in a controlled manner.

Once a change request has been logged, performing an assessment of a change, checking its impact on the project, and so on might be necessary. Make sure such assessments are documented in the project change log. A proposed change might have timetable and/or financial repercussions. Consequently, project management (together with appropriate stakeholders) must authorize any change the project team chooses to implement. The last thing you want to see is someone instigating a change that delays delivery of the software without the appropriate stakeholders, particularly the customer, knowing about the impact. Monitor the progress of a change request that is being implemented so you can close the request as "completed" when that is appropriate.

Fostering a Good Development Ethos

A key role in the project management of a software development is to foster a good development ethos within the organization. The most essential component of this ethos is a culture based on success. If each programmer believes that to deliver on time is good, you are more likely to get a "buy-in" to a project than if the programmer believes all software projects are late. A culture based on success can evolve only if that success is repeated, over and over again.

Another key aspect to fostering a good development ethos is acceptance of the "buy-in" principle. It's worth pointing out that programmers usually react well to being given responsibility. Possibly, the most important aspect of all is to follow a methodology that achieves a high degree of consistency across a team composed of many people with differing levels of ability, enthusiasm, commitment, and so on. (Remember, no one said it was going to be easy.)

Conclusion

A project is a team effort. As a team member, you have responsibilities to others, and vice versa. The success of a project is determined by the collective attitude, ability, productivity, and commitment of all its constituent personnel. A project is only as strong as its weakest component. If you think programming can be difficult, just reflect on what project management requires to turn a concept into a software product.

And, Finally, the E-MagBook

The project is still growing. Monty's looking at differently sized versions of the product. He wants one E-MagBook to hold maps and drawings, so that it can be used as a portable drawing viewer to replace huge rolls of paper. He has another version that he wants as a portable document viewer to hold all forms of scanned-in paperwork, accessible by key words. He also has a demonstration of a learning aid that provides assessment of an individual's learning ability from a question-and-answer session, based on what that person has been taught by the device. Another version on the drawing board comes with a digital camera—specifically, as a photograph album. He also wants to produce a multimedia electronic diary. In Figures 12.1 and 12.2, you can see the hardware of an E-MagBook running on the tabletop, using a 640×480-pixel display.

We now have from 4 to 12 people working on the project at any given time. And Monty's still coming up with new requirements, but they're all being handled in the same way, from concept to deployment.

There's the phone again. It's Monty once more...something about Arabic and Chinese character sets....

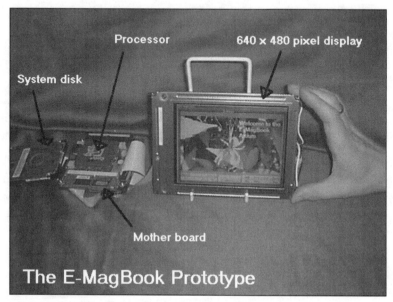

Figure 12.1
The E-MagBook internal hardware components.

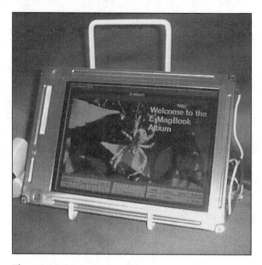

Figure 12.2
Close-up of the E-MagBook miniature display.

Appendix A
Feasibility Study

This appendix contains a record of the feasibility study I mentioned in Chapter 2. It also serves as an introduction to image and multimedia handling for readers who are unfamiliar with these aspects of VB. This Appendix will let you follow the E-MagBook case study in more detail.

The Image and Multimedia Feasibility Study

When we were in the presales stage of the project to develop software for the E-MagBook, both Julie and Archie were concerned about the complexities of handling images and multimedia files. Because neither had any experience in these areas, they would have a problem trying to estimate the amount of work required to fulfill these requirements. We had identified their inexperience as a major area of technical risk. Consequently, we had decided to spend half a day exploring the issues. In particular, we wanted to answer the following questions:

◆ How can we easily load and scale images onto defined screen areas?

◆ How can we easily load and run video clips on screen?

◆ How can we easily load and play sound or music files?

This analysis would set the scene for what we had to do. Because I had quite a lot of experience in both image handling and multimedia file use, I would try to get Archie and Julie up to speed as quickly as possible, and then we would check out the feasibility of developing code to answer the preceding questions.

A Quick Look at Image File Formats

We first had to learn a little about images. Images can be stored in a variety of file structures, the two most common being Microsoft's BMP format and what is often called JPEG format. Mixing the appropriate intensities of the primary colors—red, green, and blue—can create any color. The BMP format is a simple format in which each pixel (each addressable point on the screen) is assigned three, 8-bit values that define the intensity of each primary color at that point on the display. Mixing the appropriate intensity for each primary color at each pixel generates a screen image from a BMP file. A value of 0 represents zero intensity (black), and a value of 255 is peak intensity for a color. Pure black consists of a combined set of values of 0,0,0 (no red, no green, no blue) and white is defined as 255,255,255 (maximum red, maximum green, maximum blue). The file-storage requirements to hold images, consequently, become quite considerable. For example, if a picture is scanned at 500x500 pixels, the disk file will be 500x500x3=750,000 bytes (remember, three bytes are required for each pixel stored). An 800x600-pixel picture would require well over 1MB of disk space.

As Julie pointed out, an 800x600-pixel picture would just fit on a 3.5-inch diskette. She went on to point out that most of the images on her PC were much smaller than that. When I asked what file extension those files had, she replied that she thought their extension was JPG. This brings us neatly to JPEG. A body known as the Joint Photographic Experts Group (JPEG) has developed compression algorithms that discard color information the human eye cannot detect. In their simplest form, these algorithms take groups of similar colors and con-vert those colors to a common hue. What makes JPEG outstanding is that you can vary the amount of compression. This is not really the place to go into detail, but JPEG provides very good data compression, which leads to smaller file sizes. You must appreciate, however, that, with the compression, you lose data. The eye might not be able to see the loss; nevertheless, a reconstructed image is not as good as the original. If you want to do any specialized image analysis, you need all the data. If you're interested in only *looking* at images, the JPEG format (indicated by the JPG file extension) is more than adequate.

Samantha talked about "high quality" images that could be enlarged to reveal portions of the whole, and these images would probably be BMP files. They would likely be much bigger than the 640x480-pixel resolution available to us from the E-MagBook's screen size. So, in terms of functionality, we needed to be able to handle very large files that could be scaled to fit on the available screen area.

Under normal conditions, you wouldn't choose the development language for a project until after you had captured and analyzed the requirements and, ideally, after you had completed the design phase. However, the image and multimedia requirements had led me to believe that VB was more than up to this particular task. So, we'd use my experience to determine how we'd handle the images using VB; at the same time, we'd keep open minds, because VB might not be the final choice. We needed to keep our options open.

VB possesses two controls that display images. We could explore the capabilities of those controls and see whether they could accommodate our requirement. This approach would give Archie and Julie confidence that we could engineer a solution using VB or any other language that has similar tools.

VB's Picture and Image Controls to the Rescue

Two controls, or screen objects, handle bitmapped images in VB—the **Picture** control and the **Image** control. The **Picture** control is referred to as a "heavyweight," because it contains a lot of inherent functionality. You can load images, and you can draw graphics on the control as well, using a variety of graphical methods. As a result, and as you would expect, the **Picture** control is resource hungry. The second control, the **Image** control, is much lighter and less resource hungry—for starters, it supports no graphics.

Loading an image is easy. Let's start by setting up a browser to load a selected file into a **Picture** control. We'll set the **Picture** control so that it automatically takes on the actual size of the stored image. The code for the browser is straightforward, and you are probably familiar with it, but, just to be on the safe side, I'll go through the code in detail.

Start up a new VB EXE project on your computer. First, you need to select the common dialog box from the VB toolbar and create an instance of a dialogue box on your form. Then, drop a **Picture** box and a command button onto the form. The result should be like what you see in Figure A.1.

An important aspect of using any computer language in a commercial organization is adhering to standards. Doing so is of vital importance to quality assurance. One of our company standards is that we use Hungarian notation, so I've called the common dialog control **dlgDialog1**, the **Picture** control **picPicture1**, and the command button **cmdLoad**. Now, we need to put the code into the command button, to invoke the common dialog control to let us select a file to load into the picture control.

Place this code in the command button's click event:

```
Private Sub cmdLoad_Click()
  dlgDialog1.Action = 1
  picPicture1 = LoadPicture(dlgDialog1.FileName)
End Sub
```

And that's all we need to invoke the dialog box, allow the user to select a file name, and load the file into the **Picture** control. Try it out and see what happens.

You can use the file \E-MAGBOOK\IMAGES\DUCK_2.JPG on the CD. Alternatively, you can select any image file on your PC—BMP, JPEG, whatever you fancy; the **Picture** control supports a wide range of graphical formats. When Julie tried setting up the screen, she complained that the screen was showing her only the top bit of the image. You can see what Julie's screen looked like in Figure A.2.

Julie's control was clipping the image. The container as we'd set it up wasn't big enough to show the whole image. Now, change the **Autosize** property on the **Picture** control from **False** to **True**, and then rerun the program and load that same image. You can see the result of Julie's second attempt in Figure A.3.

Julie complained that the image was still not correct, so I told her to make the form bigger. She did so by pulling the bottom, right-hand edge of the form using the mouse cursor, increasing the height and width of the window—and, low and behold, the entire image came into view, as you can see in Figure A.4.

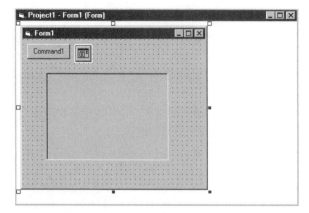

Figure A.1
First stage of image-handling prototype program.

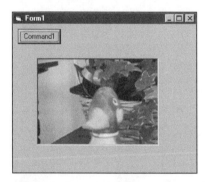

Figure A.2
Julie's screen with her first attempt at loading DUCK_2.JPG.

Figure A.3
Julie's screen with the **Picture** control's **Autosize** property set to **True**.

Figure A.4
Julie's expanded form showing the full-sized image.

At last, the screen displayed the entire image. To appreciate the inherent capabilities of this control, you need to understand what happened—all part of the learning process. When Julie first ran the program, the **Picture** control was set with the **Autosize** property set to **False**. The image was loaded into the control, which had its height and width fixed. The area wasn't big enough to show the whole image, so it looked clipped. Then, Julie set the **Autosize** property to **True** and reran the program. This time, the image loaded, and the control changed size automatically to match the dimensions of the bitmapped image. Unfortunately, the form wasn't big enough to show the whole **Picture** control. Expanding the form's size revealed the entire image.

What we've learned from this very simple exercise is that the **Picture** control's **Autosize** property will ensure that any image we load will be placed on the screen at full size. If the image is too big for the screen to hold, the screen does what you saw before the form was stretched—it shows as much of the image as it can in the available area. If the form is maximized to full screen, and the image still doesn't fit, that's it. You get to see only what the screen can fit into the available space. But that's not what we wanted. In this project, we would have images that would be much bigger than the available display area of 640x480 pixels, so how could we guarantee that the whole picture would fit into the available area?

It's All to Do with Aspect Ratio

Go back to your demo, and remove the **Picture** control. Replace the **Picture** control with an **Image** control, name it **imgImage1**, and change the code reference from **picPicture1** to **imgImage1** in **cmdLoad_Click**. Set the dimensions to approximately those

Figure A.5
Julie's form after she had changed the picture control to an image control, rerun the program, and reloaded her image.

you see in Figure A.5. Change the **Stretch** property of the **Image** control to **True**, and then run the program, and load the same image. When Julie followed these steps, her form now looked like the one in Figure A.5.

This time, the full image had been squeezed into a fixed-size **Image** control such that the bitmapped image filled the form exactly, with no attempt at keeping the aspect ratio constant—hence, the distortion.

Aspect ratio is the ratio of an image's width to its height. If you change the size of the image, either by shrinking or enlarging the image, and you make sure that the ratio of the new width to the new height is the same as the original ratio of width to height, you prevent distortion. In this case, the width had been expanded to fill the image container's width, and the height had been reduced to make the image fit in the container's height. The overall result was that the aspect ratio no longer matched the original aspect ratio, and the picture was distorted.

Scaling an Image to Fit into a Fixed Area

We were now getting close to one of our requirements. We needed to be able to load an image, regardless of its true dimensions, and make it fit into a defined screen area. That area might or might not be the full-screen capability, as dictated in the screen-format diagrams we had produced.

We first needed to define to the program the maximum area into which an image was to be placed. Then, when we loaded an image, we needed to find out the image's true size so we could calculate its aspect ratio. Next, we needed to scale the image to fit inside the container area available to us. In terms of the E-MagBook, we'd have one area defined for the Picture Album format and another for the Reference Book format.

Although we could have scaled the image with just the **Image** control, we'd use both the **Image** and the **Picture** controls. We could use the **Picture** control to give us the image's true dimensions by setting its **Autosize** property to **True** and loading the bitmapped image into it. We could then capture the aspect ratio from **picture.width/picture.height**. We needed to define where we wanted the final image to be placed, and what the maximum area available was to be. We could do this by sizing and positioning an **image** control at design time. When the program loaded, it would simply capture **image.width** and **image.height**, which define the maximum allowed values for any image that would be loaded. So as long as we captured these two values in a pair of variables at start-up time, we could subsequently use the **image** control to house selected bitmapped files.

At runtime, a file would be selected and loaded into the **Picture** control to get the image's aspect ratio. Then, we would check each of the image's dimensions in turn, to make sure they lay inside the allowed maximum values. If one did not, the dimension would be set to the allowed maximum value, and the other dimension would then be recalculated using the captured aspect ratio. After we had dimensions that were guaranteed to fit inside the allowable area, we could set the dimensions of the **Image** control to the calculated settings and load the bitmapped image into the **Image** container, which would have its **Stretch** property set to **True**. To put this into practice, you need to modify the prototype, as you see in Figure A.6.

The **Image** control is the larger of the two controls, and it defines where we want the final picture to be placed. The picture must fit inside this area, but with the same aspect ratio as the original picture. The smaller control on the form is the **Picture** control. Where we place the **Picture** control and what size we set the control to at design time don't matter. We must, however, set the **Autosize** property to **True**. The **Stretch** property of the **Image** control must also be set to **True**.

What now follows is the code we'd use to load the image, size it, determine the aspect ratio, calculate the new dimensions required for the image to fit into the **Image** container area, and then reload the image. Don't worry if you don't follow the code at first; we'll go through it in detail in a moment.

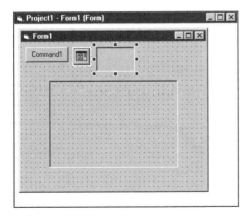

Figure A.6
The prototype form containing a **Picture** control (top of form) and an **Image** control (center of form). The **Image** control has been set to the size of the area into which all images must be displayed (that is, it defines the maximum height and width that any image may possess).

You need to place the following code in the form's general section:

```
Option Explicit
Dim sngAspectRatio As Single
Dim sngWidth As Single
Dim sngHeight As Single

Dim sngMaxWidth As Single
Dim sngMaxHeight As Single
```

Next, set up the form's **LOAD** event handler as follows:

```
Private Sub Form_Load()

  sngMaxWidth = imgImage1.Width
  sngMaxHeight = imgImage1.Height

End Sub
```

Now, enter code for the **LOAD** command-button click event handler:

```
Private Sub cmdLoad_Click()
' Capture max allowed dimensions for image display
dlgDialog1.Action = 1
picPicture1 = LoadPicture(dlgDialog1.FileName)
sngAspectRatio = picPicture1.Width / picPicture1.Height
sngWidth = picPicture1.Width
sngHeight = picPicture1.Height

Call scaleit

imgImage1.Width = sngWidth
imgImage1.Height = sngHeight
imgImage1 = picPicture1

End Sub
```

And, finally, insert the routine to perform the scaling:

```
Sub scaleit()
' Scale dimensions of image to fit inside allowed area
' on entry sngWidth and sngHeight set to original values
' on exit, they will be set to scaled values that will fit in area
' sngMaxWidth and sngMaxHeight define allowed area
```

```
' 1. Check width lies inside container
If sngWidth > sngMaxWidth Then
        sngWidth = sngMaxWidth
        sngHeight = sngWidth / sngAspectRatio
End If

' 2. Check height lies inside container
If sngHeight > sngMaxheight Then
        sngHeight = sngMaxheight
        sngWidth = sngHeight * sngAspectRatio
End If

End
```

Before you run the code, check that the **Picture** control has **.AutoSize** set to **True** and **.Visible** set to **False**. Remember, we're using the code only to size the file. We don't need to see the image while the program performs the sizing operation, we're just using this technique as a measuring tool. Also, check that the **Image** control's **Stretch** property is set to **true**.

Run the program, and load a few different images. You should find that the images load onto the screen such that they always fit within the original container area we set up at design time. Note that the **Left** and **Top** settings are the same as the design-time settings for the **Image** control, because we have made no attempt to center the bitmapped image in the container area.

By way of explanation, let's start with the data settings. Another of our VB development standards is to always use **Option Explicit**. Doing so ensures that the compiler traps any errors created by the programmer's "finger trouble," or any spelling mistakes he or she makes when typing variable names. Using **Option Explicit** saves time in the long run, even though using it means that you have to declare every single variable you use. (If you recall, in Chapter 1, we talked about quality standards. Always using **Option Explicit** and Hungarian notation are examples of programming standards. Part of quality assurance is ensuring that programmers adhere to these standards.)

We set up the following code in the general section of the form:

```
Option Explicit
Dim sngAspectRatio As Single
Dim sngWidth As Single
Dim sngHeight As Single

Dim sngMaxWidth As Single
Dim sngMaxHeight As Single
```

We had an aspect ratio (**sngAspectRatio**), two variables that would be used to set up the width and height of an image (**sngWidth** and **sngHeight**), and two variables to define the maximum values that the final versions would be allowed to hold (**sngMaxWidth** and **sngMaxHeight**). (Yet another of our programming standards is that we use variable names that are meaningful, which helps to cut down on unnecessary comments.)

Next came the form's load-event code:

```
Private Sub Form_Load()
' Capture max allowed dimensions for image display
 sngMaxWidth = imgImage1.Width
 sngMaxHeight = imgImage1.Height

End Sub
```

The form load event is being used to capture the maximum dimensions for the image on screen. The event is grabbing the most recent values that were assigned to the **Image** control at design time. This procedure is a useful trick to remember, and a neat way to define an area on screen. Set up the **Image** control where and in what sort of area you would like the bitmapped image to appear. After it has captured these important parameters, the code can do what it likes to the **Image** control. Now, let's look at the LOAD button event handler:

```
Private Sub cmdLoad_Click()

 dlgDialog1.Action = 1
 picPicture1 = LoadPicture(dlgDialog1.FileName)
 sngAspectRatio = picPicture1.Width / picPicture1.Height
 sngWidth = picPicture1.Width
 sngHeight = picPicture1.Height

 Call scaleit

 imgImage1.Width = sngWidth
 imgImage1.Height = sngHeight
 imgImage1 = LoadPicture(dlgDialog1.FileName)

End Sub
```

We obtain the name of the image as before and load it into the **Picture** control, as seen in the first two lines of code. The **Picture** control is set invisible, and its **Autosize** property is set to **True**. Consequently, the size expands to the size of the bitmapped image, even though the control is invisible. We then calculate the aspect ratio from the **Picture** control's **Width** and **Height** properties and store that calculation in **sngAspectRatio**. Remember, this is the full-sized image's aspect ratio. We also set the first attempts at the final width and height, (that is, the dimensions we will use to display the image) as the full-size measurements. Then, we call subroutine **scaleit** to alter these sizes if they are too big to fit into the maximum allowed area. The routine will adjust the values until both values are less than or equal to their corresponding maximum allowed values. The program then uses these modified values to set up the dimensions of the empty **Image** control. Note that the **Image** control's **Left** and **Top** properties are untouched. Because the **Image** control's **Stretch** property is set to **True**. when the image is loaded, the bitmapped image is squeezed into the area to fill it completely. The resulting image has the correct aspect ratio displayed in the allowed container area. Whatever the size of the image was, the final image will be scaled to fit within the defined area.

The clever programming is all done here, in the subroutine **Scaleit**, which we'll look at bit by bit:

```
Sub scaleit()
' Scale dimensions of image to fit inside allowed area
' on entry sngWidth and sngHeight set to original values
' on exit, they will be set to scaled values that will fit in area
' sngMaxWidth and sngMaxHeight define allowed area
```

As the comments indicate, the routine begins with the width and height already set to those of the full-sized, bitmapped image. At this stage, we don't know whether that size is too big to fit in the container.

```
' 1. Check width lies inside container
If sngWidth > sngMaxWidth Then
        sngWidth = sngMaxWidth
        sngHeight = sngWidth / sngAspectRatio
End If
```

First, we check the width setting and see whether it is bigger than the maximum allowed by the design-time-defined maximum width. If it is, we shrink the setting to the maximum allowed value and recalculate the height accordingly, to keep a constant aspect ratio. With this code, we have a width that is guaranteed to fit into the available area.

```
' 2. Check height lies inside container
If sngHeight > sngMaxHeight Then
        sngHeight = sngMaxHeight
        sngWidth = sngHeight * sngAspectRatio
End If

End
```

When we enter the second section, we know, for sure, that the width now fits the allowed container, so we check the height. If it fits, great; if it does not, we shrink it to the maximum permissible value and recalculate the width. This technique gets us a pair of dimensions that are guaranteed to fit inside the defined container area. Archie went a bit further. He had reduced the size of his "allowed" area to the size of a postage stamp and was loading the area with large images. We knew they were large because he had modified the code slightly. He had put in two buttons. The first button loaded the selected bitmapped image into a visible **Picture** control so that he could see the original size, and a second button control completed the process by removing the **Picture** control, sizing the necessary **Image** control, as defined earlier, and loading it. The effects were quite impressive.

This exercise made both Julie and Archie feel much more comfortable about the requirement to display an image on screen, regardless of its size. In fact, Julie thought sizing and displaying images was ridiculously simple—possibly because, with help from some VB screen objects, it is! It only looks difficult if you've never done anything like this before.

The valuable lesson here is to know your components. We've made the most out of two very powerful VB controls. It's also worth noting that we could replace **picPicture1** with an **Image** control as long as its **Stretch** property is set to **False**—in which case, its size, too, will expand to the size of the bitmapped image loaded. You can check this out by replacing **picPicture1** with another **Image** control called **imgPicture1**. Change all **picPicture1** references to **imgPicture1**, set the **visible** property to **False**, and try the program out. It should function exactly as before.

I tend to use the **Picture** control for the sizing operation because it has other properties that let us get the width and height in a variety of units, such as inches, centimeters, and pixels, which might be useful. What we've done here took about an hour in practice. Developing this code was very much a matter of someone who knows what he or she is doing imparting that knowledge to others. The alternative available to Julie and Archie would have been to read all the manuals and experiment with the controls to achieve the desired result. Obviously, this could have taken considerable time.

Hopefully, you can see how important this exercise has been. Julie and Archie now knew how a suitable programming environment, with the correct components or tools, could give them the capability to load and manipulate images as needed for the project. With this feasibility study, they could now assess the work required for image handling with a firm understanding of the underlying technology. We also knew that VB could quite readily accommodate our requirement.

Multimedia Files

If you recall, from Samantha's talk, we also had to handle AVI movie clips, WAV sound files, and MID music files. I knew Archie knew what all these things were, but Julie had no idea.

AVI is the video-clip format Microsoft developed to display moving images. We needed to be able to handle a single video clip as a possible option to the static image for both the Picture Album and Reference Book formats. An AVI file contains a data stream. From the data stream, an initial image is loaded onto the screen in a separate form. According to timing information, also held in the file, the on-screen image is updated from disk data at a rate that is sufficient to fool the eye into thinking it is looking at continuous motion. AVI formats use compression. Compression allows a large proportion of the data to be composed of change information, indicating how the initial, fully stored, image changes in subsequent frames. This approach enormously reduces the amount of data that needs to be stored. As a further attempt to decrease the amount of data in the stream, the image sizes are often kept small. The PC has to work quite hard unpacking the information and setting up the next frame quickly enough to keep the sequence running smoothly. If you use Windows Explorer to look for an AVI file on your PC and double-click the file when you find it, your default video player will play the file in a form on the screen.

Next, let's look at WAV files, which are digital recordings of sounds. Any sound a microphone can pick up can be amplified and then *sampled*. Sampling involves converting the analog voltage produced by the microphone at a given point in time to a digital value. Just as we can use a byte to define the intensity of a primary color—somewhere between black (0) and saturated red (255), for example—we can do the same with sound. A value of 0 represents no sound, and a value of 255 represents maximum sound level. However, using only 256 sound levels doesn't produce good quality sound (this quality is often referred to as *tape quality*). To get *CD quality* sound, you need to digitize to 16 bits of resolution, which gives more than 64,000 discrete, sound-level values.

The frequency at which you sample is also important. The human ear can detect sound from a few *Hertz* (that is, cycles per second) to as much as 18,000 Hertz. To capture high-quality sound, you must digitize at least at twice the highest frequency you want to record. So, CD quality requires 16-bit digitization at a sampling rate of 40,000 Hertz.

The WAV file contains one byte, or one pair of bytes, for every single sample taken. That's 80,000 bytes for a 1-second burst of sound at CD quality. Archie commented that this fact explained why, in general, WAV files tended to be so large. The content of a WAV file can be absolutely anything. A WAV file is just a digital tape recording. MID files, on the other hand, are completely different.

The MID format was set up many years ago to allow sequencers and synthesizers to record and play back sounds that they produce. A typical PC synthesizer consists of a bank of "voices," such as trombone, oboe, harp, and so on. In the synthesizing process, you set up one or more voices, and then you use a keyboard to define the notes you want to play. The MID file captures all the events on a synthesizer as and when they occur. For example, if you press middle C, the event is "Start Middle C." When you take your finger off the note, the event generated is "End Middle C." Because the events are time stamped, all you need in the file to play middle C for any time period are two, timestamped event messages. To do the equivalent in a WAV file, you would have to digitize for the full period of time, creating 80,000 bytes at CD quality for every second the note was held down. Typically, the size of a MID event message is only 3 bytes.

So, a MID file consists of sequential events, each containing the appropriate timing information to indicate when the event is to be actioned. If you use eight fingers to play a chord, you generate eight single events, which are recorded one after the other with the same timestamp into the MID file. The event stream can then be used to play back the music by directing it to a device that can translate MID event streams.

There we have it—AVI, WAV, and MID files. AVI is played onto screen in a separate form, as you can see using Explorer and double-clicking any AVI file. WAV data streams are played through a PC's digital-to-analog converter subsystem, in which the original waveform is reconstructed from the numbers onto a loud speaker. The MID data stream is directed to the PC's sequencer and results in synthesized music. Each format is handled by a completely independent subsystem. By the way, the two sound channels actually have their own volume controls.

Meeting the Multimedia Requirements

So much for the theory—let's return to our requirements in the E-MagBook. We had already determined that a given page might have either a WAV file or a MID file playing. In theory, because the two types of files are played by separate subsystems, they could be played together. In fact, we weren't sure whether Monty would require this option. We couldn't find any references in our notes to sound and music being played together or separately. So, we called Monty to clarify the situation. He was quite adamant that, because of the problems involved with trying to synchronize the two sound sources, for the time being, the requirement would be for one type or the other. But, like all good customers, he put in the proviso that the requirement might change in the future. He pointed out that music or speech can be incorporated into a WAV file—after all, it's just a recording from a microphone. So, if they wanted music and narration, they would record both together in a WAV file. But, we might have a future requirement to enable the program to play both file types at the same time. This was another future requirement that the design must consider.

To consider the feasibility of handling multimedia, we were again going to call on VB. We now had come to one of the most impressive VB components you will come across—the VB **Multimedia** control—available in the Professional and Enterprise versions of VB. Let's start by adding two **Multimedia** controls to the prototype in your sample project—one control for the video channel and one control for sound. We can play a video at the same time a sound is being played back, but this capability requires two separate instances of the **Multimedia** control, unless the sound is coded into the AVI file as an auxiliary WAV data stream. In that case, the AVI file contains a video data stream played through the video player software, and a WAV data stream played through the sound subsystem. We can accomplish all this using a single **Multimedia** control.

If separate sound and video files are to be played, two **Multimedia** controls are required—one per file. Note that, if an AVI file contains a WAV audio stream, another **Multimedia** control will be unable to play a second sound stream from a WAV file, because only one source can be connected at a time. This limitation means that, if we load and play a video file with an inherent sound track, any WAV file we have allocated to the page will not be played. Now, modify the prototype program we have developed so far so that it looks like the form in Figure A.7.

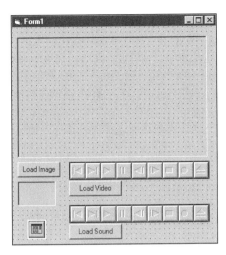

Figure A.7
Prototype form with **Multimedia** controls installed.

We still have the **Load Image** button to load bitmapped images onto the screen. We have increased the image viewing area, simply by making **imgImage1** bigger at design time, thus expanding the available viewing area. We have added two **Multimedia** controls called **mmcVideoPlayer** and **mmcSoundPlayer** at the bottom of the screen, one above the other. Below each control is the appropriate **Load** button. These three subsystems—static image display, video-clip playback, and sound playback (WAV or MID)—are all independent of each other in the prototype.

If your toolbox has no **Multimedia** control, you will have to load the control as a component. Use the Project drop-down menu on the VB menus and select Components from the submenu. A list of all the components available on the PC then appears. Look for Microsoft multimedia Control, and select it for loading. (This control is available only in the Professional and Enterprise versions of VB.) Returning to the VB design-time environment, you should now find a **Multimedia** control available in your toolbox. Create two instances of the control, as described earlier.

The code to handle the video and sound channels is simple. The **Multimedia** control serves as an interface between your program and the range of multimedia services, CD, digitized sound playback, synthesizer playback, and the PC's screen for video clips. The control uses a standard language, which the programmer can use to "command" the interface. The control also supplies a series of manual buttons that can be used to stop, start, rewind, and so on.

In the form you see in Figure A.7, the **Multimedia** controls have been set up with all their elements enabled. You'll see an Eject button, which is clearly not applicable to videos or sound generation, but which is applicable to playing CDs (which the **Multimedia** control can also help you to play).

Let's look in detail at the code required. Remember that the video is contained in a file. All we have to do is tell the control what the file name is, that it is an **AVIVIDEO**, and ask the control to play the video via the appropriate multimedia service, to which it automatically connects. We use a series of commands and set the **Filename** and **DeviceType** properties. Believe it or not, the following code is the code to load and play a video clip. Load this code into the **Load Video** button's click event handler:

```
Private Sub cmdPlayVideo_Click()

dlgDialog1.Action = 1

mmcVideoPlayer.Command = "CLOSE"
mmcVideoPlayer.DeviceType = "AVIVIDEO"
mmcVideoPlayer.FileName = dlgDialog1.FileName
mmcVideoPlayer.Command = "OPEN"
mmcVideoPlayer.Command = "PLAY"        ' Play an AVI file
If mmcVideoPlayer.ErrorMessage <> "" Then
        MsgBox mmcVideoPlayer.ErrorMessage
End if
End Sub
```

Both Archie and Julie were quite amazed that this was all the code necessary to play a video. To try it out, you need to find some AVI files on your disk. You can see the result of the program running an AVI clip in Figure A.8.

Archie and Julie were astonished. In less than two hours, we had worked out how to load and size images and run video clips using VB. As you can see in Figure A.8, an image has been loaded, and a video clip is running in its own form, which was generated by the AVI software to which the **Multimedia** control has linked the program. Let's look at the new code—for the **Load Video** control button—in detail. The first line is familiar; the second is new:

```
dlgDialog1.Action = 1
mmcVideoPlayer.Command = "CLOSE"
```

Line 1 activates the common dialog box for you to make a file-name selection. The next line issues a **CLOSE** command to the **Multimedia** control. If the channel wasn't doing anything, nothing happens; if it was playing an AVI, the command stops the action and shuts down the channel.

```
mmcVideoPlayer.DeviceType = "AVIVIDEO"
mmcVideoPlayer.FileName = dlgDialog1.FileName
mmcVideoPlayer.Command = "OPEN"
```

Figure A.8
The prototype program with an image loaded and an AVI video clip loaded and running in its own video form.

The next three lines define the type of file—AVI VIDEO—then the file name to load. The **OPEN** command primes the multimedia interface to connect to the appropriate playback software. The next line contains the **PLAY** command and starts the video:

```
mmcVideoPlayer.Command = "PLAY"        ' Play an AVI
```

Then, just as a precaution, we check the **Multimedia** control's error property. If the error message is not blank, we report the error string:

```
If mmcVideoPlayer.ErrorMessage <> "" Then
           MsgBox mmcVideoPlayer.ErrorMessage
End If
```

Like most things, "It's easy when you know how," but take a look at how much simpler playing sound files turned out to be. Here's the code for the **Load Sound**—and it's even simpler. Load this code into the Play Sound button's click event:

```
Private Sub cmdLoadSound_Click()
  dlgDialog1.Action = 1

  mmcSoundPlayer.Command = "CLOSE"
  mmcSoundPlayer.FileName = dlgDialog1.FileName
  mmcSoundPlayer.Command = "OPEN"
  mmcSoundPlayer.Command = "PLAY"
```

```
      If mmcSoundPlayer.ErrorMessage <> "" Then
                MsgBox mmcSoundPlayer.ErrorMessage
      End If
   End Sub
```

As you can see, the dialog control is activated to allow the user to select a file in the same way as before. The **File Name** property of the second **Multimedia** control is then set to the selected file name after the channel has been closed and flushed of any previous playback. The channel is then reopened with the new file onboard, and the file is played.

Both Julie and Archie pointed out that no instruction existed to tell the control what type of multimedia file to play. If you recall, we used **mmcVideoPlayer.DeviceType="AVIVIDEO"** to tell the control that the file was an AVI-formatted movie clip. In this case, we were letting the control determine the type of multimedia data stream from the file contents. The header in every multimedia file contains a description of the type of data the file holds. Interestingly, if you select an AVI file with this second control, it will load a window and run the video, having worked out that the file is an AVIVIDEO data stream. In fact, you can run two videos together, one from the first control and another from the second. Both programmers agreed that this was powerful stuff.

A Positive Conclusion

I asked Julie and Archie if they now felt more confident about handling images and multimedia files. Their replies were unanimous. The feasibility study had demonstrated quite conclusively that we could meet the requirements, as we currently understood them. Again, here are the three goals we set for ourselves at the outcome:

♦ How can we easily load and scale images onto defined screen areas?

♦ How can we easily load and run video clips on screen?

♦ How can we easily load and play sound or music files?

We now had code showing how we could answer each of the questions. That is, we could easily load and size images onto defined screen areas, we could easily load and run video clips on screen, and we could easily load and play sound or music files. These capabilities were feasible, provided the final development environment contained similar image and multimedia screen objects to those VB uses. These conditions would obviously serve as a requirement when we set out to evaluate programming environments for the project.

Julie commented that what she had thought would be the most difficult part of the development now appeared to be the easiest. I asked her and Archie to imagine how much time and effort they would have required to get up to speed with the technology without the aid of someone who had been there before. The question was sobering and prompted Julie to say that there's no real substitute for experience. Unfortunately, that's true. If you're going to use components such as the **Multimedia** control in a project, getting to know the object is absolutely imperative. Then, when you are looking at the requirements, you can match the component's capability to what's needed. Like any person who is asked to quote for a job, you must know what you can do with the tools at your disposal and be able to estimate how long a required job will take. If you have no knowledge of how to use the tools available, you don't stand much chance of getting the work without taking a huge risk. Software development is no different. To minimize the risks, you need to know your technology and try out various scenarios using that technology to ensure that it can accommodate the requirement.

In this case, the feasibility study amounted to an afternoon's work. In a large project, a feasibility study might turn into a project all its own, but its function is the same. The purpose of the feasibility study is to answer such questions as, Is it feasible to meet a specific requirement with a software solution? And a key point is that you need to do only enough work to prove the point—not actually do the job.

Appendix B
The CD Player

As we saw in the feasibility study that we performed for handling multimedia files, the multimedia control is a typical component you can add to a VB project. A multimedia control interfaces your program with a wealth of multimedia-driving software for a huge range of devices and facilities. We've already used the control in Appendix A to handle video-clip data streams from AVI files, digitized sound streams from WAV files, and event data streams from MID files. Now, we're going to connect the multimedia control to CD services to play audio CDs from a CD-ROM drive.

The data on a sound CD consists of 16-bit, digitized sound levels, sampled at high frequency to provide good-quality sound on playback. After it's connected to our program via the VB multimedia control, the CD controller can be used under manual control. To begin with, the only code we'll write will be to connect to the relevant service on your PC. From then on, you can click the available buttons to make the CD playback system do whatever you want.

New VB Project

Start a new VB EXE project, and add the multimedia control. Remember, if the component is not already on your toolbar, you will have to add it via the Components submenu from the Project drop-down menu.

Button Controls

If you recall from our previous feasibility study in Appendix A, the multimedia control has a wealth of buttons available for use. We can tailor which buttons the control shows us. For a CD, we want buttons to do the following: skip to the next track, skip to the previous track, play, stop playing, and eject the CD. All we have to do is make those controls visible and the remaining controls invisible. For the first feasibility study we did, we left all the controls visible and used only the ones that the interface itself activated. Here, we are personalizing the button array to suit the application.

Figure B.1 shows how the project form looks with a single instance of the multimedia control created. All buttons are made visible by default, and all are marked as disabled. This setup will change only after a connection is made to one of the multimedia services, at which point, the relevant buttons are enabled automatically. Tailor the control by setting the buttons you don't need to **Invisible**, until the form looks like what you see in Figure B.2. You will make the following buttons invisible: Back, Pause, Record, and Step.

Connecting

With the following code, we can use the form's load event to connect to the CD playing software on the PC:

```
Private Sub Form_Load()

  mmcCDPlayer.DeviceType = "CDAUDIO"
  mmcCDPlayer.Command = "OPEN"

End Sub
```

You can place a sound CD in the CD-ROM drive of your PC and run the program. The multimedia controls will automatically be enabled, as Figure B.3 shows. You can now play sound CDs using the buttons on screen.

NOTE: *If you try this program and experience problems, the problems might be because most PCs contain intelligent, CD-service software that takes over playing the CD "at the drop of a hat"—that is, as soon as you place a CD in the drive. The result is that you are locked out of CD services when your program tries to connect because the facility operates on a "first-come, first-serve" basis. Once control is relinquished, another program can request the service. If you experience problems, look to see whether you already have a CD-player program running; if so, stop the program, abort the*

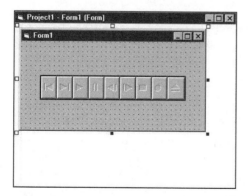

Figure B.1
Multimedia control with all button controls made visible by default after an instance has been created.

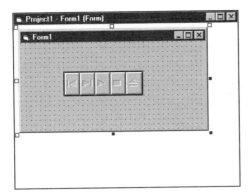

Figure B.2
Multimedia control after buttons not required for CD control are made invisible.

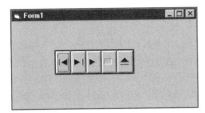

Figure B.3
Multimedia control after the CD services have been engaged.

player, and then try your program. Your default player might not only start automatically when you load a CD, but it might even take over again when you stop your program. To avoid interference, either disable the default player or, before you try anything with the test program, simply abort the default player if it is running. After the program connects, you will have no more problems until you terminate the program and try to reconnect later.

The multimedia control connects to the CD-playing service and enables all the buttons except Stop, which—as you might expect—will be enabled only when you start playing. At that time, the Play button becomes disabled. The component responds to a click event on the buttons with its own internal code. Nevertheless, as with all good objects, you can write event-handling code to add to the control's capability.

Adding a Little Color

Suppose we want to simulate a lamp or LED (light emitting diode), the little red or green lamp that you see on most electronic equipment. Let's set up a shape control as a lamp indicator, which is gray when the CD is not playing and green when it is playing. At the same time, I'll show you a neat way to set colors that you can easily make user-configurable. This information will all be useful to us in the E-MagBook project, so don't think we've digressed

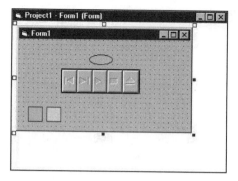

Figure B.4

Adding shape controls to emulate an LED in the CD form.

far from the project. Start by putting three shapes onto the form—**shpGreen**, **shpGray**, and **shpRunIndicator**—as Figure B.4 shows.

Set the **Backstyle** of each shape control **Opaque**. If you don't do this, you won't see the color. Of the square shapes shown in the bottom left-hand side of Figure B.4, the square shape on the left is colored gray, and the shape to its right is colored green. The indicator, which you see above the multimedia control, has been set to **Oval** using its **Shape** property. You can use the **Play** event on the multimedia control to turn the indicator green, as in the following code example.

Set up this code in the **PlayClick** event of the multimedia control, as you see here, having first followed the previous instructions:

```
Private Sub mmcCDPlayer_PlayClick(Cancel As Integer)
    shpRunIndicator.BackColor = shpGreen.BackColor
End Sub
```

To turn off the indicator, use the **Stop** event to set the shape's color back to gray:

```
Private Sub mmcCDPlayer_StopClick(Cancel As Integer)
  shpRunIndicator.BackColor = shpGray.BackColor
End Sub
```

When you run the program, the lamp goes green when the CD is playing and gray when it's stopped. Figure B.5 shows how the form looks when a CD is not playing, and Figure B.6 shows how the form looks when a CD is playing. Again, both Archie and Julie were staggered by the lack of code required to do all this.

Incidentally, because we are using shapes to set colors, we could make the two invisible shapes visible and develop a facility to let a user define, from a color palette, what color to use in the "stopped" state and what color to use in the "run" state.

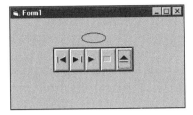

Figure B.5
Form showing a CD not being played—the oval indicator is gray.

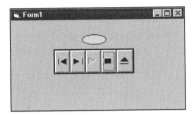

Figure B.6
Form showing a CD playing, with the the oval indicator set to green, triggered by the Play button's click event.

Invisible Components as Tools

This is the second time we've used invisible components as "tools." We used the picture control to size images, and, now, we're using shape controls to set background colors. In this situation, we've actually supplied some additional functionality by defining our own event-handling code for the **Play** and **Stop** events. Being able to define event procedures for an object gives us, as programmers, tremendous flexibility in terms of what we can make components do.

NOTE: *By the way, whenever you use color on computers, you need to remember that some people are color-blind and find it difficult to distinguish between reds and greens in particular. So, making the color settings user-configurable is a good idea. This information is useful, because I'm sure color will play a part in the editor. Situations will exist in which we need to warn the user of some condition on the GUI, and color is an ideal way to do that. You'll see what I mean later.*

Using the Multimedia Control in General

To wrap up this session on multimedia, I want to go over the detail of how to use this control so that your knowledge of the component is reasonably complete. Manipulation of a multimedia control is managed by setting properties in the usual way as well as by issuing commands to the control, as you have seen. Quite a few buttons are associated with the multimedia control, and we need to understand which ones best serve us under a given set of circumstances. Here are some notes you will find useful when development starts:

Notes on Multimedia Control Buttons

Previous

This button is used to move the player back to the start of the medium. In the case of an audio CD, this movement will be back to the start of Track 1; in the case of a video clip, the movement will be back to Frame 1, and so on.

Next

This button forces the service to go to the end of the current medium.

Play

This button causes the service to play the device connected from the current position on the medium.

Pause

This button requests the service to pause the current playback. Clicking either the Play button or the Pause button will continue play.

Back

This button forces the device to be stepped back one track or frame, depending on type. For example, on the CD audio player, the Back button has the effect of moving back to the beginning of the current track, or, if the CD is already playing close to the beginning of a track, back to the start of the previous track. If a video is in pause mode, the Back button allows the user to step back one frame.

Step

This button requests the service to step forward one frame or track.

Stop

This button stops the player.

Record

This button switches the service into record mode for devices that are capable of recording.

Eject

On devices that can eject the medium, such as the CD player, this button causes the carriage to eject and, if it's already ejected, to reinsert the CD.

Using the multimedia control, you can even record from a microphone into a WAV file and then play back the recording. This capability is a superb example of component technology at work. Gone are the days when you had to code every single aspect of functionality—now, you look for components you can purchase to do the majority of the work for you.

Components and Programmers

Archie thought that the growth of component technology might mean programmers would soon be out of work. In fact, that likelihood is far from the truth. Creating the sort of objects we've been talking about will still be a requirement. The real impact will be that programmers can develop astonishingly sophisticated systems by writing the code to manipulate these objects and handle their events in clever ways.

The project at hand is an excellent example of this relationship. Although you might be impressed by the power of the multimedia control, you'll find that we still have to write a lot of code to make the control work for us. However, the task of writing the code is greatly simplified, which means we can get on with developing a really exciting multimedia product.

Multimedia Control Properties

Now, let's look at the device type and command properties of the multimedia control. Here are some more notes to complete your current level of understanding of this component:

Multimedia Control Property: DeviceType

This property defines the service that the control must connect to.

DeviceType="AVIVIDEO"

This property informs the control that AVI files are to be played as video clips.

DeviceType="CDAUDIO"

This property informs the control that it is to connect to the service that allows audio CDs to be played from the CD drive.

DeviceType="MMMOVIE"

The Apple Macintosh system uses a different video format for movie clips than the format PCs use. The Macintosh format requests the system to connect to the appropriate service (QuickTime for Windows, for example) to play MOV files. MOV files are simply the Macintosh equivalent of PC AVI files.

DeviceType="WaveAudio"

This property is used to set up services for playing either WAV sound files or MID music files.

Multimedia Property: Command

This property is used to tell the control what to do. The commands are simple and also emulate those commands that were described on the button bar, thus providing the programmer with alternatives to using the button bar. This section provides a brief introduction to the most common commands.

Command="OPEN"

By setting the **DeviceType** property (as defined in the previous section), this command forces the control to open the appropriate service that was defined in the instruction prior to the open. This command must be executed before any of the selected services become available.

Command="CLOSE"

This command shuts down the interface to the service, thus allowing a different service to subsequently be selected from the same control via another **OPEN** command.

Command="SAVE"

When a service is used in recording mode, this command will save the recording to a disk file. The file name must be allocated to the **FileName** property of the control.

Button Command Set

For each of the button commands described in the previous section, an equivalent command can be set by the program code. These equivalent commands are **Play**, **Pause**, **Stop**, **Back**, **Step**, **Prev**, **Next**, **Record**, and **Eject**. Each command functions in the same way as I described in the previous section. These commands are issued as the following example shows, where **mmcPlayer** is an instance of a multimedia control:

mmcPlayer.Command="PLAY"

The multimedia control can connect to a host of other services, providing a highly versatile interface to multimedia services. These other services include digital video, scanners, sequencers, VCR, and videodisc. However, a word of warning: Documentation is hard to come by. In my experience, programming with the multimedia control involves a lot of "try it and see what happens" in terms of the results you achieve.

Know Your Controls

I cannot emphasize enough the need to know your controls before you use them. In the true sense of the word, the controls are sophisticated objects. They have properties, methods, and events that you need to understand in detail. Controls are your tools, but, as in all crafts, the craftspeople who use the tools must know what those tools can do for them, and how the tools work.

Appendix C
The Web Browser

The brief for the feasibility study was to answer the question, Is it feasible to integrate Web browsing technology into the E-MagBook concept? I'm going to introduce you to another astonishingly powerful object—the VB Web Browser form. The project requirement was that the E-MagBook must accommodate both local HTML pages and Internet Web sites. The E-MagBook page reference becomes an .html file reference, or a typical **http://** string or URL. To service this requirement, we needed to be able to invoke a Web browser whenever we encountered such a reference, pass the page reference to the browser, and "tell" the browser to fetch the page.

We had a discussion with Monty about the requirement, and ultimately he supplied us with an object or component that we could use to make the connection via his in-built telephone. Don't forget, this capability did not affect the current project, but, to avoid compromising our design, we needed to understand how we would achieve the connection.

Monty told us that we would set the **Dial** property on his object and wait for a **Connection** property or event to indicate that the link had been made. Once the link was made, we would need to do no more. We would invoke the browser and give it the URL from the E-MagBook Index, and the browser would connect to the Internet using standard protocol; we would just wait for the Web page to appear.

As far as the feasibility study was concerned, we must set up a program that invoked a browser and passed a URL string to it. At any time, the URL string could be changed in the program, which would then update the browser with the new reference. As you will see, we only needed to do enough programming to convince ourselves that the requirement was achievable; we didn't need to provide a full solution. From a management perspective, we had to ensure that the study didn't develop into a solution.

The VB Browser Form

The VB Browser form is another Microsoft component, and you can add it to the CD player that you developed in Appendix B. From the Project menu, Components option, select Microsoft Internet Controls. You can see this form in Figure C.1.

When you select the Microsoft Internet Controls component, two controls appear on the toolbar, as Figure C.2 shows.

The browser is the globe-shaped icon in the middle of the bottom group on the toolbar. To set up a browser, we'll use a second form and call it **frmWebBrowser**. On the second form, put a label called **lblURL** and create an instance of the Microsoft Web browser, which we'll call **brwWebBrowser**. You can see the result in Figure C.3.

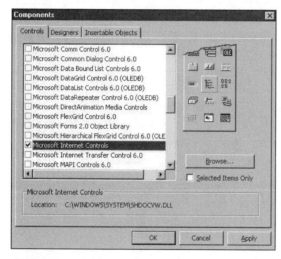

Figure C.1
Selection of the VB Browser component.

Figure C.2
The VB toolbar after the browser component has been loaded.

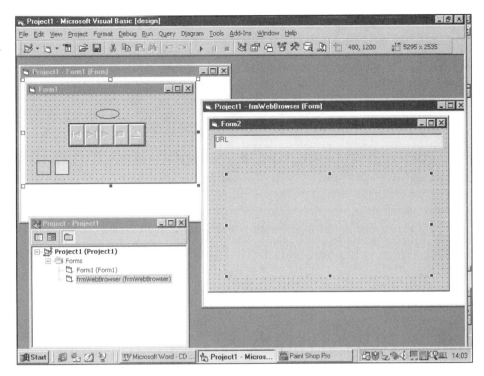

Figure C.3
The CD project modified to contain a Web browser.

At design time, you don't see much of the browser, which is the highlighted object on the second form. The code couldn't be much more straightforward, which, once again, shows the awesome power of component technology. First, we will add a text box and a button control to the main form. We will use the text box to enter a URL. We will use the button to launch the browser (if it is not already loaded) and request that it retrieve the Web page. The main form now resembles Figure C.4.

NOTE: *To set up the URL, we just type the URL into the text box. We're trying to simulate the situation in which the main program has encountered a URL by whatever means and needs to get a Web page onto the screen. So, for this exercise, we'll just enter a URL and then order the browser to fetch it.*

The code we need is ridiculously simple. To launch the browser, send it the URL, and tell it, essentially, to "go get," you need to insert this code in the button click-event handler:

```
Private Sub Command1_Click()
  frmWebBrowser.Show
  frmWebBrowser.lblURL.Caption = txtURL.Text
  frmWebBrowser.brwWebBrowser.Navigate frmWebBrowser.lblURL.Caption
  frmWebBrowser.SetFocus
End Sub
```

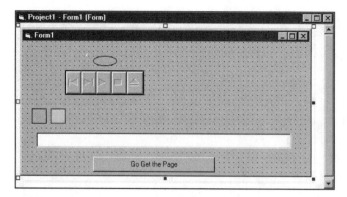

Figure C.4
The CD project main form with the text box into which a user can type a URL, and the button control that will be used to launch the browser and pass the URL to it, simulating the E-Viewer environment.

And that's it. That's all we need to do to bring up whatever URL we typed into the text box in our browser on screen.

The Requirement Simulated

Let's run the program and see what happens. But before we do that, we need to make sure the PC has an open socket to the Internet. At this stage, you simply need to invoke the software you use to make a standard dial-up connection to your Internet Service Provider (ISP). Clearly, if you want to try out this program, you must have a method to connect to the Internet. After the connection is established, you are ready to run this program. If your start-up process has invoked any browsers, terminate them, so that no browser is running when you invoke the program. Figure C.5 shows the program in operation.

Recap

Before we go any further, let's review what's happened. We connected to the Internet, so in the background we have an open TCP/IP socket to the ISP's server. We ran the program, and the first form appeared. We then entered the URL **http://yahoo.com** into the text box on the CD form, and then we clicked the command button. A tiny browser window containing the Yahoo! page appeared.

Browser and Multimedia Function

You can now stop the program and change the size of the browser form and the browser control itself. Make sure your connection is still open, and rerun the program. Start a CD, type the Yahoo! URL into the text box, and click on the button control on Form1. You should now see something similar to Figure C.6.

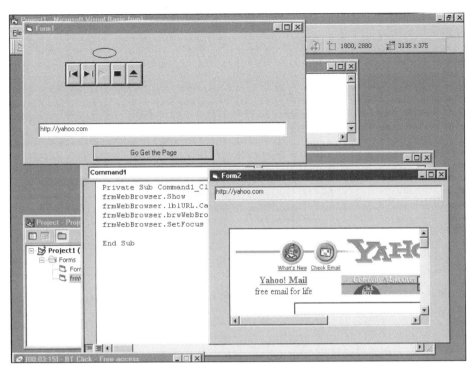

Figure C.5
The CD main form is shown on screen with a URL typed into the text box. The button has been activated to launch the browser, which has loaded the Yahoo! page.

The fact that we have the multimedia control playing a CD is reassuring in the sense that having an open connection to the Internet with a browser running does not impair the functionality of the multimedia control—not that we thought it would, but we still wanted to check it out.

Code Required in Detail

Let's go through the code. First, we ran the program with an Internet connection already made. We started the CD player, typed the Yahoo! URL in the text box on Form1, and clicked on the command button. Next, we invoked the **show** method of **frmWebBrowser** to load and display Form2, using the following line of code:

```
frmWebBrowser.Show
```

The next line of code set up the label in Form2 with the name of the URL (that action was purely cosmetic, just so we knew what was happening):

```
frmWebBrowser.lblURL.Caption = txtURL.Text
```

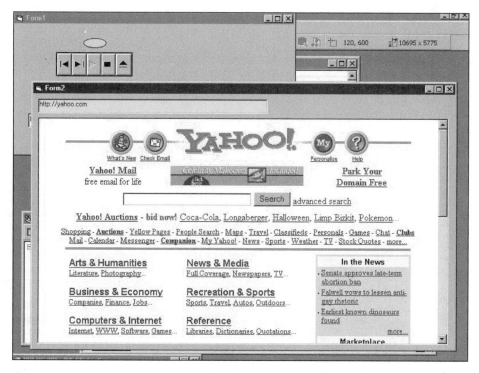

Figure C.6
Modified browser size running from CD program with a CD playing.

Next, we told the browser control to navigate to the URL defined in the label. This label could be any text string variable or object. I just happened to use the label on the second form, into which I'd already copied the URL from the text box on Form1. We just as well could have used a string variable or even the text box on the first form. We used the following code:

```
frmWebBrowser.brwWebBrowser.Navigate frmWebBrowser.lblURL.Caption
```

Finally, we made sure that the browser form had focus so that the first form did not hide it:

```
frmWebBrowser.SetFocus
```

Again, all this code and the resulting capabilities were "good stuff," and, as Julie said, "With it, you can bring the power of the Web into your own application."

More Simulation

Let's look at how we switched to a new URL. Remember, we were trying to simulate the E-MagBook of the future. The scenario we wanted to test was this: We had selected an E-MagBook page that contained a Web page reference. We extracted the URL and handed it over to the browser, which we launched if it was not already on the screen.

We can simulate this scenario by typing in a URL and clicking the button control. Type in the URL of Microsoft's Hotmail site, and then click the button control. The screen will change to something like what you see in Figure C.7.

Error Handling

But the functionality doesn't stop there. You're actually using Internet Explorer components, so watch what happens if you now break the connection and try to access a URL. Figure C.8 shows what happens.

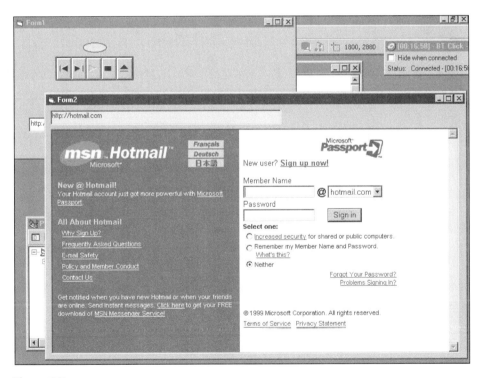

Figure C.7
Prototype now switched to Microsoft's Hotmail site.

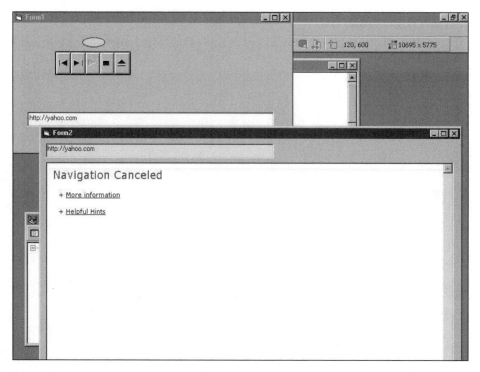

Figure C.8
The Internet connection has been broken.

The screen message is telling us that navigation has been canceled. Click More Information, and you'll see details like those in Figure C.9.

All this automatic functionality is inherent in the component that we have set up in our application. We have written only a handful of code lines to invoke and transfer URL information to the browser. According to Archie, all this functionality, programmed with a minimum of code from us, indicated one thing: "Component technology is the way to go."

Conclusion

We had now simulated enough of this requirement to convince ourselves that—at least with VB—integrating browser technology with the E-MagBook concept was quite feasible.

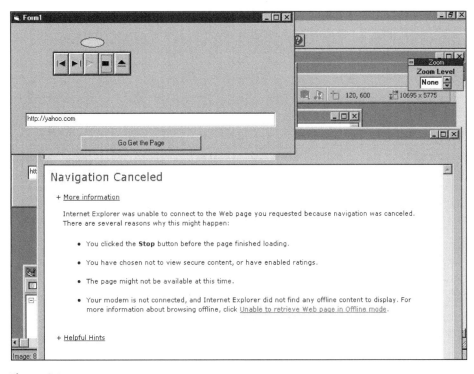

Figure C.9

Error messages from the browser.

Appendix D
More Feasibility—Drag-and-Drop

A t the start of the second day in project Week 2, we began another feasibility study. This was not a study for which we were being paid. I'd decided to do this one to help us understand another area of risk—drag-and-drop functionality—and also to give Archie and Julie a break (variation) from the rigors of analysis.

The operating system generally controls form dragging and dropping, but not the objects that have been placed on a VB form. Written code is necessary to directly handle the appropriate events and control moving objects around a VB form. You must set up drag-and-drop functionality in Workbench mode in a way that either the image or the text box can be moved around the screen. Again, we would use VB to conduct the study, regardless of whether VB would be our final choice for the development environment.

The Workbench Screen Objects

We had two objects—an image control and a text box. We would use their **.top**, **.left**, **.width**, and **.height** properties to move and size the objects. Objects also have events, and drag-and-drop involves two main events.

In terms of the first main event, when the user selects the object, he or she initially moves the mouse cursor over the object onto the pickup point and then holds down the mouse button. At this point, the target object has been selected at an offset from its origin, which we can consider being at the top, left-hand side of the object itself. (We need to know this offset for reasons that will become apparent later.) We can capture the offset in the **MouseMove** event for that object.

In terms of the second main event, we need to use the event that occurs when a dragged object is dropped on top of another object. The drag-and-drop event is triggered in the object onto which the dropping is performed.

The VB Project

To explore drag-and-drop functionality, we created a new VB project, which you can copy. We created a new form and placed an image control and a text box onto the form, as Figure D.1 shows.

The image is named **imgImage1**, and the text box, **txtText1**. We loaded a picture into the image control at design time and made it a suitable size, as shown, by setting the **stretch** property to **True** and resizing the image to suitable dimensions. (Again, we did all this at design time.) We then placed some text in the text box and set the **multiline** property of the text box to **True**. If you don't do this, then, regardless of the text box's width, all you will ever see is a single line of text.

General Declarations

To develop the code for drag-and-drop, we first set up two data items in the general declarations area of the project:

```
Option Explicit
Dim intX as integer
Dim intY as integer
```

MouseMove Event

Next, we placed the following code into the **MouseMove** event handlers for both the image and the text controls:

```
Private Sub imgImage1_MouseMove(Button As Integer, Shift As_
Integer, X As Single, Y As Single)

             intX=X
intY=Y
End Sub


Private Sub txtText1_MouseMove(Button As Integer, Shift As_
Integer, X As Single, Y As Single)

intX=X
intY=Y

End Sub
```

This code tracks the position of the cursor as it is moved around each object. As the user moves the mouse cursor onto the object, a stream of events fires, registering the new **X, Y** position each time the position changes. The **X** and the **Y** are supplied by VB, as you can see in the argument list of the subroutine, and the code places the values into the variables that we've declared in the form's declaration statement. The moment the user clicks the mouse

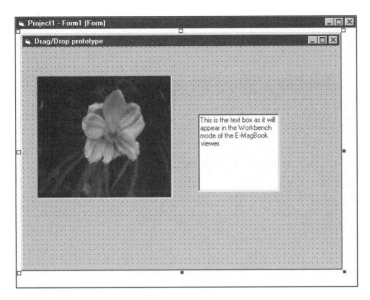

Figure D.1
The layout for the form to test drag-and-drop functionality for the Workbench.

button and holds it down to start a drag operation, the content of **intX** and **intY** reflect the previous position of the mouse cursor, which is the offset at which the control is picked up.

What happens next depends on where the user drops the object being dragged. Three possibilities, or scenarios, exist in the Workbench prototype. The dragged object can be dropped onto the form, onto the other screen object, or onto itself.

Scenario 1

To assist in the feasibility study, I had produced three diagrams, and you can see the first in Figure D.2.

If we use **imgImage1** as our example, we can pick up the image and drop it on the form or on top of the text box. The important point is that whichever object is underneath the final drop point has its drag/drop event triggered. Code must be written to cater to either eventuality. A third possibility also exists. If the drag is short, the drop might occur over **imgImage1** itself. In this case, **imgImage1**'s drag/drop event will be triggered. We now must accommodate three possible situations, and Figure D.2 shows the first one—that is, when an object is picked up and dropped onto a blank section of the form. This is Scenario 1.

In Figure D.2, **imgImage1** starts at the **initial position**. A user then picks up the image with the cursor at the crosshairs shown on **imgImage1** on the diagram and drags it to the final position, or *drop point*, where it is released. The curved line between the pickup point and the drop point indicates the movement of the image. In Scenario 1, **imgImage1** is dropped onto the main window at drop point. Remember **intX** and **intY** refer to the pickup position on

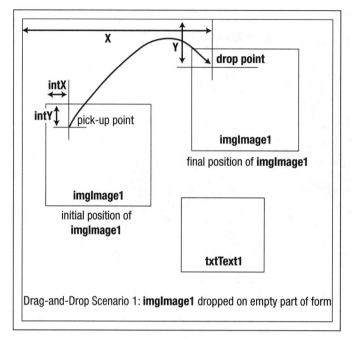

Figure D.2
Drag-and-drop Scenario 1: The object is dropped onto the form.

imgImage1. This position is measured from the origin of **imgImage1**. The drop point is defined as being at **X** and **Y**, which are measured from the origin of the object onto which the drop occurs. In this example, the drop point is measured from the origin of the form and shown as **X** and **Y**.

Drag-and-Drop Event Handler

X and **Y** are supplied as arguments in the drag-and-drop event handler. The question now is, What does the code in the form's drag-and-drop event handler look like? Let's start by looking at the following code as a solution:

```
Private Sub Form_DragDrop(Source As Control, X As Single, Y As Single)
    Source.Move X, Y
End Sub
```

The **Source.Move** method operates on the object that is being dropped—in this case, **imgImage1**. **X** and **Y** are as measured, as the diagram shows. The overall effect is that **imgImage1**'s **.left** property is set to **X** and the **.top** property is set to **Y**. This is not what we want.

If you set up the code, don't forget to set the **DragMode** property of **imgImage1** to **Auto**. Then, if you try a drag-and-drop operation with the code set up as above, you'll see **imgImage1** redrawn such that its top, left-hand corner is placed at **X** and **Y**. What we really want is for the left-hand corner to be drawn at **X-intX** and **Y-intY**, so that the original pick-up point is accounted for. We can accommodate this requirement by changing the code as follows:

```
Private Sub Form_DragDrop(Source As Control, X As Single, Y As Single)
   Source.Move (X - intX), (Y - intY)
End Sub
```

NOTE: *If you use **Source.Move X, Y**, **X, Y** defines the new origin for **imgImage1**. You need to move the origin across by **intX** and up by **intY** so that the top, left-hand corner is then drawn offset from the drop point in the same way it was offset from the pick-up point. The preceding code does this.*

*If you have trouble following this process, observe the program with the move set to **X, Y** only and see where the origin (top, left-hand side) of **imgImage1** appears when the cursor is at the drop point. Make sure that you pick up the image somewhere near its center to begin with. The only way you can get the desired effect is to pick up the image control at a point very close to its top, left-hand corner, minimizing the offset of the pick-up. Now, change the code to subtract the offsets **intX** and **intY**, and observe what happens when you repeat the exercise.*

You can also make the text box available to drag/drop on the form, just by setting the **dragmode** property to **auto**.

The Drop Zone

With both the image control and the text box set for automatic dragging, either object can be picked up and dragged to a blank section of the form. In fact, the form immediately underneath the drop point is all that needs to be blank. Whatever object lies immediately under the cursor when the mouse key is released defines the drop zone.

What you *can't* do is drop the image on the text box or the text box on the image, because no **Drop** event handler has been written for either the text or image controls. (We need to write a **Drop** event handler for every single object onto which another control can be dropped.)

We used the code **Source.Move (X-intX), (Y-intY)** for a **Drop** on the form. This code works because **X** and **Y** are always measured from the origin of the form. But, if the **Drop** object is not the form, **X** and **Y** are measured from the origin of the drop-zone object. This fact is vitally important in the next two scenarios.

Scenario 2

In this scenario, as Figure D.3 shows, we are picking up **imgImage1** and dropping it onto the text box. In this case, the **X** and **Y** provided in the text box's drop event handler are measured from the top, left-hand corner of the text box—not the main form. If we place these values in the **.left** and **.top** properties of the image control, the control will end up at those coordinates away from the form's origin. We need to add the coordinates of the text box itself.

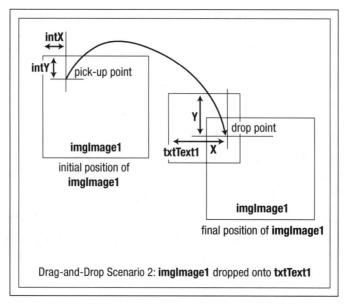

Figure D.3
Drag-and-drop Scenario 2: The image is dropped onto the text box.

Julie became quite lost at this stage, but, fortunately, Figure D.3 came to the rescue. To understand what's happening, start by setting the drop events in both controls to **Source.Move X, Y**. Run the program, pick up the image control, drag it over the text box, and release. What you will see is the image being redrawn at the wrong position. You can see this process best if you first move the text box over to the right of the form and then drag the image onto the text box. When you release the mouse, **imgImage1** will zoom off to the left-hand side of the form—in fact, at **X, Y** from the form's origin.

Calculating the New Origin

To calculate the required origin of the object being dragged onto the text control, all we need to do is change the code in the text box's drag-and-drop event to the following:

```
Source.Move (txtText1.left + X - intX), (txtText1.Top + Y - intY)
```

You still need to compensate for the pick-up offset. Look at Figure D.3 in detail. Remember that all objects are positioned on the form—regardless of what they overlay—from the form's origin, no one else's. Consequently, when calculating the **.left** and **.top** values for the newly positioned image, we must add the origin of the text control to the values **X** and **Y** to get the new position of the left-hand corner of **imgImage1** from the origin of the form. And then, we must compensate for the pick-up offset.

Julie remarked that this was simple only after she had studied the diagrams in detail. Once she understood what the **X** and the **Y** meant in the drop event, the process became clear.

NOTE: *Again, if you have trouble following this description, experiment with the code. Try* **Source.Move X, Y** *first in the text box's drag-and-drop event handler, and observe the result when you drag* **imgImage1** *and drop it on the text box. Then, try* **Source.Move (X+txtText1.Left), (Y+txtText1.Top)**, *observe the effect, and try* **Source.Move (X+txtText1.Left–intX), (Y+txtText1.Top–intY)** *again, observing the outcome. Study the diagram, and try to relate what has happened in each case with the measurements we've used.*

You can make the text box droppable on **imgImage1** by changing **imgImage1**'s drag-and-drop event to the following:

```
Source.Move (imgImage1.left + X - intX), (imgImage1.Top + Y - intY)
```

Scenario 3

You'll be very relieved to hear that the code in **imgImage1**'s drag-and-drop event handler will also handle a drop of **Image1** onto itself. Likewise, the drag-and-drop event in **txtText1** will handle the text box being dropped onto itself. Figure D.4 represents this situation.

It's All a Question of Origin

In reality, drag-and-drop functionality turned out to be a small amount of code. But, grasping what's going on is really quite difficult. If you want to be able to move an object around a screen that's full of other screen controls, you have to write a drag-and-drop handler for every single potential drop zone. And don't forget: You also need a **MouseMove** handler

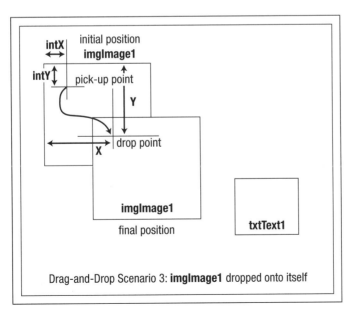

Figure D.4

Drag-and-drop Scenario 3: The image is dropped onto itself.

for every single object that can be dragged, to track the cursor as it moves across the object. After you click any given target control, the previous **MouseMove** event has faithfully recorded the position of the pick-up point.

The important factor in all this is that you appreciate which origin is which—you have the form origin, the origin of the item being moved, and the origin of the drop-zone object to consider. When you pick up an object, the **X** and **Y** coordinates supplied by the **MouseMove** event are measured from the origin of the object itself. When you drop the object, the **X** and **Y** supplied by the drag-and-drop event are measured from the origin of the **Drop** zone object, which might be the form itself, or another object with a drag-and-drop event coded. Which origin is in use when you employ the coordinates received in the call determines everything. Your **Source.Move** then must set the **.left** and **.top** properties of the item being dropped, and this position must always refer to the form's origin.

Drag-and-drop was, by far, the most complex functionality we had to face in this entire project. We'd have another look at it in design, and then, when we did the actual coding, there'd be yet another chance to see the functions in action. Despite the lack of code involved, we took a good part of the morning to digest all the information. As soon as we had it all clear in our minds, we went straight to analysis.

Appendix E
File Selection

This appendix details what Archie and Julie did to make the file-selection objects in the File Selection form prototype provide a more meaningful display for the screenshots used in the requirements specification.

The Form

First, they set up a child form in the main, editor prototype form and called it **frmFileSelection**. They placed the **Drive, Directory,** and **File** controls onto this form directly from the VB toolbox. You can see these three controls highlighted in Figure E.1.

They arranged the controls one above the other, as you can see in Figure E.2. They set up three picture controls for selecting file type (that is, **Picture, Text,** and **Sound**). If you recall, when the user clicks one of these picture controls, the default color for the file type is set in the picture control and in all the File Selection controls. The **Drive, Directory,** and **File Selection** boxes have been installed one on top of the other. Note how these boxes already show data, even in the design-time state. In the prototype, they are called **filDrive1, filDir1,** and **filFile1**.

Change Events

The big box is the File Selection control, **filFile1**. It has a property called **filFile1.Path** that is available only at runtime. This property effectively defines the path (that is, drive and directory) from which to create its displayed list. So, if the **.path** property is set to **C:\Imlib\Library1**, all the files in that directory are automatically displayed in the file list box.

filDir1 has a property called **filDir1.Path** as well, which defines its path. **filDrive1** automatically shows all the drives connected to the PC. If you select a drive, you can use the change event on **filDrive1** to set **filDir1**'s **Path** property to that drive. The **Directory** box then shows the directories available from the newly selected drive. You can use the change event in **filDir1** to set the path in the File List box, which becomes populated with the correct files.

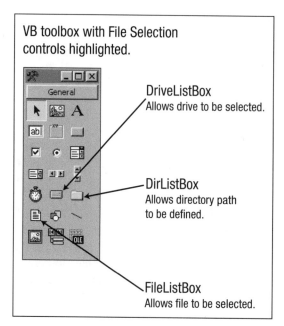

Figure E.1

VB toolbox with File Selection controls indicated.

Figure E.2

Form **frmFileSelection** with File Selection controls installed.

In this way, you can use the relevant change events to lock the **File Selection** boxes together, so a change in one always filters down to the others.

Let's consider an example. Suppose the **Directory** box shows you four possible drives: A:, a diskette drive; C:, the hard drive; D:, the CD-ROM drive; and E:, the removable E-MagDisk drive. This list is set up automatically when VB starts the application.

If you select drive E: from the list and click it, you change the selected drive. You need to let the directory control **filDir1** know about this change so it can repopulate its own list of directories. You do this by setting the code

```
filDir1.Path = filDrive1.Drive
```

in the change event of the **Drive** control. Any time you select a new drive by clicking it, you generate the **filDrive1** change event, which then executes the above line of code to change the **Directory** control's path. In other words, **filDir1**'s path changes and causes **filDir1** to be automatically repopulated with the directories of the newly selected drive.

Next, we need to repopulate the **File List** box. We do that by setting up the change event in **filDir1** to reset **filFile1**'s path. If we put the following line in **filDir1**'s change event, we cause the list box to be repopulated as well:

```
filFile1.Path = filDir1.Path
```

If, at runtime, you change the directory by clicking a new directory in **filDir1**, that action causes a change event in **filDir1**, which causes the preceding line to be executed. If you change the drive, that action changes the directory, which, in turn, changes the file list. Whatever you do, the path of the File-Selection box always shows the list of files relevant to the currently selected directory and drive.

Recap

If, at runtime, you change the drive, you actually first trigger a change event on the **Drive** control, which then modifies the path property of the **Directory** control. This, in turn, causes a change event in the **Directory** control, which is used to set the file list **Path** property, and causes an internal change event in the file list control to repopulate the file list automatically. If you change just the directory by clicking a directory displayed in the **Directory** box, you generate one change event in **filDir1**, which sets the new path for the **File List** box.

In all cases, an internal change event is instigated in the **File List** box, causing it to be repopulated with the correct file list according to which drive and directory have been selected in the other boxes. This is another one of those "simple things" that is "simple" only when you think hard about it.

Filtering

Finally, Julie and Archie put this code in the change event of the text box that was placed under the **File List** control:

```
On Error GoTo 1000:
filFile1.Pattern = txtFileFilter.Text
1000:
Exit Sub
```

All the code does is set the pattern property of **filFile1** with whatever you type into the text box. Because you *could* type garbage, we have an error trap to stop the program from bombing. Otherwise, the file selection is filtered by whatever you want. For example, if you place ***.BMP** in the box, the File Selection control automatically reorders the list to show only BMP files.

The Finished Prototype

Putting the tiny amount of code I've introduced in this appendix into the controls allowed us to set up more meaningful scenarios on the form layouts. Without this code, we would be stuck with the default setting of **C:**, which is a bit meaningless because the files have no relevance to an E-MagBook's requirements.

For example, for the Picture screen prototype, Archie and Julie set up many JPEG files in C:\imlib\library1. They set up **Drive** to be **C:** and **Directory** to be **imlib\library1**, and put ***.BMP**, ***.JPG**, and ***.TIF** into the filter. The resulting list showed the files that were present.

For the text example, they stopped the program; reset the colors; restarted the program; and set **Drive** to **C:**, **Directory** to **imlib\text**, and the file filter to ***.txt**. They then did the same thing for sound filtering on ***.WAV** and ***.MID**. Altogether, setting up the three examples of file selection that you saw in the requirements specification required about half an hour's work.

The file-selection prototype form is the only one that had any code developed for it. This exercise demonstrates how, with a minor amount of code, you can turn the prototype into something more relevant for the requirements specification. (As always, to avoid disrupting our plan, the criterion was that the amount of work involved must be minimal to achieve the desired effect.)

Appendix F
Screen Objects

Design Specifications: E-MagBook Viewer Screen Objects

You can find these screen object design specifications in Chapter 6.

Design Specifications: E-MagBook Video Form

```
frmVideoPlayer                    Main video form
mmcVideoPlayer                    Multimedia control for videos
```

Design Specifications: E-MagBook Title Index Editor

```
FrmTitleEditor                    Main form

Menu Options:
mnuFile                           dummy 'File' option
        MnuNewTitleIndex          New        Create new Index
        MnuOpenTitleIndex         Open       Open an existing Index
                                             file
        MnuSaveTitleIndex         Save       Save Index file
        MnuSaveTitleIndexAs       Save As    Save Index file to
                                             named output file

        mnuExit                   Exit       Leave program

Buttons:
cmdAdd                            Add        Add to Index
cmdInsert                         Insert     Insert into Index
cmdOverWrite                      OverWrite  Overwrite current entry
cmdDelete                         Delete     Delete current entry
```

```
cmdRelease                              Release         Release Alert state
cmdGoEnd                                >>              Go To end of Page
                                                        Index
cmdGoStart                              <<              Go To start of Page
                                                        Index
cmdNext                                 >               Go To next page
cmdPrevious                             <               Go To Previous page

Main controls:
label1 to Label5                                Holds text descriptions of input
                                                boxes etc
txtIndexFileName                        Name of loaded Title Index File
lblIndexNumber                          Number of entry on view
txtFileRef                              Data entry field for Page Index refer-
ence
txtTitle                                Data entry field for Title
txtDescription                          Data entry field for Description

Miscellaneous:
shpGray                                 Used to set Gray color
shpRed                                  Used to set alert color
shpWhite                                Used to set white
dlgDialog                               File dialogue box
```

Design Specifications: E-MagBook Page Index Editor

```
MDIfrmEdit                              main form.

Menu options:
MnuFile                                 dummy File option
        mnuNewPageIndex                 New             Create new Index
        mnuOpenPageIndex                Open            Open a file
        mnuSavePageIndex                Save            Save Index file
        mnuSavePageIndexAs              Save As         Save Index file to
                                                        named output file
        mnuExit                         Exit            Leave program

mnuText                                 dummy
        mnuSaveText                     Save Text       Save text box to file
        mnuSaveTextAs                   Save Text As    Save text box to named
                                                        file
        mnuSetFont                      Font            Set text font

mnuWindow                               dummy
        mnuEViewerSelect                E-Viewer        Switch to Viewer
                                                        form
```

mnuFileSelectionSelect		File Selection	Switch to file form

Buttons:

PicCommandToolBar			container for Command Buttons
label1		Red label	container for Index functions
	cmdAdd	Add	Add to Index
	cmdInsert	Insert	Insert into Index
	cmdOverWrite	OverWrite	Overwrite current entry
	cmdDelete	Delete	Delete current entry
	cmdRelease	Release	Release Alert 1 changed state
label2		Yellow label	container for Clipboard commands
	cmdCopy	COPY	Copy screen to clipboard
	cmdPaste	PASTE	Paste from clipboard
label3		Orange label	container for CLEAR commands
	cmdClearTextBox	TEXT	Clear text box content
	cmdClearKeys	KEYS	Clear keys
label4		Cyan label	container for Remove file ref commands
	cmdRemovePicture	Picture	Clear picture ref
	cmdRemoveText	Text	Clear Text ref
	cmdRemoveSound	Sound	Clear sound ref
	cmdRemoveAll	All	Clear picture, text and sound refs
label 5		Magenta label	container for TEXT commands
	cmdSaveTextFile	Text	Button equivalent of menu Text save

Miscceallaneous:		
DlgDialog		File dialogue box
TmrWatchDog		Watch dog timer
FrmFileSelect		File Selection Form

shpForPicture	Holds color for Picture selections
shpForText	Holds color for Text selections
shpForSound	Holds color for Sound selections
lblPicture	Object used to switch to Picture selection
lblText	Object used to switch to Text selection
lblSound	Object used to switch to Sound selection
filDrive1	Drive selection object
filDir1	Directory selection object
fileFile1	File selection object
txtFileFilter	Filter definition object
shpGray	Background color

Design Specifications for E-MagBook Software

Introduction

In this appendix, you will find all the design specifications for the E-MagBook software. Where the actual specification is located in a chapter, the appendix contains a reference to the chapter to avoid duplication. There are three main sections to this appendix.

Top-Level Design Views

References to all the top-level design views for the three programs established in Chapter 6 can be found in this section.

Data-Structure Definitions

These definitions include references to all the data structures of the three programs.

Subroutine and Function Specifications

The subroutines and functions are listed in approximately the order in which you encounter the code in the book. For example, all the specifications relevant to the viewer appear first, those for the Title Index Editor appear next, and finally, the specifications for the Page Index Editor appear.

The table of contents for the functions and subroutines presented here lists the routines in alphabetical order. The number at the end of each item designates the item/order number of the routine within the complete listing

Alphabetic list of Specifications for the E-MagBook

Use this list to find the required specification in the section "Subroutine and Function Specifications" of this appendix.

Top-Level Design Views

These design views are available in Chapter 6 and consist of the following:

1. List of functional modules required for the Mark 1 E-MagBook Software—see Figure 6.4.

2. Top-level view of the viewer program—see Figure 6.5.

3. Top-level view of the Title Index Editor program—see Figure 6.6.

5. Top-level view of the Page Index Editor program—see Figure 6.7.

6. Top-level view of the E-MagBook viewer—see Figure 6.9.

7. Top-level view of the Title Index Editor program showing the library structure—see Figure 6.10.

8. Top-level view of the Page Index Editor showing library structure—see Figure 6.11.

9. Viewer screen origin definitions—see Figure 6.13.

Data-Structure Definitions

1. Viewer Default Screen Object Origin and Dimensions Data Structure—Chapter 6.

2. Title Index and Page Index data structures—Chapter 4.

Subroutine and Function Specifications

1. DESIGN SPEC: LoadAndDisplayImage

FUNCTION: LoadAndDisplayImage(strFileRef,imgObject,intMaxW,intMaxH,intLeft, intTop)_as Boolean

VERSION 1.0: <Date>

DESCRIPTION: To load, scale, and position an image into the available image area on screen.

ARGUMENTS:

StrFileRef	Image file reference
ImgObject	Name of image control to hold picture
IntMaxW	Maximum permitted width of image
IntrMaxH	Maximum permitted height of image
IntLeft	Left coordinate of container area for image
IntTop	Top coordinate of container are for image
Function result	= True if image loaded OK
	= False if image not loaded

ACTION:

On any error **Goto LoadFail**

Set **imgObject.Visible to** False

Set **imgObject.Stretch to** False

Load image into **imgObject**

    Call SizePicture

Re-size **imgObject** according to **SizePicture** results

Position **imgObject** in center of available area

Set **imgObject.Stretch** to TRUE

Set **imgObject.Visible** to TRUE

EXIT, setting function TRUE

ERROR HANDLING:

LoadFail:

    EXIT, setting function FALSE

END:

---

2. DESIGN SPEC: SizePicture

SUBROUTINE: SizePicture(intCW,intCH,intActualW,intActualH

VERSION 1.0: <Date>

DESCRIPTION: Calculate actual size of image required to fit into defined container area.

ARGUMENTS:

IntCW	Max possible width allowed in container area
IntCH	Max possible height allowed in container area
IntActualW	On entry—holds image's full-sized width
	On exit—set to hold scaled width
IntActualH	On entry—holds image's full-sized height
	On exit—set to hold scaled height

ACTION:

Aspect Ratio = **intActualW/intActualH**

If **intActualW > intCW** then

intActualW = intCW

Calculate new **intActualH**

End if

If **intActualH > intCH** then

      intActualH = intCH

      Calculate new **intActualW**

End if

END:

---

3. DESIGN SPEC: LoadAndPlayVideo

FUNCTION: **LoadAndPlayVideo(strFileName,frmForm,mmcObject,intMaxW,intMaxH, intLeft,intTop) as Boolean**

VERSION 1.0:   <Date>

DESCRIPTION: To load and run a video clip on screen.

ARGUMENTS:		
	strFileName	File reference to video clip
	FrmForm	Name of form in which to play video
	MmcObject	Name of multimedia control for video
	IntMaxW	Maximum width of playing area
	IntMaxH	Maximum height of playing area
	IntLeft	Position of Left-side f of playing area
	IntTop	Position of top of playing area
	Function result	= True if video loaded OK
		= False if video not loaded OK

ACTION:

If any error, then Go To VIDEO ERROR

Close **mmcObject**

Set **mmcObject.devicetype** to AVIVIDEO

Load file name into **mmcObject**

Define Video form's window handle

Open **mmcObject**

Force **mmcObject** to Play video

Position **frmForm** in center of container area.

EXIT, setting function TRUE

VIDEO ERROR:

Exit, setting function FALSE

END:

---

4. DESIGN SPEC: LoadAndDisplayText

FUNCTION: **LoadAndDisplayText(strFileName, txtObject) as Boolean**

VERSION 1.0: <Date>

DESCRIPTION: To read in and display text in a text display area with correct font characteristics.

ARGUMENTS: StrFileName   Name of text file to load

TxtObject   Name of screen object to receive text.

Function result = True if file loaded OK

= False if file not loaded OK

ACTION:

Call **OpenAndReadTextIntoMemory**

If text read OK then

set Function to TRUE

Load **txtObject** from string

Else

set function to FALSE

End if

END:

---

5. DESIGN SPEC: OpenAndReadTextIntoMemory

FUNCTION: **OpenAndReadTextIntoMemory(strFileName, strText) as Boolean**

VERSION 1.0: <Date>

DESCRIPTION: Open a text file, read in line by line, and build up a string containing the complete content of the file, including carriage-return, line-feed terminators.

ARGUMENTS: StrFileName   Name of file to read in

Strtext Name of string into which text is placed

Function result = True if file read OK

= False if file not read OK

ACTION:

On any error Go To TEXT FAIL

Open file **strFileName** for Input

Blank **strText**

LOOP While Not END OF FILE

Read In next Line into **strTemp**

Strtext=strtext+strTemp+vbCr+vbLf

End LOOP

Close file

Exit, setting function TRUE

ERROR HANDLING:

TEXT FAIL:

Close file

EXIT, setting function FALSE

END:

---

6. DESIGN SPEC: LoadAndPlaySound

FUNCTION: **LoadAndPlaySound(strFileName,mmcObject) as Boolean**

VERSION 1.0: <Date>

DESCRIPTION: Load a file and play as a WAV or MID as appropriate.

ARGUMENTS: StrFileName File reference to WAV or MID file

MmcObject Name of multimedia control for playing sound

Function result = True if sound loaded OK

= False if sound not loaded OK

ACTION:

If any error, then Go To SOUND ERROR

Close **mmcObject**

Load file name into **mmcObject**

Open **mmcObject**

Force **mmcObject** to Play sound

EXIT, setting function TRUE

SOUND ERROR

EXIT, setting function FALSE

END:

---

7. DESIGN SPEC: SetUpFormat1, SetUpFormat2 and SetUpFormat3

Viewer Format Set Up Infrastructure Routines

7.1. SUBROUTINE: SetupFormat1

VERSION 1.0: <Date>

DESCRIPTION: Called to set up the Text Book screen format.

ARGUMENTS: None

ACTION:

Set any relevant data for Text Book format

Enable **txtText**

Set origin of **txtText** to origin 1

Set dimensions of **txtText** to Line1 height and Line2 width

Remove **imgImageIt**

END

7.2. SUBROUTINE: SetupFormat2

VERSION 1.0: <Date>

DESCRIPTION: Called to set up the Picture Album format.

ARGUMENTS: None

ACTION:

Set any relevant data for Album format

Enable **imgImageIt**

Set origin of Album image container to origin 1

Set dimensions of Album image container to Line1 height and Line2 width

Remove **txtText**

END:

7.3. SUBROUTINE: SetupFormat3

VERSION 1.0: <Date>

DESCRIPTION: Called to set up the Reference Book format.

ARGUMENTS: None

ACTION:

Set any relevant data for reference book format

Enable **txtText**

Set origin of **txtText** to origin 3

Set dimensions of **txtText to g_intHeight3** and **g_intWidth3**

Enable **imgImageIt**

Set origin of Album image container to origin 2

Set dimensions of Album image container to **g_intHeight2** and **g_intWidth2**

END:

---

8. DESIGN SPEC: CaptureViewerDesignParameters

SUBROUTINE: CaptureViewerDesignParameters

VERSION 1.0: <Date>

DESCRIPTION: Sets up Viewer screen-definitions data structure from design-time settings of key screen objects.

ARGUMENTS: None

ACTION:

Define origin 1's left and top parameters from Line1 and Line2 (Book and Album)

Define origin 2's left and top parameters from **imgImageIt** (Ref Book)

Define origin 3's left and top parameters from **txtText** (small text in ref)

Define origin 4's left and top parameters from **picKeyPanel** (large text ref)

Define Height1 from height of Line1 (Book and Album)

Define Height2 from **imgImageIt** (Image height in ref)

Define Height3 from **txtText** (small text in ref)

Define Width1 from width of Line2 (Book and Album)

Define Width2 from **imgImageIt** (Image height in ref)

Define Width3 from **txtText** (small text in ref)

END:

---

9. DESIGN SPEC: DisplayPage

SUBROUTINE: DisplayPage(intDisplayType)

VERSION 1.1: <Date>

CHANGE LOG: L001 **<date>**

Set up code moved out to sub **SetUpData**

CHANGE LOG L002 <date>

Design updated by Archie to set up three file text boxes at bottom of viewer when routine called with Option 1. This places the image, text, and sound file references of the page on view.

DESCRIPTION:

Option 1:According to format, display all the contents of a given page.

Option 2: According to format, update image/video, text, sound according to contents of:

>   **txtPictureFileName.Text** for image or video

>   **txtTextFileName.Text** for text

>   **txtSoundFileName.Text** for sound track

ARGUMENTS:

>   **intDisplayType** optional argument:

>   If absent, set up from Page Index record.

>   If present, set up from text objects and leave keys.

ACTION:

Call **SetUpTheData**   CHANGE LOG REF: L0001

(defines **KeysToLoad**, **PictureToLoad**, **TextToLoad**, and **SoundtoLoad** according to **intDisplayType**)

If **intDisplayType** is not present, then:

>   Set up key panel text fields with **KeysToLoad**

End If

If Text Book format, then:

>   **LoadAndDisplayText** using **TextToLoad.**

End if

If Album format, then:

>   If image, then **LoadAndDisplayImage** using **PictureToLoad.**
>
>   **If video, then LoadAndPlayVideo** using **PictureToLoad.**

End if

If Reference Book format, then:

>   If image, then **LoadAndDisplayImage** using **PictureToLoad.**
>
>   If video, then **LoadAndPlayVideo** using **PictureToLoad.**
>
>   **LoadAndDisplayText** using **TextToLoad.**

End if

If sound present, then **LoadAndPlaySound** using **SoundToLoad.**

If **intDisplayType** is not present, then:	CHANGE LOG: L0002
txtPictureFileName.text = PictureToLoad	CHANGE LOG: L0002
txtTextFileName.text = TextToLoad	CHANGE LOG: L0002
txtSoundFileName.text = SoundToLoad	CHANGE LOG: L0002
End if	CHANGE LOG: L0002

END:

---

10. DESIGN SPEC: SetUpTheData

SUBROUTINE: SetUpTheData(intAlternateDisplay, strPicture, strText, strSound, strKeys)

VERSION 1.0: <Date>

DESCRIPTION: Sets up strings to define keys and file refs according to type of **DisplayPage** required.

ARGUMENTS: intAlternateDisplay = 0 extract data from page index record

>   = 1 extract data from screen objects

>   **strPicture** contains picture file reference on exit

> **strText** contains text file reference on exit
>
> **strSound** contains sound file reference on exit
>
> **strKeys** five element array to hold keys on exit

ACTION:

If **intAlternateDisplay** = 0 then

> Transfer Index record keys to **strKeys**
>
> Transfer Index picture ref to **strPicture**
>
> Transfer Index text ref to **strText**
>
> Transfer Index sound ref to **strSound**

Else

> Keys not needed
>
> Set **strPicture** from **txtPictureFileName.Text**
>
> Set **strText** from **txtTextFileName.Text**
>
> Set **strSound** from **txtSoundFileName.Text**

End if

END:

---

11. DESIGN SPEC: VideoOrPicture

SUBROUTINE: VideoOrPicture(strFileName)

VERSION 1.0: <Date>

NOTE: Created during development of viewer <date> by Archie.

DESCRIPTION: Determines whether or not a file extension is AVI.

ARGUMENTS: strFileName—full file reference to check.

ACTION:

If **strFileName** is blank, then EXIT, setting function to -1

Extract file extension from last three bytes of **strFileName**

If extension is "AVI" then EXIT setting function to 0

EXIT setting function to 1

END:

12. DESIGN SPEC: LocateDelimiter

FUNCTION: **LocateDelimiter(strToSearch,strChar,intStartPosition) as integer**

VERSION 1.0: <Date>

DESCRIPTION: Return position of first occurrence of target character in string from start position as result of function.

ARGUMENTS: **StrToSearch** String to search

StrChar Character to search for

IntStartPosition Position in string to start searching from

Function result = 0 if **strChar** not found, else = position of **strChar**

ACTION:

Loop from start position to end of target string

> If current character = Character to search for, then EXIT setting function to position of character

End Loop

EXIT, setting function to 0

END:

---

13. DESIGN SPEC: ExtractDataFields

FUNCTION: **ExtractDataFields(strToSearch, strFields( ),intFields) as Boolean**

VERSION 1.0: <Date>

DESCRIPTION: Scans a string and returns requested number of delimited fields' data.

ARGUMENTS: **StrToSearch** Name of string array from which to extract

StrFields( ) Array to receive the data

IntFields Number of fields to extract

Function result = True for all conditions except when END of DATA found

= False if all fields contain 'END'

NOTES:

If any field is not found, then all subsequent **strFields** elements will be blank on return.

If all fields extracted are found to contain 'END', then the result of the function is FALSE.

In all other cases, it is TRUE.

ACTION:

If **intFields** < 0 then EXIT, setting function TRUE

Check **intFields** < = number of elements in **strFields( )**,

if not, then set **intFields** to actual number found

Clear output array

Loop from 1 to number of data fields requested

       Find location of next '[', If not found, then Go To NO DELIMITER

       Find location of next ']', If not found, then Go To NO DELIMITER

       Extract data from between [and] and place in output array

End Loop

Loop from 1 to number of data fields requested

       If output field <> "END" then EXIT, setting function TRUE

End Loop

EXIT, setting function FALSE (that is, END marker found)

ERROR CONDITIONS:

NO DELIMITER

EXIT, setting function TRUE

END:

---

14. DESIGN SPEC: ReadInTitleIndex

FUNCTION: **ReadInTitleIndex(strFileName) as Boolean**

VERSION 1.0: <Date>

DESCRIPTION: To open a named Title Index on disk and read into memory.

ARGUMENTS: StrFileName   Name of Title Index file to be loaded

              Function Result = True if file input OK

                             = False if not able to read in file

ACTION:

       Open **strFileName**

    If failed, then Go To FATAL ERROR 1

    Read Line1, extract field1, and verify header

If file is not a Title Index then Go To FATAL ERROR 2

START LOOP

     Read Next Line in file

     If END OF FILE Then END LOOP

     Extract Page File Reference and place in memory

     Read Next Line, Extract Title, and place in memory

     If END OF FILE Then Go To FATAL ERROR 3

     Read Next Line, Extract Description, and place in memory

     If END OF FILE Then Go To FATAL ERROR 3

     Read all lines until [END OF RECORD] is located

     If END OF FILE read, then END LOOP

END LOOP

Close File and EXIT, setting function TRUE

ERROR HANDLING:

FATAL ERROR 1—Close File, inform user file cannot be opened

EXIT, setting function FALSE

FATAL ERROR 2—Close File, Inform user file is wrong type

EXIT, setting function FALSE

FATAL ERROR 3—Close File, Inform user file has been truncated

EXIT, setting function FALSE

END:

---

15. DESIGN SPEC: PopulateCombo

SUBROUTINE: PopulateCombo(comCombo)

VERSION 1.0: <Date>

DESCRIPTION: Populates screen combo box with list of titles from Memory Index

ARGUMENTS: comCombo   Name of combo box on screen to populate.

ACTION:

Clear Combo box

Transfer all titles from in Memory Index into combo box in order.

Set combo box to display first entry in list.

END:

---

16. DESIGN SPEC: ReadInPageIndex

FUNCTION: **ReadInPageIndex(strFileName) as Boolean**

VERSION 1.1: <Date>

Change Log: L0001 Initial section made into GEN subroutine

DESCRIPTION: To open a named Page Index on disk and read into memory

ARGUMENTS: **StrFileName**   Name of Page Index file

Function result = True if file read OK

= False if file not read OK

ACTION:

Call **ReadPageIndexHeader(strFileName)** L0001

If error reported then EXIT, setting function FALSE   L0001

On any error, Go To FATAL ERROR 3

START LOOP

Read Next Line of File

If END OF FILE then Go To FATAL ERROR 4

If all fields are [END] Then EXIT LOOP

Extract Fields 1 to 8 and place in memory structures

END LOOP

Close File

Exit, set True

ERROR HANDLING:

(L0001: two error traps moved to **ReadPageIndexHeader**)

FATAL ERROR 3—Report error reading file, close and EXIT, setting function FALSE

FATAL ERROR 4—Report file truncated, close and EXIT, setting function FALSE

END:

17. DESIGN SPEC: ReadPageIndexHeader

FUNCTION: **ReadPageIndexHeader(strFileName as string) as Boolean**

VERSION 1.0: <Date>

DESCRIPTION: To open Page Index file and process header line.

ARGUMENTS: StrFileName Name of Page Index file

Function result = True if file opened and header read OK

= False if file not opened or wrong type

ACTION:

On any error Go To **ErrHandler**

Open **strFileName**

Read first line of file

Extract 3 fields from line 1

Set **g_intFormatType** according to field 1

If not recognizable format, then

report error

close file

Clear Page Index in memory

EXIT, setting function FALSE

Set default font

Override default font if fields 2 and 3 contain font data

EXIT setting function TRUE

ERROR HANDLING:

Report failed to read header

Close file

EXIT, setting function FALSE

END:

---

18. DESIGN SPEC: Workbench, Screen Objects' Events

FLOW DIAGRAM: See Figure G.1, Event handling for drag-and-drop in Workbench mode.

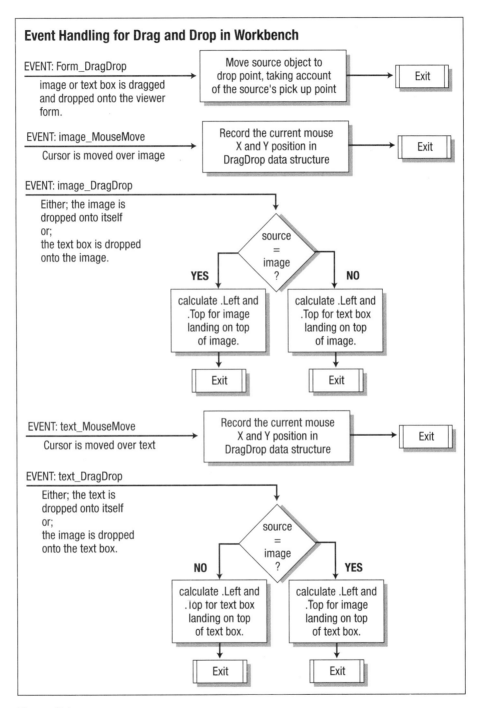

Figure G.1

Flow diagram showing drag and drop event handling in Workbench mode.

---

19. DESIGN SPEC: Workbench, ToolBar Events

FLOW DIAGRAM: See Figure G.2, Workbench toolbar event handling.

---

20. DESIGN SPEC: Workbench, Print

PRINT BUTTON EVENT HANDLER: cmdPrint_Click

VERSION 1.0: <Date>

DESCRIPTION: Arranges and then produces a screen dump of Workbench.

ACTION:

Remove Workbench tool bar

Set Workbench background color to white

Ask user if OK to print

If user cancels, then re-instate Workbench as was before entry and EXIT

Else

        Print screen dump

End if

Re-instate Workbench as was before entry

END:

---

21. DESIGN SPEC: Navigation Events

NOTE: In all the following specifications:

For Page Index navigation CP = current page number as set in **g_intCurrentPage**

For Title Index navigation CP = current entry number as set in **g_intCurrentTitle**

21.1. GENERIC BUTTON EVENT HANDLER: cmdGoStart

VERSION 1.0:   <Date>

DESCRIPTION: Brings up entry 1 of current Index

CHANGE LOG: L0001—<date> Provide consistency with **cmdPrevious**

ACTION:

If CP < 1 then Report "Index Is Empty" and EXIT

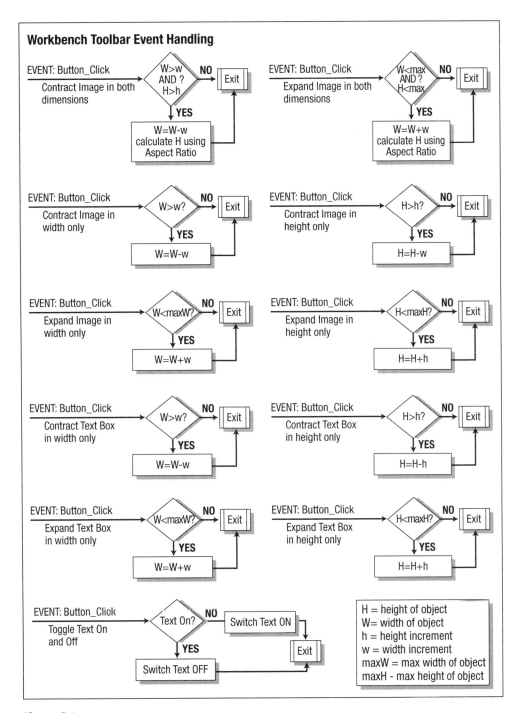

Figure G.2
Flow diagram showing toolbar event handling in Workbench.

IF CP = 1 Then Report "Already at Start of Index" and EXIT CHANGE LOG REF: L0001

Set CP = 1

Display entry 1

Set any screen comment applicable to "At Start of Index"

END:

21.2. GENERIC BUTTON EVENT HANDLER: cmdPrevious

VERSION 1.0: <Date>

DESCRIPTION: Brings up previous entry.

ACTION:

If CP < 1 then Report "Index is Empty" and EXIT

IF CP = 1 Then Report "Already at Start of Index" and EXIT

Set CP = CP - 1

Display new entry

END:

21.3. GENERIC BUTTON EVENT HANDLER: cmdNext

VERSION 1.0: <Date>

DESCRIPTION: Brings up next entry.

ACTION:

If CP < 1 then Report "Index is Empty" and EXIT

IF CP = Last Page Then Report "Already at End of Index" and EXIT

Set CP = CP + 1

Display new entry

END:

21.4. GENERIC BUTTON EVENT HANDLER: cmdGoEnd

VERSION 1.0: <Date>

DESCRIPTION: Brings up last page of current Index

CHANGE LOG: L0001—<date> Provide consistency with **cmdNext**

ACTION:

If CP < 1 then Report "Index Is Empty" and EXIT

If CP = last entry in the Index, then report "At End of Index" and EXIT CHANGE LOG REF: L0001

Set CP = Last Entry

Display entry

Set any applicable screen comment to "At End of Index"

END:

21.5. GENERIC BUTTON EVENT HANDLER: cmdGoToPage

VERSION 1.0: <Date>

DESCRIPTION: Page Index only: Gets page number from user and displays.

ACTION:

If CP < 1 then Report "Index Is Empty" and EXIT

Request page number from user

If entry is garbage, report and EXIT

If entry < 1 then

Set CP to 1, report "At Start of Index", display page 1 and EXIT

End if

If entry > Last Page Number then

Set CP to Last Page number, report "At End of Index", display last page and EXIT

End If

Set CP to entry number

Display new page

END:

22. DESIGN SPEC: Forward Search

FLOW DIAGRAM: See Figure 8.5 in Chapter 8.

---

23. DESIGN SPEC: Reverse Search

FLOW DIAGRAM: See Figure 8.6 in Chapter 8.

---

24. DESIGN SPEC: Search Index, ExamineIndex

FLOW DIAGRAM: See Figure 8.9 in Chapter 8.

---

25. DESIGN SPEC: GetIndexFileNameForInput

FUNCTION: **GetIndexFileNameForInput(dlgDialog as control, strFileName as string) as Boolean**

VERSION 1.0: <Date>

DESCRIPTION: This function solicits the name of a file required for input from the user.

ARGUMENTS: dlgDialog   name of dialogue box to activate

StrFileName   function will place the name of file selected in this variable

Result of function = False—no file selected

= True—file name provided

ACTION:

If any error, then go to Error handler

Clear **strFileName**

Set file filter to Index file types only (***.idx**)

Action **dlgDialog** for an OPEN function

Set **strFileName** from dialogue box result

If **strFileName** is blank, then EXIT setting function FALSE

EXIT setting function TRUE

ERROR HANDLER:

EXIT setting function FALSE

END:

26. DESIGN SPEC: Edit Menu Option Open

GENERIC EVENT HANDLER: Edit Menu Option OPEN

VERSION 1.0: <Date>

DESCRIPTION: The menu drop-down function OPEN for both Title Index Editor and Page Index Editor. Allows the user to select the name of an index file and then load it into the in-Memory Index arrays.

NOTES: The OPEN menu option must be disabled when the editor is in the **Level 1 Alert State**.

ACTION:

> Call function **GetIndexFileNameForInput**
>
> If function failed, then report condition and EXIT leaving currently loaded Index intact
>
> Call function **IndexLoad** with specified file name
>
> If function failed, then
>
> Clear screen objects
>
> Clear Memory Index
>
> Clear **Index Alert** status if it was on
>
> EXIT
>
> End if
>
> Update name of index file on screen
>
> Display contents of entry 1 on screen
>
> Clear **Level 2 Alert State** if it was on
>
> For Page Editor Only: switch Viewer into Page View Mode

END:

27. DESIGN SPEC: WriteOutTitleIndex

FUNCTION: WriteOutTitleIndex(strFileName) as Boolean

VERSION: 1.1   <date>

DESCRIPTION: Outputs the Memory Title Index to a specified disk file.

ARGUMENTS: StrFileName   Name file to receive Index

Function Result = True if File output OK

= False if not able to output file

CHANGE LOG: <Date> L001

Menu option SAVE needs to call **WriteOutTitleIndex** without the routine requesting authorization.

Menu option SAVE AS does require authorization. Consequently, functionality to obtain authorization has been moved out of **WriteOutTitleIndex.**

ACTION:

CHANGE L0001—Code removed

    REMOVED: Find out if file exists or not

    REMOVED: Inform user of situation and seek authorization to proceed

    REMOVED: If authorization is not given, close file, EXIT setting function FALSE

END OF CHANGE L0001

If an Error occurs, at any time, then Go To FAILED TO OUTPUT

Open File for output

Format Header line and output to file

Loop From start of Index to end

    Format Lines 1 to 3 and output to file

    Format [END OF RECORD], output to file

End Loop

Close File

EXIT setting function TRUE

ERROR HANDLING:

FAILED TO OUTPUT

Close File

Produce appropriate Error message

EXIT, setting function FALSE

END:

28. DESIGN SPEC: Save

GENERIC EVENT HANDLER: Edit Menu Option: SAVE

VERSION 1.0:   <Date>

DESCRIPTION: The menu drop-down function SAVE for both Title Index Editor and Page Index Editor. Allows the user to save the current in-Memory Index to the file name specified on the screen object that holds the Index file reference. Note authorization to proceed is *not* requested.

ACTION:

FOR PAGE EDITOR ONLY: If Viewer form is in Title Selection mode, abort function.

If Index is empty, report condition and exit

Get Index file name from relevant screen object text box

If file name is not blank then

> Output Index to file name

> If failed to output then, report error and EXIT

Else

> Invoke menu option Save As

End if

END:

29. DESIGN SPEC: Save As

GENERIC EVENT HANDLER: Edit Menu Option: SAVE AS

VERSION 1.0:   <Date>

DESCRIPTION: The menu drop-down function SAVE AS for both Title Index Editor and Page Index Editor. Allows the user to save the current in-Memory Index to a file named by the user. Authorization to proceed dependent on file status is requested.

ACTION:

FOR PAGE EDITOR ONLY: If Viewer form is in Title Selection mode, abort function

If Index is empty, report condition and exit

Get Index file name from relevant screen object text box

Using current name as a default, Get name of output file from user

(Call to **GetIndexFileNameForOutput**)

Report file condition and request if OK to proceed (call to **OKToProceed**)

If not OK to proceed, then EXIT

Output index to named file

If output failed, then report error and EXIT

Update relevant screen object with name of file just output

Clear down any level 2 Alert state that may be on

END:

---

30. DESIGN SPEC: New

GENERIC EVENT HANDLER: Edit Menu Option: New

VERSION 1.0: <Date>

DESCRIPTION: The menu drop-down function NEW for both Title Index Editor and Page Index Editor. Allows the user to create a new, blank Index.

ACTION:

Ask user if NEW is definitely required

If user wants to Abort then EXIT

FOR PAGE INDEX NEW: Request book format type, 1, 2, or 3

FOR PAGE INDEX NEW: Set up format type as requested

Clear memory Index

Clear Screen

END:

---

31. DESIGN SPEC: GetIndexFileNameForOutput

FUNCTION: GetIndexFileNameForOutput(dlgDialog as control, strFileName as string) as **Boolean**

VERSION 1.0: <Date>

DESCRIPTION: This function solicits the name of a file required for output from the user.

ARGUMENTS: dlgDialog   name of dialogue box to activate

StrFileName   On entry, this contains the name of the current Index or blank.

On exit, it contains the name of the file chosen by the user.

Function result = False—no file selected

= True—file name provided

ACTION:

If any error, then go to Error handler

Set file name for filter box default to **strFileName**

Set file filter to Index file types only (***.idx**)

Action **dlgDialog** for a SAVE function

Set **strFileName** from dialogue box result

If **strFileName** is blank, then EXIT setting function FALSE

EXIT setting function TRUE

ERROR HANDLER:

EXIT setting function FALSE

END:

---

32. DESIGN SPEC: OKToProceed

FUNCTION: **OKToProceed(strFileName as string) as Boolean**

VERSION 1.0: <Date>

DESCRIPTION: Report status of file and ask user if OK to output.

ARGUMENTS: StrFileName   contains the name of the output file

Function result = False—Do not proceed with output

= True—Proceed with output

ACTION:

Find out if file (**strFileName**) exists on disk or not

Report status (file exists or file does not exist)

If file does not exist, then ask if it should be created

If file does exist, then ask if it should be overwritten

Get response

Set function to FALSE

If response is OK then set function to TRUE

END:

33. DESIGN SPEC: Alert State Handling for the Editors

33.1. SUBROUTINE: SwitchOnAlert1

DESCRIPTION: Sets the editor into the **Alert 1 State**, indicating screen data is not same as memory.

ACTION:

Set Alert Color on main form

Disable All Navigation Button Controls

Replace DELETE Index Manipulation Button control with RELEASE Button

Disable menu options; New, Open, Save, Save As

END:

33.2. SUBROUTINE: SwitchOffAlert1

DESCRIPTION: Clears the editor from the **Alert 1 State**, now indicating screen data is the same as memory.

ACTION:

Clear Alert Color on main form

Clear Alert Color on all data fields subject to Change Handling

Enable All Navigation Button Controls

Replace RELEASE Button with DELETE Index Manipulation Button

Enable menu options; New, Open, Save, Save As

END:

33.3. SUBROUTINE: SwitchOnAlert2

DESCRIPTION: Sets the editor into the **Alert 2 State**, indicating memory is not the same as disk data.

ACTION:

Set alert color on the text box showing Index file name

END:

33.4. SUBROUTINE: SwitchOffAlert2

DESCRIPTION: Clears the editor from **Alert 2 State**, now indicating memory data is the same as disk file.

ACTION:

Clear alert color on the text box showing Index file name

END:

---

34. Event List for Change Handling

EVENT LIST: See Figure 10.3.

---

35. DESIGN SPEC: ADD TO INDEX

GENERIC BUTTON EVENT HANDLER: cmdAdd_Click

VERSION 1.0: <Date>

DESCRIPTION: Adds content of screen objects to end of in-Memory Index

ACTION:

FOR PAGE EDITOR ONLY: If viewer is not page view mode, then abort function

Get user to confirm OK to ADD

If user aborts ADD then EXIT

Increase size of Memory Index by one

Load last entry of Index from screen objects

Display last entry of Index

Clear **Alert 1** status

Set **Alert 2** status

END:

---

36. DESIGN SPEC: INSERT INTO INDEX

GENERIC BUTTON EVENT HANDLER: cmdInsert_Click

VERSION 1.0: <Date>

DESCRIPTION: Insert contents of screen object between current Index entry—1 and current entry.

ACTION:

FOR PAGE EDITOR ONLY: If viewer is not page view mode, then abort function

If Index is empty, then report condition and EXIT

Get user to confirm OK to INSERT

If user aborts INSERT then EXIT

Increase size of Memory Index by one

Shuffle all entries from current 1 to top of Index up one place

Load current entry number from screen objects

Display current entry

Clear **Alert 1** status

Set **Alert 2** status

END:

---

37. DESIGN SPEC: OVERWRITE INDEX ENTRY

GENERIC BUTTON EVENT HANDLER: cmdOverWrite_Click

VERSION 1.0:   <Date>

DESCRIPTION: Overwrite current Index entry with content of screen objects.

ACTION:

FOR PAGE EDITOR ONLY: If viewer is not page view mode, then abort function

If Index is empty, then report condition and EXIT

Get user to confirm OK to OVERWRITE

If user aborts OVERWRITE then EXIT

Load current entry number from screen objects

Display current entry

Clear **Alert 1** status

Set **Alert 2** status

END:

---

38. DESIGN SPEC: DELETE ENTRY FROM INDEX

GENERIC BUTTON EVENT HANDLER: cmdDelete_Click

VERSION 1.0:   <Date>

DESCRIPTION: Delete current entry from Index.

ACTION:

FOR PAGE EDITOR ONLY: If viewer is not page view mode, then abort function

If index is empty, then report condition and EXIT

Get user to confirm OK to DELETE

If user aborts DELETE then EXIT

If Index has only one entry, then clear Index, clear screen and EXIT

Shuffle all entries from top of Index to (current entry −1) down 1 place

Decrease size of Memory Index by one

Load current entry number from screen objects

Display current entry

Clear **Alert 1** status

Set **Alert 2** status

END:

---

39. DESIGN SPECIFICATION: Change-Handling Events

CHANGE-HANDLING EVENTS: Events for Page Index Editor, Viewer (working in the Page Index Editor environment), and Text Editor.

VERSION 1.0: <Date>

DESCRIPTION: Events specific to change handling.

3.9.1. EVENT: VIEWER FORM_Load

DESCRIPTION: Code required to lock data fields when viewer starts up. If viewer is working standalone, this code ensures that the data fields of the viewer cannot be altered by the user. The data fields are **txtText** and the **txtKeyViews** array.

ACTION:

      Lock text field against user changes

      Lock all key fields against user changes

END:

39.2. EVENT: PAGE EDITOR FORM_Load

DESCRIPTION: Code required to unlock data fields after viewer starts up, thus overriding the standalone status for the viewer when it operates in the Page Editor environment.

ACTION:

unlock text field against user changes

unlock all key fields against user changes

END:

39.3. EVENT: DATA FIELD_Change

DESCRIPTION: A data field has been changed by the user.

Applies to **txtText** and **txtKeyView(1)** to **txtKeyView(5)** in the viewer operating in Page Index Editor environment.

Applies to **txtFileRef**, **txtDescription**, *and* **txtTitle** in Title Index Editor.

ACTION:

If user does not have focus on data field, then EXIT

Change background color of data field to **Alert 1** color.

Change background of Program's main form or panel to **Alert 1** color.

END:

39.4. EVENT: Data Field_GotFocus

DESCRIPTION: User places focus on a data field.

Applies to **txtText** and **txtKeyView(1)** to **txtKeyView(5)** in viewer operating in Page Editor environment.

Applies to **txtFileRef**, **txtDescription**, and **txtTitle** in Title Index Editor.

ACTION:

Indicate user has focus of data field.

END:

39.5. EVENT: Data Field_LostFocus

DESCRIPTION: User removes focus from data field.

Applies to **txtText** and **txtKeyView(1)** to **txtKeyView(5)** in viewer working in Page Editor environment.

Applies to **txtFileRef**, **txtDescription**, and **txtTitle** in Title Editor.

ACTION:

Indicate user does not have focus of data field.

END:

40. DESIGN SPEC: File Selection

FILE SELECTION EVENT HANDLERS: For Drive, Directory, and File Selection screen objects.

40.1. FILE SELECTION EVENT HANDLER: filDrive1_Change

VERSION 1.0:   <Date>

DESCRIPTION: The contents of the Drive selection box have been changed. Set the path attribute of the Directory selection box to the new drive.

ACTION:

Set **filDir1.Path** to **filDrive1.Drive**

END:

40.2. FILE SELECTION EVENT HANDLER: filDir1_Change

VERSION 1.0:   <Date>

DESCRIPTION: The contents of the Directory selection box have been changed. Set the Path attribute of the File Selection box to the new directory path.

ACTION:

> Set **filFil1.Path** to **filDir1.Path**

END:

40.3. FILE SELECTION EVENT HANDLER: filFile1_Click

VERSION 1.0:   <Date>

DESCRIPTION: Use clicks on a file name in the File Selection form's File Selection box. File is loaded according to current file-type setting.

ACTION:

If Viewer is not in PAGE VIEW MODE, Report and Exit.

Construct full File Path and name

If SELECT MODE is 'PICTURE' Then

> Set **txtPictureFileName** to full file name

> Set Viewer **Alert 1** Status

> If Format Type = BOOK, warn user; will not show image/video & Exit

End IF

If SELECTMODE is 'TEXT' Then

Set **txtTextFileName** to full name

Set Viewer Alert Status

If Format Type is ALBUM then warn user will not show text and Exit

End If

If SELECT MODE is 'SOUND' Then

Set **txtSoundFileName** to full name

Set Viewer Alert Status

End If

If no selection made then Inform user that SELECT MODE has not been set and exit

Display Page using the Viewer text box file references

END:

40.4. FILE SELECTION EVENT HANDLER: Select File Type

VERSION 1.0: <Date>

DESCRIPTION: The user can click on one of three file-type objects at the top of the File Selection form. One object selects PICTURE mode, another TEXT mode, and a third selects SOUND mode. Clicking on one of these objects determines which type of file the three file-selection objects will choose.

ACTION:

Save Current File Type's context: Filter setting, drive setting, and directory setting.

Set screen objects to new file type's identification color: Red for Picture mode, green for text, and blue for sound.

Restore new File Type's context: Filter setting, drive setting, and directory setting.

END:

40.5. FILE SELECTION EVENT HANDLER: Filter box change event

VERSION 1.0: <Date>

DESCRIPTION: Whenever the user changes the content of the Filter selection box of the File Selection form, the change event is activated.

ACTION:

Set File selection control to new filter selection.

END:

41: DESIGN SPEC: Page Index Editor COPY and PASTE

41.1. DATA STRING SPECIFICATION: Paste Buffer viewer page copy

VERSION 1.0: <Date>

DESCRIPTION: This string contains the keys and file references of a viewer page for copying to the Windows paste buffer.

DEFINITION:

Field 1:	[E-MAGBOOK CLIPBOARD PACKET]
Field 2:	[Key(1)]
Field 3:	[Key(2)]
Field 4:	[Key(3)]
Field 5:`	[Key(4)]
Field 6:	[Key(5)]
Field 7:	[Picture file reference]
Field 8:	[Text file reference]
Field 9:	[Sound file reference]

END:

41.2. EVENT HANDLER: COPY

VERSION 1.0: <Date>

DESCRIPTION: Copies page content to paste buffer.

ACTION:

Set up E-MagBook clipboard packet from screen objects: keys, picture file, text file, and sound file references. Format up the string according to 41.1 and copy to paste buffer.

END:

41.3. EVENT HANDLER: PASTE

VERSION 1.0: <Date>

DESCRIPTION: Reads paste buffer and sets up page.

ACTION:

Read paste buffer into string.

If string is not standard E-MagBook Clipboard packet, report error and EXIT.

Set up screen keys.

Set up picture, text, and sound file references on screen objects.

Reload page according to screen references.

Set **Alert 1 State**.

END:

---

42. DESIGN SPEC: Text Save and Text Save As

FUNCTION: Menu options "Save Text" and "Save text As"

VERSION 1.0: <Date>

DESCRIPTION: Saves content of text box to disk file.

NOTES:

Making the appropriate changes, you can set up these functions following the design of the Index **Save** and **Save As** functions.

Index

What's on the CD-ROM

The *Software Project Management: From Concept to Deployment*'s companion CD-ROM contains elements specifically selected to enhance the usefulness of this book, including the following:

- Complete set of Visual Basic projects for the testing programs developed in the case study. This collection of projects allows you to follow the case study without the need to build the code line-by-line as detailed in the book.

- Set of blank Visual Basic forms for the three main programs developed in the case study. These forms can be used as the starting point for readers who *do* wish to develop the programs line-by-line as described in the book.

- Set of complete VB projects for the three programs developed in the case study for the reader who does not wish to build the programs line-by-line as detailed in the book.

- Collection of multimedia, electronic book examples. These e-books can be used with the code developed from the case study and the code available on the CD.

- All projects supplied on the CD have been set up using Visual Basic Version 6. If you wish to use an earlier version of Visual Basic, you will have to enter the code, line-by-line, as detailed in the case study, to newly created projects.

System Requirements

Software

- Your operating system needs to be Windows 95, 98, NT4 or higher.

- Professional or Enterprise version of Visual Basic 6 or Visual Studio is needed to complete the projects included in this book as these versions contain the multimedia component necessary. Ordinary versions of Visual Basic 6 can be used but video and sound facilities will be unavailable in the completed project. (Visual Basic is not provided on this CD-ROM.)

Hardware

- Any multimedia PC is suitable.

- 32MB of RAM is the minimum requirement.

- The entire content of the CD can be accommodated in less than 30 Megabytes of storage on your hard drive.

- Full multimedia capability required together with full color monitor of 800 by 600 pixel minimum resolution.